THE SAME OI

Volume Two: Co

Mike Roberts

"The old game was no doubt unscientific compared with the game of the present day, but it was a glorious game, and I look back upon my last football term as one of the happiest times of my life, when I remember wondering to myself
…if life could ever be so delightful again."
Arthur Pearson, former Rugby pupil, 1923.

ROBERTSBCN
PUBLICATIONS
2011

First published 2011
By RobertsBCN Publications
Rogent 47, 2º 2ª
Barcelona 08029
Spain

© Michael Roberts 2011. All rights reserved.

www.sameoldgame.com

ISBN- 13: 978-1463741310

All rights reserved. No part of this publication
may be reproduced, stored in a retrieval system,
or transmitted in any form or by any means,
electronic, photocopying, recording or otherwise
without the prior permission of the author.

Cover images:
Front:
An English Foot-ball Match – England versus Scotland
by WH Overend and LP Smythe (1886)*.

Back:
Football in Richmond Paddock (Melbourne Post, 1866)
Football at The Oval (The Graphic, 1878)

* By kind permission of F.Humbert www.rugby-pioneers.com

CONTENTS

1 **LAYING DOWN THE LAWS** — 7
The Football Association is born

2 **HISTORIC ASSOCIATIONS** — 25
How the FA's game became the world's game

3 **SCRUM ON DOWN** — 46
The early days of Rugby Union

4 **LEAGUES AND GENTLEMEN** — 73
Professionalism and the schism between rugby union and rugby league

5 **THE CELTIC TIMES** — 120
Irish football before the GAA

6 **PADDY POWER** — 146
The GAA and the foundation of Gaelic Football

7 **GAMES WITH FRONTIERS** — 168
The politics of the GAA

8 **GAA DAY SPORT** — 189
International rules and the possible Gaelic Australian connection

9 **ESCAPE TO VICTORIA** — 209
Early football in and around Melbourne

10 **A KICK UP THE BEHIND** — 222
The early years of Australian rules football

11 **COMING TO AMERICA** — 251
Colonial football in the United States

12 **THE NOT SO ALL-AMERICAN GAME** — 281
Early soccer and rugby in the United States

13 **DOWN ON SCRUM** — 301
Walter Camp and American football in the making

14 **THE KILLING FIELDS** — 326
American football and the issue of violence

15 **SLEEPING WITH AN ELEPHANT** — 346
The early years of football in Canada

16 **CANADIAN CLUBS** — 367
20th century Canadian football

17 **THE GAME IS UP** — 391
Conclusions

APPENDIXES — 397

INDEX — 419

BIBLIOGRAPHY — 430

1 LAYING DOWN THE LAWS
The Football Association is born

The simplest game

We don't know when ball games were first played in the British Isles. They were certainly around by the 12th century, but judging by the way explorers came across similar games among primitive and isolated cultures all around the world, logic tells us they had been around for a lot longer than that.

The term 'foteball' was first recorded in 1409. In the 1660s, Francis Willughby described a game that was most definitely an early version of soccer[1], in which the ball was kicked by teams into goals at either end of a field. There were other sports where the ball was carried, such as East Anglian camp ball, Cornish hurling and Welsh *cnapan*. But as standardisation swept across Britain, and just like stickball games came to be known collectively as 'hockey', the term 'football' came to be used as a catch-all for a whole variety of different games, whether the ball was kicked, thrown or carried.

There were four particularly important factors that affected football in the first half of the 19th century. First, there was the need for roads to be used for transport, epitomised by the *Highway Acts* of 1830 and supported by the introduction of a proper police system. There was no place for the large-scale street football festivals of the past, and games were instead transferred to the fields and delimitated plots of land.

Second, there were major developments in ball-making technology. Rustic, fragile animal bladders gave way for vulcanised rubber footballs. More durable and bouncy, they transformed the image of football from a vulgar poor man's game to something on a par with the more chivalrous sports of the time.

Third, and as a direct result of the two previous factors, football was no longer considered unworthy of gentlemen. Instead, it became the epitome of Muscular Christianity and was widely encouraged, even enforced, at schools. This new involvement of the middle classes in what until then had been the domain of the working minions led to the formation of gentleman's associations along similar lines to cricket clubs, and folk in 'higher society' felt the need to develop a more formal structure to the way the game was played.

And fourth, all this was happening just as Britain was being united by the railroads. It had been unthinkable just a couple of decades earlier, but by the 1860s it was quite feasible for a group of footballers to travel to other cities in search of a challenge. The first challenge, however, was going to be settling on a common set of rules.

---

[1] As in Volume One, to avoid the confusion of the word 'football' being used to describe different games in different countries, this book uses the term 'soccer' to describe the Association game, even though its use is uncommon in Great Britain.

An editorial in *The Field* in December 1861 sets the scene. "What happens when a game of football is proposed at Christmas among a party of young men assembled from different schools? Alas! We have seen the attempt made again and again, but invariably with a failure as the result. The Eton man is enamoured by his own rules, and turns his nose up at Rugby as not sufficiently aristocratic; while the Rugbeian retorts that 'bullying' and 'sneaking' are not to his taste, and he is not afraid of his shins, or a maul, or a scrimmage. On hearing this, the Harrovian pricks up his ears, and though he might previously have sided with Rugby, the insinuation against the courage of those who do not allow 'shinning' arouses his ire, and causes him to refuse to play with one who has offered it. Thus it is found it is impossible to get up a game."

It's not that football didn't have rules. It now had too many. Not only the schools, but adult clubs too, like Cambridge University, Sheffield, Surrey, Lincoln and Nottingham devised their own laws and stuck to them just as steadfastly. Meanwhile, football had already made it abroad, and heaven only knows what hare-brained ideas they were coming up with in America and Australia!

It was not even clear whether you should kick the ball or carry it, but when teams like Sheffield FC and Forest FC started looking for games beyond their own backyards, the need to standardise football moved from being an occasional inconvenience to an urgent necessity. Cricket was ideal in the summer, but the winter game of football was proving something of a bugbear because it involved far more physical contact and far fewer rules – and those that did exist could change from one week to the next.

Charles Thring, the Old Salopian who had tried to get everybody at Cambridge to agree to a uniform set of rules, continued to have strong views on the subject, and even wrote a book about it, *The Winter Game* (1862), where he stated that "it would be quite impossible, even if it were desirable, to induce the different schools to give up their time-honoured vanities, and to adopt a uniform game." But if they wanted to play each other, they would need to meet somewhere in the middle "lest too frequent spills and too heated personal encounters might lead to results not compatible with the dignity and honour of maturing manhood."

In his book, Thring introduces his proposal for *The Simplest Game*. It was clearly based on what he had learned from his Cambridge experience – that football was getting too complicated, and the fewer the rules the better. He also makes it clear that his idea was "an antidote to the Rugby game, which has unhappily been lately adopted by many clubs."

Thring's new rules gain massive credit for the inspired Rule 3 that says "kicks must be aimed only at the ball." But now he had reverted back to the strict offside law whereby no player could ever stand in front of said ball. So much for simplification. This law echoed the one used in rugby and which the FA would adopt more or less verbatim: "A player is 'out of play' immediately he is in front of the ball and he must return behind the ball as soon as possible. If the ball be kicked by his own side past a player, he may not touch or kick it nor

LAYING DOWN THE LAWS

advance until one of the other side has first kicked it or one of his own side, having followed it up, has been able, when in front of him, to kick it."

He also said that "hands may be used only to stop a ball and place it on the ground before the feet" and "a player may not kick the ball whilst in the air." Come again? Did he mean you couldn't kick the ball while you yourself were airborne, or did he mean you could only kick the ball while it was on the ground? It was the latter, for a comment was made in the *Sporting Gazette* in December 1863 that "neither do I concur with Mr Thring that the ball should be kept as much as possible on the ground."

His throw-ins were a bit odd too (if indeed they were thrown at all, for he doesn't specify that). Says Thring, the ball "must be returned by the player who kicked it, from the spot it passed the flag line, in a straight line towards the middle of the ground." Still, his rule must have provided an ideal solution for the time-worn problem of one team kicking the ball out, but a player from the other team having to climb over the fence to fish it out from the ticks. We've all been there.

Thring's *Simplest Game* was used in 1862 for a game between Old Etonians and Harrovians and may have convinced some influential people of its merits, but it raised just as many doubts. One of the main problems was that the simplicity of the game was precisely what the public school players did not want. They liked convoluted and complicated games. The *Simplest Game* felt like child's play in comparison. It was too simple.

Order out of chaos

The Civil War and the abolition of slavery in America, the laying of the first lines of the London underground, an outbreak of smallpox, the foundation of the International Red Cross and Charles Darwin suggesting that a human being was a kind of monkey were among the subjects dominating the press in the early 1860s. Others were more concerned with the evolution of the game of football.

The debate was not entirely focused on the elite public schools and Oxbridge. Pompous git as he was, an Etonian calling himself 'Goalstick' also considered the lower echelons, for whom he felt football needed to be simple, or else "our lusty slogging dependents of the plough or spade" would never get their heads round them. He describes the "utter hopelessness of the Rugby rules being drummed into the thick heads of our country cousins" because "we never … meet with a sufficient number of educated people in our country villages to enable the game, if a difficult one, to be adopted with zest. Our labourers are not very fond of being pulled up for little trivial errors and omissions which they don't and can't understand in a game[2]."

---

[2] Goalstick does have a point about keeping the game simple and eliminating pedantic rules. But it's a shame his motives were so un-PC, for South Wales and Yorkshire in particular are two fine examples of how a working class culture could understand the Rugby game perfectly well, and be quite good at it too.

MIKE ROBERTS – THE SAME OLD GAME: CODIFICATION

Another Old Etonian in *The Field* in 1861 felt the public school game needed to remove some of its violence if was to appeal to appeal to wider society. "The savage rouge or the wild broken bully would cause a vast sensation among our agricultural friends," he wrote.

In 1859, the editor of *Bell's Life* went as far as to say that enough was enough and he would be refusing to publish any more correspondence on the issue. Although *Bell's* didn't entirely stick to its word, most of the buck was picked up by the highly authoritative *The Field*[3], which provided more than ample coverage of a debate that was stirring up passions[4]. Most of the rumpus was mediated by a journalist called John Dyer Cartwright, making him, in many ways, one of the most influential figures in the progress towards a regulated game. He was the *Forgotten Man*, as Graham Curry titled his 2003 study.

Cartwright was convinced who they should be turning to for help. "A set of rules issued from the University of Oxford or of Cambridge would set the matter right very speedily" he offered in November 1863. He was unaware that Cambridge had just published a revision of their original composite code, but when he did secure and print a copy, he was decidedly impressed. On November 21, he wrote that "we have much pleasure in publishing these rules, framed by Cambridge men, from Rugby, Harrow, Eton, Shrewsbury, Marlborough and Westminster. The first match to be played by them was fixed for yesterday (Friday) afternoon. Our football readers who study them closely will observe that they have many very excellent features. An amalgamation of laws has not been attempted, but the rules have been framed upon the general principles of the game." He went on to list all the main public schools' rules as a comparison, to enable the reader "to see at once how far the Cambridge University rules … accord with those of any particular game."

The Cambridge rules were essentially the same as the ones their forbears had written 15 years earlier, but clarifications and modifications now included such items as a decision to finally do something about the length of the game and the number of players on each side, dictating that "the time during which the game shall last and the numbers in each side are to be settled by the heads of the sides." OK, it was start.

As well as a strict offside law that prevented any movement ahead of the ball, and throw-ins being taken with the hands, Cambridge had also adopted the Eton 'rouge' in place of the equivalents of goal kicks or corners. "When a player has kicked the ball beyond the opponents' goal line, whoever first touches the ball when it is on the ground with his hand, may have a free kick bringing the ball straight out from the goal line."

A free kick "may be taken in any manner the player may choose", which implies you could punt from your hands, but catching was now out. This was a game in which the ball "when in

---

[3] Established in 1859. It still exists today for the Tally-Ho brigade, covering 'country' sports like shooting, racing and hunting. It was willing to cover football in the 1860s, but not any more, unless to perhaps make some kind of derogatory remark at its expense.

[4] It wasn't just *The Field*. A series of six articles in the *Sporting Gazette* and numerous letters published in *The Times*, for example, also had a huge bearing on the debate.

LAYING DOWN THE LAWS

play may be stopped by any part of the body, but it may not be held or hit by the hands, arms or shoulders." So, if you couldn't hold the ball, then you had no hope of running with it, and hacking was also out, for "all charging is fair; but holding, pushing with the hands, tripping up and shinning are forbidden."

What Cartwright's article does more than anything is highlight that although the Cambridge rules were not a bad amalgam for most of the public school games, the one that really looked set to lose out was Rugby football, with its running with the ball, hacking, mauling and kicking over the crossbar. That game stood to be altered beyond recognition by any hybridisation with the 'kicking' codes, but that would not have bothered Cartwright too much, who felt Rugby "play the game splendidly; but is the game football? Might they not have as good a game with rather less violence? Certainly they might. Such a one is now offered them from Cambridge, in the construction of which two of their own players have taken a prominent part. Will they not accept it?"

They wouldn't. With hindsight, it's easy to see where things were heading. The Rugby rules were singled out more than any other for both biting criticism and unconditional praise. A 'JH' of Winchester insisted that nobody would ever be able to understand them. "Forty rules?" he scoffed. "It's 'jest awful', when the articles of the Church of England are only thirty-nine!"

But much as Cartwright liked the Cambridge game and disliked Rugby's, the problem was getting everybody to listen and act at the same time. He was convinced that what was "wanted is a headquarters for football, from which rules shall be issued and tried, revising again and again – a headquarters such as there is for cricket in the Marylebone club, and for all other sports which England claims as national. In our next paper, we shall endeavour to show that such a 'headquarters' might be easily found." We would never find out what Cartwright's plan involved. By one mighty editorial oversight, in the very next column of the same edition of the paper, there was a short article titled *Formation of a Football Association*.

The man who had finally managed to set the proverbial ball rolling went by the name of Ebenezer Cobb Morley, the captain of the Barnes club. It was at his proposal that a meeting was arranged between a selection of the southeast's most important clubs to do just what Cartwright was presumably going to propose the next week. Cartwright could have become the Godfather of football, but Cobb Morley beat him to it.

Putting a soccer in it

Some wondered why Cobb Morley was bothering. "Football can never attain the proud position among the national sports of England which its admirers so fondly look forward to, the cricket of the winter months" scorned *The Sporting Gazette* in October 1863. Following two mergers, this publication eventually became *The County Gentleman, Sporting Gazette and Agricultural Journal* and survived until 1900. Football survived a bit longer.

MIKE ROBERTS – THE SAME OLD GAME: CODIFICATION

The chosen venue for the FA's first meeting was the Freemason's Tavern in Great Queen Street, London, which football memorabilia seekers will be dismayed to learn cannot be visited now as it was destroyed a few years later[5]. It is now the site of a hotel and the New Connaught Rooms conference hall, which has at least been symbolically used on later occasions for FA meetings.

Monday, October 26, 1863 was the date that the body that still oversees the FA Cup and FA Premiership was formed. Eleven clubs were represented: Forest FC (the public school old boys who would later become The Wanderers and represented by John Forster Alcock, the older brother of Charles Alcock, who would be one of the most important administrators of 19th century soccer); No Names Football Club Kilburn (mainly Old Harrovians, many of whom seem to have also been Forest FC players, and who never did get around to coming up with a name, even though Kilburn Football Club must surely have been a fairly obvious choice. Soon after they became 'no team', though it was their representative, Arthur Pember, who was elected to be the first president of the FA); Barnes (represented by Morley who would become Honourable Secretary); the Civil Service (though they were mistakenly recorded as the 'War Office' because they were represented by a member of that department called Mr Warne, spelt Wawn in the minutes. They still exist today, playing in soccer's Southern Amateur League); Crusaders (who had originally been based around Old Etonians but had gradually introduced more and more players that never went to that school, and which typifies the gradual transition from old boy teams to more general private football clubs); Crystal Palace (not the modern-day team of that name, which was not founded until 1905, although both used the same ground, so there is at least a spiritual link); and also five teams that advocated the Rugby game, particularly Blackheath (represented by Mr Francis Maude Campbell, who would be both treasurer and chief shit-stirrer), plus Surbiton, Perceval House and two schools, Kensington and Blackheath Proprietary.

The small gathering also included a few other gentlemen from no particular club[6], and an observer from Charterhouse School, Bertram Fulke Hartshorne, which was the closest they got to getting the public schools involved. The inconvenience of a date in the middle of term and the questionable advertising were partly blamed for their absence, for the FA certainly wasn't trying to squeeze them out of things and noted the general dismay that the schools had shown so little interest. It is not clear why Charterhouse declined membership, but it is often argued there were moves afoot among the public school community to try to regulate some kind of inter-school football of their own, and Hartshorne didn't want to be seen treading on the wrong toes. Nothing ever came of those plans, but Charterhouse were still reluctant to get too involved with the FA before discussing the issue with the other schools first. All that may

---

[5] However, there are unfounded claims that the site of the first ever meeting of the FA was actually what is to this day The Freemason's Arms, which inherited the business. The claims are almost certainly wrong.

[6] *Sheffield FC: celebrating 150 years of the world's first football club* (At Heart Ltd, 2007), makes the claim that Harry Chambers was there representing Sheffield FC.

LAYING DOWN THE LAWS

be true, but I rather like Jonathan Rice's alternative explanation that the eighteen-year-old Hartshorne didn't have the guinea required for the enrolment fee.

The meeting also received a telling letter from Edwin Ash of the Richmond Club[7] explaining why they would not be attending. "As most of our men are only here preparing for the army and do not remain for any length of time in Richmond it is useless our trying to form any kind of regular club, we merely club together during the winter for the sake of playing a few matches … If the rules of the association are decided upon in time for us to use them this winter we shall no doubt adopt them whatever they may be, as it will be a great convenience to us when playing other clubs."

Richmond did indeed provide Barnes with the opposition in December 1863 for what would be the first ever match played by the Association's new rules. But despite their early interest, they found the FA's rules a bit of a let-down and gradually distanced themselves from the whole thing, preferring instead to stick to games more in keeping with the rugby theme. Indeed, it would be the selfsame Edwin Ash who would call a meeting in 1871 to get clubs together to form what would become the Rugby Football Union[8].

Not in their wildest dreams did the founders of the FA think at the time that the proceedings of those meetings in a cigar-stained upstairs room of an inn in the London of gaslights and hansom cabs was going to have an influence on cultures from Waikato to Brazzaville. But they did have a sense of purpose. Minutes were meticulously kept, and read more like the deeds for the sale of real estate than details of arguments over football rules.

One of their earliest resolutions was that "it is desirable that a football association should be formed for the purpose of settling a code of rules for the regulation of the game of football" suggesting it should be called the Football Association[9]. That bit was easy, but there were bigger issues at stake. Those present, who included advocates of both the kicking and the handling codes, now had to decide what exactly this thing called football was going to be.

---

[7] Richmond Football Club had been formed on Richmond Green, London in 1861, originally playing by Harrow's rules. Problems with pedestrians walking down a footpath through the middle of the pitch caused them to change to a different park. However, rather sadly from a historical curiosity perspective, this was probably not the result of an ancient by-law stating that the Green could only be used for cricket and bowls, as according to an anonymous Londoner in Marshall's book (1892) "it was long after the Richmond Club had migrated to its first ground in the old Deer Park that the above-referred-to prohibition of football on the Green was found to exist."

[8] Richmond would go on to become one of the south's most prominent rugby pioneers, and much later on, in 1996, they would be the first English rugby union club to go professional. However, the project proved a disaster when they lost their financial backer and were forced to merge with London Irish and start a new Richmond from the very bottom of the national amateur pyramid.

[9] To this day it is still merely The Football Association, although it only governs football in England and nowhere else. At the time it was formed, the FA did not feel the need to indicate what geographical body it was meant to be dealing with, and judging by its initial membership, probably had no grander pretension than to standardise the game for a small group of middle class clubs based in the southeast of London.

The first meeting barely touched on the nitty-gritty, and the session was adjourned until November 10. Despite much better publicity, the second meeting was hardly any better attended than the first, with the Royal Naval School being the only new recruit. The public schools were approached again, but as feared, most of them hadn't even bothered to reply to their invitations, and none of them had the slightest intention of attending. One school that at least had the decency to answer was Harrow, but their letter said "we cling to our present rules and would be sorry to alter them in any respect whatsoever", which pretty much sums up the interest the public schools were going to be showing.

So the schools were out of the picture when the Association finally turned to the delicate matter of rules. At first, it was more a question of sounding out opinions, and the minutes state that they discussed "general rules as to length of pitch, width of goals, height of goals, cross bar or tape, when a goal should be won", and a whole variety of different options for starting the game, including "rolling the ball down the centre" with none of the ideas being the kick-off as soccer knows it now. They also examined a myriad of other issues, such as "offside, touch, behind the goal-lines, hard play, hacking, mauling, holding, packs, running with the ball, fair catch, charging, settlement of disputes, boots, throwing the ball, knocking on." After this initial brainstorming session, Ebenezer Cobb Morley took it upon himself to set the different ideas in order, and vowed to be back a week later with a complete first draft of the rules.

But it was no one-man show, and the rules were not something these guys were going to take lightly. In fact, so intent were they on making sure that everything was done properly that they would meet four more times before declaring any official verdict.

Rumours of the goings-on at the FA were starting to cause ripples outside of its elite circle, and in between those meetings plenty of mail would be dropping through Ebenezer Morley's letter box offering new ideas that may have served as much to confuse the issue as to help. At the third meeting on November 17, without any new clubs attending, Morley started by reading aloud a letter from the Lincoln FC secretary, Mr Chambers, who said he would "be proud to see the day when the game of football will be played and managed upon one universal system", and enclosed a copy of their own hybrid rules based on the Marlborough, Eton and Rugby games.

Good old Charles Thring was keen to get in the act too. He had written a letter to draw attention to his *Simplest Game* and suggested the FA have a good think about merely accepting them as the new rules. Charles was keen to enrol his Uppingham School with the new association, and they would have been a hugely influential member too. However, it was the headmaster, his brother Edward, who stood in the way. Much as he was a fan of football among the kids, he felt that organising inter-school fixtures was perhaps taking things a bit too far, and that it would better to concentrate on more academic aspects of the curriculum. Fair play to him, he was running a school, not a football club!

LAYING DOWN THE LAWS

But Thring's "antidote to the Rugby game" was not what the FA was looking for. The founder members included people from all camps, and they agreed to make a concerted effort to make "provisions of the rules in force at Rugby … with a view to compromise." They weren't squeezing Rugby out. They were doing their best to create something even they would be happy with.

The key points were Rule 9 that "a player shall be entitled to *run with the ball* towards his adversaries' goal if he makes a fair catch, or catches the ball on the first bound; but in case of a fair catch, if he makes his mark he shall not run" while Rule 10 said that "if any player shall run with the ball towards his adversaries' goal, any player on the opposite side shall be at liberty to charge, hold, trip *or hack him*, or to wrest the ball from him, but no player shall be held and hacked at the same time."

Based on Morley's work and considerable amendments following much heated discussion, the meeting ended with a draft set of 23 rules to go on, which would be tidied up and collated down to 14 by Morley over the next few days, ready to be finalised at the fourth meeting a week later. That would never happen. Rules 9 and 10 were going to provoke too much controversy, and lay the foundations for the division of football into soccer and rugby.

Hands off!

Something happened that would have a dramatic effect on the FA's game plan. Assorted former public schools boys at Cambridge University had revealed their aforementioned composite game, and received glowing reviews in *The Field*. It caused quite a stir at the fourth meeting of the FA on November 24, 1863. Morley announced that he had just received a copy of the Cambridge Rules, and that they "seemed to embrace every requisite of the game with great simplicity, and before passing the laws that had been proposed it would be well they should consider every phase of the matter." A chorus of 'hear, hears' followed. These Cambridge Rules looked good. John Alcock of Forest FC pointed out that their most important benefits were that "there were several of the public schools who had taken part in the matter", they "have the support of the universities" and therefore "appear to be the most desirable code of rules for the association to adopt." He spoke sense.

With Wimbledon being the only new recruit, the FA wasn't getting much further than a seemingly interminable series of meetings at the Freemason's Tavern. Establishing contact with Cambridge was the ideal way to gain a bit of credibility and spread their message to the major academic institutions.

But despite the apparent enthusiasm, not everybody was quite so impressed, and none less so than Francis Campbell of Blackheath. The Cambridge Rules allowed neither hacking nor running in, which surely the FA had already decided were acceptable? Blackheath, fervent supporters of a tougher kind of game, were unnerved by the talk of adopting these unmanly sounding rules instead.

The meeting agreed to form a sub-committee "to enter into communication with the committee of the University, and to endeavour to induce them to modify some of the rules which appear to the association to be too lax, and liable to give rise to disputes."

Campbell wished for Alcock's bit about Cambridge being 'the code to adopt' to be changed to "appear to be worthy of consideration." Morley produced the counter-suggestion instead that they should include the words "embrace the true principles of the game with the greatest simplicity."

The minutes noted that "on a division there were eight voted for each amendment, and the President gave a casting vote in favour of Mr Morley's amendment." A motion was then proposed "that the committee to be appointed be empowered not to insist on the clause in the association's proposed rules which allow running with the ball." Perhaps they'd had one too many brandies by that point, because that clause takes some getting your head around (as it also did at the time). It seems not everyone was entirely sure whether that meant they were voting for or against running with the ball, and "several representative members of the school clubs said they had misunderstood the purport of the amendments, and therefore had not voted … the resolution had been passed without their fully understanding the matter."

Pember, no fan of the running game, seemed happy enough with the way things had turned out, brushed aside all protests, and insisted on pushing on with the agenda. But he came under pressure to allow yet another motion, this time that "the committee do insist upon hacking when running with the ball, in their communication with Cambridge." With everybody now a whole lot clearer about what they were voting for, the motion was carried by 10 votes to 9. Hacking and running with the ball were going to stay, something which neither Morley nor Pember seemed overly enthused about, and decided "that vote to all intents and purposes annulled the business of the evening."

That was only the start of it. At the fifth meeting on December 1, all hell broke loose and some of the most classic quotes in footballing history were uttered. It all started smoothly enough, with Morley updating his fellow members on his latest mail, which included a most encouraging one from Sheffield FC containing a number of suggestions based on their experiences of inter-provincial football in the North.

But the theoretically simple matter of passing the previous week's minutes was the catalyst for the daggers to finally be unsheathed. There were no photocopiers back then, so the minutes were read aloud, and here we get a taste of Morley and Pember's rather blasé view of the principles of democracy. They had a tendency to steamroll their own ideas through, and only take any notice of shows of hands when the right ones went up. Shockingly, the minutes made no mention whatsoever of the 10-9 vote to endorse running with the ball and hacking. And it was something Campbell in particular felt very strongly about indeed. Whether hacking or running with the ball were a good idea or not is one issue, but what does seem clear is that the man who held the higher moral ground in terms of democratic

LAYING DOWN THE LAWS

procedures was Mr Campbell. But democracy only works if those in power are willing to play along. Pember and Morley were not.

The hacking issue was raging in the press. It was an Old Rugbeian, of all people, who asked "why should the Blackheath men insist on hacking? It is clearly an evil … in any game played according to the new rules there seems no necessity for it, and there will always be enough casual hacking to satisfy the most bloodthirsty man that ever fought for or on Blackheath." Indeed, a third form public schoolboy wrote to *The Field* to say that "they'll find it a game that can two can play at, and I shall not be at all likely to stop and look at the law and see whether shinning is allowed … We've just been playing a match – it was awfully jolly, I got lots of kicks … The girls squeaked a bit when they saw their brothers upset, because it is in their nature to do so; but you never hear a fellow squeak even if his leg is broken." Manly words, but one wonders how awfully jolly he really would have found a broken shinbone, and whether there would really have been more squeaking than at a cheese and wine evening for the local mouse population.

What seems to have happened at the fourth meeting of the FA is that despite hacking and running being narrowly voted in a week earlier, the make-up of the December 1 meeting included far fewer supporters of a running and hacking game, maybe something Morley himself had engineered. So, it was an ideal moment to pretend the 10-9 loss at the previous meeting had never happened, and use this meeting to get hacking and running out of the game for good.

Morley observed that "hacking and running so much affects every rule, the length of the ground, the tape, the width of the goal posts, and indeed everything connected with the game that they must be looked upon as the most vital points. As far as either hacking or running is concerned, I do not mind it myself personally but … if we carry those two rules, it will be seriously detrimental to the great majority of the football clubs. I do not say that they would not play with us, but it is more than probable that they would not, and Mr Campbell himself knows well that the Blackheath clubs cannot get any three clubs in London to play with them whose members are for the most part men in business, and to whom it is of importance to take care of themselves. For my own part, I confess I think the hacking is more dreadful in name and on paper than in reality, but I object to it because I think that its being disallowed will promote the game of football … If we have hacking, no one who has arrived at the age of discretion will play at football, and it will be entirely relinquished to schoolboys."

Some pertinent remarks there from Mr Morley, and Pember agreed that hacking was "a very dangerous and painful practice, very brutal when deliberate and likely to prevent a man who had due regard for his wife and family following the game."

Such talk infuriated Campbell, who was going to respond with one of the most memorable speeches in footballing history. "Hacking is the true football game" he said. "And if you look into the Winchester records you will find that in former years men were so wounded that two of them were actually carried off the field, and they allowed two others to occupy their places

MIKE ROBERTS – THE SAME OLD GAME: CODIFICATION

and finish the game[10] ... As to not liking hacking as at present carries on, I say they had no business to draw up such a rule at Cambridge, and that it savours far more of the feelings of those who liked their pipes and grog or schnapps more than the manly game of football. I think the reason they object to hacking is because too many of the members of clubs began late in life." This was clearly a dig at Morley, who had not attended public school. "If you do away with it you will do away with all the pluck and courage of the game, and I will be bound to bring over a lot of Frenchmen who would beat you within a week's practice[11]."

His following words were the first inkling that 'rugby' supporters might break away to create their own separate code, articulated in the form of the royal 'we' no less. Stand up the real William Webb Ellis. "While you can play our game in your way we cannot play it in ours if your resolution is adopted. We have been willing to meet halfway, but ... we who are the advocates of running and hacking are in a minority. I will, however, say this, that I represent the true feeling of our club when I say that in the event of this resolution being carried out we shall not only feel it our duty to withdraw our names from the list of members of the association, but we shall call a meeting ... with the other clubs and schools to see what they think of it."

President Pember was anything but impressed by Campbell's attitude, suggesting that it was precisely his indisposition to 'meet halfway' that defied the whole ethic of the FA. "You virtually say, I will come and join your association, and will see if I can get my notions adopted, and if so go with you, but if not we will secede, and form an association for ourselves."

Campbell made one last stand. Knowing that the public schools would support him on hacking, and maybe running too, he proposed that the "meeting do adjourn until the vacation, so that the representatives of the schools ... may be able to attend." The motion was defeated, and in any case, Pember was pretty confident that "there was not the least chance of the public schools adopting the rules of any association, or, in fact, departing in any way from their own."

Campbell announced that although Blackheath "perfectly agreed with the object of the association ... at present they wished their names to be withdrawn." Charles Alcock understood their motives entirely, explaining that for such teams "the abolition of running would have meant such a radical alteration in the constitution of football, that it can hardly be a surprise to find those who had been educated in the mysteries of that particular kind of game opposed to a sweeping reform, which would have reduced them to the necessity of

---

[10] Campbell would be horrified to see football played today, when players are stretchered off the field for the most minor of injuries, or substituted just because they are feeling a bit tired.

[11] Brilliant! In that he was quite right, for the French would indeed turn out to be more than adequate soccer players. They've won the World Cup (1998) and European Championship (2000) recently, while England has had nothing major to celebrate since 1966. But the Frenchmen haven't done that badly on the rugby pitch either, with more Five/Six Nations titles than any other nation since rejoining the competition in 1947.

unlearning the lessons of their boyhood, and schooling themselves in a, to a great extent, different game." But despite the melodramatics, the Campbell somewhat surprisingly agreed to stay on as treasurer, perhaps encouraged by the promise that, in September 1864, a new meeting would be called to review the rules following the experience of the first year[12]. But running with the ball was fighting a losing battle. That meeting on December 1, 1863 was the one that ultimately confirmed the division between soccer and rugby.

As Campbell warned, not everybody went along with the FA's idea. Some continued running about with the ball in their hands and hacking each other in the shins. Blackheath would be among the founder members of the Rugby Football Union just under a decade later. But it is ironic that Campbell's defence of the 'rugby' spirit should have concentrated so much on the hacking issue, an element that was being phased out of all forms of football, for when the RFU was formed, it wouldn't allow hacking either! Amusingly, although illegal, deliberate hacking is still rife in soccer, yet these days it would be unthinkable to kick somebody in the shins in a game of rugby! It is with running with the ball where soccer and rugby's differences would ultimately lie, and perhaps if Campbell had conceded on the hacking issue and focused his attention on that instead, the story could have turned out very different.

Standard bearers

A week after the face-off with Campbell and Blackheath, on December 8, 1863, the FA met once again to pass their definitive set of rules, which had in fact already been published three days earlier in *Bell's Life in London* (see *Appendix Six*).

These were to be the rules for the first few years of FA governed soccer, but the game was still very different to the one we know now. Rule 3 says teams had to change ends after each goal, while Rule 5 says the throw-in was given to the first player to touch the ball, regardless of who had kicked it out. Throwing the ball in at right angles is an idea still maintained by rugby union today, but the FA allowed throws in any direction from 1879 because the scrimmaging and charging of players gathering in a line was getting too out of hand.

Rather curiously, they decided on goals "without any tape or bar across them." They knew about crossbars but decided not to have them. As Rule 4 tells us, goals could be scored at any height, so chipping it over the defence would have been the simple matter it still is in Australian rules. Perhaps they were just being pragmatic, and felt crossbars were more hassle

---

[12] A trial game was indeed played in Battersea shortly after the AGM that month involving teams captained by Morley and Pember, and with running with the ball allowed. It wasn't a great success, mainly because by that stage the Association had grown too attached to their invention, while most hackers and carriers had lost all interest in anything the FA was doing and were playing their own matches.

MIKE ROBERTS – THE SAME OLD GAME: CODIFICATION

than they were worth[13], while Charles Alcock claims it was a deliberate nod to the Harrow rules.

The FA imitated Cambridge's strict offside, whereby nobody could play the ball if they were in front of the point where it was kicked, and they also imported the 'rouge' idea that Cambridge had imported from Eton, and which Sheffield had also suggested, whereby if "the ball goes behind the goal line, if a player on the side to whom the goal belongs first touches the ball, one of his side shall he entitled to a free kick from the goal line at the point opposite the place where the ball shall be touched. If a player of the opposite side first touches the ball, one of his side shall be entitled to a free kick at the goal only from a point 15 yards outside the goal line, opposite the place where the ball is touched, the opposing side standing within their goal line until he has had his kick[14]."

It's fascinating to observe that this was exactly the same as rugby's idea of a try on goal (which, at that time, didn't score any points either, but merely won the right to a free kick). Rugby kept the idea, and eventually even awarded scores just for touching the ball down behind the goal, whether or not this free kick was scored (the value would increase over the years to the current value of five, last upgraded as recently as 1992). But soccer soon did away with the race to touch the ball down entirely, and simply awarded a goal kick or a corner kick depending on who touched the ball last before it went out.

And still there, as in so many early versions of early football, was the idea that you could catch the ball on the fly, make your mark, and take an unchallenged free kick, the idea revisionist Australians are now trying to say was learned from the outback tribes and was even named 'marking' after a certain tribe's word for 'catch'.

The 1863 rules had nothing specific to say about the length of the match, half-time, referees, or even the number of players in a team[15], all which were matters to be decided depending on the circumstances of the day.

The groundwork done, the FA couldn't wait to try the game out. Less than two weeks after they had been published, the rules were first tested on December 19 by Cobb Morley's

---

[13] However, the 1863 Cambridge rules had specified a bizarre goal that was 12 feet wide and 20 feet high. That was so narrow it would have been easy to defend, had it not been for the impossibility of reaching any balls flying through the top half of the goal. Scoring by kicking the ball high in the air was obviously not something to be discouraged at the time.

[14] The opening goal in the first Nottingham derby was scored in this fashion in March 1866, in which Notts Forest's WH Revis scored a touchdown, and the ensuing free kick at goal won them the game. Historians of that match aren't so clear on the result, mind, for the *Daily Guardian* clearly reports that it ended nil-nil.

[15] The FA instigated eleven-a-side when it set up the FA Cup in 1871, quite probably because that was already the number of players in a cricket team. But that was a tournament rule, and eleven-a-side didn't actually become a written law until 1923, and even today at an informal level and in practice matches, the most important thing is just to be sure that each team has equal numbers. In fact, as substitutes were not allowed until the 1950s, if ever any player was injured and unable to continue, it was the custom for many years for the opposing team to take off one of their own players as well to keep the numbers matched.

Barnes against Richmond in that failed attempt to convince the latter to join the gang. The fact that no goals were scored may have raised some concern, but *The Field* was suitably impressed, reporting that "very little difficulty was experienced on either side in playing the new rules, and the game was characterised by good temper, the rules being so simple and easy of observance that it was difficult for disputes to arise."

Forgotten fathers

Staggered by the "irradiating impact of a book, and such a small book, a book of laws put together in a pub in London by a dozen English gentleman enthusiasts in 1863," Melvyn Bragg felt compelled to make the *Rule Book of Association Football* (1863) one of his *Twelve Books that Changed the World* (2006). He ranks it right up there alongside the *King James Bible*, the *Magna Carta*, Darwin's *On the Origin of Species* and Isaac Newton's *Principia Mathematica*. Some might say that's going a little too far. Others would disagree.

Later developments of the same set of rules now govern a game that is played in every country in the world, with just one game (the 2010 World Cup Final) being watched by anything between 400 and 715 million people on television, a clever little device that would not be unveiled to the world for another 70 years. A sport that is now played in every corner of the world and to the extent that no matter how linguistically and culturally divided two children might be, the mere utterance of names like Leo Messi or Manchester United will have them grinning at each other in shared admiration for the same heroes.

But Richard Holt asks "how far should we see football not as an invention but rather as a form of cultural continuity, especially as far as the traditions of male youth are concerned? Perhaps we have taken on board too eagerly the heroic accounts of the public school men, who founded the Football Association in 1863." He does have a point. The FA did not invent football. But its formation did mark a before and after in the history of the game of soccer, but also for rugby and by extension all the world's other football codes too.

Gathered in the Freemason's Tavern were some of the most influential figures in the entire history of football, and considering the importance their decisions would have for the future of one of the biggest social and cultural phenomena in human history, it seems extraordinary that the record books have given them such short thrift. Jules Rimet, Henri Delaunay, Sam Maguire, Vince Lombardi, the Earl Grey … they all had major trophies named after them. Walter Camp in America, Tom Wills and HCA Harrison in Australia, Michael Cusack in Ireland … all are revered figures in the folklore of their own national games, while rugby fans pay homage to a schoolboy called William Webb Ellis for something he probably never did.

Yet ask a soccer fan what they know about Ebenezer Cobb Morley or Arthur Pember and the chances are that the names would mean nothing to them, and memorials in honour of what they achieved are shockingly thin on the ground.

MIKE ROBERTS – THE SAME OLD GAME: CODIFICATION

As far as Ebenezer Cobb Morley is concerned, Bryon Butler tries to set the record straight in the introduction to the *Official History of the Football Association*, observing how "on the laden shelves of the game's literature there is no more than passing reference to the man who was the 'father' of the Association. Ebenezer Cobb Morley deserves better." After all, he was secretary of the FA from its foundation through to 1867, when he became its second president. The next two secretaries (Robert Willis and Robert Graham) would also be from the Barnes club that Cobb Morley himself had founded in 1862.

So who was this Ebenezer Cobb Morley character whose fundamental role in football's history has so rarely been given the recognition it deserves? Importantly, he wasn't a member of the southern 'establishment' at all. He was a northerner, born in Hull in 1831, and it wasn't until 1858 that he moved down to London. Also unlike so many of his peers he never attended public school, which was why he was able to take a far more objective view of the respective benefits and shortcomings of the different school games and was less blinkered by the need to respect traditions in the quest for a composite set of rules.

In those days, the men who administrated the game were also the ones who played it. Morley himself would go on to score the first ever goal in a representative match, the forerunners to internationals (London v Sheffield, 1866). A fine player indeed, *Bell's Life* wrote in March 1863 that "we cannot abstain from saying that Mr Morley of Barnes and Mr C Alcock of the Forest club elicited great applause from the spectators, of whom there were a large number present." A keen sportsman, he also rowed for the London Rowing Club and founded the Barnes and Mortlake Regatta (which still exists today), he set up a small gym in the district and was also the owner of a pack of beagles and very involved in the local fox hunting scene.

Morley watched the game he had helped to build grow and grow, and was the guest of honour at the FA's Golden Jubilee dinner in 1913. He was still alive ten years later, the year 127,000 people caused mayhem at the first FA Cup Final to be played at Wembley. A year later, 1924, he died at the grand old age of 93, at 26, The Terrace in Barnes, where he had resided for sixty years. The same house where he had written the first ever draft of the official soccer rules. John Blythe Smart poignantly mused how "there is a blue plaque at 33 St George's Square, Pimilico to 'Major Walter Clopton Wingfield (1833–1912), the Father of Lawn Tennis'. Why was there no similar memorial to Ebenezer Cobb Morley?"

Thankfully there have been improvements in this respect since Blythe Smart penned those words. A blue plaque was finally placed on the wall of his long-time home by English Heritage in 2009. There are also plans for something similar in his hometown of Hull, which were originally delayed by problems tracking his childhood home. It was eventually found to be 10 Garden Square, Princess Street, but that no longer exists, so the exact location is now generating some debate. His grave in Richmond remains abandoned and derelict and persuading the FA to do something about it has proved difficult, although in June 2011 they did at least announce that "restoration of Ebenezer Cobb Morley's grave and the surrounding

LAYING DOWN THE LAWS

area has been discussed by the relevant local authorities and the FA has been advised of potential plans and possibilities for the site." Finally something is being done to honour somebody who did so much to create one of the biggest and richest cultural phenomena ever devised by humankind.

If Morley got it bad in the memorial stakes, Arthur Pember comes off worse. He was the founding president of one of the most influential sporting bodies there ever was, and the man who chaired the meetings that defined the future of soccer, and yet the football history books rarely do more than mention his name and move on. For several years Pember even suffered the wicked injustice of not even having a Wikipedia entry to his name, a travesty that has finally been corrected.

Pember was a man of little note as a sportsman, and he was representing a club that didn't even have a name and was of no particular influence. Like Morley he never attended public school, and yet despite being surrounded by some of the most prominent figures in 1860s London sport and society, he was the unlikely fellow that was elected to oversee such a crucial series of debates.

There seems to be no logical reason why Pember should have been chosen, other than he was in the right place at the right time, displaying undoubted brightness, plenty of character, and the qualities of man not shy of a challenge. Charles Alcock wrote that he was nominated because he "had taken a prominent part in the organization, as well as in the successful conduct of the inaugural meeting." But Pember also comes across as the kind of man who would throw his heart and soul into any project but quickly lose interest. Although he was still around to captain the first ever London select side against Sheffield in 1866, that was one of the last things he ever did in football, and by 1868 he had left the FA for good.

Most of what was written about the early days of football says nothing more than it has to about Arthur Pember. One gets the impression he was a man his peers would rather forget. As shown in the following chapter, under Pember's presidency, other than writing the laws of the game, the FA achieved next to nothing, and this was most probably due in no short measure to his lethargy. In 1864, rather than football, it was mountaineering that seemed to draw Pember's fascination, his ascent of Mont Blanc being his proudest achievement. On top of that, he had some pretty radical political views that would have alienated him from many of his peers, while Blythe Smart also gets the impression that in 1867 he fathered an illegitimate son while his stock broking career was going down the pan. Pember had seen enough. In 1868 he left England, and football, for good, and went off in search of a new life in America.

The football world was not at the port to see him off, and not one football historian seemed to ever care what happened to him next until Blythe Smart decided to do some impressive research, and discovered how, in New York, he carved out a career for himself as a writer for both the *New York Times* and the *New York Tribune* and later documented his experiences in a book called *The mysteries and miseries of the great metropolis, with some adventures in the country*. Participant observation was Pember's game. He had it down to a fine art, disguising himself as a commoner and getting hands on experience of the "gamblers, prison-jailers, and keepers of disreputable houses ... thieves, tramps, beggars and cub-stone singers" that populated the Big Apple. He masqueraded around the city as a beggar. He took a job as a canal boatman. He became a train driver. He joined the circus as a stable boy and ended up parading through the city dressed in knight's armour. He worked in a coal mine. He even managed to get himself thrown into the Tombs, the city's notorious prison, in order to get firsthand experience of the conditions there. He once passed himself off as a spirit medium, and even got hold of a bogus medical degree and exposed the fraudulence of the system by managing to find employment as a phoney doctor. And this was the first ever president of the Football Association!

Probably in 1884, Pember left Manhattan and went off to spend his final days in North Dakota, what was then a remote outpost of American expansion into Indian territory. It is unclear why he went there, Blythe Smart theorising that "he may have seen new opportunities ... or perhaps he went there in a spirit of adventure and discovery." He was that kind of man. He died two years later in 1886, in relative obscurity. The *New York Times* at least found space for a few lines about its former contributor, saying that "Arthur Pember, formerly a writer on the New York press, died at La Moure, Dakota, yesterday morning, aged 50 years. He was an Englishman by birth. His death was the result of kidney difficulties, supplemented by blood poisoning from a carbuncle in the lumbar region."

And that was it. The football world did not mourn his death. There was no minute's silence before the Cup Final. Back in England, there was probably nobody that knew, or even cared, that the first president of the FA was gone.

2 HISTORIC ASSOCIATIONS
The FA's game expands

Sweet FA

"History is written by the victors," writes Goldblatt, and he's quite right. The FA's own website opens its account of the events covered in the previous chapter by saying "football as we know it dates back to 1863." The typical tale of football is that from December 1863 onwards, soccer lived happily ever after and was ready to go about organising its FA Cup, followed by national leagues and international matches. That wasn't how things happened at all. The FA hadn't really achieved anything yet. They had settled rules, although truth be told, these were almost entirely copied from Cambridge University. But the real challenge was not just agreeing to a rulebook, it was getting the rest of the football community to agree to use it as well, an issue their meetings did very little to address.

The FA was going to face an uphill struggle to get itself noticed. Not one of the rather paltry gathering of clubs they got together for their first meetings would ever go on to play in the Football League. The public schools wanted nothing to do with them. In 1870, *The Graphic* was still expressing "our wish that means could be found of drawing up a set of football rules that might be used in common by all the public schools, whose respective games are now so various as to be quite unintelligible to each other. This lamentable state of things has hitherto prevented the desirable consummation of having public school matches played in London[1]." Seven years had passed, yet even on its own doorstep, the Football Association was being utterly ignored!

Rather than a tidal wave sweeping across the sporting ocean, the new FA barely raised a ripple. This would have come as no surprise to an Oxford man calling himself Non Nobis Solum who had written to the *Sporting Life* in November 1863 to warn that "I do not think the meetings in London are attended by people or clubs of sufficient influence to cause their suggestions to be generally acted upon." Barnes, Forest, No Names and their friends were no doubt "composed of very estimable individuals", but this was really the job for the public schools and universities. It may reek of snobbishness that *The Field* was so concerned in 1868 that the FA committee could "only boast of two public school men," but in that day and age, only people of a certain pedigree could get themselves heard in the right places.

The minutes of the FA's first AGM in October 1864 give a clear picture of how few real achievements it made over its first twelve months. All they reported was the sad fact that "no business was conducted." And if that sounds bad, there would not be a further entry in the book until February 1866, two years later! Writes Harvey "far from unifying football, the FA

---

[1] *Football at Rugby* in the Saturday, January 8, 1870 edition of *The Graphic*.

had left the game more divided than ever and appeared to have neither the ideas nor the appetite to change such a situation."

Perhaps their thinking had been far too wishful. Their role had been to agree to a set of rules, and they had done that admirably. From then on, they just rested on their laurels. Having published their resolutions in the papers, they came to what Morley called the "assumption that the FA had accomplished the object for which it was established," that the rest of the country would simply accept them and no further questions would be asked. Morley now realised they had been very wrong.

Their aim to create a form of football that all clubs would play had been an abject failure. They had deliberately eliminated all the hacking, running and physicality that so many footballers loved. As a result, Blackheath, Richmond and so many other influential clubs in London simply weren't interested despite the FA's worthy attempt to embrace some aspects of the rugby game.

Routledge's Handbook of Football in 1867 claimed the FA was "a band of antagonistic brethren who met together in London and attempted a compromise, but from whose efforts not much good has hitherto sprung." The FA even failed to impose its values on the few member clubs it had. The Royal Engineers may have been an important signing, but they insisted on allowing the ball to be carried in their games, and in 1866, No Names complained to the FA that arranging matches was a nightmare because only Barnes and Crystal Palace stuck to the FA rules, and even a game that year between precisely those two clubs was hampered by inconsistent interpretations of the meaning of offside.

The offside law was something clubs found particularly unsatisfactory about the FA rules, but as they were under absolutely no sworn obligation to use every single FA law verbatim, they avoided the issue by negotiating whatever rules they fancied. If two teams felt like doing away with offside, allowing a bit of hacking, or making the goals a few feet wider, the FA had absolutely no authority to stop them. Very little Association Football was played in the strictest sense. If anything, it was something better described as Association-type football.

As Charles Alcock proudly noted, not counting public school teams, there were 122 football matches played in 1866. But as Harvey notes, he omitted to mention that "the vast majority of these were not conducted under the Association's rules and the FA was almost irrelevant to the spread of football."

Other than a few timid letters to the universities, the FA aroused little interest in the provinces. Cordial correspondence was maintained with Sheffield, but no games were played, and Lincoln was its only other truly provincial member when they joined in 1863, believing that the FA's laws might help iron out some of their local problems. But they found it hard to get any local games going as folk in their area preferred something "more animated and plucky." They veered instead more towards a rugby-like game, to the extent that within a few years they had gone to the other extreme and in order to get fixtures against the new clubs emerging in Lincolnshire, they found themselves having to tone down some of the

HISTORIC ASSOCIATIONS

violence. Getting Lincoln to play by the rules proved a thankless task, and in 1866 they left the FA, with President Pember glad to see the back of a side that was "opposed to anything but hacking, throttling and other harsh practices."

The FA, whose membership was down to an all-time low of nine, had failed in its mission and looked to be on the verge of giving up entirely. In 1868, Paul Ward seemed to think they already had. "A Football Association, it may be remembered, was formed some years ago, with the avowed intention of endeavouring, out of the many sets of rules in existence at the public schools and elsewhere, to form one uniform code ... It was a praiseworthy attempt, and deserved to succeed, but unquestionably it did not ... it is certain the scheme fell though, having failed to obtain the necessary support[2]."

It would be great to take Ward along to a Premiership match today and ask if he still stood by that view. As the 1860s drew to a close, the FA was considerably more proactive. It wasn't that they did anything particularly spectacular, but compared to the absolute nothing they had done between 1863 and 1866, anything was an improvement, and the results gradually started showing. By 1868, the likes of Milford College in Wales, Leamington College in Warwickshire and Hull College in Yorkshire were on their gradually increasing membership list, and a year later, Charterhouse and Westminster both signed up for the FA. Behold, they even had a couple of public schools on their side.

What stirred the FA back into action? One reason was the injection into the FA committee of some important new blood in the form of a 28 year old called Charles William Alcock. He was one of the founder members of the Wanderers team, but until 1866 it had been his far less effective older brother John who had dealt with the administrative side of affairs. When Charles took over, it was another matter entirely, and he went on to become the most dynamic figure in 19th century soccer.

A northerner from Sunderland by birth, Alcock was secretary of the FA for a quarter of a century, from 1870 to 1895, as well as being one of the top players of his era (captaining the first ever FA Cup champions, and also the English national side in 1865). But through his involvement in the Surrey County Cricket Club, he was also instrumental in that sport, and was one of the prime movers behind the first proper international test between England and Australia in 1880. John Blythe Smart tells us that he even captained a French cricket team against Germany in Hamburg, although the details are sketchy as to how on earth that ended up happening!

Alcock's contribution to early soccer was a massive one. He had an objective mind and managed to tactfully deal with a number of delicate situations. He may have been Harrow educated, but he was from a northern 'trade' background, which helped him to appreciate both sides of the conflict between the amateur elite and the rising tide of working class professionalism. It was he who encouraged Forest FC to become the Wanderers and travel

---

[2] Paul Ward *Reminiscences of Cheltenham college, by an old Cheltonian* (1968).

around London recruiting teams to the cause. It was he who invited Yorkshiremen onto the FA committee "to further remove the barriers which prevent the accomplishment of one universal game." And it was he who instigated the first FA Cup, and also the first international with Scotland.

He also enjoyed a prolific writing career, editing bestselling football and cricket magazines and annuals right up until his death in 1907. For that reason, historians have sometimes suspected that he used his role as the great chronicler of early soccer to elevate his own status and leave a few other people out in the cold. But his writing is usually admirably honest, and Eric Midwinter argues the other way, observing that "one thinks of Charlie Chaplin or Walt Disney as the icons of cinema, or Elvis Presley as the icon of pop music, but substantial as has been the impact of these cultural phenomena, they have not, in singular form, conquered the planet as football has so decisively done. Yet soccer's progenitor is not well-known."

Had it not been for Alcock's presence, soccer may not have even made it out of the 19th century. But it was not only his arrival on the committee that pushed the FA in the right direction. There was an even more important factor, and to learn about that one, we have to go back to Sheffield.

Sheffield roars

While FA did little more than pen pushing, and not too much of that, in the north of the country, Sheffield FC had gone a long way further in standardising a soccer-like football game in South Yorkshire, and had also made playing contact, albeit not always too successfully in terms of agreeing to rules, as far afield as Nottingham, Lincoln, Leeds, Derby and Stoke. While the FA was struggling to maintain its membership in double figures, just a tiny fraction of the overall number of clubs playing some kind of football in London alone, it has been claimed Sheffield had banded together as many as 250 teams. That is clearly an exaggeration, but their membership was a lot more impressive than London's, that's for sure. Contemporary reports rarely give much indication of the attendances at matches, but reading between the lines, the only people watching games in London were a few curious passers-by, while games in Sheffield were already attracting sizeable crowds.

Some writers have tried to sell Sheffield's role in the story as a battle between north and south for supremacy in football governance. That may be an argument for football academics of the present, but it was not for the people of the time. Although the FA and Sheffield would have their occasional differences, there was little animosity in their relationship. Sheffield appreciated what the FA was doing because their own attempts to play inter-city matches were facing problems due to the established clubs in north being more inclined towards a rough-and-tumble carrying game. The two associations were united against a common 'enemy'. It was not so much a case of the differences between the Sheffield and the FA drawing them apart, as a case of the similarities drawing them together.

HISTORIC ASSOCIATIONS

On hearing about the creation of the FA in 1863, Sheffield's William Chesterman immediately put pen to paper. The letter was read aloud by Ebenezer Cobb Morley at the fifth meeting on December 1, shortly before hacking and running-in were eliminated from the London game for good: "Our committee have read with great interest the late discussions respecting the laws of football and … are anxious to enrol the club. I herewith enclose the amount of subscription … We think it very desirable a general code of laws should be established and heartily wish you success in the undertaking. I enclose a copy of our rules and perhaps you will excuse a few remarks on them. I am very much in favour of a crossbar. Without one it is sometimes very difficult for an umpire to decide and, whatever his decision, he generally displeases someone."

Chesterman would have been glad to learn that the FA outlawed running-in and hacking, for he agreed that these were "directly opposed to football, the latter especially being more like wrestling. I cannot see any science in taking a run-kick at a player at the risk of laming him for life." He also suggested "a very useful and desirable rule," which was the use of the 'rouge' system of counting 'touchdowns' in the case of a tie, which the FA did indeed experiment with for a while.

As for offside, "we have no rule at all like your No 6, but I have written in the book a rule which is always played by us." This Sheffield rule went that "any player between the opponent's goal and the goalkeeper unless he followed the ball there is offside[3] and out of play. The goalkeeper is that player in the defending side who is for the time being nearest his own goal." The FA insisted that nobody could move ahead of the ball, but Sheffield had something similar to the offside rule in soccer today[4].

Despite this contact, the two football communities remained relatively isolated. As the FA was failing to get itself noticed in its own back yard, Yorkshire was the least of its concerns for now, and they failed to realise that there was a lot they could learn from a game developed not in a London pub, but out of years of experimentation on the field. London remained aloof, but in the 1865–66 season, Sheffield even went as far as to try out the FA's no forward passing rule, but decided it made scoring far too difficult and switched back to their original method a season later.

In February 1866, the London FA opted for a major revamp of the rules. Despite outlawing hacking and carrying, the original 1863 effort had still included feeble concessions to the Rugby camp, in the vain hope that they could still win over their support, which Charles Alcock felt was the very reason why the FA was struggling to make progress. "It had become evident that to amalgamate the two classes was impossible and the Association decided to throw its lot entirely with the opponents of Rugby[5]" explained FA secretary Robert G

---

[3] This is the first known use of the term 'offside' to describe such a situation.
[4] Although forwards can have one player between themselves and the goal to make allowances for the fact that goalkeepers rarely move from between the goalposts.
[5] Robert G Graham *The early history of the Football Association* (Badminton Magazine, 1899).

MIKE ROBERTS – THE SAME OLD GAME: CODIFICATION

Graham. The new rules eliminated the free kick for a fair catch, although players could still use their hands to stop the ball on the fly. The conversion after a touchdown was also eliminated, as was the rugby-esque ban on forward passing that so many players had complained about. They actually discussed doing away with offside altogether, but eventually decided that "a player is not offside provided that he has three opponents between himself and the opponent's goal[6]," the law originally suggested by Cambridge in 1863, and which Charles Alcock felt was introduced "with a view apparently to secure the co-operation of Westminster and Charterhouse." Also, reportedly because Cobb Morley had witnessed a goal being scored 90 feet above the ground at Reigate in 1865, the FA decided a tape marking the top of the goal hadn't been such a silly idea after all[7].

How much these changes had come from the FA's own experiences, and how much they were straight copies from Sheffield's game is unclear, but Lincoln FC's secretary was convinced it was the latter. "Would it not be well for the Association to shift headquarters to Sheffield and then, under Mr Chesterman's superintendence, endeavour to frame a code of laws?" he wrote in a sarcastic letter to the FA.

Graham sent copies to clubs all around the country "and their simplicity and efficacy was met with universal approval." The law changes certainly impressed Sheffield, because just six days later, the FA received a letter requesting a challenge match between the northerners and a London team. The FA accepted, and at long last, north and south were going to put faces to names in a historic encounter played in Battersea Park, presenting the ideal chance for both sides to get together and discuss the respective merits of their games, to rouse some interest in soccer-based games in the south and also kick the wilting London FA into action. Sheffield were so keen that they were even willing for the game to be played entirely by the FA's new rules.

An influential match it was indeed, because that was the day when not only did the teams realise that they needed to agree on the standard size of the ball (a Lilywhite No 5), but it is sometimes claimed they also set precedents for the size of the pitch (120 yards by 80 yards) and playing a game over ninety minutes. The agreement was for "play to commence at 3 pm and terminate at half past 4 pm", although that may be mere coincidence, as the 90 minute rule was not the norm until the FA Cup started. Sheffield FC were a little miffed that the FA had not realised that by 'London team' they had meant they wanted to play one club not an all-star selection. They represented the social elite of Sheffield football but not necessarily the footballing elite, and got more than they bargained for from a London combination of the best players from Wanderers, Barnes, No Names Kilburn and Crusaders. That perhaps explains why the southerners cruised to a win by "two goals and four touchdowns to nil."

---

[6] Offside worked and it didn't work. Almost a decade later, in 1874, a certain WH Stacey is noted as complaining that there was always bickering about whether someone was offside or not, a situation that would, of course, be unthinkable in our modern age.

[7] It was not until 1875 that solid crossbars became a compulsory element, following Sheffield's lead.

The game was described as "a very hot one, although Sheffield were over-matched, many of the Londoners were badly knocked about."

Something that really stunned the southerners was the way the crazy Sheffield boys not only used their feet, but also their heads! Graham Williams reckons that in London "it was normal for a player to either evade the ball altogether or to protect his face by blocking the ball with his hands," but the more likely story is that the Londoners had only recently eliminated the fair catch rule, while the Sheffielders, who were more used to playing without it, had learned that if you can't catch the ball, you can always head it. It was something new to soccer, but as late as 1888, Montagu Shearman was still of the opinion that "heading savours more of clowning than of manly play, and many would be glad to see some limit placed upon the exercise."

North and south

The London v Sheffield match should have stirred the FA into taking a more hands-on approach, but a year later, the 1867 AGM was attended by just six people from a pathetic membership of ten. There was still much reminiscing about the high hopes they had all had at first, when Ebenezer Cobb Morley remembered "there was much more enthusiasm than has ever been displayed since." But now, "what was the utility of meeting again to do nothing?"

That meeting might well have been the last we heard of the FA, for there was even discussion of dissolving the association. Fortunately, one of the six, who had travelled a long way to be there, was William Chesterman, from what even Morley conceded was "the greatest stronghold of football in England," and he was there to describe the amazing progress being made in Yorkshire and to encourage the FA to do likewise.

He was no longer representing Sheffield FC, but instead the newly formed Sheffield Football Association, one of whose first projects was the organisation of soccer's first proper tournament, the Youdan Cup, run in collaboration with Tommy Youdan, the owner of the Surrey Music Hall, one of the city's top nightspots. As a major innovation, rather than ask each side to supply a match official, as was the usual practice, Youdan announced that there would be neutral umpires to make sure there was absolutely no funny business. He also declared that in the case of a tie, "the first side to score in extra time win the match," thus coming up with the 'golden goal' idea well over a century before FIFA started experimenting with it.

The widely promoted competition drew paying crowds of up to 3000 people, something extraordinary for the time. This would have raked in a reasonable amount of money for Mr Youdan, and although he probably put all of it back into the game in the form of trophies and expenses, this was perhaps the first sniff of football being a potential money-spinner. Twelve teams entered, but Sheffield FC themselves didn't bother, their interest lying more in travelling to other cities in search of new opposition than wasting their time on local fixtures with their social inferiors. The final, which Youdan himself sadly missed though illness, was

MIKE ROBERTS – THE SAME OLD GAME: CODIFICATION

between Hallam and Norfolk and ended 0-0, but the system of using rouges as a tie-breaker was still in force, and Hallam won on that count, 2-1[8].

The following year, 1868, one of Youdan's rivals, Oliver Cromwell (nothing to do with the Lord Protector, but the manager of the local Alexandra Theatre) organised his own competition, and the trophy is still on show in winning club Sheffield Wednesday's trophy cabinet.

With football booming in Sheffield, Chesterman had a lot to say at the 1867 AGM of the Football Association, and would have been disappointed to only have five people to say it to. He had three amendments to the rules to propose, none of which were accepted. The first was the use of rouges (touchdowns) as a tiebreaker, an idea which some southern clubs were already using, but the FA was having none of it and rouges would also be abandoned by Sheffield a year later and replaced by a rule the FA itself imported in 1872, whereby "when the ball is kicked out behind the goal line, a player of the opposite side to that which kicked it out shall kick it in from the nearest corner flag." The corner kick[9].

Chesterman made another unsuccessful push for London to accept Sheffield's far more lenient offside rule. Also, now London had eliminated the free kick for a fair catch, Chesterman was proposing an even more radical development whereby "holding the ball or knocking or passing it on is altogether disallowed and the side breaking this rule forfeits a free kick to the opponent's side." Sheffield wanted soccer to be limited to play with the feet only. The FA was unconvinced, but did finally agree to this in 1870 by decreeing that "no player shall carry or knock on the ball" but made an exception for this in the case of the goalkeeper, although it would still be some years before the definition of that player's role fell in line with what we know today[10].

Though Sheffield and London were collaborating, these different issues meant there were still fundamental differences between their games. Although they were keen for another London v Sheffield match, the lack of a unified code, and particularly London's much stricter

---

[8] Sheffield's game had its rouges, but it also had its rogues, for the trophy awarded to Hallam went missing some time after. It was presumed lost to history until 1997, when Hallam FC, still battling way after all these years in the Northern Counties East League, received an unexpected phone call from a Scottish antiques dealer. He had a come across a trophy and he thought it might belong to them. It did.

[9] The corner kick has not changed since then, although common sense prevailed when the goal kick was moved to where the goalkeeper usually stands, which in the modern game is the six-yard box.

[10] In 1871, Sheffield allowed anybody to handle the ball, but only within 3 yards of the goal. In 1872, the FA decided that "a player shall not throw the ball nor pass it to another except in the case of the goalkeeper, who shall be allowed to use his hands for the protection of his goal." It was generally understood that the goalkeeper could not handle the ball elsewhere on the field, and it was Sheffield that first sensed the need to drive that rule home by insisting that handling was only legal in the keeper's own half of the field. It was not until 1912 that the goalkeeper was limited to handling the ball inside his own goal area. It is also curious to note that until 1894, as the keeper could legally be shoulder barged when he held the ball, the preferred option was usually to punch it away.

HISTORIC ASSOCIATIONS

offside law, meant the idea was put on hiatus[11]. Matters were no better in 1870, when a match between Sheffield and The Wanderers had to be cancelled when the "Sheffield Association refused to play strictly Association rules." It was not until December 1871 that the fixture was finally repeated, but not without again being cast into doubt, this time because the Londoners refused to accept any compromise rules. It was only thanks to Charles Alcock that the game ever got played. Desperate for the north and south to sort out their differences for fear of the rising threat of the rugby game, he put out an unofficial side and suggested that the home side picks the rules. It turned out to be such a great success that from 1872 to 1874, the sides met three times each year, once in London using the FA's rules, once in Sheffield using the SFA's rules, and once again in Sheffield playing one half by each – although Alcock makes it clear that "the selection and management of the London team was wholly and solely in private hands, and the fixtures had in no way the official impress of the Football Association."

Those games became the highlight of the soccer year, with 6000 people at Bramall Lane in 1874 to watch Sheffield see off the southerners 2-0. Although the vast majority of the games ended with the home side winning, that may have had as much to do with home advantage and travel problems as it did with issues concerning the law book. The more the two associations played each other, the more their different rules were amalgamating into one. They were working together. At an 1874 meeting of the SFA, the minutes plainly state how they were deliberately trying to assimilate the differing rules in the north and the south, the same year that they received a letter from Charles Alcock with a series of proposals for rule changes.

In 1876, the minutes of a meeting of the SFA state that "we firmly believe there is a much greater vitality in the cutlery town's society than there is in the so-called national one of the London Association." They were probably right. The revisionist viewpoint is that almost every rule that London introduced was something they had learned from Sheffield. But Sheffield made just as many, if not more, adjustments to its own game to bring it into line with the FA's. It was not a case of one Association trying to impose its ideas on the other. The two communities liaised and developed together, and generally adopted the ideas that worked best, regardless of where they came from. Suffice to say that the traditions observed by modern soccer owe as much to Sheffield as they do to either London or Cambridge.

By the time they played their last representative match in 1876, there was little to pick between the two codes and an SFA general meeting decided it might make sense for the two associations just to merge as one. It is important to note that it was never really seen, particularly in the north, as an FA 'takeover'. It was a merger. At an 1877 meeting, the remaining bones of contention were resolved. Sheffield agreed to accept London's three-man

---

[11] But this was the year that representative county matches were instigated. Middlesex, Surrey and Kent all played matches, but perhaps due to the lack of affinity in England with people's counties, and despite the success of county cricket, the idea was never particularly popular in soccer.

offside law, and in return London accepted Sheffield's rule that throw-ins could be thrown in any direction, and not just at right angles to the touchline, and also endorsed the use of free kicks to penalise hacking, holding or worse. The two communities wouldn't always see eye-to-eye. In 1882, Charles Clegg of the SFA was understandably upset by an FA law that forbade shinguards, but even today, not everybody agrees with what the FA has to say.

Some say that rather than the meeting of the FA in 1863, it was really when they settled their differences with the SFA that soccer really became a unified code. But no matter how influential, Sheffield was just one of many cities in the provinces. It would take something else to finally turn the FA's game into the nation's game.

Up for the cup

Even today, unofficial matches will adapt some of the rules to suit the circumstances, unlimited or rolling subs being a prime example, and if there's no referee, teams might decide to do away with the offside rule. Taking off your shirt is a yellow card offence under modern soccer rules, but in the local park, a whole team might play as 'skins' in order to tell the sides apart.

All the games in the 1860s were one-off challenge matches. Neither the FA nor the SFA had any kind of authority to insist that clubs used their rules for these games, and even if they had dared to intervene, they would have been told it was none of their business. Outside of the two associations in London and Sheffield, the rest of England carried on using whatever rules they fancied. But if rather than being mere friendlies, these games counted towards some kind of competition, then common rules would no longer be a yardstick, they'd be a necessity…

Although the SFA had organised the first ever cup tournaments, these were sporadic affairs, and it didn't run any regular tournament until the SFA Challenge Cup began in 1876 in an attempt to do something about their ailing form in representative matches against teams from the south. Perhaps if the SFA had set something up earlier, it would still be the centre of the football world today, but in the end it was London and its FA Cup that would ultimately unify soccer.

It was yet another brainchild of Charles William Alcock. At the start of the 1871–72 season, he placed an advertisement in *The Sportsman* announcing "that it is desirable that a Challenge Cup should be established in connection with the Association, for which all clubs belonging to the Association should be invited to compete." He had got the idea from the Cock House Cup that he had enjoyed so much in his Harrow days, feeling something similar would be just the tonic to add some competitive spark to the soccer scene. Most importantly in the long run, it also meant that any club that wanted to get their hands on their trophy would have to play by the FA's rules.

The FA had been steadily growing up to this point, and now had 50 members, but it only managed to get fifteen teams interested in the inaugural cup. It wasn't an impressive start, but

HISTORIC ASSOCIATIONS

by October 1871, Alcock had left it a bit late, and most clubs had already sorted out their fixtures for the season, although several potential entrants were put off by the competitive element. For amateurs that merely played for the social side of things, it all sounded a little bit too serious, and they were happy enough just arranging friendlies.

The FA Challenge Cup was to be played by the time-honoured knockout system, although if games were tied, the bizarre rule was that both teams would progress to the next round. One wonders why teams didn't just pact draws to both go through! November 11, 1871 was the historic date when the first games were played in the world's oldest surviving soccer competition, and Jarvis Kenrick won the honour of scoring the very first goal in Clapham Rovers' 3-0 win over Upton Park. What followed was a haphazard affair in which three teams, Reigate Priory, Harrow Chequers and Donnington School[12] scratched before playing a match, but the sides were eventually whittled down to just the Wanderers and the Royal Engineers, who would contest the first ever FA Cup Final.

Bell's Life described it as "rather a recreation for a few public schoolboys than a truly national sport" and *The Times* didn't bother to mention it at all, but the final nevertheless attracted 2000 people to the Kensington Oval in London on March 16, 1872. Not a bad crowd for the time, especially considering the one-shilling admission charge that *Bell's Life* felt was rather excessive, although perhaps Jonathan Rice is right to be sceptical, for two thousand "seems to be the favourite estimate for all decent-sized sporting crowds in the latter part of the 19th century." In whatever case, this was nothing compared to the 20,000 who turned up to watch Eton and Harrow playing cricket at Lord's.

The Engineers, who had reached the final without conceding a goal and hadn't lost for two years, were down as 7-4 favourites, but had to play from the tenth minute with what were effectively ten men after Lieutenant Edmund Cresswell broke his collarbone. A minor problem like that was no reason for a player to leave the pitch in those pre-substitution days, and Cresswell bravely soldiered on, but was hardly in any condition to be of much use to his team. They still managed to put up a sterling fight, but eventually went down to a single goal tapped home by AH Chequer. It later transpired that Chequer was a joke name, for he was actually Morton Peto Betts, who had originally been registered as a Harrow Chequer and only switched to The Wanderers after his team pulled out of the competition. Quality … the first ever goal in an FA Cup Final was scored by a ringer!

The cup itself wasn't presented until a month later at the FA's annual dinner, and was an 18 inch embossed pot that cost £20. It came to be known as the Little Tin Idol, although its official name was, as it still is, the 'FA Challenge Cup', the original implication being that teams would compete for the right to 'challenge' the previous year's winner. So, the

---

[12] Unfortunately, I know of no evidence to prove the brilliant rumour that Donnington opted out because they had to revise for their exams. It seems more likely they withdrew after being drawn away to Queen's Park of Glasgow – a daunting opponent and a massive distance for the schoolboys to have to travel.

MIKE ROBERTS – THE SAME OLD GAME: CODIFICATION

Wanderers automatically qualified for the 1873 final, against Oxford University, but that would be the first and last time that the cup holders received a bye.

Football had a showpiece event in the FA Cup. Crowds were gathering around the field, but there was no need quite yet for terraces, and the matches were winning only a few column inches from the cricket and racing news. *The Graphic* in November 1872 found space for a few words on football at the start of the second FA season, observing how the game was "no longer confined to boys at school, but being now regularly played at the Universities and even among grey-headed men in the provinces. The game has had a revival or rather development like all other athletic sports and pastimes within the last few years. Clubs have sprung up like mushrooms, and like modern cricket clubs indulge in loud costumes and grotesque names." Football was still more of a bizarre curiosity than a part of mainstream culture.

The football community was having no more of an impact on the bigger picture than Australian rules matches played by expatriates in London today, but the FA Cup was soon the thing that mattered most to those in the select circle. Rivalries developed between the competing teams like never before, and to calm the arguments, the FA realised that they were going to have to assign neutral referees. By 1873, the men in the middle were even able to send offenders off.

Sheffield FC were so impressed by what they heard of the FA Cup that they decided to enter the third edition, that of the 1873–74 season, as did fellow northerners Shropshire Wanderers. To help them save on travel costs, these two were allowed to play each other in the first round, and after two 0-0 draws, Sheffield progressed on the toss of a coin, and then beat East London side Pilgrims 1-0 to make the quarter finals, where they went out to Clapham Rovers, 2-1. More important than the results, however, is the fact that in order to compete, Sheffield and Shropshire had no choice but to accept the FA's rules.

Other northern clubs were soon following suit. Such sides as Darwen and Notts County went into the hat for the 1877–78 FA Cup[13], the one great standardiser of the modern game. In one famous incident in 1878, the Old Etonians were drawn away to Reading, and were alarmed on arrival to learn that word had yet to reach Royal Berkshire that only the goalkeeper was now allowed to catch the ball with his hands.

It was not long before similar competitions were being run on a regional basis up and down the country. There were 2000 people watching the final of the Birmingham and District Association's cup final in 1877, the same year that Wrexham beat the Druids in the first Welsh Challenge Cup Final, while Darwen won the first Lancashire Cup in 1879. British soccer had gone cup crazy.

---

[13] These, and Reading who also entered that year, were the first teams to play in the FA Cup that would go on to become members of the Football League. Darwen, that said, dropped out in 1899 after losing eighteen games in a row, a record which still stands today (although Sunderland came mighty close to an even worse run in 2003).

Once London and Sheffield had settled their differences, the game went from strength to strength. As Montagu Shearman noted "in 1874, only one club played Association football in Birmingham. In 1876, an association of over twenty clubs was formed in the district. The rapidity with which the new class of players acquired their skill was equally remarkable. In 1877 the new Birmingham Association met London at the Oval, and were beaten by 11 goals to nil. Two years later, at the same place, Birmingham beat London by two goals to nothing."

Scotland – the final frontier

The FA Cup worked wonders for standardised soccer in England, but it also helped to establish the new code in Scotland, where folk were still going about things in their own separate way. The Scottish national soccer team arguably first took on England, captained by CW Alcock, in a 1-1 draw at The Oval, London, in March 1870. In November of the same year, they played again, England winning 1-0. The games were widely reported by the press both north and south of the border, but particularly following Scotland's defeat in the second match, there were ripples of discontent in Alba. The issue was whether these games could really be considered full internationals, for rather than drawing from any of the Scottish clubs, the Scotland team was made up of exiles living in London. In fact, it has been claimed that it was worse than that, and one player was merely picked because he had been north on a few grouse shooting expeditions, while another managed to blag his way in by pointing out that he was rather partial to a bit of Scotch Whisky.

Charles Alcock attempted to settle the issue in an article that appeared in *The Scotsman* in November 1870. "I assert that of whatever the Scotch eleven may have been composed, the right to play was *open to every Scotchman* ... and that if in the face of the invitations publicly given through the columns of leading journals of Scotland the representative eleven consisted chiefly of Anglo-Scotians ... the fault lies on the heads of the players of the north ... to call the team London Scotchmen contributes nothing. The match was, as announced, to all intents and purposes between England and Scotland[14]."

In Alcock's defence, he had indeed published a letter in *The Scotsman* in September 1870, asking to play a side made up of Scotsmen from "north of the Tweed" but had failed to get any response. But whether that meant the English therefore had the right to prefabricate a Scottish eleven out of the London expatriate community and claim to have beaten Scotland is another argument entirely.

He also wrote to the *Glasgow Herald*, suggesting a game between "the best elevens at their disposal ... in Scotland, once essentially the land of football, there should still be a spark left of the old fire." There was plenty of the old fire left, but not of the kind Alcock was proposing. The Scottish response was explained pretty clearly by *The Scotsman* in December

---

[14] Despite saying this, in his own football history, Alcock later confessed that the "eleven which represented Scotland was, in a great measure, composed of players merely of Scotch extraction, and in some cases, perhaps, of even less substantial qualifications."

of the same year, whereby "Mr Alcock's challenge to meet a Scotch eleven on the borders sounds very well and is doubtless well meant. But it may not be generally well known that Mr Alcock is a very leading supporter of what is called the 'association game' ... devotees of the 'association' rules will find no foemen worthy of their steel in Scotland." Scotland had become rugby territory, and arrangements were instead made for what would be the first ever rugby international in March 1871, which would be watched by 4000 people. It didn't look like Alcock's soccer idea was going to have too many takers up north.

As late as December 1872, the year of the first FA Cup final in London, *The Scotsman* observed that there were only about ten football clubs in the whole of the country. We know of no club in Glasgow until the Academicals were formed in 1866, a group of old boys who drew up their own set of rules, although these were clearly influenced by the rugby-like game being played in Edinburgh, and the club still exists today, playing rugby union.

With Scotland's predilection for running with the ball, few would have held out much hope for the FA's dribbling game. But there was a minority in Glasgow, and particularly the gentlemen at the local YMCA, who formed the country's oldest soccer club in July 1867, when it was announced that "tonight at half past eight o'clock a number of gentlemen met at No 3 Eglinton Terrace for the purpose of forming a football club." They deliberated different names, including The Celts, The Northern and Morayshire before settling for Queen's Park.

Struggling to find like-minded soccer clubs on the banks of the Clyde, Queens's Park pricked up their ears when they learned of the formation of the FA, and became one of its earliest non-London members in 1870. The FA probably didn't appreciate at the time just what a coup that was, and things got even more interesting when the Scots decided to enter the first ever edition of the FA Cup.

The only one of the original entrants that is still playing senior football today, Queen's Park got an easy ride to the semi finals. Donnington School twice pulled out of fixtures against them, and as there was then an odd number of teams left in the competition, and in sympathy for the considerable travelling costs, the Scotsmen were handed a bye into the semi finals, where they were drawn against The Wanderers. When Queen's Park finally did travel down to London, nobody expected much from a side that had little more experience of soccer than kickabouts on Glaswegian parks. But, as the club's minute books proudly reported "very much to the astonishment of the Londoners, who expected to carry it without much effort" the game ended 0-0, the first major 'cupset' in the tournament's history. That meant Queen's Park and The Wanderers were going to have to play a replay. The Scots decided they couldn't afford the travel costs and withdrew, but they had done enough to impress the English. Scottish soccer had potential.

International debut

Enthused by Queen's Park's fine display against the mighty Wanderers, in October later that same year of 1872, the FA noted in its pre-season minutes that "in order to further the

HISTORIC ASSOCIATIONS

interests of the Association in Scotland, it was decided that during the current season, a team should be sent to Glasgow to play a match v Scotland." His idea of 'furthering interests' is not too unlike today's summer tours of Asia by soccer clubs. The trip to Glasgow was not just a challenge, it was also a promotional exercise. The Rugby Union had been formed a year earlier, and had exploited the FA's failure to arrange a match with Scotland by organising a rugby international instead, and with resounding success. Thanks to Queen's Park, soccer now had the chance to bite back. More than a match between England and Scotland, this was a match between soccer and rugby.

November 30, 1872, was the date for one of the defining matches in soccer's history. Charles Alcock later reminisced about the experience. "Those were days primeval. To go to Glasgow – a railway journey of over 800 miles there and back – for an hour and a half's football and at one's own expense was not in a way grateful and comforting. How we did it is not as easy to say. But it was done, and plenty of fun it brought with it, even if one has to travel through the night in draughty carriages with hard seats – a severally economical style." Sadly, Alcock himself didn't get the chance to play in the inaugural game, having suffered a career-threatening injury just a fortnight earlier, but he still made the journey north to support the lads.

Finding the best Scotland team was not a very complicated affair, as they all played for Queen's Park, who supplied the entire home side. England, meanwhile, did their best to represent their whole footballing fraternity. The pick of London were joined by three players from Oxford University and one each from The Wednesday (Sheffield) and Nottingham FC. The potential of representing one's country was another carrot being dangled before players by the FA as it sought to get clubs to play by its rules.

One of the two northerners, Charles Clegg of The Wednesday, was none too impressed with the whole affair, commenting later that "none of the southern amateurs spoke to me, so I wouldn't play again." Sir Frederick Wall, commenting on Clegg's first and only appearance for England was moved to say that "the great majority of players were snobs from the south who had no use for a lawyer from Sheffield. The ball was never passed to him and nobody ever spoke to him … They did not understand him and he resented their air of superiority[15]."

The venue was a cricket pitch, of all things, the West of Scotland ground in Glasgow. Over 3500 Glaswegians (nearly twice the crowd for that year's FA Cup Final) turned out to watch, including a wee bairn called Walter Arnott, who would later go on to play full-back in the great Queen's Park team of the 1880s, and also win fourteen caps for Scotland. Arnott walked five miles to the ground, only to find that "there was no chance of getting in unless we paid at the gate. What few coppers we had among us were gone … Just when we had given up hope, we earnestly begged a cabman to accommodate us on top of his cab, and it was from that perch that I witnessed the first encounter between the two nations." And who

---

[15] Sir Frederick Wall. *50 Years of Football, 1884-1934* (reprinted 2005 by Soccer Books Limited).

wouldn't swap a lifetime of World Cup Final tickets to have been able to stand on top of that cab too?

The game ended without any score, which was hardly a great advertisement for the sport, but the general response was encouragingly positive. The *North British Daily Mail* sent a reporter who predicted that "the Association game is one which will commend itself to players who dread the harder work of the Rugby mode."

Queen's Park, thanks to their FA Cup exploits and impressive performance against the best England could offer, inspired a sudden wave of soccer playing clubs in Glasgow. Dumbarton, Third Lanark and Renton all sprung up in 1872, and Glasgow Rangers a year after that. There was to be no doubt which code the biggest city in Scotland was falling in love with. The seeds were sewn for Glasgow to become home to one of the most passionate rivalries in sport (the Celtic and Rangers Old Firm), for the city to have three of the biggest and best stadiums in the world (Hampden, Ibrox and Celtic Park), and where 149,415 people, the largest crowd ever for a European football match, would gather to watch Scotland play England in 1937.

Scotland formed its own national association in 1873, mirroring the FA in London[16] and soon the central belt of Scotland probably had a greater concentration of soccer clubs than anywhere else in the world. When the third edition of the Scottish FA Cup began in 1875, it had 49 entrants compared to just 32 for the English one. Soccer had even started making inroads into Edinburgh when Heart of Midlothian and Hibernian were formed in 1874 and 1875 respectively, although that city would remain a rugby stronghold, and to a certain extent, that still holds true today.

Despite the newer clubs, Queen's Park still managed to win ten of the first twenty Scottish FA Cups, and to this day only Rangers and Celtic have more titles. In the 1880s, they even made it to the English FA Cup Final on two occasions, 1884 and 1885, losing both times to Blackburn Rovers[17]. No fewer than seven Scottish clubs entered the 1886–87 FA Cup, with a new force in that country, Glasgow Rangers, going all the way to the semi final, but their involvement was coming to an end. English clubs were turning professional and were infuriating the Scottish clubs by plundering all their talent, and when one of the worst culprits, Preston North End, beat Queen's Park 3-0 at Hampden, the 15,000 strong crowd invaded the pitch, and the focus of their fury, Preston's Edinburgh born Jimmy Ross, had to escape the ground in disguise. That summer, any hope of more regular competition between English and Scottish clubs came to an end when the Scottish FA banned its clubs from

---

[16] This set a trend, and Ireland and Wales soon formed their associations too, the knock on effect of which was that the FA would never govern football throughout the United Kingdom, but only in England. And that paved the way for something that never ceases to irk the Catalans, Corsicans and other stateless nations: the division of Great Britain and Ireland (later just Northern Ireland) into four separate associations, and therefore four national teams.

[17] For the record, the only non-English side to ever win the English FA Cup was Cardiff City of Wales in 1927, who almost repeated the feat in 2007, losing the final to Portsmouth.

relations with "any other national association." It is somewhat ironic that nowadays it is Scottish clubs, and particularly the Old Firm, that have often voiced their desire to compete in English competitions, for had it not been for that decision, the Football League, formed a year later, would quite probably have invited Scottish involvement from the outset.

Instead, Scotland formed its own separate League in 1890, which is when Queen's Park's decline began. Being a 'gentleman's club', they vehemently opposed an idea they felt would be detrimental to the interests of smaller clubs and would encourage the evils of professionalism. They didn't join until 1900, by which time Scotland had inevitably given into the professionals too, and by then Queen's Park's amateur ethos meant they were destined to struggle. They're still in the Scottish League today, faithfully sticking by their motto *Ludere Causa Ludendi* (to play for the sake of playing), with a players' wage bill of zero, although they have lifted the ban on former professionals. Scottish soccer has a lot to thank them for.

Combined forces

It proved a lot easier for the FA to agree with the Scots on a unified set of rules than it had done with Sheffield. But that was no surprise, because the Scots had imported most of the rules from England in the first place. The only really contentious issue was the throw-in. The FA still allowed players to throw the ball however they liked, but in 1880 the Scots decided that the one-handed underarm throw meant players could hurl the ball such ridiculous distances that they invented the modern-day two-handed throw instead. This led to heated disputes when the countries next faced each other at international level, but the English eventually came round to the Scottish way of thinking in 1882.

The throw-in was one contribution Scotland made to modern soccer, but legends abound from that first ever international in 1872, and the most popular one is that the English were stunned to see that their northern neighbours were passing the ball to each other. England played a 1-2-7 system that we can only dream could exist today, with players simply getting the ball and dribbling it as far up the field as they could without being tackled, or just hoofing it upfield in a primitive kick-and-rush game. Meanwhile the Scots played a hideously defensive 2-2-6, passed the ball amongst themselves, and revolutionised the game as people knew it.

Only a brave man would argue a point like that with a Scot, but it is not clear what real evidence there is of this. The whole story seems to come from interpretations of reports like that which appeared two days later in *The Scotsman*, whereby "during the first half of the game the English team did not work so well together, but in the second half they left nothing to be desired in this respect. The Scotch team, on the other hand, though not comprising so many brilliant players, worked from first to last well together, through knowing each other's play."

MIKE ROBERTS – THE SAME OLD GAME: CODIFICATION

If the Scots played more as a unit it was probably because they were all regular team-mates for Queen's Park, while the English were from nine different clubs that didn't even share the same rulebook. However, Queen's Park had played in London half a year earlier, where the Scottish flair for the passing game was already recognised. "They dribble little and usually convey the ball by a series of long kicks, combined with a judicious plan of passing on," wrote *The Field* after witnessing their famous draw with The Wanderers.

One reason for this was that Queen's Park was one of the first clubs to systematically train, and in local games they preferred to use their own *Rules of the Field* written in 1867, which used the same two-man offside law that soccer has today, as opposed to the more restrictive three-man law the FA used from 1866.

Despite their apparently superior passing game, the Scots could only draw with their English visitors, and lost 4-2 a year later at the Oval. But from 1874 to 1886, England beat Scotland just once in fourteen attempts, and in 1882, Charles Alcock wrote that "the disinclination to pass at the proper time settled England's chances as effectively as it has done from the very first of these international contests."

Does this mean Scotland invented the combination game? Not necessarily, for we could ask why Clegg was so upset that his team-mates didn't pass to him if English footballers weren't expected to do so anyway? Clegg himself had played for Sheffield against Nottingham in January 1872 where "the only goal scored in the match was obtained by Sheffield, owing to a good run up the field by Steel, who passed if judiciously to Matthews, and the latter, by a good straight kick, landed it through the goal out of reach of the custodian."

Clegg himself later wrote that 'the combination game' was invented by the Royal Engineers, and considering his adversity to southerners it is unlikely he would say that without good reason to feel it was true. Various pre-1872 descriptions of the Engineers in *Bell's Life* speak of how they "worked well together" and "had learned the secret of football success – backing up." In one game, "Lieut Mitchell made a fine run down the left, passing the ball to Lieu Rich" and in another "Lieut Creswell … kicked it into the middle to another of his side." Sir Frederick Wall[18], the secretary of the FA from 1895 to 1934, was present at the 1872 Scotland match and spoke highly of the Scottish passing game, but nevertheless also supports the Royal Engineers claim.

Other sources have accredited Lancashire and especially Blackburn Olympic, purportedly the architects of the long ball, with its invention. Or did it all start with the 'passing on' that was so much the trademark of the Shropshire Wanderers? Or should we believe others who in 1883 believed that the Cambridge University XI had invented a whole new brand of football, playing as a team rather than eleven individuals?

There is probably no definite answer; it would have simply been a natural progression. In the early days, giving up and passing the ball to somebody else was considered the ultimate

---

[18] Sir Frederick Wall. *50 Years of Football, 1884-1934* (reprinted 2005 by Soccer Books Limited).

HISTORIC ASSOCIATIONS

cop-out, a sign of cowardice and failure, especially before 1866, when passing the ball to somebody in front of you wasn't even allowed.

The relaxing of the offside rule opened the game up to tactical changes and the gradual perfection of the passing game, to the extent that CW Alcock said in 1874 that "nothing succeeds better than what I may call a combination game" thus coining the vogue phrase in 1870s soccer. Then again, a year later, the same man was writing in his *Football Annual* that dribbling was "the most effective kind of play" so perhaps we shouldn't read too deeply into Alcock's meandering musings either.

So, perhaps we'll leave this argument with the words spoken in 1877 by England international and staunch gentleman amateur Alfred Lyttelton, who was no fan of this combination tomfoolery. When criticised by Sheffielder Billy Mosforth for not passing the ball against Scotland, he retorted that "I am merely playing for my own pleasure, Sir!" Quality response. What idiot decided that football had to be a team game?

All the world's a stage

Soccer was a far cry from a game that just seventy years earlier had been described by Joseph Strutt as one that "seems to have fallen into disrepute, and is but little practised." The *Penny Illustrated Paper*, on December 14, 1861, introduced an article on a game between Rugby and Marlborough by saying that "this fine old English sport is still preserved in many places" suggesting it was a dying breed. Just a decade later, following the first FA Cup final in 1872, Charles Alcock was moved to say that "what has been the recreation of a few is now becoming the pursuit of thousands, an athletic exercise carried on under a strict system and in many cases by an enforced term of training, almost magnified into a profession."

From the mid 1870s, soccer boomed. A crowd of 2000 was an outstanding achievement in the 1860s, but in the 1870s, attendances of 10,000 or more were commonplace. In 1876, there were 20,000 watching Scotland play Wales. Soccer was reaching adulthood, yet it was still wasn't quite the game we know today. It was certainly more physical. Royal Engineers half-back Lieutenant Ruck, admitted, for example, that many of his side's goals were scored "by hurtling goalkeepers through their own goals all ends up."

The four national FAs of England, Scotland, Ireland and Wales did have a habit of making small but unilateral modifications to the rules, which presented problems whenever they met for internationals. In 1886, they decided to resolve the issue by forming the International Football Association Board, with one voting representative from each country, and agreeing that "decisions of this board shall be at once binding on all the associations, and no alterations in the laws of the game made by any association shall be valid until accepted by this board[19]."

---

[19] This is the same body that writes the rules of soccer today, although since 1913, it has also admitted representatives from the world governing body, the *Fédération Internationale de Football Association* (FIFA,

Among its resolutions at its first meeting in 1886, the IFAB declared that the goalkeeper would only be able to handle the ball in his own half of the pitch (and wouldn't be limited to handling the ball in his own area until 1912). Deliberate handballs by other players on the goal-line were causing headaches, and in 1891, the Irish FA presented a solution that was unanimously accepted. And so it was that, in September of that year, the first penalty on record was scored by John Heath of Wolves in a 5-0 win over Accrington.

There were further changes to come, but surprisingly few. Goal nets were introduced in 1892, having been tested for the first time a year earlier in the annual North v South match. There were no 'proper' referees as we know them today until 1898. Until then they were merely judges that stood on the sidelines and were only called upon if a team made an appeal. In 1925, the offside rule was amended from a player receiving the ball needing to have three to the current two players in front of them, substitutes were first permitted in 1958 (albeit only if a player was genuinely injured), and red and yellow cards came into force at the 1970 World Cup. Apart from petty things like taking off your shirt being a bookable offence and the ban on tackling from behind that comes in at every World Cup without referees taking the blindest bit of notice, perhaps the only major change of the last forty years came about when goalkeepers were forbidden from handling back-passes in 1992.

By the turn of the century, soccer was largely the same game we know today, and we can leave its story there. We all know how it went on to conquer the world, with British travellers teaching the locals the game wherever they went, whereupon indigenous sporting traditions would be dwarfed, even doomed, by this new global obsession. How the magic of soccer and the magic of Christmas would become one as German and British soldiers enjoyed moments of humanitarian harmony during the First World War. How Hungary's emphatic win at Wembley in 1953 showed the English that they were no longer the all-conquering force they were. How the game would even be the catalyst for a war between Honduras and El Salvador. How Diego Maradona could claim to have scored with the Hand of God and for Argentinians to take him literally. How Cameroon's defeat of Argentina at Italia '90 finally heralded the realisation of Africa's potential. How Hillsborough and Heysel showed just how low football could go. How England losing to Germany for the umpteenth time can be seen as justifiable reason to go and trash the nearest Volkswagen. How the break-up of Yugoslavia showed just what a powerful propaganda tool soccer can be. How the average European would struggle to name a single historical Brazilian figure, but could recite the names of dozens of its soccer players. How, like the English pioneers that went on that mission to Glasgow to face Queen's Park, the World Cup has now become a quadrennial

---

formed in 1904). The current system is the same one agreed to in 1958, whereby representatives of the four 'home nations' are joined by four from FIFA. The voting system ensures that the British delegates are unable to modify any rules without the support of at least one FIFA member, but also that if the British associations are united any issue, FIFA is powerless to overrule them.

HISTORIC ASSOCIATIONS

trade show that in 2022 will be stopping off in the tiny Emirate of Qatar. How a top player can earn enough money from the game in a month to buy the kind of house most of us could only ever dream of, or feed a starving village in the third world for years. And how we still adore them for it, and however much they charge for pay-per-view, whatever the touts are asking for tickets, never mind the exorbitant prices of replica shirts, we still fork out the cash. Mr Strutt may have been right, for in many ways the game of football has "fallen into disrepute" but two hundred years on and counting, it is anything but "little practised."

By the end of the 1870s, the 'Association' game was known all around the country and in all walks of society. The fact a handful of elite education centres still insisted on using their own rules was no longer of any particular relevance. But no matter how widespread soccer became, its conquest was never complete. Not even by a long shot did all the football clubs in the country accept this new brand of football, and just as the ball-kickers slowly gathered under the wing of one governing body, the ball-carriers were soon gathering under another.

This split in football was not really the result of the formation of the FA in 1863. The division of football into separate camps was already evident before then, and the FA's objective was not to create a breakaway sport, but to create a composite code to stop the football community from being divided. It originally sought to create a set of rules that everybody would be comfortable with, but appeasing the Rugby supporters proved too difficult, despite some noble compromises on the FA's part in 1863 that were eventually abandoned in 1866.

Soccer spread, but found itself competing for resources and territory with what it had tried to make its ally, but eventually became its rival. Hopes of the two codes ever combining as one gradually faded, and with their futures uncertain, the two football communities would instead endure an often uncomfortable coexistence. It is to rugby and its oval ball that we turn to next.

3 SCRUM ON DOWN
Rugby heads towards union

Back to school

By the 1850s, Rugby School's game was seeping into other schools as part of the package of revolutionary ideas that were the legacy of Thomas Arnold's headmastership. Many of his former pupils and members of staff were appointed to senior positions at other schools. Arnold's liege, George Cotton, became headmaster of Marlborough in 1852 and, unimpressed by the uncontrolled way the kids were running wild in their free time, he taught them to play football by the Rugby rules. Thomas William Jex-Blake made himself a handy sideline selling copies of the tiny pocket-sized football rules booklet as a pupil at Rugby, and in adult life was principal at Cheltenham. He introduced the game, and after watching six matches proudly said that "nothing I have seen this term has given me greater pleasure. If there were more in the playground there would be less of that lounging about in the town, that dawdling dandyism that is so contemptible, and no more haunting of billiard rooms and places of still worse repute."

Arthur Haslam, the headmaster at Ripon was a former captain and head boy at Rugby and in 1884 gave a stirring speech on the benefits of *mens sana in copore sano*[1]. A later Archbishop of Canterbury, Edward White Benton, left Rugby in 1858 to become the first head of Wellington College, where he immediately introduced the game[2]. Over at Haileybury in Berkshire, an Old Rugbeian called Arthur Gray Butler, an accomplished sportsman in his day with a peculiar penchant for jumping across rivers, is said to have introduced rugby to the school in 1862[3]. Butler would get so excited by the boy's matches that he couldn't resist the temptation to pile in with them, for "an impatient movement would ensue, and cap and gown would be given to the nearest small boy, coat and waistcoat hastily placed on one of the long benches which stood against the wall of the terrace, and a figure presenting to view an immaculate shirt and a pair of red braces would be seen dashing into the fray, now emerging triumphant with the ball held aloft and at another moment bowled over in the mud like the humblest forward, eventually retiring from the fight with great detriment to his clothes but none to his dignity[4]."

---

[1] A healthy mind in a healthy body.

[2] Rugby going to Wellington was particularly important as it had such strong connections with the military, hence one of the main reasons for the popularity of the handling code in the armed forces. Wellington would be one of just two schools to attend the first ever meeting of the RFU.

[3] This story is inconsistent with the claim by a pupil that transferred from Rugby to Haileybury in the 1830s, Alexander J Arbuthnot (*Memories of Rugby and India* (1910)), who said that "I played football a good deal at Haileybury, and helped to introduce Rugby rules." That was thirty years before Butler set foot in the place.

[4] Lionel Sumner Milford *Haileybury College, past and present* (TF Unwin, 1909).

There was similar mixing with the boys at Bromsgrove, where another Old Rugbeian principal, John Collis, was described as "a plump man and was fond of catching the ball on the bounce. But he never ran. He stood stock with the ball in his arms, and the players swarmed around him like bees."

At Clifton "the games of the School began in the Winter Term of 1862 with football, organised on the Rugby system … with the help of Mr Dakyns … a very well-known 'Cap' of his day at Rugby[5]." A former Shrewsbury football captain and later master at Rugby, Alexander William Potts, was instrumental in taking the game to Scotland via Fettes College, where he was the first headmaster from 1870 to 1889. St Paul's and King Edward's in Birmingham, and both the public schools in Bedford all had both former Rugby staff and rugby-like football traditions by at least the 1860s. The Rugby game, or games at least like it, was getting everywhere. Manchester, Worcester, Radley and Bristol all preferred carrying to kicking the ball.

Very few schools didn't see the potential for including games in the curriculum. Cricket in the summer, football in the winter. It was a winning formula, and without traditions of their own, the newer independent schools almost invariably turned to the Rugby game for their inspiration. The advantages were manifold. It's a game that is often described as the perfect team sport. The nature of the different positions means that there is a role for everybody, from the bulky forwards to the fleet-footed backs[6]. And this had been tried and tested at some of the finest academic establishments in the land. It had rules they could refer to and there were enough complexities to make it a thinking man's game. It was a manly way to keep the kids occupied and burning up all that excess energy that Muscular Christianity was so concerned about getting rid of.

The Football Association's sanitised version of the game was fairly universally shunned by the schools. It wasn't the kind of game they wanted. Graham Williams explains how, at least in a British context, this has never really changed. "For many of today's football supporters their first encounter with Rugby came at secondary school" he writes. "It was there that some well-meaning teacher explained that this new and rather alien game would replace soccer for a term. Not really understanding why this should be the case, many young soccer fans had to endure a strange game in order that their 'character' might be built! Enjoyment had nothing to do with it, that was the preserve of soccer[7]."

---

[5] EM Oakeley *Clifton College annals and register: 1860-1897* (1897).

[6] That is as long as they are reasonably tough and willing to put up with some hard-hitting tackling, which affects players in every position. It doesn't take too much of a difference in size between two opposing rugby players to make it a physical impossibility for the smaller adversary to have even the remotest hope of halting the charge of a more powerful other. In soccer, even the puniest of defenders might just get a foot to the ball to even stop Cristiano Ronaldo from getting by.

[7] That's being a little harsh on rugby, a game plenty of children get immense pleasure out of. However, it's true that at many British schools, soccer still isn't even part of the physical education curriculum or has only been

Ruck and roll

Rugby School, as we saw in the previous volume, had drafted an early set of written rules in 1845. But those were really no more than a clarification of some of the more contentious issues, and were produced solely for the benefit of the boys playing the game at that school. But the same game was now being exported to schools up and down the country, despite it having no formal structure and no more of a 'governing body' than a bunch of acne-riddled schoolkids.

Outsiders started turning to Rugby School to clear up the finer points of the rules, and it became clear that it would help to have the them properly documented, which had never happened before mainly because much as football was endorsed at Rugby, there had been next to no adult involvement. This changed under the headmastership from 1857-69 of Dr Frederick Temple, a future Archbishop of Canterbury. Famously, a visitor who was somewhat taken aback by the violent game enquired whether Temple had ever stopped it. "Never, short of manslaughter" was the reply. Nevertheless, Temple did set a shock precedent. He was the first member of staff to dare to insist on changing one of the rules.

It was the way the fags had to stand in goal that he objected to, something he rightly considered a complete waste of the junior pupils' time. The school now had seven playing fields and juniors played 'little-side' games, so there was no need for them to do their apprenticeship standing about watching the older boys. But it wasn't so much the no-fags rule that upset the traditionalists as the fact that a teacher had interfered with the boys' creation.

Then in 1862, a former pupil, Francis Elliot Kitchener, returned to Rugby to work as a mathematics tutor after graduating from Cambridge, which is probably where he became aware of the need for the Rugby rules to be cleared up for the benefit of outsiders. This was precisely the period that the debate was raging in the papers about the confused state of football, and which would lead to the formation of the Football Association in 1863. In order to defend its case, Rugby was going to need to present a decent set of rules.

On the cover of a surviving copy of the result of their work, Kitchener's own writing called it the "first attempt to codify the customs." It wasn't any such thing, of course, but the 1862 version was clearly aimed at a wider audience, for although it still included such stipulations as "the walk in front of the Headmaster's House, leading to the Barby Road is in goal", a note explicitly indicates that these "are, of course, intended solely for Rugbeians." The 1862 rulesmakers were aware that they were no longer writing only for the benefit of their own peers. "Football is played on a large level field or piece of ground" they helpfully say, which could have been any piece of ground, and not just the one at Rugby School.

---

introduced fairly recently while rugby and cricket form part of a long tradition. Yet at break time, when the kids get to choose what games they play, soccer is omnipresent, and rugby barely gets a look in.

SCRUM ON DOWN

Though carrying was allowed, it was "not lawful to take the ball off the ground." It could only be carried if it was caught on the fly or bound. Once it was rolling or still, it could only be kicked. Scoring worked in much the same way as it did in *Tom Brown's Schooldays*, either by "dropping a goal or placing a goal: the former in the course of the game … the latter only after a touch down in goal. The touch down is accomplished in the following manner: any player who catches the ball, either fair or on the bound … may run with it if he can, till he gets behind the line of the goal of the opposite side, where he will touch it down as near as he can to the goal." What follows is a description of the ritual of the ball being kicked back into play from the point where the touchdown was made, and hopefully caught by one of the same team, who would place it for the nominated kicker to attempt to get the ball over the bar. Excellently "no player may stand on the goal bar to interrupt it going over."

If the ball went into touch, the procedure was exactly the same as that which was widely used in soccer at the time, whereby "the first player who touched it down, takes it and walks with it to the touch line, and throws it out at right angles to the line of touch." But there was also the weird alternative whereby, if he preferred, the player "bounds it outside the line of touch (i.e. in the field) and catches it again, and runs with it, or drop-kicks it himself."

As for tackling, it was no longer limited to just holding one arm as it was in 1845, although it's comforting to know that they outlawed "attempts to throttle, or strangle, which are totally opposed to all the principles of the game." The rules also say that "when anybody has the ball in his hands, any of the opposite side may maul him. If he cannot get free, or give the ball to some other of his side (not in front of him) who can run with it, he cries 'have it down'."

The 1862 rules are not really all that different from the 1845 originals. Much of the wording is exactly the same, but several useful clarifications have been thrown in. For example, they not only describe what a knock-on is, but explain what to do about it, namely that it "is altogether disallowed under any circumstances." But despite Kitchener's good intentions, the rules were still pretty ambiguous, and there were still plenty of complaints that anybody who didn't already have a decent working knowledge of the basics of the game found them mightily hard to comprehend, and schools and athletics clubs that didn't happen to have a former Rugby pupil handy continued to misinterpret them in all kinds of ways.

One thing the rules failed was get across the 'spirit' in which the game was played. For instance, passing the ball to team-mates was part of the game, but this was really only done in desperation, as was often the case with early soccer players. An article written by an unknown senior pupil in an 1859 edition of the *New Rugbeian* criticised "the fiddle-faddle humbug of the present day" and reminisced about the games played just two years earlier. Either the game was developing at a frenetic rate or our friend was getting more than a bit overexcited in his nostalgia for a time when "there was none of that underhand shuffling play with the ball then that there is now; no passing it along from one to the other; it was all manly and straightforward[8]."

The rules also give us an idea of the tactics of the game, and suggest the modern-day positions were slowly coming into existence. "Generally, three or four of the swiftest runners, and most expert at dropping, keep some distance behind the rest, and are called back players; some too who are clever at dodging play half-back." Our anonymous whinger in the 1859 *New Rugbeian* took objection to that too. He despaired that "nor did you see any of that shirking outside scrummages that is always going on nowadays. No one thought you worth your salt if you weren't the colour of mother earth from head to toe ten minutes after the match had begun." However, we should take this writer with a pinch of salt, because Thomas Hughes' description of the game some two decades earlier also mentioned the backs that never went anywhere near the scrummage.

Scrummages were nothing like they are today. After being mauled and yelling 'have it down' the rules say that a player "then puts [the ball] down and kicks it, and all who have closed around him ... begin kicking at the ball, and often encounter each other's shins." Our 'it wasn't like that in my day' pal delighted in the anarchy, which was "the sort of thing to make your hair stand on end. Fellows did not care a fig for the ball then except inasmuch as it gave them a decent pretext for hacking." He remembers one game in which "we'd been hacking for five minutes already, and hadn't had half enough, in fact, the swells had only just begun to warm to their work, when a bystander (confound his impudence!) kindly informed us that the ball was waiting our convenience on top of the island ... My maxim is hack the ball on when you see it near you, and when you don't, why then hack the fellow next to you." Public schools took mob football and 'refined' it into the modern game? Yeah, right...

Former Blackheath schoolboy and later RFU president Harry Garnett[9] remembered how "boots were made specially with an extra sole piece at the toe, pointed like a ship's ram, and hardened" in order to be able to hack "with the utmost violence." Once he'd seen an opponent try to defy the hackers by having the audacity to wear shin guards, and stubbornly informed his rival that "if you don't take that off, I'll hack it off." In the same article, Reverend Dykes, who had played rugby at Durham School, claimed the worst hack he ever

---

[8] Cecil Hawkins in *The Captain* (March, 1913) believed it was George Cotton of Marlborough's misinterpretation of one of the Rugby rules that led to the modern passing game. Law 26 of the 1871 rules stated that "it is lawful for any player who has the ball to throw it back towards his own goal, or to pass it back to any player of his own side who is at the time behind him." This led to players throwing the ball back to other team mates, but the argument is that the original rules only allowed the ball to be handed to another player, but not thrown. I doubt this however, because Cotton left Marlborough for India in 1858, thirteen years before the RFU rules were written, and this quote shows that the passing game was around long before the RFU wrote that ambiguous law.
[9] Speaking to the *Yorkshire Evening Post* in 1901.

received was from a future Bishop of Calcutta[10]. According to him, the ideal way to prepare for games was "solemnly hammering my shins with a poker to make them hard." The lengths people will go to.

A brilliant description of the art of hacking is provided by Arthur Pearson, reminiscing about playing the game at Rugby in the 1860s. He claimed it "was not necessarily a violent proceeding[11]" and he could "only recollect during my five years at Rugby one broken leg, one broken collar-bone, and the case of one boy who received injuries to his back, from which, however, he completely recovered", which would be no better or worse than a casualty count at a school these days. He actually describes hacking to be more of a delicate art of tripping than a form of brutal kicking, and he doesn't remember it being quite as widespread as some might have had us think. That said, Pearson does feel "it was an unnecessary adjunct to the game and was very wisely done away with" and made inter-schools matches impossible because "it was feared that the intense excitement of such matches might lead to hacking of a serious character." Even if it was "admissible among boys, hacking was eminently unsuitable for men in professions or business who might as a result have to limp to their offices on a Monday morning!"

Rugby headmaster Frederick Temple agreed. In a letter to his son, he said the game was "for boys and not men. The violence of it suits the one and does not suit the other." Having already shaken the establishment by banning the fagging system in football, he later turned his attention to the hacking. The 'hacking in', which was tripping players up as they ran with the ball, now that wasn't too bad, but it was the hideous hacking in the scrummage he didn't like, and he decided it was high time to stamp out the stamping.

Identity crisis?

As football gained in popularity not just as a school activity, but also an adult pastime, Rugby School's game was among the different codes that the Football Association sought to amalgamate into a hybrid game at its 1863 meetings. Despite being hotly defended in some quarters, hacking people over as they ran with the ball was not to be part of the code they decided on. Would that mean rugby was doomed?

No, it wouldn't. As we saw in the previous chapter, other than for a handful of clubs in London, and another pocket of teams based around Sheffield, it was not until the 1870s that the 'Association' game had any sizeable impact on football as it was played around the country as a whole.

Apart from Queen's Park in Glasgow, handling ruled the roost in Scotland. Trinity College, whose rugby team was formed in 1854, had made running with the ball the way forward in

---

[10] No Bishop of Calcutta had a Durham connection, but maybe Dykes had once played against the aforementioned George Cotton, who was a master at Rugby from 1836 to 1852, before becoming headmaster of Marlborough and later Bishop of Calcutta.

[11] In a centenary article in *Rugby Football* (November 3, 1923).

Dublin. Even in the London area, where the FA was based and presumably most influential, there were (according to Adrian Harvey's figures) 39 teams playing rugby-like games in comparison to 30 playing soccer-like games in 1870. As Montagu Shearman notes, "between 1863 and 1870 the Rugby Union game was making decidedly more way in the country than the Association game." The northwest, which had a strong Old Rugbeian tradition, had early clubs in Manchester, Liverpool and Sale. Durham School was no doubt the reason for the growth of rugby in the northeast[12] which led to the Cumberland and Westmoreland County Union becoming the second oldest after Yorkshire, where another pocket of rugby clubs had clustered primarily in Hull, Leeds, Bradford, Huddersfield and York. The southwest has always been strong Rugby country, where the likes of Bath, Gloucester, Bristol and Exeter are all strong rugby cities to this day, no doubt influenced in the old days by schools like Cheltenham, Clifton and Sherborne.

And of course there is South Wales. It has never really been made clear how rugby reached Wales, but the first clues are the games in the 1850s played at St David's College, Lampeter and Llandovery College, where former pupils from English schools had probably taken the game. But it was also strikingly similar to the traditional folk game of *cnapan*, which was still around in the 19th century, where it was once described at Llanwennog near Lampeter. Perhaps as a result of that, and in stark contrast to most of England, where Welsh rugby football really took off was among the working classes, and especially the mining community. Social reforms meant they now had the unthinkable luxury of a six and a half day week, so there was half a day left for playing games, and for huge numbers of men, a game of rugby on their one afternoon off fitted the bill. In doing so, they were sowing the seeds for one of the most passionate cradles for rugby talent in the world. Neath RFC is said to be the oldest club, formed in 1871, and Swansea, Llanelli, Newport and Cardiff all formed within the next two or three years.

It is admittedly somewhat retrospective to call any of these 'rugby clubs', as there was still no Rugby Union with a standardised code. The view that these clubs were all playing the same game as that used at Rugby School is probably wrong. Teams that preferred more of a running and hacking game, what we should call rugby-like rather than rugby *per se*, were under no obligation to get their heads around Rugby School's incomprehensible set of laws, and usually made up their own.

Rules disputes among 'rugby' clubs were as rife as they were among 'soccer' clubs, because they were essentially one and the same thing. As Adrian Harvey succinctly puts it, in the mid 1860s, "the association and rugby games might be better viewed as extreme points of a continuum rather than distinct and separate entities." The FA's Charles Alcock spoke of the

---

[12] When the Durham cricketers decided to form a rugby section, the public school had no qualms about taking them on, and it's nice to see the common sense at last on the shin-breaking issue when a report of the game says "tripping and hacking were properly forbidden, both are dangerous and there is no occasion to make what should be sport ... more risky than it is."

SCRUM ON DOWN

dribblers as 'guelphs' and the runners and hackers as 'ghibelines'. Just what he meant by those words is unclear, perhaps he was drunk, but the rugby-soccer distinction was not yet crystal clear. Games classed as 'rugby' often looked more like soccer. Arthur G Guillemard[13] said for example that "I can well remember watching the matches played by the Blackheath School Old Boys in 1857 and 1868, when they used short flag-posts for goals and had a goalkeeper in rear of the full-backs." Leeds Athletic claimed to be playing rugby, yet their game strictly forbade players from running with the ball, and there was no crossbar to score over, just two uprights, and their first outside challenge came from the soccer-playing Sheffield.

When Yorkshire arranged its first major representative football match against Lancashire in 1870, despite the predilection for rugby-based games in the county, they felt it was only right to also include four Sheffield players in the team, who may have been to blame for the fact they lost. Organiser JG Hudson was shocked to see that the Sheffielders "played as if they had never seen a rugby ball."

The first half lasted 45 minutes, the second a full hour, and although Lancashire captain William MacLaren had asked for hacking to be tabooed, because many of his men "were in situations and it would be a serious matter for them if they were laid up through hacking", it was thanks as much to their kicking of players as their kicking of the ball that the Lancastrians won the game.

There were caveman-like problems with the rules. In a classic comment regarding one of the Lancashire forwards "one of the Sheffield men grabbed the ball by the lace and hammered his opponent around the head with it." As WHH Hutchinson explained, "I had to tell him it was not provided for in the rules and he seemed surprised to learn it."

Montagu Shearman wrote that "as, however, all the players of the rugby game agreed in not allowing off-side play, few causes of dispute arose, and in general disagreements were avoided by a rule that in matches between clubs the rules of the home club were always to be adopted." But Guillemard didn't think things had been quite so smooth. "The earliest established clubs in nearly all cases laboured under no slight difficulties" he writes. "For the majority of their members had not acquired a practical knowledge of the principles of the game in early years, and had no mentor to explain to them this rule and that."

A 'wag' is something very different now, but in 1890 it was the penname used by a contributor to the *Yorkshireman Football Number* who suggested that verbal persuasion skills were often as important as footballing abilities, and "some captains would jaw away until they gained their point by sheer blarney, the opposing side giving in merely to get some more play."

The noble effort by the Rugby Schoolboys to put the laws of their game onto paper often raised more doubts than it solved. Such statements as "it is not lawful to take up the ball

---

[13] In his invaluable eyewitness account in Francis Marshall's book.

when rolling as distinguished from bounding" created arguments just waiting to happen. When exactly does an oval ball stop bounding and start rolling?

Rather than help with this, Rugby School took a surprisingly nonchalant view of the growing popularity of the game they had created. Very few clubs in the surrounding Midlands were encouraged to take it up, and the school itself played no direct part in the foundation of the Rugby Union.

Astonishingly, the school itself once said that the governance of the game in the outside world should be the responsibility of the Football Association! That was in 1867, when the FA, as part of its desperate attempt to bolster its floundering support, wrote to as many clubs and schools as it could find and tried to persuade them to take up their code. They even had the audacity to write to Rugby School, and although Rugby was obviously uninterested, the response (from a boy by the name of Ellis, but no relation) was a surprising one. Ellis said it was his wish that some kind of laws could be drawn up for everybody in the country playing football based on the Rugby game, and that "if the FA wish to complete thoroughly their good work, they might turn their attention to this subject." Crazy! That was Rugby School willingly inviting soccer's governing body to oversee their game on a national basis! That could have changed the course of history. The FA could have been like the GAA in Ireland with its hurling and Gaelic football, governing both sports on an equal footing! As the FA was quick to endorse professionalism, rugby league may never have come into being, and maybe rugby and soccer might have eventually been merged into a single code. But as it happens, the FA secretary, RG Graham, politely wrote back to tell Ellis that they simply didn't have the time to deal with the Rugby game as well.

Rugby School remained isolated. It wasn't until 1876 that they first took on outside opposition and were obliged to play by the Union rules, and it was not until 1888 that they finally adopted them for playing internal house matches. That marked the end of 'traditional' rugby at the school and two years later they finally joined the RFU. Old Rugbeians have continued to feature prominently in the game, however, and as recently as 1999, the president of the RFU, John Simpson, was a former Rugby pupil.

Towards union

As the 1860s ended, and despite having no governing body, rugby was probably far stronger in Britain than soccer. But in the early 1870s, it looked like the balance was shifting. The previously lethargic FA had now joined forces with Sheffield and Scotland, and their successfully organised cup tournaments proved influential in promoting their game far and wide. The only very loosely defined rugby game had none of that, and at the same time was getting negative press for the aggression it endorsed.

An article in *The Graphic* (November 26, 1870) listed the latest spate of injuries and suggested parents "can hardly feel quite easy at the prospect of crutches for life for their sons … the growth of public opinion … will perhaps be more efficient in bringing masters to a clearer perspective of their duty in this matter." A letter from an anonymous surgeon in *The Times* that same month had raised notorious alarm by highlighting the danger and brutality of the game. Guillemard considered it "an inaccurate and intemperate letter ... silenced very promptly by direct contradictions from several members of the school and the medical officer; but the correspondence furnished matter for criticism in the daily papers, and a number of articles were published stigmatising the game as brutal and unmanly, and one calling for instant reformation, if not total abolition ... though the leading clubs were not seriously alarmed by one writer's threat that Parliament should be moved to abolish the game, it was felt incumbent on them to place it on a recognised footing and under authoritative control."

Word was getting around that the FA's more sanitised version of football might be a more appropriate alternative[14]. It was time for the rugby clubs to join forces and fight for their cause. In December of 1870, Edwin Ash, the same man from Richmond who had turned down an invitation to attend the first meeting of the FA because he didn't have a regular enough set of players, published a letter in *The Times* explaining "that some code of rules should be adopted by all clubs who profess to play the Rugby game, as at present the majority have altered in some slight manner the game as played at Rugby School ... strangers in each match finding themselves at once at a disadvantage in not knowing the rules of the ground ... We therefore propose that all clubs ... join with us in forming a code to be generally adopted." Ash had good reason to want to see Rugby clean up its act. Two months earlier, one of his team had died of injuries sustained in Richmond's opening game of the season.

The Pall Mall Restaurant in London was selected as the venue. This monument to rugby does not exist anymore, but if you're ever by the Texas Embassy building near Trafalgar Square, do take the time the check out a plaque that honours where the birthplace of the Rugby Football Union used to be.

It all happened on January 26, 1871. All the clubs that answered the call were from the London area, and they numbered 21, which, incidentally, was roughly the same number of member clubs the FA had in London at the time.

The gentlemen that gathered in the Pall Mall were there in representation of Blackheath (who were going to behave themselves this time), Richmond (the aforementioned Ash, who contrary to popular belief never went to Rugby School, and was named treasurer), Wimbledon Hornets (now Wimbledon RFC), Guy's Hospital (that historic contender for the 'world's oldest club' prize), Clapham Rovers (who were fairly unique in that they were also a soccer club, playing one code one week and another the next, and hence earning the moniker 'the Hybrid Club'. They would win the 1880 FA Cup, yet at the same time were one of the

---

[14] There was another reason for establishing a more formal structure. As we saw in the previous chapter, the Scots had turned down the FA's challenge to a game of soccer because they preferred to play by rugby rules. The English rugby community pricked up their ears. They intended to take up that challenge.

MIKE ROBERTS – THE SAME OLD GAME: CODIFICATION

top London rugby clubs, before somewhat mysteriously dissolving in the late 1880s), Lausanne (another rugby-soccer club, who folded in 1881, and it is only speculation that they were linked in some way to the club formed in 1860 in the Swiss city of the same name), Harlequin FC (the only one of the clubs that is still playing at the highest level in England today), Belsize Park (who moved to form the successful Rosslyn Park side in 1878, although the original Belsize 'reformed' in 1971, and according to their website "have more in common with the footloose, amateur ethos and spirit of the Victorian club; indeed, many of those original members are still with us, and playing!"), school teams in the form of Wellington College (the only non-city team, from Berkshire), King's College, St Paul's and Marlborough Nomads, plus teams representing the Law Club and the Civil Service, a collection of now defunct clubs that were nevertheless influential in their time: Flamingoes, Addison, Mohicans, Ravenscourt Park and West Kent, plus two short-lived sides that promised so much more in the early days of metropolitan rugby, a side formed by Old Tonbridgians calling themselves the Gypsies, and Queen's House, whose disbandment shortly after was due in no small measure to the emigration of three key members to Canada.

One very big name was missing. Until a year earlier, what would become London Wasps had been part of the Hampstead Football Club. In 1870, and because they no longer played in Hampstead or even had many players from there, the club decided to change its name, eventually settling for Harlequins. Thinking Harlequins was a silly name for a rugby team, a breakaway faction decided to form a different club. They called it Wasps, which is not a silly name. It has been claimed that they were absent from such a seminal meeting because their representative managed to get the date wrong. That's quite feasible, although another version of the story might be in better keeping with rugby tradition. That one goes that the Wasps man accidentally turned up at the wrong restaurant, where he settled into some serious drinking and by the time he had realised his mistake, he was too under the influence to do anything about it.

Still, it's a good job that happened, because otherwise there really wouldn't be an awful lot to say about the first ever meeting of the RFU. They were all united by a common cause, and already had the Rugby School rules as a more than solid base, so there was nothing like the potential for fireworks of the first meetings of the FA. Guillemard, who was there in representation of West Kent, wrote that "everyone present was of one heart and of one mind that eventful evening, so that the labour was not protracted." Richmond were the club of influence, and their Algernon Rutter became the Union's first ever president, while Edwin Ash was both secretary and treasurer, and in Guillemard's opinion "it would be very difficult to find a man better qualified to set going a society in connection with any of our national games; he was the principal mover in getting up the meeting under notice, and its success was mainly due to his efforts."

Apart from a few very minor modifications to what were now 'laws' rather than 'rules', the only major topic for debate was whether or not to include hacking. Rugby School still

SCRUM ON DOWN

allowed the practice, but was being berated in the press for doing so. Thinking back to Mr Campbell mouthing off about the need for hacking in the Association game, it's amusing to note that one of the RFU's first resolutions was to abolish the practice too.

The hacking issue was no longer all that contentious anyway. It was already well on the way out of non-school rugby by the time of that meeting. Much of this stemmed from the rivalry between Blackheath and Richmond in the mid 1860s, with the former still enjoying its reputation for playing one of the most vicious interpretations of the rugby laws ever seen. Richmond, meanwhile, considered themselves to play 'pure' rugby and in November 1866 their captain, Edward Carleton Holmes, wrote to *Bell's Life* explaining how they had sent a circular to all London clubs pledging that "all unnecessary hacking should be put a stop to … all hacking in scrummages, except by those immediately on the ball, is contrary to the spirit of the Rugby game … that no player be hacked over except he has the ball in his hands." The suggestions were heartily accepted by almost all who read them, and just one month later, even Blackheath decided to start putting limits on hacking. By 1871, the practice had so few supporters that the decision at the first meeting of the RFU was a foregone conclusion.

The meeting itself did not agree to any definite set of laws, but rather discussed some of the finer issues and then entrusted the task of producing a draft set of rules to a three-man committee made up of the newly elected president, Algernon Rutter, plus his Richmond team-mate Edward Carleton Holmes and Leonard James Maton of Wimbledon. All three of them were Old Rugbeians, and were no doubt selected for that very reason, which rather puts paid to any revisionist theories that question how much influence Rugby School really had on the modern game.

Rugby has never been noted for the simplicity of its rules, so this was no overnight task. The three men, who were all involved in law, regularly gathered in Holmes' office at 31, Bedford Row to discuss the matter, but by the time of the first international against Scotland in March, they still hadn't finished the job. Would they even be ready for the next rugby season? Probably not, but as Guillemard put it, "most fortunately for the Union, though not for himself, Maton, the elected draftsman of the trio, broke a leg. Anxious for some employment whilst thus laid on the shelf, and accepting his colleagues' offer of a large supply of tobacco if he completed the work before he left his sofa," he got the job done. Incidentally, in his own book, Guillemard writes that much as he is honoured by claims by Montagu Shearman that it was he and Edwin Ash who drafted the original laws of the RFU, "I think it right on our joint behalf here to state our disclaimer. Maton and his two colleagues did the whole of the work." Poor old Maton, stuck at home with a broken leg for weeks on end writing the rules of rugby, and nowadays all the credit goes to a virtual nobody called William Webb Ellis!

It was not until June 22, half a year after they started, that the first copy was presented to the other members of the RFU for their approval, whereupon a number of amendments were made. The first ever edition of the 1871 rules is proudly maintained to this day by the

MIKE ROBERTS – THE SAME OLD GAME: CODIFICATION

Museum of Rugby at Twickenham. It is hand written on seventeen sides of paper, with plenty of crossing out and scribbling in margins, making some parts almost indecipherable, meaning Nigel Trueman's noble effort to provide a transcript, sometimes resorting to the 1874 amendment to make sense of the scrawls, may feasibly have taken half a year to produce as well! In all there are 59 different rules[15], and compared to the sheer simplicity of the Football Association's offering, these ones are mind-bogglingly convoluted (given in full in *Appendix Seven*).

Office 1871 was considerably more primitive than later versions, but even without the benefit of a word processor, one does wonder what Maton was doing all that time on his back. The text is considerably better structured and more informative than the schoolboys' effort, but as for major changes to the game, the only ones of import are the banning of hacking and tripping (which was one of the main reasons the Union was formed in the first place), the replacement of the elaborate system of laying the ball up for a try at goal with a simple kick (which many teams had already being doing anyway), an offside player being able to rejoin the action once play had caught up with him, the ball having to be returned to play from the point it crossed into touch, and some formal guidelines for umpiring.

Scrum dancing

There is nothing in the 1871 rules about the positions of the players, which is hardly surprising as it doesn't even stipulate how many players are on a team. The common practice at the time was twenty-a-side, and it was apparently the Oxford and Cambridge Universities in 1875 who first experimented with fifteen players and found it opened things up for more of a running and passing game than the dull affair of a mighty pack of forty men scrummaging up and down the field. Getting rid of five players also made it a lot easier to find enough bodies to make up a team and transport them to away matches, and the idea soon spread throughout the rugby community, and England's win over Ireland in February 1877 was the first to be played by national XVs.

Playing with smaller teams would also imply smaller scrummages, which would lead to a major shift in the way people played the game. The 1871 rules state that "a scrummage[16] takes place when the holder of the ball being in the field of play puts it down on the ground in front of himself and all who have closed round on their respective sides endeavour to push their opponents back and by kicking the ball to drive it in the direction of the opposite goal line."

The wording of that rule would turn out to be very important indeed. It fails to make it entirely clear how to form a scrummage. There is nothing about binding as a modern scrum would do, although the idea of linking bodies and crouching soon crept into the game. The

---

[15] And if 59 rules seemed excessive at the time, there are now about 190 pages of the things.

[16] The shortened form 'scrum' was not recorded until 1888.

1876 edition of the semi-official *Football Annual* advised against this new idea, noting how "some players are given to putting their heads down in a scrummage ... so as to look after the ball better, but it is a plan not to be commended as it loosens the mass, a man with his head down taking up the space of two. A scrummage should be formed as compactly as possible, every man pressing firmly on the man in front of him, bodies and legs close together, so as to form a firmly packed mass to resist the weight of a like mass of opponents. The great point to be aimed at being to stop the progress of the ball towards one's own quarters[17]."

In the 1870s, a scrum was simply an impenetrable wall of players hoping to make it impossible for the ball to be kicked forwards. Teams would hack away, trying to get the ball out of the scrum, which was not as easy thing to do because the simple option of kicking or heeling it backwards was illegal. Rule 22 clearly states that any player who "in a scrummage gets in front of the ball" was offside. And if the rules state that an offside player is "out of the game and shall not ... in any way interrupt or obstruct any player", then by definition, as soon as the ball was played backwards, the players in the front row were technically offside and also obstructing players, and therefore violating the rules. England international Charles Marriot remembered exactly that when he mused how "in the old days the obstructionists would have been swept away with a little wholesale hacking, or unceremoniously hauled out for off-side play[18]."

Getting the ball into open play was very difficult. Some teams opted for 'foiking' the ball, which was to hook it sideways out of the scrum, or otherwise they might use a tactic invented at Bradford that involved getting the ball to one side and then 'wheeling' the scrum, which if done properly could get around the offside rule.

But it was all very confusing, and these grey areas about what was legal and what was not caused no end of problems. Arthur Budd wrote that "scrummaging was then the real article. It meant carrying the pack by superior weight and propelling power, and was not at all badly described by the definition which is still to be found in our present code, and which speaks of a scrummage as taking place when the ball is put down, and 'all who have closed round on their respective sides *endeavour to push their opponents back, and by kicking the ball* to drive it in the direction of the opposite goal line.' I cite this definition because it affords a graphic illustration of the magnitude of the change which has occurred since those days in the style of play. In 1870, the above definition presented a very fair picture of what a scrummage was; now [1892] it depicts exactly what a scrummage is not. Then, men pushed

---

[17] In Frank Marshall's book, Arthur Budd, who started playing at Clifton in 1872, played five times for England, and went on to become president of the RFU in 1888, commented that in the early days "a player who could not take and give hacks was not considered worth his salt, and to put one's head down in a scrummage was regarded as an act of high treason."

[18] Cited in CW Alcock *Football* (1894). American football, as we shall see later, was faced with exactly the same problem, and more than any other factor, it was the difference in their methods for tidying up the scrummage that made today's American game so different to rugby.

MIKE ROBERTS – THE SAME OLD GAME: CODIFICATION

straight ahead might and main, while to heel out was regarded as unfair and discreditable; to-day, they never by any chance do the former, while they do not scruple to do the latter at their own sweet will ... this *modus operandi* is extremely unfair, and entirely opposed to the spirit of the offside laws, seeing that the bulk of the scrummagers are in front of the ball. It has, however, by general consent been admitted as legitimate, and it is, I am afraid, too late to protest against its continuance."

All this eagerness to get the ball into the open was the direct result of smaller teams, and therefore fewer forwards involved in scrums. Now that it was much easier to get the ball into the open, teams found that rather than pushing the scrum up the field to gain ground, it made far more sense to quickly get it to the backs and for them to advance by running with the ball. No doubt influenced by soccer, teams soon learned the benefits of passing the ball among the backs. The whole essence of rugby had changed, and by the early 1880s it had come to resemble much more the game as it is played today.

The failure of players to release the ball, which invariably led to unsightly mauls, was what rule 18 sought to address by insisting that "in the event of any player holding or running with the ball being tackled and the ball being fairly held he must at once cry down and there put it down." Montagu Shearman himself played in a game shortly before the new rules were drafted in which "the heavier side, when one of their own men was collared, used the tactics of never calling 'down', but of shoving the whole of the opposite forwards down the ground until the accidental or intentional 'tripping up' of the whole scrimmage by the side losing ground necessarily caused a halt, and the ball was then at last put down. The 18th law was especially framed to deal with this abuse."

But writing a rule was one thing, another thing was getting teams to abide by them. Even today, the releasing of the ball remains one of the most contentious issues in rugby. Guillemard witnessed how Rule 18 was commonly "disregarded, and one often saw as vigorous a maul in midfield as if the ball were in goal. On one memorable occasion a maul of this kind was timed as lasting for ten minutes, the only object of the struggle being the privilege of putting the ball on the ground in the centre of the scrummage. Many spectators of the rougher class considered, judging from their excited shouting, that this feature of the game was more attractive than the most brilliant of runs, the cleverest dribbling, or the prettiest drop at goal."

Trying times

In 1871, a 'touch down in goal' still won you nothing more than a 'try' at scoring over the posts. By the 1880s, people began to realise that all this was something of a lottery. A team could dominate a game, and win considerably more 'tries' than the other, but ultimately it all came down to the kicker. If he didn't actually convert any of those 'tries', all that effort counted for nothing, while if their opponents were lucky enough to have a particularly good

SCRUM ON DOWN

kicker, they could often win a game by winning just one 'try' and converting it[19]. And this was at a time when kicking was even more of an art then than it was now. Getting a synthetic, waterproof Gilbert Synergie to float gracefully over the bar is one thing, getting a sodden blob of mud-soaked leather to do the same was another matter entirely.

Montagu Shearman wrote in 1888 that "place-kicking is never so good as it is with schoolboys, and the result was that in very many matches no goal was scored from the tries which were gained, and it became a common thing for a match to remain 'drawn', although one side had secured several tries. As an example of the absurdity of the system it may be mentioned that the present writer played in one match when nine tries were obtained by one side, and yet the match was declared drawn."

We mustn't forget, however, that goals could still be kicked from the field, but with the play so congested by the scrum, this was usually suicidal, and would more likely mean surrendering the ball to the opposition. It made more sense to get the ball over the line and kick on goal that way.

The first proposal to award some kind of score for tries whether or not they were converted was mooted by the RFU in November 1875. The motion was rejected, but they did agree that "a match shall be decided by a majority of goals, but if the number of goals is equal or no goals be kicked, by a majority of tries." So, the try-count was to be used as a way of settling draws. This was basically the same idea as the system used at Eton and in Sheffield's soccer, only they called a try a rouge, which was also the term used at Cheltenham School for their rugby-based game. However, as Charles Burton Barrington pointed out, "a touch down was only a deciding factor when there was nothing else, but that was not looked upon as a real victory[20]."

A points system was again proposed and rejected by the RFU in both 1881 and 1882, but one place where one was implemented with resounding success was nowhere in Britain, but in America! The Ivy League colleges were reshaping rugby into their own national code of football, and in 1882 decreed that four touchdowns took precedence over a goal kicked from the field. Before long, American 'rugby' would be almost entirely focused on scoring touchdowns rather than goals. There was a similar shift in British rugby, but only later.

The South East Lancashire Cup dabbled with a points system in the mid 1880s, awarding 4 points for a try, 8 for a converted try and 6 for a drop goal. There was also got one point for a 'minor', which was when the defending side touched down in their own goal[21]. In London,

---

[19] This issue may not exist any more due to points being awarded for tries whether converted or not, although with penalty kicks playing such an important role, having a good kicker remains a huge advantage in modern rugby.

[20] Cited in Trevor West *The Bold Collegians: The Development of Sport in Trinity College, Dublin* (Lilliput Press, 1991).

[21] That's an idea that still exists in American football, called a 'safety', which in 1882 had been deemed equivalent to a touchdown.

the United Hospitals Cup was soon proclaiming that three tries equalled one goal, and Cheltenham had its own system whereby "a match shall be decided by a majority of points. A goal shall equal three points, and a try one point ... Where a goal is kicked from a try the goal only is scored[22]."

It was Cheltenham's method that was finally imitated by the RFU, in the wake of a county match in 1886 in which Yorkshire had scored four tries but missed all of their conversions in gale force winds, and instead Andrew Stoddart fluked a late drop goal for Middlesex to win the game. Now that tries had a value of their own, the focus of the game began its shift away from the goalposts. To being more like American football, one could argue.

The scoring system was changed again in 1891. A try was deemed to be worth two points, a converted try worth five points, a field goal four points and there were also three for the new idea introduced in 1888 of a penalty goal (as is still the case now, the value of penalties never having changed). The proposal was controversial, but was met with widespread approval, G Rowland Hill, a year later, going as far as to say that "it is eminently satisfactory that this general approval has been obtained. It will be very unwise to do anything that may interfere with this unanimity unless the very strongest reasons arise for it[23]."

There would be interference though. That status quo only lasted for two years, when in 1893 the try now scored three points and the conversion two, the first time the try was actually worth more than the conversion that followed it.

Rugby went for a fresh start after the Second World War, and the drop-goal's value was reduced from four to three points, meaning drop-goals, penalties and tries were now all worth the same (although the try offered the chance to add two more points from the conversion).

In 1971, the try was upgraded to four points, and that was the first time that it was ever worth more than any other form of scoring, and it was made even more important in 1992, when five points for a try was introduced. It's funny to think that the five-point try was implemented as a way of making sure teams stuck to the essence of rugby, scoring tries, although when the RFU was originally formed, tries weren't worth anything at all[24].

The Code War

The creation of the RFU in 1871 meant the standardisation of a new sport, but the people of the time didn't necessarily see things that way. Both the RFU and the FA's games were generally referred to as 'football', and it was more a case of two rival governing bodies and

---

[22] Expressed in more modern terms, a try scored one point and a conversion another two.

[23] Again cited by Frank Marshall.

[24] To avoid complication, we have skipped mentioning another form of scoring, called the 'goal from mark', which was not abandoned until the 1971 reform, having been worth three points, except between 1891 and 1905 when it was worth four. This was scored when a player 'marked' the ball by making a fair catch and shouting 'mark', and then had the option of a free, unchallenged kick, which could be at goal if he wanted – and which is very similar indeed to one of the most basic plays in Australian Rules.

two different sets of rules for the same game. Both games appeared in the same football columns of the newspapers, sometimes without even specifying which particular sets of rules were being used.

Clubs couldn't afford to be too picky when it came to choosing opposition. The captain of the Manchester Association Football Club put it nicely in 1877 when he said "I think that I may safely say that there is not any district in which the inconvenience of having two different codes of Association rules is felt more than here, where if a club adopt one, no matter which, it is obliged to get matches with clubs playing the other, and has to play different rules, when away, from those which it plays on its own ground[25]."

A good example of the kind of situation is the following report of a game in 1871 between Garrick of soccer-playing Sheffield and the visiting Free Wanderers from rugby-playing Manchester. The home spectators were far from impressed by what they saw.

"It was arranged" explains the report, "that each club's rules should be played on its opponent's ground, so that a novelty was provided for the lovers of football in Sheffield, the Rugby rules being played here for the first time ... The peculiarity of these rules is that it is next to impossible to give a foul, as a player can pick up the ball and run with it, knock it on, kick it, or throw it to another when likely to be tackled. If, however, he has the ball in his possession, an opponent seizes him round the neck, legs, or any portion of clothing that first presents itself to his grasp. Others then come up, and unless he cries out 'Have it down', he is quickly prostrated and rolled on or sat on, as the case may be. Several cases of deliberate hacking, or, in other words, kicking at an opponent's shins as he is running with the ball, did not convince either us or the spectators of the superiority of the Rugby over Association rules. They are quite suitable for schoolboys, who are proverbially impervious to accident, but we should have thought adults would prefer a game with more skill and less roughing ... a decidedly unfavourable opinion of the Rugby rules was formed by the spectators ... a detailed account of the play is simply impossible, consisting as it did of wrestling, strangling, running with the ball under one arm and striking opponents in the face with the disengaged hand[26]."

Even today, despite being the fourth biggest city in England, Sheffield has no team playing at the highest level of either the union or league code. Sheffield did not want rugby, but instead looked to promote soccer elsewhere in Yorkshire. In 1876, a Mr Dignam of the Football Players Accident Society is noted in the SFA's minutes suggesting the teams play exhibitions in rugby playing towns, indicating a drive to get Yorkshire teams to take an interest in playing something a bit safer.

Graham Williams offers pages and pages of examples of teams playing by other codes than the ones they were used to. We only have space here to mention a few. For starters, there was

---

[25] Stuart G Smith in *The Field* (March 1877).
[26] "Copied from a Sheffield newspaper" by Frank Marshall.

Southend FC's constitution in 1870, which included the trickily worded rule that "any club challenging this club, plays by the club rules, but if this club sends a challenge we play the rules of the club challenged[27]."

It was still a widespread practice to even play half a game with one club's rules and the other half by the other's, one famous case being the game between Sheffield and the Royal Engineers in December 1874. It has even been claimed that this was origin of the half-time interval[28]. Villa Cross Wesleyan Chapel Cricket Club's first game in 1875 involved playing one half of soccer and one half of rugby against a mainly rugby playing club. They were cagey about it, renting rather than purchasing a soccer ball, but they decided they preferred the Association game. They made the right choice, eventually going on to win the European Cup as Aston Villa in 1982.

Williams quotes a preview in the *Staffordshire Sentinel* of 1873 that claims that before a match against Stoke "it is only fair to mention that the Crewe men are not used to the Association rules, but will have the chance of turning the tables in the return match, which will be played according to the rules of the Rugby Union."

The cricketers playing on Stoke Green in Coventry played something resembling soccer in their off-season until they were invited to play Allesley Park College in 1873, and were asked if they fancied playing half the game by the rugby rules that the students were rather partial to. The Coventry lads were impressed, and out of that Coventry RFU was born.

The Midlands was a soccer stronghold, and to illustrate the problems for rugby in the area, EB Holmes notes in Marshall's book that "in the early days so difficult was it for the Moseley Club to obtain fixtures without having to travel a long way from home, that they arranged matches with the Wednesbury Strollers, an Association club of some repute, on the understanding that a game under Association rules should be played at Wednesbury, and that in the return match at Moseley, Rugby Union rules should be adhered to."

But the soccer being played in Birmingham was not the FA's game. The Birmingham and District Association was formed in 1875 to promote just that, but for many years the actual clubs insisted on playing instead by a compromise code they had invented, a loose amalgamation of local varieties of football.

---

[27] The practice of teams of different codes playing each other might seem decidedly odd to us these days, but one place where something along such lines still exists is North America. In areas along the border between Canada and the USA, particularly in the west, high schools from the different countries play each other, and the usual tradition is that when the Canadian school is at home, they play by the Canadian rules, and when the American school is at home, they play by American.

[28] That is certainly a possibility, but with a tea or beer break being an essential element of Victorian society, it is more likely that intervals were programmed so that the players could get some refreshments and a well earned rest. Also, in order for both sides to benefit from any irregularities in the slope of the pitch, unfair breezes, sunlight or so forth, it was originally a common practice for teams to swap sides after each goal. This probably got a bit tiresome in high-scoring matches, and players realised it made more sense just to change once, after the interval.

SCRUM ON DOWN

Even Preston North End originally started out playing rugby. They were used to travelling to face teams elsewhere, because the newer football clubs in the immediate vicinity seemed to have opted for the Association rules. In 1878, they finally gave the kicking game a try against Ealing, decided it wasn't all that bad, and ten years later were the first ever national soccer champions.

Hull FC was formed in 1865, originally playing some kind of hybrid game that involved running with the ball and was therefore more akin to rugby. But getting to Yorkshire to find opposition proved difficult, so in the early days they had to make do with soccer matches against the sides in Lincolnshire. William Hutchinson remembered how "we played any mortal code possible with other clubs away from home so long as we could get a game of some sort[29]."

Bradford was essentially a rugby club, but as late as 1873, their fixture cards noted that they still kept aside certain dates for Association practice. In the haphazard football climate of the 1870s, there was no telling what kind of rules you might be playing from one week to another. Middlesbrough FC, who were always staunch supporters of the Association code, played their first match in 1876 against a rugby club called Tees Wanderers, who insisted on playing by the rugby rules, but gallantly offered not to use their hands!

You can imagine the moaning all this would have caused. A team travels for three hours on a cramped train, only to get there to find half the squad whining at their captain "not bloody Sheffield rules again! That's the third time this month … I thought you said we were going to be playing rugger today…"

Historians have often tried to 'map' how the rival codes expanded, but it's a largely futile exercise due to the lack of logic, as reflected by a comment in *The Times* in 1880 that "the distribution of the game is sporadic and curious. The seed of one or other game has, for no visible reason, settled in some districts and been wholly driven out in others. In Nottinghamshire and in Sheffield, the Rugby game is regarded with contempt; but nothing else is played round most of the large towns in Yorkshire, while the same game again is largely predominant in Lancashire."

By the 1890s, cross-code matches had as good as become a thing of the past. This was partly because rugby had shifted so much away from kicking that the two codes now bore few similarities. But also, both codes had expanded in popularity so much that it was no longer such a chore finding local opposition that played by your chosen code. No longer in need of each other, the soccer and rugby communities grew apart. There was room for them both.

---

[29] In a 1900 interview with the *Yorkshire Evening Post.*

Socca and rugger

This is as good a point as any to interject on the origins of the word 'soccer'. It's a word the British rarely use, other than to scorn it as an ugly Americanism. But they're actually wrong to say that. The name 'soccer' as opposed to 'football' may now be associated with America (and also Oceania and to a certain extent Ireland), but its origins are as English and tea and biscuits.

The exact origin of the phrase has been attributed to Charles Wreford Brown, who attended Charterhouse and Oxford before going on to captain England at soccer in 1894 and 1895. When asked if he played 'rugger', his witty reply was "no, soccer", and the name stuck. That story cannot be substantiated, but 'soccer' made its first written appearance in 1889, spelt *socca*[30], and in 1891 as *socker*[31] and eventually soccer[32] in 1895. The shortened form most likely came about because 'Association Football' was a bit of mouthful when there was a need to differentiate the game from the many other forms of football floating around at the time. Newspapers took to the habit of shortening it to 'Assoc.' (it's also been suggested that 'ass.' was out the question because it looked a bit rude). It was a common practice among the gentlemen of the day to add the '-er' suffix to anything, so you had a fiver, a tenner, a copper, brekkers and of course, rugger.

In no small measure because the rugby community would soon be more concerned with the difference between 'rugby union' and 'rugby league', the word 'football' was dropped from most rugby talk. It was just 'rugby', leaving Association as the only significant game to be commonly called 'football' in Britain, and 'soccer' gradually faded from everyday usage.

But the name 'football' in America, Australia and Ireland was used to describe their own national forms of the game, so when referring to the Association game, they still needed to differentiate it as 'soccer', and still do today. But the word's origins are unquestionably English. Quibble no more. Because that, ladies and gentlemen, is fact.

Test matches

In Scotland, Edinburgh Academy, the Royal High School and Merchiston Castle had all been playing competitive football with each other from 1858 onwards, and Loretto School and Fettes College joined them soon after. The latter was headmastered by Alexander William Potts, and there is no doubt that it was to his former school, Rugby, that Scottish football turned to for its earliest inspiration.

It was certainly a rugged affair, and played on rugged land. James Walvin quotes a Scottish writer who asked "what did they care about ridges or furrows or that it was difficult to see the

---

[30] When Ernest Dowson's *Letters* was published, in which he wrote, "I absolutely decline to see socca' matches."

[31] *Lock To Lock Times* (October 24, 1891): "A sterling player, and has the best interest of the 'socker' game at heart."

[32] *19th Century* (November 1895): "When the boat-race, sports, and "soccer" are in most men's minds."

lower goal posts when you were at the other end[33]?" and describes a game in which a horse and plough were used to mark the boundaries of the pitch.

Loretto's Hely Hutchinson Almond later recounted how "so little did any of us masters or boys then know about it that I remember how, when Lyall ran with the ball behind the Merchiston goal, the resulting try was appealed against on the ground that no player might cross the line whilst holding the ball. The previous rule at Merchiston had been that he must let go of the ball and kick it over before he touched down. It must be said in excuse for this and other similar sins of ignorance, that the only available rules were those printed for the use of Rugby School. They were very incomplete, and presupposed a practical knowledge of the game[34]." Matches were consistently interrupted by disputes over different interpretations of the rules, and it was not until 1868 that these were largely resolved by the publication of what became known as *The Green Book*, of which, sadly, no copy survives.

The first contact between Scottish and English clubs came about as a result of Charles Alcott and the FA's challenge in 1870 that led to the bogus soccer international in London against whisky-drinkers and grouse-shooters. As we saw in the previous chapter, the 'real' Scots claimed they were unable to field a decent soccer side because all of their clubs played rugby, and so it was the newly formed RFU took up the challenge instead and sent a team north for the first rugby international, played at the Edinburgh Academy in Raeburn Place in March, 1871. The fact that the organisers struggled to find a time that the local cricket pitch wasn't being used suggests inauspicious beginnings for a tie that would eventually come to be called the Calcutta Cup, although the reportedly 4000 strong crowd that turned out to watch indicates more than healthy interest in rugby in 1870s Scotland.

The match was played twenty-a-side, and the England team (half of which were former pupils of Rugby School) opted to play with a selection of 14 players from the London clubs plus three each from Manchester and Liverpool (which weren't actually affiliated to the RFU at the time). That made for a rather makeshift England outfit in comparison to the carefully selected squads of later years, and as a result they struggled to contain a set of Scottish players that were more used to playing together.

The Scots did not know what to expect, but as the great Robert 'Bulldog' Irvine, who played that day, wrote in Marshall's book how "the Scotch leaders felt that they could not be so very far behind their opponents, and at all events, better to know the truth than to be set down as inferior, as it were, by proxy" although "many of us entered that match with a sort of vague fear that some entirely new kind of play would be shown by our opponents, and that they would out-manoeuvre us entirely."

---

[33] Walvin unfortunately never reveals his sources, so I have no idea where the quote comes from.

[34] Hely Hutchinson Almond, headmaster of Loretto, in a chapter on his experiences of early Scottish football in Francis Marshall's book. A passionate Muscular Christian, who had first played rugby at Oxford University he wrote in 1893 that football was "productive of scarcely anything but good," and was so influential on Scottish rugby that in 2007 he was a very posthumous nominee for the second year of the IRB Hall of Fame.

MIKE ROBERTS – THE SAME OLD GAME: CODIFICATION

The RFU's trio of lawmakers still hadn't got round to finishing the first draft of the official rules, so there was not yet any standardisation of the game on just one side of the border, let alone both. Not surprisingly, the first attempt at an international test was blighted by several disagreements over what went and what didn't.

Arthur Guillemard notes that the two teams arranged for the match to "be played for two periods of fifty minutes each, that no hacking-over or tripping-up should be allowed, and that the ball should not be taken up for a run unless absolutely bounding, as opposed to rolling." Nowhere is it mentioned whether said ball itself was oval or round, and the oval ball was not made compulsory until 1892.

Irvine notes that playing without hacking was something of a novel experience for both teams that day, and several players couldn't contain their instincts. "As blood got up, it began to be muttered, 'Hang it! Why not have hacking allowed?' It can't be prevented far better have it.' The question hung in the balance. The teams seemed nothing loth. The captains (Moncrieff and F Stokes) both looked as if they ought to say 'no' and would rather like to say 'yes', and were irresolute, when Almond, who was umpire, vowed he would throw up his job if it were agreed on, so it was forbidden, and hackers were ordered to be more cautious."

The home side won by one goal and one try to one goal, and deservedly so according to Guillemard, who said that "the Scotch forwards were distinctly quicker on their feet, and in better training than their opponents" and in describing one incident, it is tackling in American football rather than rugby that comes to the modern mind. "Finlay had got well away with the ball, and was sprinting towards the English goal at a hundred yards' speed, when Osborne, folding his arms across his chest, ran full tilt at him, after the fashion of a bull charging a gate. Both were very big, heavy men, and the crash of the collision was tremendous, each reeling some yards, and finally falling on his back. For a few seconds players and spectators alike held their breath, fearing terrible results, but the two giants promptly resumed their places, apparently none the worse."

The arguments reached their peak in the second half when a scrummage was ordered five yards from the line. Even though under the English laws it was not allowed, the Scots merely drove the entire scrummage over the line and grounded the ball for a try, which was awarded and duly converted for the only score of the game.

The referee that day was Loretto headmaster Hely Hutchinson Almond who, many years later in Marshall's book of 1892, gave us a quote that many modern-day referees might secretly identify with. He had the gall to claim that "I do not know to this day whether the decision which gave Scotland the try from which the winning goal was kicked was correct … I must say, however, that when an umpire is in doubt, I think he is justified in deciding against the side which makes the most noise. They are probably in the wrong."

One of the biggest problems umpires had was getting anybody's attention among the mayhem, for it was not until 1885 that a rather useful innovation was introduced. G Rowland Hill wrote in Marshall's book about how "the wonderful success which has attended its introduction must cause those who had the experience of umpiring or refereeing prior to this time, to reflect how it was possible that they were able to carry on their work at all; the difficulty of letting players know when an appeal was granted, and the uncertainty as to the decision of the referee caused endless stoppages and confusion. Few things have done more to improve the game than the whistle system."

Not that having whistles meant that referees were suddenly able to stamp their authority on the game and earn widespread respect. Hill moaned that "the treatment of referees, much to be deplored, is becoming worse … the exhibition of discontent to which referees are subjected after a game is over is most painful. Continually one is told of a wrong decision given by such and such a referee. This grumbling and growling is a species of disease from which, we regret, all classes of players are suffering." Rowland, dear man, well over a century has passed since you scribed those wise words, and it woes me to report that absolutely nothing seems to have changed in that respect. Anybody who runs an amateur football league will fully sympathise with Hill's lament that "there is an increasing demand for referees who are qualified to act, but there is a decreasing desire on the part of such men to undertake the post. The task is a most difficult one under the most pleasing conditions, but it is an intolerable one if the referee is not treated properly."

The early England v Scotland matches were revolutionary not just for football, but for world sport in general. When the first games were played, not even cricket had managed that. Granted, English teams had regularly toured Australasia, but these were just groups of travelling gentlemen, not teams picked to represent the best in the country. It wasn't really until England toured Australia in 1881–82 that there was a proper international test between the countries.

After England and Scotland, Ireland[35] was the next Union to form, playing their first game against England on a rain-sodden Oval in 1875. England won by two goals and a try, a scoreline that flattered the roughly assembled Irish team. Writes another contributor to Marshall's 1892 book, JJ McCarthy, "such an enterprise, and such a twenty! They had never previously seen each other; the twenty a-side game was absolutely unknown in Ireland, and some of the team did not turn up at all … and the whole lot were immaculately innocent of training … The late football editor of *The Field*, HO Moore, asserted that he could whip up twenty Irishmen, then resident in London, who would make hares of this pseudo-Irish

---

[35] Ireland was still united to Great Britain at the time, and the political divide into Northern Ireland and the Republic was almost half a century away, but from 1874 to 1879 the island had two separate unions. The Irish Football Union operated in Leinster, Munster and parts of Ulster (basically the modern day Republic), while the Northern Football Union of Ireland operated around Belfast (modern day Northern Ireland), and for that first game with England they compromised by picking ten players from each. The rival unions eventually settled their differences in 1879, and although soccer split into two separate associations following the partition of 1922, rugby to this day maintains one association and one national team for the whole of Ireland.

twenty." Isn't it great how he considers the Irish that actually lived in Ireland to be the 'pseudo' team!

Wales joined the international fold in 1881. Oddly enough, although rugby was by far the bigger game in the Principality, a Welsh national soccer team had faced Scotland five years earlier in 1876, when the selection of only one player from South Wales caused a storm of protest, fuelling the divide between rugby in South Wales and soccer in the north[36]. In their first international outing, the Welsh were thoroughly outmatched by England, who won by eight goals and 6 tries to nothing, which in modern terms would equate to a 69-0 hiding. It was in that match that one throw by Lennart Stokes was deemed illegal by the umpire because it was so long it was simply 'not football'! The rout had been a rude awakening, but the Welsh were quick learners, and within a year had claimed their first international scalp in Ireland, winning by 2 goals and 2 tries to nil. Wales would not beat England for the first time until 1890. But what a happy day that must have been.

What these teams played would have been recognisably rugby to us today, but there were still plenty of changes to come. Montagu Shearman wrote in 1888 how "rather more than a dozen years ago we saw a shoving match between rival teams of Scotchmen and Englishmen which was dignified by the name of an 'international match'. A quarter of a hundred of heavyweights appeared to be leaning up against each other for periods of five minutes or thereabouts, while occasionally the ball became accidentally disentangled from the solid globe of scrimmagers, and the remaining players then had some interesting bursts of play between themselves while the globular mass gradually dissolved."

One of the practices that had yet to be abolished was that of 'scragging', which Shearman explains "consisted in the twisting of an opponent's neck round, with a gripe of the arm, to make him cry 'down', if he had any available voice." Delightful.

Shearman felt that in 1888, the game had only recently developed from what he calls its 'shoving' era into the 'passing' era, explaining that "it is only in the last few years that the science of passing has been so far cultivated as to make the game of today distinctly different from what it was in 1880 or 1881. It is difficult to fix a precise period at which the game changed, and long and low passing into the open became the predominant feature of the play as it undoubtedly is at the present time. The style of playing a game alters so slowly ... Probably the playing public were converted to the new style by the wonderful play shown by the Oxford University team between 1882 and 1884. Certainly, since that time up to the period of writing, passing has been all the rage, no player apparently being ever satisfied now to run half a dozen yards without passing the ball ... If one comes on to a field before play has commenced, the men waiting for the game are not taking drop-kick practice, or dribbling

---

[36] Marshall noted in 1892 that "Rugby football is confined practically to the southern counties of Wales, and the four great clubs [by which he meant Cardiff, Swansea, Newport and Llanelli] have been the developers of home-made talent by continually playing and replaying amongst themselves. This concentration of strength in a comparatively small area, and with a few leading clubs, has given Welsh football a style of its own."

the ball about to 'keep their feet in', as was their wont before the rage for passing came in, but are now to be seen playing at catchball, and slinging the ball from hand to hand, not high in the air, but about the level of the hands from the ground ... It is also obvious, however, to us that the passing system is capable of being brought to a far greater state of excellence than it has reached at present; and when, if ever, some professional team appears in the field, they may pass with as marvellous accuracy in all weathers as their brethren of the Association game carry out their passing and heading."

Rugby being rugby though, with rules only the referees seem to fully understand, the disputes continued, and the Welsh, Scots and Irish were getting increasingly perturbed by the way the English seemed to think they had a God-given right to run the game. Referee HH Almond, who was at the thick of it, later commented in 1892 that the crux of the issue was that the Scots had originally "adopted the English rules and any changes in them subsequently made by England in bulk, and hence afforded a precedent for the claim on the part of England of a sole right to legislate, which caused such a stir some years afterwards."

It was some stir. The arguments reached an almighty height in 1884 when England scored a try against Scotland, a decision that the Scots hotly protested because the scorer, Kindersley, had only collected the ball after it had been illegally knocked back by one of the Scottish team. The English claimed that the try should stand because not only was knocking back perfectly legal by English rules[37], but even if it had been an infringement, the Scots had made no appeal and thus the try should stand by virtue of the advantage rule[38]. There was utter confusion, and it was eventually decided that the game should continue, and that it would be left to the two national unions to decide what to do about the disputed try.

A series of hot-tempered letters were exchanged, with RFU secretary GR Hill issuing a statement that read "my committee much regret this result, but they are firmly convinced that the abandonment of the match is a matter far less important than upholding the principle that a referee's decision is unimpeachable."

This was something of a last straw for the SFU and their Irish and Welsh brethren, who were fed up to their teeth of being bullied by the decisions of the English Union. The following year, Scotland refused to play England at all and instead set about forming the International Board along with Ireland and Wales, self-proclaiming themselves the new overseers of the laws of the game and rugby in general.

---

[37] The basic argument was whether a 'knock on' was only illegal if the ball was sent forwards. James Alexander Gardner, secretary of the SFU, argued his point by saying that his committee "at once accept the ruling of the Referee that the ball was 'fisted' by a Scotchman, but they entirely dissent from your reading of Rule 26. They consider that 'knocking on', the technical expression for what is commonly called a 'fist', includes knocking forward, knocking to the side, and knocking backwards. Striking the ball with the hand in any direction they believe to constitute a knock-on, and thus to be illegal."

[38] The English argument is not helped at all by the fact that they were lost in a temporary time warp, as the advantage law wasn't officially introduced until 1896, although it was already becoming a custom, if not in Scotland.

MIKE ROBERTS – THE SAME OLD GAME: CODIFICATION

The Scots informed the English that they would withdraw their dispute over the 1884 result if the English were willing to join them in forming a four-way union. Not giving much of a hoots-mon about the 1884 result, the English RFU refused to have anything to do with them, claiming that the one vote per country system was hardly fair on them, as they had so many more clubs, and should therefore enjoy greater representation. Probably just to test the waters, the RFU started making minor modifications to their rulebook, which the IB steadfastly refused to accept, and deemed that IB rules should apply for all international matches, which effectively meant no international rugby for England in 1888 or 1889.

The argument between two very stubborn sets of people was doing nothing but damage to a game that was already under serious threat from the formation in 1888 of a fully professional soccer league in England, which was drawing huge crowds and unprecedented media attention. English rugby needed a solution fast, and called upon Lord Justice Clerk Kingsburgh (the second most senior judge in Scotland) and, of all people, the president of the Football Association, Major Francis Marindin[39], to arbitrate.

Marindin was not the kind of man the Scots could hope to get too much support from. As referee of the 1887 FA Cup semi final, Marindin showed his true colours when he said to the West Bromwich side "are you all Englishmen? Then I have great pleasure in presenting you with the ball. You have played a very good game and I hope you win the Cup." WBA's opposition that day was the almost entirely Scottish Preston North End.

With Marindin involved, it comes as no surprise that it was largely the English that came out on top. The decision was to form the International Rugby Football Board as the sport's governing body for all international play, which it was deemed "shall consist of twelve members, six of whom shall be elected to represent England, two to represent Scotland, two to represent Ireland, and two to represent Wales." The English voluntarily reduced their number of members from six to four in 1910. Based in Dublin, what was renamed the International Rugby Board in 1997 is still rugby union's global governing body today.

A major rift had been averted. For a moment, it had looked as if the rugby world was going to end up being split into two different factions, and who knows what that could have meant? Well, we do know actually, because just a few years later, there was going to be another major difference of opinion in the rugby world, only this time, there was to be no compromise.

---

[39] Marindin was one of the giants of the times when the leisured classes had dominated English soccer, and played for both the Royal Engineers and the Old Etonians. This caused something of a problem for him in 1875, when his two sides met in the FA Cup Final, and he did the diplomatic thing and sat the game out, although there are claims that this is but a folk legend, for the Major was really posted elsewhere that year and couldn't have played anyway. Whatever the story, every other time he played in the final his side lost, so the poor guy never collected a winner's medal! Marindin went on to become one of the first great referees in world soccer, as well as being knighted for his work to promote safety on the railways and developing London's first electrical lighting system.

4 LEAGUES AND GENTLEMEN
Professionalism and the schism between rugby union and rugby league

Different strokes

Soccer thrived on its early popularity and did not take long to realise its potential not only as a form of leisure and exercise, but also to commercialise itself as a form of entertainment. From the 1870s onwards, its cup competitions grabbed the attention of the masses, but all that 'pot-hunting' was kept at arm's length by the rugby community, which (quite rightly as it turned out) felt such things would only encourage cheating and professionalism. Rugby wasn't totally averse to competitions – the United Hospitals Challenge Cup was inaugurated in 1874 and still exists today, but apart from representative County Cups, in which only the Lancashire versus Yorkshire matches ever really managed to capture the imagination, there was no formal national competition in English rugby union until the RFU Club Competition[1] was created in 1971. It wasn't until the Courage Leagues were set up as late as 1987[2] that there was any formal nationwide structure[3]. What is now the Six Nations has been going since 1883, but although fans did like to work out who had won using a soccer-inspired points system, there was no trophy or official recognition for the winners until the 1993 edition. Soccer's first World Cup was played in 1930. Rugby didn't follow suit until 1987. In soccer, it was winning trophies that mattered. Rugby clung onto its gentlemanly spirit of playing for pleasure. It was played by the players for the players, and perhaps paradoxically, in what is often heralded as the ultimate team sport, the biggest accolades were not collective but individual, in the form of the honour of being selected to appear for your county or country or in other representative matches.

By the 1880s, British soccer's leagues and cups were of such massive consequence that the players and administrators were too engrossed in their own affairs to have much interest in what might have been happening to football elsewhere in the world. While soccer stayed at

---

[1] Originally with neither a trophy or sponsor, this later became the John Player Cup (1976), Pilkington Cup (1989), Tetley's Bitter Cup (1998), Powergen Cup (2001), EDF Energy Cup (2001) and is now the LV Cup, otherwise known as the Anglo-Welsh Cup, which following many changes of format is now only contested by teams in the English Premiership and the four Welsh regional teams.

[2] Prior to this, newspapers would publish merit tables, but without a standard fixture list these were very subjective. The Courage Leagues have evolved since 1987 into today's national structure, with the Premiership at the top of the pyramid system.

[3] Following the introduction of professionalism in 1995, the whole ethos of the game changed so much that the once-shunned pot-hunting became so relevant that the Guinness Premiership in England had a champion of the regular league, and also a champion of the daft play-off system, which ensured a showpiece final at Twickenham to end the campaign.

home, it was left to the rugby players to travel on increasingly more ambitious foreign tours. Given rugby's more international outlook in the late 19th century, it might seem peculiar that it was soccer, rather than rugby, that became the truly 'global' code of football. But much as rugby's travels helped to foster interest in the game worldwide, the pioneers had a somewhat blinkered idea of what the 'world' meant, and rarely looked beyond the commonwealth nations of South Africa, Australia and New Zealand for opposition[4]. Rugby remained centred around its traditional core of top-tier nations, and although Italy and Argentina have finally been invited to join them at the top table, little has changed in that respect today.

The FA was remarkably insular in its outlook, but without them even having to try, their game spread with almost no resistance from the oval code. Rugby was a complex game that required careful instruction in many rules that were based as much on tradition as common sense. The FA, instead, had created a deliberately simplified game, and outside of the Anglosphere, it was the more immediate and natural kicking code that caught people's fancy when it was introduced to them by such missionaries as Thomas and James Hogg, who formed the Buenos Aires Football Club in 1868, or the workers at the Rio Tinto Company who formed Spain's oldest club in Huelva in 1889.

Back home, rugby was also being dwarfed by soccer. This did not have to happen, and probably would not have happened, had the RFU taken a different stand against a wave that was rising in the north and rapidly sweeping south. Soccer was relatively quick to surrender to the clubs that wanted to exploit the potentialities of football to ensure packed stadiums every weekend. The RFU stood its ground, and in doing so, voluntarily allowed soccer to win the battle for commercial domination of football virtually unchallenged. But not everybody in rugby agreed with the RFU's principles. The dissenters broke off relations and went their separate way, creating a division in the game that still exists today. For the outcome of the infamous schism would be rugby league, and is to that code that our attention now turns.

Football crazy

However, we shall begin our study of the origins of rugby league by returning to soccer. There is reason behind the madness. To properly understand how rugby league came about, it is also important to understand how the Football Association dealt with the same issues.

Football culture sprang up from nowhere. The *Ten Hour Day Act* of 1847 had literally set the ball in motion, summed up perfectly by cotton spinner Moses Heap when he says "for a while we did not know how to pass our time away. Before it had all been bed and work; now

---

[4] There was very little contact with the USA, where it was the collegiate game, which made wholesale changes to the rugby rules from the 1880s onwards, that was the dominant code. Canadian rugby was also being americanised and although there was a tour of Britain by a Canada team in 1902-1903, the British Lions did not play in Canada until 1959, for an unofficial test in Toronto on their way back from the antipodes.

in place of 70 hours a week we had 55½. It became a practice, mostly on Saturdays, to play football and cricket, which had never been done before[5]."

The working classes flocked to the seaside, to the music halls, and to the sports grounds. As social journalist Tommy Wright wrote in 1867, "the working half of Saturday is up at one o'clock, and that wished-for hour seems to come round quicker on that day than any other … the workmen, with newly-washed hands and their shop jackets or slops rolled up under their arms, stand in groups waiting for the ringing of the bell, it is a sight well worth seeing, and one in which the working man is, all things considered, perhaps seen at his best. He is in good humour with himself and fellow-workman … When the bell rings the men leave the works in a leisurely way that contrasts rather strongly with the eagerness with which they leave at other times; but once outside the workshop gates, the younger apprentices and other boys immediately devote themselves to the business of pleasure. They will be seen gathering together in a manner that plainly indicates that there is 'something in the wind[6].'"

Not everybody thought handing so much leisure time to the working classes was a good thing. The *Illustrated London News* in 1863 forewarned of the potential difficulties of affording "more holidays to the working classes without at the same time diminishing their means of subsistence", and despite the positives of day-trips for families to the beach, not everybody knew how to make proper use of their free time. The rowdiness of public holidays was eyed with caution as bars were drunk dry and wages were squandered in the brothels, by gambling on fist-fights and other vices.

Organised sport provided the solution. As Arthur Guillemard wrote in 1892, "players of the present day may well ask how the young men of thirty years ago passed their Saturday afternoons in the winter. The answer is not easy to find, but it must be remembered that in those days a half-holiday on Saturday was by no means the general custom, and a very large number of offices were not closed until four o'clock, so that outdoor exercise by daylight was possible to but a few. Hockey was but little played, and I am by way of thinking that, if there was no ice available for skating, most men adjourned to billiard-rooms or went straight home and smoked or slept until dinner-time. We live a more vigorous and healthy life now."

The church was quick to react, and embarked on a mission to channel all that excess energy and leisure time to positive benefits, and mirroring the Muscular Christianity that had done so much good in the public schools, it set its sights on getting the working classes playing organised games[7].

---

[5] This mill worker from Rawtenstall, Lancashire kept a diary from 1824 to 1913 and provides a wonderful insight into the life of the 19th century working class. Previously cited by Graham Williams and Tony Collins.

[6] Thomas Wright *Some habits and customs of the working classes* (Tinsley Brothers, 1867).

[7] Peter Lupson (*Thank God for Football!* (Azure, 2006)) noted that 12 of the 38 teams that had played in the soccer's English Premiership had religious origins. His book has chapters on Aston Villa, Barnsley, Birmingham City, Bolton Wanderers, Everton, Fulham, Liverpool, Manchester City, Queen's Park Rangers, Southampton, Swindon Town and Tottenham Hotspur.

Everton was formed by boys in the Bible class at St Domingo's Methodist Chapel in 1878. Manchester City was the brainchild of Anna Connell, the 25-year-old daughter of the rector of St Mark's Church, to provide an alternative to street-fighting among the local lads in the disease-riddled slums. The Trinity Church was behind the Small Heath Alliance (later Birmingham City) in 1875, St Luke's Church in Blackenhall was the origin of Wolverhampton Wanderers, St Mary's Church founded what would become Southampton FC (still known today, of course, as The Saints), and Bolton started life as Christchurch FC in 1874, the first president being the vicar who ran the local Sunday School, Reverend John Farrall Wright. From this, one might get the impression that early footballers were a bunch of god-bothering bible bashers, but generally they were nothing of the sort. The folk of the cloth may have hoped that through sport they could attract some new members to their congregations, but it was football not prayer that these people were after.

The Nether Green Sunday School in Leeds was a fine example. An article in the *Yorkshire Post* in 1893 explains how "matters have been left too much to the management of the players themselves, with the result that, contrary to the original intentions of the officers of the school, the team is largely composed of those who have no connection with it." Within a few years, most of the 'religious' clubs had shaken off their holy patrons. The future Bolton Wanderers, for example, soon cut the Reverend Wright out of the picture and relocated to a pub, both then and now a considerably more popular venue than a church for footballers to gather, with the landlords' offer of a brew considerably more attractive than the chance for expert guidance with the scriptures.

Other clubs grew out of the factories, mills, railways and mines. Cray Wanderers FC, who are still plying their trade on a semi-professional basis in the Isthmian League are regarded as the oldest truly 'working class' football team in the world. The club was formed by people working on the London, Chatham and Dover railway line from 1858 to 1860, and in their spare time they enjoyed nothing more than a good kickabout. But the 'working class' origin is doubtful. Stoke City and Crewe Alexandra are also popularly acclaimed to be clubs formed by railway workers, Coventry City by employees of a cycle factory, Arsenal by workers at the Royal Arsenal in Woolwich and West Ham was the creation of staff at the Thames Ironworks, but the groundwork was usually done by the gentlemen who oversaw the operations, and it was only later that manual labourers proved themselves worthy of playing alongside their superiors[8].

Clubs like Derby County, Middlesbrough, Sheffield Wednesday and Sheffield United started out as offshoots of cricket clubs, although the more widespread interest in the newer sport meant that it would soon be the football sections that were keeping the cricketers afloat.

Wherever your local team's origins lay, it was not long before not only playing it, but also watching it became an institution. It was a win-win situation for everybody. The players

---

[8] The North Staffordshire Railway Company workers that formed Stoke City, for example, were almost all former Charterhouse pupils.

LEAGUES AND GENTLEMEN

obviously thrived on becoming local celebrities and getting to pull all the best birds in town. For the local authorities it was opium for the masses. If it was football the mob wanted, then it was football they were going to get. Bread and circuses. If the mob had aggression to vent out, then it was far better vented out on a fellow bunch of grown men running around after a ball of leather than on, well, the local authorities.

Football had come along at just the right time; it was building up a sense of pride in newly formed industrial communities. Without the local football club, it might have been very difficult for anybody to sense any pride for the vermin-infested hovels they inhabited, especially as a large percentage of the population was made up new arrivals that had abandoned distant homes to move to the cities in search of work. For the people of Blackburn, Bolton and Burnley, football was a source of unity and identity.

It had once been the church that gave people something to believe in. Now that role was being taken over by football. Players were worshipped like Gods and football grounds became the new temples.

Pro evolution soccer

For the people running the clubs, football became a tidy little earner. Nothing even remotely like the money-spinning bandwagon it is in our modern day and age, but there was money to be made all the same. When clubs realised that not only did people want to come to watch the matches, but were willing to pay for the privilege too, the first rudimentary stadiums were erected. Big matches were attracting crowds upwards of 10,000, and the gate money was generating clubs much more income than they had budgeted for, and while some gave it all away to charity, we can be sure than many, if not most, found 'better' uses for all that cash.

By the 1870s, the idea of hiring professional players, as was already widespread in cricket, became a viable proposition. We say today that football has lost its soul because clubs sign foreigners rather than nurturing domestic talent, but even back then clubs were using financial incentives to attract players from elsewhere. In soccer, that 'elsewhere' meant, more than anything, Scotland, the Brazil of the Victorian period, from whence there seemed to be a never-ending stream of porridge-powered talent to entice down south with the offer of decent jobs with local firms. Very decent jobs indeed in some cases.

As usual, it was Sheffield who were ahead of the rest of country, with Peter Andrews (of Heeley) and James Lang (of The Wednesday) being considered the first Scottish exports in 1876. Lang himself later claimed to have been the first, for "Peter did not go to play football. He was sent to Leeds on business by his firm, and, after being there for some months, became connected with the Heeley club[9]." This was not quite the same as Lang's move south, whereby "I had played for Glasgow against Sheffield the previous February, and

---

[9] *The First Anglo-Scot James J Lang* in the *Sunday Dispatch* (November 4, 1922).

MIKE ROBERTS – THE SAME OLD GAME: CODIFICATION

between that match and the one at Kinning Park, the Sheffield people seemed to have come to the conclusion that I might be of use to them. I am not going to say that I crossed the Border to play for nothing, because you would not believe me if I did." Although Lang did have a position at Fearnehough's Knifeworks, it was all very iffy, with his most important duty seemingly being to sit around all day reading the newspaper. Amazingly, while all this was happening, he also managed to conceal the fact that he was blind in one eye following an industrial accident in 1869.

These two were just the first of many 'Scottish professors', as they were known, to make the pilgrimage south in search of under-the-counter payments. Sheffield wasn't their only destination. Over in Lancashire there was an island of soccer in the midst of rugby country centred around Darwen, Blackburn, Preston and Bolton, and it was there more than anywhere, that Scottish imports were amassed. There were so many Scots in British football that it was plain obvious that most of them were reaping extra benefits for being there, and some Lancastrian clubs even went as far as to place ads in the situations vacant columns of the Scottish press. Burnley, for example, had nine Scots in 1883, and the whole affair led one contemporary observer to comment that the "employment of the scum of Scottish villages has tended, in no small degree, to brutalise the game[10]."

Darwen signed one of soccer's earliest stars from Partick Thistle, Fergus Suter, in 1878. Suter had actually started out as a rugby player, but didn't take long to realise, like many after him, that much as scrummaging around after an oval ball was fun, kicking a spherical ball around the park had financial benefits to offer. He was known to be applying for work in England as a stonemason, so Darwen was an odd destination considering there wasn't much call for men of that trade there. As it happens, he soon gave up his work in masonry, apparently because the unfamiliar English stone was so hard that it was causing his hands to swell. The club flatly denied that they were paying him. Out of work, poor Suter must have been struggling enormously to get by as he helped Darwen to some scintillating achievements in the FA Cup. Suter then decided he'd like to go and play for local rivals Blackburn Rovers. He had no regular income, yet rather than beg for survival on the Lancastrian streets, he won three FA Cup winners medals and became a local hero everywhere but at Darwen, the club he had neglected. Nobody ever managed to prove Suter was paid to play, though it is obvious that he was. Men like him already knew how it worked – when asked, deny everything. Catch me if you can.

Catching Darwen as they came in and out of the bank was one thing, but catching them on the football pitch was no easy matter either. Their 1879 FA Cup meeting with the Old Etonians was legendary. The northerners, who the *Blackburn Standard* noted "belong entirely to the working class", were facing a side that included such legendary figures of the

---

[10] Cited by Graham Curry.

LEAGUES AND GENTLEMEN

leisured elite as Major Francis Marindin and Arthur Kinnaird[11]. Early football had rarely seen such an extreme case of rich versus 'poor', but Darwen bounced back from 5-1 down to seal a dramatic 5-5 draw, the last four goals coming in the last quarter of an hour. Some game.

The embittered Old Etonians played the dirty trick of refusing to play extra time, insisting instead on a replay, and in London rather than Lancashire. The northerners had to raise £175 for the long journey back to the capital, with the small consolation that the Etonians chipped in with a fiver but the rematch also ended in a draw and another unreasonable insistence on not playing any extra time[12]. The Etonians won the second replay by a handsome 6-2, but the significance of Darwen's stand was not lost on the masses. The *East Lancashire Cricket and Football Times* was delighted that "Darwen has done more than any club from the North of England has done before." But they were just the start of it.

Under the counter payments were not just a magnet for outsiders; they were also something many local players wanted. It was all very well for the middle and upper classes, who could play soccer where and when they fancied, but when clubs started picking players from the proletariat, there was an obvious problem. These players had jobs to do for six or more days a week, and finding the time to play matches, let alone train or travel to away fixtures, was no easy matter. For your average working class footballer, the only way to play was by taking time off, and few could afford to do that. Miners, for example, were only paid for the time they actually spent on the job, so any time spent playing sport was lost time. Not putting in the hours not only meant less pay, but it also inevitably meant that you'd be first in line for the chop whenever the boss needed to 'restructure' his staff. And that's not to mention the huge risks of injury players were taking week in week out by playing sports at a time when sick pay was something nobody even dreamed would ever be a legal right.

---

[11] Soccer has rarely known anybody quite like Kinnaird, a Londoner but who was fervently proud of his Scottish parentage. A man of immense charisma, his nine cup final appearances (playing anywhere from goalkeeper to centre forward) and five winner's medals still stand as records. He has been called football's first great hero, to the extent that his fans once took the place of his horses and pulled his carriage to the ground. Despite being frightfully posh and owning large estates in Scotland, he was much loved throughout society for such projects as the London Polytechnic for the education of the poor. He was a strong supporter of the old school hacking, and Major Marindin was allegedly involved in a cracking exchange with the Lady Kinnaird, who was concerned that that her husband would come home from the football one day with a broken leg. Replied Marindin "don't be alarmed, for if he does, it will not be his own!" The *Athletic News* once wrote that "Lord Kinnaird used to say that he played four or five matches a week and never grew tired, but he added, late in life, that he would never have been allowed to stay on the field five minutes in these latter days. Nevertheless, he was fair, above board, and was prepared to receive all the knocks that came his way without a trace of resentment." A legend as a footballer, Kinnaird then went on to be one of the game's greatest administrators, spending 33 years as president of the FA and guiding the sport though immense changes right up until his death in 1923, just months before the opening of Wembley Stadium.

[12] The *Darwen Cricket and Football Times* reported that "Darwen, anxious to have the tie settled, made strong representations to play an extra half-hour. As on the former occasion, this was positively declined by the Etonians."

MIKE ROBERTS – THE SAME OLD GAME: CODIFICATION

Professionalism was illegal, and so the evidence was hidden, making it is hard to tell now how rife it really was in English soccer in the early 1880s. But it is safe to say that there was a lot of it, and Darwen's famous cup run was just the first indication that football was no longer only the plaything of the zany wealthier classes with their staunch defence of the amateur ethos. Those people could not hope to draw on the kind of mass support that the working men's team could gather from their local communities.

But although the bitter southerners took the higher moral ground and blamed it all on the money, they were also being outclassed by a new breed of footballer. The 1882 FA Cup Final was a yardstick event. Blackburn Rovers became the first working man's club from the north to reach the final, losing to the Old Etonians with a team that included three weavers, a spinner, a dental assistant, a plumber, a cotton operative and an iron foundry worker[13]. It would be the last time a strictly amateur member of the old guard ever won the cup. It was the public schools' last stand, or handstand perhaps, as Arthur Kinnaird famously celebrated the win by doing one in front of the pavilion.

Blackburn Olympic would follow their neighbours to the final a year later, but went one better by winning the thing, the decider being scored in extra time by a humble cotton spinner called Jimmy Costley. Olympic were helped by the fact that their opponents, once again Kinnaird and his Old Etonians, played most of the final with ten men after future England captain Arthur Dunn was forced to retire through injury, but the match reports suggest that the Etonians were simply outclassed by the northerners' ability to switch the ball from wing to wing with a cunning passing game. "The sinewy plebeians played skittles with the much more formidable looking sons of the aristocracy" went one report, and future FA president William Pickford reckoned "their tactics simply wore the Etonians off their legs."

Despite the glowing reviews of the Olympic passing game, there was also fierce criticism of their rough play. "On more than one occasion did the spectators (even their own friends) express their disapprobation at the charging from behind, holding and tripping tactics employed" wrote *Bell's Life*, although other reports imply the Etonians gave as good as they got in what can't have been the prettiest game of football ever played.

The *Eton College Chronicle* accepted defeat gracefully, but couldn't resist a jibe at their victors, for "so great was their ambition to wrest the cup from the holders, that they introduced into football play a practice which has excited the greatest disapprobation in the South. For three weeks before the final match they went into a strict course of training, spending, so reports says, a considerable time at Blackpool, and some days at Bournemouth

---

[13] However, Graham Curry still exercises caution with the "over-simplified notion that northern teams were necessarily composed of men employed in mundane occupations." Just because a team was from the north does not necessarily mean they were all millers and miners. Blackburn Rovers, for example, seemed "more middle class … though their playing membership appears to have involved a mixture of social classes." But although their founder members included former students of Harrow and Malvern College, by 1882 the team included four notable 'Scottish professors', including former Darwen man Fergus Suter.

and Richmond. Though it may seem strange that a football eleven composed of mill-hands and working men should be able to sacrifice three weeks to train for one match, and to find the means to do so too, yet when we reflect on the thousands who attend and watch matches in Lancashire, and so swell the revenues of the Clubs, and on the enthusiasm of the employers of labour in the pursuits of successes of their countrymen it is not so surprising."

Nevertheless, the victory was heralded as one for the working masses, or "a northern horde of uncouth garb and strong oaths" as the *Pall Mall Gazette* described the flat-capped throng that descended on the city that day, suggesting that neither southern prejudice towards the north, nor the northern talent for decorative use of the vernacular have changed much in over a century. The writer added, in further reflection of the political correctness of the time, that a tribe of Sudanese Arabs wouldn't have been any less amusing. But as Bryon Butler observes, "Blackburn could afford to smile. Some would even have known that the writer was the Lancashire-born son of a dedicated Rovers supporter."

Allegedly, after the final had been won, SA Warburton, the captain of the winning Blackburn side, was told that the cup looked like a tea kettle, to which he replied "Ey lad, but it's very welcome in Lancashire. It'll have a good home and it'll ne'er go back to Lunnon." He wasn't far off the mark. *The Accrington Times* felt "now that the Cup itself has gone out of London, the time has come for the great football centres of Lancashire, Sheffield and Birmingham to be properly recognised by the Association authorities." The balance of soccer had shifted; it now belonged to the north.

A period of domination followed for the northern and midland clubs. Blackburn Rovers won the next three finals, and by the end of the century both the main clubs from Sheffield and Nottingham, plus the likes of Preston, Wolverhampton, West Bromwich and even Bury had been able to celebrate titles. Sadly the future was far less rosy for the original northern champions. As Rovers got stronger and more professional, local rivals Olympic faded into the background, and in 1889, just five years after winning the north's first FA Cup title, they folded with barely a whimper.

The cup would only go back to the capital once in the next forty years, when the professional Tottenham Hotspur won it in 1901 (and even that team included three northerners, five Scotsmen, two Welshmen and an Irishman). But technically speaking the 'tea kettle' that had so amused the Olympic players never did go back south, and we've got Aston Villa to blame for that. After they won it in 1895, it spent some time on display in William Shillock's sportswear shop. As the proprietor himself later explained, "I pictured myself a ruined man. I seemed to see myself a hated individual man – to see my business boycotted. What was this heinous crime of which I was guilty? Why, I was the man who lost

MIKE ROBERTS – THE SAME OLD GAME: CODIFICATION

the English cup!" Yep, on September 11, 1895, some Brummie tea-leaf half inched the FA Cup, and it was never seen again[14].

A replica trophy was made, which was presented to outgoing FA president Lord Kinnaird for keeps in 1910, and the current trophy has been with us ever since, although the original is now so delicate that since 1991 it is a replica that has been presented to the winning captain.

Pros and cons

Professional soccer was on the rise. In 1881, Charles Alcock recognised that "it will be well for those who have the interest of the game at heart to recognise the existence of a problem that will in all likelihood have to be mastered before long[15]." He and the Football Association were going to have a tough time in the early 1880s.

In 1882, the FA started taking a more lenient attitude towards clubs that wanted to compensate their players for financial losses as a direct result of playing soccer, but any player "receiving remuneration or consideration of any sort above his actual expenses and wages actually lost" would be banned. Accrington became the first casualty when they were thrown out of that year's FA Cup[16], but they seem to have been more scapegoats than anything else. Otherwise, the FA did surprisingly little to clamp down on an omnipresent practice, partly because it was so difficult, but perhaps also because although they wanted to appear to be doing something to appease the 'gentlemen', their primary concern was to develop the sport. After all, in February 1884, some of its council even proposed that the easiest solution would be to simply legalise professionalism. The proposition was shot down, but the tide was obviously changing.

The middle class amateurs didn't like the sound of this, but neither did the Scottish association, which was understandably miffed at all their best players being snapped up by the English and demanded to know what the FA planned to do about it. Partly to support the Scots and partly to dissuade professionalism, a ban was placed on all non-Englishmen from playing in the FA Cup.

The real crunch came in 1884, when Preston North End put London side Upton Park out of the FA Cup. A claim was made that that the game should be void because Preston were obviously using professionals. It was never made clear exactly who had lodged the protest,

---

[14] 68 years later, in 1958, a homeless 83-year-old called Harry Burge stepped forward to confess that he was the thief and that he had melted the trophy down to make counterfeit coins. But with twisted irony, his problem was convincing anybody that he really had been the criminal, and that he wasn't just making it up!

[15] In fact, much as professionalism was vilified as the greatest evil of the modern game, there was nothing really new about it. To cite just two examples, way back in 1773, the *Leeds Intelligencer* reported on a game played at Walton in Yorkshire for twenty guineas, and the *Northampton Mercury* in 1765 mentioned how "a prize of considerable value" was contested.

[16] Somebody apparently not connected to the club had "offered inducements" for James Beresford to stay at Accrington. Ironically, the tell-tale tits were local rivals Darwen, who weren't even drawn against them, and who were no angels themselves given the whole Fergie Suter saga!

LEAGUES AND GENTLEMEN

but it certainly wasn't Upton Park, who were embarrassed by whole affair. There had been prying eyes observing Preston's antics for some time, and when Charles Alcock wrote to inform the club that they were investigating, the prosperous owner, Major William Sudell[17], shrugged and said, well, yeah, of course he paid his players, and so did all the other clubs. How else was he expected to keep up with the likes of Blackburn Rovers? "We were supposed to have trades of course" wrote one of the players, Georgie Drummond, years later. "I was reckoned to be a painter, Jack Ross did a bit of slating, and Jimmy Ross a bit of plumbing … But work never interfered with football. We could always get off when we liked – when we did work."

Following the Upton Park incident, Sudell found his club thrown out of the Cup, and probably suggested a convenient part of the FA's anatomy where they could insert their trophy. Preston bitterly felt they had been made the scapegoats, and the *Preston Herald* responded by accusing Bolton Wanderers of having fourteen imported professionals, Hailwell ten and Burnley eight.

The peeved Sudell announced that he was going to form a rival body instead. There were plenty of takers. He rounded up no fewer than 31 clubs in the northwest and midlands, all of whom were either paying players already or were very keen to do so, and held a meeting in Manchester to form the British Football Association. Unless the FA acted quickly, its power to govern the sport would be swept from under its feet.

Rather like UEFA today dealing with the potential threat of a European Super League, the FA's biggest fear was the loss of the breakaway clubs, who were the ones with the best players, the biggest followings and the finest facilities. They would be left with the amateur clubs and the public school old boys that, frankly, Joe Public had lost interest in. The future of soccer was in the north, and the FA knew that only too well.

In January 1885, some 200 delegates of the FA gathered at the Freemason's Tavern to discuss the problem. Two of the most outspoken promoters of the amateur cause were Harry Chambers of Sheffield FC, who was fuming at being dictated to by these upstarts from Lancashire, and Charles Crump of Birmingham, whose words were shouted down as hypocritical. William Sudell gave a stirring speech that "there were men who had played in Lancashire as professionals who were now figuring in Birmingham as amateurs, and the authorities of Birmingham must be aware of it."

Oddly, by now even some of the most outspoken southern amateurs were changing their tune. Charles Alcock explained that "I cannot be called a supporter of professionalism, for when I played football it was played only by amateurs, but until professionalism is legalised

---

[17] A shrewd mover with a win at all costs mentality, Sudell was putting together his team of *galácticos* well over a century before Real Madrid coined the expression, and in his role as treasurer he would also play his part in the development of the Football League. But his downfall was not an elegant one, for later in life he'd be serving time in prison for fraud, having been convicted of covertly using funds from his cotton mill to finance his football club.

MIKE ROBERTS – THE SAME OLD GAME: CODIFICATION

the deadlock which now exists will continue. I consider that veiled professionalism is the evil to be repressed, and I am sure it now exists in nearly every football district, 'pure' Birmingham not excepted. Professionals are a necessity to the growth of the game and I object to the idea that they are the utter outcast some people represent them to be … I object to the argument that it is immoral to work for a living, and I cannot see why a man should not, with that object, labour at football as at cricket."

A motion was presented to legalise professionalism. It was defeated, but only narrowly, and the writing was already on the wall. It would be a different story at a similar meeting in July of the same year, when Francis Marindin sold his and soccer's soul as he penned the immortal words that "it is now expedient in the interests of association football to legalise the employment of professional football players, but only under certain circumstances."

Those circumstances included restrictions to regulate how money was spent and where. The 1886 FA Cup rules included such new items as "no professional be allowed to play for more than one club in any one season" and "professionals must be born or have lived for at least two years within six miles of the headquarters of the club they sign for."

The life of a soccer professional was not one of riches. The severe regulations left them almost entirely at the mercy of the cotton lords who ran the clubs, who were hardly renowned for their generosity when it came to wage-earners, no matter how sharp their football skills. While professionalism had been illegal, players were free agents with considerable bargaining power. Now they were bound to the club owners and a minimum wage, and no longer free to decide on their own destiny. Not until Jimmy Hill successfully won his campaign to have the £20 maximum wage scrapped in 1961 would footballers enjoy true freedom, and although their conditions were considerably better thereafter, it was not until the Bosman Ruling of 1995 that players were able to move freely to another club at the end of their contract.

The amateurs did all they could to ensure that professionals got as much leper treatment as they could humanely get away with. One FA official was once moved to say that it was "degrading for respectable men to have to play with professionals," no paid player could sit on any FA committees, the first professional to appear for England, Blackburn Rovers' James Forrest, had to wear a different coloured shirt, and there was the case of amateurs Lindley and Walters making their point by sailing for an international in Ireland on a different boat. Right up until the turn of the century, the selectors of England national teams were laughably biased in their choices, with numerous amateurs getting to play for their country when everybody knew full well that there were far better professionals getting overlooked.

But ultimately, amateurism was fighting a losing battle[18]. Soccer had become a business.

---

[18] The FA appeased the amateurs by creating the Amateur Cup in 1893, but although the first edition was won by the Old Carthusians, it eventually became the domain of the lesser working men's teams that didn't have the resources to go fully professional. Instead, the Arthur Dunn Cup for old boys teams was set up in 1902, which is

The human league

The most immediate problem facing professionalized soccer was finding the right matches to play. Knockout competitions hardly gave clubs the regular competition they or their fans wanted. Supporting your local side was pretty rubbish if they had been knocked out of every major tournament before the Christmas tree had gone up. Another problem with cups was that in the early rounds, the biggest clubs were obliged to play sub-standard opposition, when they would much rather have negotiated exhibition matches that fans would be more interested in paying to see.

No self-respecting fan in those days would be complete without his club's fixture card in his pocket, but they were not the most reliable of objects. Clubs still moan today about inconsistencies in FIFA's 'unified calendar', but it was far worse when they had no idea which cups they would still be playing in, or when they might lose half the squad to any number of county or representative matches, and also had to work the season around the players' cricket schedules. Clubs vied to secure matches with the most attractive opponents they could, and this often meant cancelling games at will, and the pre-match gossip was often less about who was going to win, but whether both teams would even turn up[19].

It was a Scot called William McGregor who came up with the solution. Hailing from Perthshire, he had never been a player himself, saying "I tried it once when I was young and had to take to bed for a week." But when he moved down to Birmingham to open a draper's shop, he found he loved watching the game, and in particular Aston Villa. He was aware of the problems with fixture lists, and after Villa had had games cancelled on five consecutive Saturdays, he was moved into action. He circulated a letter explaining how "every year it is becoming more and more difficult for football clubs of any standing to meet their friendly engagements and even arrange friendly matches. The consequence is that at the last moment, through cup-tie interference, clubs are compelled to take on teams who will not attract the public. I beg to tender the following suggestion as a means of getting over the difficulty: that ten or twelve of the most prominent clubs in England combine to arrange home-and-away fixtures each season[20] ... This combination might be known as the Association Football

---

still played today. In the early days it even shunned penalty kicks, believing it a travesty to suggest that 'decent' people would ever break any rules deliberately.

[19] This was not just a soccer problem, it affected rugby too. In 1886, the *Wigan Observer* describes the fear among the organisers of financial disaster when the Wigan ground was almost empty shortly before the game with Wakefield Trinity. But "it is quite evident that Wigan people are wise in their time and like to see a team turn up before going into the ground, consequently when the Trinity players arrived in the town there was a great rush to the field."

[20] It is often said that McGregor's inspiration came from learning about the conference system used by American baseball, and several contemporary quotes support this (see Andrew Zimbalist and Stefan Szymanski *National Pastime: How Americans Play Baseball and the Rest of the World Plays Soccer*, Brookings Institution Press, 2005). The evidence that McGregor was listed as treasurer of the British Baseball Association in 1891 and that Aston Villa even had a baseball team also lend far more credence to the story than the counter-claim

Union, and could be managed by representatives from each club. Of course, this is in no way to interfere with the National Association; even the suggested matches might be played under cup-tie rules ... I am only writing to the following - Blackburn Rovers, Bolton Wanderers, Preston North End, West Bromwich Albion, and Aston Villa, and would like to hear what other clubs you would suggest."

The venue for the meeting was originally to be Anderton's Hotel in London, on the eve of the FA Cup Final. However, as all ten of the invitees were from the north, the meeting was moved to Manchester on April 17, 1888. The venue was the Royal Hotel, which no longer exists, but you will find there is a red commemorative plaque on The Royal Buildings in Market Street.

McGregor's suggestion to call it the Association Football Union was dropped because the word 'union' reminded too many people of rugby, and instead it was to become the 'Football League', despite some concern that it might lead to confusion with the Irish Land League political movement. The word 'English' was deliberately omitted because the organisers were open to the idea that perhaps one day they could persuade Scottish, Irish or Welsh clubs to join as well.

As for how a football league could work, they eventually settled on two points for a win and one for a draw (with some clubs arguing that drawn matches should be worth nothing). That system remained the norm for more or less a century, before three points for a win gradually crept into all competitions in the early 1990s.

Not everybody jumped at McGregor's idea. Clubs were worried all this might mean missing out on prestige friendlies, could prove too costly, and might mean pushing their luck too far with the FA. One major outfit that preferred to keep its distance was The Wednesday from Sheffield, a rare occasion when South Yorkshire missed the footballing boat, while Nottingham Forest was another surprise absentee.

Rather than the standard of football, it was the standard of attendances that mattered for inclusion (*The Athletic News* damned the whole project as "mere money-making speculation"), and the twelve clubs that played in the first ever season of the Football League in 1888–89 were Accrington, Aston Villa, Blackburn Rovers, Bolton Wanderers, Burnley, Derby County, Everton, Notts County, Preston North End, Stoke, West Bromwich Albion and Wolverhampton Wanderers[21]. There were six teams from the North and six from the

---

that he got the idea from the County Cricket Championship, considering the CCC didn't even have a proper league structure until the 1890s.

[21] The only one of the original twelve that isn't still playing there or thereabouts in the present day 92-club League system is Accrington. Contrary to popular belief, there is no connection between the modern day Accrington Stanley and the founder members of the football league, Accrington FC. Strictly speaking, neither is there really any connection between the former Accrington Stanley that went bust in 1962 and the modern day Accrington Stanley that was founded in 1968.

Midlands, and not one from the south. As late as the turn of the century, Arsenal and Luton would still be the only southerners in the competition[22].

And here's one for those who think soccer just isn't what it used to be, with teams no longer taking competitions like the FA Cup as seriously as they should. The same thing was happening in the first ever season of the Football League. Stoke and Bolton, for example, fielded reserve teams and crashed out early doors respectively to little Warwick County and Linfield of Belfast (Irish sides entered the FA Cup back then), while Everton didn't even bother turning up for their game with Ulster FC. Not that the Football League didn't have teething problems of its own. The early seasons were blighted by what the *Official History* describes as the 'casual and haphazard' organisation of the fixtures, with games frequently being cancelled because teams missed their train connections or were unable to get a side together.

The first edition of the Football League was won by the almost all-Scottish Preston, or The Invincibles as they were appropriately nicknamed for they didn't lose a game in the process; a feat that nobody thought could possibly be repeated until Arsenal's incredible 2003–04 season. But Preston topped it all off by winning the FA Cup as well, and did so without letting in a single goal.

Despite forming a breakaway association, what is important is that the Football League never sought to invent a new game. They played by exactly the same rules as the FA, the teams continued to participate in FA endorsed competitions as well, and League players remained as eligible as anybody else for places in representative and international sides. The FA and the League worked together, even though the relationship was never going to be a comfortable one, all the way through to 1992 when the FA itself gained control of the top flight of the Football League and rebranded it as the FA Premiership.

But it's curious to wonder what might have happened to soccer had the FA stood its ground on the amateur issue and the northern clubs had gone ahead with their British Football Association, leading to a definitive split rather than the compromise that was negotiated. Soccer would have been run by two rival governing bodies, one amateur, the other professional. And driven by professionalism, would the northern clubs have felt the need to modify the way the game was played as it sought to improve its market appeal? To the extent

---

[22] This was partly because professionalism was slow to develop in the south, but not entirely. The Royal Arsenal seemed to be employing a curiously large number of former members of Scottish and Midland football clubs by the late 1880s, and clubs like Millwall, Southampton and Tottenham would be following suit soon after. Arsenal went openly pro in 1891 and joined the Football League, while other professional clubs in the south formed the Southern League in 1894. This league grew in stature as a rival body, to the extent that Tottenham, in 1901, became the only non-league team to ever win the FA Cup. But some context is needed here, as there were really two separate leagues operating, and what we now call the FA Community Shield was originally an annual play-off between the northern and southern champions. But the northern league was generally much stronger, and particularly as transport got quicker and cheaper, southern clubs gradually started defecting to the extent that in 1920, the two competitions merged as one.

Working class heroes

In the 1860s, rugby was still a recreation rather than a spectacle. Onlookers were more of an inconvenience than something to be encouraged. Guillemard describes this beautifully when he tells us how "the crowds on these unenclosed grounds were a great nuisance, for they invariably … excepted to keep in touch, and the clear field of play was often not more than some thirty yards broad. Then did the wily half-back see his opportunity, and dive into the thick of the shouting throng … to dodge amongst the flying spectators in such a way as to have one or more of them between himself and his would-be tacklers … so persistently did some of the least civilised of the crowd stand between the full-backs and the ball that on one occasion at Blackheath my colleague, whose zeal sometimes outran his discretion, after vainly expostulating with a burly blacksmith … knocked him several yards in the direction of the touch-line, behind which the injured one was careful to remain for the rest of the afternoon, nursing his jaw and venting threats of slaughter. In the matter of keeping the field of play clear things have improved wonderfully during the past twenty years, as nearly all clubs play in enclosed grounds where ropes and stakes can be utilised, but in old days the Metropolitan Board of Works forbade the use of them on the heaths and commons under their management."

Soccer clubs appreciated the benefits of people wanting to watch them play, but the rugby community was more sceptical. In November 1884, on the eve of soccer's acceptance of professionalism, the *Manchester Guardian* predicted that "with the introduction of professionals a new departure is taken. The first effect of the change will be to make the Rugby game the aristocratic one, and the Association game will probably die out in the South of England, where it is already declining in favour[23]."

The *Manchester Guardian* had failed to notice that northern rugby was going the same way as soccer. The *Yorkshire Post* wrote in 1889 how "this rugby football movement, which commenced in Yorkshire with the 'classes' and first drew its strength from the public schools and middle classes, has finally, like other movements and fashions, good or bad, spread downwards to the 'masses'."

Old Rugbeians may have been the driving force behind the spread of the game, but the bulk of the best players were inevitably going to come from the hordes of men at the mills, in the factories and down the pits. Pure mathematical logic tells us so, there were millions of them. And like their soccer-playing brethren, the northerners were, generally speaking,

---

[23] That, of course, was assuming professional soccer would never catch on in the south, which of course it eventually did. Even so, although clubs like Portsmouth, Southampton and Norwich City have had their moments, outside of London soccer has no major strongholds in the south.

LEAGUES AND GENTLEMEN

considerably less classist about the way they ran their clubs. In Leeds in 1864, a rail clerk called Henry Irwin Jenkinson, who later enjoyed some success writing walking guides, placed an ad in the *Leeds Mercury* saying "Wanted: a number of persons to form a football club for playing on Woodhouse Moor for a few days a week from 7 to 8 o'clock am." There were soon some 500 people involved, with no particular emphasis on class distinctions. At Hull, they accepted plumbers, glaziers and other blue collar workers from the outset, and over in Rochdale the same club that is the Hornets today was formed in 1871 by a magistrate and other important businessmen, but who took an 'open door approach' to membership, and also charged admission to their games almost from day one.

The only condition was that players were expected to pay anything from one to ten shillings for membership, for as in amateur clubs today, subs were required to cover different expenses. This hardly suggests that they were set up as a social service, like many church sponsored soccer clubs were, and many manual labourers would have struggled to find that kind of money, but as long as you paid your fees, it didn't matter much to the northerners who you were. A northern rugby player was valued far more for the way he played rugby than where he stood in the social pecking order.

But these players were going to face the same problems their soccer playing cousins were encountering, namely trying to find a way of fitting the game into a horrendously long working week, while if the risks of injury and having to foot your own medical bills were high for soccer players, playing a full-contact sport like rugby was akin to financial suicide.

The solution was to provide the less wealthy players with a helping hand. The *Yorkshire Post* in 1873 described a tournament in Leeds that quite openly offered £15 to the winning team and 15 shillings to each player, so it seems odd that there was such horror at a story in the same paper six years later described as "such a startling statement as … we can hardly give credence to." The revelation was that "a certain well known Yorkshire club has in its ranks a paid man." It would later be revealed that the heinous crime had been committed by Wakefield Trinity, and the player was Teddy Bartram, one of the sport's brightest talents and a former professional cricketer. His defence was not helped much by the fact that he was getting £52 a year from his somewhat vague position as 'assistant secretary', and had also been 'lent' money by the club.

Such situations were fairly new to Yorkshire rugby in 1879, and the immediate reaction was to lift, word for word, one of the MCC's cricket rules that stated that "no gentleman ought to make a profit by his services … but that if any gentleman feel difficulty in joining the match without pecuniary assistance he shall not be barred from playing by having his actual expenses defrayed." Expenses could be covered, but all other payments were illegal.

Blackheath's Arthur Budd made the RFU's position on professionalism patently clear in the 1886 issue of the *Football Annual*. "To take a very close analogy, mark the progress of events in the sister game" he wrote. "Only six months after the legitimisation of the bastard we see two professional teams left to fight out the final Cup tie. To what does all this tend?

MIKE ROBERTS – THE SAME OLD GAME: CODIFICATION

… I am correct, I believe, in saying that in the whole of the North of England and the Midlands there is not a single amateur football eleven. What does this mean? Why that the amateurs in those districts have been out-classed, and been submerged by professionals, and have now to seek other modes of recreation than Association football for their leisure … we would ask all who have the welfare of the game at heart to consider what would be the effect of recognised professionalism in the Rugby game … Gentlemen who play football once a week as a pastime will find themselves no match for men who give up their whole time and abilities to it. How should they? One by one, as they find themselves outclassed, they will desert the game, and leave the field to professionals. And what sport, we would ask, has thriven when supported by professionals only? Why, none."

It was obviously ridiculous for Budd to reckon that every single soccer club in the north was professional, which would defy financial logic. And just because the working class teams were beating the toffs at their own game, there was no reason for the latter to stop playing it altogether. Montague Shearman felt it was a case of sour grapes, and as far as he was concerned, the gentleman amateurs could like it or lump it. "It would be strange, indeed, were gentlemen to desert a game as soon as they met with a reverse from the 'players'" he wrote. "But apart from this we think the Rugby Union authorities are wrong for quite different reasons. Were gentlemen forced by any rule to meet opponents whom they disliked, we could well agree with him; but no club need ever play with any clubs but those it chooses, nor in the Rugby game, where there is no national cup tie, is there any moral obligation for a club of gentlemen to meet any crack club of 'players' to try conclusions."

But such handpicking of opponents was not so easy in Yorkshire, where Shearman notes in the same publication that "it is almost in Yorkshire alone that the 'cup tie enthusiasm' has taken hold of the spectators of the Rugby game." Arthur Hudson, a Leeds wool manufacturer, had invented the Yorkshire Challenge Cup in 1877. "We will make football the game for every boy in Yorkshire and Yorkshire shall be able to play the rest of England and beat it" he proudly proclaimed as he donated a trophy, *t'owd tin pot*, but no medals, because that would have had too much of a whiff of professionalism to it.

Just like soccer's FA Cup, having more of a purpose to matches sparked off a fresh wave of enthusiasm. Eight thousand people turned up to watch Halifax's first cup tie, and when they faced their first away trip, to beat Wakefield Trinity, they took five hundred fans with them. When the two clubs met again in the following year's final, 12,000 people saw Trinity get their revenge.

There was a huge rivalry between these two teams. Press reports frequently mention crowds of supporters gate crashing matches and the police being hopelessly under-prepared to react. Referees were lynched, and in 1879, Halifax supporters were so bitter about defeat to Wakefield that they attacked their train and almost overturned the carriage. Among the bones of contention were suspicions surrounding halfback Rufus Ward's switch from Trinity to

LEAGUES AND GENTLEMEN

Halifax, apparently because his girlfriend lived there, although others were sure he had been tempted there by a sneaky backhander, a practice known at the time as 'kidnapping'.

Local rivalries in Yorkshire became so intense that it was as much about the winning as the taking part. Arthur Hudson was most perturbed by all this bickering, and announced in 1881 that he might ask for his trophy back because he was so upset at the way it had turned "football clubs into organisations for the collection of very large sums of money (which there was reason to fear was not always disbursed in the best manner) and football grounds into the recognised haunts of betting men."

And it also meant the amateur clubs, just as Budd had feared, were soon pushed into the background. Hull White Star's working men's club was soon outclassing the elitist Hull FC, and the same was the case with the all-embracing York Melbourne, who eventually swallowed up the dwindling remnants of the public school old boys playing for York FC when the sides merged in 1882. Some sides, like the original Leeds club, simply refused to enter the cups and only played their social equals, and eventually faded into insignificance as a result.

There were no cup competitions in Lancashire, but even there middle class teams came under increasing pressure to prove their worth, and it was telling that when Manchester's gentlemen finally agreed to take on the 'Colliers' from Swinton, they were beaten by a try to nil. Despite persistent requests for Lancashire to set up its own rugby cup competition, the governing body steadfastly clung onto its old ideals. Eventually it was down to the semi-autonomous West Lancashire and Border Towns Rugby Union to start the county's first cup competition in 1886 – Wigan, St Helens and Warrington were among the entrants. Lancashire provided several of the founder members of soccer's Football League in 1888, and a year later its rugby clubs felt they had no option but to imitate that and establish their own league. Crowds started flocking to games in their thousands. Had Lancastrian rugby saved itself from soccer in the nick of time?

Montagu Shearman didn't think so, saying that "it is strongly felt that the Rugby Union game, with its collaring and throwing to the ground, its scrimmaging and its collisions, is naturally so rough that not the least occasion should be given for allowing warm partisanship to lead to ill-temper, and ill-temper to brutality … The present writer has seen various Rugby Union cup ties, and never left such a match without feeling strongly that they are an abomination."

Pro life

The RFU's Arthur Budd also felt that cups and leagues bred competitiveness, which in turn bred professionalism and unfairness. "The Rugby Union Committee finding themselves face to face with the hydra, have determined to throttle it before it is big enough to throttle them" he said in something akin to a declaration of war.

91

MIKE ROBERTS – THE SAME OLD GAME: CODIFICATION

Throttle it they set out to do. While 'veiled professional' soccer clubs in the north went to Scotland in search of potential talent, the rugby clubs scoured South Wales for similar supplies. Dewsbury were probably the first club to spot this happy hunting ground, and from the mid 1880s they were well accustomed to the sound of the Welsh accent. Most notorious were Cardiff's William Stadden and Angus Stuart in 1886, who had been so taken by the touring Dewsbury lads and their tales of a Yorkshire market town with a booming trade in recycling old woollen items into heavy blankets and uniforms that they could not resist the temptation to move north. It was surely no coincidence that Mark Newsome, who offered them work at his spinning plant, was also captain and president of the local rugby club, and would later be a leading campaigner for more permissive laws on the payment and movement of rugby players.

But despite the accusations of professionalism, nothing could be proved. There was nothing in the rules to stop somebody getting a job in a different town, and therefore also finding a new rugby club. But the RFU was suspicious about what was really going on, and later that year of 1886, for clubs like Dewsbury to give players a 'helping hand' in their search for employment would be deemed an illegal practice. The RFU also penned into their rules the stipulation that "a man will be a professional and debarred from playing if he receives from his club or any member of it any money payment whatsoever, even for secretarian work or labour for his club[24], any recompense for loss of time, any training expenses." The rules were now harsher than ever.

There were fireworks on the way. The witch-hunt against professionalism often reached ludicrous levels. Cleckheaton were suspended in 1888 for the atrocity of offering free cloth to its players as a way of encouraging them to continue training through the summer. It is possible that it was not so much the cloth that bothered the authorities as the training, something regarded as 'dishonourable', almost cheating. It reeked of professionalism, as did the playing of games in the summer, and in 1890, the YRU suspended eight clubs for such repulsive overindulgence.

Another famous early case was that of Welsh international brothers David and Evan James, or the 'curly haired marmosets'. In March 1892, they both left Swansea to play for Broughton Rangers in Manchester. Speaking to the *Clarion*, the Broughton secretary claimed "you know how things are in Swansea. Trade is bad and the wages … not of the highest. So they came to Manchester in search of employment. Is there anything extraordinary in that?" Actually there may have been. The same paper spoke to a contact in Wales who reckoned the duo "were idolised in Swansea but their demands were too exorbitant." The RFU investigated the case, and although they failed to find any evidence that the Taffs had been paid, they were convinced that they had asked for money, which was bad enough in the RFU's book. They wouldn't be allowed to play again until the ban was overturned in 1896.

---

[24] The 'labour for the club' bit ruled out the loophole cricket clubs were using to 'conceal' professionalism by pretending to employ players in administrative roles.

LEAGUES AND GENTLEMEN

Not everybody was willing to tolerate the sheer absurdity of it all. In 1890, Ted Southall, who was called before the YRU committee on suspected professionalism on the grounds that he was also the secretary of the Leeds Cricket Club simply told them where they could stick their committee and announced that he'd rather give up the game than face their show-trial.

Heckmondwike had three England internationals including the great Dicky Lockwood, who was almost certainly earning a wage, and were banned for three months when they failed to explain how it was that despite the huge crowds they attracted, their books claimed that their gate takings had never been any more than twenty quid. It was also a bit odd how all the players that joined the club found work at the same factory. Even odder than that, their players were allotted 4d each for refreshments at players' meetings. This was fine in theory, but Francis Marshall was a little concerned about the frequency of said gatherings. In just one month in 1888, he calculated that they must have had 60 of them. Quality!

The whole farce would make a wonderful setting for a sit-com. There was an incredibly generous, and quite possibly fictional, gentlelady in Harrogate, who sent the most lavish of Christmas presents to the players, while by an amazing stroke of fortune, the weekly winners of the lottery at the Elland club were always the players themselves.

In 1892, Tadcaster actually banned one of their own players, England international William Bromet, for singing in the bar after a game and passing around a hat to collect 12 shillings. Another popular way of covertly employing players was to put them in charge of local pubs. Either that or in the 1890s, somebody had spotted that people with experience of pulling pints were also ideally suited to rucks and mauls. Bradford's 1893 Yorkshire championship winning side contained no fewer than eleven publicans.

Testimonial matches are played these days in honour of long-serving players, but in the 19th century they were used to raise money in the form of a 'golden handshake'. It was obviously illegal, but a player that was about to retire anyway was hardly going to be too bothered about being banned by the Union. Wakefield's Teddy Bartram, rugby's first proven professional, was in his thirties by 1889. He could have played on for a few more years, but preferred to take up the offer of a full honours testimonial. That meant he could never play rugby again, but also put an extra £50 in his bank account.

In Wales, a collection fund run via the Cardiff Coal Exchange in 1896 managed to raise 'hundreds' of pounds as a gesture of thanks to the nation's first great superstar, Arthur Gould[25]. The tricky argument was that none of this money had, in theory, come from any club or union, and if the Welsh populace was willing to bond together and hand cash over to Gould by their own free will, was this really professionalism? The RFU certainly thought it was, and severed links with the Welsh Union, who took advantage of what would be a year in the wilderness to present the now retired Gould with the title deeds to a house.

---

[25] Although professionalism seemed to exist on the biggest scale in Lancashire and Yorkshire, it was not limited to those two counties. Other than South Wales, there were also investigations into alleged cases in Scotland, the Midlands and the South West too.

MIKE ROBERTS – THE SAME OLD GAME: CODIFICATION

Presenting a player with real estate was an extreme example, for most cases of 'professionalism' were little more than an extra coin or two in the pitiful wage packets being paid to manual labourers. One wonders how much, deep in their hearts, the middle class rugby community was really bothered about surrendering the Corinthian values of amateurism as they were about the potential knock-on effects of letting their social inferiors get involved. For them, rugby was all about mixing it with their fellow old boys, and enjoying the high-brow social gatherings that followed the games. It was a game for gentlemen with money, status and leisure time, just the things that they were so hell-bent on preventing the less privileged from getting their grubby hands on. The amateurs simply didn't like the idea of being swept aside by flocks of uncouth blue-collar workers and their thousands of uncultured followers from the nondescript suburbs of northern factory towns.

The *Yorkshire Post* in 1889 felt that the presence of working class rugby players "has led to the corruption of the sport, which has in some districts tended to drive gentlemen out of the field." One reassuring letter went that "as our club is pretty nearly free from the working-class element, you have nothing to fear about a rough or noisy game[26]." And another comment went that "it was an ill day for the game when the northern labourer diverted his attention from quoits and rabbit coursing and pigeon flying and turned it to football ... the lower class player is the greatest adept at breaking laws when the referee is not looking[27]." The RFU didn't want these people, and for them to even be paid for the privilege of staining their sport was a concept too grotesque for words.

Arthur Budd was adamant that if the working man "cannot afford the leisure to play a game, he must do without it. How many splendid athletes are never heard of again when they leave their universities and schools, because they have to follow avocations which will not allow them to play football matches, which necessitate one, two, or three days' desertion of their profession?" His argument, and not necessarily a poor one, was that members of the wealthier classes that had no time for games simply had to do without them – should it not be the same for the working classes too? He reckoned there would be public outcry if a stockbroker took a couple of days off to play football and even demanded payment to compensate for the work he was missing. Yet that is exactly what the working man wanted.

But Montagu Shearman smelt the rat of hypocrisy. He writes that "we must still confess that we prefer a man who plays for money and says that he does so, to a gentleman who receives liberal sums for 'expenses'."

He had a valid point. After all, if paying rugby players for their services was really the issue, then how come in 1887, staunch amateur Arthur Budd's own Blackheath players were paid £4 a head to travel up from London to play Bradford? And why were the ultimate

---

[26] Quoted by Frank Marshall from a Londoner on the subject of Goole FC and a potential fixture with York in 1882.
[27] From a chap called Creston in the *Fortnightly Review* in 1894.

LEAGUES AND GENTLEMEN

bastions in amateur values, the Corinthians, charging opponents £150 for the honour of a game?

And what was that tour of Australia and New Zealand all about in 1888, perhaps one of the worst shows of two-facedness the RFU has ever displayed? The plan sent the first ever British trip to the Southern Hemisphere in the form of a 20 man squad of Englishmen (all but one northerners) on a 35-match tour of Australasia, including some games by the Victorian rules. It was a mammoth undertaking, the whole thing taking no less than thirty weeks, and one of the players, Alfred Shaw, later had no shame in admitting that "we arranged the trip in the hope of making money." Admittedly, the RFU had always maintained that they would only ever endorse a trip to Australia if they were fully satisfied it was a non profit-making venture, and this clearly wasn't. But although they refused to have anything to do with it, this would prove easier said than done.

The first problem was a member of the touring party called Jack Clowes. He played for Halifax, who had recently beaten Dewsbury, a side that appealed to the RFU after the game on the grounds that Clowes was a professional being paid to go to Australia. Clowes was indeed willing to admit that he'd been offered £15 to tour, but by the time he had been declared a pro and banned from playing it was too late. He had already set sail! It meant he'd be part of the English touring party, but would not be allowed to play a single game.

The trip was not much of a success for the captain of the English side, Bob Seddon, who was tragically drowned in a boating trip while down under, but for everybody else involved it was probably not just a once-in-a-lifetime chance to wander among kangaroos to the sound of didgeridoos. It is unlikely that there was a single member of the squad that didn't come out of the trip with a healthier bank balance. With reports of relatively minor players bagging anything from £90 to £200 for their efforts, one can only wonder what bonuses were collected by the likes of replacement captain Andrew Stoddart, who was offered a £50 cheque just to join the tour, with more to follow, it seems.

When the players returned, it was to be an embarrassing episode for the RFU. All of the players were temporarily banned while an investigation was conducted. It would have been easy to simply hand out punishments to all those avaricious working class players, but at the same time they had the rather delicate subject of some rather over-generous 'expenses' being paid to 'gentleman amateurs' of such high standing as Stoddart. There was only one thing for it. In order to save face, the RFU simply asked all of the players to sign an affidavit making it clear that they had not made anything out of the tour. In other words, everybody was encouraged to lie and the RFU decided not to press charges and instead brush the whole dirty affair under the table. At least Clowes' ban was conveniently wavered. This was just the first of many episodes of over a century of shamateurism in the rugby union game.

Big issues

Whether it was right or wrong to condemn professionalism, doing so was playing into the hands of the Football Association, who had legalised the practice in 1885. With the attraction of cup competitions, and the possibility of earning money from football, it was not so much the respective merits of the two codes as games as it was other issues that caused a conspicuous drift away from rugby and towards soccer.

As Lancashire's *Oldham Evening Chronicle* put it in 1890, "the association game is slowly taking our best men, as it is only likely that they will play where they can be paid." AA Sutherland wrote in the *Clarion* in 1892 that "less than ten years ago not a single association club could be found either in Manchester or district" but he could now name several clubs that once "stood up high in rugby circles" but were now playing the association game. "The conservatism evinced by rugby footballers in the Palantine is astounding and those who profess to look after the best interest of the game are content to sit while the tide of association football makes great inroads into the stronghold of the rugby game."

It was clear to him that it was time for rugby to move with the times. Two years later, in 1894, the same man was bemoaning the "lamentable want of brains or honesty ... people are getting heartily sick and tired of the whole thing ... there are two courses open for the clubs to take – either amateurism or professionalism ... What we do want, and pine for, is the honest official bold enough to give prominence to the wishes of the majority of the working men players, and strike out for professionalism."

Sutherland was not the kind of man to mince his words. He did not even feel the issue of expenses was worth considering. Why meet half way? "What the working man requires is hard cash for services rendered, and in view of the money the clubs make, his demand is fair and legitimate."

Was it time for rugby to follow soccer's lead and endorse professionalism? If it wanted to keep up with soccer, it didn't really have much choice. But it was a divided issue. An 'Old Player' wrote in the 1889 *Football Annual* that "the rugby game is losing ground among the working class and association is spreading in its place, owing to the pecuniary advantages from the latter game. The loss of followers of the grand old game is regrettable, yet looking at the present state of all professional sports, we cannot but think that this possible loss is far preferable to legalising professionalism."

Apart from the morality, there was concern about the economics of professional football. Nobody was sure that rugby would really be able to compete with professional soccer, and not everybody was sure that professional soccer had been such a wise financial move either. It would be a long time before multinationals were willing to pay big bucks to advertise on shirts that would then be packaged off for sale to pay-per-viewing fans in the Far East. 19th century clubs could charge spectators an entrance fee, and perhaps get a bit more out of them by flogging refreshments or offering lottery tickets, but they were by no means raking in a fortune, and it was often only thanks to the support of wealthy patrons looking for a way of securing popularity ahead of the local elections that many could afford to operate at all. Slipping the odd brown envelope in a pocket or two was one thing. But having the entire squad queuing up each week for their wage slips was going to put quite a strain on the resources, especially when many clubs were struggling to get by as it was.

There were other reasons for opposing professionalism. Soccer man Charles Clegg felt that "if professionalism is allowed it will only be placing greater power in the hands of betting men and encourage gambling" and that could lead to teams accepting backhanders to throw games as well as win them – something that had already brought about the downfall of boxing as a respectable sport.

And then Rowland Hill makes a powerful point in Marshall's book when arguing that professional football was not like cricket, a more sedentary game a man could play well into middle age without too much risk of injury. He explains that "professionalism … is injurious to the individual who becomes a professional. A man finds for a time that it is more remunerative to play football than to follow his regular occupation. He is induced in many cases to give up his work at an age the most important in his life for forming habits of industry; he does not realise that a man cannot play for many years in sufficiently good form to earn good wages from the game. After a time his play falls off and he has to go. He has got out of the way of work, and lost valuable time in which he should have been learning a trade."

In the 21st century, the morality of professionalism is rarely considered an issue, but the aspect Hill highlights is still a major concern. We all know the players that have forged glittering careers in the game. But those who are raking in thousands of notes a week are just the tip of the iceberg. Beneath them are hordes of others slogging it out in the minor clubs and leagues, often struggling to make ends meet. Some may be lucky enough to one day get signed to a big name club, some may go on to get work in football coaching or administration, but many others find themselves going into their thirties and the twilight of their football careers with nothing to put on their CVs apart from the fact that they are good at kicking a ball.

It was the same in the 19th century. Wray Vamplew notes that of the 250 newly signed professionals for the 1893-94 soccer season, only 20 percent had their contracts renewed the following year, and only 12 were still playing four years later. Football has always been a precarious career choice.

Insurance was also an issue in the 1880s. The amateurs' attitude was that if you were injured on the football field, you took it like a man. Nobody was forced to play football, and if you did get seriously hurt, it was your own stupid fault. To expect to be compensated financially was frankly obscene. But as well as the morality of it, there was also the fear that insurance was basically professionalism under another guise, and clubs could not be trusted not to use the system as another way of bending the accounts. The RFU eventually bowed to pressure in 1886 and allowed a maximum of ten shillings a day in insurance payments, a

MIKE ROBERTS – THE SAME OLD GAME: CODIFICATION

paltry sum, and such payments could only be made via *bona fide* insurance companies, thus preventing payments to players in the form of false insurance claims.

Professionalism also threatened to put an end to the community base of football teams. Here we can go back to Arthur Budd, who felt professionalism "leads to the wholesale importation of players of repute from other districts or, it may be, countries, to the exclusion of indigenous ability. Is this sport? I say, certainly not. It is nothing more nor less than handing over success in the game to the best capitalised club. If you could give me the wealth of the Duke of Westminster and professionalism in Rugby football to boot, I would in a very short time produce the most formidable fifteen in the United Kingdom. They should be called the 'Charing Cross Crusaders', though, probably, on their arrival from the North the majority would have to make inquiries as to the whereabouts of that metropolitan centre … One can understand people becoming enthusiastic over a *bona-fide* club, that is, a club composed of players who have been born or reside in the district but it is past my comprehension to understand how eleven men, transported from various points of the compass, can inflame with partisanship the natives whom they are actually excluding from the team which they ought themselves to be representing."

Today, Budd is probably turning in his grave as soccer and rugby clubs employ players that sometimes don't even speak the same language as their fans, but who still queue up to buy replica shirts with their names on, as a replacement for last year's design, which carried the name of a different player that is now earning twice as much at a club on the other side of the world.

If Budd had a point at the time, then over a century later he most certainly does when he decries "the vanity of those people who can deceive themselves with the hallucination that renown accrues to Birmingham, Nottingham, or Preston by victories earned through the prowess of imported Scotsmen who have as much to do with either of those cities as I have with Jerusalem."

You may also start coming round to Budd's way of thinking when you hear him comment far-sightedly that "three days a week are as much as anybody can play, and then only for an hour and a half at a stretch. This brings the total of the week's play to four and a half hours. Allowing for training and practising in addition to this, the greater part of a man's time would still remain unutilised. The profession of football, then, means a life of idleness while it lasts."

A different league

But the RFU was based in London, where football of either form was still a relatively low-key affair, hence making professionalism impracticable. Even if the clubs had endorsed it, there simply wasn't the public interest to make it work. For the major games played at the Oval, even for the internationals with Scotland and the annual North v South games, they'd be lucky to get 2000 people coming through the gates. In the south, it was playing sport that

LEAGUES AND GENTLEMEN

mattered. Merely standing around watching others play was the pathetic antithesis of Muscular Christianity. Not so in the north, where the Lancashire v Yorkshire game of 1878 in Halifax was watched by 14,000. As Charles Alcock wrote in his *Football Annual* that year, "it will be a great day for the Union if a third that number can be got together at an international match in London."

The RFU was clearly out of touch with developments in the north, where the debate over the future of the game was taking place against the background of social revolution. The proletariat were making a stand. They were striking in the mines, they were striking in the mills, they were striking in the gasworks and they were striking in the docks. The mob was rising, there was rioting on the streets, and if that wasn't enough to trouble the middle class patience, not only did they want the working day reduced and their wages increased, but they wanted to be paid for playing football too!

Having cited the Reverend Francis Marshall's book on numerous occasions, it is now time for the man himself to enter our story. He was the personification of the fight against professionalism, and never tired of writing lengthy articles in the press to condemn its evils, whilst preaching the values of the Muscular Christians Society he had helped to found. He was once described as "the one being in the world who had been known to pulverise an opponent with a single blast of two words – SIT DOWN!"

His arch-rival was Mr James Miller, the president of the Yorkshire branch of the Union, where Bradford and Leeds had just been exposed for paying players, and where an accusation from the Cumberland County Union of an unnamed Yorkshire club poaching one their players through the offer of money had led to Lancashire and Yorkshire combined threatening to withdraw from the RFU if it dared issue any punishment.

Relations with the south had been in gradual decline since 1887, when the RFU had refused to admit Mark Newsome, a man who was suspiciously supportive of the working class cause, onto its executive. Until this point, Yorkshire had, if anything, been the most vehement union in the pursuit of professionalism, and had been the first to draft laws illegalising it. But by the 1890s, and with the Yorkshire game increasingly more working class influenced, the newer members had very different views to their predecessors.

There is a famous cartoon of the period in which Marshall says to Miller "Oh, fie, go away naughty boy. I don't play with boys who can't afford to take a holiday for football any day they like!"

To which Miller replies "Yes, that's just you to a T; you'd make it so that no lad whose father wasn't a millionaire could play at all in a really good team. For my part I see no reason why the men who make the money shouldn't have a share in the spending of it."

Sentiments echoed by somebody called Nomad in the *Yorkshireman* in 1893, who felt that if players "are not fit subjects for remuneration, then … the thousands that flock to witness their performances ought not to be charged with any admission fee." He made the very valid analogy of comparing the footballer's situation with that of actors in the local theatre. Nobody was suggesting that the actors should not get paid.

With the northern clubs pushing for some kind of professionalism to be made legal, the 1893 AGM of the RFU at the Westminster Palace Hotel, London promised to be a lively event, and the YRU even laid on a special train to visit eleven northern towns and collect potential supporters. Although the twelve carriages were by no means full, there weren't too many seats going spare.

Defending his motion that "players be allowed compensation for *bona fide* loss of time" Miller gave a powerful speech. "Why have we brought this proposal forward?" he said. "Simply because of the changed conditions under which Rugby football is now played … Formerly it was played only in public schools, the Universities, and by the favoured classes, but the game has become the favoured winter pastime of the young working class men in this country. This is particularly the case in the great industrialised centres of the North of England. The Union, unfortunately, still declines to recognise this new type of player. We recognise him in the North and we treat him differently to what we would have done some years ago. The question is one … which we in the North have to deal with and which people in the south seem to know nothing about. The working man has to leave his work and lose his wages to play for the benefit of his club, his county or his country, but he received no recompense for the loss of earnings. Was that fair, right or reasonable? These men naturally ask why they should have to play on such disadvantageous terms compared to the solicitor, the stockbroker, the clerk or the undergraduate. Why should they take part in these matches at a loss to themselves? I have no desire to make football a source of profit to the player, but equally it was not meant that players should play it at financial loss to themselves. If it was legitimate to refund expenses, why not refund lost wages? We wish to remove an injustice, and we have the true interests of the game at heart as much as anyone in this room. Please don't pooh-pooh it simply because it comes from a county which is not always a savoury morsel to others. In concluding, I believe that if the proposal was carried it would be the strongest barrier against professionalism that has yet been devised."

Mr. Rowland Hill, the Secretary of the RFU, replied to the proposal by commenting that "if the resolution is passed it must inevitably lead towards professionalism. What this resolution means is paying men of playing football. What would be the effect on the working man? The temptation to play rugby was too great already. The opportunities were so many that a man may be away a whole week, and thus earn his wages without doing a single stroke of work. Mr Miller has not given us one practical suggestion as to how his scheme would be carried out[28]. If carried it must break up the Union, and much as I regret this it would be preferable to have division than professionalism."

---

[28] Hill seems a little short-sighted here, for soccer had been professional for a full ten years by the time he made his speech, and was surely the perfect example that, yes, professional football could work.

LEAGUES AND GENTLEMEN

The debate raged on, generally regurgitating everything that had already been given ample coverage in the press. At least it gave some people the chance to put a face and voice to the arguments, but nothing was said that was likely to have changed many minds. When it went to the vote, broken time soundly lost by 136 votes to 282 to the motion that "this meeting, believing the above principle to be contrary to the interests of the game and its spirit, declines to sanction the same." Despite all the efforts to pack northerners on the trains to help usher the professionalism bid through, if they had been around at the time, Paddy Power would have paid out the moment the first man walked through the door.

The legitimacy of the vote has been called into question. The RFU had gone to great lengths to ensure the amateurs were always the majority. The story goes that they came armed with 120 proxy votes against professionalism, which meant the northerners never really stood a chance. It has also been suggested that several of the southern clubs were just made up for the occasion and that rather than their usual one vote each, each of Oxford and Cambridge University's many colleges were treated as separate entities too. However, Tony Collins gets the impression that these conspiracy theories were cooked up later, for there is no contemporary evidence that any of these accusations were true. All kinds of other rumours were circulated. That several northerners had been so disgusted by the debate that they walked out before the voting started. That others were still wandering around London trying to work out where Westminster Palace Hotel was. That not everybody travelling south had any intention of attending the meeting at all and just fancied the chance for a subsidised trip to the capital. That many members of the Lancashire contingent may have been uncomfortable with the idea of siding with the RFU, but were far less comfortable with the idea of being left on their own with the Yorkshiremen.

Whatever the causes, it was patently clear that if the supporters of broken time were going to get their way, they weren't going to get it through democratic negotiation with the RFU. Just to make sure the northerners never caused trouble again, the following meeting of the Rugby Union amended its rules to say that "the name of the society shall be called the 'Rugby Football Union' and only clubs comprised entirely of amateurs shall be eligible for membership, and its headquarters shall be London where all general meetings shall be held." So there.

False horizons

Having got what they wanted, the RFU followed on with even stronger measures to make sure payments to players were driven out of the game. The cheats were exposed left, right and centre, largely thanks to the hordes of rugby puritans up and down the country that seemed more intent on grassing on opponents to the authorities than beating them on the field. Leigh was the first big club to suffer. For allegedly paying their Welsh imports, they were moved to the bottom of the league table and banned from charging gate receipts at games. Salford soon met the same fate, but rather than be made scapegoats, they presented cases against other clubs for the same offence. One of those, Wigan, was soon in the sin-bin too. Before too long, there would hardly be any top flight club in Lancashire that was not helping the LRU with its enquiries.

All of this undermined the credibility of the northern game in much the way that doping charges affect cycling today. The RFU even went as far as stating that "the burden of proof of innocence lies on the club or person charged." In other words, guilty until proven innocent. It's a wonder they didn't announce that they would only let possible professionals off the hook if they could survive an hour's dry-roasting at the stake. It was a contentious clause that the RFU would eventually be forced to retract when it was pointed out to somebody that medieval justice systems didn't hold in any walk of modern society.

The RFU's argument in the south was clearly not compatible with the situation in the north, where it was no longer a matter of whether rugby should be professional or not, but a matter of what should be done about a game that clearly already was. The idea of severing ties with the RFU was mooted again and again, but that was an extreme the northerners wanted to avoid at all costs. Although they operated against working class backgrounds, the men in charge were middle class businessmen that had no desire for any kind of split from the Union, and were as determined as the RFU to find a way of holding things together. A north/south divide in rugby was the last thing the sport needed at a time when it was already starting to play second fiddle to the Association game. One of the FA's greatest achievements was the way it had united the whole country under one body. Somehow or other, rugby had to do the same[29].

The RFU might have thought that it had got its way, but the situation would prove untenable. Crushing sanctions gradually led the northern clubs to stop paying their players, who had no option but to return to work, leaving clubs without players, matches being cancelled and northern rugby heading nowhere, and heading there very fast indeed. The more the authorities were successful in eradicating payments in rugby, the more it made the clubs realise that unless things changed, they had no hope of survival.

The RFU upped the ante in 1895, when they placed a blanket ban on entrance fees. They also stamped out the blatant marketing ploy of playing 13-a-side matches in the hope of making them more appealing to spectators. They'd be changing the names of the clubs to things like the Tigers, Bulls and Sharks next! That major clampdown had the reverse effect.

---

[29] Also, division was vehemently opposed to the national psyche of the time. As Tony Collins so rightly observes, this was a period when the once heavily regionalised British landscape was developing a stronger sense of national unity than ever before. National newspapers, national rail networks, national retail stores, national sports competitions. The seeds of what we now call globalisation were being sown on a national level. A man who took a train from Hull to Bristol would no longer be faced by such culture shock as he would have done fifty years earlier. He would see familiar products in the shops, he would see people reading the same papers, and he would see people playing sports by identical rules. Disunion was not what rugby wanted.

LEAGUES AND GENTLEMEN

The RFU had pushed its luck that little bit too far. One more straw and the northern camel's back would snap.

The north in union

On August 29, 1895, the representatives of 21 northern clubs met at the George Hotel, Huddersfield[30]. The clubs were (from Yorkshire) Batley, Bradford, Brighouse Rangers, Dewsbury, Halifax, Huddersfield, Hull, Hunslet, Leeds, Liversidge, Manningham, Wakefield Trinity and (from Lancashire) Broughton Rangers, Leigh, Oldham, Rochdale, St Helens, Tyldesley, Warrington, Wigan and Widnes. Stockport also agreed to join the union that day, for even though they couldn't attend, they were able to state their intentions thanks to yet another handy little invention that was changing the way we lived, the telephone, and Runcorn also joined in time to play the first season.

All but one of the assembled clubs[31] decided that to "live honestly under the proposed new rules of the English Rugby Union was a moral impossibility and much as we regret the severance from the parent body, the bulk of the far-seeing football enthusiasts are unanimous in their opinion that the time has come to kick against the ridiculous rules and demands of the Old Lady."

As the *Huddersfield Examiner* reported the following day, their first motion was "to form a Northern Rugby Football Union, and pledge themselves to push forward without delay its establishment on the principle of payment for *bona fide* broken time only." The *Hull Daily Mail* wrote that the clubs were "to be commended for throwing off the cloak of hypocrisy, conceit and subterfuge, and standing out for those essentially English characteristics – honesty and straightforwardness." As opposed to those shady, dishonest foreigners.

In its first year of existence, 1895–96, the National Union imitated what professional soccer clubs had done in 1888, and cricket in 1889, by creating the Rugby Football League, which was also played on a home and away basis. It turned out to be too overambitious a project. The extensive travel proved a heavy burden, and especially with droves of new clubs seeking admission, for the next few years the League was divided into the Yorkshire and Lancashire championships. In 1901–02 the two counties were united again, and although there have been numerous changes in system, with different divisional and play-off ideas being introduced over various periods, the top flight has always basically been the same one that since 1996 has been known as the Super League[32].

---

[30] The George Hotel still stands today, opposite the railway station.

[31] Dewsbury asked to be given more time to think things over, and eventually opted to remain with the RFU. After two poor seasons, they decided to defect to the Northern Union in 1897, where they didn't win a single game and only scored two tries all season. Rugby obviously wasn't their thing, and the next season, they took up soccer. What is now the Dewsbury Rams rugby league club was formed a year later in 1898.

[32] The knockout tournament, the Challenge Cup, was introduced a year after the League in 1896-97, and barring the war years has been played every season since. In its first edition, Batley defeated St Helens 10-3 in front of

MIKE ROBERTS – THE SAME OLD GAME: CODIFICATION

It was because of this that the professional clubs came to be known as those that were 'playing in the league' as opposed to those that had stayed 'with the union', and as the codes went their separate ways, modern parlance started differentiating between 'rugby league' and 'rugby union'.

But although the creation of the Northern Union has since been championed as the triumph of the lower classes, at first it wasn't quite as all-embracing as one might imagine. The NU knew that rugby only offered very short-term prospects, and rightly wanted to encourage players to realise that life was not just about egg-chasing but egg-nesting as well. So, it did not immediately endorse professionalism, and actually imposed hefty fines and suspensions on any offenders. All it allowed was a fairly measly six shillings a day, and only for genuine loss of earnings. Otherwise, players had to have full-time employment outside of the sport, and those that belonged to 'unrespectable trades' were far from welcome[33].

Much of the concern in the build-up to the sanctioning of broken time payments had been that it was only meeting the problem half way. The critics were proved right. They had only moved the goalposts slightly, and as expected, the shift from money for expenses to money as compensation for lost wages merely served to make life even easier for the balance-book chefs, who cooked up more or less identical controversies to the ones before the formation of the NU. The authorities seemed to spend their entire lives investigating the veracity of players' real jobs, and dished out bans wherever they spotted any irregularities.

Two particularly poignant examples of the daftness of it all were TD Davies of Leeds, who suffered the misfortune of being sacked from his job on the Thursday before a match and being expected to find a new job in time to play the following day, and R Petrie of Seaton who was in trouble for missing a day's work even though he had never made a claim for payment from his club in the first place!

The NU, thanks to its unpractical regulations, was becoming a farce. You can almost imagine fans looking bemusedly indifferent as the latest star back from Swansea was unveiled, but partying in the streets to celebrate the acquisition of an Oxbridge lawyer specialising in labour laws. He wasn't much cop in a ruck, but with his knack for spotting inconsistencies in rival players' work schedules, he could make a win out of even the most resounding of defeats on the field!

So extreme were the NU's controls that some clubs now found it harder to satisfy their players than they used to, albeit illegally, under the auspices of the RFU. It was common

---

a crowd of 13,490 at Headingley. In 1929, and because it was the only place that could seat enough people, the final was played at the new Wembley Stadium in London, which, apart from a few exceptions due to unavailability and the recent reconstruction, has been the home for the final ever since, even though it is nowhere near the rugby league heartland in the north.

[33] What the NU described as *bona fide* employment did not include just about any kind of work involving the pub trade, which included the commonly semi-invented position of 'billiard marker', who kept score for the players. It was bit of an unfair blanket ban that must have affected scores of *bona fide* publicans and barmen, but the NU was aware how close the association was between breweries and rugby clubs.

LEAGUES AND GENTLEMEN

knowledge that the NU limit of six shillings a day wouldn't be enough to entice any Welshmen up north, as they were able to get much more than that back home in the form of under the counter payments from their RFU clubs in Glamorgan. Any Welshman that moved north was only doing so because he was being offered a lot more than the legal maximum.

Rather than wallow in their improved conditions, teams and players seemed just as discontent than ever, and the first years of the NU were blighted by a series of strikes. Some players weren't getting their money (their clubs probably finding they didn't actually have it), others wanted more, and others still were disappointed to find that their payments weren't in cold hard cash but were merely in kind, while the most burning issue was the way several clubs, such as Wigan, paid the backs more money than the forwards, given that they were the players the fans really parted with their money to see.

It clearly wasn't working as well as the NU had planned, but the system huffed and puffed along for a decade. Matters finally came to a head in an infamous Challenge Cup encounter between Leigh and Wigan in 1905. Leigh beat Wigan, but Wigan discovered something dodgy in a Leigh player's working status. The game was replayed, and this time it was Wigan's turn to win and Leigh's turn to produce evidence of something suspect regarding a Wigan player's employment.

The NU decided Wigan would qualify for the next round, but would not be able to keep any of the gate money from their next game (against Halifax), but the farce was lost on nobody. By the end of the year, the NU was fed up to the teeth with all this tomfoolery, and realised the only sensible solution would be to stop flogging a dead horse and just allow outright professionalism. And that's exactly what they did.

Change of rule

So, how was the RFU going to respond to all this? Not very well, as it happened. Players, officials or clubs that were associated to the Northern Union in any way were subjected to severe sanctions. No NU players would be allowed to play for any international rugby union teams ever again, and the RFU even imposed hefty penalties on its own members who played for or against teams in the NU.

Those people holding out hope that the RFU could still prevail in the north managed to go about things in exactly the wrong way. Rather than seek compromise, they created an environment in which very few people were left with any option other than to join the NU whether they liked it or not. Any YRU team that dared challenge an NU side to a game was immediately banned. In the case of Horbury, including a player in their line-up that had previously played against a team that included an NU player was enough to warrant a suspension.

You had to be incredibly careful who you chose to play. Goole FC probably thought they were safe when the cast of the Little Red Riding Hood pantomime challenged them to a match. Nobody thought to shout 'behind you' as a YRU official pointed out that the

MIKE ROBERTS – THE SAME OLD GAME: CODIFICATION

thespians had recently played a charity match against NU club Batley. Oh no they didn't. Oh yes they did!

The Northern Union managed quite nicely without the RFU's blessing. The RFU's membership in Yorkshire and Lancashire fell from 240 clubs in 1890 to just 25 by the turn of the century, with a paltry eleven teams entering the once great Yorkshire Cup. But the NU's real rivalry didn't lie with the amateur southerners. All that struggling to contain semi-professionalism had done Yorkshire and Lancashire rugby no favours in its battle with soccer, and had done little to curb the practice of rugby clubs and players defecting to the rival code. By 1905, you would have been hard pushed to find a city anywhere in England that didn't have a well-supported soccer club, and that meant the Northern Union strongholds too. Wigan, Leeds, Hull… from west coast to east, soccer was hammering rugby into the ground.

Mark Newsome, who would even become RFU president in 1902, had no qualms about switching his Dewsbury club from rugby to soccer in 1897. One of the most poignant examples was Barnsley, where in 1898 the local rugby trophy, the Beckett Cup, was handed over to the soccer clubs. There was no point continuing their rugby competition because there were no rugby clubs left to play in it.

But the most celebrated case was that of Manningham, the first NU champions. With soccer keen to make inroads into rugby-mad Bradford, the city was actually offered a place in the Football League even though it had no soccer club, ground or players. Unable to resist the temptation, Manningham turned their backs on rugby and became Bradford City in 1903. They had been big fish in a small pond in the NU, while in soccer terms they were nobodies, but within weeks they had become the flagship team for Bradford, where thousands had long craved a proper soccer team, and their gate receipts boomed. The city's big rugby club, Bradford, looked on with envious eyes. In 1907, in what was known as the 'Great Betrayal', most of their players decided to switch to soccer too, and became Bradford Park Avenue[34].

The provincial nature of rugby league didn't help. The Football League was a national affair, but the NU only operated in one region. Neither did the NU's proletariat image encourage the affection of middle class patrons, who like them or not, are handy things to have. And soccer worked better as a spectacle. When the FA had drafted its first rules in 1863, they were clearly seeking to create something simple with broad public appeal, and the result was a more immediate and marketable game than this thing called rugby, which was

---

[34] Bradford City won the FA Cup in 1911, but have rarely lived up the potential of being located in England's 11th biggest city. Park Avenue fared worse and forever lived in their shadow, finally going bust in 1974. They reformed in 1988, but in the lowest echelons of the English pyramid. But despite the Great Betrayal, a stalwart group of rugby players refused to switch to soccer and formed Bradford Northern, who will be more familiar today as the Super League's Bradford Bulls. Super League Grand Final wins for the Bulls in 2001, 2003 and 2005 are testimony of rugby league eventually coming good in the foothills of the Pennines.

LEAGUES AND GENTLEMEN

little more than a blubbering mass of heaving man flesh, coupled with rules and scoring systems that spectators struggled to get their heads around.

It was all pretty dull if you happened to be sitting on the other side of the pitch and didn't have a clue who exactly had the ball underneath that bundle of male testosterone. An article written in the *Yorkshire Post* in 1891 felt that "the association game is no doubt in a healthy state and this has sounded the death knell to Rugby football. Why is this? Simply because the public want a game where they can see plenty of the ball." And Harry Beardsell bemoaned how "the spectators had to be content to hear the shouts and desperate grunts of the pack of humanity that struggled for possession of the ball most of the afternoon[35]." If the NU wanted a constant supply of northern bums on northern seats, they were going to have to do something to make rugby a bit more interesting.

When soccer went professional, the Football League maintained its relations with the FA and continued to use the same set of rules. It was a different matter with the northern rugby clubs. In the very first year, 1895, one small change was made to the RFU's rules, whereby, during a scrum, the scrum half was not allowed to advance beyond his own forwards until the ball came out. This helped get the ball quickly into open play because there was nobody to interfere with the pack that won the scrum. A year later, the NU made a further modification by awarding penalties for deliberate knock-ons. Neither change made a huge difference to the way the rugby was played, but now they had started changing laws, where were they going to stop?

1897 saw the first major overhaul. First, the lineout, which had a habit of leading to nothing more than unsightly mauls, was scrapped. A soccer style throw-in was one suggested alternative, but they eventually agreed on a 'punt out' from touch, although like in the RFU rules, teams also had the option of requesting a scrum. That punt out proved a bit of a disaster, as teams would just hoof the ball up the field, and the charge to grab it caused so many injuries that the idea was abolished in 1902, making a scrum the only option when the ball went out of play.

But 1897 was also the year that the NU completely changed the scoring system. Drop goals were devalued from four points to two and penalty kicks from three points to two, meaning that the try, still worth three points, was now the most valuable way of scoring[36], something that would not happen in American football until 1912, and not until 1971 in the case of rugby union!

Following other minor modifications over the years, in 1903 the NU decided that only a penalty kick could be kicked into touch 'on the full' (i.e. without bouncing). Scathing 'unionist' EHD Sewell was particularly amused by this innovation, which it considered "by

---

[35] Speaking to the *Yorkshire Evening Post* in 1900. It was Beadsell who, in 1871, scored the first ever goal for Yorkshire against Lancashire, and what would remain the only one until 1883.

[36] The scoring system used at present in rugby league is 3 points for a try (5 in union), 2 for a conversion (also 2 in union), 1 point for a drop goal (3 in union) and 2 for a penalty (3 in union).

MIKE ROBERTS – THE SAME OLD GAME: CODIFICATION

far the most idiotic ordination ever passed by man for the utter ruination of a capital sport … the man is not yet born who … can so manipulate the ball with his foot as to make it bounce into touch[37]."

Then in 1904, teams were limited to placing just three players in the front row of the scrum (previously there had been no limit), but it was in 1906 that the NU decided to introduce a couple of changes that would imply the real split between the two codes, and which led to most of the characteristic traits that differentiate it from the union game today[38].

The debate that fifteen players on each team were too many to produce fast, flowing play had been going on for over a decade by now, while the potential financial saving of having to pay fewer players was also a factor. Twelve-a-side games were already the standard at junior level, and several experimental and exhibition matches had been played with differently numbered teams. Even so, John H Smith still felt that, when in 1906 the NU finally agreed to implement the idea of removing two forwards (the flankers), there was "much adverse criticism; but the condemnation of the theoretical stage was speedily withdrawn … and no responsible Northern critic has now a word to say against the advantages claimed for the reduced side."

It is curious to note that the downsizing to 13 players happened a quarter of a century after the American colleges had first started playing rugby 11-a-side, one of the first changes that would eventually lead to the separate code of American football. But this was not the only possible American influence on rugby league.

The chaotic pile-up of bodies in rucks or mauls was another issue addressed in 1906, the *Wakefield Express* having revealed that in three seasons in the 1890s there were "71 deaths, 208 broken bones and 158 other injuries" from playing rugby in Yorkshire alone. The iconic 'play-the-ball' rule was introduced as the solution, whereby if any player that was brought to ground or 'held', rather than scrum required by the RFU's rules, that player had to immediately put the ball back into open play by getting to his feet and rolling the ball backwards with his feet to another player. John H Smith justified this rule change as being "in order to minimise the liability of injury to players which might result if it were legal to kick at the ball while players are lying on the ground in the immediate vicinity." But it also meant that the Northern game was no longer a lumbering spectacle of two packs heaving it out with each other, but instead made the most out of its running with the ball potential.

The idea was strikingly similar to the 'snap' that Walter Camp had introduced to America twenty-five years earlier as a way of getting the ball back into open play as quickly as

---

[37] EHD Sewell *The Northern Union Game: Is it football?* in *Amateur Sport Illustrated* (1908).

[38] To the uninitiated, even today rugby union and rugby league don't really look all that different, and players often play both codes. The basic notions of tackling, running with the ball and not throwing the ball forwards are essentially the same, and you still score points for scoring tries, drop goals, penalties and conversions, although different amounts. But there are other differences between the games, which we shall explore on the next few pages.

possible, but although there may have been some American influence, observers at the time considered it to be a return to rugby's original roots, such as an article in New Zealand that said that "the most excellent rule, that was obliterated from the earlier laws of the Union has again been introduced, that a player, when collared, must put the ball into play[39]."

Another idea that was seriously discussed by the NU was a switch from an oval to a soccer-style round ball. Rugby league legend Dicky Lockwood was one of the most outspoken advocates of the idea, the belief being that it would make it easier to dribble with the feet. The idea never went through, being rejected because it was felt a round ball was too hard to punt and pass (although this never seems to have caused too many problems in the GAA), but if it had, then one wonders whether it mightn't have been a better idea just to scrap the NU altogether and join the FA!

The NU's president John H Smith reflected that "alterations have been made in the laws governing the actual playing of the game – almost all of which have been framed with the object of improvement viewed from the spectacular standpoint[40]." But rugby union diehards looked at what was going on with scorn. "The play of the working classes has not … gained one whit in the finer points which distinguish the intelligent player from him who relies on his stamina and physique" observed Frank Mitchell.

However, it's amazing to notice how many of the derided changes eventually made their way into the union game as well. Rugby union would also eventually make tries worth more than goals (which Sewell felt the NU had done "rather from a desire to be different than for any other reason"), would also copy the 'bounce to touch' rules that Sewell found so silly, would also limit the number of forwards in the front row to three, would also prevent the scrum half from standing on the opposite side of the scrum, and rugby league was also first to scrap both the 'goal from mark' and the 'field goal', which was scoring by kicking a loose ball on the ground over the posts.

It wasn't until the 1960s, when rugby league hit on a depression and found attendances were dwindling, that it decided on another major overhaul. One of the big problems was that due to 'play-the-ball' a team could be tackled as often as it liked and still got to keep the ball, and the maintenance of possession at all costs was preventing teams from taking risks. Bill Buckley, president of the New South Wales Union in Australia voiced his concern about the way "the craze for possession of the ball at all costs has resulted in vital laws of our game being ignored," which was blamed for St George winning eleven consecutive premierships. This was the same problem that American football had been obliged to address way back in 1884 when it introduced the 'downs' system to oblige teams to gain a determined amount of ground in a certain number of plays. British administrator Bill Fallowfield came up with rugby's solution, and readily admitted that his inspiration came from the American game.

---

[39] *The Truth* (November 10, 1906).
[40] *Northern Union Football* in the *Encyclopaedia of Sports & Games published* (1912, reprinted by Sri Satguru Publications, 1988).

MIKE ROBERTS – THE SAME OLD GAME: CODIFICATION

But rather than 'downs', his idea was the four-tackle rule, whereby once a team had been tackled four times in a row (it would become six in 1983), it had to concede possession to the other side. Perhaps the code's most distinguishing feature of all was successfully trialled and became law in 1967.

Another of the reasons for bringing in the limited-tackle rule was to try to cut out the number of scrums in the game. Their entertainment value from a spectator's point of view was questionable, and the fact so much scoring was coming from penalties awarded for scrum infringements was taking so much of the fun out of the game.

From the 1970s, the rugby league scrum began to decline in importance, serving more as an excuse to remove the forwards from the game and open up the rest of the field than anything else. There is no rule in rugby league that says that a scrum cannot be contested (i.e. the packs push against each other), but it rarely, if ever, happens, rendering it largely pointless, and it has often been suggested the game should do away with scrums altogether and just restart play with a tap kick.

An insular world

As clubs throughout Yorkshire and Lancashire turned professional, the most likely scenario would have been for teams in other counties to start following suit but, with surprisingly few exceptions, clubs elsewhere stayed loyal to the RFU. It is hard to explain why that was the case. Certainly, even with large numbers of supporters, professionalism in the NU struggled, and for clubs elsewhere, it often wasn't a viable proposition. Rather than playing professionally in their hometowns, players and officials looking to make money out of the game headed north. It is also tempting to argue that although NU clubs were openly professional, there was just as much money changing hands, albeit illicitly, in the RFU.

Also, although the northerners were proud of their creation and their defiant stance against the amateurs, the rest of the country was less inclined to replace their game with this new form, which had done away with so much of the running creativity by the backs and replaced it with play-the-ball, which invariably saw one charging advance by the forwards followed by another. Rather than adopt rugby league, non Yorkshire or Lancashire clubs were more likely to condone professional rugby union, which they have always believed to be the 'true' game. That is eventually what they would do, but not until the century was almost over.

Rugby league found a few takers in the northeast region of Tyneside. Wallsend RFC were the first, South Shields entered a team around the turn of the century, as did Newcastle in 1938, but they didn't rejoin after World War Two. In the Midlands, Coventry were thrown out of the RFU for paying players in 1909, and turned to the NU as an alternative until World War One put a stop to that. There was also a period when it looked like rugby league was going to take off in London, where three clubs[41] attracted decent support in the 1930s, but

---

[41] Highfield (1933-34), Acton & Willesden (1935-36) and Streatham & Mitcham (1935-37).

LEAGUES AND GENTLEMEN

that promise also proved short-lived[42]. Rugby league was virtually non-existent in either Scotland or Ireland until very recently, and even now it is only played on a very small scale, and their national sides are almost entirely made up of ex-pats and players that qualify by the 'granny rule'.

The most logical place for rugby league to triumph was South Wales. Like in the north, here was a similarly industrial region where the bourgeoisie had fewer qualms about the working classes joining in with their games of rugby. The Welsh did dabble with professionalism. Merthyr Tydfil and Ebbw Vale joined the NU in 1907, and Aberdare, Barry, Mid Rhondda and Treherbert followed soon after. But the experiment didn't work. The Union game had become the unofficial religion of South Wales, and fans showed nothing but aversion to this bastardised form. With many clubs in Wales based around small mining communities that had little in common with the expanding urban conurbations of the north of England, there just wasn't the kind of support base to generate the gate money rugby league needed to survive. By 1912, no clubs were playing rugby league in Wales.

Nevertheless, Wales would still feel the effects of the new code. Its players frequently came from humble backgrounds, and the temptation of 'going north' and being paid to play was often too big. Gareth Edwards writes that "any rugby union player 'taking the shilling' as it came to be known, to go north, knew he would almost certainly be consigning himself to the world of the leper. He would be banned from rugby union clubhouses even when he returned to his family's roots and could expect … a blank stare and silence from his former playing colleagues in the amateur code[43]." Anybody with a rugby connection and northern accent was the focus of suspicion in South Wales, for NU scouts were to be treated with both fear and loathing, such as one from Wigan who ended up being hurled into the sea in Penarth.

It was their severed ties with the RFU over professionalism that led the French to take an interest in rugby league in the 1930s. But whereas union was seen as the establishment's sport, league was considered socialist, and the Vichy regime (the French government under Nazi rule) was keen to quash it. Word came from Berlin that the sport was to be banned, and union chiefs stormed league clubs and made off with everything, balls and kit included. Even

---

[42] Rugby league finally made it to London in 1980 when Fulham soccer club entered a team. Despite a promising start, the club later struggled and after a period as the London Crusaders became the Broncos in 1994 in association with the Australian club from Brisbane. Then in 2005 they teamed up, in an unprecedented move, with powerful union club Harlequins, and are still going very strong in the Super League.

[43] Welsh international scrum half 1967-1978, and often said to the best union player ever, in his insightful *Tackling Rugby* (Headline, 2003). Major Welsh losses to the 13-a-side game included Arthur Daniels, David Watkins, Scott Quinnell and Jonathan Davies, but the phenomenon was by no means limited to the men of the valleys. Just to cite some notorious examples, England lost Mike Coulman and Martin Offiah, and Ireland lost Ken Goodall, although it was in Australia where rugby union struggled most to hold onto its players. And much as it is often said that Welsh rugby union suffered more than any other nation through the loss of players to rugby league, England and Australia surely suffered more through such a large amount of their young populations going straight into league without ever playing union at all.

though the ban was lifted after the war, it was not until June 1991 that players were allowed to use the word 'rugby' to define their sport (French Republic documents stating that it could only be called *jeu à treize* ('game of thirteen'), and the wounds still haven't healed, with claims being made for seized assets during the ban.

That, and the reacceptance of France by the Home Nations, meant that much as rugby league exists to this day in the country[44], it is very much the lesser of the two sports, with some 10,000 players compared to union's 215,000.

Rugby league remained focused on Yorkshire and Lancashire, and other than mild success in France, failed to conquer Europe. But on the other side of the world, it would be a very different story.

Up and under

In Australia, the arguments over the legality or not of paying players were just as rife as they were elsewhere. With 52,000 people paying to go through the turnstiles to watch Australia play the All Blacks in 1907, the players knew there was money being made somewhere, and quite rightly wanted to know why some of it couldn't be used to help players like Alick Burdon, who had broken his arm playing the game but was refused any kind of financial compensation.

As it happens, broken time payments, though strictly speaking illegal, were already widespread. It was no secret, for example, that when Newtown's Harry Hamill announced that he couldn't play for New South Wales against the English tourists because he had to work, the offer of fifteen shillings worked wonders in persuading him to reconsider. The rugby heartlands of New South Wales and Queensland were also under threat of losing their players to Australian rules football, which had already endorsed professionalism and was expanding around the country. In many ways, Australian rugby only presented an amateur face to appease the English administrators of the game, but at ground level, did all they could to ignore the regulations.

But the story of rugby league down under begins not in Australia, but New Zealand, in 1906, at the Wellington post office, the workplace of a rugby player of minor importance, Albert Henry Baskerville. One of his colleagues had a coughing fit, and in doing so dropped a copy of the *Athletics News*, whereupon Baskerville noticed among the phlegm that it contained a report on a professional game of rugby played in England that had attracted over 40,000 people[45].

---

[44] Following the failed Paris Saint-Germain Project in the 1990s, the Catalans Dragons from Perpignan joined the Super League in 2006, capitalising on the game's relatively large following in the southwest of the country.

[45] It does sound like this tale has been flowered up a little, because being the author of a book titled *Modern Rugby Football*, one would imagine Baskerville was already fairly wizened up on all things rugby without the need of his colleague's choking fit.

LEAGUES AND GENTLEMEN

There were already mutterings of discontent among the Kiwi rugby community, which were fuelled in particular by the hugely successful All Black rugby union tour of Britain, which had raked in a profit of £9,962 for the organisers, while the players themselves had only received about a tenner each for their efforts. You don't need a degree in applied mathematics to see that something wasn't quite adding up.

One of those disgruntled players was winger George William Smith, and he and Baskerville assembled what was not far short of the best rugby squad the country could muster and announced they were off to Britain to play games against Northern Union clubs. The New Zealand rugby authorities could ostracise them as much as they liked, but they were going on tour to make money.

Before they set off on their mammoth voyage, Smith and Baskerville's side travelled to New South Wales, where the Aussie press immediately dubbed them the 'All Golds', as opposed to the 'All Blacks', in mockery of the way their visitors were being paid to be there. However, when the games proved to be a massive hit, the Australian promoters were only too happy to reap their own financial benefits and start discussing plans to implement professional rugby in their own country. A meeting was called at Bateman's Crystal Hotel in Sydney in August 1907, and the New South Wales Rugby Football League (NSWRFL) was formed. The first season started in 1908, and has been played every season since. It is now the NRL, which has the highest attendance figures for any club rugby tournament in the world, and if it hadn't been formed, it seems highly unlikely that rugby would have been able to stop Australian rules from becoming the number one sport all over the country.

The NU had recently changed the laws for the professional game, but these were still unknown on the other side of the world, and the three tests at the Sydney Showground were all rugby union. So, when the All Golds got to the northern hemisphere, having convinced Herbert 'Dally' Messenger, Australia's biggest rugby star of the time to join them[46], they needed a crash course in the new rules before taking on their first opposition, Bramley, in October. It wouldn't be until January of the following year that the All Golds played the first ever international rugby league test, which didn't involve any Englishmen at all. It was played against Wales, at Aberdare (whose local club would be joining the NU later that year), and the home side won in front of a crowd of 20,000. But the All Blacks soon got the hang of the new game, and although 19 wins in 35 matches was not exactly a whitewash of their British opponents, the long and tiring schedule, plus injuries picked up along the way, did pay their toll. They won two of three tests played against the full Great Britain side at Leeds, Chelsea and Cheltenham, which were odd choices of venue, considering that of the three, only Leeds is actually in the north. The games were a success, with the tourists collecting 70% of gate receipts, at a minimum guarantee of £50 for mid-week matches and £100 for Saturday games. By today's exchange rate, that was a small fortune and a

---

[46] And in whose honour the NRL still awards the Dally M Medal for Best Player in the NRL.

considerably better deal than the three shillings a day the Australian rugby union team was getting to cover their out-of-pocket expenses on a similar tour at roughly the same time. To make matters worse, the union players stood accused of being professionals, and had their already paltry allowances reduced in punishment. Not surprisingly, thirteen of the touring Wallabies defected to rugby league as soon as they got back home.

There was no stopping the All Golds, and by May 1908 they were back in Australia, and singing the praises of the new rules they had learned in England. This time they were in the next state up from New South Wales (that'll be Queensland, which the first rugby league British Lions tour would be visiting a few months after). A game in Brisbane served to kick start rugby league there, in the shape of the Queensland Rugby Football Association[47]. The All Golds' visit to Brissie ended in tragedy though, with tour leader Albert Baskerville dying of pneumonia. Internationals between New Zealand and Great Britain today still play for the Baskerville Shield in his honour[48].

Rugby league proved a major hit in Australia, and has been the dominant code in the country ever since. But surprisingly, considering the All Golds' efforts to promote the game, rugby league has always played second fiddle to union in New Zealand. Baskerville's death can't have helped matters, neither could the fact that most of the All Golds were so good that they were snapped up by British clubs in the Northern Union[49], and those that didn't were immediately stripped of their playing status by the NZRFU.

The NZRFU was so influential in all walks of life in the country that it successfully crippled any attempt to establish professional rugby at the root. New Zealand had such a small and disperse population that it would have been hard to support professional rugby anyway. But as British Lions manager James Baxter famously observed in 1930, "every town must have its sewer," in reference to the Auckland area, where rugby league has a considerable following, and which since 1995 has provided the base for the first Kiwi side to play in Australia's NRL, the New Zealand Warriors (formerly the Auckland Warriors).

---

[47] Games between New South Wales and Queensland, the 'State of Origin' series, are still among the best you can hope to see in any code of football.

[48] The centenary of the 1907 All Golds Tour was commemorated in 2007 when the touring New Zealand team played a 'Northern Union' select side at Warrington, with the Kiwis winning 25-18 in a game played using the scoring system of a hundred years earlier. To add to the authenticity, the New Zealanders even invited one of the greatest Australian players of all time, Andrew Johns, to play the role of Dally Messenger (fittingly Johns is the only player to win the Dally M Medal three times). Sadly, Johns was forced into retirement earlier in the year with a neck injury, and the token Aussie would instead be Queensland front row Steve Price.

[49] Including the outstanding centre Lance Todd, one of the finest players to ever live. Todd was originally signed by Wigan and five years later went to Dewsbury for £400, an astonishing amount for the time. His legendary status was sealed in the 1930s when, as a manager, he led Salford to three national championships, and his name stays with us forever in the form of the Lance Todd Trophy awarded to the best player in the Challenge Cup Final.

The strained relationship

To quote the Northern Union president, John H Smith in 1905, "the Northern Union is sometimes referred to as a moribund organisation, and there are those who express the belief that its extinction is only a matter of a few more seasons. Probably this is, in some instances, a case of pious wish rather than an expression of honest conviction[50]." It turns out that Smith was very right, for although many have wondered how rugby league managed to survive when it was only played in such a small area of the country, the real question we should be asking is how rugby union managed to hold out when it was a strictly amateur sport.

Although the RFU shrugged the schism off as a minor loss, it was anything but. It meant the surrender of the two most important strongholds of British rugby, Yorkshire and Lancashire, and by 1904, the Northern Union had more member clubs than the rest of the country combined. After the schism, it would take England a full 18 years to win the international championship, the forerunner of what is now the Six Nations.

It destroyed any hope of rugby union competing financially with professional soccer, for just where the FA was strongest, the RFU had almost no influence at all. And when professional football clubs started appearing in the south, they obviously opted for the FA's code. Rugby wasn't even available as an option.

Rugby union remained the code of choice at schools, and adults continued to play for the love of the game. For most of over a million rugby union players in England alone, as they crawl out of bed on a Saturday morning and nurse their hangovers and check their beer guts, professionalism is hardly going to be an issue. Rugby union was never going to go away, and in most of the country people were only aware the league game existed at all because the BBC showed matches on Saturday afternoon (which was a cue for everybody outside of Yorkshire and Lancashire to switch over to the wrestling on ITV).

Rugby union and rugby league continued their uncomfortable coexistence through the 20th century, often reaching laughable proportions, such as the case in 1959 of Michael Jopling, the Conservative candidate for election in Wakefield, being invited by league club Wakefield Trinity to take the honorary kick off at one their matches. The local union club decided that that meant Jopling had been 'professionalized' and duly made him a *persona non grata*[51].

Even today relations are strained at the best of times, and there is no doubting which side Sean Fagan is barking from when he concludes that "the split would also ensure that rugby union would forever polarise itself as a middle-class game and live its 'amateur' lie for a further hundred years."

---

[50] In the *Book of Football* serialised in 1905 and 1906.

[51] But there was also room for compromise, one major example being the case of the Second World War, when the RFU said it was okay for servicemen to play league in civilian life, and union in the forces, and two games were even played between players of the two codes, and despite playing to union rules, the league players won both.

Despite its apparently outward insistence on defending its amateur ideals, accusations of 'shamateurism' in rugby union were rife, and league supporters would spend the 20th century delighting in exposing any shreds of evidence of money changing hands in the RFU.

Sport as an industry was growing, and professionalism had become both logical and ethical. If there was money to be made from sport, then it was only fair that the athletes themselves should get a share of the spoils. By the 1990s, the only sport in the Olympic Games that still refused entry to professionals was, and still is, boxing. Soccer was already into its greed-is-good Premiership and Champions League phase, American football was moving silly money, there was even professional darts and ten pen bowling, and World Series Bottom Burping was probably beginning to see the potential, and yet rugby union stayed amateur.

Stadiums were packed to the rafters for internationals, the likes of David Campese, Jonah Lomu and Will Carling were household names, even in the royal household in the case of the latter, there was rugby union merchandising everywhere, and huge deals were being struck for television rights to show games. The Lions would be off on tour around the globe for weeks, and between the build-up and the games themselves, playing at the World Cup took over two months out of a worker's year, if not more. Rugby was still proudly parading its amateur virtues around the world, and yet just how amateur it really was, and just who was making money and who wasn't, we couldn't be sure.

Matters came to a head with the *Relations between Rugby Union and Rugby League* report published by the National Heritage Committee and calling for an end to the 'shamateurism' that was so blatantly present in the union game. An investigation by the International Rugby Board itself had been forced to confess that "breaches of the amateurism regulations were wholesale."

Paris. August 1995. Exactly 99 years and 364 days after the Northern Union had made its historic decision to endorse broken time payments, the IRB announced that it was going to allow professionalism too. It was as significant a moment as any in the history of the football codes and only coincidence, of course, that the announcement also managed to completely undermine the media's interest in rugby league's centennial celebrations.

None other than the British parliament would be moved to speak on the subject. The Culture, Media and Sport Committee on *The Future of Professional Rugby* in 1995 declared that "although rugby union had been ostensibly amateur since its birth, the regulations prohibiting professionalism were not, in practice, enforced. Governing bodies 'turned a blind eye' to breaches of the regulations. Professionalisation removed the major barrier between rugby union and rugby league, the very obstacle that had caused the split that formed the two codes one hundred years previously. Since that split, the two codes had remained separate, distinct and, at times, antagonistic … The absorption of professionalism into rugby union in the Northern Hemisphere was dictated by the reality of shamateurism at the highest levels of the game, particularly in the Southern Hemisphere, where the pretence of amateur status had become severely undermined and unsustainable."

Rugby re-union?

Rugby union had to reinvent itself to cope with the demands of professionalism, and in the British Isles one wonders how it would have coped without the help of zealous promotion on Sky TV. Tries were upgraded to five points and the bonus point system was introduced to encourage attacking rugby. The rules are still up for scrutiny, and the Stellenbosch University laws are gradually being introduced to make the game simpler and more consistent.

Its internationals may have attracted huge crowds and media attention, but only the real diehards took an interest in the game at club level. Market forces had caused the geography of soccer to shift to the big city clubs with the colossal fan bases, but many of the top rugby union clubs were based in small towns on the periphery. Could places like Gloucester, Limerick and Pontypool really support professional rugby?

The first club in England to turn fully pro was Richmond in 1996, but it proved a financial disaster, and they ended up having to merge with London Irish, while West Hartlepool and London Scottish were also early casualties. Scotland could only support three professional teams, Edinburgh, Glasgow and Borders, which would later be reduced to two. Wales had a wonderful tradition of small-town clubs, but professionalism needs huge crowds in purpose-built stadia, not social gatherings of pipe-smoking pensioners on tiers of concrete, and the clubs were eventually whittled down to four artificially created franchises: Cardiff Blues, Llanelli Scarlets, Newport Gwent Dragons and the Ospreys from the Neath-Swansea region. Ireland was the biggest success story, where its clubs based on the four provinces of Munster, Leinster, Connacht and Ulster provided something the fans could identify with. But as none of Scotland, Wales or Ireland had the infrastructure to support their own professional leagues, they opted to combine forces and form the Celtic League, which at the time of writing had become the Magners League and been extended to Italian clubs.

Rugby union clubs in Australia were going to face stiff competition from the NRL sides with their proud histories. The New South Wales Waratahs, the Brumbies (Canberra) and Queensland Reds were formed as state teams to play in the new Super 12 tournament in 1996, and the eight-team Australian Rugby Championship was set up in 2006. Not even South Africa and New Zealand managed to cope with professionalism without having to invent new clubs, where their national championships still continue, but they field newly created franchises in what is now called Super Rugby.

Professional rugby union has certainly put a check on players defecting to the other code, and as expected, several rugby league 'turncoats' have been tempted back into union (Allan Bateman, Scott Gibbs, Scott Quinnell and Brad Thorn, to name just four, though the latter, a

New Zealander, eventually went back to league). And it's even started working the other way, with rugby league players opting to move to union[52].

It was also widely predicted that the professionalization of rugby union would be the death knell of rugby league. Outside of Australia, what hope could there be for a game that in England is almost entirely confined to the 'M62 corridor' between Liverpool and Hull? The widespread opinion was that people only played rugby league at all because they could get money from it, and now union was professional too, league was doomed. That has not proved to be the case. For the time being at least, rugby league has continued to thrive as much as ever, while rugby union is still picking up the pieces it dropped over a century ago.

In fact, rugby league, if anything, has benefited from the professionalization of its rival code. Union players are no longer discriminated against for having a go at rugby league, there has been an upsurge in interest at amateur level, and just between 2002 and 2004 there was a reported 94 per cent increase in registered rugby league players.

While not decrying the benefits of either code, it's a shame that the infamous schism ever had to happen. In overall terms, separation was more negative than positive for both sports, and meant the division of players, resources and even territory. Nigel Trueman puts it brilliantly when he says "rugby could and would have been a single code and it's only the fact that the officiators of the Union game staunchly stuck to the amateur ethos introduced in 1886 come what may that created and maintained the split. The labelling of the Northern clubs as rebels or splitters when they were really left with only one course of action open to them is an injustice which can never be undone. It therefore seems to me that the blame, if blame has to be apportioned, needs to reside with the higher levels of Union administration who presided over the game for 100 years where little was done to improve the game in terms of coaching, spreading the game, encouraging competition, developing referees, allowing participants in the sport to profit from writing books, etc. and for what? The principle of amateurism?"

The reconciliation has been welcome. England now play rugby league internationals at Twickenham, something unthinkable only a few years ago, we had the fascinating Bath v Wigan clash of the codes matches in 1996, when the sides played each other at both games[53] and top coaches are now adapting their experiences in one code to that of the other, and all for the good of both games.

---

[52] Jason Robinson was one of the first and most successful converts, followed later by the likes of England rugby league captain Andy Farrell joining union club Saracens in 2006, and Wendell Sailor, who would go on to play for the Wallabies. Code hopping has become commonplace. You had Wales' Iestyn Harris who went from union to league and back again twice in his career. Henry Paul left his native New Zealand to play league in England, switched to union and even played for England at it, before going to Harlequins to play league. Ireland's Brian Carney (who started out playing Gaelic football) was tempted away from union to play league both in Australia and England, before going back to Munster and rugby union.

[53] Under league rules, Wigan beat Bath 82-6. Two weeks later the return match under union rules was held at Twickenham, and Bath won 44-19.

LEAGUES AND GENTLEMEN

Amateurism versus professionalism is not the issue anymore. The 1895 schism is no longer relevant. It's about the rulebook. It's about the fact that while they were divided over payment, the two rival unions went and changed so many rules that we've ended up with two different versions of what should have remained the same game.

It is unfair to blame rugby league for this. In fact, although union fans adamantly maintain that their game is the true great grandson of the game as it was originally played, and rugby league is a modern bastardisation, over the years, their game has almost certainly imported far more ideas from rugby league than vice versa!

For the foreseeable future, rugby will stay divided. Maybe one day it won't be so much about 'union' or 'league', but it will once again be about the love for rugby that both codes still share, albeit in different ways. Maybe one day they will both sit down at a table together and carry on where they should never have left off in 1895, and sort out a compromise set of rules.

As I write, plans are being made for an as yet unconfirmed game between Australia's two national rugby teams, the Wallabies and the Kangaroos. The rumoured hybrid rules for what would be a 12-a-side game include: "Tries are worth four points and conversions are for two. Field goals and penalties are worth two points ... league play-the-ball rules when teams coming out of their own half. Six tackle limit ... ruck and maul rules when teams enter opposition half with the football ... contested five-man scrums. The traditional rugby front row to be taken out of the equation ... a place kick to start the game and for restarts[54]."

With both codes facing financial concerns, maybe that is the way ahead for rugby. Brisbane Broncos, Llanelli Scarlets, Canterbury Crusaders, the Catalans Dragons, Melbourne Storm, Leeds Rhinos, the Free State Cheetahs and Leicester Tigers would all be playing the same sport, and what a healthier thing rugby would be for it.

Maybe one day, the rugby world will live happily ever after and just laugh about the mess their forefathers made of that brilliant invention that was created so many moons ago on the Bigside grass of Rugby School.

---

[54] *The Age*, May 23, 2010.

5 THE CELTIC TIMES
Irish football before the GAA

Gael force

Until the world's leisure industry was swamped by Irish theme bars, and along with it the chance for the unwashed masses to enjoy Setanta and RTE's live coverage of matches, most people outside of Ireland had never even heard of Gaelic football (*peil ghaelach* or *caid* in Irish), let alone seen it played. That has now changed, and we now know that those strange replica shirts worn by the holidaymaking Irish have nothing to do with soccer teams.

For those unfamiliar with the game, it is played on exactly the same field as hurling, with the same H shaped posts with a 'soccer' net beneath the crossbar. It also uses the same scoring system: three points for getting the ball into the opposition's goal and one for scoring 'rugby' style over the crossbar and between the posts. Also like hurling, all games are played over 70 minutes at senior level, and matches are 15-a-side.

The play is somewhere between soccer and rugby. The ball is not unlike a soccer ball, and can either be kicked with the feet or punched with a clenched fist, rather like serving a volleyball. Catching the ball is part and parcel of the game, but it cannot be picked up directly from the ground, as was also the case with early rugby. Gaelic also shares a lot in common with Australian rules football, in that it is a form of soccer in which the ball can be caught but there are limitations on how much you can run with it. In Gaelic, you can only travel four paces. However, players can advance further by 'soloing' the ball, which involves dropping it to their feet and kicking it back into their hands, or they can bounce it on the ground (but never twice in a row).

Unlike soccer or rugby, if the ball goes into touch, it is kicked back in, not thrown, and where soccer awards a corner kick, Gaelic has a kick from the 45 metre line opposite the point where the ball crossed the goal line. Tackling is not as tough as it is in rugby, but considerably rougher than soccer. There are no two-handed tackles, and neither is there any pushing, tripping, shirt-pulling or attempting to wrest the ball from an opponent, but shoulder-barging, for example, is permitted.

It all adds up to a sport that rouses passions like no other in Ireland, getting 34% of the total sports attendances in the Republic[1], while the All Ireland Final is usually the most watched

---

[1] Figures for the Republic only, from *Social & Economic Value of Sport in Ireland* (Irish Sports Council, 2005). Hurling gets 17% of attendances, soccer 16%, and rugby 8%. Soccer's low score can partly be attributed to the relatively low profile of the League of Ireland, because when it comes to television viewing figures, soccer matches involving English and Scottish clubs attract higher overall audiences than Gaelic football does.

THE CELTIC TIMES

sports event of the year[2] and more Irishmen are playing members of Gaelic football clubs, 13% of the male population, than they are for any other type of sport[3].

Gaelic football is an inherent part of the culture of a country whose history has always been shaped by its proximity to Great Britain, which governed the island for eight hundred years, and still controls the six counties of Northern Ireland. It wasn't, and still isn't, a situation that many if not most Irish people appreciate. And for some in the late 19th century, the problem went deeper than that. They didn't like their football being governed from Britain either. So it was that in 1884 the Gaelic Athletic Association (GAA, often pronounced *gargh*) was formed to write the rules for football as it was played in Ireland. Or perhaps we should rephrase that to the rules for football as it was *going to be* played Ireland. That's because although it is hard to dispute that forms of football had been played in Ireland for just as long, and maybe even longer, than they had been on the larger island to the east, it really isn't all that clear how much the game the GAA unleashed upon the Irish nation in the 1880s was really based on ancient traditions, and how much it was something that was simply made up so that they could show they were different to the British.

Diarmaid Ferriter comments on the "dearth of suitable analytical historical material" on the GAA, and on how before giving a lecture on the Association at University College, Dublin, a colleague and firm GAA stalwart warned him that "with you the GAA is not in a safe pair of hands[4]." That was not an untypical response to outsiders prying into the GAA's past. Ferriter senses that "the GAA has been touchy about its history and unduly sensitive to criticism" and adds that the little literature available on the subject is invariably "sanitised and uncritical," painting over the cracks and taking liberties with the truth to present a self-congratulatory image of Gaelic games.

That could be because almost every academic word that has ever been written on the GAA has been supplied by fervent supporters of everything it stands for. Hardly anybody else has ever bothered to take an interest. But the crying need for a less biased review of the story is already creeping into Irish academia[5], and what we'll try to do on the next few pages is take an objective look at the origins of the GAA, filter out the blarney, and find out how the sport really came about.

---

[2] And when it isn't, that's usually because it's topped by the All Ireland Hurling Final, as was the case in 2010, when soccer's World Cup Final only managed third.

[3] Although soccer is the most widely played sport in the Republic, with 17% of all males playing the game as opposed to 8% for Gaelic, but that's including 5-a-side and social play, as opposed to being a member of a formally organised club.

[4] In his introduction to the multi-authored *The Gaelic Athletic Association 1884-2009.*

[5] As reflected by historian John Murphy at the beginning of the 125th anniversary DVD, *Part of What We Are - A History of the GAA* (Motive Television, 2008) when after describing the ancient origins of hurling he adds, almost with a scorn that "Gaelic football is to some extent a creation of the GAA."

Green parties

Eoin Kinsella reckons the relative lack of early football references in Ireland was because of a "perception that it was a less skilful or exciting game than hurling[6]" and that this "dissuaded poets and commentators alike from writing about football." We can't be sure how right that assumption is, but the stickball game does seem to have been a far more intrinsically Irish pastime that football ever was.

But there was football in Ireland, and what is commonly dubbed as the oldest reference to it was found in the *Irish Plea Rolls*[7] for 1308, which tell how "it is found by the jury that, whereas William ... in the town of New Castle of Lyons, was playing at ball with men of that town, and the ball was struck in the direction of John, who was standing near to watch the game. John ran towards the ball, which William was following in pursuit, and met him so swiftly that he wounded William in the upper part of his right leg with a knife ... which ... unfortunately without John's knowledge pierced its sheath and so injured William, to his damage of five shillings. And the jurors, being asked if John did this from ill-timed zeal ... say that it was not so, but that it was for the purpose of playing that he ran towards him to hit the ball ... that William and John at the said time and before that were fast friends, and that John did not wound William knowingly."

It really is bizarre just how many cases there are in history of people being injured and even killed by playing ball, not so much because of the danger of the game itself, but because of the curious insistence on playing while carrying their weapons. However, all this report tells us is that the protagonists were 'playing at ball', and whatever they were playing, it was no more likely to have been a form of early football than any other ball game, perhaps hurling.

Football hardly abounds in Irish records of the first half of the millennium, but by 1518 even the priests were playing it, and Archbishop Rokeby was anything but impressed to learn of it. Among the regulations stipulated in his *Red Book of Ossory* "the playing of football by clergymen was forbidden under a penalty of 3s. 4d. to the Ordinary, and 3s. 4d. to the repair of the parish church."

This was just a decade before the historic Galway Statute of 1527, which we met in the previous volume decreeing that "at no time to use ne occupy ye hurling of ye litill balle with

---

[6] In *The Gaelic Athletic Association 1884-2009.*

[7] A fascinating document, here we also learn the tales of folk like Adam Sott who "was eating oysters in a tavern, he threw an oyster shell over his shoulder, which struck a wall, and the shell rebounded and struck Maurice ... in the left eye, by which he lost the sight of it [of the eye, not of the oyster, we assume]." Or there was the foolish Mabilla, the lady in the case where "John Clement and other shepherds shot arrows at a mark, near which Mabilla was seated, and the said shepherds instantly asked Mabilla to move away from the mark, which she refused to do. At length John Clement shot towards the mark with a blunt arrow, which was deflected by the wind to Mabilla and against the will of John Clement struck her on the head and wounded her so that she died."

THE CELTIC TIMES

the hookie sticks or staves, nor use no hand balle to play without the walls[8], but only the great foot balle", whereby the English rulers implied that 'hookie', by which they presumably meant something like hurling, and handball were the favoured sports of the Irish, and therefore not to be encouraged among the foreign settlers.

On the banks of the Boyne in County Meath, as reflected in *Iomain na Boinne,* a poem written in an old dialect of Ulster Gaelic by wandering minstrel Seamus Dall Mac Cuarta, they were abidingly playing 'the great foot balle' in a match played on October 28. Sadly we don't know of what year. Scholars seem to feel it would have been between 1670 and 1712, but have missed the rather obvious flaw that the text mentions King George I, who wasn't crowned until 1714 and reigned for 13 years. It's a long, rambling ode, so we'll only provide some highlights here, for rather than telling us about the actual game, Seamus spends most of his time waxing lyrical about the majestic heroism of the men of Slane and Boyne and mocking their feeble opponents, believed to be from nearby Duleek:

"The best of victories to the strong boys of the Boyne;
And they will have it every time against hundreds
And as twelve of them hit their shoulders together
With skill up on the pitch.
My heroes that would sweep away teams like driving away birds
The crowds going wild with the ball;
That was natural because of the pleasant gifted men
That were in front of the bean-eating coxcombs.
Noble and Gaelic, victorious and gifted
Are my heroes that shattered the host
And that hit the ball high up the pitch
Rendering them unable to do the work…
…And three sons along with the true blood of O'Reilly,
Very comely in position in the goal[9]…
…Like that were George and the boys of the Boyne
Driving the ball[10] past the worthless and lamentable men…
…Who would destroy every band that might gather to play
Against them with a goal, without an hour's respite[11]."

---

[8] When they say handball, they probably don't mean anything like rugby, and neither does the form of handball played under the auspices of the GAA have much to do with the game called handball which appears in the Olympic Games. Irish handball is rather like squash, in that it is played against a wall, but using the hands without a racket. In principle, it is similar to the game of *pelota* played in the Basque Country, and given the history of trading between Ireland and Spain, it is possible that they shared a common root.

[9] This may be a suggestion that some sort of goalkeeping or at least positions were involved.

[10] This bit has been translated in some versions as "kicking the ball" but I am reliably informed by Irish speaking friends that the original expression, "*ag cur balla,*" doesn't make any specific mention of the feet being used.

MIKE ROBERTS – THE SAME OLD GAME: CODIFICATION

The only reason for assuming that this was football is that there is no specific mention of any sticks being used, but as the game is called *iomain*, a term commonly used in Scots Gaelic to describe shinty, they possibly did.

If travelling English bookseller John Dunton is anybody to go by, football was the exception rather than the norm in 1698. It was then that he wrote that the Irish "do not often play at football, only in a small territory called Fingal near Dublin, where the people use it much and trip and shoulder verie handsomely[12]." Dunton must have been mistaken with his claim that the game was only played in Fingal, but it seems unlikely that it was particularly widespread in Ireland at the time.

Then in 1720, we come across the finest piece of ancient Irish footy literature of all, which belies its rather unimaginative title of *A Match at Football*. The bard was a lawyer named Matthew Concanen, who two years later left for England and rarely wrote about Irish matters again. His burlesque describes a game played at Swords, County Dublin, between:

"Six men of Soards (a goodly sight!),
their active limbs, all loosely clad in white"
and "six lusty lads of Lusk … their bodies light,
their aspects chearful, and their dresses white;
A ribbon in his cap, of azure hue,
distinguish'd each bold champion to the view."

So we had a game where the players wore a kit, although there was a bit of a colour clash, and it was ribbons in caps that they used to tell each other apart. Concanen provides a detailed description of The Green where the game was played, down to the trees and flowers and all, which is all very nice but a bit irrelevant to our interests. He also tells us how a crowd of "bold youths arrang'd on either hand, around the field in decent order stand" to watch the game and how:"   The buxom lass,
reclines her weary'd limbs upon the grass;
there laid at ease, receives her lover's treats,
or makes new conquests, or old vows repeats."

Gotta love those buxom Irish lasses. The poet dedicates most of the next part of his work to lengthy descriptions of each of the players, all of whom seemed drawn from the labouring classes. It gives us a fascinating idea of the life and times of early 18th century Ireland. We had Neal and Cabe, "whom poverty sent forth from the bleak regions of the rugged North", while for a certain Terence "all that he hopes his labours to beguile, is from bright Norah one approving smile."

Judging by this poem, impressing the watching maidens was a major incentive to play early Irish football, but when they finally set their minds to it, there seems to have been an

---

[11] We can only guess, but Seamus seems to be telling us that one goal would win the game, and that scoring said goal in less than an hour was quite some accomplishment.
[12] John Dunton *Teague Land: or A Merry Ramble to the Wild Irish* (1698).

THE CELTIC TIMES

impressively solid structure to the game. One player was "both swift of foot, in artful grappling skill'd", another "at good defence his chiefest talent lay", while of surly Dick, the miller, we are told there were "few better skill'd than him to play the game, or toss the football with a surer aim."

The player pen-pics over, Old Hobbinol is charged with informing the crowd that "the victor's lawful prize" will be "six Holland caps", while the losers ("yet shall the vanquish'd not contend in vain") get the consolation prize of a pair of gloves each, which was nice, but not half as nice as the fact that the local squire would be laying on a "cask of humming beer." We'll leave it to the imagination as to whether, 39 years before Arthur Guinness first poured his truly marvellous brew, the fact that the beer was 'humming' was a good or a bad thing. We'll assume it was good.

The game can't have been too poorly viewed by the local authorities, because the ball itself was "the present of your Lords", and we are also told what it was like:

> "To outward view, three folds of bullock's hide,
> with leathern thongs fast bound on ev'ry side:
> A mass of finest hay, conceal'd from sight,
> conspire at once, to make it firm and light."

Moving on to the basics of the game and:

> "At this you'll all contend, this bravely strive,
> alternate thro' the adverse goal to drive:
> two gates of sally bound the spacious Green,
> here one, and one on yonder side is seen.
> Guard that ye Men of Soards, ye others this,
> fame waits the careful, scandal the remiss."

Well, that sounds as football-like as you could hope for. On to the early throw-up, the job of Old Hobbinol who   "flung the ball:

> The champions crowd, and anxious wait its fall.
> First Felim caught, he pois'd, and felt it soft,
> then whirl'd it with a sudden stroke aloft:
> with motion smooth and swift, he saw it glide,
> till Dick, who stop'd it on the other side,
> a dextrous kick, with artful fury drew,
> the light machine, with force unerring, flew
> to th'adverse goal; where, in the sight of all,
> the watchful Daniel caught the flying ball;
> He proudly joyful in his arms embrac'd
> the welcome prize; then ran with eager haste,

> with lusty strides he measur'd half the plain[13],
> when all his foes surround and stop the Swain;
> They tug, they pull; to his assistance run,
> the strong-limb'd Darby, and the nimble John:
> Paddy, with more than common ardour fir'd,
> out-singled Daniel, while the rest retir'd:
> At grappling, now, their mutual skill they try,
> now arm in arm they lock, and thigh in thigh[14];
> Now turn, now twine, now with a furious bound,
> each lifts his fierce opposer from the ground."

There's plenty more where that comes from, but Concanen does go on a bit, so we'll leave it there. It's epic stuff. What he describes is a game with goals at either end of a field and that involves both kicking and throwing the ball. In the Ireland of 1720, we have something that is as much like rugby football as anything we know of in England at the same time.

A caid of magic

Dall Mac Cuarta's *iomain* was one of the old Gaelic words used to describe early football games, while another, *caid*[15], is still sometimes used by Kerry old-timers to describe modern Gaelic football. The common story goes that in the 18th century it was particularly common around Kerry, and even more specifically the Dingle Peninsula. This theory seems to have grown out of a 20th century thesis, *The Traditional game of Caid* by Father W Ferris of Glenflesk, Killarney, on the basis of the memories of an 80 year old interviewee, who had played *caid* in an enclosed area with arch-shaped goals, while there was another wilder game played after Sunday mass, and which involved plenty of wrestling, ball-carrying and other malarkey.

Renowned RTE commentator Michaél Ó Muircheartaigh claims *caid* was played cross-country between parishes with few rules about the number of players on each side. It was essentially a carrying game in which "the winning team was the team that brought the ball home … it was said that *caid* provided the basis for rugby[16]." That may well be, and this has indeed been mooted in studies of the origins of the oval code, but only as a distant

---

[13] It's interesting to observe what Daniel did. He ran with the ball in his hands, a full 103 years before William Webb Ellis purportedly did so for the first time.

[14] All that arm-locking suggests a rugby scrum or something very like it.

[15] The name, so the theory goes, comes from the Irish word *cadairne* meaning testicle, although there is no evidence of such 'balls' ever being used. They did use the good old pig's bladder, though, which was revolting enough.

[16] *Sport in the Rural Community* at the *2nd annual Fr John Aughney Memorial Lecture* (May 2000, Leighlinbridge).

THE CELTIC TIMES

possibility. *Caid* has no greater claim to antiquity than Cornish hurling, Welsh *cnapan* or English campball, which were played at roughly the same time.

Staying in 18th century Ireland, in 1706 a group of young men in Waterford made the mistake of accepting a challenge. The opposition turned out to be a naval press gang who snapped up twelve of the fittest and finest for a seafaring career they would rather have gone without. "A grate match at footeball was played between married men and bachelors[17]" at Dangan, County Meath in 1731, a game was played on the frozen River Liffey in 1741, there was even an international of sorts in 1757 when "a match at football was played in the Artillery Ground between twelve Irishmen and twelve Yorkshiremen … which was won by the former, they having won every Gole. There were several large bets depending[18]" and in 1797, aristocrat and revolutionary Edward Fitzgerald observed a game in which "Kildare's tall strong twenty men wore white linen shirts."

A poem by Redmond Murphy an tSléibe, called *Léana an Bhábhúin,* describes a 12-a-side game played in County Louth in 1740. Running with the ball was permitted here too, and the tale tells of how one of the poet's own relatives was injured by being slung against a pile of rocks, and died sixteen days later.

In December 1790, students at the Irish College in Paris "repaired for recreation to the Champ de Mars, and commenced a game at football – not the *jeu au balon*, as is incorrectly stated by Prudhomme, and which consists in thumping a large inflated ball with the feet from one player to another – but regular down-right football, after the Irish fashion[19]." The text doesn't offer an explanation of what that game was like, but when Charles O'Reilly of Louth accidentally kicked the ball and knocked over a sacred statue, the ensuing scuffle with the French led to six players being incarcerated for the afternoon.

Football was no more popular among those who preferred a more placid life than it was in Britain, and matches are often described in a negative light. Patronage of football was not always the way to go about earning respect. In 1797, the wonderfully named Valentine Lawless (the 2nd Baron Cloncurry no less) described how Wogan Browne lost his Justice of the Peace status for kicking off a football match in the Clane area. *Sleators's Public Gazette* reported in 1759 how a man fractured his skull and lost half of his nose in a football incident near Finglas Bridge. A game near Sandyford in 1789 led to "bloodshed and battery", in what is now Baggot Street in Dublin in 1754 the "riotous proceedings" of a football match were stopped by "the arrival of a guard of soldiers and a posse of constables", and in similar fashion at Drumcondra in 1774, a regiment of foot soldiers was sent in "to disperse a riotous mob who weekly assemble there to play football."

The *Hibernian Journal* reported in 1780 on how a well-known Dublin watchman called 'Clubby' was ordered to "prevent idle disorderly persons from playing at football." But yer

---

[17] Paddy Mehigan *Gaelic Football* (Dublin, 1941).
[18] *The London Chronicle*, December 24, 1757.
[19] Andrew O'Reilly *The Irish abroad and at home: at the court and in the camp* (1856).

MIKE ROBERTS – THE SAME OLD GAME: CODIFICATION

man got a little carried away with his duties, and "shot an innocent man, a baker from Church Street, with a blunderbuss." He was convicted to Newgate Prison for his rashness, and rightly so.

Like in Britain, it was not so much the football itself as the tendency for games to lead to riots that concerned the powers that were. In 1802, Sir Richard Musgrave felt that the mob that "used to assemble in the environs of the capital, particularly at Harold's Cross, under a pretext of boxing or playing at football[20]" were actually gathering to fuel rebellion, the same reason his colleague James Gordon was concerned about Catholics "assembling on such other pretences as funerals and matches of football[21]."

Irish eyes are smiling

Ó Muircheartaigh explains that football struggled to develop in Ireland due to an Act passed in 1385 banning all sports but archery, and which was not repealed until 1845. The image of Irish football struggling for centuries despite English attempts to quash it is a popular one in GAA circles. But as we saw in the previous volume, despite hurlers proving troublesome from time to time, and whatever a 14th century decree might have said, there is very little evidence that the British took any objection to Irishmen playing stickball as long as it didn't cause trouble. The same goes for football.

Considering how much effort the English put into preventing their own people from playing different sports, the Irish got off pretty lightly. But like in Britain, football in early 19th century Ireland was not helped by the Industrial Revolution, and the country had such additional concerns as its struggles against British occupation, severe famines and the diaspora of its people abroad. The labouring classes were going to get precious few opportunities for any kind of field sports, and indeed it was noted in Country Antrim in 1838 that "the taste for amusements … declined as the pressure of the times has increased."

But contrary to what might be expected, while football was on the verge of disappearance in England, it was in considerably better health on the Emerald Isle. In England, it was noted in 1823 of football that "the Sabbath, though confessedly an improper one, was the day on which it was generally practiced … These meetings which were common all over this country thirty years ago are now very rare[22]." But the same author reckoned that "in some parts of the north of Ireland, they still flourish in their pristine vigour … It is usual in some parts of Ireland in a contest between two counties, to make a choice of the best twelve men in each … The ball is then thrown up so as to preserve the equality of the parties, and an instantaneous struggle to throw each other and reach the ball first immediately takes place. As that party which gains the most falls will outnumber the other at the first onset, the greater prospect of ultimate success is thus determined by the previous wrestling. Contested in this

---

[20] Richard Musgrave *Memoirs of the different rebellions in Ireland, from the arrival of the English* (1802)
[21] James Bentley Gordon *History of the Rebellion in Ireland in the year 1798* (1801)
[22] W Litt *Wrestliana: An historical account of ancient and modern wrestling* (1823).

manner, football would prove an attractive amusement in any part of the kingdom." Football was alive and well in Ireland, and if they were organising representative county teams, it must have been surprisingly well-structured at a time when, according to the author, it was becoming a thing of the past in England.

Sentiments echoed by a contributor calling himself JRP, writing in *Hone's Every Day Book* in 1841, who had seen Irishmen playing football regularly in English fields around Islington, and offers that "I believe as is usual in the sister kingdom, county men play against other county men … some fine specimens of wrestling are occasionally exhibited in order to delay the two men who are rivals in pursuit of the ball. Meantime the others get on with the combat. The arrival of the ball in the goal is greeted with a lusty shout."

And John Fisher Murray felt "Germany has her heart set upon strong beer, tobacco and the *valtz* … Scotland has her bagpipe, her toddy, her golf, her curling matches, and her reels. Ireland her hurling matches, jigs, wakes, and football playings. England her cricket, her rural dances, sports, and fairs[23]." As late as 1843, this English writer believed football was a typically Irish thing.

In 1835, JD Herbert remembered "the plagues of Dublin – that of bull-baiting, dog-fighting, throwing at cocks, wrestling, football playing and boxing matches. All those gymnastic exercises and vile sports were practiced with impunity to the odious actors and abettors[24]" and in 1837, English traveller Jonathan Binns, after stating the obvious that "the Catholics and Protestants do not appear quite so sociable here as in other places" commented that the former were not good churchgoers, which he attributed to the fact that conducting services in Latin meant they were "unable to derive any benefit[25]." They would arrive at church just to catch the end of the service "and in the afternoon they play at football and other games."

In volume one, we came across the football played at Stonyhurst College in England. Being a Catholic school, about a third of the students were from Ireland, and children from the two countries would play each other. "The Irish were marshalled on one side of a large field, and the English on the other. When they became heated, the boys showed a spirit of antipathy, which reminded one of the feuds of the two nations. In general, the English were successful because they showed more prudence and self-control. The Irish were so precipitate and headlong as constantly to miss the victory when they were on the point of gaining it[26]."

If any of those Irish footballers went on to complete their education at the Maynooth university village in County Kildare, they were in for disappointment, because a description of the extreme strictness at that institution tells us that in fine weather, students "are permitted to play at ball, or possibly at prison-bars, in a gravelled court, but they are strictly

---

[23] John Fisher Murray *The world of London* (1843).

[24] JD Herbert *Irish varieties, for the last fifty years: written from recollections* (1835).

[25] Jonathan Binns *Miseries and beauties of Ireland* (1837).

[26] *The New Monthly Magazine* (1823).

MIKE ROBERTS — THE SAME OLD GAME: CODIFICATION

prohibited from amusing themselves with foot-ball, as that game is not deemed decorous for lads of seventeen[27]."

Ireland clearly still had a footballing culture of its own as late as the 1840s. As explained in a later chapter, at roughly the same time, the first known references to football played in both the Australian cities of Adelaide and Melbourne were played by members of the Irish community. There were also Irish sports clubs in America, the oldest on record being a hurling club in San Francisco in 1853, although Paul Darby[28] is jumping the gun when he describes the Irish Hurling and Football Club, established in New York in 1857, as a 'GAA' club three decades before the Association was formed.

Shamrucks

We find an interesting quote in 1892 from Irish rugby man JJ MacCarthy, who is rather offish in his comment that football "was played after a very primitive fashion by the peasantry of the west and south over a hundred years ago, and at times matches between rival parishes remained undecided until the representatives of one were able to carry the ball home by force. Any method to prevent this capture was permissible, sticks, sods, and stones being freely used, and many serious injuries were sustained on both sides. It was in about 1868 that the game began to assume some civilised shape[29]."

Football may have been more widespread in Ireland than England in the early 19th century but times had changed. Victorian culture adopted a whole new approach to the wild folk games, and football was now played on delimitated fields with structured rules. These innovations were also going to affect the way the Irish played football. There is no evidence that the British enforced their new footballing ideals on the Irish people. If the Irish had preferred to ignore rugby and soccer and stick to their own rules, they were quite free to do so. But that would not happen until some four decades later, when the GAA was formed as a backlash against the Irish population's willingness to adopt the English rules rather than make up their own.

It was particularly via the education system that the English rules were introduced to Ireland, and Trinity College, Dublin[30], played a prominent role. The first evidence of football there goes way back to 1811 and a poem by Edward Lysaght, who suggested:

"Dear C-if-id, play football no more, I entreat,
The amusement's too vulgar, fatiguing and rough
Pursue the same conduct you've followed of late
And I warrant, ere long, you'll get kicking enough[31]."

---

[27] *The Quarterly Review* (1828).

[28] In Cronin, Murphy and Rouse's book.

[29] In Frances Marshall's 1892 work.

[30] The source of much of the information on football at Trinity is courtesy of Trevor West's *The Bold Collegians: Development of Sport in Trinity College, Dublin* (Lilliput Press, 1991).

The oldest record of a football club at Trinity College dates to December 1855, when the *Daily Express* announced that "a match will be played in the College Park today (Saturday) between original and new members of the club. Play to commence at two o'clock College time[32]."

From that date on, there is ample evidence of football fixtures among Dublin students, including Internals v Externals, Fair Hair v Dark Hair, Football Club v Boat Club and Cheltenham Boys or Royal Schools v The Rest to name but a few, while the first game against a non-university side was against Wanderers[33] in 1860. *The Irish Times* of October 28, 1867 mentions a series of three games played against the military, where for the first two games the University agreed to play by the Eton Rules (one win each), and then cruised to an easy win in game three when they decided to switch to the Rugby code.

The main man behind football at Trinity College was the 'father of Irish rugby', Charles Burton Barrington, although he never claimed to have introduced the game. Instead, he suspected his own uncle, Charles West, who attended Rugby School before 1850 and was "the East in *Tom Brown's Schooldays* ... might have had a hand in it ... when this Old Rugbean went out to play in the Park for the first time, the game may have seemed to him peculiar but it never occurred to him that it was anything else than Rugby of sorts ... the whole thing was very loose, two fellows were made heads, tossed for first choice and then picked their team from the bystanders who happened to turn up[34]."

Barrington did not go to Rugby, and was introduced to football at St Columba's College, where "we played a sort of soccer game. On one afternoon a man called Strickland appeared and played in our game. He belonged to the TCD[35] football club, we heard, but who brought him the boys did not know. He played as we did. On making a catch, though, he ran with the

---

[31] A footnote to the original publication of the poem explains that "at the time when Ned Lysaght was in Trinity College [c. 1780] the fellow-commoners considered themselves superior beings to the pensioners; and of course they were above taking any part in the amusement of football which was then played every evening in the College Park. It so happened that a pensioner whose name was C-lf-ld had been vain enough to associate entirely with fellow-commoners, and, of course, never deigned to play at football, until one evening when he accidentally condescended to do so; scarcely had he made the attempt, when some of his fellow students (pensioners) indignant at his past folly, soon tripped up his heels, to the no small gratification of the whole assemblage then present, but to the mortification of C-lf-ld and his companions."

[32] The mention of 'original' members suggests the club was actually formed before 1855. Dublin University FC still exists today. And although they were by no means the first ever football club, they certainly have a valid claim to be the oldest club in existence that has a continuous, uninterrupted and documented history, and when the option arose later in the century, the code they would settle for, and the one they still play now, was rugby.

[33] The Wanderers were probably former students, and unlikely to have had anything to do with a well-known Dublin club formed ten years after.

[34] This and all other Barrington quotes are from a series of letters exchanged later in life with rugby historian Edward J McCartney Watson and cited in Trevor West *The Bold Collegians: The Development of Sport in Trinity College, Dublin* (Lilliput Press, 1991).

[35] Trinity College, Dublin.

MIKE ROBERTS – THE SAME OLD GAME: CODIFICATION

ball, but when collared and downed would not let the ball go. Our big boys had difficulty in getting it from him. This incident would show that TCD did run with the ball in 1859. Anyhow our masters made him drop it."

But when Barrington himself went to Trinity in 1867, we learn that the Football Club, despite existing, can't have been all that big a deal. He writes that there were "no cycles, no golf, no hockey, no anything, only card-playing, billiards, whiskey-drinking, and a stilted social life. There was, however, a little desultory football, with no particular rules to speak, or kit. A good little chap called Wall was running the show. I started away and pulled things together, made a good club out of it with the rules of Rugby School, and we were very successful for it caught on at once. I have a photo of our First XV by me, and we are a queer-looking lot judged by modern ideas. We had caps made in Rugby too, but there was no-one in those far-off times to play against. The match of the year was against the Medical School. Sometimes too the Dublin Garrison boiled up a team to play us. We played matches among ourselves, 'pick up' twice or three times a week … The Club was really a great success and did introduce the Rugger game into Ireland … The club had no rules, written or unwritten. They just played and ran with the ball, no touch line, no goal lines, our only parpanalia [sic] being the Rugby goal posts. These were all sufficient for the simple tastes of those days in Dublin Football. A Rugbean brought in the new idea of Rules. Rugby itself though had no written rules! They were traditional, like the British Constitution or the Secrets of Free Masonry."

We know he was wrong there, Rugby School had written its rules over twenty years earlier, but he was none the wiser so "Wall sat gravely at his little table. A small dark wiry hardy chap with a short black beard and kindly dark eyes. He wrote and I dictated. Gradually and gradually as one could remember them the unwritten laws that govern the immortal Rugby game were put on paper."

These were the same laws that appeared the *Cricket Annual* from 1868 onwards. For all intents and purposes, they were the same rules as the ones used at Rugby and any minor discrepancies would eventually be ironed out when the RFU issued its own official laws three years later in 1871. Like the RFU, Trinity outlawed hacking[36], and as mathematician Arthur Garves, who played with Barrington, later explained "passing was against the rules – it was called hand ball … and as there was no passing one often saw very fine long runs – sometimes even three-quarters of the length of the ground, with wonderful swerves and dodges ... in every respect the game was more individual and scientific than it is today."

The influential Wanderers FC was formed in 1870, and also still exists. Their own website explains that they were formed "by some former members of Dublin University FC" and

---

[36] A practice Barrington had experienced at school, where they even "had what was called a Hallelujah at the end of a House Match ... The ball was then taken away. All the players went into the scrum and hacked each other away dutifully for five minutes. That was the finish and all went to their houses to hot water, footpans, tea and baked potatoes."

132

were so called because they "had to seek opponents outside of Ireland, as there were no other Irish clubs at that time." Obviously they would have preferred to play by the Rugby rules, but like in England, any kind of football club would have sufficed for the sake of a game. But football clubs were still an alien concept in Ireland, although before long MacCarthy noted that that football teams did start appearing, with "Dublin University, North of Ireland, Catholic University, Rathmines School, Belvedere College, Clongowes College, and Tullabeg College being almost the only organisations which recognised any discipline in their play." There does seem to be a hint in this sentence that there were other clubs that played a less disciplined form of football than the Rugby code, and he tells us that "the two last-named colleges had methods of their own, which mainly consisted of dribbling, an art which they brought to a pitch of perfection never excelled in an Association International match. They used to play on gravel, and the ball, which was made by the college shoemaker, was about double the size of an orange." School traditions varied in Ireland as much as in England, but there is no evidence that these games had anything to do with ancient forms of Gaelic football.

Irish football clubs were not being converted to rugby. They were being formed to play rugby. The Irish Football Union was founded to govern football in November, 1874, and there was controversy, but not regarding the rules. The Rugby rules were accepted with little argument, and the upset was about how Dublin had gone ahead and formed the Union without consulting Belfast first. The first club in the north, the North of Ireland FC was founded by cricketing old boys from Rugby and Cheltenham in 1868, and just weeks after the IFU was formed, Dublin's Wanderers were severely beaten by them. The Northerners, disgruntled that Dublin had self-proclaimed itself the headquarters of Irish rugby, sulked off and formed their own separate union instead.

Soccer kicks in

Although it was sweeping across England, Scotland and Wales, the Association game didn't find its way across the Irish Sea until 1878, a full 15 years after the London FA was formed. It was a Belfast man called John McAlery, after watching the game while on his honeymoon in Scotland, who first arranged for two teams, Queen's Park and Caledonians, to play a soccer match in his home city. The local press was astonished to see as many as a thousand people turning out to watch a weird game in which the players headed the ball "like a pack of young goats."

RM Peter's response was that "Belfast has always been, and most probably will continue, a stronghold of Rugby football; and although the majority of the spectators evinced a decided preference for the Rugby code, still there were not a few who were much impressed with the scientific beauty of the dribbling game." McAlery was one of the latter, and within a year had placed an ad in the *Belfast Newsletter* looking for players to join what would become Ireland's oldest soccer club, Cliftonville FC.

MIKE ROBERTS – THE SAME OLD GAME: CODIFICATION

Rugby had had a decade's head start on soccer in Ireland, and the first Ireland rugby international had even been played against England in 1875. Therefore, Cliftonville had no choice but to turn to local rugby team Quidnuncs for their first opposition, and lost 2-1. Soccer may have been unknown in Belfast, but it would soon catch on, and within a year Balmoral Academy had a team, while Knock Lacrosse Club, and both the Albion and Windsor Rugby Clubs were more than happy to try out the new game. The Avionel side proved a particularly significant addition to the Belfast soccer scene, being formed by Glaswegians building a new distillery, and it was the close links between Belfast and the northwest of England and Scotland that really helped soccer culture explode in the north.

There was no stopping McAlrey and by 1880 he had formed the Irish Football Association (playing by "the Scotch rule book") and in 1881 his Cliftonville side was beaten by Moyola Park in the final of the first Irish FA Cup. Still not satisfied, and less than five years after the first game of formalised soccer had been played on Irish soil, he assembled an Ireland team in 1882 to take on the mighty England. He was trying to run before he could walk, for the Irish were played off Bloomfield Park in Belfast to the tune of a 13-0 defeat, which still stands as both England's biggest ever win, and Ireland's biggest ever loss.

Wanted: Gaelic football

The first report of a football match in the newspaper *Sport* in 1881, describes a game played in Longford, probably some kind of rugby judging by the description, that was watched by "rustics who had never seen the game before" and who, when they saw one of the home players fairly tackled, in their ignorance thought they were witnessing an assault and "rushed in on the ground and knocked over a couple of Dublin men ... and a free fight all round was prevented with difficulty." Rugby and soccer, or anything like them, were unfamiliar games in the Ireland of the early 1880s, when there wasn't a single apparent utterance that there might have been an Irish form of football to defend against the increasing popularity of rugby and soccer in the country. And certainly not one that was played by anything even remotely resembling a national standard, something which any self-respecting sports historian knows could not possibly have been achieved without generating a considerable amount of documentary evidence.

Richard M Peter's tome, the *Irish Football Annual*, edited in 1880, makes for telling reading, and it is important to note that it was written less than half a decade before the appearance of the GAA. In the first major yearbook of football in Ireland, Peter, the Honourable Secretary of the Irish Rugby Football Union, invited 56 different secretaries of Irish football clubs to provide reports of how their seasons had gone by providing results of matches and other anecdotes. These were more or less all the football clubs the country could offer at the time, although there were eleven others he had no contact address for, while references to other teams in the different reports suggest that there were other groups of people that could raise some kind of team from time to time.

THE CELTIC TIMES

The yearbook contains over 150 pages of reports of clubs from all over Ireland (from Dublin, Clare, Galway, Tipperary, Belfast, Cork, Wexford, Armagh and others). A common theme is that many of the clubs had only recently formed and were struggling to get people with no previous football experience used to it.

Although it is called the 'football' annual, and the game is frequently referred to by that name, almost all of the clubs Peter lists were affiliated to the IRFU. However, he also includes a section on soccer for "as the Association Game of football has now been introduced to Ireland, and as there is every prospect of it, ere long, becoming a very general pastime at least in the northern districts" it was "deemed worthy of record."

The president of the IRFU, WC Neville, contributes six insightful pages on the situation of football in Ireland, and his comments on soccer really get our eyebrows fluttering. "An effort made lately to introduce into Belfast the Association Code of Rules signally failed" he writes, though as later events turned out, this may have been more wishful thinking than actual fact. "Any renewed efforts at such an innovation will, I hope, meet with a like fate; not that the Association game is not a fine and skilful one, but because, even at present, we have too few players to let their attention be frittered away in various directions."

Neville was not knocking soccer as a game. His objection was that in a country with a relatively small and disperse population, the last thing rugby needed was for its players to start drifting away to soccer. Well, perhaps not the very last thing, because his frustration would probably have gone into overdrive when he learned that some of his countrymen were plotting to set *yet another* code of football loose on the country.

If Neville had been aware of any native kind of football, it seems extraordinary that he would not have mentioned it with a similar lack of enthusiasm. But he does not. Instead, he states that football in Ireland was only in its sixth year because "for all practical purposes we may date the origin and progress of Irish football from the winter of 1874–75" and even then, most of the action had been centred around Dublin, for elsewhere "despite the efforts of individual clubs … the game, as a winter pastime, could scarcely have been called 'racy of the soil'."

Understanding Ireland

Questioning the historical accuracy of Gaelic football tends to get its supporters on the defensive. So entwined is the GAA in Irish culture that any criticism is interpreted as a patronising slur. It is common knowledge in Ireland that their game forms an important part of the nation's heritage – anybody who tries to deny that is a paddy-bashing moron on a par with a Danish cartoonist drawing pictures of Mohammed.

To understand just why the Irish should feel so strongly about defending their own football, and their national identity, means delving into the history books, and understanding why the Irish have more than enough reasons for the chip they bear on their shoulder when it comes to their cousins on the neighbouring island.

MIKE ROBERTS – THE SAME OLD GAME: CODIFICATION

Relations between Britain and Ireland had never been healthy, and in the lead-up to the formation of the GAA in 1884, just the latest in eight centuries of unpleasant episodes involving the two countries were still fresh on many minds.

One hundred years earlier, at the close of the 18th century, Ireland had been an autonomous state, although its Parliament was effectively nothing more than a puppet-government run by the British. The apartheid imposed upon the natives was gradually being retracted as part of the process of Catholic Emancipation. Among the discriminations against Catholics (and the years the laws were repealed) were a ban on marriage with Protestants (1778), a ban on being educated abroad (1782), a ban on working as teachers (1782) and a ban on holding firearms (1793, the same year Catholics finally got the right to vote). There were even bans on Catholics taking custody of orphans, and although they could build churches, they had to be made of wood and not near any public roads.

Considering its past history, this was a time of relative peace and reconciliation in Ireland. Meanwhile, many Protestants no longer felt like the colonialists they were before, and came to consider themselves Irish too. And so it was that the French and American Revolutions served as the inspiration to believe that Ireland's time had come and the United Irishmen drew upon support from both religions in the drive to form a non-secular, truly independent state.

Theobald Wolfe Tone (often regarded as the father of Irish republicanism) stated that the goals were to "substitute the common name of Irishman for Protestant, Catholic and Dissenter" and to "break the connection with England, the never failing source of all our political evils."

The Irish Rebellion was a bloody one, and from an Irish point of view, it failed. Wolfe Tone committed suicide rather allow the British to carry out their death sentence on him, and the Rebellion ultimately only served to make matters considerably worse for Ireland. The British were as delightful in their way of dealing with the issue as they had been so many times in the past. Rebels were hung, burnt alive and gang raped in some of the most gruesome massacres Ireland has ever endured. The rebels themselves were no more caring in the way they dealt with their captives, and as it turned out, the worst Irish atrocities were committed by Catholics and Protestants against each other as the realities of war showed it was going to be a lot harder than many had hoped for the two religions to live side by side on a troubled island. As a result of the three-month Rebellion, some 30,000 people lost their lives, and thousands more were deported to Australia. In fact, these massive deportations of Irish people have often been cited as one of the most obvious reasons for suggesting Gaelic and Australian football might share a common root.

Great Britain decided it needed to exert total control over Ireland and made the two a single country by the Act of Union of 1801. Not even the Irish Parliament, dominated by Protestants as it was, existed any more, and Irish MPs were elected instead to sit at the British Parliament in Westminster.

THE CELTIC TIMES

The positive side of this for the Irish was that as they were now direct subjects of the Crown, they could enjoy the same privileges as British people. They did indeed. Just like the poor of Victorian England, they got next to nothing. With so little being done about the abject misery being suffered by the working (and not working) millions on their own doorsteps in the urban monstrosities being created by the Industrial Revolution, the British authorities were hardly going to be any more considerate about Ireland. They controlled it, but were aloof about helping it develop. It was no fun being poor back then. It was even less fun being one of the Irish poor.

The Irish population doubled in the first half of the 19th century, and as farms were handed down through the generations, the land had been divided so much between heirs that these plots were no longer enough to support a family. That was if you could hold on to your land at all, because Protestant landowners had a habit of enclosing large areas of land for intensive cattle grazing, and anybody that happened to live there was simply moved aside. Again, this was not really persecution of the Irish; it was persecution of the peasantry. The authorities were doing exactly the same thing to their 'own' people in England.

Ireland was hit by famine (the worst one, but not the only one, from 1845–49), as well as epidemics of typhoid, cholera and dysentery, which saw a million die and a million more flee to Britain, North America or Australasia. Throughout the second half of the 19th century, its population was almost halved. The British government didn't seem to care much. At the worst of the famine, Prime Minister John Russell simply declared that it wouldn't do to have the Irish thinking they could live off handouts from England, and opted instead for a few timid and unsuccessful attempts to try to make Ireland economically sustainable.

Other nations did show they cared, and sent what charity they could, and it is perhaps poignant to observe that although her government seemed unmoved by the Irish plight, Queen Victoria did make a personal donation to the cause. But Victoria's generosity was not as great as one might have expected of woman in her position, and this is where Drogheda United soccer club make an unexpected appearance in our tale. The story[37] goes that the Ottoman Sultan Abdülmecid wished to send £10,000 to support the Irish farmers, but was advised by the British ambassador in Istanbul that as the Queen herself had only sent £2,000 (later reduced by half), it would be diplomatic not to send any more than Her Majesty. The Sultan instead sent five shiploads of food to Dublin, but apparently the British administration refused the vessels permission to land. The Turks eventually secretly docked at Drogheda, and the local gratitude for that is still displayed in the form of the Turkish star and crescent on Drogheda United's club crest.

The Irish peasant class was decimated by the tragedy, and the few that survived went on to become locked in the Land Laws as they fought to reclaim farmland from the outsiders that

---

[37] Backed up by Thomas P O'Neill in *The Threshold* magazine in 1957.

MIKE ROBERTS – THE SAME OLD GAME: CODIFICATION

had forcibly taken it over. Uprisings, such as that led by Thomas Francis Meagher and his Young Irelanders in 1848, were common but unsuccessful.

The tide in 19th century Ireland is typified by Isaac Butt, an Orangeman, Tory MP and fervent opponent of Irish nationalism who was persuaded by events during and after the famine to totally change his political views and establish the Home Rule League, which drew all the different nationalist groups together as a single united political force that started lapping up votes, winning no fewer than 54 seats in the British Parliament in 1874.

Butt died in 1879, and his mantle was largely taken over by an Anglican landowner, Charles Stewart Parnell, who formed the equally influential Irish Parliamentary Party (IPP) in 1882, two years before the formation of the GAA. Of British ancestry and wealthy stock, Parnell was once described by William Gladstone as the most remarkable person he had ever met. Such were his political achievements that historians even speculate that had Parnell not died, Ireland would have achieved home rule much earlier and such horrors as the Easter Rising and Irish War of Independence would never have had to happen. Revered among all walks of Irish nationalism, even Sinn Féin, the 'uncrowned king of Ireland' used peaceful, political measures to wield the Irish influence in London. His downfall would ultimately not be a political one, but the revelation that he had been having a long-term affair with an English woman called Katharine (Kitty) O'Shea, the wife of a fellow MP, and had even sired three of her kids. His political career would be blighted by the scandal, and he died of a heart attack brought on by rheumatic fever in 1891. He didn't even get a gravestone until 1940, but when it was laid, there was no need to carve more than just one word … Parnell.

Others had less time for diplomacy with the British authorities, and adopted a more hard-line approach, the leaders in that department at the time of the foundation of the GAA being the Irish Republican Brotherhood (IRB), or the 'Fenians', who sometimes collaborated with the IPP, but generally favoured a more direct course of action (i.e. armed revolt against the British, what some people would call 'terrorism' today, and indeed the IRB would have a lot to do with the origins of the Irish Republican Army (IRA) in the 20th century). In 1867, they attempted full-on armed rebellion, but this was crushed fairly easily by the British. The movement was still around in the 1880s with a series of dynamite attacks on British cities, and the British Chief Secretary for Ireland, Lord Frederick Cavendish, was assassinated in 1882. History does not suggest that the IRB counted on an awful lot of support among the Irish people. The Catholic Church certainly opposed its violent methods, although it is also fair to say that public declarations of support would probably not have been the best idea, given the fear of reprisals by the British.

'Penal servitude' was generally the punishment for activity in support of the IRB. This involved forced labour in prison camps, which often served no purpose whatsoever. It meant treading mills all day that contained nothing but sand or carrying cannonballs up and down the prison yard. Penal servitude was not something many people were keen to do. If you supported the IRB, you didn't make too public a point of it.

Culture clubs

At least at first, the GAA did not originate out of any rebel movement, but out of the desire to fire new life into Irish culture. The events of the 19th century had had a devastating effect on the Irish language, which by 1850 had become the minority tongue. William Butler Yeats, George Bernard Shaw and Oscar Wilde were just three of the great 19th century Irish writers, but all were writing in English. By the end of the century, *Gaeilge* barely existed outside of a few vernacular-speaking communities, or *Gaeltachts*, on the western coast.

The sentiment is brilliantly conveyed by a landmark lecture given by Douglas Hyde[38] in 1892, *The Necessity for De-Anglicising Ireland.* It's a shame there's no room to print the whole address here, because you won't hear many better displays of oratory brilliance, but the gist goes that "I should also like to call attention to the illogical position of men who drop their own language to speak English, of men who translate their euphonious Irish names into English monosyllables ... we have lost the notes of nationality, our language and customs ... The Irish race is at present in a most anomalous position, imitating England and yet apparently hating it ... This awful idea of complete Anglicisation, which I have here put before you in all its crudity is, and has been, making silent inroads upon us for nearly a century ... We must strive to cultivate everything that is most racial, most smacking of the soil, most Gaelic, most Irish, because in spite of the little admixture of Saxon blood in the north-east corner, this island is and will ever remain Celtic at the core ... We must create a strong feeling against West-Britonism[39], for it ... will overwhelm us like a flood, and we shall find ourselves toiling painfully behind the English at each step following the same fashions, only six months behind the English ones; reading the same books, only months behind them; taking up the same fads, after they have become stale there, following them in our dress, literature, music, games, and ideas, only a long time after them and a vast way behind. We will become, what, I fear, we are largely at present, a nation of imitators, the Japanese of Western Europe, lost to the power of native initiative and alive only to second-hand assimilation ... I would earnestly appeal to every one, whether Unionist or Nationalist, who wishes to see the Irish nation produce its best ... because upon Irish lines alone can the Irish race once more become what it was of yore – one of the most original, artistic, literary, and charming peoples of Europe."

These ideas were still tied in with the greater end of securing Home Rule, for as Mike Cronin explains "Ireland could not begin working towards some ideal of political home rule if culturally it had ceased to be Irish ... Without a cultural conception of what it meant to be Irish ... then home rule, should it come, would be a meaningless achievement."

And it was against that background that Michael Cusack founded the GAA to defend Irish sporting interests against the spreading British influence, and he did so with brilliance.

---

[38] Who would form the Gaelic League in 1893 to promote Irish culture and would eventually be the first president of an independent Ireland in 1938.
[39] 'West British' is a derogatory term used to describe pro-British people in Ireland.

MIKE ROBERTS – THE SAME OLD GAME: CODIFICATION

Michael Cusack

Michael Cusack (in Irish Mícheál Ó Ciosóg) was born in County Clare in 1847, at the height of the famine. It is difficult to think of any single person in the history of any of the codes of football who was quite so fascinating and intriguing as this veritable dichotomy of a man. Eoghan Corry, the founder of the GAA museum, describes him as an enigma, adding how "somewhat appropriately, even the site of his birthplace in Carron, restored by the GAA in 1984, is disputed."

With struggles against British occupation raging in the background, this self-made son of a poor herding family went on to work as a teacher, finally making it to French College (now Blackrock College, Dublin) in 1874. He later established his own Civil Service Academy, which established an excellent reputation for training young boys for entrance into universities and the civil service and also firmly established his position among the *nouveau riche*.

In the great tradition of Victorian gentlemen, Cusack was a sporting all-rounder. He played handball, he rowed, he was Irish champion at putting the 16 pound shot in 1879 and 1882, and he was also a huge fan of football, which he encouraged among his pupils, who drew up their own rules, which were soon to be replaced by a more established set.

We referred earlier to the *1880 Football Annual*, in which there is a curious lack of any reference to any native Irish form of the game. But Cusack gets a mention. He had formed Cusack's Academy Football Club, who in 1880 had just enjoyed their first successful season, and was affiliated to the IRFU. They played in Phoenix Park, Dublin and must have looked terrific in what they called their 'Joseph's Coat' colours. A crash of drums, a flash of light, and we find that the rugby club was being run by a "hard working forward" by the name of Michael Cusack, and "under the leadership of such a sterling lover of the game as Mr Cusack, they may reasonably expect to be even more successful next year." As it happens, the Academy team didn't have much of a future at all, but that wasn't necessarily a bad thing for its players. Cusack's Academy earned itself such a fine reputation for producing brilliant scholars who went on to find excellent jobs that the rugby team was constantly left struggling for players, and folded after just a year. Cusack started turning out for the Phoenix Rugby Club instead.

There is no sport more quintessentially British than cricket, nor one less in keeping with the GAA's principles, so it is unusual to find young Cusack was devoted to the game. In his later years as a prolific journalist, he would often write with obvious passion about the beauties of the sport, saying that Ireland should have cricket clubs in every parish, and in *The Shamrock*, in July 1882, just two years before the formation of the GAA, that "you may be certain that a boy who can play cricket well will not, in after years, lose his head and get flurried in the face of danger."

In 1881, Cusack was advocating that "English standards of excellence be accepted" in Irish athletics, and also criticised the congress of the Society for the Protection of the Irish

Language for being "too nationalist." Members of the Royal Irish Constabulary (RIC), the British police force operating in Ireland, would later be ostracised by the GAA, yet in 1882, Cusack was actually campaigning for the Dublin Athletic Club to do away with its rule prohibiting policemen from being members. He was doing so in the company of Owen Harte, a member of the RIC and a close friend, and schoolmaster John Huston Stewart, a Protestant.

Cusack's name has often sat uncomfortably in the GAA annals, and his cricket and rugby-playing past is something most GAA histories prefer to brush under the carpet. But Cusack's love affair with 'English' sports was soon to come to a bitter end. 1882 seems to have been the watershed year, when his life underwent a remarkable turn, and by the end of it, the same man who had been happily filling column inches with such copy as advice on cleaning cricket bats and storing them properly though the winter months would be ordering the good people of Ireland to turn their backs on the very sports he himself had done so much to encourage, calling rugby "a denationalizing plague" that carried "on through winter the work of ruin that cricket was doing through the summer."

Before then, it doesn't seem to have occurred to him that all this importation of English ideals may have equated to cultural imperialism, or that sport meant anything more than a form of healthy exercise. However, something was stirring in him, and the suddenness of his switch from Anglophile to Anglophobe is just one of the intriguing mysteries surrounding the man. But 'impulsive' is as good an adjective as any to describe the founder of the GAA, and in this case, the impulse may have come from one of the forgotten figures in this story – a man called Pat Nally.

Not on my Nally

When he formed the GAA, Cusack was merely building on something that had been brewing for some time. Forming an Irish sports association was nothing new. Cork journalist Denis Holland may have been the first with his attempts to set up native sports clubs from 1858 onwards, a project that came to nothing when he emigrated to America. Other ventures included the Dublin Amateur Athletics Club of 1867, Henry Dunlop's Irish Champion Athletic Club of 1872 and also his Amateur Athletics Association of Ireland in 1881, and Val Dunbar's Irish National Athletics Committee of 1877. Cusack himself had been involved in six of those projects, but these were about embracing British sports culture, not rejecting it, or creating anything new and intrinsically Irish. One suspects Cusack was rewriting his own history when he later wrote that "in that modest state of life and feeling, I was invited to sit on the Council of the Irish Champion Athletic Club. Desiring to make the acquaintance of all Ireland, I accepted the honour without thanks. I was a good listener in those far-off days. I soon realised that my colleagues were viciously West British. I let them die. Soon after we started the Dublin Athletic Club. The Amateur Athletic Association of Britain was to be our model. Nothing was to be done in Ireland without the sanction of England ... I revolted. The majority tried to expel me. I expelled them, and started on my own account."

By the early 1880s there were over a hundred different athletics meetings being held around the island, with various combinations of running, jumping, throwing and cash prizes involved. One of these was at Balla, and was traditionally held each year on the grounds of local landlord Sir Robert Lynch-Blosse. He was not a popular man, and in 1879 there was outrage in support of the Dempsey family, who after two years of poor crops were unable to pay a £26 debt and were to be evicted from their cottage. A rally of Land League activists, including Charles Parnell and Michael Davitt, descended upon Balla, but their protests proved so ineffective that the events were hushed up as they were deemed poor publicity for the effectiveness of such activities. Instead the rebels clubbed together to raise the £26 and paid to keep the Dempseys in their home.

Lynch-Blosse was upsetting folk, and the Irish nationalists wanted nothing to do with the athletics meet he was patronising, and instead held their own alternative games, the National Sports of Mayo, on Pat Nally's farm, patronised by Parnell himself, although the big man didn't actually attend. With banners proclaiming 'God Save Ireland', plenty of nationalistic music and some 2000 people involved, the most symbolic event was the 300 yard race for labourers. That was something Lynch-Blosse would never have tolerated, for under the English AAC rules, athletics meetings were solely for the enjoyment of people of the ruling Protestant ascendancy, and common labourers were anything but worthy participants.

Nally, a leading Fenian and one of the finest all-round sportsmen in the country, went on to make quite a name for himself as a promoter of nationalist sports meetings. Probably sensing Cusack would be a useful vehicle for getting his ideas heard in Dublin, the two first met in 1879, and a year later Cusack organised the first National Athletic Meeting in the capital. But although some more traditional Irish sports were included in the programme, the main motive was to take control of athletics away from the landlords and allow artisans and nationalists the chance to "make an effort to preserve the physical strength of our race."

Writing in the *United Irishman* in 1889, Cusack went as far as to say that Nally was the one man more than anybody else that had influenced him to go on and form the GAA. If he had had the chance, Nally himself would probably have been the man to do just that. But in 1882, after living in hiding in England under an assumed name, he and six of his colleagues were arrested on charges of plotting the murder of land agents. The evidence against him was questionable, but Nally was sentenced to ten years incarceration, and died of ill health at Mountjoy Prison in 1881. He would end up becoming the only man never to be directly involved with the GAA to have a stand named after him at Croke Park, the Nally Stand, which was knocked down as part of the 2003 redevelopments. It was put back together in Tyrone, but a section of the terraces at Croke Park still honours the Nally name today.

The Gaelic mission

Michael Cusack's rhetoric seemed to wander in one direction and then the other, but he seems to have been far more of a cultural revolutionary than a political one. It is not clear

THE CELTIC TIMES

how much sympathy, if any, he really had for the Irish Republican Brotherhood, or the Invincible Violence group that was doing the rounds in his time. Religion was certainly not a motivation, not one Cusack quote ever suggests he had anything against Protestants, and many of them he considered friends and allies, along with several unionists. But as a fluent Irish speaker, he had long been impassioned by the defence of the native language and culture against the constant threat of Anglicisation. He was the most active member of the Gaelic Union for the Preservation and Cultivation of the Irish Language, founded in 1880.

But the idea that Irish games were also under threat from Anglicisation didn't seem to have dawned on Cusack until Pat Nally started putting ideas in his head. And with Nally behind bars, it was down to Cusack to pick up the baton. "The idea of doing for our national pastimes what my colleagues were doing for our national language was taking firmer hold of me day after day" he later wrote in the *Celtic Times*. "I was living with the men of Erin of pre-Christian times. In spirit I hunted with Fionn's invincible hosts from Antrim to Kerry. I hurled with the Fenians of sixteen centuries ago from Tara to Killarney. I resolved to bring back hurling." This man could write.

In *United Ireland* in January 1885, he wrote of how his people were "being driven like famished rats back to their wretched cabins by the administrations of an infamous Curfew law." They were ready for something to believe in, something to feel proud of, and with a spin doctor like Cusack at the helm, Gaelic sport was going to be the Messiah they yearned.

As we saw in volume one, one of Cusack's first projects was indeed to put his mind to reviving the declining game of hurling, and it was his involvement with the Metropolitan Hurling Club that convinced him that there was some yardage to be gained with this 'Irish sports' idea, writing in his own *Celtic Times* in 1887 that this was the club "out of which the GAA sprang." Some saw the man with the immense beard as something of a loon, others welcomed his ideas with open arms, but for good or for bad, he was certainly making a name for himself with what was dubbed somewhat disdainfully in 1883 as his 'Gaelic mission'.

His ideas were famously unleashed upon the nation in a celebrated article titled *A word about Irish athletics*[40]. He wrote that "no movement having for its object the social and political advancement of a nation from the tyranny of imported and enforced customs and manners can be regarded as perfect if it has not made adequate provision for the preservation and cultivation of the national pastimes of the people. Voluntary neglect of such pastimes is a sure sign of national decay and of approaching dissolution.

"The strength and energy of a race are largely dependent on the national pastimes for the development of a spirit of courage and endurance. The corrupting influences which, for several years, have been devastating the sporting grounds of our cities and towns are fast spreading to the rural population. Foreign and hostile laws and the pernicious influence of a hitherto dominant race drove the Irish people from the trysting places at the crossroads and

---

[40] Which appeared in the October 11, 1884 edition of the nationalist newspaper *United Ireland.*

143

MIKE ROBERTS – THE SAME OLD GAME: CODIFICATION

the hurling fields, back to their cabin where, but a few short years before, famine and fever had reigned supreme. In these wretched homes … the Irish peasant too often wasted his evenings and his holidays, in smoking and card-playing."

It's inspiring stuff, but despite his interest in ball sports, the focus of Cusack's ire was actually Irish athletics (as in track and field). He continues that "a few years later a so-called revival of athletics was inaugurated in Ireland. The new movement did not originate with those who have ever had any sympathy with Ireland or the Irish people. Accordingly labourers, tradesmen, artists, and even policemen and soldiers were excluded from the few competitions which constituted the lame and halting programme of the promoters." It is difficult not to imagine the Pat Nally influence on these words.

"Two years ago every man who did not make his living either wholly or partly by athletics was allowed to compete. But with this concession came a law which is as intolerable as its existence in Ireland is degrading. The law is, that all Athletic Meetings shall be under the rules of the Amateur Athletic Association of England, and that any person competing at any meeting not held under these rules should be ineligible to compete elsewhere.

"The management of nearly all the meetings held in Ireland since has been entrusted to persons hostile to all the dearest aspirations of the Irish people. Every effort has been made to make the meetings look as English as possible – foot-races, betting, and flagrant cheating being their most prominent features. Swarms of pot-hunting mashers sprang into existence. They formed Harrier Clubs, for the purpose of training through the winter, after the fashion of English professional athletes, that they might be able to win and pawn the prizes offered for competition in the summer.

"We tell the Irish people to take the management of their games into their own hands, to encourage and promote in every way every form of athletics which is peculiarly Irish, and to remove with one sweep everything foreign and iniquitous in the present system. The vast majority of the best athletes in Ireland are Nationalists. These gentlemen should take the matter in hands at once, and draft laws for the guidance of the promoters of meetings in Ireland next year. The people pay the expenses of the meetings, and the representatives of the people should have the controlling power. It is only by such an arrangement that pure Irish athletics will be revived, and that the incomparable strength and physique of our race will be preserved."

One man who read Cusack's words with interest was a renowned athlete from Carrick-on-Suir, Tipperary, called Maurice Davin. You don't get too many like him these days. An amazing all-rounder, he had broken world records for running, hurdling, jumping and weight throwing, and was also an officer for his local Rugby and Cricket Club. He saw the appeal in what Cusack was saying. Back in 1877, he had discussed much the same problem in the *Irish Sportsman* when he wrote that "the laws under which athletic sports are held in Ireland were designed mainly for the guidance of Englishmen, and they do not deal at all with the characteristic sports and pastimes of the Irish race."

144

THE CELTIC TIMES

A few days after Cusack's article in *United Ireland*, Davin replied in the letters column of the same paper by saying that "it is time that a handbook was published with rules, etc. for all Irish games. The English Handbooks of Athletics are very good in their way but they do not touch on many of the Irish games which although they are much practised, are not included in the events or programmes of athletic sports. Weight-throwing and jumping appear to be going out of fashion in England; but such is not the case in Ireland, although those events are too often left out of programmes of what might be called leading meetings. I have some experience of those things, and see numbers of young men almost daily having some practice. It is strange that for one bystander who takes off his coat to run a foot race, forty strip to throw weights or try a jump of some kind."

Davin also comments on the 'professionalism' that Cusack was so uncomfortable with, but feels this was not so much an English infection as a common problem of concern on both sides of the Irish Sea. "I thought we in Ireland were pretty free from the abuses you mention. I know they are said to be a great blot on the sport in England, but I understand the management there are doing all they can to remedy it."

But he also makes an intriguing reference to football: "Irish football is a great game and worth going a long way to see when played on a fairly laid out ground and under proper rules. Many old people say hurling exceeded it as a trial of men. I would not care to see either game now as the rules stand at present. I may say there are no rules and therefore those games are often dangerous. I am anxious to see both games under regular rules."

It is curious that he should mention 'Irish football' here. At least in his mind, there was a local alternative to rugby and soccer, but one that lacked any rules.

All told, Davin makes for refreshing matter-of-fact reading compared to Cusack's impassioned but impetuous bluntness and often contradictory rants. Davin was from a wealthy family of Tipperary farmers with a river haulage operation, and was unquestionably the more demure of the two. But it is important to note that neither gentleman ever condemned rugby, soccer, cricket or any other British sports as bad. Quite the contrary, they rarely suggest anything but admiration for them and willingly used them as their models. The motivations for the GAA were not so much a backlash against British imperialism as they were a reaction to the way the Irish people themselves had so readily accepted the imported rulebooks without making any concessions to their own sporting traditions.

To sign off, Davin pledges that "if a movement such as you advise is made for the purpose of reviving and encouraging Irish games and drafting rules, etc. I will gladly lend a hand if I can be of any use." Davin would indeed lend a hand, and would go on to be Cusack's greatest liege in the foundation of the GAA.

6 PADDY POWER
The GAA and the foundation of Gaelic football

Meeting of minds

It's ironic, but rather than be imperialistic about their sporting conventions, the British were actually quite the opposite. As Richard Holt writes "the spread of sport in Europe was not the result of an English campaign to convert Europeans to football or rugby. In sport as in other aspects, the British held aloof in splendid isolation."

Neither the Football Association nor the Rugby Football Union ever promoted their games as being inherently British, nor did they seem particularly bothered about other countries adopting their rules or not, which makes it all the more remarkable that they were so successful. Football was not embraced because it was British, it was embraced because people liked it. Vodka came from Russia, spaghetti from Italy and ivory from Africa and folk liked those things too.

Perhaps if they had gone on a cultural crusade to force the rest of the world to accept its sporting ideals, the Brits would have been met with greater resistance. That is not to say that some weren't wary. In France, Grousset formed his *Ligue Nationale de l'Education Physique.* In Italy, the fascists invented their alternative form of football called *volata* and Germany preferred to encourage its *turnen* gymnasiums[1]. But none of these projects inspired the masses quite like the English football codes did. However, the GAA was going to be very different. It produced exactly what they wanted, and supported it with some of the most brilliant marketing in sports history.

There was to be no messing around once Cusack and Davin got their heads together. On August 26, 1884, the former wrote to the latter to say "the paragraphs on athletics in *United Ireland* are exploding like shells in the enemy's ranks. Of course they know it is my doing and therefore the paper is not likely to hang fire soon … The Irish Association with its members must be formed before the end of this year. The Association could organize the whole country within the year 1885. We could then safely hold the projected national gathering in 1886. The business must be worked from Munster. Suppose we held a meeting of delegates in some central place in Tipperary on the 1st of November next … then the education of the people could start in earnest."

A circular was placed in *Freeman's Journal, United Ireland* and the *Irish Sportsman* stating that "you are earnestly requested to attend a meeting which will be held at Thurles on the 1st of November to take steps for the formation of a Gaelic Association for the preservation and

---

[1] In response to the *turnen* and the Germanisation of their culture, the Czechs established the *sokol* gymnastics movement in 1862. It was not just about mass calisthenics, but also about promoting the Czech identity in their political struggle for independence.

PADDY POWER

cultivation of our National Pastimes and for providing rational amusement for the Irish people during their leisure hours."

November 1 was no random date. This was date that the mythical forest-dwelling Fianna warriors had supposedly died, but they could still be called upon for much appreciated help in times of need. The formation of the GAA was that time. Dramatic stuff, but not only did the Fianna fail to put in an appearance, but neither did a lot of other people.

The meeting point was Hayes's Commercial Hotel in Thurles, County Tipperary, the idea being to then decide where to actually hold the momentous meeting. Being Irish, and there being a bar handy, they didn't opt to go to too far, and simply plumped for the billiards room next door.

In his own report published in *United Ireland*, Cusack described "a well attended meeting." He was never shy when it came to bending the truth, because rather than that, the first meeting probably got a pretty feeble turnout.

Along with Cusack, Davin and McKay there was something of a mixed bag of folk. Representing Cork Athletic Club was John McKay, who also wrote for the *Cork Examiner*, where he reported that "the meeting was poorly attended and several important athletic clubs in the South did not send a representative but perhaps this was due to the fact that the notice given was very short." He names just six men, but adds an etcetera that implies there were others.

There was another journo in John Wyse-Power, for Waterford's *Leinster Leader*, but also a member of the Naas and Kildare Club and a noted Fenian. And there was Joseph Kevin Bracken, a stonemason and former cricketer from Templemore, who would go on to be one of the best respected early GAA referees. He was also a fervent IRB supporter yet, ironically, and typifying the bizarre complexities of Irish politics at the time, he would also be the father of Brendan Bracken, who would become Winston Churchill's closest friend and a member of the British Cabinet during World War II.

There were also two men whose involvement with the GAA never went any further than their attendance of that meeting, Joseph O'Ryan (a solicitor and, like his friend Davin, from Carrick-on-Suir) and perhaps most curiously of all, Thomas St George McCarthy, an inspector in the British police force. It does seem odd that there should have been a police officer there, but McCarthy, a former pupil of Cusack's and who had recently won his first international cap for Ireland's rugby team, was probably only there out of purely sporting interest, and not a spy as some theorists have suggested, even though his father was a senior Tipperary magistrate. In fact, Marcus de Búrca's study of the man's later life[2] suggests he was something of a subversive who was regularly reprimanded for disobeying orders. What his presence reveals most of all is how Cusack and Davin were happy to open the GAA's doors to each and every one of the people that made up the complex patchwork of Irish

---

[2] Marcus de Búrca *The Curious Career of Sub-Inspector Thomas McCarthy* (Tipperary Historical Journal, 1988).

MIKE ROBERTS – THE SAME OLD GAME: CODIFICATION

society. But Eoghan Corry may be right in suggesting that the poor turnout at the Commercial Hotel may have been because anybody with a strong IRB connection would have beaten a fairly hasty retreat once they realised there was an RIC police officer sitting in the room[3]!

The meeting decided to name their new society the 'Gaelic Athletic Association for the Preservation and Cultivation of our National Pastimes'[4]. It wouldn't take long for them to realise that was a bit of a mouthful, and within weeks they had cut it down to the more palpable Gaelic Athletic Association (*Cumann Luthchleas Gael* in Irish). There does not appear to have been any mention of either Gaelic football or hurling at that first meeting. The focus was entirely on athletics, and establishing the GAA as the Irish governing body for the sport. John McKay's report in the *Cork Examiner* explains that the GAA would "regulate the management of all meetings, frame rules of their own for the government of such meetings, and put an end once and for ever to their being bound by the rules of the English AA Association."

This, in principle, wasn't a hugely controversial move. After all, several sports, soccer and rugby included, had their own separate associations in Ireland, and for all his criticism of the EAAA's influence in his country, Cusack actually declared himself an admirer of theirs and pointed out that the GAA "could not do better than adopt somewhat similar rules." But he did want to see the high jump, long jump and throwing the 16 lb and 56 lb weights included on the athletics schedule, his concern being that English athletics concentrated too much on the track and too little on the field. And with retrospect, the GAA can be commended for their role in shaping athletics as we know it today, for all those disciplines, or something very like them, now form part of any standard athletics meet.

Cusack also read out several letters of support he had received[5], in particular one from Michael Davitt, one of the Irish nationalist celebrities of the period and very much the Irish face of the Lands Wars[6]. It was shortly after he had been released from prison for the third

---

[3] Any move to create something Irish in defiance of Great Britain would have naturally attracted the more nationalistically minded sympathisers. Sport may have been the only item on the agenda, but as John Murphy claims (in *Part of What We Are*, Motive Television for Setanta Sports, 2008), the "founding fathers" at that Thurles meeting were "largely Fenians" and, in the same video, journalist Eugene McGee agrees when he says "it was clearly obvious that if you were involved in the GAA at the time, you were … certainly a nationalist if not a fanatical nationalist. That's how the GAA got its source, really."

[4] Cusack's original suggestion was actually to call it the Munster Athletic Club.

[5] Other enthusiastic correspondents included Morrison Miller, organiser of the Caledonian Games, Kimmersley Lewis for the Welsh nationalists, Professor Roehrig in the name of Irish Americans, and a Mr Lynch representing the Irish in Australia.

[6] Davitt had only one arm following an accident at work in a cotton mill when aged just nine, for which he received no compensation, and as a result he was a staunch supporter of labour rights. He also became a prominent Fenian rebel, which earned him a period of exposure to the cruelties of Dartmoor Prison. After his release, he rose through the ranks of the Land League that was fighting for the cause of the Irish tenants being exploited by their landlords. In County Mayo, he once led a campaign to ostracise a particularly vilified

PADDY POWER

time that Cusack's GAA caught his eye, and in his letter, he asked "why not make an effort to revive the Tailteann Games? A national festival could be organised to come off at some historic spot, at which prizes could be awarded for merit."

The Tailteann Games were a sort of Gaelic Olympics that had died out in the late 12th century following the Norman invasion. If they were to be revived, finance was not considered an issue. The GAA believed they could fund the project with money from Irish Americans, and in any case, judging by the experience of the recent Caledonian Games at Ballsbridge, a major athletics meeting could rake in a tidy profit.

As it turned out, the Tailteann Games idea was one the GAA would lay to one side for the time being, and wouldn't become a reality until after the foundation of the Republic of Ireland, when they were first held in 1924, and repeated in 1928 and 1932.

Patrons of the art

Much has been made of the first meeting of the GAA in Thurles, but it was actually a fairly inconsequential event. Marcus de Búrca observes that, "there is no evidence, apart from Davin, that the others played an active part in starting the GAA" and in the _Celtic Times_ in May 1887, even Michael Cusack conceded that "for all practical purposes there were only two men at the meeting." Rather than a meeting, it was more of a declaration of intent to the press.

One of the main conclusions made by the relative nobodies gathered in Thurles was that they weren't going to get very far unless they secured the support of some more influential figures. As Cusack had written shortly before the GAA was founded "although I am not a member of the National League, I think I am not without influence with several of its leading members ... I have found it to be utterly hopeless to revive our national pastimes without the assistance of the leaders of the people and I have not hesitated to urge my claim with a persistence that brooks no refusal. After a protracted struggle I won all round."

Thanks to that, they could already count on the backing of the aforementioned revolutionary Michael Davitt, and would later acquire the patronage of his arch-rival Charles Parnell, the leader of the nationalists' governmental wing, the Irish Parliamentary Party[7].

---

landlord by the name of Charles Boycott. Shops refused to serve him, he was ignored in the streets, the mail service wouldn't even deliver his letters, and the landlord could eventually stand it no more and went back to Britain. The story got so much press coverage on both sides of the Irish Sea that Charles' surname entered the English language as the verb 'to boycott'. It was for pranks like these that Davitt ended up behind bars two more times, yet as his life progressed his attitudes changed dramatically and he turned his back on his Fenian past, took a seat in the British parliament and started preaching the gospel of non-violence and peaceful negotiation, to the extent that none other than Mahatma Gandhi cited Davitt as one of his greatest inspirations.

[7] On December 17, 1884, Parnell wrote the following letter to the GAA: "Dear Sir, I have received your letter of the 11th instant. It gives me great pleasure to learn that a 'Gaelic Association' has been established for the preservation of National Pastimes, with the objects of which I entirely concur. I feel very much honoured by the resolution adopted at the Thurles meeting and I accept with appreciation the position of patron of the

MIKE ROBERTS – THE SAME OLD GAME: CODIFICATION

This would prove a very useful alliance indeed, for Parnell's National League had branches all over the country and offered the ideal framework for a little networking. If the GAA could persuade Parnell (and they did) to get each of these to set up athletics clubs, they'd have people playing Gaelic games around the country in no time. It wasn't so much that the founders of the GAA were political, it was more that politics offered them the perfect way to get their message to the people.

Next on their quest for support among the upper echelons of the Irish hierarchy was that hugely influential institution in Ireland, the Catholic Church. And in that respect there was no better contact than the Archbishop of Cashel, Thomas William Croke, the man after whom the great temple of the GAA, Croke Park[8], would be named in 1913. Croke was one of the most liberal-minded clergymen of the era and famous for his passion for Irish culture and sport. His letter in *United Ireland* in December 1884 makes it more than clear that the GAA could not have asked for a more enthusiastic sponsor. Let it go, Croker...

"One of the most painful ... and ... one of the most frequently recurring reflections that, as an Irish man I am compelled to make in connection with the present aspect of things in the country, is derived from the ugly and irritating fact that we are daily importing from England, not only her manufactured goods, which we cannot help doing, since she has practically strangled our own manufacturing appliances, but, together with her fashions, her accents, her vicious literature, her music, her dances and her manifold mannerisms, her games also and her pastimes, to the utter discredit of our own grand national sport and to the sore humiliation, as I believe, of every genuine son and daughter of our old land.

"Ball playing, hurling, football kicking according to Irish rules, 'casting', leaping in various ways, wrestling, hand-grips, top-pegging, leap-frog, rounders and tip-in-the-hat and all such favourite exercises and amusements among men and boys may now be said to be not only dead and buried but in several localities, entirely forgotten and unknown. And what have we got in their stead? We have got such foreign and fantastical field sports as lawn tennis, polo, croquet, cricket and the like ... For my part, I should vastly prefer to behold, or think of the youthful athletes whom I used to see in my early days at fair or pattern, bereft of shoes and coat, and thus prepared to play at hand-ball, to fly over any number of horses, to throw the 'sledge' or the 'winding stone' and to test each others mettle by the trying ordeal of 'three leaps' or 'the hop-step-and-jump'.

"Indeed if we continue travelling for the next score years in the same direction as we have been going for the same time past, condemning the sports that were practised by our forefathers, effacing our national features as though we were ashamed of them, and putting on with England's stuffs and broadcloths, her 'masher' habits and such effeminate follies as

---

Association which has been offered to me. I need not say that I shall do anything I can to render the working of the movement a success. I am, yours very truly, Charles S Parnell."

[8] The stadium was not purchased by the GAA until 1913, but what had previously been the Jones Road sports ground was used for Gaelic sports more or less from the day the GAA was founded.

she may recommend, we had better all come and public abjure our nationality, clap hands for joy at the sight of the Union Jack and place 'England's bloody red' exultingly 'above the green'."

Croke certainly has a wee dig at the Brits here, although it's really the Irish he is criticising for embracing the foreign games so enthusiastically. But perhaps he's being a bit harsh. Rather than forsaking Irish culture, it was all part of the 19th century process of sporting standardisation. Hand-grips, top-pegging and tip-in-the-hat must have been wonderful country traditions, but 'sport' in the 1880s meant something very different to what it had done 30 years earlier.

Much as he reviles croquet, and although the rules were indeed written in England, Ireland played its parts in the game's origins. Something called *crookey* was played at Castlebellingham, County Louth in 1834, a year before the first use of the modern spelling was recorded in Dun Laoghaire! And despite his opposition to the Englishness of polo, that was hardly an English game, seeing as it had been played for centuries throughout Asia and never made it to England until 1869. Also, as Croke despised the idea of the English game of cricket being played in his country, he felt people should play rounders instead, although there isn't a jot of evidence that rounders was ever a peculiarly Irish tradition, and let's not even get started on leap-frog.

But it's interesting that Croke mentions "football kicking according to Irish rules." Like Davin, Croke was also convinced that there was an Irish form of football, but unlike Davin, he also believed it had its own rules, and the Irish should revisit them rather than adapting their footballing ways to the regulations dictated by the British.

Archbishop Croke's speech struck a chord with the Irish people, and also with Cusack, who described his famous letter as "that of a man who knows that we can keep back the demoralising and prostrating tide that is rushing through the ill-concealed sewers which are the homes of the vile and treacherous things that work during the night." When somebody can be as prosaic as that, who's going to dare to argue?

Mixed response

Quite a lot of people as it happened. The nationwide reaction to the GAA's emergence on the Irish sports scene was hardly one of people leaping (in various ways) for joy. People may not have been too keen on British rule, but one thing they did like were the games, and this idea that they were too 'British' had not occurred to them before.

The Irish Cyclists' Association said they "could not allow themselves to be dictated to, or bossed in the way proposed" and urged athletics and cycling clubs all over the country to support them in their opposition to how "this association at a meeting held at Thurles … at which seven gentlemen were present, passed rules presuming to dictate to the whole body of Irish athletes … The Gaelic Athletic Association does not command the confidence of Irish athletes, and that this meeting refuses to recognise the right of such an unrepresentative meeting to make laws governing athletes in Ireland[9]." EJ Macredy at Trinity College sensed that the GAA was about politics, not sport, and suggested Irish athletes should do all in their power to "quash the Gaelic Union" and JA Christian of the Irish Amateur Athletic Union was anything but impressed with an association he considered to be "putting through rules purporting to govern all athletic sports."

Over in Britain, the press was mocking the funny Irish and their silly ideas. *The Daily Telegraph* reported on the foundation of the GAA by commenting that an "Olympic Games for Ireland hardly seems a serious proposition, yet this is the objective of a new society just started by the Archbishop Croke … and others of the National Party in the sister isle. We may be sure that an agrarian offence is no disqualification for a competitor."

Cusack responded with his usual venom, claiming the GAA was set up "by about a dozen Irishmen, not a single one of whom has, as far as I am aware, ever aspired to the position of leader in the ranks of Irish nationalists." Well, maybe not 'leader' as such, but... The *Telegraph* article he described in *United Ireland* to be "as vile a production as has ever been evolved out of the wilful lie. Your representative will at all times be perfectly welcome at our meetings, but it may be necessary for him to be acquainted with the Irish language if he wants to report our war shouts on the hurling field."

The second meeting of the GAA, held at the Victoria Hotel, Cork on December 27, 1884 showed a clear shift towards less athletic affairs. Eoghan Corry feels the GAA "was founded by sportsmen with a passing interest in politics, rather than politicians with a passing interest in sport," but whatever the intentions of the merry band of gentlemen that gathered for the first meeting of the GAA, given the turbulent climate of 1880s Ireland, it was difficult to keep politics out of anything, and something with the potential of the GAA was not going to be an exception. From its low-key beginnings, at its second meeting, the GAA invited all 25 members of Parnell's Irish National League onto its central committee.

This was quite possibly a concession to Parnell's concerns about the notable IRB presence in the GAA. But Irish politicians and clergy were a notably fiery and vociferous breed, and bringing them on board wasn't always going to give the organisation the best of names. The British police certainly watched with suspicion, and it is records of their investigations that give us much of our information on the political makeup of the early GAA, as long as we remember that these were not the most impartial of documents. The GAA's first social event in January 1885 commemorated Scottish poet Robert Burns in an attempt to promote fellowship between Irish and Scottish 'Celts', which Dublin Castle was concerned might be "treasonable activities" organised by "a thinly masked Fenian conspiracy." Eoghan Corry notes police records cynically observing in 1887 that the GAA provided "a good opportunity of a general communication of all the leading conspirators in the country" and how "the growth of the GAA was hardly to be accounted for by a sudden love of athletics." And yet

---

[9] *Freeman's Journal*, 25 January 1885.

among all the national tunes, God Save Ireland banners and harp motifs, most of those fears were unfounded. There is little or no evidence that the GAA itself has ever directly done anything more 'troublesome' than arrange sports contests and celebrate being Irish. Some of its members may have caused the odd bit of bother for the British, but making the assumption that somebody was an revolutionary just because they were in the GAA was as ridiculous as supposing today that anybody seen entering a mosque is a terrorist.

Although the second meeting of the GAA was attended by at least four representatives of leading Dublin-based clubs, there was still a notable southern bias in the early membership. As Cusack has warned Davin in October 1884 "don't bother your head about Dublin. The place couldn't well be worse than it is. We'll have to look to the provinces for men. Dublin will have to fall in or keep up the connection with England." It was a shrewd move. The clubs in the capital were happily gathered in Val Dunbar's IAAA, run by the same family that also published its affairs in its *Irish Sportsman* newspaper, a publication that not surprisingly didn't always show its patch-grabbing rival, the GAA, in the best of lights. In 1886, Cusack described the IAAA in *Freeman's Journal* as a "ranting, impotent, West British abortion," but he knew that its presence would make it difficult for the GAA to get a solid foothold in Dublin. Dubs will be Dubs, and it is no easy thing for folk from elsewhere in the country to persuade them to change their ways. At least in its formative years, the GAA would find more support in the provinces, and to certain extent, that still holds true today.

The IAAA was affiliated to the British union, which refused to acknowledge the rebel GAA. The Dunbars, however, did see the potential of their association agreeing terms to simply amalgamate somehow with the GAA, but Cusack wasn't in the mood to negotiate with the 'enemy'. In his typically to-the-point style, he replied that "I received your letter this morning and I burned it." At the third meeting of the GAA, held back at Hayes's Hotel, Thurles, on January 17, 1885, it was agreed that "any athlete competing at meetings held under other laws than those of the Gaelic Athletic Association shall be ineligible to compete at meetings held under the GAA'.

But the only people that were really losing out through this standoff were the Irish athletes themselves, who were torn between being accused of turning their back on the Irish cause, or missing out on lucrative competitions. Even Archbishop Croke realised that his earlier attack on foreign sports had been a bit over the top. In *Freeman's Journal*, he commented that he hadn't given the matter enough thought when he made his famous speech that had already become the GAA's equivalent to the Lord's Prayer, and admitted that "it did not strike me at all at the time, nor does it strike me now, or form any part of my design, absolutely to discharge, and even denounce, all sports and pastimes that are not national. As a patron of the GAA ... I would respectfully suggest to the committee of management of the GAA the advisability of modifying their rules ... to allow all qualified athletes to compete for their prizes."

MIKE ROBERTS – THE SAME OLD GAME: CODIFICATION

Later in 1885, Cusack agreed that the ban on athletes also participating in IAAA events was wrong, and it was somewhat cryptically declared that "the GAA prizes are now open to all. We shall see where the best athletes are. Our movement is a national one. He who is not a nationalist, I use the word advisedly, no matter what his religion or politics may be, need not come near us except for a prize. Our prizes are open to all honest men."

In April of the following year, the IAAA also bowed to popular pressure to allow GAA athletes to compete in their events, and a major meeting was held at what is now University College Cork involving entrants from both associations.

The rival bodies would coexist in varying degrees of harmony for decades, but the instability had a negative knock-on effect on Irish track and field, which had been so strong when the IAAA and GAA were founded, but suffered from a divided architecture, and subsequently wasted much of its potential. Of particular note was the failure of Pat O'Callaghan's world hammer record to be internationally recognised as such and the rift even caused Ireland's absence from the 1936 Olympic Games in Berlin (which with retrospect probably wasn't such a bad thing).

Ultimately, the GAA probably did more harm than good to Irish track and field. But Cusack and Davin had more than athletics in their sights. Quite feasibly inspired by the knowledge that the Americans and Australians had invented their own national rules for football, the third meeting of the GAA was the moment for Ireland to do the same.

Making a game of it

As Garnham puts it "for sportsmen more eager to take a game that had the image of an Irish hero more closely associated to it, hurling was the obvious choice ... football in any form was not perceived as truly Irish enough to warrant much attention from the GAA ... the new football code would have trouble establishing for itself a niche and an identity within Ireland. Amongst existing football players it had to compete with the comparatively well-established rugby game and the novelty of the association code."

As we saw in volume one, Cusack had long been keen on promoting hurling as an Irish alternative to the English game of hockey, and that was always going to be an early priority for the GAA. But with the rugby versus soccer code war raging on, the addition of a third set of Irish-made rules to an already knotty issue was a bold move. But it was football, not stickball, that was catching the imagination on both sides of the Irish Sea, and perhaps there was the worry that hurling, like hockey, would struggle to compete with the football codes. To a certain extent that was the case, because it would eventually be Gaelic football and not hurling that would come to command the greatest interest, despite it being the less 'traditionally Irish' of the GAA's two biggest creations.

The English hockey rules were only known at a few elite institutions in Dublin, while despite being an 'endangered species' Ireland's hurling tradition still existed, and only needed a more organised structure to push it in the right direction. Football was different.

154

The rugby game was already widespread and soccer was gaining in popularity. Archaic games like *caid* may have once existed, but these unregulated folk pastimes were now just a distant memory, and there is no evidence that there had ever been anything even remotely resembling a national form of football in Ireland until the GAA presented its rules in 1885. And although those rules (shown in *Appendix Eight*, as published in *United Ireland* on February 7, 1885) may have been connected in some remote way to native Irish traditions, they were clearly far more influenced by the achievements of the RFU and FA in England, and particularly the latter.

In fact, the original blueprint for Irish football was almost identical to soccer. In 1885, "a goal is scored when the ball is kicked through the goalposts under the cross-bar." The H-shaped goal and the scoring of overs would be a later invention. The only real differences between this game and soccer were little more than token adjustments to the number of players on a side (anything between 15 and 21) and the length of each half (half an hour), which were more than likely introduced in defiance to having to accept English standards than any association with Irish traditions.

It had taken English footballers decades of bickering and arguments to settle such issues as handling, hacking, pushing, scoring, free kicks, out of play and so on, and even so, there was still irresolvable division between soccer and rugby. But a group of diametrically opposed Irishmen were able to agree to rules for two different sports practically at one sitting. It is almost as if the exact content of the rules was the lesser issue, what really mattered was that they weren't the English ones.

Nevertheless, the English influence is everywhere to be seen. The original FA rules for soccer in 1863 made no mention of neutral referees, different coloured shirts, goalkeepers, tossing coins for ends, changing ends at half time, playing a set number of minutes per half, goal kicks, throw-ins, sending players off or marking the top of the goal with a crossbar. These came about over years of trial, error and heated debates. Yet all these late 19th century innovations had all somehow time warped their way back into ancient Irish tradition as well!

Nicholas Mason makes the same observation, saying that "Gaelic football à la Davin and Cusack was no more the true game of the Irish countryside than Association football was the true game of the Northern English village – it had become an artificial, though probably far more enjoyable, version of the old traditional game, and the new rules owed everything to laws tried and found effective by the players of 'foreign and fantastic field sports'".

The only major divergence from the English code was the total absence of any kind of offside law, which was a no-brainer when it came to creating something that shunned English public school traditions, but is also very likely to have been more akin to the way the Irish liked to play their football. And the absence of offside and therefore sanctioning of forward passing clearly removes the most immediate link to rugby. In fact, although Gaelic football is often described as a mixture of soccer and rugby, the original 1885 were so far removed from the complexities of scrums, offside, knocking on, tries on goal, mauls, rucks and lineouts that

MIKE ROBERTS – THE SAME OLD GAME: CODIFICATION

it is hard to see where the connection lies. Rugby was already well established in Ireland by 1885, and it was probably too late to attempt to replace it with something else. But although soccer was now the more popular code in England, it was still only new in Ireland, and that looks to have been the market that the GAA wanted to focus its efforts on.

For that is what early Gaelic football was – soccer. Not only was there no H-shaped goal, but the original rules made no mention of hand-passing or the characteristic soloing of the ball as it is carried and bounced about the pitch. In fact, the basic issue of carrying the ball, which had caused so many problems and ultimately division in English football, apparently wasn't a topic for discussion at the GAA's first rules meeting. They had nothing to say on the matter, which is so extraordinary that it's tempting to believe the GAA was undecided and waited until April 1885 before adding the rule that "the ball must not be carried."

Neither is there anything about the ball being round or oval, surely another basic issue that would have needed addressing. As it happens, rugby balls were more common earlier on (probably simply because they were easier to come by) but spheres gained in favour and became standard in 1901.

The idea was certainly not to promote a violent game. It was declared that "pushing or tripping from behind, holding from behind, or butting with the head shall be deemed foul and players so offending shall be asked to stand aside and may not afterwards take any part in the match," although apparently this so incensed Cusack that he was once quoted as saying that they may as well stop using their hands at all and "then we have the Association game." From that comment, it's tempting to believe that the Association game was exactly what some early GAA players wanted, and Cusack was adamant that they weren't going to get it!

But the 1885 rules were only very basic, and clearly not brilliantly thought through. Although the thrown-in and goal kick are present, there is no mention of what happens when in soccer a corner kick would be awarded. But the rules for hurling, published at the same time, do say that "if the ball is driven over the goal-line by a player whose goal it is, the opposite side shall have a free puck on the ground twenty yards out from the goalposts" and by 1889, that rule was also being used in Irish football.

The hurling rules make for interesting reading[10] because although now the two GAA codes are played on the same pitch, this would not have been possible in 1885. The football pitch was "120 yards long by 80 in breadth," which was only half the size of a hurling field, which was "at least 200 yards long by 150 yards broad, or as near to that size as can be got." Not only that, but the hurling goal consisted of "two upright posts, twenty feet apart, with a cross-bar ten feet from the ground" while football's was much smaller at "15 feet apart, with cross-

---

[10] Most of the basic hurling rules would look familiar enough to players today, although they may be a little surprised by rule 11, which states that "if the ball is driven over the side-line it shall be thrown in towards the middle of the ground by the referee or one of the umpires; but if it rebounds into the ground it shall be considered in play."

bar eight feet from the ground," and hurling games lasted a total of "one hour and twenty minutes" and football games just "one hour."

Patriot games

So where did these rules come from? The bog-standard history that has been copied and pasted onto numerous GAA websites reckons that the rules were based on those of the Commercials club based around Cannock's Drapery Store in Limerick, but I have never seen this supported with any evidence. While for all other codes of football, the evolution of the rules was widely documented and hotly debated in many quarters, those for Gaelic football seem to appear out of thin air in January 1885. We do know that they were basically the work of Maurice Davin. Séamus Ó Riain[11] describes how he accumulated press cuttings over the years about developments in the rugby and soccer rules, and used them as his inspiration for making up a new set for the Irish. A detailed explanation of how any of the ten original rules came about and why they were so peculiarly Irish does not seem to exist, and probably never did. They weren't British, and that's all that really mattered.

Not to knock the GAA or its games, for the former is a wonderful institution and the latter is a terrific game, but on their own website the GAA had the gall to claim that "Gaelic football can be described as a mixture of soccer and rugby, although it predates both of those games[12]." This is simply not true. There is absolutely no evidence to show that football was an Irish game before it was a British game, and as for soccer and rugby in their modern codified forms, it is frankly ridiculous to claim that Gaelic football could possibly be older. In fact, if it hadn't been for the FA and RFU, it is unlikely that the GAA's game would ever have existed at all, and even if it had, it would undoubtedly have been very different.

Speaking in Galway, and quoted in the *London Times* in March, 1891, Charles Parnell once accused the enemies of the GAA as having "nothing to rest upon but a foundation of lies and hypocrisies." But when it comes to bending the truth, the GAA might have a little to answer for too. For historians to fail to recognise the contributions of Charles Alcock, Ebenezer Morley, Edwin Ash and so many others to the evolution of modern Gaelic football is an insult to all they achieved, for it was their ideas for the modernisation of football that were lifted by Cusack and Davin, who merely played around with a few of the rules and passed them off as their own invention. The GAA had every right to play football by whatever rules it liked, but to claim that in doing so they were conserving a 'national pastime' from the infiltration of English culture is nothing but audacious hyperbole. If there really was any link between the ancient ball games played in Ireland and the GAA's modern game, then those links were forged not in Ireland, but in Britain.

---

[11] In his biography *Maurice Davin, (1842-1927): First President of the GAA.*
[12] This claim seems to have disappeared in the latest version of the website, although the original text was lifted to over a hundred GAA related sites where it still survives.

It is an issue that is generally skirted around with a few mumbles and embarrassed clearings of throats among the GAA faithful. There is no finer case in point than the late Jack Mahon's *History of Gaelic Football*. He writes that "despite much opposition, poor organisation, and bad management at times, the GAA came into being in 1884 and Gaelic Games spread like wildfire." Just like that! In a mighty tome of 247 pages, the entire foundation of the GAA and its codification of football fit neatly into one 23-word sentence!

The *Official Guide to the GAA* (effectively its constitution and rules and last revised in 2007) states that "those who play its games, those who organise its activities and those who control its destinies see in the GAA a means of consolidating our Irish identity. The games to them are more than games – they have a national significance – and the promotion of native pastimes becomes a part of the full national ideal, which envisages the speaking of our own language, music and dances. The primary purpose of the GAA is the organisation of native pastimes and the promotion of athletic fitness as a means to create a disciplined, self-reliant, national-minded manhood. The overall result is the expression of a people's preference for native ways as opposed to imported ones.

"Since she has no control over all the national territory, Ireland's claim to nationhood is impaired. It would be still more impaired if she were to lose her language, if she failed to provide a decent livelihood for her people at home, or if she were to forsake her own games and customs in favour of the games and customs of another nation ... Today, the native games take on a new significance when it is realised that they have been a part, and still are a part, of the Nation's desire to live her own life, to govern her own affairs[13]."

Well over a century later, with Gaelic games now well established traditions, it may be valid to ask why Ireland should "forsake her own games and customs in favour of the games and customs of another nation." But in 1885, if there were any surviving traditional forms of football played on the Emerald Isle, then the GAA most certainly forsook them in favour of something that, other than a few academic changes, was almost entirely based on ideas imported from abroad.

The belief that the GAA's rules constitute a 'national pastime' was driven into Irish consciousness, and then on to the rest of the world. Gaelic football was demonstrated in 1990 at the first *Journée Internationale de Jeux et Sports Traditionnels* that took place in Carhaix (Brittany), and was also on the agenda of traditional sports at the 2004 Forum of Cultures in Barcelona. And good luck to the Barcelona Gaels, good friends of mine that I will always support, but there isn't really anything either ancient or traditional about the arts of soloing, hand-passing and scoring overs, none of which were even mentioned in the original rules written in 1884! The Gaelic game is no more 'traditional' than American football. In fact,

---

[13] Other orders are that "the National Flag should be displayed at all matches. Where the National Anthem precedes a game, teams must stand to attention facing the Flag in a respectful manner. Penalty: €500" and "Irish paper shall be used for all official documents and correspondence. Documents not complying shall be ruled out of order."

bicycle polo, which was allegedly invented in 1891 by an Irishman, Richard James Mecready of County Wicklow, might have a better claim to being an ancient Irish sport!

Prairie fires

The GAA's new rules for football were printed in nationalist newspapers, and a pamphlet was made publicly available at the remarkably decent price of sixpence a copy. And whatever the fictitious claims being made about its origins, there is no question that the game was a good one, and if it was going to get the Irish doing exercise and feeling good about themselves, then it was all positive. One article puts it brilliantly by explaining how until the GAA came along "everything was lonely and stagnant, and the young men in their idle hours loitered in dull fashion by the street and fence corners. In a few months how different things became! The country was soon humming with interest and activity, the ambitions of the young men were aroused, every parish had its newly-formed hurling or football team, prepared to do or die for the honour of the little village ... The brawls and fights so common heretofore disappeared from our midst. The young learned that skill and self control were better and nobler than quarrelling and fighting, and that deft handling of the *caman* was more to be admired than to trounce a brother Irishman with fist or cudgel[14]."

From there, in Cusack's words, "the Association swept the country like a prairie fire." The first AGM of the GAA was held in October 1885 and reported that over the year "150 sporting meetings were held throughout the country – athletics, hurling and football." By February 1886, *United Ireland* claimed that "those who frequent the Phoenix Park on Sundays now find almost every available batch of ground swarming with football players and hurlers."

Douglas Hyde himself opined in his famous 1892 lecture that "I consider the work of the Association in reviving our ancient traditional game of *camán* or hurling, and Gaelic football, has done more for Ireland than all the speeches of politicians for the last five years."

But much as football clubs were being founded up and down the country, one of the GAA's earliest problems would be getting the new teams to play the game the way they wanted them to. Cusack wrote in his *Celtic Times* of a game in 1887 that attracted a disappointing crowd and where "there were at times during the contest a half-dozen of the hurlers lying with their faces on the ground resting themselves, while the side-your-own system was in full operation," by which he meant you played according to your own rules.

Football's flimsy set of rules didn't help matters, and caused no end of problems as teams travelled elsewhere in the country and found their opponents had totally different interpretations – usually due to confusion between the Gaelic game and rugby. The *Westmeath Nationalist* in 1893, for example, speaks of a game in which a player "hugged the

---

[14] Written by JB Dollard of Ontario, Canada, in a reminiscing piece about his younger years in Ireland and published in the *Gaelic Athletic Annual* (1907).

MIKE ROBERTS – THE SAME OLD GAME: CODIFICATION

ball under his arm and in right true rugby style ran towards the Mullingar goal." Mullingar seemed to be constantly at odds with teams that didn't play the game properly, including one complaint in the *Westmeath Examiner* about a game played in Dublin the same year that was "simply indescribable as the Dunleary men began to play under rugby rules and they pulled down the visitors whether playing the ball with the hands or the feet."

The GAA was faced by the same problem the FA had faced when they first released their rules. They didn't really have any authority to dictate to anybody how they were supposed to play football. But the organisation of a competition would ensure they would have to fall in line. In 1887, both Gaelic football and hurling were able to hold an All Ireland Championship for the first time (but not the finals, because due to administrative squabbles, neither game would get played until 1888), and the county-based structure caught the imagination immediately. As Michaél Ó Muircheartaigh[15] puts it, "as far as rural Ireland was concerned, the initiation of the All Irelands in 1887 was part of the biggest social revolution in the country. A growth took place immediately … Clubs began to spring up everywhere. It was now possible to have local heroes. Up to then heroes were distant figures – they might have been politicians or clergy. This was the first time people were acclaimed within their own county."

Unlike today, the first All Irelands weren't played by truly county teams, but by the champion clubs of each county[16], of which only 12 of the possible 32 entered the first edition (just five for the football competition and eight for the hurling).

The Commercials won the Limerick championship by default when their opponents in the final, St Michaels, were not allowed to field five of their first team because they were rugby players, and marched on to beat Young Irelands of Louth in the final, 1-4 to 0-3[17], played at Clonskeagh in Dublin. It was a relatively low key event, without there even being a trophy to play for, and the winning players were not presented with medals until many years later, in 1912. And despite the cheering crowds when they returned home, the victory hardly sparked a Gaelic football revolution in Limerick. The county would only ever win one more All Ireland championship, in 1896, and by the end of the century rugby union ruled along the banks of the Shannon Estuary, where it is still disproportionately popular in comparison to the rest of the country.

In the meantime, hurling was also enjoying its inaugural All Ireland championship. And Thurles, whose players were described by the *Celtic Times* as having "the speed and dash of the Fianna of ancient Ireland", were strongly fancied and beat Twomileborris in the Tipperary final, which was played with both teams barefoot.

---

[15] Speaking in Leighlinbridge and cited in *The Nationalist* (Friday, May 19, 2000).

[16] A new law was introduced in 1892 whereby the champion club from each county was allowed to select players from the other clubs in their county to play with them in the All Ireland championship, and it was not until the 1923 championship that the entrants were truly county-based selections.

[17] Points scores were recorded, but for the time being were only tie-breakers.

PADDY POWER

Thurles qualified for the All Ireland Final, which was played at Birr, County Offaly against the Meelick club from Galway, who drafted in a few ringers from neighbouring teams. They were fairly inauspicious beginnings. When it looked like Thurles weren't even going to show, the Meelick lads withdrew to the pub. Several ales later, with the Meelick boys sufficiently 'locked' as the Irish would say and about to tuck into a hearty meal, the Tipps finally arrived, and the game went ahead after all. One Meelick player, a certain John Lowry, was so cheesed off to be made sub after walking 20km to get to Birr that he apparently spent most of the game coming on and interfering with the play! Being the town where the GAA had been founded, it was fitting enough that it was Thurles that claimed the first of many Tipperary hurling championships, beating Meelick 1-1 to 0-0.

New directions

Gaelic football was still in the process of inventing itself. Although the original GAA laws were strikingly similar to those of soccer, they soon started developing towards the modern game played today.

The first three recorded trial games of football using the new laws, two in Kilkenny and one in Kildare, all ended scoreless. The lack of point-scoring was going to be one of the first issues that needed addressing. Unless the GAA could make the games more interesting, they would go down no better than a turkey glove puppet at the Eurovision Song Contest. In 1886, to encourage scoring, the goal in both football and hurling was widened to 21 feet. But two further 'point posts' were added 21 feet to either side. The rule was still that "a goal is won when the ball is driven between the goal posts and the cross bar", but teams also recorded the number of 'points' that were scored when a shot missed the goal but still passed either over the bar or to the left or right of the goal but still between the two outer posts. However, for the time being these 'points' only counted as tie-breakers after a game ended tied on goals.

The idea was nothing new. It takes us back to the 'rouge' used many years earlier in Sheffield soccer, and Australian football had been using a similar tie-break system of recording near misses, called 'behinds', since 1866. It may not be coincidence that the Irish distance of 21 feet was exactly the same as the one which the Australians used. Behinds didn't become part of Australian scoring until 1897; five years after the GAA had already done the same by declaring that five points were equal to one goal. In 1895, this became three, which is the same as it is now, although it was not until 1910 that the 'point posts' were moved inwards to the edge of the goals themselves, thus creating the typical H shaped Gaelic football goal, with 3 points for scoring under the bar and into the goal (which now had a net) and one point for scoring over the bar[18].

---

[18] In his influential *How to play Gaelic football* (1914), Dick Fitzgerald, one of the finest players of the era and after whom Kerry's stadium is named, wrote how "in other forms of football, such is the constitution of the rules governing them, there is often too much of the element of luck. In the native game, however, there is no such preponderance of luck, and this is to be accounted for by the fact that the rules provide the two kinds of

As Chad puts it "this radical surgery was quite contradictory behaviour from an association that continued to argue that their sport had centuries of tradition[19]." He does have a point!

Getting teams to turn up was also an issue to the extent that it was not until 1910 that an All Ireland season managed to start and finish in the same year. A problem that is still common in all sports at grass roots level today was that of having enough players ready at the scheduled time. It was for that reason that the number of players on a GAA team was gradually reduced over the years, even as low as 13 at one stage before finally settling on 15 in 1915.

Having had five years to experiment, the 1889 rules for Gaelic football included a number of changes that made the game considerably more like the one we know today. But many of the new rules were more or less imports from soccer, such as free kicks and the way that after throwing in from touch "the thrower must not play it himself until it has been touched by some other player" and "neither goal nor point can be scored from a throw in from the side line."

But some rules really catch the eye. One was that players guilty of violent play "shall be ordered to stand aside for such time as the referee may think fit", possibly the first example of the sin-bin idea being applied to a ball sport. Another said that "if a player be hurt and unable to play ... the referee shall allow his side to take in a man in his place." Substitutes! Here Gaelic football was indeed ahead of its time. Allowing common sense to prevail and permitting a replacement for an injured player would not come into force in soccer until 1965[20], putting an end to such scenes as the 1956 FA Cup Final when Bert Trautman played the last quarter of an hour with a broken vertebra in his neck.

Of major importance is Rule 10, which stated that the ball "may be caught when off the ground, and the player so catching may kick it in any way he pleases, but must not carry or throw it." What Gaelic football had introduced was the 'fair catch' rule, which had been part of the original 1863 FA rules but was scrapped in 1866, but which still survives to this day in the form of 'taking a mark' in the Australian game. But although throwing and carrying were out, these rules state that "the ball may be struck with the hand." The hand pass was born[21].

---

score." A fair point, until we remember that, with the exception of soccer, all of the world's different football codes allow for more than one type of scoring!

[19] On his highly entertaining www.convictcreations.com website.

[20] Substitutes had actually been used in soccer for much longer (as early as qualifying games for the 1934 World Cup, in fact) but only in certain competitions and only by mutual agreement between the two teams. Rugby union followed soccer's suit shortly after, with Scotsman Ian Mcrae becoming the sport's first ever substitute in France in 1969. Australian rules allowed one player on the interchange bench from the 1930s, which has increased over the years to four, and substitutions are now unlimited (the players rotate as in basketball).

[21] But despite this, some teams seem to have preferred to take a soccer-style approach to Gaelic football, and as late as the 1913 All Ireland final, "Louth were noted for passing the ball on the ground and for a 'soccer' style of play. Kerry, on the other hand, used a traditional catch, swing and kick style." (Cited on the official Croke Park website at www.crokepark.ie).

PADDY POWER

It is curious that the new sport of Gaelic football included so many archaic elements of soccer, such as the 'fair catch' and the counting of 'near misses' as a tiebreaker. The form of football played in Ireland from the mid 1880s shared a lot in common with the soccer that was promoted by the FA in England in the 1860s, but which had been modified considerably over the two decades that followed. The folk at the GAA, unhappy with the new Association code creeping across to their island, claimed that their new game was based on the way they remembered football being played in Ireland before the arrival of the foreign games. But had they perhaps been a little misguided? Was the football they remembered really just soccer as it was played not just in Ireland, but also England, in the 1860s, with its catching of the ball and rouges? That explanation for the origins of Gaelic football actually makes a lot of sense, and would also explain the uncanny similarities between the Irish and Australian games.

The 'fair catch' rule is followed by a note that "there is nothing wrong in this rule to prevent the player throwing the ball a little in front to allow himself more freedom in kicking it." It was out of this that one of Gaelic football's most defining traits would grow. The solo run.

It is here that the sport found its own William Webb Ellis in Seán Lavan, who would revolutionise the sport with his legendary run for Mayo against Dublin at Croke Park in 1921. A class footballer, Lavan demonstrated that day a curious loophole he had spotted in the laws. You can't carry the ball as in rugby, but with a bit of skill, how's about throwing the ball a short way forwards, then meeting it again with the foot to kick it back into the hands, and then repeating the movement over and over again to advance up the pitch? Off stormed yer man, hand to toe, toe to hand, hand to toe, toe to hand and he scored a point at the end of it. The referee disallowed the goal, but it sparked off heated debate in GAA circles. After all, technically, Lavan hadn't done anything wrong.

Seamus O'Malley, who would captain Mayo to their first All Ireland crown in 1936, was there that day. "It was the first solo run I ever saw" he later said. "And to the best of my knowledge the first exhibition of the skill in Gaelic football. As time went on it came to be accepted and used by players across the land."

Irish Independent sportswriter John Hickey's later comment that he was also at that game "to see the great sprinter Seán Lavan playing football" has cast doubts on when Lavan really made that famous run. For although Lavan did achieve great things on the running track, he didn't win any major athletics titles until 1923, two years after the supposed day that Hickey witnessed "the protestations to the referee that a culchie from Mayo is making his own rules." So impressed was Hickey to see what he was convinced was a revolution in the way the game was played that "at the end of the game I scampered onto the pitch and touched Seán Lavan's jersey."

The exact day it happened may be beside the point, for there is little doubt among Irishmen that Lavan was the man, and in 1996 a plaque was erected in his native Kiltimagh to commemorate the town's famous son.

163

Cusack's fall from grace

Despite the booming success of his creation, the man without whom the idea of the GAA may never have arisen in the first place, Michael Cusack, was pushed out of the picture surprisingly early on. By 1886, just two years after the GAA had been founded, Cusack was no longer part of it. Historians will argue about how that happened, but it was basically a case of an outspoken, controversial figure making too many enemies, even out of people that should have been his allies, and pushing his luck that little bit too far.

The *Irish Sportsman* was the paper run by the Dunbar family, with whom Cusack already had a feud running over the IAAA they endorsed. The argument reached its height with the publication in 1885 of a poem satirising the founder of the GAA, which went:

> "If he ever gets a pass for his much neglected class,
> What an awful fluke 'twill be,
> Then at every Gaelic meeting,
> You have no chance of competing,
> Except Irish you can speak,
> And pronounce the Celtic names,
> Of the Grand Olympic Games,
> We have pilfered from the Greeks."

Considering the way Cusack had managed to insult just about every important person in Ireland in his scathing newspaper columns over the years, it was a bit hypocritical of him to sue the *Irish Sportsman* for libel after this went to print, but he won his case and pocketed £12 for his troubles.

Upsetting the *Irish Sportsman* was not the most diplomatic of moves, but with its IAAA background, it was never going to be the most supportive publication of the GAA anyway. For Cusack, losing face with the most influential paper in the country, *Freeman's Journal*, was a far less tactful move. He and its owner Edmund Dwyer Gray had never quite seen eye to eye on many things, but Cusack started raising the ill-feeling to unnecessary levels when he was reputedly either directly or indirectly behind a series of attacks on the *Journal* for anything from comments printed in the paper criticising his refereeing, for not giving enough column space to GAA games and events, for being biased in the way they had reported on the Cork teams that insisted on rugby rather than the GAA game, and for failing to report on an important speech given by Archbishop Croke.

While Cusack was urging the people not to support "papers hostile to the National Pastimes", Gray was dumbfounded at this opposition, claiming they had always been fully supportive of the movement. Croke, a close friend of Gray's, got involved here and agreed that the GAA had no right to turn the nation against *Freeman's Journal*, and that in fact it had been he himself who had asked Gray not to publish his speech because he wanted to doctor some of its content! He also, quite rightly, told Cusack that it was not exactly in either his or the GAA's interests to be hanging out his dirty washing quite so publicly.

Cusack was not a quick learner. He then had a letter published in which he warned Croke that "as you faced the Pope, so I will, with God's help, face you and Gray." It was as if he liked playing the victim and causing trouble for trouble's sake. Croke's response was that as long as Cusack stayed in control of the GAA, then he would not be having any further part of it.

Ultimately, over petty, pedantic issues, Cusack had managed to lose the support of much of the press and one of his most important patrons, and was hardly going about promoting the best of names for his Association. He also fell out with Michael Davitt, and as Paul Rouse muses "it does not seem outlandish to imagine that Cusack would have managed a similar dispute with Parnell, had the latter not died so prematurely."

Cusack made a public apology, and by a vote of 38–14 in April 1886, the GAA council decided to forgive him for his thoughtless outbursts. But matters with Cusack didn't improve, and his over-inflated ego and inability to control his temper eventually got the better of him. Writes Marcus De Búrca, "obliged to face his opponents alone in Dublin because his executive was largely scattered throughout the provinces, he became more dictatorial in his style of management and resentful of criticism from any quarter ... He was always treading on someone's toes, suggesting ignoble motives, and only happy when quarrelling. If the GAA did not quickly find a new secretary, Cusack would wreck it."

At the same time, there were others rubbing their hands with glee as the founder of the GAA brought about his own downfall with such imprudent class. Cusack may not have been too gifted at presenting a good personal image of himself, but his idea of creating a new face for Irish sports had gone down an absolute storm. Almost overnight, it had become one of the finest symbols of Irish nationalism. It was something any political movement would have been delighted to get involved in, and as it happened, the GAA had willingly invited the church, Parnell's National League and most particularly the Irish Republican Brotherhood to get involved. At first Cusack had seen potential in using the political network to get his own ideas heard. The tables had turned. The political network was now interested in using the GAA for the same reasons. Cusack was ultimately a small fry, playing a game that had got too big for him. He would have to go. Going into the next GAA meeting, the writing was on the wall.

He again tried to defend himself, but never stood a chance. He had no option but to resign, and turned instead to journalism, launching *The Celtic Times* in 1887, for which he wrote almost all the content. It proved a wonderful platform for his eccentric style of nationalistic writing, promoting Irish language and culture while dealing with a delicious pot pourri of topics from cookery to the apparently ancient Irish pastime of chess. Its other primary concern was slagging off everybody at the GAA.

MIKE ROBERTS – THE SAME OLD GAME: CODIFICATION

The Celtic Times faced immediate opposition in the form of *The Gael*, published by the GAA itself, which in the late 1880s was little more than the IRB in another guise. *The Gael* would go on to become the standard for news on developments in Gaelic games, but in Cusack's words, it was "the organ of idiocy and illiteracy; the organ of a spurious patriotism; and the organ of all that is mean and contemptible. Away with the filthy thing!"

They were hard times for poor Cusack, for while all that was going on, his academy in Dublin was also in the process of closing its doors for the last time. Sadly, *The Celtic Times* lasted just a year, before it was forced to fold due to poor circulation figures, with Cusack reportedly pawning his watch in a desperate attempt to get the January 21, 1888 edition onto the streets. And then in 1890 he lost his beloved wife Margaret to tuberculosis.

But the fall-out didn't entirely mark the end of his ties to the organisation. We know he refereed a game on the site of the future Croke Park in July 1896, and also attended some GAA conventions, the last in 1906, when he had fallen on such hard times that the Dublin County Board agreed to give him £50. In November of that year, at the age of 59, he died of a chronic kidney disorder, which would not have been helped by his heavy drinking. The day of his funeral, writes Marcus De Barça, "was a dull murky day in Dublin, an ideal excuse for not attending a funeral. Yet the GAA, to whose leaders one suspects their founder had become something of an embarrassment in recent years, turned out in force to swell the cortege to Glasnevin cemetery. By a stroke of luck, the hurlers of Tipperary and Kilkenny were in town for a game and, wearing mourning rosettes and with camans reversed, they marched alongside the hearse all the way from the Cathedral. Behind them came a hundred hurlers from Dublin, the county where he had begun the hurling revival and where he had always had his most loyal associates in the GAA."

Despite their troubled relationship, the GAA turned out to show their respect for the man who started it all. The Cusack Stand at Croke Park still bears his name, but some might argue that not enough has been done to honour the man's legacy. As Michael Foley wrote in the *Sunday Times* in December 2006, on the 100th anniversary of his death, it is shocking that his name is not held in higher regard in modern Irish history. "In a year that saw Samuel Beckett plastered all over the media and cultural outlets of the land to mark the centenary of his birth … the anniversary of Cusack's death passed almost unnoticed. Did the founding of the GAA have any less impact on Irish life than *Waiting for Godot*?"

Ultimately he should be remembered as a man whose demise was brought about by the fiery passion he put into everything he did. Paul Rouse's description is worth repeating here, when he says "at his best, he was extraordinary and brilliant, capable of great warmth, humour and generosity. But Cusack's flaws were as outlandish as his talents. He was impetuous on a cartoonish scale. He thrived on confrontation and managed to find it in most quarters … to succeed in being ejected from a thriving organisation you yourself have founded suggests a considerable talent for making enemies."

The belief that James Joyce, in his classic work *Ulysses,* based the character of Citizen on Cusack has no supporting evidence. He was probably a very different man to the one GAA romanticists believe in. Even though he wrote in 1899 that "I resolved to be a Fenian. In order to be a Fenian, I had to be a hurler," those are the kind of comments he would make one day, then contradict the next. He was primarily a sporting rather than a political revolutionary, even though he sometimes liked to think he was one of the latter. The real political revolutionaries were the ones that were going to take his place. The next seven secretaries of the GAA, right up to 1924, would all be members of the Irish Republican Brotherhood.

7 GAMES WITH FRONTIERS
The politics of the GAA

Power struggles

In 1886, *United Ireland* praised Charles Lynch for establishing a club in Shrule, saying "we cannot too earnestly comment the patriotic conduct of Mr Lynch who has given free access to his lawn to the Gaelic football players of his parish." Promoting football was no longer just about promoting physical exercise and the competitive spirit. It was patriotic.

Keep politics out of sport? Not on your Nelly, "our politics being essentially national, so should our athletics" proclaimed an article in *The Irishman* in 1884, and quoted again in Ibrahim Rashad's *An Egyptian in Ireland* of 1920, which provides a fascinating outsider's account of the country in the early 20th century. Rashad loved Gaelic games and their political connotations, commenting that "if any two purposes should go together, they ought to be politics and athletics. The Irish people knew that well long ago."

If the minutes are anything to go by, early GAA meetings were as much like political conventions as they were gatherings to discuss sporting issues. This was hardly surprising. Undercurrents of revolution were rife in the Ireland of the time, and where better to go recruiting new blood than the association that gathered some of the fittest and most nationalistically minded men in the country[1]?

Historian John Murphy states "it was the GAA players who provided the rank and file for the volunteers and freedom fighters, there's no doubt about that. Nevertheless, the ruling authorities in the Association tried to steer clear of taking sides[2]."

It was at the November 1886 convention that the GAA really started getting political. Under Cusack, the executive was mainly composed of people associated in some way with sports, which included Protestants and police officers. Politics was a means, but not the end. The mood was shifting.

Following the 1886 reshuffle in the wake of Cusack's farewell, half of the GAA executive consisted of known IRB activists. The leader of a failed Fenian rising back in 1849, John O'Leary, was made a patron, his acceptance letter going on about how "when we've skill our strength to wield, let us take our own again[3]", and events were held to raise funds to erect a memorial to the Irish revolutionary Charles Kickham.

---

[1] This was neither the first nor the last time that this kind of situation would arise in relation to football. Look no further than the exploitation of soccer hooligans in the former Yugoslavia to fuel the war there, as so brilliantly described by the opening chapter of Franklin Foer's *How Football Explains the World* (2004).

[2] In *Part of What We Are* (Motive Television for Setanta Sports, 2008).

[3] Citing *Our Own Again*, by revolutionary poet Thomas Osborne Davis (1814-1845), who also penned one of the most famous Irish rebel songs of all, *A Nation Once Again*.

GAMES WITH FRONTIERS

There was the uncomfortable situation, however, of the presence of a large number of Parnellites too. The GAA's first ever constitution tackled the issue of politics in the association by stating that "the Gaelic Athletic Association shall not be used in any way to oppose any national movement which has the confidence and support of the leaders of the Irish people." That's a cleverly ambiguous sentence. It doesn't really say anything about whether they were pro Parnell or pro IRB, or neither or both, because there is no explanation of who exactly they were referring to by 'national movement' or the 'leaders of the Irish people'.

Amid a background of rising tension on the streets as the police tried to curb the violence brewing between landlords and their tenants that couldn't pay the rent, the GAA met again in 1887 and decided to ban the British backed Royal Irish Constabulary (RIC) from membership of the GAA "in consequence of their action towards the people throughout the country," adding that "this resolution not to apply to the army or navy" although the armed forces would eventually be banned too.

An irate hurler wrote to Cusack's *Celtic Times*[4] to protest that "there are no just grounds on which members of the RIC can be thus boycotted. It is a body principally composed of small farmers, and which can count within its ranks men in whose bosoms there burns the fire of patriotism no less brilliant and no less intense than is to be found in the breast of any man who ever swore fidelity to the cause of Ireland. The brutality of the force on certain trying occasions was the exception, not the rule, and instances are on record in which kind-hearted members of the police contributed to the support of impoverished tenants whom they reluctantly helped to exterminate ... Every liberal-minded Gaelic man should raise his voice in protest ... It will, otherwise, have the effect of excluding some of our best men from the arena of Gaelic Athletics ... Having thus seen the many blunders made by the present Executive ... I think every effort should be made to rescue the Association from their hands, and to place it in the hands of men who will be competent to guide it properly."

None of this was the working of the GAA's president, Maurice Davin, nor of founder member John Wyse-Power, who resigned as assistant secretary in protest. Davin hadn't even been able to attend the meeting, but when he found out about this exquisite display of counter-productivity, he too resigned from his position, claiming he had little other option. It seems to have been the last straw for a man who had never had any other agenda than getting the Irish playing sport. He was upset at how the GAA had degenerated into little more than a branch of the IRB, operating in a dictatorial fashion with what he described in *Freeman's Journal* as "threats of personal violence to members who seem to differ from the present executive."

---

[4] More than likely it was Cusack himself masquerading as one of his readers, as he was wont to do. The letter is certainly written in his typically fiery style.

Chaos in Thurles

From there, as Eoghan Corry puts it, matters "vacillated from farce to comedy" with the 600 or so clubs around the country sharing contrasting views of what the GAA stood for, and the papers doing their best to milk the controversies for all they were worth. It all reached boiling point at the rancorous November 1887 Convention in Thurles, at which prominent revolutionary Patrick Neville Fitzgerald was being promoted as chairman amidst such cries as "only men ready to die for their country should be at the head of the GAA." The less radically minded Dublin clubs were refused access to the meeting, soon to be joined outside by one of the fiercest of Fitzgerald's opponents, Father Scanlan of Nenagh, and his fellow priests.

It was a near riot, it was madness. The ousted parties gathered in a neighbouring hotel and organised a meeting of their own, while the GAA meeting proper seemingly descended into little more than a rally against both Parnell and the Catholic Church.

However, it was never made clear exactly what happened at that notorious convention of 1887, for there is so much contradictory evidence. Are the British police force's documents really the most reliable of sources? They often appear to have been more about providing the RIC with what they wanted to hear rather than factual truths. Indeed, although the cops came to the conclusion that "after Thurles we may look upon the GAA as a purely Fenian society", Eoghan Curry writes that "recent examination of the files suggests that many of the suspects made unlikely Fenians and local constables may have overestimated the extent of IRB infiltration." Curry claims there is counter-evidence that the GAA never had any intention of making an IRB man its president, and that there were just as many members of the IRB attending the counter-meeting outside.

We will probably never know what really went on that day, but *Freeman's Journal* was most upset to learn of it. It admired the spectacular progress made by Parnell, Croke et al's "constitutional methods to obtain the legislative independence of the country" and felt "the only possible method of defeating the otherwise assured success of Home Rule" was to support the IRB men that had infiltrated the GAA to "encourage the young men of Ireland to enter into secret associations for revolutionary purposes", a "revolution which has practically no chance of success ... When it comes to the point that a man like Dr Croke has publicly to disassociate himself from the Association which he fostered and practically created, then we say it is time for every man connected with the Association to pause and consider whither he is going."

Whether the IRB was good or not for Ireland depended on your point of view, but most of the 50,000 or so members of the GAA were actually far less interested in using the association to plot revolutions as they were in playing Gaelic games, which had become almost an afterthought, with competitions for the All Irelands suspended while the chaos was going on.

The situation was obviously untenable. Fitzgerald called upon a familiar face as mediator, when stating in an address to his executive that "I would respectfully ask His Grace, Archbishop Croke, to consult the other patrons and see if an amicable understanding could not be come to. It is not a time for division amongst any class of Irishman."

Maurice Davin was reinstated as president of the GAA, and many of the 'Fenian section' were asked to step aside. Croke was reunited with the Association, and did his job well. By January 1888, he was able to write a letter to the latest GAA convention in Thurles congratulating them on reconstructing the GAA and placing it "on a solid and satisfactory basis, as well as on the becoming and brotherly feeling that has manifested itself so conspicuously." His Grace instead now urged the members to look at a more pressing issue, "the grave matter of drink in connection with our Gaelic sports," requesting that "in selecting the locality for such sports, the immediate neighbourhood of public houses be specially avoided."

Almost certainly to the detriment of the GAA, Davin's second term only lasted a year, after which he resigned in the wake of not a political, but an economic fiasco. He had come up with the brainwave of taking 50 men to play exhibition games in America, expecting to raise something in the region of €50,000. Instead, the tour ended with him having to find £400 (about €400,000 by today's exchange) just to pay for his men to sail home. The Americans had been far less enthusiastic about watching Irishmen running around hitting a ball with a stick than Davin had expected, and the project was not helped by mismanagement, appalling weather, a presidential election raging in the background, and the GAA getting itself mixed up in a touchy dispute between the rival governing bodies of American athletics. With the players not even earning enough money to pay their hotel bills, almost half of them never even returned to Ireland, some even going on to compete for the USA at the first Olympic Games in Athens in 1896. Far from solving its cash flow problems, the GAA was now more in the red than ever, and Davin and his harebrained 'American Invasion' took the blame.

If Davin had stayed longer, the story might have been different, but as it happens, his post was taken by prominent revolutionary Peter Kelly, clearing the way for yet another IRB takeover. *The Times* (September 1888) reckoned that although there was no proof of "members having been discovered engaged at drill, using their hurleys as muskets … the public are in no way deceived by its ostentatious pretence to be non-political."

Within a year of its foundation, in 1884, the GAA already had over 600 member clubs, and had almost three times that number by the end of the decade. But by the early 1890s, the figure had fallen to around 220, and almost all in the south, with hardly any GAA presence at all in either Connacht or Ulster. Attendances at some of the earliest GAA finals were as high as 9000, but by the 1890s, the novelty was wearing off and they were lucky to get more than a few hundred coming through the gates, and the once flourishing GAA was now £850 in debt. One report claimed that "interest in the GAA is beginning to flag. Last year the sports held at Tralee, Killarney etc were very largely attended but so far the Tralee meetings this

MIKE ROBERTS – THE SAME OLD GAME: CODIFICATION

year show a great falling off. The members are beginning to suspect the leaders of using funds for their own purposes and are becoming restive under the frequent demands for subscriptions. It is probable that ere long several clubs will cease to exist except on paper[5]."

The GAA idea had been fun while it lasted, but interest was now shifting back to rugby and the new attraction of soccer. The blame for this seems to rest entirely on the way that the GAA was constantly sidetracked by political issues, rather than concentrating on setting up a decent sporting infrastructure, the real *raison d'être* of the GAA and the one area where opinions were united. What hope was there for a hurling tournament in 1892 that only three counties entered? Or for the teams to arrive for the 1893 final only to discover that nobody had even bothered to cut the grass? The *Irish Sportsman* in 1891 bemoaned a violent sport that was bordering on the dangerous and little more than "a helter-skelter, hit-or-miss business carried in without any attention to rules at all."

And so began yet another campaign to kick politics out of the GAA, and for it to focus on the good of sport and sport alone. A Meath man, Dick Blake, was appointed secretary in 1895, and turned out to be an excellent choice, for he saw himself as a footballing reformer rather than a political one, focussing his efforts on making the game safer. It was he who proclaimed "the advisability of forgetting their party politics when they entered the athletic field. If the clubs wished to name themselves after any distinguished Irishman, that he be none who is taking part in the present unfortunate dispute in the country" and all political discussion was banned at GAA meetings. Although he would only last three years in the job before being ousted, like Davin, in the wake of a financial controversy, he and his associates can largely be thanked for getting the GAA back on the right track, and membership has increased on an almost annual basis ever since.

Foreign sports

Being one of three different football codes in a country of just four million people, Gaelic football faced tough opposition, and would come into direct and sometimes hostile conflict with the rising tide of soccer, which was filtering through in Ulster, where there has always been a larger concentration of Irish people of Protestant-British extraction. Since the 1880s, soccer has been the number one sport among that group, where passion for the game is as great as anywhere else in the United Kingdom and *God Save the Queen* is sung before Northern Ireland internationals with a greater verve than even at England matches[6].

---

[5] Police files on the links between the IRB and GAA in County Kerry (April 12, 1890). This investigation describes how the IRB patrolled GAA matches looking for new recruits.

[6] The only reason Northern Irish football has failed to be either fully professional or particularly competitive is due to the small size of the region, and any decent player will move to England or Scotland to play. Internationally, Northern Ireland did reach the 1982 and 1986 World Cup Finals, but other than that, they are generally also-rans on the international stage.

GAMES WITH FRONTIERS

Cliftonville is the only major club in 'Norn Iron' that has mainly Catholic supporters, but the sectarian rivalry associated to Rangers and Celtic is as rife in Ulster as it is in Glasgow.

Had it not been for the GAA, it seems unconceivable to imagine that by the 1890s, there would not have been soccer clubs forming left, right and centre from Galway to Dublin and from Donegal to Cork. As it happened, it would take a lot longer than that for soccer to become anything more than an afterthought in most of the country. Northern Irish Catholics were generally encouraged to play GAA, something which to a certain extent still holds today. The six counties of the north have a fine record. Armagh and Tyrone have both won the All Ireland title in recent years, and Down and Fermanagh are also traditionally strong.

The GAA offered many bonus attractions, not least the presence of beer tents and bookmakers in the grounds, something the other codes would never have condoned. GAA matches were often held back to back, with one or more games of both hurling and football thrown in for the price of one entry fee, and the patriotic displays of dancing, poetry and so forth made for what was often a more varied, glamorous and altogether Irish experience than anything soccer or rugby were offering.

One of the motives for soccer's failure was the GAA's sanctioning of games on Sundays, something the Protestant church had outlawed in its 1695 *Sunday Observance Act*, which decreed a hefty fine of twenty shillings, or otherwise a two-hour session in the stocks, as punishment for "tumultuous and disorderly meetings, which have been, and frequently are used on the Lord's Day, under pretence of hurling, commoning, football-playing, cudgels[7], wrestling, or other games, pastimes or sports on the Lord's Day." A major bummer when Sunday was the only time most working men would ever get the chance to play games at all.

But although they may have objected in the Middle Ages, by the time of the GAA, the authorities had more important priorities than sending footballers to the stocks for disrespecting the Sabbath. Rather than any official prohibition, Sunday observance was generally respected by soccer clubs because they themselves considered it not to be the done thing. Even today, when television schedules spread fixtures across the whole weekend, you will hear disgruntled soccer fans pining for a return to traditional Saturday afternoon football[8].

In reality, Sunday football was not an act of defiance by the GAA. It was just something they didn't particularly make an issue of, and no official declaration was ever made on the matter. It's also shady how much this was a Protestant/Catholic affair, for there were plenty

---

[7] Cudgels was a form of stick fighting, often used as a safer alternative for sword fighting practice, and popular among young men throughout Medieval Europe. 'Commoning' was an anglicised way of saying *camán*-ing, in other words, a precursor for hurling. Sport on the Sabbath would prove a contentious issue for centuries, and it was not until 2004, when gambling laws were relaxed, that Northern Ireland hosted its first Sunday horse racing meet.

[8] One of the main reasons for this all over Britain was that Saturday was the traditional day for going to the local stadium to watch the top teams play, and Sunday was left free for 'social' and 'amateur' matches.

of Catholic priests that were also concerned about the Sabbatarianism issue, or even the idea of playing football full stop, no matter how Irish the rules. As it happens, one of the main voices to come out in support of the GAA playing on Sundays was its Protestant vice-president William Houston Stewart, possibly because of the practicalities of avoiding a clash with rugby and soccer matches.

The Ulster Protestants didn't quite see things the same way. Sundays in the first decade of the 20th century saw a serious of riotous attacks on GAA players and spectators, and a riot in Lisburn even led to investigations by the British Parliament. The RIC police force, who were of course banned from playing Gaelic games, somewhat ironically came out to protect players on several occasions.

Typically of Ulster, Sunday observance was only the pretext. The real issue was sectarianism and for some Protestants any excuse to have a go at the GAA was a good one. Further trouble was caused by the Great Northern Railway company, who decided to make life as difficult as they could for the GAA by cancelling or rescheduling services – with one major casualty being Fermanagh, who lost their first ever All Ireland semi final by default in 1907 because they couldn't get a train.

Soccer struggled to catch on in the south. Although there were clubs in Dublin and some of the provinces from the late 1880s, practically all of the public, media and playing interest was focused on the GAA and rugby union. As late as 1920, when Ireland was partitioned into North and South, only two clubs in the Irish Football League were from what would become the Republic, and never had there ever been more than four players from the south in the same Ireland national team.

Outside of Ulster, the GAA's biggest competitor was not soccer but rugby, a game that, undaunted by its new rival, continued to gain popularity among the middle classes, progressing in Ireland on a very similar scale to the other home nations. The power of the oval code was going to a very tough nut for the GAA to crack. It already had an established tradition in the country when Gaelic football was but a twinkle in Cusack's eye. Ireland played its first ever rugby international against England in 1875, losing by one goal, one try and one drop goal to nil (11-0 by modern scoring methods). It wasn't until their eighth test that the Irish even managed to score a point, but they finally got their first win in their 15th international appearance, and it was against England in 1887.

After just witnessing the magic of getting one over the English on the field of play, the rugby community was hardly in the mood to switch to this new sport being promoted by the GAA, and one that seemed to have been deliberately designed to isolate them from playing the English, Scots and Welsh, which was, and still is, one of rugby's greatest attractions. Not only that, but Gaelic football may have offered a valid alternative to soccer, but with no carrying or throwing of the ball and no scrummages it was less likely to tempt away potential rugby players.

GAMES WITH FRONTIERS

The GAA transformed rugby from a pleasant manly game into a slur on the nation. There can be no finer case in point than JF Murphy and his Lees Club in Cork. Murphy was one of the earliest vice-presidents of the GAA, but although he agreed with its principles, he still much preferred the old rugby rules and stuck with them. His place on the committee didn't last long. Ousted from the GAA, Murphy went ahead and formed his Munster National Football Association based in Cork, and a GAA convention was most alarmed to hear that these "opponents of the GAA … are playing football under rugby rules." As it happened, the MNFA would eventually accept the GAA's rules once they had undergone their first major revamp, which probably not through coincidence had moved away from soccer and more towards rugby.

Nevertheless, other clubs were still struggling to get to grips with the idea that football was not rugby any more, and for some years 'tries' were still being noted in the scores of matches governed by the GAA. Ballymore actually became the first champions of any GAA county championship, Wexford's, on the back of an aggregate total of eight tries for and three against, and a report of the first All Ireland Final mentions that there was a 'scrummage'.

Rugby gained a particularly strong foothold in County Kerry, and Killorglin Rugby Club, was "able to hold their own against the best in Munster[9]". However, two teachers from Dublin, Jack Murphy and Tom Cronin, persuaded the players to form a new club, Laune Rangers, and align with the GAA. Although they now called the game *caid nua*, obviously associating the GAA game to the ancient Kerry sport, and therefore considering it more nationalistic, they took far longer to entirely break from rugby and accept the new rules. But the side made it to the All Ireland final of 1891, and Kerry, or 'The Kingdom' as it is known, has gone on to become the most successful Gaelic football county of them all.

In 1892, JJ MacCarthy[10] described the lay of Irish land in football terms quite nicely, almost a decade after the emergence of the GAA. "Football in Ireland may be said to consist of three parts: Rugbeian, Associationist, and Gaelic. The rule of play in these organisations has been denned as follows: In Rugby, you kick the ball; in Association, you kick the man if you cannot kick the ball; and in Gaelic, you kick the ball if you cannot kick the man … The Associationists are mainly confined to Belfast, where they form a body which it would be as difficult to convict of professionalism as it would be for them to prove that they are amateurs." It goes without saying that MacCarthy was a rugby man.

His feelings about the Gaelic game were particularly scathing and sarcastic, yet mildly amusing too. "The Gaels are a free and festive community, who have their headquarters at Clonturk Park, Drumcondra, co. Dublin … This park is conveniently situated between Glasnevin graveyard and the Mater Miserecordia Hospital. A man has been known to pass from the football field direct to the hospital, and from the hospital to the cemetery; another

---

[9] Letter by Patsy Begley (July 1944) cited in Kieran Foley *History of Killorglin* (Killorglin History & Folklore Society, 1988).
[10] Opening his chapter on Irish rugby in Francis Marshall's book (1892).

175

match being then got up to raise funds for the benefit of the next-of-kin, thus running the risk of killing a few more for the benefit of the deceased! Gaelic football, which is almost exclusively played on Sunday, flourishes enormously all over the country, and its most important rule is that no man who has played Rugby shall be permitted to participate until he has purged himself by two years' abstention from the pseudo-Saxon game."

The GAA had decided a little enforcement would be required, and as early as 1887, Maurice Davin successfully proposed a ban on GAA players dabbling in any of the 'foreign' codes.

In many ways, they were shooting themselves in the foot, for this meant that if any GAA member was ever caught playing rugby, then he was condemned to having to do so for at least the next two years! All this really did was help ensure the healthy survival of Irish rugby, while at the same making it impossible for GAA clubs to scout potential talent from the most obvious of sources – local rugby clubs.

However, despite the conflict of interests, Eoghan Corry makes the valid point that "in provincial towns and urban centres, the two sports professed an admiration for each other's values and the management of their own affairs ... even in exclusion there was empathy. GAA players were banned from playing rugby union, rugby union players were banned from playing rugby league. Both understood the dynamic[11]."

Nevertheless, the rule sat uncomfortably, possibly doing more damage than good, and following a protest by rugby and cricket playing Corkman Tom Irwin in 1896, the GAA decided to do away with its ban, although that reprieve would only last for six years before the rule was reinstated.

Soccer also offered something that neither the GAA nor rugby union were ready to condone, and which would pose a new threat to both codes. Professionalism. Gaelic footballers could barely resist the temptation of the odd game of soccer if they stood to be paid for the privilege[12]. The loss of players to the professional code was one of the main

---

[11] This comparison to the union/league dispute leads us on to instances of bans issued in other sports that were no better or worse than what the GAA did to soccer/rugby players or British soldiers and policemen. It would be considered outrageous if the GAA banned foreigners, but that was normal in soccer competitions throughout Europe until the European Union deemed that it contravened the Treaty of Rome in 1978, and even after that it was common practice to limit the number of foreigners that could play at any one time until the Bosman Ruling of 1995 ended all restrictions, at least on Europeans, while rugby also has strict laws to regulate foreign imports. In American baseball, black players were forced to play in the Negro Leagues. As late as 1945, the MLB voted 15-1 to keep blacks out and it was not until 1947 that, amidst much furore, the great Jackie Robinson first played for the Brooklyn Dodgers. American football never had an official racial policy, but the American Professional Football Association had only thirteen African-American players between its inception in 1920 and 1933, and by 1934 it had none. Canadians know all about the great Ulysses Curtis, Tom Casey, Johnny Bright and Warren Moon, black players that escaped to the less discriminatory CFL. And that's not to mention what Apartheid meant for black rugby and soccer players in South Africa.
[12] One such defector, James Reilly, who became a soccer goalkeeper, is reputedly the man who instigated the rule that keepers can only handle the ball inside their own penalty area.

reasons for the ban on foreign games being reintroduced in 1902, the infamous Rule 27, which read that "any member of the association who plays or encourages in any way rugby, football, hockey or any imported game which is calculated to injuriously affect our national pastimes, is suspended from the association." They went as far as the formation of Vigilance Committees, whose job was to patrol 'foreign' sports grounds and seek out GAA men among the players or spectators.

As always with these bans, farcical situations were spawned. In 1913, the Sinn Féin Lord Mayor of Dublin was not invited to the All Ireland Football Final because he was also the Honorary President of Leinster's soccer association. But Rule 27 reached its height in 1938. Douglas Hyde, a man who had done much for the GAA and had helped Cusack to form the Gaelic Union for the Preservation and Cultivation of the Irish Language, and had himself formed the highly influential Gaelic League for the same purpose, was stripped of his GAA status. He had just become the president of the country, and made the mistake of accepting an invitation to attend an Ireland international soccer match against Poland.

It was not a great sympathy winner. On December 19 that year, the *Irish Times* screamed that "the notion that the game by which a round ball is kicked only, and not punched as well as kicked, is detrimental to the national culture, is of course, the most utterly childish form of humbug ... their little victory over President Hyde will be Pyrrhic, because the head of the State will continue to be the representative of all the people, and not of any clique, however large it may be."

Much drama has been made of that 'unfortunate incident', as it has of the infamous Jimmy Cooney case of the same year, in which Tipperary were thrown out of the All Irelands merely because their man had gone to watch a rugby match[13]. Then there was Waterford hurler Tom Cheasty, who received a six month ban in 1963 for attending a dance organised by a soccer club, while one of Ireland's finest ever soccer players, Liam Brady, was expelled from his school when he preferred to captain the Irish Under 15 soccer team rather than turn out for the school GAA team.

There was constant opposition to the ban, influential journalist John D Hickey writing in 1962 that "the rule is a mockery rather than a cornerstone of the association. All over the country the rules are openly flouted." Votes to do away with it were a regular item on GAA agendas until it was finally voted out in 1971, to almost no opposition, and with most members unable to think of any valid reason why it should be kept. Since then, GAA players are free to play as much rugby or soccer as they like, and it's almost certainly been more beneficial than detrimental to the Irish game. GAA players that opt to play one of the rival codes, or even attend one of their matches or functions, can now return to the Gaelic game

---

[13] That wasn't strictly what happened. Cooney had already served his three-month ban for his sins, but there were irregularities with his paperwork due to his GAA registration having been processed while he was officially banned. Despite being advised not to play him against Clare, Tipp did so anyway, and were stripped of their win when an enquiry adjudged that they had fielded an ineligible player.

without fear of ostracism. The potential of making a good living in England means the GAA will continue to lose players like Kevin Moran, Niall Quinn and Steve Staunton to the soccer pitch, but at least GAA clubs are now free to draw from the ranks of soccer and rugby clubs – two Sligo Rovers soccer players were immediately snapped up by their county GAA team just two months after the rule was revoked. Where things bode less well for the Irish games however, is that, as Eoghan Corry notes "as a result of the removal of the ban, GAA schools embraced rugby and soccer. So far no traditional rugby school has started playing GAA."

As the century drew on, soccer's popularity throughout Ireland grew and grew, and it was the advent of television and the globalisation of sport that meant so many Irish could resist the temptation no more. The GAA may have had its county championships, and Gaelic football may have been just as good a game, better in many opinions, but soccer could offer a kind of glamour that the insular and isolated world of the GAA could not. Soccer had its World and European Cups, it had Pele and Cruyff, and it even had Glasgow Celtic, which could offer an opportunity for venting out your sectarian ill-feelings in a far more wicked way than any Gaelic football match ever could.

Soccer was perceived less and less as an imperialistic, money-grabbing evil. A lot of Irish came to think that the GAA had got it all wrong. Along came Liam Brady, Frank Stapleton and David O'Leary in the south, and the late, great George Best in the north. Ireland was getting the soccer bug.

June 12, 1988 was the greatest turning point of all. In the European Championship, the Republic of Ireland faced England at the Neckarstadion in Stuttgart. Ray Houghton[14] scored after six minutes. Graham Taylor's pitiful English side failed to conjure up a reply. The rest, as they say, is history. What the GAA had dreaded had finally happened. Ireland had never seen anything quite like it before. The whole country took to the streets, tears flowed for joy, and the Irish nation celebrated its finest sporting hour as one. No All Ireland Final had ever managed to generate scenes quite like that.

A former World Cup winner for England, Jack Charlton, became a national hero as he guided that fine Irish side to its first ever appearance at the World Cup in 1990, and took them there again in 1994, followed on both occasions by astonishingly huge swathes of emerald-clad supporters. But when it happened, the GAA found it wasn't quite as painful as it may have feared. They had resisted soccer for the best part of a century, but when soccer finally did find its way into Irish cultural heritage, it didn't lead to any reduction in the numbers of people either playing or watching Gaelic football, though it did perhaps inspire

---

[14] Ray Houghton is in fact Scottish and ironically only four of the Ireland team that started that day (Pat Bonner, Frank Stapleton, Kevin Moran and Ronnie Whelan) were *bona-fide* Irishmen. Most were British born players that qualified for Ireland through having Irish blood in the family. It is testament of the expansion of soccer in Ireland that, two decades later, the 'granny rule' is now rarely exploited, yet Ireland is still one of the world's strongest teams.

the GAA to start thinking about rebranding its image and reviewing a few of its somewhat antiquated opinions.

Rebel rule

No code of football is as closely associated with nationalism as the Gaelic game. That is not necessarily a bad thing, so it is almost absurd that so many people seek to deny it. The GAA's outwardly apolitical image was certainly not helped by nationalist politicians being so keen to be photographed throwing up the ball at important games. There was nothing very apolitical sounding about the Galway GAA's proposal in 1913 that its clubs should set up rifle clubs "for the purpose of training an army", or to the number of branches of the Irish Volunteers associated to GAA clubs. Eoghan Corry also notes how Croke Park was used for Irish Volunteer drills, and how rebel song *A Nation Once Again* was sung at the 1914 GAA congress.

The names of prominent politicians and convicts are a regular feature in GAA nomenclature. "Besides reviving our national sports" wrote future Irish president Douglas Hyde in 1892, "the GAA has also revived the memory of many great and good Irishmen." A Special Branch investigation of 1890 into GAA activity in County Meath identified 31 different clubs. Every single one of them had an IRB-related name, as did 19 of the 25 clubs in Longford[15].

The politics involved in the three codes of football played in Ireland hit on a watershed moment with the outbreak of the First World War in 1914. With Ireland still not an independent state, British involvement in the war would mean Irish involvement too. But the GAA preferred not to let the war affect their business and carried on regardless, although there were certainly contrasting views among its members about the correctness of doing that. While proceeds from some games were reported as being donated to wounded soldiers, other GAA members were keen to dissuade Irishmen from supporting the British forces.

Soccer in Ireland never ceased completely during the Great War, although several major competitions were suspended or reformatted – the general feeling being that soccer was good for keeping up morale through difficult times, while the most Anglophile of the three codes was rugby, and the IRFU's reaction to the war was to immediately cease the playing of all games and in Dublin they even formed the Irish Rugby Football Union Volunteer Corps[16].

---

[15] Although the GAA instigated a rule in 1925 to prevent political figures being used in club names, little heed was taken of it, especially in the north. Casement Park in Belfast is named after Sir Roger Casement, a prominent member of the IRA. In 2006, GAA president Nicky Brennan paid a visit to the Kevin Lynch club in Derry, named after a member of the Irish National Liberation Army who died on hunger strike in 1981. The Derry Intermediate Championship is named after James Sheridan (20), John Bateson (19) and Martin Lee (18), Provisional IRA members killed when a car bomb exploded prematurely in 1971. And the name of the All Ireland trophy they are all competing for is the Sam Maguire Cup, named after a prominent member of the IRB!
[16] Those that went to war with the Royal Dublin Fusiliers were sent to Gallipoli in Greece, where the mission was to gain control of Istanbul, the capital of the Ottoman Empire. Australasian involvement in that battle is still

MIKE ROBERTS – THE SAME OLD GAME: CODIFICATION

Rugby's position often got a few unconvincing looks from the more extreme elements of Irish politics. There was a war memorial at Lansdowne Road, yet the Irish flag was not flying, although it is fair to say that the fact that even after partition the national team has continued to feature players from both north and south tends to contradict its supposedly unionist posture.

The rugby playing volunteers that were stationed back in Ireland chose a most unfortunate moment to organise a training march. It was Easter Monday, 1916, the day of the outbreak of the Easter Rising. The war with Germany was seen as the ideal moment for the Fenians to act, the adage being that 'England's difficulty is Ireland's opportunity'. What followed was the biggest rebellion against British rule seen in the country since 1798, and which paved the way for over a decade of violence that eventually led to the establishment of the Irish Free State. The volunteers marched straight into the middle of the Rising, making a natural target of themselves, and six of them lost their lives that day.

Of the sixteen executed leaders of the 1916 Rising, six were prominent members of the GAA, whose president James Nowlan was among those arrested, a man who had said two years earlier that members of the association should "join the Volunteers and learn to shoot straight." The leader of the rebellion, Patrick Pearse, also had a GAA history, once saying "I am certain that when it comes to a question of Ireland winning battles, her main reliance must be on her hurlers. To your camans, o boys of Banba!" Several Dublin clubs, including The O'Rahilly, Seán McDermott and Peader Macken were named after fallen Irish heroes of the Rising. Such was the extent of GAA involvement in the rebellion that Kerry, in 1917, had no option but to withdraw from the championship because so many of their players were in prison.

However, Paul Rouse makes the argument well that historians have tended to overstate the political edge of the GAA to the detriment of what it has achieved in sporting terms. "Inevitably, every organisation in Ireland was influenced to some extent by the political identity of the people who formed it … to suggest otherwise would be a nonsense … but by focusing entirely on the politics of sport and by reducing an understanding of Irish sports to mere associations of Fenians or of Saxons is absurdly simplistic[17]."

The GAA was the obvious choice for any nationalistic minded Irishman looking to play sport, but that does not mean that the GAA itself should in any way be targeted for blame or praise for the events of early 20th century Ireland. To say that getting young Irish people playing football and hurling was akin to preparing them for war is blowing things out of proportion. Even though a large number of its members were rebels, and were honoured in death, there is no real evidence that the Association as a body propagated any political or violent actions.

---

remembered in the form of ANZAC Day. It was one of the bloodiest and cruellest moments in the entire war, with 100,000 Allied and 20,000 Turkish deaths – including many of Ireland's finest rugby players.

[17] In Alan Bairner's book.

There were two opposing forces at work – those that wanted the GAA to be associated to the conflict, and those that did not, and although the latter generally had the final word, there were certainly enough of the former to earn the GAA a reputation that it never actively sought.

Diarmuid Ferriter puts it succinctly. "We often think of the GAA as being associated with some of the major milestones in Irish Republican history at that time, the 1916 Rising, later on the War of Independence and the Civil War. And perhaps there's a tendency to exaggerate how green, how nationalist, the GAA was as an organisation in retrospect. But if you go back to the early 20th century, in particular when the Irish Volunteers was formed in 1913, the GAA doesn't want the Irish Volunteers in Croke Park, it doesn't want them drilling on their grounds … They didn't necessarily have the same gung-ho, nationalist, republican attitude that they were deemed to have in retrospect[18]."

But the British authorities didn't see things that way, and following the Easter Rising their suspicion of the GAA intensified. Gaelic sports received little governmental encouragement, with an entertainment tax being slapped on gate receipts. Martial law in the form of the *Defence of the Realm Act* meant authority was required for any large gatherings of people, which was fully applicable to GAA sports, while soccer and rugby matches were never considered a problem. GAA clubs openly defied the authorities by refusing to apply for the required permits, leading to such events as the 1918 game between Cavan and Armagh, when bayoneted troops stormed the 3000 strong crowd. In August of the same year, no fewer than 2000 illegal GAA matches were played at the same time throughout the land, a stance that ultimately led to the permit rule being waivered.

Sunday, Bloody Sunday

Many may have opposed it, but Rule 21 stayed in force for 96 years. That was the one that said "members of the British armed forces and police shall not be eligible for membership of the Association", while members of the GAA were also banned from attending social events organised by such people.

British military personnel made for such improbable GAA members that the rule may have seemed rather pointless, but there were cases, such as the 1905 All Ireland Final between Cork and Kilkenny, which had to be replayed when it was revealed that Cork keeper Daniel McCarthy was a reservist for the British Army. One of the most celebrated instances, many years later, was that of Sean McNulty, an All Ireland Minor Champion with Down in 1977, who later joined the Royal Ulster Constabulary and was therefore obliged to give up the game he loved. Yet McNulty showed no remorse, and openly declared that he perfectly understood why the rule existed.

---

[18] In *Part of What We Are* (Motive Television for Setanta Sports, 2008).

MIKE ROBERTS – THE SAME OLD GAME: CODIFICATION

The Rule survived in the GAA's books until November 21, 2001, when it became largely redundant following the formation of the Police Service of Northern Ireland, which embraces both Catholics and Protestants, Nationalists and Unionists. The PSNI now even fields its own GAA team, who play the Irish Republic's police force, the *Garda*, for the annual McCarthy Cup (named after the member of the RIC who attended that first ever meeting of the GAA).

Rule 21 has finally gone, but its disappearance was not without controversy. Many argued for years that it was an unnecessary symbol of the GAA's political alignment. For others, it ran a lot deeper. Fresh in the memory was the occupation by British forces of GAA grounds in the early 1970s. Fresh in the memory was the name of hurling referee and administrator Frank Corr, shot dead in July 1972. Fresh was the memory of Francie McCaughey, looking to purchase a pitch for his local GAA club, but shot dead in Tyrone in 1973. Of Aidan McAnespie, shot dead on his way to play Gaelic football in Tyrone in 1988. Of Sean Brown, a member of Bellaghy Wolfe Tones club in Derry, and who regularly laboured to build better structures at the ground to protect it from Loyalist attacks that had burned it down twice, but who in return for his efforts was shot dead by British paramilitaries in 1997.

But if there is one event with which Rule 21 will always be linked, and one that forever associates Gaelic football with the Irish struggle against the horrors of British occupation, then it was what happened on November 21, 1920. If Gaelic football had lacked a 'true' history, on Bloody Sunday it sure as hell found one. A day that may have nothing to do with the origins of the Gaelic game, but which exemplifies everything it stands for.

The War of Independence was in full swing. The Irish had finally declared themselves independent of British rule and had set up their own parliament. The British had responded by sending paramilitary forces to quash the rebellion, and their methods were so brutal they even attracted the condemnation of King George V.

The GAA played on regardless, and on that fateful day Dublin were to meet Tipperary at Croke Park in an exhibition match to raise funds for the volunteers, which went somewhat against its supposedly apolitical stance. It raised the suspicions of the authorities, who particularly had their eyes on the Tipp players following a brawl on the train to Dublin, which resulted in two British paramilitaries being thrown off. Knowing they could expect trouble for that, the team opted to split into different hotels, and two of the players, Michael Hogan and Tommy Ryan, who were noted volunteers for the Irish Republican Army, were given special protection by a fellow IRA man in the capital.

They couldn't have picked a worse moment to create hassle. The same night, the IRA's Chief of Intelligence, Michael Collins[19], was busily plotting the following morning's assassination of a group of what the British called intelligence officers, but the Irish deemed spies, including members of the notorious Cairo Gang, so named because they had proven their worth in Egypt and Palestine during the First World War.

---

[19] Who had originally been recruited to the movement by Sam Maguire, after whom the All Ireland trophy is named.

GAMES WITH FRONTIERS

The sickening events later on that day often overshadow the fact that what the IRA did on the morning of November 21 was unashamedly horrific in itself. British officers were murdered around Dublin in almost simultaneous fashion in scenes not unlike the sequence of killings in *The Godfather*, many in the cold light of day and in front of their wives and families. 14 people were killed (including one wife) and a further six wounded. Some of the dead were suspects that were never proven to have any connection to politics, and some of the evidence that they were spies was shaky at best, but in general it was a major coup for the IRA against British intelligence in Dublin.

Collins showed no remorse, later saying "my one intention was the destruction of the undesirables who continued to make miserable the lives of ordinary decent citizens. I have proof enough to assure myself of the atrocities which this gang of spies and informers have committed … my conscience is clear. There is no crime in detecting in wartime the spy and the informer. They have destroyed without trial. I have paid them back in their own coin." Whether the victims deserved what they got is not for us to discuss here. What is certain is that the further victims later that day did not.

There was considerable unease in the city following the morning's killings. The Dublin branch of the IRA suggested it might be a better idea to cancel the game, but the plan was rejected as that would have been as good as the GAA holding up their hands and admitting they had been responsible for the bloodshed. So, the game went ahead as planned, and getting on for 10,000 people passed through the turnstiles. For the British security forces, the IRA and the GAA were one and the same thing. They wanted reprisals for what had happened that morning. Although there is no evidence to support the claim, it is said that the officers tossed a coin to decide whether to loot Sackville (now O'Connell) Street, or raid Croke Park, and it was the stadium that lost. An aeroplane fired a red flare over the ground, while down below, 15 truckloads of paramilitary troops and two tanks closed in.

There was some kind of skirmish outside the stadium, apparently involving a group of ticket-sellers that in the British eyes were acting suspiciously by running away from the military presence – although in the Ireland of the time, and anywhere else for that matter, that was a perfectly natural thing to do. If you see a tank approaching, you don't normally hang around to watch. That weak motive seems to have been the only reason for the atrocity that followed. *Freeman's Journal* reported that "spectators were startled by a volley of shots fired from inside the turnstile entrances. Armed and uniformed men were seen entering the field, and immediately after the firing broke out scenes of the wildest confusion took place. The spectators made a rush for the far side of Croke Park and shots were fired over their heads and into the crowd." At first, the people assumed the British were only firing blanks, but with horror, they soon discovered that the shooting was for real.

As panic ensued and the British forces overreacted in appalling fashion, no fewer than seven people were killed instantly, while a further five would die later from their wounds, and two more were trampled to death by the fleeing crowd. The dead included three Dublin

MIKE ROBERTS – THE SAME OLD GAME: CODIFICATION

boys aged just 10, 11 and 14. They included Jane Boyle, whose death was witnessed by John Scott, the man she was due to marry five days later. And they also included one player, Tipperary's Michael Hogan, shot in the mouth, and surely not coincidentally also one of the team's two known IRA volunteers. An unnamed priest described to *Freeman's Journal* how "I found poor Hogan lying on his back in a pool of blood. His feet were on the playing pitch, and his body on the gravel walk."

The other known volunteer, Tommy Ryan, was later captured by the troops, stripped naked, and marched back to Croke Park, where Eoghan Corry writes "an ambulance man went around the ground with a bucket picking up pieces of bone and in one case a length of thigh, and the Tipperary players were rounded up and threatened, before they were set free by an officer who told them he feared he could not restrain his own men's thirst for blood."

It was one of the most shameful episodes in the entire history of British occupation of Ireland, and a public relations disaster, which they unconvincingly attempted to justify in a press release claiming that their intelligence officers had learned that "a number of men came to Dublin on Saturday under the guise of asking to attend a football match between Tipperary and Dublin. But their real intention was to take part in the series of murderous outrages which took place in Dublin that morning. Learning on Saturday that a number of these gunmen were present in Croke Park, the crown forces went to raid the field. It was the original intention that an officer would go to the centre of the field and speaking from a megaphone, invite the assassins to come forward. But on their approach, armed pickets gave warning. Shots were fired to warn the wanted men, who caused a stampede and escaped in the confusion."

Despite such timid efforts to justify what had happened, even in Britain there was widespread condemnation. It was argued that the massacre was the result of ordinary police officers taking matters into their own hands and "was carried out without orders, was indiscriminate, and unjustifiable" in the words of Major-General Boyd, the officer commanding Dublin District. However, the "secret and v. urgent" order to raid Croke Park that day seems to contradict that argument. It states that an officer "will warn by megaphone all people present at the match that they will only leave the ground by the exits. Anybody attempting to get away elsewhere will be shot." Any claim that there were no orders to shoot was a lie.

Bloody Sunday saw too many innocent people die. Ireland was struck by grief, and Michael Hogan's body, dressed in his football kit, was followed by a massive crowd to his grave in his native Grangemockler. His name is honoured to this day by Croke Park's Hogan Stand.

Football was suspended until 1922, when Dublin and Tipperary fittingly made it to an emotional All Ireland Final at Croke Park, won by Tipperary, 1-6 to 0-2.

On December 6th of that same year, the Republic of Ireland became an independent state. It was the dawn of a new era. But peace was still a long way off in Ireland. The six Protestant dominated counties of the north remained under British rule, as they still do today.

Off the field

The other hot potato is the infamous Rule 42[20], which effectively bans the playing of soccer or rugby on GAA facilities. Exactly what this rule means has been left open to interpretation, and despite common belief, it never said that 'foreign' sports were banned from GAA facilities. The exact wording is that "all property including grounds, club houses, halls, dressing rooms and handball alleys owned or controlled by units of the Association shall be used only for the purpose of or in connection with the playing of the Games controlled by the Association, and for such other purposes not in conflict with the Aims and Objects of the Association, that may be sanctioned from time to time by the Central Council." This is followed by a similar rule stating much the same thing in that "grounds controlled by Association units shall not be used or permitted to be used, for horse racing, greyhound racing, or for field games other than those sanctioned by Central Council."

When the GAA say they are refusing access to their facilities to games 'not in conflict with the Aims and Objects of the Association', all they are really doing is protecting their own interests. The GAA and its clubs have built the grounds, so why should soccer and rugby get to use them, especially when there has been so little love lost between the codes down the decades?

It was a far less controversial a rule than the fuss surrounding it warrants. After all, any field hockey club that has laid down a brand new Astroturf pitch is likely to be reticent about soccer players traipsing all over it. And rugby has a long history of keeping its grounds soccer free. Twickenham in London has never hosted a soccer match, and rugby fans would be horrified to see it happen, and staunchly opposed Fulham's bid to use it when their Craven Cottage stadium was being refurbished. It was not until the opening game of the 2000 World Cup that the ground hosted its first game of rugby league, in which Australia beat England.

In Wales, Riverside FC, founded in 1899, occasionally played at the Cardiff Arms Park until 1910, when they moved to Ninian Park, and became Cardiff City. It would not be until 1989 that the Welsh FA, who for decades had been doomed to playing international matches in the small-scale surroundings of Ninian Park and Wrexham's Racecourse Ground, finally persuaded the WRU to allow soccer to return to the National Stadium, when Wales entertained West Germany.

And in Scotland, Murrayfield had only ever been used for rugby union until it hosted the rugby league Challenge Cup final in 2000, and no soccer was played there until Hearts decided their own Tynecastle Stadium was too small for UEFA Cup matches and switched to Edinburgh's bigger venue for the game in which they beat Portuguese club Sporting Braga 3-1 in September 2004.

The GAA's showpiece stadium in Dublin, Croke Park, did host sports other than those that came under its auspices. The first time was 1946, when a game of American football was

---

[20] Now Rule 44 following amendments to the constitution.

played by US servicemen on the way home from the Second World War. This may seem as un-Irish an event as Croke Park could have hoped to stage, but with 40 million Americans being of Irish descent, it was seen as a way of paying tribute to them[21].

In 1997, the NFL's Pittsburgh Steelers and Chicago Bears played an exhibition match at Croke Park, the first time any professional team sport had been played there, although in 1972, another sport, boxing, had witnessed the great Muhammad Ali defeat Al 'Blue' Lewis at Croker, and the pugilists weren't doing it for free[22].

Cynics have often singled out these events as hypocritical exceptions to the GAA-only policy, but if we go back to the original wording of Rule 42, we find that the GAA was quite willing to accept activities that were "not in conflict with the Aims and Objects of the Association." There's a grey area here that leaves room for manoeuvre, and as neither American football nor boxing were deemed to be treading on any GAA toes, there was no reason why they could not use Croke Park, or indeed for concerts to be given by such English acts as The Police and Robbie Williams.

But soccer and rugby were a no-go area, and those sports' finals and internationals were played instead at the much smaller Lansdowne Road. That all changed in 2005 with the controversial temporary overruling of Rule 42. The reason was the upgrading of Lansdowne Road, which started in 2007 and was completed in 2010, resulting in the ultra-modern 51,700 capacity Aviva Stadium. The problem was that while the brickies were at work, Irish rugby and soccer internationals were going to be left without any suitable venue anywhere in the country. There were two options. One was to play games abroad, almost certainly somewhere in the UK, the other was to somehow persuade the GAA to back down on Rule 42, and lease them Croke Park for a few years.

It was one of biggest talking points in recent Irish history. Tim Carey wrote that "as a historian I try to be neutral on the matter of Rule 42. There is a possibility that it would lose something if opened up to other sports. Its uniqueness would be lessened – that would be a concern. And there are difficult issues for different people. Take for example the fact that the Hogan Stand is named after someone killed on Bloody Sunday. The thought of an English team then playing in front of that stand may be impossible to take for some. But being

---

[21] The same sentiments lay behind the Shamrock Classic, played between NCAA college teams that were selected specifically because of their historical Irish connections. In 1996, Notre Dame beat the United States Naval Academy in front of 38,651 at Croke Park. This game was the Fighting Irish's 33rd win in a row against Navy, and set the record for the longest winning streak over an annual collegiate opponent, which would eventually be stretched to 43 before a dramatic Navy win in 2007. The two teams plan to return to Croke Park in 2012.

[22] One great anecdote from that game was when Ali, on arrival in Dublin, insisted he wanted to see where the black people hang out. "There aren't any" was the reply, in a time when Dublin had practically no racial minorities.

pragmatic I would like to see other sports there on an intermittent or short term basis – something that would not affect the overall symbolism of the place[23]."

A cacophony of opinions reverberated throughout the island. Michael Greenan, vice-president of the GAA, told *The Guardian* that "say you were Tesco, and Sainsbury's couldn't open for some reason and they came to you and said, 'Can we sell our groceries at your shop?' You would tell them to get lost, of course you would." But in the same article, senior GAA member Tommy Kenoy expressed a different view that it was "time to move on. We live in a different age. Ireland is a multicultural society." Indeed, times had changed. Irish sport was no longer forcibly divided into GAA and 'foreign' communities. The people that wanted to somewhere to play soccer and rugby internationals were fellow Irish citizens who were as supportive of the GAA as the next man or woman.

On April 16, 2005, the historic motion to temporarily relax Rule 42 was put to the GAA Annual Congress, and it was carried by 227 votes in favour to 97 against, just 11 votes more than the required two-thirds majority.

And so it happened. An amendment was made that "Central Council shall have the power to authorise the use of Croke Park for games, other than those controlled by the Association, during a temporary period when Lansdowne Road Football Ground is closed for the proposed development."

Other than for the traditionalists, this was a win-win situation all round. The GAA would make around a million euros a game from leasing its facility to the IFA and IRFU, who in turn, thanks to the additional ticket sales alone, would be able to rake in a tidy profit themselves. The problem now was that some people, generally those that didn't really feel too happy about public funds being invested in football stadiums (the Irish government supplied €190 million, more than half the cost of the project), were asking why, if rugby and soccer could be played at Croke Park, the city should waste money redeveloping Lansdowne Road at all?

February 11, 2007, was a momentous day in the history of Irish sport. Ireland's home game with France in rugby union's Six Nations was played at Croke Park, the party atmosphere at the biggest stadium to ever stage a match in the competition being cut short by a late French try to win 17-20.

But two weeks later came the one so many GAA purists had been dreading. Ireland were to play at home to England. 87 years after Bloody Sunday, the English were coming back, to play rugby of all god-damned things, and there was major concern as to what the reaction would be to *God Save the Queen* being played over the Croke Park tannoy.

There was a gathering of protesters outside the stadium. Out came the banners. 'Remember Bloody Sunday', 'Mick Hogan murdered by crown forces', the rather witty 'Ireland 32,

---

[23] Tim Carey *Croke Park: A History* (The Collins Press, 2008), an updated edition of the 2004 version, produced to include the story of its temporary acceptance of rugby and soccer.

England 0', and the one the British press picked upon with glee, which read 'No to Foreign Games' and was being held up by a man wearing, of all things, a Celtic soccer shirt!

Sinn Féin Vice President Des Dalton was there, and stated that "this isn't an anti-rugby protest. We object to the political symbolism of bringing a team representing a country that still occupies part of Ireland to play a game in Croke Park", and as for the playing of the British anthem, "you have a sense, even from people who aren't die-hard republicans, that it will still stick in their throats."

The British authorities even suggested the English players should lay down a wreath at the Hogan Stand, but the idea was rejected, as the potential animosity that the British had taken so long to conjure up any kind of apology might cause more trouble than it was worth.

As things happened, both sets of fans not only respected each other's national anthems, but even heartily applauded them in what turned out to be a wonderful day not only for sport, but for Anglo-Irish relations in general. And playing at Croke Park certainly seemed to do the trick for the Irish players, who ended up beating England by the biggest margin ever, 43-13.

Former Irish international Trevor Ringland perhaps summed the occasion up better than anybody. He said "we know about the history and the conflict, but we're trying to create a different future in this century. I like what Abraham Lincoln said. 'I destroy my enemies when I make them my friends.'"

In March of the same year, soccer was played at Croke Park for the first time ever, when the hosts faced Wales in a Euro 2008 qualifier, winning 1-0 thanks to a goal from the appropriately named Stephen Ireland.

The temporary opening up of Croke Park did nothing to damage the GAA. Interest in the game and attendance figures are as high as ever, and bringing some of the finest sportsmen in the world to Croke Park, including the German and Brazilian soccer teams, provided a wonderful global showcase of what the GAA has achieved over the years

In 2011, there was another visitor to Dublin. On Elizabeth II's historic first ever visit by a British monarch to the Republic of Ireland, Christy Cooney, president of the GAA, welcomed her with words unthinkable not so many moons before. "Your Majesty, on behalf of the members of the Gaelic Athletic Association throughout Ireland and across the world, I am delighted to welcome you to our headquarters at Croke Park." One wonders what Michael Cusack would have made of that. Times have changed for Gaelic football, but it is still something for which the Irish people can feel immensely proud.

8 GAA DAY SPORT
International rules and the Gaelic – Australian connection

Sporting cousins

When explaining to an Australian pal that I was writing on the origins of Australian rules football, he laughed that the 'research' can't have been that hard. "Basically", he scoffed, "some Irish people moved to Australia, played Gaelic football, and changed the rules a bit". You've gotta love the Aussies. While the rest of the football world argues about whose version is the most ancient, the ones that probably have the strongest claim of all seem quite happy to hand the credit to somebody else!

Indeed, the idea that Aussie Rules is a bastardisation of the older Irish game imported by immigrants from Ireland is often assumed so obvious that it isn't even worth debating. The champion of confusing the popular anecdote with historical fact, Rudolph Brasch, writes that the game's roots "have been traced to Irish immigrants, gold diggers of the 1840s. In their spare time they improvised the wildest of games that they based on whatever they remembered of hurling and Gaelic football back home." Or as Norman Giller puts "down under in Australia, the Irish influence was so strong, particularly in the Melbourne area, that they took to Gaelic football and matched it with an aboriginal game and came up with Australian rules football."

We've already looked at the *marngrook* connection and come to the conclusion that if there was an aboriginal influence on Aussie Rules at all, then it was only very, very small. And the fact of the matter is that, even though fans of Gaelic and Australian football seem to like the idea that their two games share a common history, the direct connection is a lot easier to disprove than it is to prove.

But it's easy to see why this idea came about. The two sports are uncannily similar in many ways. Soccer is about the feet, while American football and rugby are almost entirely about the hands, but in Gaelic and Aussie rules, both the hands and the feet are used in far more equal measure. Both games put limits on running with the ball, and in neither game are you allowed to throw it. In Australian rules you have to bounce the ball once every fifteen metres (in rugby country, they call it cross country basketball), while the soloing of Gaelic is pretty much the same thing. And in Australia, the ball is propelled by a handpass, which involves holding the ball in one hand and punching it with the clenched fist of the other, and is not unlike Gaelic football's open hand tap. In both sports, you can also opt to kick the ball instead.

MIKE ROBERTS – THE SAME OLD GAME: CODIFICATION

Other similarities include the way that neither sport has an offside rule. Although Gaelic starts with a throw-up and Aussie rules with a bounce-down, the basic idea is the same. And in both sports you can either score a full on goal, or are otherwise rewarded for a near miss.

The bare essentials being so similar, it is no wonder that modern-day Australians living in Ireland have often been able to cure their yearning to play the game they enjoy back home by fitting in very nicely indeed with the local GAA club, while Irish emigrants to Australia have done likewise by replacing their thirst for Gaelic football by nurturing a new liking for the Australian game. The GAA being strictly amateur, there has never been much incentive for professional Australian footballers to take up Gaelic, but there have been significant moves in the other direction.

Ron Barassi is one of the most influential figures in Australian football history. One of the finest players of the 1950s and 1960s, he went on to also become a revolutionary coach and is still one of the country's most famous media personalities. Where he comes into our story was the 'Irish experiment' that has largely been attributed to him when he was coach of Melbourne. In the mid-eighties, he had spotted the potential of tempting Irish footballers down to Australia to learn the game and maybe one day go on to make money out of it.

Adverts were placed in the Irish press, and several candidates answered the call, the most notable being a 1984 All Ireland Minor Football Championship winner with Dublin, Jim Stynes. He didn't know the first thing about the Australian game, but within a year he was on the other side of the world and playing for the Demons' youth team. He was not the quickest learner, but the selectors kept their faith, and he made his senior debut in 1987, as Melbourne made their way to the Preliminary Final. There they were leading Hawthorn in the last minute when Stynes made the naïve error of running across a free for the opposition, which resulted in a match-winning 15 metre penalty for Hawthorn!

They were cursing the Dubliner for that, but he more than made up for it in his later career. He went on to become one of the finest players ever to appear for Melbourne, making the second highest number of appearances ever for the club, playing an AFL record 244 consecutive games at one point and in 1991 becoming the first and only overseas winner of the Brownlow Medal, awarded to the 'best and fairest' player of the regular season.

After retiring, he became an anti-racism officer at the AFL, a direct result of his astonishment at the amount of abuse he suffered throughout his playing career for being a foreigner. The Victorian of the Year of 2003 became chairman of Melbourne FC in 2008, a role he still held at the time of writing despite fighting a battle with cancer.

Stynes is no doubt the finest example that a player of one code can make the grade in the other. But there have been others, including Sean Wright, who was at Melbourne alongside Stynes, and Kerry's Tadhg Kennelly who moved down under in 1999 to play for the Sydney Swans and among much media hype became the first Irishman to win an AFL Premiership medal in 2005. But despite this moderate success of GAA imports, the Irish invasion many predicted in the wake of the Jim Stynes phenomenon has yet to be manifested.

GAA DAY SPORT

But despite the many semblances between the two games, there are also some fairly blatant differences. For a start, the Aussie rules pitch is famously oval, while in Gaelic it's rectangular. The ball is a different shape too. The Aussies have a rugby-esque oval (the correct term is 'prolate spheroid'), while the Gaelic game uses a soccer-like sphere. A game of Aussie rules is divided into four 20 minute quarters and has 18 players on each side, while Gaelic is played over two 35 minute halves and is 15-a-side.

Those are technicalities, but Aussie rules is also considerably more physical and allows full-on tackling as long as it is above the knees and below the shoulders, while in Gaelic the best you can get away with is blocking, or 'shepherding', the player in possession of the ball. No such limitations in Oz. Down there you can block whoever you like, as long as they are within 5 metres of the ball.

In Gaelic there is a goalkeeper, but in Australia there is none. Australia has its characteristic 'marking', by which you get a free-kick if you catch the ball after it has travelled 15 metres, but there is no such rule in Gaelic, and while in the Aussie game you can pick the ball up off the ground, in Ireland you can only kick it up with your feet.

Australian and Gaelic football may share many basic principles, but they are also very different. And although it may be true that Gaelic footballers have managed to make the switch to the Aussie code, there are many, many more that have moved from Gaelic to soccer (Kevin Moran, Neil Lennon, Niall Quinn, Martin O'Neill and Steve Staunton, to name but a few), or rugby (Brian Carney, who played union and league, Rob Kearney, Geordan Murphy and Moss Keane, to name but four).

Joining forces

Nevertheless, enough similarities were spotted between the two codes to produce one of the most fascinating sporting creations of the modern era: International Rules Football, also known as 'inter rules' in Australia and 'compromise rules' in Ireland, or, to make matters more complicated, *peil na rialacha idirnáisiunta* in Irish.

The idea was a great one. Both sports are played almost entirely within their respective countries, making the outlet of international competition wishfully impossible thinking. There was never any point forming an Irish international team because they had nobody to play against, while although there had been a tradition since 1947 of selecting the All-Australian Team, modelled on American All-Star teams, it was a purely symbolic gesture, because no other country could possibly put together a team good enough to give them a decent game. But what if the Irish and Australians were to amalgamate their respective versions of footy to invent a brand new sport that met somewhere between the two?

It was not a totally new idea. Australian rules had actually been involved in previous cases of hybridising its code with other forms of football in order to widen its playing horizons. The south-eastern state of Victoria is the homeland of the Australian game, but although they had a healthy cricketing rivalry with New South Wales to the north, when football season came around, there was a sporting divide between the two. NSW, and its capital Sydney, was rugby country.

Towards the end of the 19th century, the impossibility of football clubs from the two states playing each other led the rugby folk in NSW to consider certain compromises to the Victorian game, such as getting rid of scrums and allowing players to catch a mark, but the RFU in London, which governed the sport, was having none of it. As the years went by, and both sports went professional (rugby as rugby league), they also showed increasingly greater interest in their respective markets, and moves towards an agreed set of football rules for Australia as a whole became more and more serious.

The matter reached a head in 1914 when England played NSW in a rugby league international at the MCG in Melbourne. Officials from the NSWRL and the Australian National Football Council actually sat down together and worked out a set of composite rules. It was to be played on an oval field, it had rugby's 'H' shaped posts and no behinds, with tries scoring two points and all goals scored from the field or from conversions scoring one. Offside would work like in rugby league (but only in an area 35 yards in front of the opposing goal), so there would be no forward passing (the ball could be thrown as well as punched), and tackling was basically the same as in rugby too.

Those rules give the impression that it was the rugby contingent that would have come out of it best but concessions to the Victorian game included the elimination of scrums (the game re-started with a bounce-up), the mark rule, and there being nothing wrong with a knock-on as long as that same player retained possession after.

It looked like they were perfectly serious about it, and had it not been for the outbreak that year of World War One, when hybridising football codes was suddenly the last thing on anybody's mind, the merger of Australian rules and rugby league may well have happened.

The idea was as good as forgotten, and it was not until 1933, when the national rugby league team, the Kangaroos, were in Melbourne and were invited to dinner by VFL officials, that everybody probably had one too many to drink and the idea resurfaced.

Rugby league historian Sean Fagan sums up the mood of excitement generated by the renewed interest in a hybrid code as he quotes three contemporary commentators. A Mr Hickey said "if a NSW team, playing a truly national code, could travel to Perth playing en route in Melbourne and Adelaide, I doubt whether the ovals would be able to accommodate the crowds. The financial possibilities are unlimited. There are excellent features in both codes that could easily be adopted", a Mr More felt it was time to "search for a game for Australia, and forget about England" and a Mr O'Connor joyously proclaimed that "if the brilliant, spectacular features of Australian rules were combined with the hard, solid features of rugby league we would have a game with which to storm the world."

The expectations were so high, with people on both sides of the footballing divide preparing themselves for the imminent Universal Football League, that it is surprising that the idea eventually passed away with barely a whimper.

A trial match was played at the Sydney Showground in August 1933, but although the game was meant to be played 14-a-side, they only managed to muster 24 bodies, and reports are mixed as to whether it was considered a success or utter confusion as the players tried to come to terms with the combination of two sets of rules that turned out not to be quite as compatible as had been hoped.

Plans were in place for further exhibition matches to get the Australian public used to the new future of football in their country, but that game in Sydney was probably the only one that ever got played.

The rugby leaguers were particularly apprehensive. After all, they probably stood to lose a lot more than they could gain. There may have been potential benefits on offer in states where the Victorian code was dominant, but by changing their rules, they were cutting themselves off from the international rugby community, and that mattered a lot more to them than the possibility of a few games in Melbourne and Geelong.

Jersey Flegg, President of the NSWRL, decided the composite game was something best forgotten, saying "even if they retained 90% of league rules, and only 10% of the other rules, it still would not be rugby league. There is nothing in common between league and any other game ... If they want a new game, get out of our game and form their own."

That was about as far as it went for Australia's attempt at a truly national game, but it was not just rugby that could have combined forces with Aussie Rules. That same year of 1933, Melbourne's *Sporting Globe* mentioned a meeting held between the VFL and soccer chiefs to discuss a possible amalgamation of their two bodies. Composite rules may not have been on the agenda, but the sharing of grounds and other facilities certainly was.

A decade later, in 1943 and following the bombing of Pearl Harbor, there were something in the region of 30,000 American soldiers stationed in Melbourne. Partly in an attempt to win back the favour they had lost among the local male populace by wooing away their ladies, the Americans decided to put on football matches.

But the sexually-frustrated locals were frankly bored by the rigidly structured and stop-start nature of the American game, while attempts to get the Americans playing by the Australian rules failed because the Americans simply didn't have the kicking skills to match their hosts.

One Ern Cowley, who must have had plenty of spare time on his hands being the baseball editor at the *Sporting Globe*, came up with a brilliant compromise to get the Americans and Aussies playing together. The latter continued catching 15 yard kicks to call their marks, but the former were allowed to throw it instead, as they were used to doing in their code. The hybrid game was called Austus, and the novelty factor drew considerable crowds to the many matches that were played.

There was much excitement at the time that a new bond had been created between the two sports, but despite plans to continue the link, once the American soldiers went home the idea was forgotten, probably never to surface again.

Galah days

The seeds of International Rules were sown in 1964, when the GAA first picked up on the idea that it might be fun to play an Australian team, but although they issued an invitation to clubs to come north and play them, nothing ever came of it.

Then in 1967, former Aussie rules umpire Harry Beitzel was in London on business[1], and happened to catch the All Ireland Final on the telly. It seems odd that Gaelic football was being shown on one of the only three terrestrial television channels in the UK at the time, as neither the BBC nor ITV have traditionally shown much, or better said any, interest in the game, but apparently Beitzel did see it, and was fascinated by how similar it was to the game he was so closely involved with back home.

He went about putting together an Australian team to travel to Ireland. They were nicknamed the 'Galahs', not because the name sounds like GAA or Gaelic, as one might suspect, but because of comments in the Melbourne media that the garish suits the players wore resembled the distinctive pink and grey plumage of an indigenous Australian cockatoo.

After a two-point win in a warm-up against a Dublin Civil Service team on October 28, 1967, the next day the Galahs faced the real challenge, Croke Park and a Meath team that had recently been crowned All Ireland champions. Although the popular conception is that the 1967 Galahs tour was the first time International Rules was played, that wasn't really the case. The games were played to GAA rules, the only exception being that the ball could be picked up in any way, and not just with the feet as in Gaelic.

So, a bunch of Australians had arrived in Dublin to play the Irish at their national sport? They had never played it before, and the team they were going to play was none other than the national champions! Was this some kind of joke? 23,000 people went along to watch that day, and none of them really knew what to expect.

The outcome was one of the most staggering sights Croke Park has ever witnessed. The Australians were brilliant. They played Meath off the park, winning 3-16 to 1-10 (i.e. 25-13). The professional visitors were simply too big and too fit, and even though they weren't allowed to tackle the way they were used to, their tactics and dazzling teamwork would give the Irish plenty of food for thought and sparked off a minor revolution in the way Gaelic football has been played ever since.

A midweek match in London failed to materialise, and instead a rather shambolic exhibition of Aussie Rules against ex-pats in England was played at Crystal Palace. But the Galahs were the talk of the town back in Ireland, and a second match was arranged at remarkably short notice on the following Saturday, once again at Croke Park, and this time against Connacht champions Mayo in front of 20,000. The Galahs again taught the locals a thing or two,

---

[1] Having retired from umpiring due to injury, Beitzel was now well on his way to becoming one of the sport's most renowned broadcasters, and had a few business interests on the side. In 1994, one of these involving some dodgy dealings for a lottery organisation would see him ending up in jail, although in his favour he did forcefully deny that he ever knowingly did anything wrong.

GAA DAY SPORT

winning 2-12 to 2-5, before rushing off to America, where New York had a fine Gaelic football team of their own, and finally put an exhausted and jet-lagged Aussie side to the sword by thrashing them by a resounding 4-8 to 0-5. That was an ugly game best forgotten, with 9000 spectators witnessing the first of many overcharged affairs involving Australian rules players and foreign opposition. The game degenerated into little more than a brawl, with New York narcotics detective Brendan Tumulty breaking his thumb in the process of planting a nose-breaking punch on the face of none other than the great Ron Barassi.

It had been a humbling experience for the GAA in general, but it was Meath who were left particularly shell-shocked. So, they jumped at Beitzel's invitation to travel to Australia the following year and seek their revenge[2]. Off they went on a five-match tour, where they played in Perth, in Melbourne against the Galahs in front of 18,000 people, in Sydney, in Adelaide, and finally against the Galahs again, but this time at the Carlton Oval, where there were 12,000 in the crowd to see Meath end the series with their pride restored after winning five out of five and scoring a remarkable total of 26-43 points to a combined reply of just 3-29 from the Australian opposition[3].

Unhappy by the way Meath had swept aside all and sundry as they made their triumphant march across Australia, Beitzel put together an even finer touring side than he had done in 1967 for what was heralded as the Australian Football World Tour a year later, which even included exhibition games in Romania and another at Wembley. The games in Ireland were again played to Irish Rules, and included draws with Kerry and Meath and a win against the All Ireland champions Down at Croke Park.

It was Kerry's turn to go down under in 1970, where they won all seven games in Australia, even when using the oval Australian ball for half of one game, and also travelled to New York and New Zealand. Beitzel brought another team of tourists up north in 1978, winning every game bar one with Kerry, who would go on another Australian tour in 1981, winning all three games to keep their unbeaten record against antipodean opposition intact.

Composite rules

At their 1982 Congress, the GAA was unanimous in its support for a motion proposed by Meath's Pat O'Neill to try to formalise the growing links with what was then still known as the VFL. The idea was the first ever full international between Ireland and Australia to celebrate the GAA's centenary year in 1984.

---

[2] As described in Peter McDermott's terrific account _Gaels in the sun: a detailed account of Meath's historic trip to Australia, March 2-24, 1968_ (Drogheda Independent, 1968).
[3] Nobody has ever managed to work out why it is that the travelling teams so often have the upper hand when Irish and Australian football teams meet. The only explanation seems to be that the tourists are more focused on the task at hand, having been drawn away from their usual routines with nothing else to focus on for a few weeks, while the home sides only have to take a day or two out of their normal lives to get ready for the task, and are invariably caught underprepared.

MIKE ROBERTS – THE SAME OLD GAME: CODIFICATION

Not surprisingly, the issue of rules cropped up. Fair dinkum, playing on a different shaped pitch, with a different shaped ball, and not being able to tackle, mark or score behinds did put the Australians at a slight disadvantage. The Australians may not have minded playing a few exhibition games under the Gaelic rules, but if international pride was to be at stake, then they wanted a few concessions.

In 1974, Nicholas Mason feared that the possibility "that the Irish and the Australians might agree on a composite game which both can play is very remote." Thankfully he was proved wrong, for ten years later the Irish and Australians did agree to meet midway, and a set of rules was drawn up. It was no longer Gaelic football, it was no longer Australian football, it was a brand new hybrid sport, and it was called International Rules.

The rules devised for the 1984 series are, despite a bit of tweaking, essentially still the same today. The Irish get to use their round ball, and the game has to be played on a rectangular pitch as an Aussie rules oval simply wouldn't fit in Irish stadiums. Like Gaelic, it's played fifteen-a-side and includes a goalkeeper, and games last 72 minutes (divided into four quarters of 18 minutes), which lies roughly in between the length of games played in either code and, as in Aussie rules, there are unlimited substitutions.

The scoring cleverly combines the systems used in both games. It uses Gaelic's H shaped goals, but also two typically Aussie behind posts on either side. Scoring into the goal gets you the maximum six points, getting it over the bar scores three, while there is one point for each 'behind'. Major concessions to the Australians include the addition of 'marking', and how the ball can be collected off the ground any way a player likes. And the game is officiated by one Irish and one Australian referee on either side of the pitch.

So, everybody happy, up came the elite of Victorian football for a three-test series against the best the GAA had to offer. Sadly, the very average crowd of 8000 at Páirc Uí Chaoimh, Cork for the opening fixture hardly suggests that the Irish were falling over themselves in the battle for tickets. Instead, the battle would take place on the field, with one particularly ugly scuffle in the third quarter. Despite all the hard work that had been put into creating rules that both sets of players would feel comfortable with, in an incredible instance of short-sightedness, none of the laws of the new game said anything about what kind of tackling would be deemed legal.

In Gaelic football, grabbing a player around the waist and throwing him to the ground is just not the done thing. It is in the Australian game. In fact, the player being tackled could have a free called against him if he doesn't release the ball in time! It doesn't take much to imagine the chaos, and with the Irish being subjected to a considerably more physical game than they were used to, the visitors emerged victorious to the tune of a 70-57 win.

The Irish soon got the hang of this tackling malarkey though, winning 80-76 at Croke Park a week later in front of 13,000, a crowd that more than doubled for the decisive test at the same venue, and where Australia clinched the series with a 76-71 win, against the lively background of another punch-up and three sendings off.

GAA DAY SPORT

The tackling issue was in dire need of straightening out. The Irish spectators were bemused by the sheer lack of refereeing consistency, while Australia's coach, John Todd, made enemies wherever he trod by putting the Irish aversion to proper tackling down to the fact that they were a bunch of wimps.

Sadly, it would later transpire that the fights were not so much related to teething problems with the rules. They were merely setting the tone for things to come. Unfortunately, International Rules has often proved little more than a veiled excuse for a bunch of Paddies and Aussies to kick the shit out of each other!

In 1986, it was the turn of the Irish to travel, and the opener at the WACA in Perth gave the locals the chance to enjoy the unseemliness into which this new hybrid sport could descend. Five players were sent off in an Australian win. But disappointed with their results in 1984, the GAA had put considerably more planning into their team, and it showed. They went on to win the next two matches and the series, although the poor crowds of around 10,000 in Melbourne and Adelaide again suggested that the general public still needed convincing that this game had something to offer.

Australia won the 1987 series in Ireland by two games to one, but refereeing controversies again blighted the tour, and there was yet another win for the tourists in 1990, when Ireland won two of their three games in Australia, although crowds were now as low as 7000 and increasingly less media interest in the matches took much of the momentum out of the project. It would not be until 1998 that the two countries would meet again.

Only a decade had passed, but sport had changed considerably and was less about filling stadiums as it was about filling TV schedules. The AFL now governed the Australian game in place of the old VFL, and clubs were relocating to rugby league strongholds in search of new sources of income. International Rules was keen to jump on the gravy train, with Fosters for the Aussies and Coca Cola for the Irish financing its comeback and a major effort was made to milk the hybrid game for all it was worth. Everything was taken so much more seriously than before, and the added interest for AFL fans was that their teams would now be directly based on the All Australian Team, meaning the 'fantasy' team would now become a flesh and bone reality.

Australia and Ireland agreed to meet each other on an annual basis, alternating the home country for each series, in which the winner would be the side with the best aggregate score from two matches.

As each year went by, the meetings generated more and more interest among the viewing public. The opening game of the first series of the modern era, at Croke Park in 1998, attracted just 22,000, but since then attendances in Ireland have almost consistently been bigger each year, to the extent that the games in 2006 were played in front of a sell-out crowd at the Pearse Stadium in Galway and then at Croke Park, where for the first time there was not an empty seat in the house as 82,127 watched the Australians turn around an eight point deficit to win the series.

MIKE ROBERTS – THE SAME OLD GAME: CODIFICATION

Interest increased in Australia too, where the AFL stuck to their word that they would make a proper effort to promote the games. There was a massive 64,326 at the MCG in 1999 (a bigger crowd than even the All Ireland Final that year), while in 2003, the Subiaco Oval in Perth was the stage for the first sell-out game down under.

Four of the first five series were won by the touring team, but that curious phenomenon gradually changed, and from 2003 to 2005 the home team came out on top, the run only being broken by that Australian win in 2006. Disappointed by recent performances, the Aussies had decided to do away with the practice of simply fielding the All Australian Team, and instead hand-picked a team of players that were felt to be the best suited to the international rules, and the results showed.

Controversies over the rules persisted though, the main bones of contention being the method for advancing the ball (how far it can be carried and whether bouncing or soloing is allowed or not) and, of course, tackling, an area that has always been disturbingly monochrome. And although the new corporate-logo-and-all International Rules Series got off to a promising start, with the players managing to contain their behaviour for most of the early matches, matters slowly deteriorated, and the fisticuffs did not take long to make a comeback.

The second test of the 2005 series at the Telstra Dome in Melbourne was a particularly unsightly affair, with Australian captain Chris Johnson being sent off after at least three cases of high tackling. It was great entertainment … sorry, let's rephrase that, it was disgraceful … and once again the matches were attracting the headlines for all the wrong kind of reasons. The Aussies argued that Johnson was merely responding to the low contact being made by the inexperienced Irish tacklers, to which the Irish press responded in unison that the Australian players were just a bunch of thugs.

It was in Ireland in 2006 that matters really took off. The first game in Galway saw Graham Geraghty viciously sticking his knee into the head of Australia's Lindsay Gilbee, while Carlton's Brendan Fevola was sent home after he grabbed an Irish barman in a headlock while out on the town, which did nothing to cool the tourists' bad-boy image.

The Aussies had not forgotten Geraghty. In the second test, Danyle Pearce of Port Adelaide decided he deserved a timely reminder for what he had done to Gilbee, and a hideous tackle left the Meath player unconscious in an ambulance. The Irish, who also suffered a broken nose, were quick to accuse the Australians of thuggery, although a head-butt causing serious bleeding to Australia's Ryan O'Keefe hardly made them an innocent party in the incidents that led Irish coach Sean Boylan to call for the series to be scrapped. The GAA issued a statement that they "would put on record the basis of structure, rules, their implementation and penalties on which the future of any Series must be considered. This document will be brought back to Central Council for decision after which it will be forwarded to the AFL for their consideration. If the Gaelic Athletic Association's terms, as outlined in this document, are acceptable to the AFL, then discussions on the future of the Series could take place."

GAA DAY SPORT

In other words, the GAA was pulling out unless the Australians accepted their amendments. There were no matches in 2007 and it looked like International Rules was going to be on a hiatus for the foreseeable future. But neither association wanted to see it die, and after far stricter laws were introduced to curb the violence, Ireland travelled to Australia in 2008 and won by an aggregate score of 102-97. Thankfully, there were no major discipline problems, and it seems that the Series is back with us for good[4].

The Irish diaspora

Apart from bringing two geographically distant takes on football together, what International Rules has also done is add impetus to the theory that the two sports must share some kind of common history, to the extent that it is now often accepted as fact. The *Oxford Companion to Sports and Games* states that Australian rules is "manifestly based on the old-time Kerry pastime of *caid.*" Professor John Molony's *Penguin Bicentennial History of Australia* patently explains how "the Victorian goldfields in the 1850s gave rise to a unique code of football based on the Irish game." One quote advocating the Gaelic theory is so clever and authoritative sounding that it seems to feature in every discussion of the subject. It states how the presence of aspects of the Irish game "in Victorian football may be accounted for in terms of a formative influence being exerted by men familiar with and no doubt playing the Irish game. It is not that they were introduced into the game from that motive; it was rather a case of particular needs being met[5]."

We have to be cautious when listening to many of these people, and ask whether it is sports or Ireland that fascinates them more. The author of the latter quote is a lecturer at Macquarie University in Sydney, and just about all of his major published works seem to be on Irish, rather than Australian affairs. John Molony is also fiercely proud of his Catholic Irish background. Another promoter of the Irish link was Patrick Farrell (1933–2003), who was known for his histories of Roman Catholic and Irish influences on Australia, while another name that frequently crops up is that of another proud Irish-Australian, Chris McConville. Irish historians are not a species to be trusted without a very large pinch of salt gripped between your fingers.

To the support the idea, what we need first is evidence of a large Irish presence in Australia around the 1850s, and particularly in the Melbourne area of Victoria, which was when and where the sport came into being. And there can be little doubt that if it was Irish people you wanted, then outside of Ireland itself, at that time there were few places where you were going to find more than Victoria.

---

[4] In fact, the Australians are keen to get a Tri-Nations series going that includes South Africa, a country where Australian rules has started to make significant inroads. There is also potential for the United States to field a side (New York enters a 'county' side for the All Irelands, which has occasionally done surprisingly well).

[5] From Barry W O'Dwyer's *The Shaping of Victorian Rules Football* which appeared in *Victorian Historical Journal* (1989).

MIKE ROBERTS – THE SAME OLD GAME: CODIFICATION

One of the British methods of dealing with the problem of rebellions and uprisings against their presence in Ireland entailed shipping dissidents south. Lots of them. Between 1791 and 1867, some 40,000 Irish convicts arrived on Australian shores.

Those were the immigrants that had little choice in the matter, but also between 1840 and 1914 some 300,000 other settlers arrived from Ireland in search of a better future as Australia was transformed from a prison colony into a land offering much more promise than the bloodstained island back home. And if it was promise you wanted, then the discovery of gold near Ballarat in 1851 provided plenty of that. In one of the largest gold rushes the world has ever seen, the population of Victoria exploded over the next decade from 76,000 to 540,000, which was a rise from less than a fifth to almost half of the total population of Australia. From being considered the butthole of the planet, all of a sudden there were few better places in the world to be than the colony of Victoria. The state was producing one third of the world's gold, and people wanted in, with the two largest incoming communities coming from Ireland and China. Even today, about one in ten Australians identify themselves as being of Irish descent.

The common image of the Irish in colonial Australia is one of second class citizens, which is entrenched in such figures as Ned Kelly, the son of an Irish convict and a notorious and iconic outlaw who finally perished at the gallows of Melbourne Gaol in 1880 for multiple murder. There are tales of Irish living in marginalised poverty, and of Gaelic being considered a conspiratorial tongue, the speaking of which was castigated in any number of horrific ways. The reality was probably a lot less grim. In fact, at the very time that Ned Kelly was fighting for his cause, 80 per cent of the Victorian police were Irish-born, and many Irish rose to prominent positions and played a fundamental role in the development of the colony.

But whatever their social status, Irish there were aplenty, making up roughly one in four of the Melbourne population, so it seems only logical that they should also play a fundamental role in developing the Australian variety of football.

Did they play football? You bet they did. The earliest known reference to football in the colony immediately to the west, South Australia, was part of the St Patrick's Day celebrations of 1843 when it was announced that "a few of the colonists from the Emerald Isle intend this day enjoying themselves in honour of their Saint with a game of football. After which with their friends they hope to regale themselves with a portion of an ox to be roasted whole opposite the Market House, Thebarton, this day at 2 pm[6]."

Ten years later, the Irish football connection was still strong in what is now a suburb of Adelaide. Patrick McCarron, landlord of the Foresters and Squatters Arms, published an ad in the paper whereby "twelve men of Westmeath offer to play at football twelve men from

---

[6] *The Southern Australian* (March 17, 1843).

any of the counties in Ireland, or six each from two counties, at Thebarton on Easter Monday. Play to commence at 12 o'clock[7]."

If that's not exciting enough, the first recorded evidence of football being played in Melbourne involved what is typically referred to as the 'Irish Picnic' of July 12, 1844. Any Irishman knows the meaning of July 12 – it is the date of the Battle of the Boyne in 1690, deposed King James II's failed attempt to save Roman Catholicism from the rising power of Protestantism in Britain. In many ways it is the same battle that is still being fought on the soccer field today whenever Celtic meet Rangers in Scotland.

The anniversary of the war is when so many Protestant 'Orangemen' enjoy marching around in celebration of the victory and generally getting on the tits of the Catholics. To this day it causes grief in Belfast, and there were plenty of Protestant Irish in the Melbourne of 1840 ready to keep the tradition going on the other side of the world, even though the truth has to be said that, in the main, Australian Irish of both religions generally put their historic grievances behind them and made a new start in a new country.

In July 1844, the Melbournian Catholics appealed to the local authorities to do something about the nasty marching, but the latter preferred not to get involved for fear of creating even more trouble. The Catholics responded by playing a hurling match instead (some say comforted in the knowledge that if need be, their hurley sticks could be used for thumping something other than the ball). The *Port Phillip Gazette* reported on the event the day after saying "the Hurling Match and Picnic was attended by about 200 persons each carrying a *shillelagh* of formidable proportions. Sixty special constables were sworn in on the morning, duly furnished with batons and authorised to quell any outbreaks that might arise."

Morning Herald reporter Edmund Finn recalled how "the Special and Regular constabulary were accordingly stationed on the ground near the present Spencer Street Railway Station, but they enjoyed a pleasant sinecure simply as 'lookers on,' for there were no casualties to report beyond a few barked shins accidentally occurring … the hurlers had a glorious days fun and footballing was for the first time introduced as an afterpiece[8]."

That's the first ever mention of football in Melbourne, and it was played by Irish and in a context as pro-Irish Catholic as you could hope for. Not much more than a decade after that, Tom Wills and his pals would be drawing up the first ever set of official rules for the game. Now, how much more evidence do we honestly need to prove that Australian football descended from the Irish game?

The evidence does seem very convincing. And yet extraordinarily enough, if we look closely at the way Australian rules developed, there is very little evidence whatsoever to support the Irish theory. There are three main problem areas. First, if there really was a Gaelic influence, it seems extremely weird that nobody ever mentioned it. Second, early

---

[7] *Register* (March 28, 1853).

[8] In *The Chronicles of Early Melbourne*, a bumper tome published in 1888 and recording much of what had gone on in the city in the mid 19th century.

MIKE ROBERTS – THE SAME OLD GAME: CODIFICATION

Australian rules didn't really have much in common with the Irish game at all. And third, and most importantly of all, Australian rules was developed in the 1850s, but as we discussed in the previous chapters, there is very little solid evidence that Gaelic football existed in its modern form until the GAA drew up its rules in 1884, a good three decades later.

To H- with your rules!

Let's look at the first problem. The early days of Australian rules were actually quite straightforward. Most of the 'mystery' is the result of people insisting on inventing alternate versions of a well-documented story.

As the 19th century progressed, Victorian football started filling more and more pages of the local press. There are pages and pages of the stuff. And with a quarter of a million Irish flowing into Australia by the end of the century, you would have thought that one, just one of them, might have mentioned that he had spotted a similarity between the local breed of football and the game that was played back home. But that was not the case. In a place where a quarter of the population was of Irish heritage, these immigrants remained peculiarly determined to keep the connection a secret!

Counter evidence includes a letter written by James Thompson to fellow football pioneer Tom Wills in 1871, where he writes how "I turn now to football, which I am sorry to see has degenerated into horse play riot. You may remember when you, Mr Hammersley, Mr T Smith and myself, framed the first code of rules for Victorian use. The Rugby, Eton, Harrow and Winchester rules at that time came under our consideration."

This kind of talk is common among the scribblings of the founders of the Australian games. They were well aware of the different sets of rules that were being debated back in Blighty. Tom Wills had played football at Rugby School, while many of his peers had also played similar games in England, and they often documented their different influences.

There is no evidence that they also discussed the merits of any Irish game. As Blainey puts it, "if the numerous Irish settlements in Victoria really rejoiced that their native game was conquering the parklands of Melbourne, many of the English immigrants, wary of the Irish and their customs, would have deliberately shunned the new game and retreated to what they saw as English versions of football. There was no such retreat by English purists." He notes that in 1885, there were reportedly 10,000 people watching a hurling match in Sydney. That was the game that prevailed among men of Irish descent, and not football.

You would have thought at least that Thomas Henry Smith, being Irish and one of the seven gentlemen that sat down to discuss the first ever Australian rules, would have thought to mention it at some point. He was a Protestant from County Monaghan who had studied at Trinity College, Dublin, so he would have been more familiar with the rugby game, which was popular there, but would surely have been aware of any Irish forms of football too.

The fact that there was only one Irishman on the original committee is also telling, for if Gaelic was so influential, where were all the Irish when this was going on? In fact, Geoffrey

GAA DAY SPORT

Blainey notes that despite the proliferation of Irish in 1850s Melbourne, there are surprisingly few Irish names on the early team-sheets, that "in 1880 not one of the dozens of senior and suburban football teams in Melbourne and Geelong wore the green of Ireland" and that it was "Protestant schools with headmasters from England and Scotland" that were prominent football-playing institutions in the early days. The first Catholic school to achieve anything of note was the now non-existent St Patrick's, and that was for going the whole 1877 season without scoring a single goal.

Blainey's damnation of the Gaelic theory throws more and more fuel on the fire. He points out that the first president of the governing organisation was a Freemason not a Catholic, that the meeting to revise the first laws was held at the Freemason's Hotel, a place rarely frequented by the Irish, and that wherever you look, there was a distinctly un-Irish feel to the whole thing.

In contrast, there was a remarkably strong presence of Scots. The first big football match in Melbourne was played in 1858 at Scotch College, umpired by Glaswegian John Macadam. Another Glaswegian, Alexander Bruce, sat on the first ever rules committee. The first trophy was the Caledonian Challenge Cup in 1862. The influential Essendon club was set up by the McCracken family from Ayrshire. It is also common knowledge that early Scottish soccer and rugby clubs disliked the English offside law, which could explain its absence from the Melbourne game.

However, reading between Blainey's lines, one senses that he is on a personal crusade to debunk the Irish 'myth' once and for all, and we also have to ask how relevant, for instance, the un-Irishness of the Freemason's Hotel really is.

Because although the official lawmaking was in the hands of an elite group of gentlemen, the place the game was really being invented was on the field of play, slowly and gradually in ongoing discussions featuring anonymous contributors whose ideas and comments have long since been lost in the mists of time.

In fact, there *are* references to Irishmen playing football, and especially in the goldfields, where a newspaper article in the 1850s told how "those Irish, abetted by Irish privates in the local garrisons, played a game that seemed a combination of many games, including football, wrestling and general rough house." Blainey himself distinctly states that at the Ballarat club "judging by their surnames most were Irish."

An article in *The Australasian* on June 12, 1869, describes a game of football that showed how "the rules are few and simple, and easily understood by the most unsophisticated of Irishmen." Leading on from that, it's perhaps not so much what the Irish gave to the game that matters as much as what they took away from it. Let us explain.

TW Marshall, secretary of the Victorian Football Association after it was formed in 1877, made the eye-opening comment that although most early players were English, "still not a few hailed from Ireland and Scotland, all eager to refresh their memories with games of their faraway homes. Englishmen of course played Rugby, Scotchmen a nondescript game ...

while Irishmen contented themselves by yelling and punting the ball as straight as a die heavenwards. Each man played a lone hand or foot, according to his lights, some guided by their particular code or rules, others by no rules at all[9]."

And check this one out, Irish connection cynics! Here's Henry Colden Harrison, the father of Australian rules himself, telling us in his own memoirs that "as Captain, I once protested that such tactics were against the rules, but the only satisfaction I got was the forceful reply, 'to H- with your rules! We're playing the – Irish rules'"

The Irish are mentioned in a condescending tone in these quotes, but what they suggest is that the English were adamant that the game should include all the complexities of a rugby-like game, while the Irish showed blatant disregard for such unnecessary convolutions as offside and were into a less structured, more free-flowing game, which is what Australian football became. The Irish insistence on playing football the way they preferred it was probably not unlike the kind of arguments that might have been brewing back home, and which eventually led them to form their own association in the GAA.

Perhaps it was the Irish presence more than any other that inspired the multi-national settlers not to do the logical thing and adopt any of the fledgling codes that were breaking through in England, but to go their separate way and create a 'game of our own'.

Let's do the time-warp

The strongest argument against the Irish connection is in the timeline. It is only natural for us to assume that Ireland, being the older nation, at least in 'European' eyes, would have the older game, and that it would have been taken south by Irish settlers.

But when Michael Cusack and his cronies met in Thurles to write the rules of Gaelic football in 1885, a quarter of a century had passed since the first set of rules had been written in Australia, most probably in 1858, maybe earlier. South Yarra were already holding aloft the first Challenge Cup trophy in 1865, while it would be another 22 years before the Commercials of Limerick would be proclaimed Irish champions in 1887. If Victorian football got its act sorted out that much earlier than Gaelic, then it suddenly becomes very difficult indeed to fathom how the Irish game was supposed to have influenced the Australian one. Australia did not need the Irish game to learn how to play a soccer-like game that involved catching the ball. There was also a 'fair catch' in soccer until 1866.

It seems to have been due to ignorance of this time paradox that the Gaelic 'myth', if that is what it is, was so widely accepted for so long. In a nutshell, Australians are aware that theirs is a relatively young country and are often as surprised as anyone to learn that their game is, at least in an 'officially sanctioned' sense, possibly the oldest football code of them all.

---

[9] TW Marshall in Mancini and Hibbins' revisitation of football pioneer Henry CA Harrison's memoirs *Running with the Ball. Football's Foster Father* (1987).

GAA DAY SPORT

Now that we have the fairly obvious problem of the dates sorted out, and outsiders are beginning to wonder how much of Gaelic football's historic past was merely cooked up along with the corned beef and cabbage among the North Tipperary silver mines in 1884, some have put the shoe on the other foot and suggested that in fact, it was probably more likely that it was Melbournian football that influenced Gaelic.

It's a conceivable theory. After all, thousands of the people that travelled south did not go there permanently. They were attracted there by the gold rush, and whether or not they had managed to pan their fortunes out of the dust, many eventually returned back home, and would have brought with them tales of the football they had played down south. With soccer and rugby fighting their code war for football supremacy, there was little room for talk of the Australian game to have much of an impact in Britain. But Ireland, whose football culture was comparatively primitive, was a different story.

The people that eventually founded the GAA would have been fascinated to learn about events in Australia. Down there they didn't play football the British way. They had invented their own game. And it was great. What's more, there would have been other Irish returning from America with tales of how the colleges had invented their own rules for rugby. If Australia and America could invent their own forms of football, then why weren't the Irish doing the same?

One of the most commonly cited pieces of evidence to back up the claim takes us back to Archbishop Thomas Croke. He had actually spent some time in the antipodes, when he was appointed second Bishop of Auckland, New Zealand, in 1870, and stayed there until 1875.

Now the Croke link is a very tenuous one indeed. For a start, the geography is a bit skew-whiff. Although the people of the Northern Hemisphere tend to lump the two together, New Zealand is not Australia. It's over 2000 km away. But just as Croke was preaching the biblical gospel in Auckland, Victorians were preaching the football gospel in New Zealand, especially after the Otago gold rush of 1861, which saw a massive wave of movement from Victoria to New Zealand, either in the shape of frustrated prospectors heading off in search of new opportunities, or merchants, clerks and tellers keen to reinvest the knowledge and profits they had acquired in Victoria into a new economy.

Football was played in New Zealand from at least the 1860s, and although we can't be sure what kind of rules they played by, there must have been some Victorian influence. Christchurch FC was founded as early as 1863, and their rules included something about bouncing a ball every four yards, which does sound like an idea they may have got from Australia.

We also know that there were at least two early football clubs in what was the biggest city in New Zealand in the 1870s, Dunedin. The club that bore the city's name was Scottish influenced and played a form of rugby, while the Union Club, despite the name, had more of an Australian feel to it, and their finest player answered to the name of Cleverdon and was from St Kilda, Victoria. The first properly documented evidence of a match being played in

MIKE ROBERTS – THE SAME OLD GAME: CODIFICATION

the city was in 1876, when these two clubs met in a match in which the first half was played by rugby rules and the second by Victorian. There was apparently another side playing by the Victorian rules (or something like them) in the gold-mining town of Balclutha, a 70-mile journey away by horse-drawn coach, but that was about as far as it went for the Australian game in New Zealand in the time leading up to Croke's return to Ireland in 1875, and all of those towns were on South Island, while Auckland is right up at the top of North Island, which had far stronger trade links with Sydney than Melbourne and where any football played in the 1870s was almost universally of the rugby variety. Victorian football would make further inroads into New Zealand as the century wore on[10], but given the time, the early 1870s, and the place, Auckland, it is highly unlikely that Archbishop Croke would have learned much about it. Besides, the Archbishop's role in the origins of Gaelic football was more as a patron and he is unlikely to have had much input into the actual rules of the game.

The Croke claim is unconvincing, but it is a little known fact that Michael Cusack himself had a sister, Mary, who emigrated to Australia. And fascinatingly, on December 13, 1867, there is a record of a 21 year old called Michael Cusack, born in Carron, Clare, son of Matthew Cusack and the late Bridget Flannery, passing through immigration in Sydney and on their way to visit his sister[11]. It is odd that in none of the copious amount of journalism that Cusack churned out over the years does he ever mention that he went to Australia in the year of the Fenian Rising. But he did. Cusack had family in Australia and would have had at least some knowledge of Australian football.

Chickens and eggs

The idea that Irishmen returned from their antipodean adventures with new ideas to contribute to Gaelic football is not to be discounted. And if there is any truth in the theory, then it is hardly surprising that the GAA never advertised the fact. After all, if they were going to pass off their somewhat spin-doctored invention as an 'Irish' game, it would have defeated the object to let on that they had copied ideas from a British colony!

---

[10] It was in the 1880s, and well after Croke was back in his home country, when Victorian football really gained popularity in New Zealand, with something in the region of 115 clubs. From 1888 to 1889, the famous touring Maori side that won 78 out of 107 matches in New Zealand, Australia and the British Isles were happy to play several games to the Victorian rules when in that state, and amazingly beat the greatest team of the era, South Melbourne (now the Sydney Swans). But the rising tide of rugby union eventually proved too much for Aussie rules in the land of the long white cloud, and by the end of the First World War, there were no clubs left in the country. Particularly due to television coverage in New Zealand of the VFL (and now the AFL), there has been something of a resurge in interest, but Australian rules football is, and probably always will be, a minority sport in New Zealand.

[11] Oddly, on this document Michael is recorded as being a labourer who was able to read but not write. Of course, he was a qualified and practicing teacher, and obviously could write, but the other personal details on this document seem to make it patently clear that this is the right man.

GAA DAY SPORT

But the coincidences that both games used an oval ball (until the GAA switched to a sphere in 1910), allowed running with the ball albeit with certain restrictions, and allowed the ball to be either kicked with the foot or hit with the hand can perhaps be explained by the way that both the Australian and Irish codes were born out of a similar context of combining, rather than dividing, the handling and the kicking games. This was for different reasons. The Australian game was created before soccer and rugby had split, and merged ideas from both, while the GAA wanted to invent something that could replace both those games at one fell swoop and seemingly drew on their memories of football as it was played before the FA and RFU standardised two separate codes. Basically, the same pre-division type of football that had formed the basis for Australian football. Both the Australian and Irish codes hark back to the days when soccer-like games still allowed catching of the ball, and they both wanted a more free-flowing game that eliminated the rigid offside and tiresome scrummaging of the English codes. The result would have been two football cultures that shared a lot in common.

However, it is the 'overs' and 'behinds' of the respective codes that start making us wonder whether there are too many similarities to write off as mere coincidence. 'Overs' were not a part of the original Irish rules. Behind posts were added to the Irish game later, and perhaps it was no accident that when they were, they were placed at the exact same distance of 21 feet apart as they had already been in the Australian game for some time (only later were the outer posts moved inwards to create Gaelic football's characteristic H shaped goals). Although it does not explain the equal distance, nor the curious happenstance that both sports record the number of goals separately from the number of overs or behinds rather than doing the obvious thing and just adding up the total score, there may also be a valid explanation for why these two sports both chose to give points for scoring goals and also bonuses for coming close.

It comes down to both games having no offside rule. Although, in principle, doing away with offside should encourage open, attacking play, that isn't always how it works. The offside rule in soccer offers the security for the last line of defence to move all the way up to the halfway line, otherwise several players would be obliged to stay at the back to keep an eye on any number of rival 'goal hangers'. It obliges a team to work the ball up the field and then break the defence with through balls rather than just hoofing long balls up to the waiting forwards. By doing away with offside, both Irish and Victorian football faced the problem that teams actually found it harder to score goals, and both games came up with the idea of a second, wider scoring area, in both games originally as a tie-breaker and eventually as a bonus point. And if the idea shared a common root with the Sheffield 'rouge', then it's particularly telling that the Yorkshire game was another version of football that had no offside rule! Ireland and Australia maintain the idea to this day, but one wonders if the absence of an offside law would make for quite such entertaining games if teams didn't have the option of scoring goals by kicking the ball way above everybody's head from the kind of distance soccer players really only score from by sheer fluke.

207

MIKE ROBERTS – THE SAME OLD GAME: CODIFICATION

Historian Geoffrey Blainey seems keener than anyone to dispel the myth of the Irish-Australian connection. He writes that "today's similarities tell us little about the complicated history of each game. Just as two games can grow apart over time, so they can become more alike over time. At one period, Australian football and Gaelic football grew apart; in another period they converged in spirit more than in rules. Australian football in the first years had virtually no likeness to Gaelic football as played today. It is the modern versions of Gaelic and Australian football which give rise to the dubious belief that the two codes are first cousins or even father and son."

Until further evidence comes to light, we may just have to stick with Blainey's version of the events, but it is nevertheless tempting to believe that there is a connection that history has forgotten to tell us about.

But before we move on to the most established and easily proved theory – that the Australian game was British in origin, we should end this chapter with the wise words of Martin Flanagan[12]: "Whose game is it, you ask? The blackfellas say it's theirs. The Irish claim they invented it and poor old HCA Harrison went to the grave swearing it was British. If you want my opinion, it's a bastard of a game (swift, bold and beautiful) for a bastard of a people."

Put like that, is there any need to carry the debate any further?

---

[12] Author of the romantic novel on the life of Australian football pioneer Tom Wills, *The Call*.

9 ESCAPE TO VICTORIA
Early football in and around Melbourne

The granddaddy of football

"I have played both Rugby and soccer and I have seen the American game at its best, but I consider that the Victorians' system has some points that make it the best of all – certainly from the spectacular point of view[1]." Who's saying that? It's Sir Arthur Conan Doyle of all people, creator of Sherlock Holmes.

And with those noble words of introduction, we turn to Australian football. Or better put, we turn to the traditional view of its origins, for in most of the standard literature, the possible Aboriginal or Irish contributions are largely ignored or delivered a sharp torpedo punt out of the oval. Having respected both the potential merits and more probable shortcomings of both those theories, we concentrate here on what seems to be the most obvious scenario.

And that tells us that Australian rules, though the most geographically distanced of all the different codes, and created in the continent with the shortest history of western settlement, actually has a surprisingly valid claim to be both the oldest code and the truest to the original spirit of antiquated forms of football.

That seniority perhaps largely came about because of Australia's geographic and historical position when football was being codified back in the motherland. While the FA and the RFU were fighting their Code War for supremacy in Britain, doing their best to convince different clubs and regions to take up their structured forms of the game, in a small and distant part of the world, the state of Victoria in southeast Australia, an isolated community of less than half a million people, was largely unaffected by all that quibbling and just got on with it.

It was one thing to convince the whole of the British Isles to do away with local traditions for the sake of a national standard, and another matter entirely to convince the handful of teams in a geographically secluded community that had very few local traditions to be sidetracked by.

Before we go any further, it is important to make something vehemently clear to non-Australians, to whom this might come as a surprise. When we talk of Australian rules football, we are not really talking of a game that has intrinsically historical roots throughout the country as a whole. We tend to imagine the colonial Australia of the 19th century as one happy family. But that was not strictly the case. Small settlements sprang up all over the continent, almost entirely on the coast, with much of the inland territories not explored until sometime later. Out of these came a series of what we could call 'semi-autonomous states',

---

[1] Arthur Conan Doyle *The Wanderings of a Spiritualist* (Hodder & Stoughton, 1921).

all of which were initially more tied to the British government than to each other, and communication between the communities in Victoria, New South Wales, Tasmania, Queensland the other regions was surprisingly limited. There would be no rail link between Melbourne and Sydney, for example, until 1883. Each state grew separately, and when they did start coming together, there was as much rivalry between them as there was a mood of them all belonging to the same, great Australian nation.

The creation of Aussie rules was not a nationalistic issue. Cricket, football and other British sports were imported and welcomed. But soccer and rugby as separately recognised sports didn't really exist until the 1860s. Rugby in particular would thrive on the east coast, but in the colony of Victoria it would be met with resistance. The Victorians had jumped the gun. They had already written their own rules in the late 1850s, and built a footballing culture around them that was possibly unrivalled anywhere else on the earth at the time.

It was not until 1901 that the colonies all came together under a single federal government, and with that in 1906 came the new Australian Football Council's campaign to promote "one flag, one destiny, one football game." The idea was to drive home the concept of 'Victorian' rules being 'Australian' rules. In those parts of the country that had preferred to embrace the rugby game, that idea was not always going to be too well received.

Going for gold

The indigenous Wurundjeri had been fishing, hunting and gathering around the mouth of the Yarra[2] for at least 30,000 years when in the early 1800s they started receiving unexpected visits from a peculiar race of white-skinned people. Having sized up the territory, these odd people decided it would be a handy place to establish a convict settlement in 1803, a plan that was abandoned within a year due to the lack of freshwater.

It was a slow start for Melbourne. Aside from a few whalers, sealers and sheep farmers, there was little or no white activity there until July 8, 1835, when an entrepreneurial farmer named John Batman wrote in his journal that "I am glad to state about six miles up found the River all good water and very deep. This will be the place for a village." He arranged a 'treaty' with the locals whereby in return for 40 blankets, 30 axes, 100 knives, 50 pairs of scissors, 30 mirrors, 200 handkerchiefs, 100 pounds of flour and 6 shirts, the aboriginals would allow him to establish his new settlement on their land. Although it may seem like he was conning them, which he probably was, it was at least honourable of him to offer some kind of compensation rather than just forcibly remove the natives, as was the usual practice whenever white settlers gathered any pretences of expansion.

Marvel Comics fans will be devastated to learn that the settlement didn't stick with its original name of 'Batmania', and decided to name itself in honour of the British Prime

---

[2] The Wurundjeri called it Birrarung. The name *yarra* actually meant 'waterfall' but the early European settlers misunderstood that this was the name of the river.

Minister, Lord Melbourne, instead. As more and more settlers arrived, footballers had Superintendent Charles La Trobe to thank for the huge parks that were preserved as Melbourne grew in sixteen years from nothing into a town with a sizeable population of 23,000 in 1851, with the wool trade fuelling most of the local economy.

Everything changed that year. The Melbournians struck gold. The rush that followed saw getting on for half a million people flood into the newly declared separate colony of Victoria, including some of Britain's best educated people overseeing the gold-seeking process. What twenty years before had only been home to a few grazing sheep was now one of the biggest cities in the British Empire, yet even then there was a shortage of labour to cope with the boom. With the working classes enjoying so much more bargaining power than they might have had back home, the stonemasons of Melbourne are believed to have been the first sector in the world to benefit from the 'eight hours of work, eight hours of recreation and eight hours of rest' principle, which gradually spread to other trades as 'Marvellous Melbourne' became what was described as a 'working man's paradise', reportedly offering the highest wages in the world. Some 80 per cent of the new arrivals decided their lot was much better here than back in Blighty, and they stayed to form part of one of the most thriving communities on the planet. Besides, the weather was much nicer, too.

Its university was set up in 1865, a grand city library was opened in 1866 and work began on the cathedral in 1868. The Wurundjeri wept into their 200 handkerchiefs as they saw their home and lives transformed by the relentless expanse of the British Empire. A century and a half later, this place is now home to getting on for four million people, the second biggest city in Australia.

It was against that frenzied background that football arrived in Melbourne, but with so much else going on, it is not surprising that the occasional scratch game failed to hit the local headlines. There was nothing unusual or newsworthy about football being played in Australia, where the oldest documentation of the game goes back as far as 1829, when there can't have been many more than 30,000 Europeans on the whole island. Captain Collet Barker, a commander at the remote Raffles Bay settlement in the Northern Territory, wrote on July 24, 1829 that "our men this morning having got a bladder from a buffalo that was killed had a fine game at football for half an hour & seemed to enjoy it. Football at Raffles Bay, Latitude 113!!!"

This finding beats what was originally thought to be the oldest documented claim to football on the continent by just one week. That dates from July 15 of the same year, although unlike Barker's offering, it suggests that the sport had already been around for some time. The *Sydney Monitor* described how "the privates in the barracks are in the habit of amusing themselves with the game and the ball can be daily described repeatedly mounting higher or lower, according to the skill and energy of the bold military kickers thereof. It is a healthy amusement, and much played in Leicestershire."

211

Writing on the Queen's Birthday celebrations of 1840, the *Sydney Herald* reported that "there was also a game of football attempted, which gave rise to sundry scuffles and broken shins to boot." But other sports were usually considered far more worthy of ink than people kicking balls around in a park. Like in Britain, rowing, athletics and prize-fight boxing quenched most of the sporting thirst, and descriptions of hunting expeditions were a far more captivating use of column inches. As early as 1838, Melbourne was already celebrating its first horse racing meet on Batman's Hill, and no settlement of the British Empire was complete without a cricket club, and Melbourne established its own that same year.

The earliest printed mention of football in Melbourne itself was the game in July 1844, mentioned in the previous chapter and played along with a hurling match by the Irish and really only of interest to the papers because of the unfounded fears of sectarian violence.

A year later, in 1845, the *Port Phillip Herald* noted that "a football was kicked while the greasy pole was being climbed" at the temperance picnic on Emerald Hill and in 1849 there was to be a fair that would end with "a grand match at the old English game of football."

In 1850, the city arranged its first ever Melbourne Gymnastic Games, which involved most of the standard running, jumping and throwing events, plus something called the 'hitch and kick', which was an old Scottish contest that involved leaping to kick a hanging ball. It is no doubt a tragedy that not one person entered the event, otherwise who knows where the art of hitching and kicking would stand in Australian sporting culture today. But the festivities were "all to be concluded with a match of football, 11 a side" though sadly the game never went ahead, and was replaced by a 'kick over' competition.

Why it was cancelled, we cannot say, but it can't have been through lack of interest, because when the rescheduled match was played a fortnight later, some 200 people gathered to watch, and both the *Argus* and the *Herald* carried stories, telling us that the players were "professional gentlemen, publicans and their sons, self-employed tradesmen and some others, probably farmers" and that they each contributed ten shillings to the purse. The *Herald* informs us how the prize was "to be awarded to the first eleven to secure a goal. After a little trifling in the way of a pony race, the long talked about game of football came off, and excited very considerable interest and amusement and led to a struggle which thoroughly used up several of our leading athletes." Another "grand football match, twelve a side" was advertised shortly afterwards, the prize this time being a silver watch. It's cute to imagine that there were twelve to a team because each winning player got to wear said timepiece for a month each! The reports don't tell us too much about what the games entailed, but at least we know that it was common practice to have an equal number of players on each team, and the winner tended to be the first team to score.

Tom Wills was still running around the fields of Rugby when all this was going on, and as yet we have not heard a whiff of the other 'father of Australian football', Henry Colden

ESCAPE TO VICTORIA

Antill Harrison. Instead, the two pioneers were Frank Stephen[3] and Dalmahoy Campbell, or just 'Dal' to you and me, a stock and estate agent, who HCA Harrison says in his memoirs was a "heavily built man, and was justly regarded as one of the most powerful men in the colony." One of his many fields of expert knowledge was the whisky of his native Scotland, but he was much more than that. He would also become a prominent founder of the Australasian League, which campaigned against the deportation of criminals to his adopted home. As bonzer as you could wish, in the first Gymnastic Games, he won £5 and immediately offered it back as a prize in a running event, and the following year donated a barrel of porter to the spectators. His interest in football would never flounder, and in 1860, when the Aussie code was more established, he would be the first ever captain of Collingwood.

Following the success of their early ventures, Campbell and his aide Stephen weren't going to let as important an event as the declaration of Victoria's independence from New South Wales pass them by without a football match. The Separation Sports and Games Carnival was declared, and the organisers turned to the delightfully named kitty, the General Rejoicing Fund, for financial backing. Unfortunately, their application was turned down on the brilliantly un-PC grounds of such an event "only being of interest to the lower classes."

Undeterred, the football went ahead anyway, 12-a-side for a prize of £15 and according to the *Morning Herald* of November 19, 1850, "the lists were soon made up and the ball set in motion by Mr Dal Campbell. To attempt to describe the state of the game at any particular period would be impossible, the play being all on one side. Instead of being worn out by their previous exertions, it appeared that new life was infused into the players and the winners were cheered loudly and heartily at the last kick."

All this may have sounded like great fun, but it faced rivalry from Henry Conway up at the Traveller's Rest, who was advertising "a Goat Race ridden by boys all booted and spurred, Greasy Pole Climbing, Catching the Soaped Pig, two hundred pigeons to be Shot At, and a Rat Catching competition in which three hundred trained rats will perform." It was all too good to be true, as in fact it was, because the *Herald* reported the next day that "a considerable number of persons collected to witness the performance, but though the people were there, the goats, rats, pigeons and spurred boy jockeys all forgot to put in an appearance and the consequence was a general 'sell'."

Football was included with less success at the 1851 Gymnastic Games, where we are told that the "match was unfortunately held over to the last day and amidst heavy rain and a pelting gale did the adventurous lovers of field sport persist in the amusement ... Mr Dalmahoy Campbell chose ten for his side, and Mr George Were an equal number for his. Sometimes the apple, or rather ball, of contention was flopped into the middle of a pool of

---

[3] Stephen, born in St Kitts in the West Indies, was a renowned runner. Incidentally, the term 'old hat' has been attributed to Stephen, which he originally coined by referring to how certain politicians thought so little about what they were doing that they would vote for an old hat.

213

water and the whole lot got a good dunking. The event was not concluded, owing to the bad weather and the stakes were refunded."

Early football in Melbourne generally formed part of 'village fair' events on public holidays, organised along similar lines to the folk footy in Europe. It would have also started creeping into the school system. Melbourne's schools were well stocked with masters from excellent academic backgrounds, many of whom were firm advocates of the role sport could play in a masculine upbringing.

Over at Scotch College, a teacher named Harvey, who it is believed had come from Rugby, is recorded importing six footballs from England, and a tiny note discovered by Mancini and Hibbins in the journal of Dr John Bromby, headmaster of the C of E Grammar School, mentions a game of football on June 5, 1858 in which his boys defeated William C Northcott's St Kilda Grammar. Bromby had been educated at Uppingham School (where football had proved such a valuable method for dissuading kids from pocket billiards) and also, like Northcott, at Cambridge. He would have been just the kind of man to want to encourage football among the pupils, given his peculiar obsession with showing off his manliness with the shovel and axe in front of the little boys.

Bromby offers no more clues about the rules the schools used for that match than we have for the games played by Victorian men in the 1850s. But reaching some kind of agreement must have been even more of a pressing issue down under than it was back in Britain, where schools and villages were still only playing football among themselves in accordance with long-established local traditions. In Melbourne, people were converging from all over the British Isles, meaning that all their contrasting ideas about football were coming together too. Back home, it was only at universities that this kind of thing was likely to happen. Down under, the standardisation of football customs mattered just as much to the working classes, which may explain why the Victorians tackled the issue so much earlier than the British.

Wills and boom

The person popularly believed to have been the promoter of organised football is Thomas Wentworth Wills, who we already met in Volume One. He had excelled as a teenage footballer at Rugby School, and on returning to Melbourne in 1856, would have been keen to see how the football he knew from England could be adapted to his homeland. In fact, he once wrote that "this manly game was first introduced into the Colony by the writer in 1857, but it was taken too kindly until the following year." That was something of a bold claim, because we know for sure that football was played in Melbourne while he was still in England, and it wasn't until July 10, 1858 that *Bell's Life in Victoria* published a letter from him, one of most significant pieces of writing ever scribed on the topic of Australian football.

"Dear Sir. Now that cricket has been put aside for some few months to come, and cricketers have assumed somewhat of the chrysalis nature (for the time being only, it is true), but at length again will burst forth in all their varied hues, rather than allow this state of

ESCAPE TO VICTORIA

torpor to creep over them and stifle their now supple limbs, why cannot they, I say, form a football club, and form a committee of three or more to draw up a code of laws? If a club of this sort was got up, it would be of vast benefit to any cricket ground to be trampled upon, and would make the turf firm and durable, besides which it would help those who are inclined to become stout and having their joints encased in useless super-abundant flesh.

"If it were not possible to form a football club, why should these young men who have adopted this new country as their motherland – why, I say, do not they form themselves into a rifle club, so at any date they may be some day called upon to aid their adopted land against a tyrant who may some time pop upon us when we least expect a foe at our own very doors. Surely our young cricketers are not afraid of a crack of a rifle when they face so courageously the leather sphere, and it would disgrace no one to learn in time to defend his country and hearth. A firm heart and a steady hand and a quick eye are all that are requisite, and with practice all these may be attained.

"Trusting that someone will take up this matter and form either of the above clubs, or at any rate some athletic games, I remain, Yours truly, TW WILLS."

Wills' butterfly metaphors suggest something of a frustrated poet, but his letter tells us so much about the origins of the Australian game, and also some of the misconceptions, that it is worth analysing in depth.

It has been argued that Wills was using a bit of cunning here, for rather than directly promote football, he was cleverly coaxing support for it by persuading the most influential sporting community in the city, the cricketers, that it would be good for them. But as he had become the secretary of the Melbourne Cricket Club in 1857, one wonders why he would have needed to write to the papers to get that kind of message across.

The theory simply doesn't fit with what we know about Wills and his life, which he surrendered to his obsession for cricket. Although he will always be remembered for his contribution to football, cricket played a far more important role in his life. He was one of the finest players of his time, and a Victorian victory over its more powerful cricketing neighbour New South Wales was a far more imperative crusade to him than anything that could be achieved through football. In his letter, he was clearly not advocating football for football's sake. He was extolling the benefits it might offer to his true love, and not just for the players, but also for keeping the grass trim[4].

Football histories often choose to ignore the second half of the letter, where if football wasn't possible, then this supposed visionary for the game says he would have been just as happy setting up a rifle club[5], or any other 'athletic games' for that matter.

---

[4] A neat idea, though it is hard to believe that the groundsmen at the cricket club would have been quite so convinced by his suggestion that the boots of two score grown men trampling on the crease was going to be a good thing for the cricket green

[5] The idea of a rifle club may appear to the modern reader to have precious little to do with playing football, but hunting was a big thing those days, and life in Victoria was not unlike the American wild west of the same era.

MIKE ROBERTS – THE SAME OLD GAME: CODIFICATION

Although he makes it clear that if they did opt to play football, then they would need to decide upon a 'code of laws', he does not make the remotest suggestion that these rules should serve to create a revolutionary Australian code. He just seemed to consider it normal practice for any new club to agree rules, like they did in England.

It is also poignant that he trusts "that someone will take up this matter and form either of the above clubs." Despite being secretary of the MCC, Wills does not hint that he would be the man to do the groundwork. As it happens, being an avid drinker and gambler, he lasted less than a year in his administrative post, leaving the club's entire possessions stashed away in a tin box in the pavilion and according to the MCC's minutes later that year "some remarks of a severe nature were made by the President relative to the non-production of the books by the late[6] secretary, TW Wills, Esq." Things were hardly going well for the man, and his father even threatened to disinherit him, for away from the sports field, his son's career in law was an abject failure.

After lending a helping hand with the early development of Victorian football, Wills then disappeared from the scene altogether in early 1861, when he moved north with his father Horatio to Brisbane and spent the year travelling with sheep flocks on a 250 mile trek to a new station at Cullinlaringo. It was here that a life-changing incident occurred. The *Australian Dictionary of Biography* tells the story: "A party of Aboriginals settled into a camp nearby. Little attention was paid to them; they were friendly, seemed harmless, and had free run of the station. Wills [senior] and his people settled to a regular routine, with a rest after each midday meal. In the early afternoon of 17 October the peace of the station was broken by a woman's scream; Wills, resting in his tent, picked up a pistol and fired at an Aboriginal but was battered down with tomahawk and nulla-nulla. With tragic speed eighteen other people were killed. Only three men on the station escaped death. Thomas Wills and two stockmen were away from the station[7]. It was the worst massacre of white men in the history of Australian pioneer settlement. Wills' careless, lavish display of food, firearms, blankets and clothing had excited the greed of the Aboriginals. Study of the station habits made the raid an easy matter; it was not resisted because there was no preparation against attack. After the massacre the Aboriginals hastily plundered the stores, wagons, tents and huts, and hurried to the ranges. They were followed by a large party of police and settlers, trapped in a valley, and shot down."

And much as an invasion of Australia may seem an unlikely prospect nowadays, in the 1850s it was a major concern. Distant as it might have been, Australia was still effectively part of Britain, and as Geoffrey Blainey tells us "the war in the Crimea, in which Britain and France and Sardinia fought on the side of Turkey against the Russian Czar, had ended only two years ago; and during the war there was widespread fear that a Russian warship would suddenly appear at Port Phillips Head and capture ships that were about to carry away the new-mined gold to England."

[6] Despite the use of the word 'late', Wills was not dead. 'Late' in those days was used to simply mean 'departed' but not necessarily 'departed from this world'.

[7] Which is how Tom Wills survived the slaughter.

ESCAPE TO VICTORIA

Tom Wills may have survived the massacre, but it was something that would scar him for life. He eventually resumed his football and cricket careers when he returned to Victoria in 1863, but where football was concerned, he was no longer any kind of authority, and was not on the committee that revised the laws in 1866.

Far from the Corinthian spirit associated to most sporting visionaries, Wills was probably disliked, even despised, by many of his colleagues. In the AFL's 150th anniversary publication, Gillian Hibbins hardly gives him a glittering review when she writes "he was in fact an overbearing and undisciplined young man who tended to blame others for his troubles and was more interested in winning a game than in respecting sporting rules." On his return to the MCG as a Collingwood cricketer, Wills was subjected to booing from the crowd, accused of cheating with an unorthodox high bowling method, and was at least once involved in a fist fight.

Although he was from a wealthy family background, and very well educated, cricket was the only thing he had ever really bothered to put his mind to. He was the archetypical flawed genius, one of life's wasters, and as his business career went down the pan, he went down an unthinkable road for any amateur sporting gentleman. He exploited cricket for money, and turned professional.

His life revolved around cricket and alcohol, or even better, the two at the same time. He lived off his cricketing reputation, becoming the eternal hanger-on, scrounging money and drink wherever it could be found, mismanaging his affairs, and as his ability faded with the years, he degenerated into a feeble caricature of his former self. He never married, though he did have a mysterious *de facto* wife in Sarah Theresa Barbor, of whom little is known, but who doesn't seem have taken her responsibilities any more seriously than Tom did. Whatever his early contributions to football, these were as good as forgotten as his short life drew closer to its end. Indeed, when he donated a trophy for an 1876 tournament between Geelong and Ballarat, *The Footballer* described him as "the veteran cricketer."

His life ended in tragedy. No longer the athlete he used to be, the bottle became his closest friend. It was a deeply disturbed and suicidal man who was ushered into Melbourne Hospital in May 1880, aged 44, with his condition described as delirium tremens – hallucinatory madness brought on by alcoholism and depression. Wills fled the hospital and made for home, having decided it was time for him and Sarah Barbor to end their lives. Terrified by her partner's madness, Sarah hid all the knives and weapons in the home, but overlooked a pair of scissors on the mantelpiece. Tom found them, and in full view of his beloved, pierced himself several times in the chest. Later that same day, he was declared dead.

At a time when suicide was still viewed as the ultimate disgrace, Tom Wills was buried on top of a hill at Heidelburg, following a short and private funeral. There was no pomp or ceremony, and although gushing obituaries appeared in all the newspapers, his family barely mentioned his name again.

MIKE ROBERTS – THE SAME OLD GAME: CODIFICATION

An appeal by the Melbourne Cricket Club to raise the money to erect a headstone for one of its most famous members only managed to collect the paltry figure of one pound. Wills' grave was left unmarked and abandoned until the MCC returned to the site over a century later to find it smothered in weeds and dirt. This time the club did pay for and erect the same headstone that still stands there today, honouring in gold letters the "founder of Australian football and champion cricketer of his time."

Melbourne storm

Despite making some important contributions to early football in Melbourne, Wills played no bigger a part in the foundation of the Australian game than several other characters. History has probably inflated his role beyond what it really was, and if any Melbournian footballers of his era were around to see his statue outside the MCG today, they would probably struggle to understand what he had done to deserve such adulation.

They might even suggest the statue be changed to one of somebody very few Australians are likely to have heard of. He was the man behind the first serious attempt at a game of senior football in Melbourne, and his name would continue to pop up in association the game for several years. Enter Jimmy Bryant, the proprietor of Bryant's Parade Hotel, just over the way from Yarra Park and now the site of the MACG Hotel. He was the first cricketer to ever play professionally for Melbourne, having previously played in his native England for Surrey, and he would also be one of the star members of the Victorian XI. Whether influenced or not by Tom Wills' letter of three weeks earlier, the publican announced via *Bell's Life* on July 31, 1858, that he "will have a ball on the Melbourne cricket ground, or adjoining portion of Richmond Park, to-day, at one o'clock." Football in the park would mean food and drinks in the pub afterwards, and it is unlikely that Bryant was not aware of this excellent business opportunity.

His advert was answered by "a number of gentlemen interested in keeping the muscles in full vigour during the winter, and also anxious for an occasional afternoon's outdoor exercise." It would be some time before footballers would actually be permitted to play on the hallowed turf of the MCG, Richmond Paddock being the expanse of land just outside. The huge pitch could have been anything from 500 to 800 metres long, making it unlikely that the whole of it was even visible from any single point, and the rugged terrain would have been riddled with pebbles and obstructed by gum trees, which may have been used as goalposts.

Brief announcements of football matches would appear in the local press on a regular basis over the following weeks.

The games didn't come without their teething problems. Dr Bromby of Melbourne Grammar noted in his diary how a game involving some of his pupils against a team of men from St Kilda "came to an untimely end" when some of the men "began to fisticuff", apparently "irritated that after an hour and a half's struggle they were unable to kick." HCA

218

ESCAPE TO VICTORIA

Harrison later reminisced about those old days, saying "it was a rather go as you please affair at first but a set of rules was gradually evolved which experience taught us to be the best."

It was on August 7, 1858, that the *Melbourne Morning Herald* proclaimed that "a grand football match will be played this day, between the Scotch College and the Church of England Grammar School, near the Melbourne Cricket Club ground. Luncheon at the pavilion. Forty a side. The game to commence at twelve o'clock."

This game, more than any other, has gone down in folklore as the one where it all began for Aussie rules, although later discoveries have shown that this game was probably far less significant than was previously thought. Bromby's journal now proves that the C of E had played at least one game before, and the men's match organised by Jimmy Bryant had been played at the same venue a week earlier.

The Grammar School's nominated referee was none other than Tom Wills, as immortalised in a statue of him overseeing two schoolboy players that stands outside the MCG. Scotch College's umpire was John Macadam, who with his flowing red hair was one of the outstanding characters of the early Melbourne scene. A native of Scotland, and a teacher of chemistry and natural science at the school, Macadam would later go on to become a senior politician, and it is also after him that the macadamia nut takes its name. The fact that he volunteered to umpire this match suggests that he may have already known something about football from his youth in Glasgow and Edinburgh.

The *Melbourne Morning Herald* reported on the game the following Monday, saying "Richmond Park was unusually lively on Saturday. Under the auspices of a fine day and their respective magnates, the juvenile presbytery and episcopacy came out uncommonly strong. Both masters and boys appeared to reach the acme of enjoyment, and most jubilant were the cheers that rang among the gum trees and the she-oaks of the park when Scotch College obtained a goal. This event occupied nearly three hours in its accomplishment. The compliment was shortly reciprocated by the opposition, who made a grand effort to do the deed. Evening's anxious shades cut short the amusement which, to judge from the evenly balanced scales of results and the apparently inexhaustible physique of the combatants, must have been interminable."

The fact that it took three hours to score the first goal suggests a congested game involving a huge pack huddled over the ball as it slowly made its way up and down the park, far more reminiscent of modern rugby than the game seen in the AFL today. And it was long, for if they had started at twelve and finished as "evening's anxious shades" poetically drew in, then even accounting for a stop for refreshments, the little mites must have been at it for six hours or more.

Just like cricket matches, which were afternoon-long affairs carried over several days, the contest was resumed two Saturdays later. This time neither side scored, and a third match played a fortnight later also failed to produce any goals, so the series was declared a tie. But that was just the start of this particular rivalry. Even today, and as the inscription on the

MIKE ROBERTS – THE SAME OLD GAME: CODIFICATION

trophy reads, "the Cordner-Eggleston Cup for football is awarded for an annual perpetual competition between Melbourne Grammar School and Scotch College who first played Australian Rules Football on 7th August, 1858."

To claim that game was 'Australian Rules Football' is going a bit far. Yes, the schools played football in Australia and most certainly observed some kind of rules, but it would be more accurate to say that this, and matches like it, were instrumental in unleashing the chain of events that would lead to the game Australians now have to go with their hot pies and cold drinks. In fact, with Wills being a former Rugby pupil and Macadam having studied at Edinburgh, where a rugby-like game was popular, it is most likely that, following the confused attempts to get football games going in the adult community, these two gentlemen were using the schools match to experiment with or maybe even promote the rugby game.

Football was gaining support, and perhaps the first match to really set the pulses going came when Melbourne were challenged by the gentlemen of South Yarra, which was then a small but prosperous village beyond the limits of the city itself, and whose team was eminently middle class, with plenty of the players familiar with football, having played at some of the poshest public schools in England. They were probably thrilled to learn that the sport was picking up a following in this remote outpost of the Empire, and this match is the first recorded case of two teams from different parts of the city arranging to play each other. September 25, 1858 was the date, and Melbourne kicked the only goal in what was probably the last match of Victorian football's first 'season', with the more important business of cricket about to get under way.

The following year, when the cricket season was over, talk amongst the sporty folk of the city started drifting back to football. The previous season may have been somewhat disjointed, with matches arranged on an ad-hoc basis, but it had undoubtedly been huge fun, and there may even have been an enthusiastic few that were almost glad the cricket was over so that they could get back to the rough and tumble of the footer field.

But the enthusiasm can't have been that great, because according to *The Argus* of May 16, 1859, when the members of MCC arranged their first football meeting of the new season, "in consequence of the small numbers of players present during the early portion of the afternoon, the captains departed from their original intention to a certain extent."

Bell's Life, on May 21, tells us more. "The first game of the season was played on May 14 between teams captained by Mr Bryant and Mr Smith. It was more of a scratch than a strict match owing to there being no fixed rules of play. Some of the parties engaged followed the practice of catching and holding the ball, while others strenuously objected, contending that the ball should never be lifted from the ground other than by the foot. The difference of opinion did not prevent the enjoyment of the sport for the greatest good humour prevailed."

William Hammersley would disagree that the humour that prevailed was entirely a good one. He remembered that "when the game first started in Victoria, it was a very rough game and no mistake. My shins now show honourable scars and often have I had the blood

ESCAPE TO VICTORIA

streaming down my legs. No wonder, for hacking was permitted and no objection taken to spiked shoes. Black eyes don't look so good in Collins Street[8]."

Hammersley was referring to that same game in May 1859, when he tells us that differences of opinion regarding the handling or not of the ball were not the only issue at stake, and that "after a severe fight in the old Richmond Paddock when blood had been freely drawn and some smart raps exchanged and a leg broken, it occurred to some of us that if we had rules to play under it would be better." A very valid point.

Curiously, these accounts tell us that the two real bones of contention were the issues of hacking and running with the ball. The same two issues that would give the Football Association so much to talk about in London. But those debates wouldn't happen for another four years. In 1859, if the Australians were going to do anything about it, they were on their own.

---

[8] Writing in the *Sydney Mail*, years later on August 25, 1883.

10 A KICK UP THE BEHIND
The early years of Australian rules football

A game of our own

The opening day of the football season not having gone half as well as they had planned, *Bell's Life* of May 21, 1859 explained what the frustrated footballers did next. "A preliminary meeting of gentlemen interested in the game was subsequently held at the Parade Hotel with the object of forming a Football Club. A list of 51 members was submitted and from amongst them the following were selected as Committee to draw up rules, etc, – Messrs Wills, Hammersley, Bruce, Smith and Wray. Mr Sewell was appointed Treasurer and James B Thompson secretary of the Club. A deputation was also appointed to wait on the Grounds Committee of the Melbourne Cricket Club to obtain permission to play on the reserve at such times as may hereafter be arranged."

It is interesting that Wills' name was listed first, as it was in another account by William Hammersley[1], a Cambridge graduate from Surrey and a prominent cricketer who went on to become a no less prominent journalist. Thomas Smith was an Irishman who had studied at Trinity, where the Rugby rules were so popular, and who Hammersley informs us was a "Master in the Scotch College, a rattling fine player and a splendid kick, but of a very peppery nature." James Bogne Thompson was another Cambridge graduate. He worked as a journalist for *Argus*, and once quipped that the eradication of roughness from football was like the Humane Society taking over football, so he would no doubt have presented a defence for hacking.

Thompson later claimed that it was just these four who had framed the rules, which is in keeping with Hammersley's version of the events. However, they were signed by seven men, the other three probably ratifying the others' work. The first of these was the treasurer, Mr Sewell. Alex Bruce was probably there because without somebody called Bruce, well it just wouldn't be 'Stralian, would it? But for unknown reasons, Thomas Wray, the MCC's Honorary Secretary who was mentioned in the *Bell's Life* article as one of the potential committee members, passed on his chance of fame. His name was missing on the document, with that of T Butterworth featuring there instead.

Being at the Parade Hotel, it seems more than likely that publican and football promoter Jimmy Bryant would have had some input too, although he probably didn't mind too much what rules they used as long as they consumed his food and drink afterwards.

It is also important to note that the mightily relevant figure of HCA Harrison was nowhere to be seen. His contributions to the game still belonged to the future. He was married to

---

[1] Hammersley explains that they decided they had little choice but to "adjourn to the Parade Hotel close by and think the matter over. This we did, with the following results; several drinks and the formation of a committee consisting of Tom Wills, myself, JB Thompson and 'Football' Smith."

Wills' sister Emily, making them step-cousins, and their shared passion for sport obviously brought them very close. But while Wills preferred to concentrate on cricket, Harrison remained at the heart and soul of football throughout its formative years. Not only was he one of the finest players of his era (captaining Richmond, Melbourne and Geelong), eventually retiring at the age of 36 in 1872, but he also went on to become the first vice president of the Victorian Football Association, chairman of Melbourne FC between 1897 and 1907, and the first chairman of the Australian Football Council in 1905. Right up until his death in 1929, he remained one of the most influential figures in the game, and the 'father of Australian football' mantle was one he was more than happy to accept, and perhaps exaggerated at the expense of others in his self-congratulatory autobiography, *The Story of an Athlete* (1923).

But just like with Wills, we can also question how much Harrison really contributed to the origins of the game. He did administrate the sport for many years, but he wasn't there at the beginning, and like Wills, tended to push the game more in the direction of rugby. In fact, Australian football seems to have come into being more despite Wills and Harrison than because of them. Thomas Smith was so annoyed in 1876 to read an article on the origins of Melbourne FC in *The Australasian* that failed to mention his own name yet gave credit to Harrison that he wrote an angry reply to say "Mr Harrison had nothing to do, directly or indirectly, with its formation." As Mangan poignantly asks "the roles of Wills and Harrison in the development of Australian rules seem to have been singled out for recognition … why have the other three – Hammersley, Smith and Thompson – been ignored almost completely? … That Wills and Harrison were Australian, rather than English, no doubt was a powerful part of their attraction, particularly in the 1880s and 1890s when Australian nationalism was making itself felt."

In trying to decide what the best rules for their purposes were, all four of the main committee members had some kind of experience of English versions of football to draw from. Hammersley mentions that "Tom Wills suggested the Rugby rules, but no one understood them except himself[2]" while Thompson wrote in a letter to Wills some eleven years later that the "Eton, Harrow and Winchester rules at that time came under our consideration."

The main problem with the different English rules is that they were all so damned complicated, a problem the FA would also have to sort out in London. The English public schools may have had their nostalgic reasons for maintaining their hots, bullies and scrums, but on the southern coast of Australia they were causing nothing but confusion. As Hammersley put it, what they really needed was "to draw up as simple a code of rules, and as few as possible, so that anyone could quickly understand them."

---

[2] *Sydney Mail*, August 25, 1883.

MIKE ROBERTS – THE SAME OLD GAME: CODIFICATION

Apart from what they knew from England, their other main reference would have been what they had learned more locally. All four would have seen what worked and what didn't among Victoria's mish-mash of settlers from different backgrounds.

Football was not just being played in Melbourne, but also in nearby Geelong, Bendigo and Ballarat. As Geoffrey Blainey so nicely puts it "each isolated club was like a railway with its own distinct gauge or width of rail, and only when the separate railways seemed likely to meet each other at a new junction was a common gauge and a common list of rules essential." That common gauge would indeed eventually be the set of rules laid down at Jimmy Bryant's Parade Hotel in May 1859, but at the time *The Laws of the Melbourne Football Club – As played in Richmond Paddock* do not suggest any greater ambitions than an attempt to invent a game they could play happily, and safely, among themselves. It was a game for the people of Melbourne Football Club, not necessarily even Melbourne as a whole, let alone Victoria, and certainly not Australia as a united nation, a concept that barely existed at the time.

There was nothing particularly nationalistic about their motives. Unlike the GAA in Ireland or the Italians with their *volata*, Australian football was not a rejection of British traditions. If there had been such a thing in Britain as a standardised football rulebook, then there is little doubt that the people of Melbourne would have willingly adopted it. When Melbourne and Geelong met to contend the first Challenge Cup in May 1865, "the Queen's Birthday was fixed for the first match", which hardly suggests an aversion to all things British, and cricket, rugby and other aspects of British culture were welcomed with open arms. The founding fathers did famously say they were going to establish "a game of our own," but those words have since been taken out of their original context. They merely meant that they needed something other than the confusion of conflicting versions of football being played in Britain.

And so they came to their decision, and their ten original rules of football were handwritten on paper and stored carefully forever. Well, not quite. They would eventually be tucked away in an old tin trunk, and would remain there for over a century until 1980, when the curator of the MCC Museum, Bill Gray, discovered them. They are now one of the most treasured exhibits, but the unearthing of the original rules was relevant for the value of the item rather than the content it revealed, for although the discovery was likened to that of the Holy Grail, a few days after they had been drafted in May 1859, the rules had already been printed for posterity in *Bell's Life* (shown in full in *Appendix Nine*).

There is a common argument that Victorian football was an offshoot of rugby, but a comparison with the different rulebooks of the time makes it clear that if the Victorian game drew any inspiration from English public schools, then they drew that from the Eton or Harrow games. The pioneers hint at that in several quotes, and had no reason to lie about their sources, nor any particular need to use underhand methods to sneakily push through rugby traditions at the expense of any others. These are just daft theories put forward by

A KICK UP THE BEHIND

Australia's rugby community today to deride the rival code as a poor man's version of their own.

If rugby had really formed the basis of the Victorian game, then it makes no sense that they had no offside law, which renders a huge number of rugby's rules about lineouts, scrummages and forward passing irrelevant. Neither did they do the obvious thing and go for H shaped goalposts, as mentioned in *Tom Brown's Schooldays*[3]. The original Victorian goals had no crossbar. They were just two posts like those used in early soccer before the crossbar became an established feature in 1866. Tom Wills was probably shouted down on this one. Six years later, at a poorly attended meeting of Melbourne FC in 1865[4], he made a push to have the crossbar introduced, suggesting "nothing to be considered a goal unless the ball was kicked between the posts and over the cross bar without touching the timber." The vote was tied, and had the man in the chair, GJ Shoosmith, not voted to maintain the status quo, history could have been very different. What we do learn from this is how, rather than the father of Australian football, it might be better to describe Wills as the father of Australian rugby that never was.

It takes as keen an eye to spot any similarity with rugby as it does to spot any differences between the Melbourne game and the kind of soccer regulated by the FA from its formation in 1863 until its major revamp of the rules in 1866. Both games were about kicking the ball, not running with it, but did allow catching, and both games discouraged the rough physicality of scrummaging.

An article by somebody calling himself 'Free Kick' in *Bell's Life* in 1864 picked up on this connection, saying it was a "very curious coincidence" that the recently published FA rules in England were so similar to Melbourne's, speculating that a copy of the Australian rules might have been the inspiration for the English equivalent. But it's a free kick against the writer here. It is well documented how the FA decided on their original rules, which were clearly a modified form of the Cambridge University rules written in 1856, three years before the four Australians, two of which were Cambridge graduates and who had very possibly played or watched the hybrid student game on Parker's Piece, wrote their own. And the Melbourne rules are so similar to Cambridge's that the only new ideas the FA could have imported from Australia were the scrapping of the offside law and the use of kick off posts, neither of which they did.

At face value, the absence of any mention of an offside law is the only really distinctive feature of the original Australian game. The first RFU and FA rules employed strict

---

[3] Which was widely read in Australia at the time, and was referenced in a July 1865 report in *Bell's Life* whereby "Fleming, for the fourth or fifth time this season, executed a clever drop-kick, which sent the ball flying between the posts as cleanly as 'Old Brooks' of Rugby fame could have desired."

[4] Where we get another hint at Wills' impatience, for although it was suggested the meeting be adjourned due to "few members being present on a dark and stormy night", Wills merely retorted that "members would have been there if they had been interested enough."

MIKE ROBERTS – THE SAME OLD GAME: CODIFICATION

regulations that generally ensured that each team stayed behind the ball. It took six separate clauses in the rugby rules to explain how offside worked, while in soccer offside was far stricter than it is now, with forward passing to other players illegal. But the kind of football played in Sheffield had no offside rule. In fact, while the Cambridge rules are similar to the original Melbourne game, the oft-overlooked Sheffield game was practically identical[5].

If Melbourne's rejection of an offside law was really such a revolutionary break from the general trend, then it seems surprising that it was not the subject of more contention. An article in *Bell's Life* in 1859 did comment with horror on the amount of 'sneaking' that this game seemed to involve. The writer suggested that some kind of law should be introduced to deal with it, but in Australia they were having none of it. I find it hard to agree with Robin Grow's theory that this was because "it would have been impossible to enforce an offside rule with players dodging around gum trees, gullies and spectators." He speaks as if England was some kind of perfectly proportioned land that lacked any such inconveniences.

Another theory exists that although it was frowned upon in Britain, in Australia the 'goal sneak', or 'goal hanger' in modern day parlance, was the hero. The lack of an offside rule was, we are told, in keeping with the Aussie psyche of the opportunist and the chancer. It's a nice image anyway.

Going oval

An Australian rules pitch is unlike that of any football code. Rather than being rectangular, it is oval. So it may come as a shock to Australians to learn that that was not always the case. There are plenty of clues to that in the 1859 rules. It would have defied geometric logic to mark out an oval shaped pitch that was 200 yards wide, while the references to a 'row of posts' marking out a 'line' from which the ball should be thrown at 'right angles' all point to something distinctly quadrilateral. No, in 1859, the field was most definitely oblong, and all of the contemporary images and descriptions of the game support that.

What's peculiar about the 1859 laws is that they do stipulate a width for the pitch, yet its length was down to the captains to decide, as was the width of the goal. Geoffrey Blainey argues that this was probably because they would just pick two pairs of handily placed gum trees as their goalposts, but it seems odd that they would take the trouble to stake out such an accurate touchline and go to such lengths to get hold of footballs imported from England yet they couldn't find four simple poles to stick in the ground as goalposts, and even odder that in none of the many press reports of early games do we get any mention of goals being

---

[5] On this one there is something of a straw-clutching theory in Henry Creswick, who played first class cricket for Victoria alongside Tom Wills and had emigrated from Sheffield in 1840. As Sheffield FC weren't actually founded until 1857, and is it is only speculation that Henry was related to one of the club's co-founders Nathaniel Creswick, then this doesn't seem to be the most likely source of Australia's lack of an offside rule, but with thousands of English emigrating to Melbourne in the 1850s, it is safe to assume that at least some of them were veterans of the Sheffield football scene.

scored between gum tress. What seems to make more sense is that as the goals themselves made it reasonably clear where the goal-line was, they only had to mark out the width.

Australian football's characteristic pitch came about when the game was moved from the paddocks of the Melbourne suburbs to the confined, and ovoid, space of the Melbourne Cricket Ground. But HCA Harrison's claim in his memoirs that "the first game on the MCC Ground was that played in 1869 against the Victorian Police Force" misled historians for years. Contemporary newspapers tell us that football had actually been played at the MCG more or less since the word go.

Alf Batchelder's research has brought the traditional view of early Melbourne football into question, for he finds that a whole decade before the game Harrison alluded to, in July 1859, and just two months after the rules were written, an announcement in *The Argus* was saying that "a ball will be ready on the MCC ground to-day, at one o'clock, when all good 'kicks' are expected to put their boots on and show." Batchelder mentions other instances when not only was football played at the MCG, but that Harrison himself was on the pitch! By way of example, a story in *Bell's Life* in 1861 explains that "on the Melbourne cricket ground, in the presence of about 600 spectators, the Geelongese were under the command of Mr Rennie; Mr HC Harrison being captain of the Melbournites."

And let's have none of this arguing that what they really meant was not the Cricket Ground *per se*, but the patch of land outside. *Bell's Life* in May 1860 makes it perfectly clear that the game was played inside and not outside the MCG when it said "the Melbourne cricket ground, which had been selected as the rendezvous (notwithstanding that the secretary had stated that it would be utterly spoiled for cricket) was well roped off."

Here's the fun bit. Whenever the use of cricket pitches could be secured, and although it seems bizarre to us today, the early footballers did not use the whole oval, but 'roped off' a rectangular area in the middle of the field! In July 1859, an issue of *Bell's Life* describes a game played at the MCC where "the long-talked-of football match between the Melbourne and South Yarra Clubs was commenced on Saturday afternoon, upon the Melbourne Cricket Ground, which was allowed to be used for the occasion. As far as roping off the arena and posting flags went, all that could be desired was effected by Mr Bryant, who has for a long time had the catering for the MCC; but it was distinctly understood that the pavilion – or, at any rate, the verandah of the pavilion – was to be set apart for the ladies."

Later that month "the Melbourne cricket ground, roped off as before, was again the battlefield", but in August "the use of the Melbourne cricket-ground was not accorded, in consequence of the late rains, and the necessity for having the turf in good order for the ensuing campaign, so that the ordinary space was marked off in the adjoining portion of Richmond Paddock."

The main reason for objecting to regular use of the MCG was the damage that football caused to the grass, and with most of the footballers also being cricket players, they were

MIKE ROBERTS – THE SAME OLD GAME: CODIFICATION

among the first to appreciate that. Also, during the off-season, the MCG was often closed for maintenance and re-surfacing, so games on it would have been out of the question.

Batchelder finds that the MCC minutes over the years mention very few applications for football to be played on their field, but when they did get them, although there were inevitably a few murmurs of discontent, provided it didn't rain, permission was rarely refused. Concern for the ground can't have been that big when, in 1861, and just three days before England were due at the MCG for the first international test between the countries, the Highland Games were held there and included horses galloping all over the shop!

The footballers were usually willing to find other venues than plush cricketing lawns for their matches, even though this was not always the easiest thing to do. HCA Harrison was consistently at loggerheads with the authorities as he sought permission to remove the gum trees from their preferred paddock, and Robin Grow explains the problems the players had with the 'corporation' who "banned cabs from picking up passengers there, and locked all the gates to Yarra Park ... it erected a fence across the middle of South Yarra's arena, served fencing contractors at Carlton's Prince's Park with a writ of trespass, and lopped a section off the East Melbourne ground."

The *Geelong Chronicle* of 1863 remarks that Yarra Park was only missing "a few hurdles to make a splendid course for a pedestrian steeplechase, the water jumps being already provided." As late as 1875, in an article in *The Footballer*, Tom Jones, no doubt wishing he could play on some green, green grass of home, lamented how "bowling has its roods, cricket its acres, and racing its hundreds of acres, but football not an inch of land it can call its own."

But as football grew in popularity, it became more and more apparent that playing on random plots of grass simply would not do, especially when a big crowd was expected, which was not always a good thing. In one game, "the consequence was that considerable inconvenience was experienced by the players from the presence of spectators, who invariably, when they have the chance, assert their freedom by getting as much in the way as possible, either careless of the annoyance they occasion, or forgetful that an equally good view could be obtained by standing outside the bounds[6]."

The Australasian in June 1869 was enthused to report on a game between Melbourne and the Garrison in which "the announcement that it would be played on the Melbourne cricket-ground, to which a small charge for admission would be made, attracted a considerable number of spectators. It is desirable that all important matches should be played in an enclosed ground, as, in spite of all the notices and warnings to the contrary, the public will always insist on encroaching on the space set apart for a grand match. Ropes and flags are useless to stop the nuisance, and the only remedy is an enclosed ground, where the playing portion can be kept clear."

---

[6] *The Argus* (August 1, 1859).

A KICK UP THE BEHIND

Pressure was put on the cricket clubs to start conceding permission for football to be played on their grounds more frequently. In 1869, Melbourne returned to the MCG, this time to face Her Majesty's 14th Regiment, and the spectators were again charged a small entrance fee. Harrison was wrong again to claim that this was the first time spectators had paid to watch footy, but was probably right in asserting that the "gate money was so much that the committee began to think the risk to the ground was worthwhile." Cricket was cashing in on the new craze. Money talks, and cricket clubs started relaxing their views, and even actively encouraging footballers to use their facilities.

But the pitch was still rectangular. A 'plan of playground' published in *The Footballer* in 1876 was still clearly quadrilateral, and the 1877 rules still specified the length and width of the field, and also differentiated between the 'kick-off' when the ball was kicked behind goal and the umpire throwing it when it went out of bounds. The turning point seems to have been a game between Melbourne and Carlton in June 1877, when they decided that instead of roping off of a rectangle, they would use the whole field. The idea was a resounding success, for using the cricket boundaries also kept encroaching spectators at bay. Australian football's famous oval field was born!

As for another of Victorian football's icons, there is nothing in the 1859 rules about the shape of the ball. In all of the earliest drawings of Victorian football the ball is clearly round and all early match reports refer to a "leather sphere." James Thompson was actually shocked when he saw Tom Wills turn up one day with an oval ball. He quipped in *The Argus* that "next year we may expect to have patent octagonal or parallelopipedal cricket balls, or some geometrical monstrosity equally inapplicable to the required purposes."

The choice was probably more down to whatever sort they could get at a time when decent balls still had to be shipped in from England. With round balls seemingly more popular and suited to the game than oval ones, especially when players were required to start bouncing it on the ground and catching it again, it seems unusual that the Victorians should have eventually made the switch, which after such leniency for two decades was regulated in such strict fashion in 1867 to the "No 2 size Rugby (26in in circumference)." The most likely reason for doing this was the increasing interest in rugby elsewhere in the colonies, which meant an accessible supply of oval balls from England. Whether Victorians liked it or not, the oval ball was in.

Behind the times

Other distinctive elements started creeping into the game as it slowly shifted from its soccer-like origins towards the game we know today. The whole affair was a process of experimentation, a small change here, a slightly bigger change there, and it is simply impossible to pinpoint any single moment in history when the game Wills and his companions regulated in 1859 transformed into the distinctly Victorian game.

MIKE ROBERTS – THE SAME OLD GAME: CODIFICATION

A good example of how that happened are the 'kick off' posts, which originally marked out a much larger version of the modern-day goal square, which, as Rule 5 explains, was the area from which the defending team restarted play whenever it had been kicked 'behind' the goal. In the 1866 rules, these posts clearly still marked the area for the 'kick-off' whenever the ball crossed the goal-line at any point, similar to the six-yard box and goal-kick in soccer. But by 1874, this law had been modified. Now the defence only got such a kick when "the ball is kicked behind goal within the kick-off posts." If the ball crossed the goal-line outside of the kick-off posts, the result was a throw-in, just as it was when the ball crossed the touchline (at the time, still delivered by one of the players).

This is assumed to have had something to do with the gradual shift towards the oval field, which would have implied the loss of any corners to mark the boundary between kicking the ball over the goal-line or touchline. Strangely, however, the oval pitch would not become the norm for at least another three years, but perhaps the 1874 rulesmakers had cleverly modified the rules in anticipation of that tendency. But it was also around this time that it became common practice for the stattoes of the time to note not just how many goals were scored, but also how many times the ball missed the goal but did go inside the outer markers. In the case of drawn matches, this was a useful way of gauging which side were at least the 'moral' victors[7]. It would not be until 1897 the newly formed Victorian Football League decreed that 'behinds' would be directly counted in the scoring, being worth one point while normal goals got six, the same system used today.

The 1859 rules make no mention of the length of the game, and the general idea was simply to play until somebody scored a certain number of goals. There was obviously flexibility here. Having already scored the only goal of the first Melbourne v South Yarra match of the 1859 series, our friend Wray did it again, what *The Argus* described as 'double first' ("an event which was the signal for a little reinvigoration in the Pavilion"). This created something of a dilemma, as "according to the original agreement, the victory was won by Melbourne when the second goal was kicked", which basically meant the game was over while the sun was still high in the sky. In reflection of the informality and gentlemanliness of the game back then, "the captains, however, came to the understanding that the first three, and not two, goals should be considered decisive."

This relaxed method of deciding the outcome of matches can't have proved overly satisfactory, because by May 1860, times were being stipulated for the end of play. *Bell's Life* explains how "the captain of the Melbourne team wanted to cut the game short", but Tom Wills, playing for Richmond and as obstinate as ever, "stoutly refused to accede to the

---

[7] It is probably no coincidence that the Cambridge Rules had used the term 'behind' in the law that explained how "the ball is behind when it has passed the goal on either side of it." And the idea was not unlike the 'rouge' that such English football communities as those at Eton and Sheffield had experimented with (the Eton rules were published along with the Melbourne rules in the 1859 *Australian Cricketer's Guide*), so it's very likely that there was some kind of mutual influence here.

proposal, and determined to play on until the time agreed upon – a quarter past five." His insistence paid off when Richmond grabbed a late equaliser.

The 1859 rules make no mention of the ball-up at the start, instead there was a kick off as was common in the English games. And there was still no ball-up over two decades later. When the 1877 rules were written, there was a "kick off from the centre point", but in a strangely inconsistent fashion, "when the half time arranged for play has expired, the players shall change ends, and the ball be thrown in the air by the field umpire in the centre of the ground."

And when the ball went out of play in 1859, it was to be thrown back in at right angles, which was the way it was done in most forms of English football too. There was no boundary umpire to throw the ball back if it hit the ground first, and there was no free kick if the ball went out on the full.

Making a mark

Perhaps one of the best explanations of how soccer and Aussie rules, so similar at first, drifted apart, is what happened regarding the mark. Nowadays kicking the ball for somebody else to catch it in their hands is one of the basic elements of the Australian game, while it has no place whatsoever in soccer. But that was not always the case. Until 1866, the FA copied Cambridge's earlier the rule that "if a player makes a fair catch, he shall be entitled to a free kick, providing he claims it by making a mark with his heel at once; and in order to take such kick he may go back as far as he pleases, and no player on the opposite side shall advance beyond his mark until he has kicked." The term 'mark' was even used in the explanation.

English soccer quickly abandoned the concept, and there was considerable opposition in Victoria to the idea too. "I hope yet to see the 'free kick' system (it might almost be called nuisance) abolished, save in case of breach of rules" wrote James Thompson in 1860. "It seems ridiculous to have the whole field stopped, and frequently with no chance of advantage to either side, just to let an individual be momentarily the centre of attraction and make a guy a hero of himself, according as he is a good or bad kick[8]." But the system was maintained and developed into one of the game's defining arts. 'Free Kick' in his May 1864 article in *Bell's Life* was all in favour of it, writing that "it makes the players on each side smarter when the ball is near the goal … when the kick is made, the ball generally takes an upward course, thereby causing that most enlivening scene, a charge on both sides to get first catch or kick at the falling ball. Without this catching and free kick, the game would be much tamer." It has generally been said that high marking was an element that came into Australian football later, but this description suggests that something like it was present from the start. After all, Free Kick believed football made for "capital training for cricket", and catching flying balls is about the only thing the two sports really have in common.

---

[8] *Victorian Cricketer's Guide* (1860).

In the 1870s, with a win at all costs mentality creeping into the game, teams spotted a handy loophole in the rules. The 'little mark' became the subject of major controversy. What it involved was a player claiming a mark, and then kicking the ball a tiny distance to another player who would claim a mark of his own. And so on up the pitch. This clearly wouldn't do, and the response was to introduce a rule saying the ball would have to travel at least six yards (about five and a half metres) before a mark could be called (the distance now being considerably longer at fifteen metres).

Popular legend has it that Essendon's Charlie Pearson was the creator of the high mark in the 1880s. An article in *The Argus* once said that "while Mr Pearson takes risks with his rocket-like leaps into the air, who knows but that this may be a new revolution in high marking. What a thrill the game would become as a spectacle if all players tried out this new idea. Perhaps in years to come we will see players all over the field sailing up in the air in this 'Pearson-like' fashion." By saying this was 'a revolution in high marking', the article itself is saying that it was not high-marking in itself that was new, but Pearson's way of doing it. Although he may have been a fine exponent of the art and taken it to another level, he could not possibly have invented anything new, because match reports for the last three decades had been referring to them. Way back in 1862, a *Bell's Life* report of a game between Melbourne and Geelong tells how "one Melbourne youth jumped wonderfully high in the air and caught the ball .... and called 'mark'."

Running away with it

Rugby, of course, was a whole lot more liberal regarding what you could do with your hands, but the Melbourne game preferred to go soccer's way and prohibit throwing entirely. But one thing that the 1859 rules fail to make very clear is whether or not players were allowed to run with the ball as they could in rugby. They probably couldn't, but nobody felt the need to mention that in writing. A modification to the rules in 1860 makes amends by stating that "it shall not be run with in any case." But the more rugby-minded among the footballers were reluctant to take too much notice. Several early 1860s references clearly suggest that although it was illegal, there was plenty of running with the ball going on, such as *Bell's Life's* sportswriter in 1864 who was most upset to observe that "frequently a player would run 20 yards with ball in hand. This may be in accordance with Rugby rules but certainly is not with those of Melbourne" Running with the ball has been cited as one of the most likely indicators of a rugby origin for Aussie rules, but rather than a legal part of the play, it was discouraged and eventually outlawed from a very early stage.

A compromise of sorts was reached in that players were allowed to run with the ball, but they had to bounce it on the ground as they went, a law that they seemed to find difficult to get players to uphold, with HCA Harrison himself reportedly one of the worst culprits, often showing a fine Webb Ellis-esque disregard for the rules and pelting about the pitch with without bouncing the ball once.

A KICK UP THE BEHIND

Said to be the fastest player in the city, and weighing in at well over 13 stone, a charging Harrison was not something to be taken lightly, and being captain of Melbourne, he seemed to think he could get away with anything he wanted. But he met his match in JE Clark of Royal Park in 1865, who decided that if Harrison could do it, then he would do it too. Clark ran even more than the bounce-less forty yards or so that Harrison was renowned for covering, and finished the run with a kick at goal. Clark's captain, Theodore Marshall, writing a year or so later, remembered with glee how Harrison had protested that such a run was not fair, Marshall explaining that "I simply wanted to settle once and for all how far a man should be allowed to run with the ball without bouncing it. After consultation it was agreed that the ball should be bounced at least once in every ten yards, and so this important point in our game was brought about[9]."

Where Melbourne did follow the rugby game of the era was in allowing tripping and pushing, although it drew an early line when it came to hacking, which Cambridge's soccer rules had also condemned. Early Australian rules was, by almost all accounts, a rough game, and here again we find Harrison causing trouble. In 1870, there was major outcry when he deliberately took out an Albert Park player and then jumped him while he was on the ground. Harrison's famous response was that "football is essentially a rough game all the world over, and it is not suitable for men-poodles and milksops[10]." He felt the game featured far too many "old women in disguise."

The Australasian in May 1869 mentions that the only way to "inflict summary vengeance" on the new breed of player, the 'dodger', was to employ "scuffing, holding and shirt-tearing." The 'dodger', meanwhile, "in trying to get away, and refusing to let the ball drop, would naturally look for assistance to his side, who would try to force him from the grip of his opponent; many from both sides would rush in, and ... would be mixed up in an indescribable heap of legs, arms, bodies and heads."

But a month later, the same newspaper was clearly more impressed with Melbourne's approach to the game than that of their more rugby versed opponents from the Garrison, who had "improved very much in the game, and if they could be induced to forego hugging and hitting, and to trust more to good kicking and dexterity in dodging, they would play a game more in accordance with what football is understood to be in Victoria ... A scrimmage from which half-a-dozen men emerge in a semi-nude state may be very amusing, and in some people's breasts may cause pleasant reminiscences of Donnybrook, but it is not football according to recognised rules, and is only calculated to beget ill-feeling, but we suppose it is useless to draw attention to what has been pointed out so often before without effect."

Victoria may have regulated the game first, but rugby had since arrived on the shores of Australia, and a rift developed between those who preferred the purely Victorian game, and those who were keen to see elements of the other thrown in. In his letter to Tom Wills of

---

[9] TS Marshall *The Rise and Progress of the Australian Game of Football* (1865).
[10] *The Australasian* (July 30, 1870).

MIKE ROBERTS – THE SAME OLD GAME: CODIFICATION

1871, James Thompson lamented how their "noble and manly game" was fit only for "the roughs of Little Bourke streets and the wharves", which indicates that even though the original designers of the game had wanted to create something that rejected the violence more associated to the rugby game, they had not necessarily succeeded.

The 1866 revised rules suggested that "in case of the ball being forced (except with the hand or arms) between the goalposts in a scrummage, a goal shall be awarded." In 1872, this was amended, and goals could only be scored by kicking, although the 1874 rules were still defining the scrummage as something that "commences when the ball is on the ground, and all who have closed round on their respective sides begin kicking at it[11]." This was undoubtedly a major element of the early game, and the overall weight of a team was as much a decisive factor as any individual kicking skills. All of this seems to have happened just as HCA Harrison was becoming the most influential man in Victorian football but when the Victorian Football Association was formed in 1877, the game was dramatically shifting away from the similarities to rugby that the 'father of Australian football' would probably have preferred to keep. One of the umpire's most important roles was to "stop all attempts at scrimmages", all hacking and tripping was now prohibited, and "pushing with the hands or body is allowed only when a player is in rapid motion within five or six yards of the ball. Holding a player is allowed only while such player has the ball in hand."

Wizards of Oz

The rules written, football in Melbourne was ready for its first season, and in July 1859, *The Argus* report of the game between Melbourne and South Yarra at the MCC happily proclaimed that "it is worthy of notice that the game was conducted throughout with the most perfect good feeling on both sides, and that in each case of acknowledged infringement of the Melbourne rules, a 'free kick' was conceded without a murmur." Likely story.

Victorian football had been invented, and William Hammersley, writing much later in 1883, proudly proclaimed that he and his friends in 1859 had produced "the rules under which the game is universally played in Victoria and most other parts of Australia," that they were deliberately simple "so that anyone could quickly understand them" and he was "sure that neither the Rugby or Association rules will ever supplant them."

A year after helping to draw up the original rules, James Thompson found himself publishing the annual *Victorian Cricketer's Guide*[12]. Here he described the lay of the

---

[11] Although it is said that Australian football never had an offside law, there must have been at least the seed of one in these scrummages where players "closed round on their respective sides."

[12] After the previous editor, William Fairfax, had quit the job after making a loss on the two previous editions. As a financial benefit, the *Guide* was no better for Thompson, but it's good for us, because his inclusion of a small section on football provides invaluable reading. He offers a series of fascinating *Hints to Footballers*. It's hard to work out whether they are tongue in cheek or not, including one that "if an adversary is running with the

footballing land in the colony at the time. "Football, as played in Victoria, is now fit to run alone. I have accordingly omitted the Rugby and Eton rules, because we seem to have agreed to a code of our own … The new rule, which prohibits lifting the ball from the ground and running with it, has worked most satisfactorily. The games have been better contested and the difficulty of obtaining goals made greater … Football in and about Melbourne promises soon to be as much an institution of the wet as cricket is of the dry season. Last season several new clubs sprang into existence, for instance the Richmond, the Collingwood and the University, nor did any of the old ones exhibit any symptoms of decline. The Melbourne Club, by whose rules … the game in Victoria is now universally played, still retains its supremacy, having suffered but one defeat throughout a long season, and then from having a weak side."

These were not just the oldest Australian football clubs. They were some of the oldest of any code or nationality. In fact, in 1859, there may well have been more established football clubs in Victoria than the whole of Britain.

The English granddaddies of soccer, Sheffield FC, had only been formed in 1857. Soon after, what went on to become rugby clubs were formed in Liverpool, Blackheath and Edinburgh. Earlier claims, such as Barnes and Guy's Hospital, are based on some pretty dodgy evidence. The oldest British example of a football club that is still playing in the top flight these days is Sale Rugby Club, formed in 1861, and it is rare for there to be any teams in soccer's English Premiership that were formed any earlier than the 1870s, although at the time of writing Stoke City (formed in 1863 as the Stoke Ramblers) are a rare exception.

But formed way back in 1859, the Melbourne Football Club is still in the AFL. Also formed in 1859 was the Melbourne University Football Club, which only exists today when it plays inter-university matches, while the university otherwise fields a variety of different amateur teams. The Williamstown Club appeared in 1862 (the current day Williamstown FC formed two years later), South Yarra FC was founded in 1864 (who merged with the St Kilda Cricketers Club in 1873 to form the AFL's present-day St Kilda FC), while the most successful club in the history of Australian football, Carlton FC, came about in 1864. The likes of Essendon (1872) and Collingwood (1892) may have been latecomers by Australian standards, but are still a lot older than most major clubs playing any other code of football.

Desert cats

However, Graeme Atkinson[13] asserts that the clubs formed in Melbourne were actually predated by others elsewhere in Victoria. He maintains that two years earlier, in 1856, no

---

ball, kick him over unceremoniously if you can't knock it out of his hand" and "never allow boys to play amongst men. They spoil the game, no one likes to rush them and yet they are almost certain to get hurt."

[13] In his *Everything You Ever Wanted To Know About Australian Rules Football, But Couldn't Be Bothered Asking* (Five Mile Press, 1981).

MIKE ROBERTS – THE SAME OLD GAME: CODIFICATION

fewer than six clubs were established in the Geelong area[14], namely Barwon, Bellarine, Corio Bay, Flinders, Kardinia and Moorabool. Should anybody ever come across a copy of something called *The Footballer's Australian Almanac* printed in 1951, which was apparently his source material, it would be interesting to know if it offers any explanation of how this could all have been the brainchild of 1856 and 1857 champion player Tommy Wills of Corio Bay, if we know for a fact that he was still playing cricket in England at the time!

There is some potential in the Geelong argument, for the city does have an admirable footballing tradition, where in the formative years, the players were fervently proud to play by their own set of rules. But we have no specific evidence of footy's presence in the rival city before April 1859 when Stitt Jenkins suggested a club, but not necessarily the first club, should be established in the town. He was a fervent supporter of the temperance movement that was all the rage at the time, promoting sport instead of booze, and the *Geelong Advertiser* agreed that "the game is one of the healthiest and easiest that could be adopted by persons cramped during the week by desk or counter service and standing in need of a little bracing exercise." In July of the same year, the *Advertiser* commented on a meeting at the Victoria Hotel to discuss arrangements for a game, where it was agreed that a committee would be set up after the match, presumably with the discussion of rules high on the agenda.

Geelong was certainly going it alone, but there is no reason to believe that they were creating their own rules in any kind of reaction to those being devised in Melbourne, or anywhere else for that matter. More probably, they weren't aware that any other rules even existed, for not even the idea of travelling the few miles along the coast to play games in Melbourne was a realistic possibility yet.

Geelong's separate football culture was probably a short-lived thing. If 1859 was the year of the first surviving record, that was also the year that *The Argus* reported how "in Geelong, football has been taken up enthusiastically, and we learn that the GDF purpose playing by the rules of the Melbourne Club[15]."

A year later, in 1860, Tom Wills really did move to the area, joined shortly after by HCA Harrison, and the two undoubtedly exerted as much of an influence on the Geelong game as they had already done in Melbourne.

---

[14] Located further to the west along the shores of Port Phillip, the same bay as Melbourne, there were already 454 people living in Geelong as early as 1838, making it the larger of the two settlements at the time, and the story goes that when gold was found at Ballarat in 1851, false maps were provided to prospectors by Melbournians that wrongly implied that their town was the best gateway to the goldfields. If that had not happened, Geelong would probably have become the major city in the region. But Geelong still grew, to around 23,000 people in the 1850s, and in 1857 the first rail link connected it to Melbourne.

[15] The Geelong Football Club is still around, now called the Cats and playing in front of over 40,000 fans a game. After winning their sixth Premiership in 1963, they then lost five Grand Finals before finally celebrating a return to glory in 2007 when they won by a record margin of 119 points against Port Adelaide Power, and won the title again in 2009.

Apart from the Geelong counter-claim, there is also the popular idea that the real origins of Australian football lie far from the urban centres, and out on the goldfields. It is much more quaint to imagine how men arrived in their thousands to put their hopeless lives in Europe behind them in search of the dream of Australian gold, and it was there, shaded from the baking sunshine by the dust clouds, that the gold-diggers spent their evenings perfecting a game of football that reflected the wild, rugged and open nature of the promised land. Records of football on the goldfields do indeed rival those from the city in the antiquity stakes, but the evidence suggests that, like in Geelong, the former adopted the Melbourne rules and not vice versa.

The two main goldfields were at Bendigo and Ballarat. At Bendigo, the first evidence of football was a club called Sandhurst, formed on June 3, 1961 and whose secretary was the same James Thompson who we know was in Melbourne two years earlier helping to draw up the original Melbourne rules. After a haphazard practice match, they faced a team of volunteer soldiers in a game that was carried over two days from June 15 to June 16, with Sandhurst scoring the only goal. A game on June 29 had to be abandoned because the field became unplayable as more and more people gathered for the celebrations of the Feast of Saints Peter and Paul.

But 40 km west in Castlemaine, evidence not discovered until 2007 revealed that their local club was formed on June 15, 1859 at the Supreme Court Hotel, and played its first game a week later on the Barkers Creek cricket ground. That makes it the second oldest football club in the country, and they still compete today in the Bendigo Football League.

In Ballarat, the fourth biggest city in Australia at the time, shopkeeper John Little was advertising footballs imported from England as early as January 1860. In April of the same year, the Ballarat Athletics Club announced a long list of sporting activities for its meeting, and squeezed in at number 18 was a football game. On New Year Day 1862, the Wesleyan Sabbath School played cricket, and as what seemed to be a side-attraction, others "employed themselves at football", while the same year the trade unionist Eight Hours and Early Closing Association organised a football game that "furnished amusement and exercise."

By 1862, there was certainly a senior team in action, playing on a paddock next to the cemetery, where the players "cannoned against each other" to such an extent that one player dislocated a shoulder and the game was called off.

So, there is no denying that early football was played on the goldfields, and also Geelong, and quite feasibly even earlier than in Melbourne. But there is less certainty that the football they played was of any particular relevance to the early development of Australian rules football.

Victorian to Australian

The natural progression would have been for the Victorian game to go on to conquer the whole country and become the national code as occurred in America. But it didn't. This

MIKE ROBERTS – THE SAME OLD GAME: CODIFICATION

unique breed of football remained almost entirely confined to Victoria for most of the 1860s. It would eventually spread to the other colonies, but by that time, footballers also had the option of adopting the newly written British rules for soccer and rugby. And just because the Victorian game had been created in the antipodes did not necessarily mean it was going to be the automatic choice.

South Australia is the state immediately west of Victoria, with Adelaide as its capital, and that was the next colony to take an interest in the football craze. In April 1860, the *South Australian Register* announced a plan to form a football club at the Globe Inn[16], and the following Saturday a game was played before "a large muster both of members and spectators" and one team "obtained one or two more goals than their opponents."

The paper was obviously going to have to learn to improve on in its sports reporting skills. Its reports of matches generally preferred to concentrate on the names of the dignitaries in attendance than details of the actual matches, which were often limited to just naming the captains and giving the scores. Despite games going on until it was too dark to carry on, all we know for sure is that the early Adelaide game rarely produced many goals and doesn't seem to have been the most organised of affairs. A meeting was held in March 1873 between the three main teams in the city (Port Adelaide, Adelaide and Kensington), and they convened to agree upon a set of rules, so we can assume that there were no established ones before that. They are said to have been modelled on soccer, but the problems persisted. A game between Port Adelaide and Kensington in 1873 ended in such confusion that they couldn't even agree who had won, and a game between Port Adelaide and Adelaide in 1875 degenerated into little more than an argument over the rules.

As the decade wears on, we start getting a clearer idea of what South Australian football was like, and the early goal posts make it clear that whatever they were playing, Aussie rules it was not. It had almost identical posts to rugby's 'H' shaped variety, with an excellent addition. As well as the wooden crossbar 8 feet from the ground, there was a rope 8 feet above that. Goals were scored by kicking the ball between the two, which must have provided an interesting challenge.

There seemed to be other elements of rugby influence, in that players could run with the ball as much as they liked, and unlike in Aussie rules, players were not obliged to release the ball when they were tackled. But by 1876, there seemed to be a shift, which was when the game adopted two free-standing posts. The South Adelaide captain happened to be a former Carlton man in George D Kennedy, and maybe there is something in the fact that the leading club in the state that year was called 'Victorian'.

Enter Richard Twopenny, an Englishman who had played the rugby-like game at Marlborough, and turned out to be a more than handy new recruit for Adelaide, being their

---

[16] Blainey finds it hard to believe the story that HCA Harrison was in town in 1860 to promote the game, partly because Harrison was not yet a major figure on the football scene in that year, and partly because it is odd he would not have mentioned such a pivotal moment anywhere in his memoirs.

A KICK UP THE BEHIND

leading scorer that season with the mighty total of one goal. He was made captain the following year and it was he who suggested the time had come to form a South Australian Football Association and abandon their forlorn attempts to establish some kind of rules and just adopt the Victorian ones instead. He had been soundly impressed with them on a visit to Melbourne, writing in his *Town Life in Australia* that "I feel bound to say that the Victorian game is by far the most scientific, the most amusing to both players and onlookers, and altogether the best."

His hope was to get some matches organised between the two colonies, and his wish came true in August 1877, when both Melbourne and St Kilda braved several days of sea voyage to reach Adelaide and play a series of three games against local opposition. Crowds in excess of 3000 turned out at Adelaide Oval to see how the superiority of the Victorian players was painfully evident. In July 1879, Victoria sent its first ever representative side to face South Australia, where *The Australian* was glad to see "all club jealousy completely banished … for the honour and fame of the colony." Enough had been done to sow the seeds of a long-lasting friendship, and the Victorian code has been the dominant one in South Australia ever since.

Just over the Bass Strait from Victoria lies Tasmania, which until 1855 was still known as Van Diemen's Land. That too proved to be a happy hunting ground for the Victorian game. Football had existed on the island for some time, the earliest known reference appearing in *The Courier* in February 1851, when a festival in Hobart was offering prizes for such sports as cricket and hurley, as well as other events like 'jumping in sacks' and a fascinating sounding 'jingling match'. Football was a fair way down the schedule and confined to the 'in addition' section, ranked in importance alongside 'climbing the pole for a hat' and the terrific 'running for pigs with a soaped tail'. Two years later, in August 1853, the Richmond Jubilee to commemorate "the cessation of transportation to Van Diemen's Land" included 'foot-ball' among the numerous festive events mentioned in *The Courier*, and although a year later the 'Richmond Ploughing Match' was grabbing all the attention, "a foot-ball and other sports will take place during the day."

The constant low-billing hardly suggests these games were taken very seriously. However, by the time of a report that appeared in the *Hobart Mercury* in 1866, football was an altogether more high-profile affair. This match had "a good attendance of spectators and some capital play. The first goal was won after about an hour's tussle … but at about half past four o'clock the rain came down so sharply as to prevent a continuance of the game." By 1871, the *Mercury* was able to proclaim that "football reigns supreme in the various academical playgrounds throughout the colony."

Tasmania had strong links with Victoria and received less direct immigrants from Britain than most parts of Australia, but all their footballing ideas were not necessary brought to them from Victoria. Sean Fagan writes that as late as the 1870s reports in Tasmania "refer to the two goal posts having a cross-bar, goals not counting unless over the cross-bar,

MIKE ROBERTS – THE SAME OLD GAME: CODIFICATION

unrestricted running with the ball, on-side rules, 'scrimmages ensued for some time', kick-offs from half-way, and place kick 'tries at goal', amidst other matches that included mentions of the awarding of a mark from a team mate's kick, bouncing of the ball while running, no off-side laws, and 'a drawback to the early matches in town has been the variety of rules' between the clubs[17]."

For several years, there was a conflict between local, rugby and Victorian interests, and if a proposed visit by a touring English side had come off in 1879, rugby may well have prospered on the island. But in May 1883, *The Sydney Mail* wrote that the Tasmanian Football Association had finally managed to standardise its game through "particularly the abolition of the crossbar and the assimilation of the laws to those of Victoria," and a month later was saying that "it may be stated the Victorian game is played everywhere in the 'tight little island'."

And they were good at it. Their rose, primrose and black uniforms may not have looked too macho, but the Tasmanians managed to teach the Victorians a thing or two, giving clubs like Geelong and Carlton such a beating that *The Australian* was moved to remark that "whilst we might, with regret, permit our neighbours from the other side of the gutter to forge ahead of us in political or mercantile matters, we are not true Victorian if we give in to them at football."

The other stronghold of the Australian game is Western Australia, although things were not always that way. The Australian Rugby Union's website claims that in Perth "there are reports of early games of rugby between the army and the crews of visiting ships being played at Barrack Square in the city in the 1820s." It is certainly conceivable that they played some form of football, but less conceivable that it was 'rugby' in the strictest sense, since the game barely existed in a defined form at the time.

A regiment of soldiers that had only three months previously been playing in Melbourne enjoyed a game of football in Perth in 1868, but even if that game was played to the Victorian rules, it failed to spark off a Western Australian love affair with them. In the ensuing years, it was rugby that became the stronger code in the state, and although there were two clubs in the early 1880s, the Unions and Swans, playing the Victorian way, they were a curious exception to the norm.

But by the end of the decade, the pendulum swung unexpectedly the other way. Wealthy Perth families were in the habit of sending their kids to the posh schools in Adelaide, where Victorian rules was strong, and there was also a strong current in the local press against the excessive violence involved in rugby. This, coupled with a massive population flow westwards following the discovery of gold in the colony, led to such a boom in the popularity of the Victorian game that one of the leading rugby clubs, Fremantle, decided to switch codes

---

[17] In *Rugby in the Colony of Tasmania* at www.colonialrugby.com.au.

in 1885. Other clubs soon followed suit, and virtually overnight Australian rules was the dominant code in a region where it had never looked like standing a chance.

Clash of the codes

By 1883, the game was spreading with such success that the Intercolonial Football Conference was founded, and one of its earliest decisions was to try to bin the term 'Victorian' football, and promote it instead as 'Australasian', which suggests they were confident the game would eventually rule supreme not only in the colonies of Australia, but all over Oceania. But although some parts of Australia were converted with relative ease, others were less easily convinced.

It was in New South Wales and Queensland that Australian rules hit upon the biggest barriers. The simplified version is that rugby had got there first, which to a certain extent is true, but when the Victorian code started moving north, there was plenty of potential for expansion in a region where football of any description was nothing like as massive as it was in Victoria. The earliest claim to any kind of team in the eastern states was the Sydney University Football Club[18] in the mid 1860s, but the Southern Rugby Football Union (SRFU), the *very* southern branch of the British RFU, didn't form to officially decree that football should be played by the Rugby rules until 1874, claiming there were twelve clubs in Sydney. Not bad, but this was nothing like the number in what at the time was the considerably larger city of Melbourne, where if we believe what Mr Twopenny had to say, there were about eight times more clubs and ten times more spectators on any given Saturday.

In Sydney, football was the domain of a hardcore clique from the established classes, many of whom were public school old boys, and among whom there was a far more conservative association with British values than the liberal go-our-own-way mood of the more vibrant football scene in Melbourne. They knew all about Victorian football, but the elite preferred to turn a deaf ear to the mutterings that they should take the former's lead and include more drop kicking and less of rugby's tedious scrummaging.

When the Victorian Football Association was formed in 1877, one of its main motives was to start getting some intercolonial games organised, as was already common between cricketers. They were aware that the SRFU was more rugby inclined, but still sent them an enthusiastic letter suggesting that if the rules were likely to be a problem, then they could play one game using one set and another using the other.

Sydney was not up for it. They replied that "after mature deliberation, it was decided not to entertain the proposal at present, the Union being of the opinion that the intricacies of the 'Off and Onside' rules of the Rugby game were far too difficult to be readily understood in

---

[18] Although both the rugby and Aussie rules community like to lay a claim to that one, the chances are whatever rules the students played by, they were a bit of both and a bit of neither before settling for rugby in 1869.

such a brief space of time to ensure perfect harmony … and that the contest had better bide the time when the rules in the respective colonies had become assimilated." The assumption was that sooner or later, and somehow or other, Sydney and Melbourne would eventually be playing the same kind of football[19].

There was going to be a lot of time to bide, and one club that wasn't prepared to wait an eternity was the Waratah team[20], who defied the SRFU and invited Carlton up to play them, saying they had no qualms about giving "the public an opportunity of deciding on the merits of the respective styles of play." No doubt egged on by one of their top players, W Newing, who had starred for Carlton a few years before, Waratah seemed keen to prove the point that the Victorian rules had something rugby could learn from, and in 1882 actually switched to that code for a while.

A crowd of 3000, the biggest to date for a football match in Sydney, assembled in June 1877 to watch Waratah beat Carlton 2-0 in the first game in the series, played by the rugby rules. Carlton "struggled in the most valiant manner to cope with the difficulties" in a game in which most of the players were often "piled one on top of the other on the ground."

Far fewer were in there two days later to see the same sides go at in a way Carlton understood better, and the visitors easily won 6-0. It seems those who had seen both matches "were unanimous in their preference of the game as played under the Victorian rules." A year later, Waratah travelled for a couple of return matches in Melbourne, and this time things were more competitive. The rugby match was drawn, and Carlton won under Victorian, but it was anything but the rout of the previous year.

Encouraged by such success, the VFA once again approached the SRFU in search of intercolonial matches, but were given the nonsensical reply that there was no venue in Sydney "for matches of so great interest", and the SRFU's vice-president Thomas Arnold (an Old Rugbeian but no relation to the former headmaster), unabated by the news of the successful Waratah v Carlton clashes, considered the idea "almost frivolous." Arnold was already toying with the idea of representative rugby matches with Australia's other major rugby community, Queensland, and also with New Zealand and maybe even tourists from Britain. With all that to look forward to, he wanted to know nothing of the pesky Victorians and their silly rules.

But the kinky sounding 'Leather Stocking' in the *Sydney Mail* tells us there were plenty in the city with other ideas, saying "it is pretty well understood ... that there are scores of

---

[19] It should be noted that the first tour of Australasia by a British select team in 1888, over a decade later, included 19 games played by the Victorian rules and rather than face difficulties, the tourists won six of them and drew another. It clearly was possible for rugby and Victorian teams to play each other, if they wanted.

[20] 'Waratah' is the name of an indigenous flowering shrub, which would eventually become the nickname of the NSW representative team from 1882 onwards, and then the fully professional NSW Waratahs when Super 12 began in 1996.

A KICK UP THE BEHIND

footballers ... who play the Rugby game under protest as it were, and who would gladly welcome a radical change in the present method of playing football."

The rugby crowd had inherited their 'us and them' attitude from their northern hemisphere colleagues, but there was also a strong element of interstate rivalry involved too. As 'Orange and Blue' put it "the great objection to the rules in New South Wales was that they were styled the Victorian Rules of Football. Had they been dubbed the Scandinavian rules, well and good, but Victorian – perish the thought!"

The 'rebels' in NSW that preferred to go with the Victorian code grouped together as the NSWFA, but by 1881 they still only had about five clubs in the whole state, compared to rugby's thirty or so, and the schools were all playing rugby. After sending a side down to get soundly thrashed 9-0 in Melbourne, the NSWFA's big chance came when they were even allowed to use the Sydney cricket ground for the return match. 5000 spectators came to see it, but Aussie rules in Sydney probably blew it that day when they were humiliated 9-1.

Those defeats did Victorian rules more harm than anything else. Australians, from whichever part, do not like losing. Being so severely outclassed at the Victorian game merely convinced the Sydneysiders that rugby was the game for them, and when Melbourne FC came on a three-match tour later that year, winning all three games easily, they preferred to look the other way. If anything, the NSWFA was just the wakeup call rugby in New South Wales needed. As Leather Stocking put it, if it hadn't been for the threat of Victorian football, rugby in Sydney "might have gone on for years in the same humdrum style", but instead it went from strength to strength. Rugby had to be strong, or it stood be overthrown by the Victorians.

Further north, in Queensland, there was something of a Victorian football community developing, with Ipswich and Brisbane playing the game from 1870, and the _Australasian_ once noted how some clubs had "discarded the rugby rules" to play "the more popular Victorian game." Queensland and Victoria were just too far apart in the 1870s for any regular footballing contact, and having the rugby-minded New South Wales in between didn't help. Nevertheless, Ipswich even managed to beat a touring Essendon side, who reported back to Melbourne on some fine progress being made in Queensland. This battle for supremacy with rugby was dealt a cruel blow in 1887, when a meeting of the Independent Schools voted by just one vote to go for rugby rather than Victorian, apparently put off by the idea that a sport passing itself off as 'Victorian' was hardly in the interest of Queenslanders. That decision was largely influential when the state decided to form its own governing body for football and opted to side with the SRFU. It was downhill from there on for Aussie rules in Queensland, and when South Melbourne faced a Queensland select on Albion Park in 1888, the visitors' 6-17 to 1-0 annihilation of their hosts speaks volumes. By the end of the century, the Victorian rules were practically unheard of in the Sunshine State.

And so it was. Australian rules thrived in Victoria, South Australia, Tasmania and Western Australia, but the east of the country was destined for a rugby culture. And so it stayed for

243

MIKE ROBERTS – THE SAME OLD GAME: CODIFICATION

most of the 20th century, and to a large extent the sporting geography of 19th century Australia still holds true today.

Reciprocal imperialism

Whatever the code, in the first half of the 20th century most countries developed nationwide football competitions. But not so Australia, where football leagues were based around states. The distances involved and the fiercely regional nature of Australia have been blamed, but the real reason was that the country was divided between Australian football in the west and rugby in the east (where rugby league superseded rugby union as the dominant code following the advent of professionalism).

The fortunes of the respective sports followed very similar patterns, whereby originally it was one particular state's competition that was vastly stronger than the others. In the case of rugby league, this was the New South Wales RFL, set up in 1908, and which apart from a few clubs that came and went, never really had any teams from outside of Sydney itself until as late as 1982, when Illawarra Steelers and Canberra Raiders[21] joined. Queensland, meanwhile, had its own Brisbane Rugby League (BRL), which despite the name, was effectively a state-wide competition. However, proximity to NSW did not help matters, and any decent rugby-playing Queenslander would soon be packing his bags and heading for the richer and better supported league in the south.

Australian football's fate was comparable. South Australia and Western Australia had strong championships of their own (even today the SANFL gathers an average of 3000 spectators a match), but Victoria and especially Melbourne remained the hotbed of the sport, and was the natural destiny for any aspiring Australian footballer whatever his origin, especially when Carlton, Collingwood, Essendon, Fitzroy, Geelong, Melbourne, St Kilda and South Melbourne broke away to form the Victorian Football League in 1896[22].

As the 20th century wore on, and especially thanks to the dawn of television, the VFL started seeing the potential of expanding beyond the Victorian border. It was in 1982 that a controversial move occurred when the struggling South Melbourne opted, to the devastation of its fans, to relocate to the rugby league heartland and become the Sydney Swans. It was a successful move, with the antics of the flamboyant high marker Warwick Capper, blond mullet, pink Ferrari and all, helping to boost attendances to an average of 25,000 a match.

The Swans project provided the impetus for the VFL to consider further expansion, and two further non-Victorian sides were admitted in 1987 in the form of the artificially created

---

[21] The latter, being from the Australian Capital Territory were strictly speaking the first non-NSW member, but the ACT is really just a political enclave located entirely within New South Wales.

[22] Before that, the VFA had simply announced its Premier Team at the end of the season based on the results of exhibition matches. It is never very clear what criteria, if any, were applied to make a decision that would make voting for the Eurovision Song Contest seem perfectly fair in comparison.

franchises of West Coast Eagles based in Perth[23] and a team from the other 'rugby league' state, Queensland, the Brisbane Bears[24].

In 1990, the VFL rebranded itself as the Australian Football League, something akin to soccer's English Premiership suddenly deciding to rebrand itself the European Super League and invite the top foreign clubs to join. But the AFL was something of a misnomer considering it didn't feature any clubs from South Australia. The SANFL, dating back to 1877 and not just the oldest football league in the country but also the world, was soundly unimpressed when its biggest club, Port Adelaide, started showing an interest in defecting to the AFL. The bitter row still raises tension in South Australia, whereby the SANFL stepped in with a counter-bid, the formation of a brand new franchise team, Adelaide, and offered to provide them with the finest infrastructure and financial backing the state could offer. It was a bid Port Adelaide could not possibly match. To add insult to injury, Port suffered the loss of several top players to the new franchise[25].

Six years after the VFL had moved beyond its borders for the first time, the NSWRL started following suit in 1988 by bowing to the pressure to allow two Queensland clubs to join, Brisbane Broncos and the Gold Coast-Tweed Giants. Then in 1995, the league also followed the VFL's lead and rebranded itself Australian Rugby League, bringing on board two more Queensland teams, plus the Western Reds from Perth, and even the Auckland Warriors from New Zealand.

Things got messy when a breakaway Super League threw the cat among the pigeons, a storm that was eventually calmed in 1998 with the creation of National Rugby League, which included a new franchise in Melbourne Storm. The home of Australian football was now also the home to a rugby league club! How things had changed, and a year later, in 1999, Melbourne were crowned NRL premiers. If that wasn't a bizarre enough scenario, in 2005, the Sydney Swans defeated West Coast to win the second of three consecutive AFL Grand Finals that didn't feature any team from Victoria at all.

---

[23] Although their inclusion meant the best Western Australian players could now be kept in the state, the historic clubs in the WAFL were naturally less enthusiastic to see the new franchise stealing their limelight and potential revenue. West Coast became the first non-Victorian team to win the Grand Final in 1992, and have gone on to become one of the most successful teams of the modern era.

[24] The Brisbane Bears are now the Brisbane Lions following a merger in 1996 with the Fitzroy Lions, a club that had a 113 year history behind it before the move. The spread of the Victorian code to new parts of the country has its positive aspects, but at the same time it is tragic to see clubs with so much history fade away in the good name of progress. It comes as little consolation to former Fitzroy fans to know that Brisbane won three back-to-back titles from 2001 onwards.

[25] Port Adelaide did eventually join the AFL in 1997, and it was nice to see that instead of another artificial franchise, the AFL was welcoming on board a team with a vintage that honours Australian rules' historic roots, even though Port were forced to dispose of their Magpies moniker, because Collingwood, also the Magpies, objected. Port came good in 2004, when they won their first AFL title, a historic occasion when their Grand Final against Brisbane was the first in which neither side was from Victoria.

MIKE ROBERTS – THE SAME OLD GAME: CODIFICATION

Elements of the east-west rivalry between the two codes do remain, but are far less pronounced now that the balance of football in Australia had shifted more towards personal preferences for one code or the other than the rivalry between regional traditions. But the shift in power away from the rugby league teams in Sydney and the Australian rules teams in Melbourne also comes down to those cities having to support so many traditional community-based teams, while the new franchises, often with huge financial backers, can draw on the support not just of whole cities, but sometimes entire states.

Newcomers Canberra and Brisbane won five out of the first seven premierships after the NSWRL's first expansion in 1988 to 1994. When Geelong won the AFL Grand Final in 2007, they became the first Victorian winner since Essendon in 2000, but in the meantime, Melbourne Storm (ranked the most popular sports team in Melbourne by a Roy Morgan Poll) were appearing in four consecutive NRL Grand Finals, winning two of them. There were plenty of Aussie rules stalwarts with smug grins on their faces when the Storm were stripped of those titles for breaching salary cap regulations in one of the biggest scandals ever to hit Australian sport.

Tie me socceroo down

So, what about soccer? Why did it never become part of Australian sporting lore? The answer is that it did, but perhaps it got there too late to ever become the first love anywhere in the country. The Victorian rules were written four years before the FA's, and especially in the 19th century, the two games were so similar that soccer was never really needed as an alternative. Even in NSW and Queensland, the few clubs that rejected rugby would usually see the Victorian game as the second best option. How could there be any room for soccer when there were already two codes vying for supremacy?

British rugby teams were visiting Australia from a very young age – the first (though unofficial) Lions Tour was in 1888, when a twenty-one man squad, almost entirely English, played 35 matches in Australia and New Zealand (which included 21 games played by the Victorian rules, and the tourists won six of them).

If British soccer teams had taken the trouble to tour Australia, then perhaps the clubs playing by the Victorian rules might have considered the Association rules instead. An official invitation was sent to the FA as early as 1886, but nobody answered the call. One of the main reasons must have been that while Northern Hemisphere rugby teams had to travel to the other side of the globe in search of international opposition, soccer was all over Europe by the turn of the century. Australia was simply too far away and too bereft of decent soccer clubs to bother with when there was greater potential for overseas soccer tours just a short ferry-ride away in Belgium.

However, soccer's presence in Australia was far greater than most history books have given it credit for, and there were a pioneering few who did lay foundations for the game. One of those was John Walter Fletcher, who in August 1880 formed the 'Wanderers' in Sydney to

A KICK UP THE BEHIND

play by the Association rules, and even enrolled his team with the FA, although he was a little ambitious with his hope that they would be able to supply him with regular fixtures. Indeed, for his first game later that month, he had to make do with opposition from King's School's rugby players for the first known game of codified soccer in the country, played on Parramatta Common.

Where soccer particularly thrived was in the burgeoning coalmining regions, which attracted numerous immigrants from England, Scotland and Wales, especially Ipswich in Queensland and Newcastle and the Illawarra in NSW, where soccer is still uncharacteristically popular.

Comments in the press that soccer was played by "old country enthusiasts" and "imported men" suggest that it was usually confined to newer arrivals, and contrary to its later image, it was considered the more aristocratic game. One of the earliest clubs, Balgownie Rangers of Wollongong, formed by a Scotsman called Paul Hunter sometime in the early 1880s, still exists today. In 1883, NSW and Victoria played their first intercolonial match in Melbourne, where only about 200 people turned up to watch what *The Argus* reckoned bore "about the same relation to the Victorian game that bowls does to cricket. It is not nearly so rough as the Victorian pastime, nor so exciting to the spectator; but on the other hand, the tactics are far less likely to provoke ill feeling and deliberate ill-usage." But despite a few condescending remarks from longer established Australians, the two camps generally cooperated, and the MCG seems to have had few qualms about allowing its facilities to be used for soccer matches.

It was not until 1925 that a touring English side made it to Australia. Their captain and only amateur, WC Caesar, told *Pals Magazine* that "I don't desire to say anything against your Australian game, but it is too much like Rugby to take my fancy, and Rugby, as you know, is certainly on the rough side. British Association football, on the contrary, is purely scientific football. There is practically no roughness in it. It is a matter of skill in controlling the ball with the feet and using your brains to get the best results ... As a rule, under the rugby or Australian code, a boy needs to be fairly robust to play, but the game of soccer does not call for quite so much strength."

But even more interesting are the comments made in the same article by SA Storey, chairman of the Australian Football Association. Soccer not historically big in Australia? The facts he presents shed some doubt on that. "In Sydney, there are 140 soccer school teams or 20 more than play rugby, which is the dominant code in New South Wales" he tells us. And this was 1925! "Altogether Sydney has 400 soccer clubs with 6,000 players. In Adelaide 44 clubs play the Australian game and 37 play soccer. In Queensland it is the only game that stands a chance of rivalling rugby league, while in Western Australia it is making strides." Judging by these figures, although there was no single state where soccer was the number one sport, in terms of total figures, it may well have been the most widespread of all!

MIKE ROBERTS – THE SAME OLD GAME: CODIFICATION

Interestingly, Victoria was the only state in which soccer struggled, but even there not everybody felt that the VFL was the be all and end all, as this article in a 1921 edition of *The Sporting Globe* suggests: "Soccer football was first introduced into Victoria in the 80s, but after 3 years it died down to almost extinction. This was due in a large measure to the migration to various parts of the Commonwealth of those who were responsible for the inception of the game. In 1908 a body of enthusiasts from the old country … met with a view to resuscitating the game and their efforts met with success … until 1914, when in common with other sports it experienced a setback owing to the war … at the present time soccer is in a better position than ever before in Victoria. There are 22 teams engaged in competition and the membership list is in the neighbourhood of 600."

Although Hakoah drew upon the Jewish community, most of the Victorian teams were British influenced, but Roy Hay notes how "one or two continental players began to appear, including Schaufelberger of St Kilda, a member of the Swiss Consular Staff in Melbourne, while Melbourne Welsh signed Larenzo, a new arrival from Italy[26]."

This was just the start of a soccer boom assisted by the biggest influx of immigrants since the gold rush, over 36,000 in the first half of the 1920s, many coming from post-war Britain in search of a new start. But although these brought more soccer into Australia than ever before, Rugby and Rules were now the games of the establishment, and frictions started to emerge. Hay quotes a Mr C Ensby who remarked on "the feeling that appeared to exist among a certain section of the public that the 'soccer' club was there to oust the Australian game." There was probably a fear of Aussie rules getting swallowed up beneath the wing of the expanding force of soccer, which by the 1930s was already holding World Cups, while the Australian game had not even managed to convince everybody in its own country.

It was after the Second World War that the face of football in Australia really changed, when waves of immigrants, particularly from Greece, Italy and Eastern Europe, streamed into the country, and often preferred to stick to the soccer they knew. Whether this was because they did not want to integrate, or whether the 'Anglo' Australians did not make them overly welcome, is a matter for debate, but it was probably a bit of both. The newcomers expanded soccer's presence but also tarnished its social prestige in a country where multiculturalism has not always been to everyone's taste.

It didn't help that they also imported their rivalries from the Old Continent. It is impossible to underestimate the impact the Europeanization of Australia had its soccer scene. Clubs sprung up that were firmly attached to ethic roots, or others were taken over by certain immigrant communities. Geelong Soccer Club was renamed IAMA (the Italian Australian Migrants Association), Richmond was essentially a German club, Melbourne was Hungarian, and then there were Polonia (Polish), South Melbourne Hellas (Greek), Slavia

---

[26] Roy Hay *British Football, Wogball or the World Game?: Towards a social history of Victorian Soccer* in John O'Hara (ed.), *Ethnicity and Soccer in Australia, ASSH Studies in Sports History,* Australian Society for Sports History, 1994, amended 2005)

(Czechoslovak), Juventus (Italian), JUST (Serbian) and others. They even set up the 'New World Cup', played for the first time in 1955 by teams representing Holland, Italy, Hungary, Scotland, Croatia, Germany, England, Macedonia and Ukraine. None of this went down too well with the locals, and Roy Hay notes how soccer rapidly switched from the sports pages of the *Geelong Advertiser* to the section dealing with 'New Australians'.

Johnny Warren, who played for the 'Socceroos' in their first ever World Cup appearance in 1974, titled his memoirs *Sheilas, Wogs, and Poofters*, which pretty much sums up where soccer stood on the social scale. Soccer was now 'wogball' and shunned as a plaything for immigrants. Children unable to get into the Rugby or Rules teams faced the humiliation of being sent to play soccer instead and the media did little to encourage this most un-Australian of sports. It was more interested in condemning the violence and inter-ethnic rivalries it spawned than the games themselves, and this negative coverage, though sometimes warranted, was rarely impartial.

Writes Hay, "violence associated with Australian rules was just as rife in the 1950s and 1960s ... Fights at the main VFA game between Port Melbourne and Yarraville were continued outside the ground after police had intervened in June 1952. For every soccer incident I find in this period I can trace something associated with football, which is reported in a very different manner. The violence in both may be condemned, but there is no racist or xenophobic content in the latter ... in 1952 one match and its aftermath received 102 column inches at a minimum over six weeks, at a time when the normal soccer report ran to around 10 ... The only occasions when Ballarat soccer was reported in Geelong in 1959 that I have come across occurred when there were attacks on referees."

Soccer was there, but very few 'real' Australians either wanted it or wished to recognise it. Hay describes how "a Greek youngster in Adelaide recalls going down to the soccer club on the morning before a game to earn sixpence by clearing the pitch of broken glass, which had been strewn there to hinder the playing of soccer." But there are now more people playing soccer than any other code of football in Australia, and as second and third generation immigrants have become more and more assimilated into mainstream Australian culture, so has soccer, with television coverage of European games also raising the profile of the sport. Ox Tam, the agency which monitors TV viewing figures in Australia, stated that 3,474,000 people in the country watched the 2002 FIFA World Cup Final, more than the 3,425,000 who watched that year's AFL Grand Final. A Channel 7 survey in March 1999 revealed that AFL was the favourite code of 30% of Australians, rugby league weighed in with a mere 12% and rugby union a paltry 4%. Soccer, meanwhile, topped the list with 37%!

The 'wog' element is fading. In 2005, the country established its first pro league, the A-League, which at a sweep eliminated all remnants of 'ethnic' clubs and created a new one-club, one-city format. The same year, Australian soccer really hit the limelight when the national side finally made it back into World Cup Finals by beating Uruguay on penalties. Soccer attained a higher profile in the country than ever before at Germany 2006, with the

Aussies making it through to the last sixteen. Parks in the major cities were flooded with crowds watching giant screens, and the game with Italy was the most watched TV show of the week. All that was missing was the win, for a fine Australian display was thwarted when Italy won thanks to a very dodgy penalty decision. Australia wept at the injustice of it all. At last, the country had been properly welcomed to the cruel world of soccer.

In recent years, Australian football culture has been turned upside down and inside out. Melbourne champions of rugby league? Sydney champions of Australian rules? And the whole country going nuts over a soccer match? Our minds go back to the response the Victorians received in 1877 when they asked their rugby playing brethren in New South Wales if they fancied a game. "The contest had better bide the time when the rules in the respective colonies had become more assimilated" they were told. It would appear that time has finally arrived, but not in the way anybody would have imagined.

11 COMING TO AMERICA
Colonial football in the United States

Beginner's Guide

At least at face value, of all the codes in the football family, the North American variety is the one that most went out on a limb. With players decked out like stormtroopers, with lines and numbers painted all over the field, with plays that last mere seconds before everything comes to yet another standstill and meaning sixty minutes of football ends up taking over three hours, and with all eleven players on a team being substituted when possession gets turned over to the other side, it looks positively alien to followers of any other form of football.

The protective gear is always the first weapon to be drawn when it comes to mocking American football. Haven't these guys seen rugby? That's a real man's game, where they don't need to wear padding and helmets when they go in for the tackle[1]. Laugh the rugby boys may, but suffice to say that there is no code of football in which the force of contact is anything like as intense as it is in American football, with 130 kilos of muscle-meat pounding in at full pelt from your blind side. Punching, kicking or leading a tackle with your helmet are out, but aside from that, pretty much anything goes. Take the padding out of American football, and you're looking at legalised murder.

If the pads, the helmets, the pompoms and the incessant commercial breaks aren't enough, then it's the unfathomable complexity of the rules that really get the cynics scoffing. But although outside of America, very few people have the faintest idea what is going on, the sad thing is that that is usually because they have never really bothered to try. As it happens, American football is relatively simple. For a foreigner to understand, all it takes is an open mind and a willingness to accept that a lot of elements of the American game may be different, but that doesn't have to mean they are wrong, right, better or worse.

For the sake of those who still gaze at the screen in a state of mystified confusion when they are invited to a Super Bowl party in early February, here is a crash course on the basics.

American football is an eleven-a-side game, but is far more forgiving than any other code when it comes to substitutions. Unlimited changes can be made from a bench of 45, so what

---

[1] The argument will run and run in Internet forums, and statistics alone are insufficient to prove the comparative deadliness of different sports. However, hospitals in the United States treated 8361 people for rugby injuries in 1998, compared to 355,247 for American football, which is a surprisingly high rate for rugby considering it is very much a minority sport in the States. But comparisons are meaningless, especially when we remember that they are rendered irrelevant purely because the Americans wear padding to reduce the chance of injury. There are lies, damned lies, and there are statistics, and some studies have actually come to the conclusion that the sport that involves the highest risk of death is actually fishing, although the suggestion that horse racing is the most deadly sport is, I believe, more convincing.

generally happens is that when a team has the ball, and are the 'offense', they will field a completely different set of players to when they are the 'defense'. What the offense has to do is move the ball up the field towards the opposition's end zone, and what the defense has to do is stop them. When the game starts, one side has to kick the ball forwards to the other team. Game on. Simple enough so far.

But rather than a free-flowing game, it is much more structured. The basis of advancing the ball is what are called 'downs'. The American football pitch is exactly 100 yards long, and lines across it mark each five yard interval. When a team gains possession (i.e. becomes the offense), they have four chances to advance the ball at least ten yards. If they manage to do that, they get another four downs from the spot they reached in the previous play. If they run out of downs, possession gets turned over to the other side. So, on the final down, the usual tactic, rather than attempting a standard play, is to attempt to kick a field goal (over the bar and between the uprights) for three points, or at least kick the ball as far away from your own end as possible.

Each down starts with one group of players from each team, usually eight, gathering face to face on either side of last point where the ball was dead. This is called the line of scrimmage. The other players assume tactical positions elsewhere (but always behind the ball). The one in the middle of the offense, the centre, 'snaps' the ball back to the player behind him, who is the all-important quarterback, the lynchpin of almost every move in the game.

So, the 'snap' is rather like an uncontested scrum, something rugby league fans will be familiar with, and from here on the game works in more or less identical fashion to rugby. But whereas a rugby team will try to hold onto possession as it battles to move the ball up the whole field, there is not much point doing that in American football. Instead, the quarterback will quickly pick out a runner, usually one of the specialists called 'running backs', who will immediately try to 'rush' the ball forwards, and as long as he completes the ten yards, his team has reached the 'safe haven' of a first down.

Other than ten-yard downs, the other huge departure from rugby is the fact that not only is the forward pass legal, but that pass can be caught by a player who was ahead of the ball when it was thrown. The limitation is that the offense can only do this once, and only once, in any single down, and the pass has to be met with a clean catch in the air, and only by what are known as 'eligible receivers', which generally means the players that did not form the line of scrimmage. If the ball is caught, the receiver can continue running with the ball as far as he can, but so can any defender able to intercept the throw.

The basic aim of the game, of course, is to carry the ball into your opponent's end zone, or catch a forward pass there, which is a touchdown and worth six points[2]. All touchdowns are followed by a conversion. There is a choice here, and unless they desperately need the points,

---

[2] Drop goals are also a possibility, but with Doug Flutie of New England's successful attempt in 2006 being the first in over sixty years in the NFL, they are not something you will see anything like as often as you would in rugby.

teams will almost always go for the option of a simple kick to goal in front of the posts for one point, rather than taking the far trickier option of running the ball over the line for two[3].

And that, albeit with the complexities removed[4], is what American football is all about. It may look alien to those weaned on other sports, but its core elements are not that far removed from what can be found in other forms of football, and most especially the game for which a group of Rugby School pupils wrote down the first rules in 1845. Which should come as no surprise. After all, that was the starting point for the American game too.

The founding fathers

No matter what fancy claims have been made, the origins of American football do not lie with the Pilgrim Fathers and their Thanksgiving celebrations at Plymouth, Massachusetts in 1621. However, ball games were played by the early settlers, as revealed by the journals of William Bradford[5], the governor of the Plymouth Colony and a staunch bah-humbug Puritan who insisted that his people would have to work on Christmas Day, for there was nothing in the Bible that supported the idea that December 25 was the day Jesus was born. Technically speaking, he was right. But led by the rebellious Thomas Morton, the settlers pestered Bradford so much, claiming it was against their consciences to work on the holy day, that their governor finally gave in and granted them a day off.

Taking a holiday was one thing, but when Bradford returned to camp later that day, he was horrified to find that the men enjoying their Chrimbo break were "in the street at play, openly … some were pitching at the bar … and some at stool-ball[6] and such like sports." At carnival time things were just as bad. "They also set up a maypole, drinking and dancing about it many days together, inviting the Indian women for their consorts, dancing and frisking together like so many fairies, or furies, rather; and worse practices." It was horrific stuff, but at least it was nice to see some respectful interaction between the settlers and the settled. Edward Winslow was there, and the events are well documented in his *Mourt's Relation*[7] of 1622, where he mentions how "amongst other recreations, we exercised our arms, many of the Indians coming amongst us, and among the rest their greatest king Massasoit[8], with some

---

[3] A system players of the Eton field game will find uncannily familiar.

[4] There is also the rare and complex scoring method of the safety, which usually involves a player being tackled in their own end zone, meaning the other side gets two points. It's rare, but you can even have teams deliberately downing the ball in their own end zone and conceding two points via an intentional safety.

[5] William Bradford *Of Plymouth Plantation, 1620-1647.*

[6] Stool-ball was an early form of baseball, and it is that sport, rather than football, that seems most deserving of its place in this part of American folklore.

[7] Full title *A Relation or Journal of the Beginning and Proceedings of the English Plantation Settled at Plimoth in New England.*

[8] It is curious, and purely coincidental, to note that the building that would later witness most of the meetings that debated the early rules of American football would be Massasoit House in Springfield, Massachusetts. The Massasoit that Winslow mentioned was the leader of the Pokanoket people, and a major player in early

ninety men, whom for three days we entertained and feasted, and they went out and killed five deer, which we brought to the plantation and bestowed on our governor, and upon the captain and others."

The Puritans detested such merriment in their quest to escape the decadence into which England had declined and build a new land based on an ideology that thoroughly rejected just about anything that didn't involve outright piety towards God and where all but the hard graft was considered sinful. Proletariat sports and games had not always been overly popular among the powers that be in England, but the very thought of them sent shivers down the spines of the Founding Fathers of America, who saw them as no more than the first step towards the even greater evils of gambling, dancing and sexual promiscuity. The Sabbath and other holy days were much more sober affairs than people were used to back in England. Benjamin Rader notes that "New Englanders celebrated none of the traditional holidays, excluding Sundays. In 1640, Massachusetts imposed a fine upon anyone who fasted, feasted or refused to work on Christmas Day" and not even "unnecessary and unseasonable walking in the streets" was allowed. An English traveller, Joseph Bennett, felt that Sunday observance in Boston "is the strictest kept that ever I yet saw anywhere[9]." Nobody could even leave the town on that day, not that there was much point, as everything was closed anyway. Down south things were no better, where the Virginia House of Burgesses banned all forms of Sunday amusements in 1619, and wouldn't allow actors to even set foot in the colony. Making servants work was also a punishable offence, which would have been great for them if only there had been anything they could legally do to enjoy their spare time. Not even a quick game of cards was an option.

William Penn set up the Quakers movement in Pennsylvania, and those guys were even harsher when it came to clamping down on "rude and riotous sports." In *No Cross, No Crown* in 1669 he wrote that his people should not "eat, drink, play, game and sport away their irrevocable precious time, which should be dedicated to the Lord." All such sins were banned in 1682, and again in 1716, when the Quakers said they objected to "races, either on horseback or foot, laying wagers, or ... any gaming or needless and vain sports and pastimes." Charleston, South Carolina was famed for its promiscuousness, but even so, as late as the 1750s, a German traveller wrote that on Sundays "no shop may keep open, watchmen go about who lay hold upon anyone idling in the streets[10]."

The Dutch, who were laying claim to land from Rhode Island down to Delaware (New York was formerly called New Amsterdam) showed a similar lack of enthusiasm for

---

European settlement. If it hadn't been for Massasoit's support, the Pilgrims would have probably perished in a hostile terrain, but instead traded peace and land with the Pokanoket in exchange for alliance against their own enemies, the Narragansett.

[9] Joseph Bennett *History of New England* (1740).

[10] Gottlieb Mittelberger *Journey to Pennsylvania in the year 1750*. The good news for slaves was they weren't allowed to work either.

anything that was not related to the building of the nation and the veneration of the Lord, but were perhaps not quite so extreme about it, because they did have bowling, boat races and their golf/hockey game called *kolven*[11].

If the prospects for an American sports culture were grim enough already, then the 1730s and the Great Awakening, when God-bothering went into overdrive, painted an even poorer picture. The Puritans and Quakers were a barrel of laughs compared to the party pooping Evangelicals, one of whose chief promoters was George Whitefield, who travelled back and forth between the Americas and Europe preaching his ideas. His report from a visit to Annapolis, Maryland, in 1739 sums up his opinions on sports. "Some of the company, I believe, thought I was too strict … they were very strenuous in defence of what they called innocent diversions; but when I told them everything was sinful which was not done with a single eye to God's glory, and that such entertainments not only discovered a levity of mind, but were contrary to the whole tenor of the Gospel of Christ, they seemed somewhat convinced."

Yeah, right. How much notice the common folk really took of people like Whitefield is open to debate. After all, the fact that the religious leaders went to such lengths to eliminate pointless pleasure from American life suggests that it was still going on regardless – and they were ultimately fighting a losing battle

Teams America

In its early years, America was made up of small, compact settlements that were relatively easy to control. As late as the early 18th century there had been practically no movement any more than a hundred miles inland from the Atlantic coast, while by 1790 there was still no city anywhere in the country with a population greater than 50,000.

But the pattern was changing. By the 1750s, over a million Britons had emigrated to North America, and another two million or so would be following them over the next two decades. These vastly outnumbered the French colonists, of which there were less than 100,000 in New France when it was carved up by Spain and Britain in 1763, but both sets of people were coming from countries where there was a strong sporting tradition.

European religions had generally become far more tolerant of folk pastimes, with some monarchs like James I of England openly encouraging them, and the newer arrivals were far less keen on being indoctrinated by the religious extremists. Irish, Greeks, Italians, Poles and

---

[11] They also had the delightful sport of gander pulling, in which the poor geese were hung by their feet and contestants had to leap, perhaps off a horse or from a boat, and grab the bird's neck to pull off its head. The sport eventually spread throughout the colonies. It may now sound like something barbarous that belongs to a bygone era when people were so much less civilised than they are now and cruelty to animals was just a part of life. However, if you chance upon the towns of Lekeitio or Markina in the Basque Country (Spain) at carnival time, you can still see this glorious tradition being practiced today, although animal rights activists recently won their battle for dead birds to be used.

MIKE ROBERTS – THE SAME OLD GAME: CODIFICATION

other new nationalities were sailing across the Atlantic in search of a better life, and they weren't going to be preached into changing their ways by these pompous clergymen.

Hanover Country Fair was established as early as 1737 and included all the things the Puritans had done their damndest to keep away from the New World. There was "a prize of five pounds for a horse race, a cudgelling match for a hat, a fiddling contest for a fiddle, a quire of ballads to be sung, a wrestling match for a pair of buckles, and a pair of handsome silk stockings … given to the handsomest young country maid." Now that's more like it! Whether the authorities liked it or not, the immigrant workers were determined to enjoy themselves as they pleased, and handing out silk stockings to country maids seems about as enjoyable a pastime as life could offer!

In a land where almost half the population was young unmarried men, an extraordinary number of these people were free of any family responsibilities, and it wasn't just the silk stocking sellers who were doing a roaring trade. Alcohol boomed – in Boston in 1737, roughly one man out of every twenty five made his living from the sale of liquor. Despite early attempts to create a law abiding and devout nation, it was the bawdy, drunken lifestyle that was rife in the brothels and taverns of America. In 1751, a clergyman described in the *Virginia Gazette* how the taverns were filled with "the very dregs of the people … where not only time and money are vainly and unprofitably squandered away, but what is worse … prohibited and unlawful games, sports and pastimes are used, followed and practiced, namely cards, dice, horse-racing and cock-fighting, together with vices and enormities of every other kind."

There were big changes on the way, and none more so than the American Revolutionary War (1775–1783), in which the Thirteen Colonies that made up what was known as British America rebelled against the crown and eventually gained their independence from it. With that came major cultural changes, and the creation of a new American identity that though still very god-fearing, was far removed from the old Puritan ideals, and certainly the animosity towards sport.

In a 1777 order to his brigadier-generals, the commander-in-chief of the American revolutionary forces, George Washington, agreed that "gaming of every kind is expressly forbidden, as being the foundation of evil, and the cause for many a brave and gallant officer's ruin." But he meant gambling, for he added that "games of exercise for amusement may not only be permitted, but encouraged." He was all in favour of "teaching the men the use of their legs, which is of infinitely more importance than learning the manual exercise."

The late 18th century saw a leisure revolution in America. The games that had once been scorned were now the height of sophistication among the middle classes, who ostentatiously whiled away their time with such sports as hunting, boating, racquets (tennis), bowling, quoits, horse racing, cricket (eventually baseball) and billiards. Slavery had much to with this change of attitude. After all, hard work had once been upheld as the great virtue of North America, but now that imported blacks, who barely qualified as human beings, were being

COMING TO AMERICA

forced to do the physical, hand-dirtying menial labour, hard work suddenly didn't have quite the same respectability to it.

But although the wealthier classes found sports to be the ideal means for flaunting their status, if the common plebs got up to anything similar, they were immediately viewed with suspicion, for surely it was little more than an excuse for alcohol and gambling. Not that the gentry weren't partial to a wee tipple or flutter themselves, but as ever, there was one rule for one class and one rule for the other.

The Lyceum movement was busy setting up its 900 or so venues that had spread throughout America by the 1830s, promoting art, literature and science, but despite such good intentions, that was not what the people wanted. They wanted dance halls, they wanted Phineas Barnum's freak shows and circuses, and they wanted sports.

Among the common mass, an underworld gaming culture developed, and there was not much the authorities could do to stop it. Pennsylvania was one of the strictest states of all, but so general was "disobedience to this law and so great the contempt of public authority, that a stranger passing through our country would rather suppose we had a law enjoining sports and diversions on Sunday, under heavy penalty, than one forbidding them … what is to become of a country where the laws are thus openly insulted and violated by every man at his pleasure[12]?"

Violence played a big part in these games, frequently involving the torture or slaughter of animals. One particular favourite was ratting, in which punters wagered on how a long it would take a dog to kill off an entire pit of rats. All kinds of animals from goats to roosters and dogs were pitted against each other in battle. In 1824, seven or eight dogs were set on a bull for the entertainment of the masses and "they soon tore his ears off, and shockingly lacerated his head which made the poor thing bellow hideously and run about in every direction to the length of his chain, maddened with pain. In ten minutes he had killed one dog and lamed others; when I turned away in disgust[13]." That traveller was not the only person to be disgusted by such cruelty. The idea that animals were to be exploited for human mirth was widely rejected as uncivilised, and by 1828, New York had outlawed blood sports, to be followed over the following years by most of the other north-eastern states.

But it wasn't just animal violence that thrilled. It was human violence too. Fist fights and American culture went hand in hand. Philip Vickers Fithian described impromptu battles that were often the result of settling scores over women or whatever matter in which "every diabolical strategem for mastery of bruising, kicking, scratching, pinching, biting, butting, tripping, throtling, gouging, cursing, dismembering, howling &c is allowed and practised[14]."

---

[12] Jacob Rush *Charges, and extracts of charges, on moral and religious subjects* (1803).

[13] Joseph Pickering *Emigration, or no emigration; being the narrative of the author, (an English farmer) from the year 1824 to 1830; during which time he traversed the United States of America, and the British province of Canada, with a view to settle as an emigrant* (1830) .

[14] Philip Vickers Fithian *Journal & Letters of 1773-1774.*

MIKE ROBERTS – THE SAME OLD GAME: CODIFICATION

These were watched by a crowd of people that Fithian refused to accept were human beings. "I know not how they came by their form, by the help of which they are permitted to associate with men, unless it has been … by an intermixture of the meaner kind of devil with prostitute monkeys … I think all such should be deemed by the community infectious, and suspended at least any kind of intercourse."

Prizefighting was all the rage. Places like Kit Burns' Sportsman Hall in New York were America's answer to the coliseum, where although illegal, bare-knuckle fights went ahead regardless, often enjoying considerable press coverage and vying for massive stakes, with the most famous names heralded as the folk heroes of their respective ethnic groups.

John Cox Stevens was one of the biggest pioneers in exploiting the potential of sport and his offer in 1835 of a thousand dollars to any man who could run ten miles in an hour drew upwards of 20,000 people to the Union Course on Long Island. That set things rolling for 'pedestrianism' to become a mass spectator sport, involving running races where the athletes were paraded in the kind of showbiz fashion now associated to WWE wrestling. The *New Orleans Delta* in 1850 reported on a fifteen mile footrace watched by "the most miscellaneous crowd of men, women and children, loafers, wharf rats, fourierites, agrarians, gentlemen, niggers, vagabonds, and outside barbarians that have rejoiced in fresh air and the sight of green fields since the day when Adam mounted on his first pair of breeches!" They knew how to write back then, that's for sure.

Horse racing was also drawing unprecedented crowds. In 1823, the much anticipated race between the champion horse of the north, Eclipse, and the south's Sir Henry attracted 20,000 people to New York and was described by English traveller William Blane as stirring up more interest than a presidential election.

Boating was another huge draw. In 1824, somebody managed to count the 50,000 onlookers lining the Hudson River to watch the Whitehall Aquatic Club win a rowing match for a thousand dollars against the visiting British crew of the frigate *Hussar*. Mass spectator sport had hit North America.

The spirit of the times

Curiously, however, there is little or no mention of football while this is all going on. By 1831, America had its first sports paper in the form of *The Spirit of the Times*, which was based on *Bell's Life* in London, primarily covering angling, baseball, boxing, cricket, foot racing, fox hunting, horse racing, rowing and yachting. There would be no football column until 1882. There was no major move either to encourage or prohibit football – the upper classes would not have considered it gentlemanly enough, the lower classes simply didn't seem interested.

By the early 19th century, athletic pursuits were all the rage in the British Isles. From the elite at the public schools down to the workers emerging from the factories and mines, football and other sports were rivalling drinking, gambling, fist-fighting and picking up cheap prostitutes for popularity. But the average American had no interest in doing sport, and was far happier betting on the outcomes of the few that did.

In 1838, an English traveller called James Silk Buckingham noted that in Boston "the vigorous exercise required for the young, in cricket, hoop, football, running, leaping and wrestling is almost unknown" and "the same degree of paleness and languor is observable in the boys at public schools[15]." Two decades later, and in the same city, British consul Thomas Grattan didn't feel matters had improved when he wrote how "every man is born middle-aged in every city in the Union ... The interval between their leaving school and commencing their business careers offers no occupation to give either gracefulness or strength to body or mind. Athletic games and bolder field sports being unknown ... all that is left is chewing, smoking and drinking ... They have no breadth either of shoulders, information or ambition[16]."

Oliver Wendell Holmes was no more impressed when, in *Atlantic Monthly* in 1858, he observed that "such a set of black-coated, stiff-jointed, soft-muscled, paste-complexioned youth as we can boast in our Atlantic cities never before sprang from the loins of Anglo-Saxon lineage." *The Spirit of the Times* was also aware of the problem. "The object of education is to make men out of boys" it said in 1857. "Real live men, not bookworms, not smart fellows, but manly fellows."

The yanks were a bunch of wimps. Somebody had to beef them up, and the transcendentalists were the guys to do it. These were times of changing attitudes – the temperance (opposition to alcoholism), anti-slavery and women's suffrage movements worked hand in hand with the transcendentalists to cleanse America of its many woes.

The father of the movement, Ralph Waldo Emerson, had plenty to say on the matter in his *Conduct of Life* (1860), a wonderful rant of a book that explains the theory of how it is down to each individual person to make themselves better, and how there is so much more to that than merely reciting chapters of the Bible and being able to quote the classics. He's basically telling Americans to get off their arses.

"The boy hates grammar and loves guns, fishing rods, horses and boats" he explains. "Well, the boy is right. You are not fit to direct his bringing up if your theory leaves out sports and gymnastic training. Archery, cricket, gun and fishing rod, horse and boat are all educators and liberalizing influences. So are dancing and street-talk. These aids will serve your child as well as books ... Provided always that a child is teachable (we are not proposing to make a statue out of sawdust), football, cricket, archery, swimming, skating, climbing, fencing and riding all are lessons in the art of power, which is really the main business of every child to learn."

The transcendentalists would have a huge impact on popularising sport in America, but although Emerson does mention football, that particular game was still anything but

---

[15] James Silk Buckingham *America, historical, statistic, and descriptive: Volume 2* (1841)
[16] Thomas Colley Grattan *Civilized America* (1859).

mainstream in his day. In the year he was writing, 1860, football was already becoming an established participant and even spectator sport in Britain and Australia, but hardly a word had been written about it in America.

It was a low-key game for little boys, which only warranted any kind of mention in print when it caused disturbances by being played in the streets. Two of the earliest such instances were in Massachusetts, where in 1657 it was noted in Boston that "people playing foot-ball in the streets would be charged 20 schillings for such offense" and a century later in 1762 in the Witch City of Salem, it was ordained that "no person shall kick a foot-ball in the publick places, streets or lanes." As in England, football was not a sin in itself, it was playing it on the road that irked[17]. The *Boston Repertory* in 1802 registered a complaint about "boys playing foot ball on the streets of Boston. They should be playing on the Boston Common." The *Colombian Centinel* in 1818 reported that ball play on the public highways was a fineable offence, the penalty being 50 cents, and at Worcester, Massachusetts it was declared in 1812 that "the Selectmen be directed to forbid any playing of ball, rolling of hoops, or any kind of play in the public highway … a practice so frequent and dangerous, that has occasioned many great and repeated complaints[18]."

Just to the south, in Hartford, Connecticut, the council decreed that "no person or persons shall play with the ball, either foot-ball or fire-ball, where horses are liable to be frightened. They shall forfeit one dollar." In the same state, Norwich also issued a law banning street football in 1827, and the *Evening Post* in New York in 1828 wrote that "let any one visit Washington Parade, or indeed any of the fields in that neighborhood, and he will find large groups of men and boys playing ball and filling the air with their shouts and yells. At present the annoyance has become absolutely intolerable … and ought to be put an end to without delay."

The forgotten game

Occasional references to early football in America have been found. William Bentley wrote in 1791 that "before winter comes on the Foot Ball, which is differently pursued in different places. In Marblehead, even heads of families engage in it, and all the fishermen while at home in this season. The bruising of shins has rendered it rather disgraceful to those of better education, who use a hand ball, thrown up against an house or fence instead of the Foot Ball, which is unfriendly to clothes, as well as safety. Such is the usual succession of puerile diversions[19]." In 1823, the Irish Hibernians were reported to celebrate St Patrick's with a game of football on Augusta Common in Georgia, watched by some 300 people, and in 1841,

---

[17] Although, on a more positive note for football, a 1768 reference states that the sport was allowed on the street in front of Roxbury Grammar School, near Boston.
[18] *Collections of the Worcester society of antiquity* (1881).
[19] *Diary of Dr William Bentley, 1784-1792.*

COMING TO AMERICA

the public square in Cleveland, Ohio was the scene for a game played by a large number of men and boys.

These references tell us next to nothing about the nature of these games, but here we can turn to a charming article in a 1902 edition of *Outing* magazine, written by Yale alumnus Clarence Deming and titled *The Three Ages of Football*. The third age was the modern era he was writing from, the second age was the period when college football was in development, and the first age was when what he called 'old football' was played. Deming is describing games he tells us he had played himself half a century before, which would have been around 1850.

He takes us on a trip down memory lane to a New England village where "an old-fashioned football game is in full cry … on each side are fifteen or twenty players, ranging from the callow city twelve-year-old … to the young man betrayed as 'day scholar' from the farm by his rough homespun and angular cowhides. For there is democracy of ages as well as conditions in the game, even the schoolmaster, maybe, leading one side and taking his full share of the knocks. There are no bleachers, no applauding crowd, no single spectator even, save as some passing rustic on his oxsled may cast his eye on the game and sigh vaguely for the days when he, too, was young; nor is the game itself that refinement of scientific force … But it is an allround breezy and 'open' sport; young and old are in it with no worse peril on the snow than a rasped shin, painful but transient; and the action is lively and incessant from the opening 'cant' up to the last instant that the ball strikes the boundary fence that serves for a goal or the school bell clangs its sharp veto on the play.

"Out of bounds meant the side fences, whether far or near, while, in lieu of goal posts, stood the wooden fences, whether the ball went over or against. The squad of many-sized players chose sides, one side 'canted' the ball; each side tried to drive the ball to the opposite fence and there the old game was, in its simplest terms.

"But it had its fine points and its touches of science. Caught on the fly or first bound the ball gave the player a free kick, and this developed into a trick called the 'toe catch'. In making a toe catch the player by a deft and quick movement of the toe tossed the ball in air, took it on a short fly, and won his kick. If the modern football man calls that trick 'dead easy' and laughs it to scorn, let him test it alone and then measure the feat in the mêlée of a game and in front of a dozen charging players.

"Running with the ball was severely interdicted in old football (with accent on the 'foot') and thus there came in another test of skill. It was 'babying,' or as the verb was then, 'puggling' the ball by short, quick foot taps, holding it in possession and taking it from or past an opponent, a sort of boxing of the ball with the feet which gave much range for deft work and was acquired only with long practise and some natal gifts. The crack 'puggler' was the kingpin of the old football squad and, if he joined with his art the toe catch, he was a double star of first magnitude in the game. Usually he was some young football genius of the

261

MIKE ROBERTS – THE SAME OLD GAME: CODIFICATION

farm, with thews hardened by toil, his natural skill polished by several football winters and his thick boots a welcome substitute for pads."

This is a glorious piece of writing, and one that shows us that, ignored by contemporary writers, football was alive and well. And judging by Deming's description, it was a game that had been brought over from Britain. It was basically the same kind of soccer that the FA was about to standardise. There was no running with the ball, not because it was something they were too daft to think of, but because it was strictly 'interdicted'. This was a game with the feet, in which dribbling was what they cutely called 'puggling'. As in early soccer, the fair catch on the fly was there, which would win a free kick.

It is remarkable to notice that Deming has to explain all these concepts, even though all of them were basic elements of other codes of football around the world in 1902, some even played in America, yet codes that this writer seems to have been blissfully unaware of.

Reading Deming, one gets the impression that he is harking back to better times, when football was an altogether simpler and more beautiful thing. He writes that "the vision of the writer goes back through many phases of football; the latter day power of dodging halfback, forceful plunger, and long punter are not forgotten; yet not one of them, if memory does not betray judgment, surpasses the work on the field of the oldtime puggler at his best, when he came out of the thick of the game with the ball as much in possession as though it were in hand and when, with no such aid as modern 'interference', he boxed it through a line of resisting players."

Deming's article also provides some useful background into the early development of the ball. "In its first estate it was a case of calfskin, shaped and seamed by the rural cobbler and fitted with a gash and eyelets for lacing. Into this was put a pig's bladder that, blown up, tied up, and duly laced in, made a ball, by queer historical precedent, the analogue of the orthodox football of to-day. Its variations of form were novel and gauged by the dexterity of the cobbler. Sometimes it was egg-shaped, sometimes oblate, more often seamed with angles or corners and a kind of cross between cube and globe, resulting in strange antics in its conduct on the field. The bladders collapsed easily and the great problem was the renewal of supply (a problem easily solved in midwinter, when pig killings were common, but deepening as spring drew near, when the whole football quad had to turn bladder hunters), old-fashioned football, in this phase, antedating a modern corner in pork. When early spring came the best we could do sometimes was to stuff the leather with hay and keep up play with a ball which, if not resilient, at least didn't burst every football day. Later there was another and quite as impressive pattern of ball. It was imported from the city, made of pure rubber, of vast diameter, blown up by brass pipe which turned a screw and, after vexing trials, locked the air in." He means the first commercially produced balls, which exploited Charles Goodyear's invention of vulcanised rubber in 1855.

But this text, rather than providing the missing link between British soccer and American football, is merely a testimonial to the final hour of the kicking game in Deming's country's

COMING TO AMERICA

heritage. Rather than being the game that subsequently gave birth to American football, these were the fading remnants of a form of football that most of America was going to turn its back on.

The Oneidas

What was traditionally considered the oldest football club in America, the Oneida Football Club, was formed in Boston in 1862 by a 17 year-old called Gerritt Smith Miller, a young man of wealthy stock who hailed from the hamlet of Peterboro in Madison County, which was founded in 1795 and named after his grandfather, Peter Gerritt Smith[20].

There is no finer description of the football played by the Oneidas than one written half a century later by one of its members, James Lovett. Setting the scene, he describes his childhood home as a "far different place from the Greater Boston of today … it is doubtful if the youth of the present day begins to realize how very different it actually was. There was not a single business house within its limits tall enough to require an elevator, and if there had been, an elevator was no more thought of then than a telephone[21]." In a world where the town crier was still the most immediate source of information, his fascinating nostalgic musings recall the days when the favourite amusements were follow my leader, I spy, sledging, snowball fights, baseball, marbles, picking fights and, in fascinating detail, football.

When Gerritt Smith moved into town in 1860, Lovett considered the newcomer "a most valuable addition to our boy world", though not responsible for inducting the locals to football for "at the time that Miller entered this school it had a fine football team, upon which he at once took a prominent place." The school in question was run and named by a Mr Dixwell, a highly reputable institution, which on the football field did battle with the English High and the Public Latin School. And boy did Lovett love it. He describes a game in 1861 against the latter in which "the goals were Beacon Street Mall upon one side, and the path leading from Flagstaff Hill to Charles Street upon the other." That day, they decided to break from tradition and play the best of five instead of three, with Dixwell's coming back from what would normally have been a 2-1 defeat to equalise at 2-2 before the author, who had "loafed around with his hands in his pockets during the first four games … finally woke up and finished the game, after forty-seven minutes, by kicking the winning goal."

---

[20] The Oneida Indian Nation, as the PRFA says "had been a tribe of Iroquois Indians long gone from the Boston environs, but the boys liked the heroic aura of the name." In fact, there was more to it than that. Peter Gerritt Smith originally leased the 50,000 acres of his estate from Oneida Chief Skenadoah, and features in the village include Oneida Creek. His son and Gerritt Smith Miller's father was a campaigner for the abolition of slavery who ran for president in 1848. He was once described as "one of the most under-chronicled figures in American social reform" and was held in high regard by his son, for much of the information that has survived about his deeds comes from a donation of papers he personally donated to Syracuse University. Gerritt Smith Miller himself would be a major philanthropist in later life, particularly known for his role in the women's suffrage movement.

[21] James Lovett *Old Boston Boys and the Games they Played* (1907).

The Oneida Club was formed in 1862, and all but three of the members were from Dixwell's, with the others picked from the other schools. It was basically an all-star select of the finest players on Boston Common, which created something of a problem when seeking opposition of similar quality. "In fact, we were never beaten" writes Lovett. "And what is more remarkable, no combination ever made a single goal against us."

However, the games were low-key affairs and only once do we know of the local press taking any interest in their activities. In November 1863, the *Boston Daily Advertiser* saw fit to publish a mere five lines on a 12-0 win for the Oneidas against an unnamed group of challengers.

Lovett also provides enough juice to paint a reasonable picture of a game that resembled soccer when he tells us that "in one game Ned Arnold and one of our opponents were both running at top speed towards each other, intent only upon kicking the ball, which lay about midway between them." American football it was not. "In the old game there were no 'touchdowns' nor was the ground marked off by lines of any kind; in fact, there was no 'gridiron', nothing but straight football, and by straight football I mean that from the time of the 'kick-off' there was no cessation, no 'let-up' (except when the ball went out of bounds, and then it was at once brought back and put into play again), until one side or the other landed the ball over any part of the opponents' boundary line ... I, personally, am sadly ignorant of the modern game of football, and will let those wiser than I comment upon and discuss its merits as compared with those of the old game, open, full of stirring episodes, and intelligible at any stage to every onlooker."

But neither was the Oneida's game pure soccer for if Lovett is anything to go by, there was plenty of rough and tumble involved too. "I remember once seeing some boy ... overtake and spring upon the back of Tom Nelson, who was running with the ball; no doubt he thought thereby to down Tom and get the ball away from him ... On another occasion I was chasing one of Dixwell's boys who had the ball and was a very fast runner. Finding I could not catch him, I made a flying leap of some ten or twelve feet and landed between his shoulders." Those are the kind of antics that belong on the rugby field.

The way Lovett describes their interpretation of the offside law is very much in keeping with the way football of either form was played at the time in England. "Lurking, known to-day as being 'off side', was considered by fair-minded boys as an offense not to be countenanced for a moment, even if the boy guilty of it was on one's own side. It was a trick very rarely resorted to in those days, in which a boy tried to sneak around in among the enemy and wait for his own side to kick the ball his way, when his chances for getting it past the opponent's full-back were much increased. Our law was to keep moving towards the ball, wherever it might be."

One thing that is certain is that the balls the Oneidas used were spherical. Anyone who doubts that can go to the National Soccer Hall of Fame in Oneonta, NY, to see one, treasured though a little deflated over the years, and inscribed with the date, November 7, 1863.

From the above evidence, Roger Allaway concludes that "my own guess is that what they were playing was a hybrid, neither fully soccer nor rugby. But it is only a guess. I don't know, and neither, I think, does anybody else[22]." The PRFA offer that "to call the Oneidas the inventors of American football is surely giving the little devils more than their due. Their game allowed running under certain circumstances, but it was still essentially soccer."

Whatever their game was, the Oneidas folded just two years later, probably because the main instigators moved on to university, but they would proudly take their achievements at battering the other local schoolkids to their respective graves. No fewer than seven members of the original team were still alive to attend a ceremony in November 1925 at which a monument was placed on the Boston Common where they used to play all those years before.

It is still there today, next to a walkway near Beacon Street, and states that "on this field the Oneida Football Club of Boston, the first organized football club in the United States played against all comers from 1862 to 1865. The Oneida goal was never crossed." The last surviving member of the Oneidas, Arthur Sherburne Hardy, after a distinguished life as an engineer, novelist and US ambassador to several European countries, died in 1930.

Correcting history

So the Oneidas were 'the first organized football club in the United States' were they? They weren't actually, but nobody knew any better than that in 1925. And thanks to the work of a remarkably small number of researchers, and Mel Smith deserves particular commendation, we now know that by 1863 there was nothing particularly unique about what the Oneidas were doing.

A decade earlier than the Oneidas, in 1854, the *Spirit of the Times* had written that the St George FBC in New York had been founded in 1843, probably as a winter activity for members of the cricket club, and played "quietly once a year." In 1851, a company in Philadelphia was recorded as selling India rubber footballs, and would not have been doing that unless they felt there was a market of local footballers ready to spend money on them.

By 1855, Smith finds that Irishmen had formed football clubs in the forms of the Boston Cork Spinners and the Baltimorans, and in 1858 it was also Irish settlers that were behind the formation of a club in St Louis, Missouri. Hartford and New Britain in Connecticut also had town teams in operation that year, as did the local Trinity College, and not only have the results of some of their games survived, but also a set of eight rules for a 20-a-side game, the earliest known football rules written in America. These specified that the ball could not be carried, but could be caught, which earned the right to a free kick. Offside meant strictly staying behind the ball at all times, and if the ball went out of play, it was kicked back in by the first player to get it. It sounds very like the game the Oneidas played and also the Cambridge and later FA games in England.

---

[22] Roger Allaway *Were the Oneidas playing soccer or not?* (2001 at http://homepages.sover.net/~spectrum/oneidas.html).

MIKE ROBERTS – THE SAME OLD GAME: CODIFICATION

Judging by the name, the East Baltimore Hurling and Football Club, founded in 1860, was also an Irish project, and they had at least one club to play in the city, for the Cottage FBC had formed a year earlier, when there are also records of a Clover Hill FBC in New York, who may have played a friendly with the Brooklyn Polytechnic.

We know games were regularly played in Boston, but the nearest we get to any precise details is that Mr Dearing's team won a match on October 19, 1843. Another game was played on Thanksgiving Day in Columbia, Philadelphia in 1857, but all we know is that a town team played another local one.

All these teams were founded long before the Oneidas first kicked a ball in anger, and so limited is the information on any of them that we can be certain there were plenty of others for which there is no surviving record.

Wherever we look, it was universally a kicking game that was providing so much enjoyment, and that meant in academia too. They were kicking, not carrying, the ball at Transylvania University, Kentucky in 1832 and at Amherst College, 1834 graduate Henry Ward Beecher "with his square-toed boots … was the chiefest kicker of his time[23]." But it was there, in the colleges, from whence American football would eventually be spawned.

Ivy towers

The establishments that had by far the greatest hand in transforming football into the game America knows today were the ones forming part of what is known as the Ivy League[24]. The term popularly refers to the elitist selectivity of these eight colleges, and especially to the pioneering role they played in the development and promotion of intercollegiate sport, and is taken from the ivy that typically grows on the walls of the antique buildings. The oldest known use was by Stanley Woodward in *The New York Tribune* in 1933, when he wrote of the football season that "a proportion of our eastern ivy colleges are meeting little fellows another Saturday before plunging into the strife and the turmoil." However, the expression itself was probably not Woodward's own invention.

Back in England, although there was once nationwide fascination whenever Oxford and Cambridge competed against each other at sport, most people had stopped caring by the 20th century, and events like the Boat Race are now viewed as curious relics that have survived from the country's sporting past. But in the US, intercollegiate sport is still almost as passionately followed as the professional variety, and attracts similar television audiences. And much of this springs from how the hierarchy among universities in North America is a far less decided affair than the Oxbridge duopoly in the UK. The Ivy League was all about

---

[23] Joseph Howard *Life of Henry Ward Beecher, the eminent pulpit and platform orator* (1887).

[24] These are, in order of the dates they were founded (although in some cases they were known by other names for several years): Harvard University (1636), Yale University (1701), University of Pennsylvania (1740), Princeton University (1746), Columbia University (1754), Brown University (1764), Dartmouth College (1769) and the only one founded after the colonial era, Cornell University (1865). All of them are in the northeast.

COMING TO AMERICA

the top colleges vying for supremacy. Although more academic matters were obviously important, the promotion of their athletes and sports teams was seen as the ideal method for getting them into the media spotlight. American football emerged against this ultra-competitive background, and was also fuelled by the inherent violence of 19th century college life.

In his *A Collection of College Words and Customs* (1856), Benjamin Homer Hall provides priceless snippets of information, anecdotes, traditions, expressions and other typical goings on at the major colleges of the era. He dedicates a fair amount of coverage to the plight of the poor Freshmen. First year students were the dregs of the college social ladder, of a similarly lowly status to the fags at English public schools.

He quotes a speech by Yale President Theodore Dwight Woolsey in 1850, describing how in what were already bygone days a "remarkable particular in the old system here was the servitude of Freshmen (for such it really deserved to be called). The new-comers (as if it had been to try their patience and endurance in a novitiate before being received into some monastic order) were put into the hands of Seniors, to be reproved and instructed in manners, and were obliged to run upon errands for the members of all the upper classes. And all this was very gravely meant, and continued long in use. The Seniors considered it as a part of the system to initiate the ignorant striplings into the college system, and performed it with the decorum of dancing-masters. And, if the Freshmen felt the burden, the upper classes who had outlived it, and were now reaping the advantages of it, were not willing that the custom should die in their time."

In 1764, the Yale rules stated that Freshmen were, among other things, "obliged to perform all reasonable errands for any superior, always returning an account of the same to the person who sent them. When called, they shall attend and give a respectful answer; and when attending on their superior, they are not to depart until regularly dismissed. They are responsible for all damage done to anything put into their hands by way of errand."

It was not a pleasant life for the Freshmen, but one found a cunning way of rebelling. "A Freshman was once furnished with a dollar, and ordered by one of the upper classes to procure for him pipes and tobacco, from the farthest store on Long Wharf, a good mile distant. Being at that time compelled by College laws to obey the unreasonable demand, he proceeded according to orders, and returned with ninety-nine cents' worth of pipes and one pennyworth of tobacco." What a star!

Freshman servitude was a tradition at all 18th century colleges, and although most of them had officially abolished the practice by the turn of the century, remnants of it survive to this day. Hazing, as it is called, is still rife in American colleges, usually as part of induction rites to enter fraternities or sports teams. One particularly notable example was recorded on video to the horror of the nation in 2003 at Glenbrook North High School near Chicago, and it happened at a junior girls' football match. Football there was none, but plenty of paint, urine, faeces and animal guts being smothered on the girls. Even more tragic was the death of Matt

Fight Fiercely, Harvard

Harvard, located in Cambridge, Massachusetts, is the oldest institution of higher learning in the United States, and was already two centuries old (who are these fools that say America has no history?) when in 1841 they published the latest edition of the brilliantly titled *Customs of Harvard College, which if the Freshmen don't Observe and Obey, they shall be Severely Punished if they have Heard them Read*. And it is here that we find the earliest known reference to college football in America, for rule 11 states that "Freshmen are to find the rest of the scholars with bats, balls, and footballs." Homer Hall tells us where said balls could be found. "A few years prior to the Revolution", which would have been the early 1770s, among the different food and drink on sale in Harvard University Buttery were "articles used in the play-grounds, as bats, balls." The date is particularly telling, because it was not until 1842 that we learn of William Gilbert spotting the market for selling footballs outside Rugby School, by which time balls had already been on sale at American colleges for over half a century!

While there were rules aplenty for the Freshmen, including the places they were allowed to 'mingo' (take a leak), the school governors also issued their own regulations, which applied to everybody. And one of those in the 18th century stated that "no scholar shall play football or any other game in the College yard, or throw any thing across the yard," which implies that although the hallowed yard was out of bounds, football was fine elsewhere.

Professor Sidney Willard reminisced about his days at Harvard, where the real sporting attraction in the 1790s was wrestling. "Beginning with these puny athletes, as one and another was prostrated on either side the contest advanced through the intermediate gradations of strength and skill, with increasing excitement of the parties and spectators." It is with regret that he ends his passionate description with the words "wrestling was, at an after period, I cannot say in what year, superseded by football; a grovelling and inglorious game in comparison[25]."

Homer Hall explains that football was played on the Delta, "a piece of land in Cambridge, which belongs to Harvard College, where the students kick football, and play at cricket, and other games. The shape of the land is that of the Greek Delta, whence its name."

In 1833, Marshall Tufts described football at Harvard from a personal perspective, and didn't exactly ooze enthusiasm. "What was unmeetest of all, timid strangers as we were, it was expected on the first Monday eventide after our arrival, that we should assemble on a

---

[25]Sidney Willard *Memories of Youth and Manhood* (Cambridge, 1855).

COMING TO AMERICA

neighboring green, the Delta, since devoted to the purposes of a gymnasium, there to engage in a furious contest with those enemies, the Sophs, at kicking football and shins[26]."

Harvard's brutal encounter between the Freshmen and the 2nd year Sophomores[27] probably resurfaced, this time with a ball, in the 1820s. One former student fondly remembered "the commensurate excitement of kicking and pounding one's very best friend." This was the same bit of fun described in an anonymous poem published in the *Harvard Register* of 1827:

"The college clock struck twelve – that awful hour,
When Sophs met Fresh, power met opposing power …
… with warlike ardour for a deathless fame,
Impatient stood – until the football came."

It rambles on and on this poem does, describing a game played with a "well-blown ball" where "shins advancing meet advancing shins." Although at one point a Freshman called Hector had "fire in his eye and football in his hands," this and the many other descriptions of early Harvard football suggest the game was essentially about kicking, if not necessarily the ball. It was basically soccer, but without the rules.

In 1849, what Hall calls a 'class poem' offers another poetic description:

"The Delta can tell of the deeds we've done,
The fierce-fought fields we've lost and won,
The shins we've cracked,
And noses we've whacked,
The eyes we've blacked, and all in fun."

It often seems the whole purpose of the exercise was just to beat the living daylights out of the Freshmen. The Sophs were at an immediate advantage because they knew each other, and hence knew who the new students were, while the Freshers probably didn't have a clue who they were playing for or against! But although it was a dramatic introduction to college life for the newcomers, it also gave them a chance to prove their worth, and players that performed well set themselves on good course for a respected position on the Harvard social scale. There were even a few dramatic moments when a surprise was pulled off. On three occasions from 1800 to 1860, the Freshmen actually managed to win a game (i.e. score a goal), though each time the Sophs still won the overall series.

However, John Blanchard provides a number of contemporary quotes that show how football was actually played "every day in good weather after afternoon prayers" and these games seemingly lacked the brutality of the traditional start-of-year battle. He reaches the conclusion that "there were no special rules; the endeavor was to kick the ball (although it might seem to have been an opponent) over the opponent's goal without being hampered by

---

[26] Marshall Tufts *A Tour Through College* (1833).

[27] For the Sophomores to take on the Freshmen newcomers is a tradition that has survived to this day at many colleges, and also in the form of events like basketball's Rookie Challenge between the NBA newcomers and the second year Sophomores.

MIKE ROBERTS – THE SAME OLD GAME: CODIFICATION

such modern restrictions as offside, holding, tripping, etc., but there is some evidence that the ball could not be carried: it had to be kicked[28]."

It seems to have been in the second half of the century that Harvard football became more of a carrying game and John Blanchard tells how, in 1858, the "sophomores who it is said were by custom given the ball, endeavored to carry it through the solid phalanx and over their goal line." Tom Brown's rugby-playing exploits in *Tom Brown's Schooldays* may have been behind this, for it was a massive hit in the US, where it would be into its sixteenth printing by November 1858. The author, Thomas Hughes, actually visited Harvard in 1870, and it was in an article he wrote for *Every Saturday* that the earliest written use of the term 'Bloody Monday' to describe the annual hazing-fest appears.

Bloody it was indeed, and the college authorities had little enthusiasm for the tradition. The June 1858 edition of *Harvard Magazine* was particularly scathing and noted that rival college Yale's own Freshmen-Sophomores game had been banned, and suggested Harvard should follow suit, explaining how "we see, on the one hand, a numerous body of disciplined men, confident of success, stimulated by their defeat in the former year … On the other hand, a squad of awkward Freshmen, hurried to the field on the third day after their first meeting, distrusting each other, with no bond of sympathy, with no expectation of success, awed by the united phalanx opposite, ignorant of the bounds, of the rules of the game (if there be any), ignorant even why they are there, scattered, irresolute, impotent … The best proof, however, of the unfair and cowardly nature of the game is found in the fact that … the Sophomores avenge their drubbing of the year before on – whom? Their late antagonists, the Juniors? O no! Whom then? Why on those who have given them no offence, but are in a fit condition to be imposed upon, bullied, and knocked generally."

By July 1860, the Harvard administration decided enough was enough. The games had to stop. The response among the students to the prohibition of their violent custom was honoured with a mock funeral, in which the ball was carried to its grave in a coffin, where "we have met together upon this mournful occasion to perform the sad offices over one whose long and honored life was put an end to in a sudden and violent manner. Last year at this very time, in this very place, our poor friend's round, jovial appearance (slightly swollen perhaps) and the elasticity of his movements gave promise of many years more to be added to a long life," but "the enthusiastic cheers, the singing of Auld Lang Syne, each student grasping a brother's hand, all, all, have passed away and will soon be buried with the football beneath the sod, to live hereafter only as a dream in our memories and in the college annals[29]."

But although the game was supposedly dead and buried, the students weren't that easy to subdue. 1864 in particular saw plenty of ugly incidents when the Sophomores tried to get the

---

[28] John Blanchard *H Book of Harvard Athletics: 1852-1922* (though not published until 1923).
[29] Speech quoted in John Langdon Sibley's *Private Journal 1846-1882*.

game going according to old tradition. College officers moved in to stop it, which ended with the Freshmen getting off lightly as many of the Sophs laid into the officers instead!

Following up the prohibition was not going to be an easy matter. The games often went ahead regardless, but came to resemble less and less football and more and more a riot. At some point they realised that they didn't really need the ball at all. The idea of scoring goals went out the window, and the players started concentrating their efforts on the brawling instead – as if that hadn't been the case all along! In 1876, it was described simply as a "mock foot-ball match ... the point of the contest was in the opportunity which the better organized Sophomores had of making foot-balls of the Freshmen, who had not yet learned to tell friend from foe[30]."

The 'game' persisted until the end of the century. The *New York Times* in October 1894 reported that "Bloody Monday dies hard; but Harvard Sophomores were milder this year. There were a few mock battles, in which no one was hurt." The story goes on to explain how the police had been called in for the last two years to control the disturbances, although the "institution had been gradually dying a natural death with the advance of civilization." The police presence had simply turned the focus of events, and by October 1904, *The Times* was reporting that the battle was being fought by different armies. "Although there was no rush between the freshmen and sophomores at Harvard this evening, 'Bloody Monday' night was fittingly celebrated by the police force of Cambridge and gangs of Cambridge boys." It was not until 1917, when the First World War meant there were far more serious battles to be fought, that the Bloody Monday tradition was finally laid to rest.

But while Bloody Monday was raging on in the background and degenerated into nothing more than a scrap, other football games carried on untroubled. A player of this kind of football later remembered that "during the 1850s and 1860s, the College played a game that had been played for many years in the preparatory schools of Massachusetts, particularly those of Boston[31]." In the same book, it is explained that "in the autumn of 1871 we all got together and began to play what was known as the 'Boston game' in which we were all trained and experienced ... We played at first on Cambridge Common to which for a while no objection was made by the city authorities. I doubt if any of us knew, or had ever heard of the origin of Bloody Monday, or of the fate of football in previous years, or of the edict of 1860. So we had no reason to anticipate ... any objection on the part of the College authorities and naturally none came, as the prohibition only related to the annual sophomore-freshman contest."

This was the game played by the Oneidas, who were attending the same prep schools for Harvard that this writer mentions, and who in 1864 even issued a challenge to the Harvard Freshmen (some of whom would have been their friends), although the game apparently never went ahead. And one of the most important things about the Boston Game was that

---

[30] Horace Scudder in *Harvard University* in *Scribners Monthly* (1876).
[31] Morton Henry Prince, Class of 1875, in *The H Book of Harvard Athletics* (1923).

MIKE ROBERTS – THE SAME OLD GAME: CODIFICATION

unlike most forms of football in the States, in this one, the ball was carried. And the fact Harvard liked carrying the ball would prove very important at a pivotal stage in our story.

Tigers and bulldogs

At another college, Princeton[32], a game "much practiced ... with balls and sticks ... is low and unbecoming of gentlemen and students ... attended with great danger to the health by sudden and alternate heats and colds and it tends by accident almost unavoidable in that play to disfiguring and maiming those who are engaged in it[33]." Life there at the start of the 19th century, where even sleigh riding was banned, was no barrel of laughs, and slovenly behaviour and general drunkenness and disorderliness seem to have formed the essence of the social scene until the 1820s, when they started playing a game they called 'ballown' that involved some kind of batting of the ball with the fists and was reported being played between teams whose names started from A to L and those from M to Z on the field next to Nassau Hall.

Where the 'ballown' name came from was never recorded, but it is curious to wonder whether there is any connection with a variety of games played over the centuries in England that went by similar names. In 1611, John Florio defined the Italian game of *calcio* as "a kind of play used in Spaine and Italie like unto the play at ballone[34]." In his 1606 play *Volpone* Ben Jonson writes how "whilst others have beene at the balloo, I have beene at my booke." Around the same time the poet Thomas Randolph was pondering how "foot-ball with us may be with them baloome" and John Donne spoke of the way "baloun, tennis, diet, or the stews, had all the morning held."

In 1630, Gervase Markham described something called 'baloone' that was a "strong and mooving sport in the open fields, with a great ball of double leather fild with winde, and so driven too and fro withe the strength of a mans arme arm'd in a bracer of wood, eyther of which actions must be learnt by the eye and practise, not the eare or reading[35]." It was the *American Mechanics' Magazine* in 1827 that spoke of "another kind of foot ball, or more properly speaking, *balloon*, which was formerly played by our gentry before the civil wars in Charles' reign." It originated in France, and was basically the same as the *jeu de paume*, in which the hard, heavy ball was batted with the hands using a brace as protection."

In 1801, our good friend Joseph Strutt was convinced that what he spelled 'balloon' and involved a "wind-ball or leathern ball filled with air, after the fashion of the later form of football, but struck with the hand or fist, is as old as the time of the Romans, by whom it was termed *follis*."

---

[32] Situated midway between New York and Philadelphia, after relocating there from Elizabeth in 1756, and which was officially known as the College of New Jersey until 1896.

[33] John Frelinghuysen Hageman *History of Princeton and its institutions: Volume 2* (1879).

[34] In his *Queen Anna's New World of Words*, which was an Italian-English dictionary published in 1611.

[35] Gervase Markham *Country Contentments: Or The Husbandmans Recreations* (1630).

COMING TO AMERICA

It would seem that Princeton's 'ballown' was probably more associated to that than football, and it is interesting that Strutt uses the present tense, as if to say that the game was still played even if ignored by the written word, and about to make a fleeting attempt to return to the public eye in New Jersey! Hall's comment that "the game of shinny, known also by the names of hawky and hurly, is as great a favorite with the students as is football at other colleges" suggests that football was never of much importance to early Princetonians.

In New Haven, Connecticut, we find another of America's great academic institutions, Yale University, whose football we first learn of thanks to 1797 graduate Charles Goodrich, who wrote that "foot-ball was our common sport, almost every day in good weather and very often twice daily and I forget if more. We had three lines in front of the college buildings down to the road that crossed the Green by two meeting houses if I remember. Of the three lines the two outside were eight or ten rods apart. We would begin on the middle line and if the scholars were generally out on both sides, whenever the ball was driven over one of the outside lines, the party on that side were beaten, and the other party enjoyed the shouting. There was no delay of the game by choosing sides, the parties were divided by the buildings in which they severally roomed."

The game was powerful enough to stir up the passions of the anonymous poet who scribed:

"There were yellings and shoutings and wiping of noses,
Where the hue of the lily was changed to the rose's,
There were tearing of shirts, and ripping of stitches,
And breaches of peaces, and pieces of britches."

College rules in 1822 said that "if any student shall play at hand or foot ball in the college building or in the college yard … he may be fined not exceeding fifty cents," so instead games were played on what was called The Green, though use of that land led to a fascinating confrontation in 1841, when a game coincided with the local fire department wanting to use the area for a drill. The firefighters won the battle for the rights, but the following day the students got their revenge by invading the field and wrecking their engine!

Richard Hurd picks up the story by explaining that "about 1840 there sprang up an annual game of football between the sophomore and freshman classes, which has survived to the present day in the form of an annual 'rush'. To call this class scrimmage football is a decided stretching of the term, as may be judged from the contemporary description of a game whose participants, attired in a unique grotesqueness of style, and with faces painted in all imaginable hues, formed wedges and phalanxes, and charged and scrambled with a most healthy rivalry, but in whom all knowledge of football was evidently lacking[36]."

But Hurd may have been too quick to condemn, for Clarence Deming was even able to cite the rules of "the old game on the Green", which he says were "of unknown date but almost certainly printed during the thirteen years following 1840." Signed by a 'graduate' they state

---

[36] Richard Hurd *American College Athletics. II. Yale University* (published in *Outing* magazine in 1889).

that "the players are to be divided into two divisions as nearly equal as possible … In the test game between the Sophomores and Freshmen, the Freshmen have the first warning. According to custom, it (the game) consists of five trials, the side that gets three games being the winner … In the last two trials, the Seniors assist the Sophomores and the Juniors the Freshmen[37]."

There was certainly a rugby element to the play, for "the brick walk on Temple Street and the fence upon College Street are two side bounds. If anyone picks up the ball over these side bounds or, picking it up anywhere in the field, can run with it over these bounds, he has a right to a kick at the place where it went over." However, "if the ball is caught it must be kicked from the place; the catcher has no right to run with it" and "if the ball is upon the ground, it must be kicked upon the ground; no one can pick it up and bound it; but he can run with it to either side bound as specified.

In 1848, the college authorities showed their first signs of wanting to prevent the game from being played, but it was actually pressure from the Freshmen, who were ultimately 'demolished mercilessly', that saw it go ahead as normal. A year later there was no game, but it was back in 1850, and still going in 1852, when a report published in the *New York Times* shows that anarchic as Yale's game might have been, it did have a structure, rules and even umpires: "The freshman gave the first kick and then a general rush was made for the ball around which they formed a dense crowd for fifteen minutes, each class striving with their utmost ability without gaining a single rod. At this crisis the ball was kicked from the crowd over the side-bounds, where anyone who can get it has the right to one kick. A sophomore obtained this right but, not being expert himself, he communicated the ball to the leader of his class, a powerful fellow, who ran several rods with it when he was overtaken by a more athletic freshman, but succeeded in throwing the ball nearly over the goal. One or two more kicks and the umpire decided that the sophomores had won the first game. After contesting the second game for nearly an hour the umpires finally decided that one of the freshmen having caught the ball was entitled to a kick at it. This the sophomores were unwilling to allow, but claimed a victory and challenged the freshmen to commence a third game. The freshmen determined to abide by the decision of the umpires and refused to commence the third game until the second (as they claimed) ended. Darkness ended the fierce conflict. Hundreds of spectators witnessed this trial of strength in which the combatants evinced as much interest and invincible courage as was exercised on the plains of Mexico by the American soldiers; and it is also worthy of note that in the contest also one brave hero fainted and was borne bleeding from the field."

In 1853, Deming explains that "the Freshmen on the fateful afternoon, put 131 men into the field and the man was evidently 'queered' for his college course who didn't show up on the Green. The Sophomores had but eighty-nine men, but with their added year of age, heavier

---

[37] Clarence Deming *Yale Yesterdays* (Kessinger Publishing, 1915).

COMING TO AMERICA

and more brawny than the Freshmen. Many of the combatants had stripped to their undershirts. Others wore fantastic clothes and false mustaches, and red paint and lampblack in streaks and blotches made their faces hideous."

But the game was reduced to a shambles "when a Freshman got the ball at the edge of the big scrimmage and with a clear field before him, ran the ball to the Sophomore goal line. The Freshmen sung their paeans of victory, but the Sophomores claimed that the ball struck the South fence and refused to play on unless the claim was allowed ... Verbal football promised to continue until darkness, the three umpires couldn't agree and two of the three resigned after declaring the match a draw." The onlooking ladies sided with the Freshmen's claim and presented them with a floral bouquet, although the Sophomores claimed in the series of vicious articles that appeared in the Yale press over the following weeks that the flower incident had actually been staged by the Frosh.

That bitter argument is given as one of the reasons why the old Yale game died out, although others have been offered. One goes that in 1855, the Freshmen opted not to play, and got away with it, and when they themselves became the Sophomores a year later, they also decided not to bother with the game. By neither accepting nor issuing the challenge, they had effectively put a temporary stop to football at Yale. Meanwhile, Hurd reckoned that "owing to a lack of grounds, the students having been forbidden to play on the city green, the annual game was given up in 1858, and football was dead until 1870." And Clarence Deming maintains that "old-fashioned class football sang its swan song in 1856 by decree of the Faculty, just after it seemed institutional and vitalized. Seen from the landscape viewpoint of half a century, the prohibition of the Faculty is to be criticised justly. In abolishing the annual class game, the Yale authorities did away with one of the salient things which lent outline, depth and picturesqueness to the academic life; which, in physical harmfulness, was to the football of today as a game of checkers ... If there had been more football in the fifties, there would probably have been less hazing in the sixties."

In whatever case, football went on a hiatus of at least a year at Yale, and the version that arose at the same place in the 1870s probably bore very little direct relation.

Agitating bags of wind

In the 1880s, and mainly because of their dominance of college football, Harvard, Yale and Princeton would come to be known as the Big Three, but the other five members of the Ivy League also had their football games, as did others that did not belong to the elite grouping[38].

Columbia University in New York had some kind of ball game from 1824, when there is a mention of boys kicking a ball around as a "campus diversion" involving "seniors and

---

[38] The earliest Mel Smith has found evidence of was Phillips Exeter Academy in New Hampshire, where future US Secretary of State Daniel Webster described how he and his colleagues would rest at the Glass House after playing the game in his only year at the Academy, 1797.

MIKE ROBERTS – THE SAME OLD GAME: CODIFICATION

sophomores lining up against juniors and freshmen[39]" and not many years later of how "on Saturday afternoons, in the fall of the year, a few students would meet in the 'hollow' on the Battery, and play an irregular game of football, generally without teams or 'sides' as they were then termed; a mere desultory engagement[40]."

The University of Pennsylvania had football of some form from around 1840 and there are passing mentions of the game at Brown University in Rhode Island from as early as 1827 being "an annual violent clash between the freshman and sophomore classes. The sport, banned by President Sears in 1862, became very popular with all the classes when it was reinstated in 1866, and then reverted to its former status as a freshman-sophomore encounter[41]."

When Cornell University enrolled its first students in 1865, football was a natural ingredient on the menu. As GL Lohmes tells us in his article in *Outing* in 1890 "football was played the first term of college, but possessed very few of the finer points which have distinguished the game of late years. The number on a side varied according to previous agreement, ranging from twenty to whole classes." Such was the enthusiasm that the players immediately sought permission from their president Andrew White to face Michigan in Cleveland, which was about half way between the two colleges. They received a reply that has gone down in American football folklore. There was absolutely no way White, who was far more interested in rowing regattas, would "permit thirty men to travel 400 miles to agitate a bag of wind."

In terms of footballing sophistication, the place that seems to have been far ahead of the rest was Dartmouth College[42] in Hanover, New Hampshire. Sport was not high on the authorities' agenda in 1771, when Eleazar Wheelock said it would be good if students diversions "may be turned from that which is puerile, such as playing with balls, bowls, and other ways of diversion … for want of an opportunity to exercise themselves in that which is more useful … the practice of some manual arts, or cultivation of gardens and other lands at the proper hours of leisure."

Despite Wheelock's noble intentions, gardening has never been a major leisure pursuit at Dartmouth, and a more enthusiastically welcomed idea was announced in 1826, when the authorities gave the green light for "the playing at ball or any game in which ball is used on the public common in front of Dartmouth College." Football was at liberty to become a part of Dartmouth life, and "a very picturesque and exciting game they made it. Now in a long

---

[39] *A History of Columbia University 1754-1904* (Columbia University Press, 1904).

[40] Charles Haynes Haswell *Reminiscences of an Octogenarian of the City of New York (1816 to 1860)* (Harper, 1896).

[41] Martha Mitchell *Encyclopedia Brunoniana* (Brown University Library, 1993).

[42] Dartmouth football was the subject of a splendid article written by Scott Meacham in 2006, and which is the source of many of the following details.

COMING TO AMERICA

array, now in solid knots, now in scattering groups, and now sweeping like a cyclone, with its runners even more effective than its rushers[43]."

This might be the earliest suggestion of college football in the US that was anything more aesthetically pleasing than a glorified fight. But if the Freshman writing in 1846 was anyone to go by, there were few rules to restrict the levels of violence, and "such rushes you never saw. It is the rule to push over every opponent you are able and sometimes small folks stand a small chance in the crowd[44]." And it was still used as a handy method of giving the Freshmen an early taste of Dartmouth hazing. The chants of 'Freshie! Football!' in the build up to games were, for the Freshmen, not unlike being called into the gladiator arenas of Imperial Rome. An 1853 Freshman later remembered how "we furnished footballs for the college, and occasionally, with a most praiseworthy philanthropy, we permitted our own bodies and limbs to be used as substitutes, in this way taking great pains to furnish amusement for the upper classes[45]."

Two decades later, in 1868, "football was simplicity itself. You ran all over the campus, and when, as, and if you got a chance you kicked a round rubber ball to the east or to the west. You might run all the afternoon and not get your toe upon the ball, but you could not deny that you had had a fair chance, and the exercise was yours and could be valued by the number of hot rolls consumed at the evening meal[46]."

If you 'kicked a round rubber ball', then to all intents and purposes, this was a variant of soccer, but like the different games at the English public schools, it shares some elements, lacks others and throws in a few idiosyncrasies of its own.

The boundary of the field was marked by the limits of The Green itself, which was 375 feet wide and 550 feet long. It is curious that they chose to play across the width rather than the length of the pitch, but at least that got around the need to worry about a rule for when the ball went out of touch, as that would have been very rare indeed. A game started with what was more or less a standard kick off, which like at so many US colleges, was called 'warning the ball', and a game was won by kicking the ball over the fences at either end of the field, and could sometimes happen in a matter of minutes, so several games were usually played back-to-back.

But by 1868, football, hazing and violence in general at Dartmouth had gotten so out of hand that "for a year the faculty in its inscrutable wisdom debarred this highly useful game because of abuses, as they thought, in the manner of playing it." But the early 1870s was a

---

[43] John Henry Bartlett, John Peral Gifford *Dartmouth athletics: A complete history of all kinds of sports at the college* (1893).

[44] Quoted by Leon Burr Richardson in *History of Dartmouth College* (1932).

[45] Daniel A Crosby, quoted by Charles Arms Carleton in *Class-Day Exercises of the Class of '57 in Dartmouth College* (1858).

[46] Professor Edwin J Bartlett *A Dartmouth Book of Remembrance: Pen Sketches of Hanover and the College Before the Centennial and After* (1922), also the quote on the following page.

277

time when all the big colleges were starting to frame more civilised forms of football, and Dartmouth was no exception. It was the author of the previous quote, future professor Edwin Julius Bartlett, who was so desperate to see the game reinstated in 1871 that "in my junior year I was one of a committee sent by the College to ask the President please couldn't we play the game again if we would be good; and he, after taking counsel, said yes."

It was agreed that football could be continued at Dartmouth, as long as such evils as forcing the Freshmen to pay for the balls and then kicking them with spiked boots were eliminated. Instead they drafted strict rules, and games were to be overseen by an umpire to make sure there was no funny business.

The 1871 rules drafted by Bartlett and his committee (see *Appendix Ten*) provide a fascinating relic of early football in America, but not 'American football' as such, for this game clearly discouraged ball handling and physical contact. Meacham agrees that the Dartmouth students were aware of the new rules that were emerging in Britain, but they devised a very different set from those that would be observed by the teams entering the first edition of the FA Cup that same year. Rather than adopt the British laws, which they had no particular reason to do, they adapted them as they saw fit. For instance, former player Albert Perkins Tibbets notes that "there were no off-side rules, practically all of both teams were ahead of the man who kicked off[47]."

Later that year, *The Dartmouth* noted with pleasure that football was being played again, but that now "there were no rushes or rows to speak of; the games were fairly conducted; and we see no reason to doubt that the difficulties attending foot-ball in previous years have now been so far obviated that it can go on in future without any squabbling."

Dartmouth stuck to its own game for many years, but from 1881, when it started to take on the other colleges, the Big Green was going to have to learn to play the new intercollegiate rules. American football. Meanwhile, what became known as Old Division Football underwent reverse evolution into its violent past.

There is a telling comment in *Dartmouth Literary Monthly* of October 1886 about "the gradual degeneration of the good old game of football, which has so long been a feature at Dartmouth. Three years ago the Frater and social games were the chief sport of the cool, breezy fall days; but now, alas! The game has become no more than a cheap imitation of rugby, kept alive not for itself, but for the convenient opportunity afforded for the meeting of Sophomores and Freshmen. Many of the rules have been forgotten, the good 'kicks' are dropping out each year and in five years more the game will have passed entirely away, to be recalled only as a tradition by gray-haired men."

The author was right to be concerned. Despite the noble attempts in 1871 to structure the game, it declined into something that was no more like football than the annual 'rushes' at other colleges. But at least the tradition was maintained much longer at Dartmouth than

---

[47] Albert Perkins Tibbets *Football at Dartmouth*, (in *Dartmouth Alumni Magazine*, 1915).

COMING TO AMERICA

elsewhere, for it was last recorded as late as 1948, by which time it was a sad relic of the college's own attempt to create a codified form of football that Meacham rather touchingly describes as "something of an evolutionary dead-end to the Anglo-American family of football codes."

Old world and the new

Like in England, football in America in the 1860s was taking off in various directions. In some form or other it was being played by schools, colleges, villagers and townspeople. Most of these games went more in for kicking, others like the Boston Game allowed handling. But although the traditional Freshmen versus Sophomores games were often just an excuse for (dis)organised carnage, to the extent that you could have taken the ball out of the game and nobody would have noticed, and in some cases they did, even at the colleges there were other kinds of football that were played in a far more structured and regulated manner.

From 1861 to 1865, life tried to meander on while the Civil War was raging in the background, with 620,000 soldiers and who knows how many more civilians perishing[48]. And it was in the middle of all this, in 1863, that the FA was formed in London to draw up the first attempt at nationally established rules for football.

News of this did seep through to American society. Beadle & Company in New York published the rules in 1866 in its *Dime Novel* series. The earliest game we know to have been played in America in strict accordance with the FA rules was that in October 1866 between Carroll College and the local townspeople of Waukesha, Wisconsin, won 5-2 by the collegers (who only had 22 players compared to the 25 for the town – the original FA rules not having had anything to say about how many players were on a team).

These were not times when the Americans were particularly likely to want to import traditions from the Old Country. In 1876, the USA was celebrating a century of independence from the British Crown, in which relations had been cool at the best of times. The presence of the British dominion of Canada in the north was particularly uncomforting. The British government generally stayed out of the Civil War, but was more inclined to support the Confederate rebels in the south, and at one point had 11,000 troops stationed in Canada ready to pounce, while a diplomatic crisis known as the 1861 Trent Affair almost led Britain and the USA to engage in direct combat. That wasn't the end of it, as late as 1895 the two countries almost went to war during the dispute over the Venezuelan border with British Guiana.

The 1908 Olympic Games in London were particularly revealing of British animosity towards a breakaway colony that was becoming bigger and more powerful than its former masters, and developing imperialistic ideas of its own. The American flag was missing from

---

[48] The crux of the war was the slavery issue, a practice that had been outlawed in the north, and in opposition to Abraham Lincoln's plans to do the same in the south, the eleven pro-slavery states decided to break away from the USA and form the Confederate States of America.

279

the Opening Ceremony, and the refusal by Martin Sheridan, the American flag bearer, to dip his flag before the royal box (because "this flag dips to no earthly king") has led to a non-dipping to royalty tradition that has continued to this day. The Games continued with a number of seemingly unfair calls against American athletes – including one in the 400m which saw the four-man race being re-run. Three of the athletes, all Americans, refused to compete, and so Britain's Wyndham Halswelle raced the final on his own. Not surprisingly, he won. As did Italian marathon runner, Dorando Pietri, but he was famously helped to the finishing line by kind British officials – who were no doubt aware that the man following immediately behind, Johnny Hayes, was an American. Pietri was later disqualified and deprived of his medal, but Queen Alexandra presented the Italian with a gold cup instead.

However, such animosity was not the reason why American colleges developed their own form of football, or why they preferred baseball to cricket. It had nothing to do with nationalism or any kind of rejection of British ideals. America could quite feasibly have become a soccer-playing nation, but simply wasn't interested enough. Americans clearly liked a more violent contest than the English FA's rules could offer, and this would affect the development of the game in the country. The students in particular would probably have agreed with the British clubs that were ignoring soccer and playing a more physical game, but the RFU would not set its code on an established footing until 1871, and for the time being, rugby was relatively unknown in the United States.

So, the soccer rules failed to catch on where it mattered, and even when they did, rather than copy them verbatim, the Americans were more inclined to adapt them to their own tastes. And why should we expect the Americans of the 1860s to have adopted the London FA's rules anyway? It is not as if the whole of the British Isles was unanimously welcoming them with open arms either. By 1868, the FA still only had 30 member teams. It took the best part of two decades to finally win over the nation, and even then, many schools and colleges still played their own games, and half the country still insisted so vigorously on their handling code that the Rugby Union was formed to oversee a totally different game. One which the Ivy League colleges would find considerably more to their taste...

12 THE NOT SO ALL-AMERICAN GAME
Soccer and rugby arrive in the United States

Cannon and balls

The origins of American football should perhaps not be placed not on land, but on water. In 1843, Yale University created a boat club, believed to have been the first proper sports club at any American college. Harvard soon followed suit and in 1852 the two universities met for the first major stateside intercollegiate sports event, a rowing race at Lake Winnipesaukee, New Hampshire. The passion with which these regattas were received by student and non-student populations alike would sow the seeds for the thriving future of intercollegiate sport.

This was roughly the same time that baseball was emerging as America's first great team ball sport. It is curious how this new game came to replace cricket, which as late as the 1860s had around 500 clubs in some 100 American cities. Similar bat and ball games like stoolball, rounders and others with such colourful names as 'one old cat' also held their ground, but although clubs were formed, they were informal affairs that rarely survived more than a year or two. Enter the Knickerbocker Base Ball Club, formed in New York in 1845 by Alexander Cartwright, who over a century later, in June 1953, the United States Congress would officially recognise as the true inventor of modern baseball, as opposed to the infamous Abner Doubleday 'myth'. That may be bestowing more credit on the Manhattan bookseller than he really deserved, for it was much more complex than a one-man show. His club may have pioneered the diamond and many of the basic rules, but they ultimately did no more than create a slightly more organised structure for what was commonly known as the 'New York Game'. But America likes its folk heroes, and if they couldn't have Doubleday, then Cartwright holds a good enough case as a replacement.

Dozens of fledgling clubs followed the Knickerbockers' lead, and within a decade they were everywhere. Baseball grew so big and so fast that it had its first professional team, the Cincinnati Red Stockings, as early as 1860, and by 1871 the National Association had organised the first pro league.

Desperate for any chance to get one up on each other, it was inevitable that the students would be among the first to start reaching for their bats. In 1859, the first known match between two colleges was played by Amherst and Williams. That was just the start of it. By 1870 almost every college in the land had its team and intercollegiate competitions were all the rage – all this at a time when American football didn't even exist yet!

One such ballgame was played in 1866 between Princeton and nearby Rutgers, which the former won by a massive 40-2. Rutgers, the eighth oldest university in the USA, but which

MIKE ROBERTS – THE SAME OLD GAME: CODIFICATION

never quite made Ivy League status, was humiliated by the defeat, and decided to gain its revenge by making an unprecedented suggestion – they challenged Princeton to a game of football! Both colleges had been experimenting with the game for some time. Princeton had moved on from their old ballown game and were now kicking an India rubber ball, while football at Rutgers had been the doing of an enthusiastic player-teacher, Chester Hartranft, who got a group of youngsters to club together and buy a ball, and gave them a fighting bird called the chanticleer as their mascot.

John W Herbert, one of the Rutgers players, was still around in 1933 to provide his invaluable recollections of the build up to the day. "To appreciate this game to the full you must know something of its background" he said. "The two colleges were, and still are, of course, about 20 miles apart. The rivalry between them was intense. For years each had striven for possession of an old Revolutionary cannon, making night forays and lugging it back and forth time and again. Not long before the first football game, the canny Princetonians had settled this competition in their own favor by ignominiously sinking the gun in several feet of concrete."

Losing a baseball match was one thing, losing the cannon was another. Rutgers had scores to settle, and captain and spokesperson William Leggett, who would later become an important member of the clergy in the Dutch Reformed Church, issued his challenge to the Princeton baseball captain, William Gunmere, who later became Chief Justice of the Supreme Court of New Jersey.

Princeton were well up for it, and a historic date was earmarked for what many consider American football's date of birth, November 6, 1869, as celebrated when Rutgers defeated visiting Princeton 29-0 in the 'centennial' game in 1969. But that claim is stretching it a bit. It is probably safer to say that it was the date of the first 'intercollegiate football match', although even that may not be strictly true, because Princeton had actually played several informal games against the neighbouring Theological Seminary from the late 1850s. Also, games had been arranged between Columbia and both the Polytechnic Collegiate Institute and Adelphi Academy in spring 1869, and although there is no record that they ever got played, there is no reason to believe they didn't, and hopefully with more success than an Adelphi game a year later that was abandoned when a 14 year old boy stole the ball!

Nevertheless, on a blustery November day, the Rutgers students welcomed their Princeton rivals at New Brunswick train station. While the rest of the players checked out the local billiard hall, a meeting was held by the captains to hurriedly agree on a set of rules, largely based on the ones the home team, Rutgers, played by. The venue was a plot of land that is now occupied by the Rutgers gymnasium, and the action was overseen by four judges and two referees. The teams had no particular kits, they just wore what they were wearing, but the Rutgers team did tie scarlet stockings around their heads like turbans to help the players and the hundred or so spectators perched around the edges of the field atop a wooden fence tell the teams apart. The goals were two posts, eight paces apart with no crossbar.

THE NOT SO ALL-AMERICAN GAME

Herbert continues that "the players lined up on each side; the organisation of the twenty-five being the same on each side. Two men were selected by each team to play immediately in front of the opponents' goal and were known as the captains of the enemy's goal." Such blatant goal-hanging suggests there was no offside rule in this game.

"The remainder of each team was divided into two sections, the players in one section were assigned to certain tracts of the field which they were to cover and never leave. They were known as 'fielders'. The other section was detailed to follow the ball up and down the field. These latter players were known as the 'bulldogs'. They were easily recognisable in the evolution of the game as the forerunners of the modern rush line … Though smaller on the average, the Rutgers players, as it developed, had ample speed and fine football sense. Receiving the ball, our men formed a perfect interference around it and with short, skilful kicks and dribbles drove it down the field … None thought of it, so far as I know, but we had without previous plan or thought evolved the play that became famous a few years later as the flying wedge[1]." That's interference in the modern American football sense, i.e. protecting the player in possession of the ball by obstructing the players around him. Off the ball tackling was something both English codes opposed, and the American insistence on keeping it part of the game would be one of the most important reasons for their game going off at a different tangent. And Rutgers used that method to score the very first intercollegiate goal.

"Next period Rutgers bucked, or received the ball, hoping to repeat the flying wedge. But the first time we formed it Big Mike[2] came charging full upon us. It was our turn for surprise. The Princeton battering ram made no attempt to reach the ball but, forerunner of the interference-breaking ends of today, threw himself into our mass play, bursting us apart, and bowling us over. Time and again Rutgers formed the wedge and charged; as often Big Mike broke it up. And finally on one of these incredible break-ups a Princeton bulldog with a long accurate, perhaps lucky kick, sent the ball between the posts for the second score.

"The flying wedge thus checkmated, Rutgers might have been in a bad spot had not Madison Ball, '73, come through. He had a trick of kicking the ball with his heel. All the game he had been a puzzle to the Princetonians. The ball would be rolling toward the Rutgers goal, and, running ahead of it instead of taking time to turn, he would heel it back. He made several such plays, greatly encouraging his team. Then he capped all this by one tremendous lucky backward drive directly to Dixon, standing squarely before Princeton's goal ... Dixon easily scored, giving us a one-goal lead. Big Mike again rose, however, in a berserk

---

[1] The 'flying wedge', which we'll be coming back to later, involved a pack of players forming into a V shape around the player in possession of the ball, and charging ahead of him to offer protection as they violently fended off approaches from opposing players.

[2] *The New Brunswick Daily Fredonia* reported how "our neighbor Princeton sent her chosen twenty-four stalwart men and one Goliath to combat our twenty-five striplings." It was this character, Big Mike, that they meant.

endeavor, and, getting the ball, he called the Princeton men into a flying wedge of their own and straight-away they took the ball right down the field and put it over.

"The fifth and sixth goals went to Rutgers. The stars of the latter period of play, in the memory of the players after the lapse of many years, were Big Mike and Large. Someone by a random kick had driven the ball to one side, where it rolled against the fence and stopped. Large led the pursuit for the ball closely followed by Michael. They reached the fence on which students were perched, and unable to check their momentum, in a tremendous impact they struck it. The fence then gave way with a crash and over went the band of yelling students to the ground.

"Every college probably has the humorous tradition of some player who has scored against his own team. This tradition at Rutgers dated from this first game, for one of her players, whose identity is unknown, in the sixth period started to kick the ball between his own goal posts. The kick was blocked, but Princeton took advantage of the opportunity and soon made the goal. This turn of the game apparently disorganized Rutgers, for Princeton also scored the next goal after a few minutes of play, thus bringing the total up to four all."

The account is fascinating. It is evident that as this was the first proper game of football most of these players had ever been involved in, and because they were playing to rules agreed upon in the hours leading up the three o'clock kick off, they were practically inventing the game and its associated tactics as they went along. But where does it fit into football's evolutionary tree? Revisionists are probably right to argue that this kicking game was nothing like modern American football, but with all that thumping around of opponents, it was hardly soccer either, and Herbert clearly comments on several innovations that would later become part of modern American football, but not soccer. It was more of an adaptation of basic soccer that the two colleges developed to suit their own tastes. But not everyone's, for rumour has it that a miserable old Rutgers professor cycled by the field at one point and got off his bike to wave an umbrella at the players, yelling that "you men will come to no Christian end!"

The November 1869 issue of the Rutgers student rag, *The Targum*, wasn't massively impressed by this early attempt at college football either, and "to describe the varying fortunes of the match, game by game, would be a waste of labor for every game was like the one before. There was the same headlong running, wild shouting, and frantic kicking. In every game the cool goaltenders saved the Rutgers goal half a dozen times; in every game the heavy charger of the Princeton side overthrew everything he came in contact with; and in every game, just when the interest in one of those delightful rushes at the fence was culminating, the persecuted ball would fly for refuge into the next lot, and produce cessation of hostilities until, after the invariable foul, it was put in straight. To sum up, Princeton had the most muscle, but didn't kick very well, and wanted organization. They evidently don't like to kick the ball on the ground."

THE NOT SO ALL-AMERICAN GAME

It was thanks to their short, low kicking game that Rutgers were ultimately able to thwart Princeton once and for all and grab two late scores to avenge the loss of the precious cannon with a 6-4 win. The game over, it was time for the after-match celebrations, which *The Targum* said involved "an amicable feed together. At 8 o'clock our guests went home, in high good spirits, thirsting to beat us next time, if they can" while *The Daily Fredonian* said "a bountiful entertainment was prepared for our Princeton friends at the favorite resort in Church Street known as Northrop's where mine host and his estimable lady know how to get up a good supper."

Nice and jolly, and in stark contrast to a comment made by one of the Princeton players, William Preston Lane, admittedly more than six decades after the match, when he remembered with less gleaming eyes how Rutgers "ran us Princeton men out of town. I never found out why they did that. But we don't ask any questions. When we saw them coming after us, we ran to the outskirts of New Brunswick and got into our carriages and wagons and went away as fast as we could[3]."

Whether the event had ended with the two sides enjoying an evening of male bonding, or whether it had ended with the Princeton players fleeing for their lives, the two sides were back at it a week later, this time in Princeton, and this time they played by the Princeton rules, which involved a few subtle differences. This time the players were allowed to catch the ball in the air and claim a free kick – which may have been a Princeton tradition, or may just have been something they had decided would help them beat the smaller but nippier Rutgers dribblers.

They had also come up with a neat trick to go with it, because this time they decided to advance the ball using a series of short kicks and fair catches, the same 'little mark' tactic that was emerging around the same time in Australia. Rutgers' dribbling game was also thwarted by a dodgy valve in the ball, which kept losing air, meaning it never managed to stay spherical for more than a few kicks at a time. Princeton cruised to an 8-0 shutout, and plenty of arguments ensued. The game was attracting far more attention than the college authorities felt it deserved, and they decided it would be wise to step in and announce that the deciding game three would not be going ahead as the students had planned. Unfortunately for Rutgers, it would be sixty-nine years before they ever beat Princeton at football again.

Great experimentations

But although that rubber match never went ahead, those two games between Rutgers and Princeton had already laid the groundwork for the future of football in the United States. In 1870, Rutgers were invited back to Princeton, and lost, and that was also the year that Rutgers brought a third college on board.

---

[3] Associated Press article in various newspapers, including *St Petersburg Evening Independent* and *The Reading Eagle*, November 22, 1933. Lane's version seems to be the inconsistent one. His memory was obviously hazy, for why does he say they ran for their wagons, if other reports say the players had arrived by train?

MIKE ROBERTS – THE SAME OLD GAME: CODIFICATION

Football was gaining in popularity among the mere 125 students at Columbia, which had such a tiny campus, then on 49th Street, that it was almost impossible for the poor lads to find anywhere to play. The *Columbia Alumni News* described how they received an invitation to travel to New Brunswick and face Rutgers in November 1870. They accepted and the game was played twenty-a-side, and after half an hour's scoreless play, they decided to do away with the goalposts altogether and declared that all they had to do was get the ball across the opposition's line. That produced a flood of goals, but mainly for Rutgers, who won 6-3.

Despite the introduction of Columbia to the fray, the boom in intercollegiate football was going to have to wait. We could call 1871–72 a 'year of transition'. Neither Rutgers nor Columbia managed to get any games off the ground despite the latter even issuing a challenge to Yale, and Princeton managed nothing more exotic than three wins against the Seminarians over the road, who never really provided anything more than practice opposition. But outside of the elite universities, football was spreading. This was also the first year we have any record of football happenings on the Pacific coast, where Oakland High took on San Francisco Industrial School to celebrate Christmas, and a year later the University of California was mustering a representative team to play outside games.

In 1872, college football was back with a vengeance. Columbia's loss to Rutgers had in no way dented their morale, and they faced them for a rematch, in a game that introduced another innovation to the game. Perhaps after reading *Tom Brown's Schooldays*, which had now been around for well over a decade, they introduced a crossbar, and the idea was now to kick the ball over it, giving the game at least some flavour of rugby as opposed to soccer.

Columbia had caught the football bug, and they threw in a game with little Stevens Tech before providing the first ever opposition for Yale, where football rushes were supposedly replaced with something more orderly by a student called David Schaff, the son of Swiss born theologian Philip Schaff. David, who would later carve out a successful career in theology of his own, had apparently learned of rugby from English pupils at Kornthal School in Germany, although the game he and his Yale peers enjoyed was more like soccer.

Yale's first attempt at setting up a game with another college had been with Princeton, but the distance between the two proved too difficult a factor to overcome. They accepted Columbia's more local challenge instead, the venue being their own Hamilton Park (where they had moved after a run in with the police for playing on New Haven Green). An amazing souvenir of this, the first ever all Ivy League match, was uncovered recently in the scrapbook of one Nathan Tyler, a Yale student at the time, in the form of the match programme, which was auctioned off in May 2007 for the tidy sum of $24,000. It includes details of all the players and the now common two referees and four judges, plus a column of nine spaces where members of the four hundred strong crowd could record the names of the scorers, there being nine gaps because the game was won by the first team to score five goals. It was also said to be the first time entrance was charged, 25 cents a head, and the game attracted such interest that several papers sent reporters to cover it.

THE NOT SO ALL-AMERICAN GAME

The *New York World* wrote how Columbia's team "entered upon their work lightly clad and distinguished by light wrappers and blue caps, while their rivals were dressed in all ways, and presented an appearance not unlike that with which Yale men are wont to seek the scene of the annual rush … As the excitement slacked, a youth might be seen retiring behind an adjoining fence to replace a dilapidated pair of pants."

After over two hours of play, and with darkness closing in, Yale had proved that appearances can deceive by winning 3-0, and Tim Cohane in *The Yale Football Story* (1951) describes how "at dinner that night, the rival players compared bruises and toasted each other. The evening in later stages became hilarious to the point where shattered crockery and glassware decimated the modest profits from the gate receipts." Yale had been welcomed into the football fraternity, and that was sign enough that things were starting to get serious.

Come together

By the end of 1872, most of the Ivy League colleges had had a go at setting things straight by drafting basic rules for their games. The earliest seems to have been Edwin Julius Bartlett and his committee's attempt at Dartmouth, where alumnus Albert Perkins Tibbets had once written that "the one rule that was observed, and that had the most influence on the style of play, was that a fair catch entitled a man to a place kick without interference[4]." But by the time official rules were written in 1871, the fair catch was gone, and instead it was declared that "it shall be considered foul when the ball is caught on the bound, or fly, or picked from the ground." Dartmouth football was clearly following the English FA's lead, first by including the fair catch in what was otherwise soccer, and later eliminating it, as the FA had done in 1866.

However, the Big Three all still allowed the ball to be caught on the fly in the early 1870s. When Princeton wrote their rules in October 1871 (see *Appendix Eleven*) they decreed that "any player catching the ball after it has been kicked or knocked and before it touches the ground shall be entitled to a free kick," although "no player shall throw or carry the ball." Also, despite all that interference in the game with Rutgers in 1869, the rules now said that "no holding shall be allowed except when the player has the ball in possession" and "no tripping shall be allowed, nor shall any player use his hands to push an adversary."

David Schaff's Yale rules (see *Appendix Twelve*) were formalised in October 1872, and these too were more like soccer than rugby, for "no player shall pick up, throw, or carry the ball on any part of the field" although the rule that "when the ball is caught in the air an adversary may strike it from the hands of the player so catching" tells us the ball could be caught, but in this case did not win a free kick. As for physicality, "no tripping shall be allowed, nor shall any player use his hands to push or hold an adversary." The goals were two posts placed eight paces apart, and there were other soccer elements, such as the throw-

---

[4] Albert Perkins Tibbets *Football at Dartmouth*, (in *Dartmouth Alumni Magazine*, 1915).

in (though only at right angles and the ball could only be played after it had touched the ground).

Harvard's game, for between ten and fifteen players only, and drafted in December 1872 (see *Appendix Thirteen*), was more or less the same, but involved kicking the ball over a rope that ran the length of the touchline at a height of about five feet. It included the curious rules that "any player is allowed to catch or pick up the ball. No player is allowed to run with the ball or to baby the ball unless pursued by an opponent, and then only while so pursued" and that "no player is allowed to throw or pass the ball to another player unless pursued by an opponent." It sounds fiercely complicated, but a former player later explained how "it may seem curious that this rule worked, but it did. The reason is that the pursuer always called out when he stopped chasing and if the runner did not at once also stop, the cry was taken up by the whole pack of opponents. He was then obliged by tradition to go back to where he was at the crucial moment, before kicking. It is obvious that under this rule there would develop the tactics of a player of the same team running by the side of the player with the ball, who, when tackled, passed the ball to his running mate, who in turn could run if chased, otherwise he must kick or throw the ball[5]."

As well as allowing running with the ball, albeit only when being chased, Harvard was also the only one of these four to have an offside law, which was also described with knotty wording, whereby "any player when on the adversary's side of the ball must either walk toward the ball, or must walk toward his own goal in a line at right angles with that goal. Any player not complying with this law shall be considered as lurking, and shall not be allowed to touch the ball until he has reached a point on his own side of the ball." Despite including many elements of soccer, and not allowing "striking, hacking, tripping, nor butting," Harvard's game was the only one that clearly included at least the seed of rugby.

What obviously would not do was for every college to carry on with this practice of inventing their own rules, and Princeton led the way by suggesting it would be a whole lot simpler if they reached some kind of common agreement. Columbia, Yale and Rutgers, the three universities that had the most experience of intercollegiate matches, were all invited to an October meeting, and they had also got wind of Harvard's growing interest in football, and asked if they would be interested in attending too.

This was where a major turning point in American football began. Harvard weren't interested. Their captain, Henry Grant, was abrupt and patronising in his pooh-poohing of Yale's suggestion for unified rules and wrote back to inform them that "Harvard stands entirely distinct by herself in the game of football. You perhaps wonder on your side at our rules; but I assure you that we consider the game here to admit of much more science, according to our rules. We cannot but recognize in your game much brute force, weight and especially 'shin' element. Our game depends upon running, dodging and position playing,

---

[5] Morton Henry Prince, Class of 1875, in *The H Book of Harvard Athletics* (1923).

THE NOT SO ALL-AMERICAN GAME

i.e. kicking across field into another's hands[6]. We are perfectly aware of our position in regard to other colleges. I assure you we gave the matter a fair discussion last spring. We even went so far as to practice and try the Yale game. We gave it up at once as hopeless[7]."

Harvard player Morton Henry Prince later explained that in his college's game "a player was permitted to pick up the ball, run with it, throw it, or pass it. He could also seize and hold an adversary to prevent his getting the ball. Quite contrary to this were the Yale rules, which were essentially the same as those of Princeton, Columbia, and Rutgers: no picking up, carrying or throwing the ball was allowed, nor was holding or pushing with the hands. The game was all footwork … kicking was the predominant feature of the game."

Harvard did allow some handling of the ball, but their game was not rugby. As a Harvardian of time explained, "there were many points of difference from the Rugby game. It was eminently a kicking as distinguished from a running and tackling game. The rules ... existed only in tradition. We went to work to learn the Rugby game, but I should question if there were three men in college who had ever seen the egg-shaped ball. A drop kick was an unknown and incredible feat, and the intricacies of off side, free kick, put out, and such commonplaces of the game seemed inextricable mysteries to novices like us[8]."

Judging by Grant's tone, Harvard's aloofness was as much about snobbery and a refusal to adjust any aspects of their game to those of supposedly inferior academic institutions as it was about real issues with the laws. Fact is, Grant was blasé about the whole affair, and ended his letter by telling Yale, quite extraordinarily, that "I would send you a copy of our rules but we do not have a spare copy." One doubts that it would have taken Grant longer than ten minutes to quickly scribble down the mere fifteen Harvard rules if he had felt that way inclined, but he just didn't seem interested.

Columbia elected delegates to attend the meeting, but due to sloppy organisational skills they never showed up, sending a message that they'd be happy to along with whatever rules the others came up with. Which meant that eventually it would only be students from Yale, Princeton and Rutgers that sat down at the Fifth Avenue Hotel in New York on October 19, 1873 to form the Intercollegiate Football Association and decide upon a set of twelve common rules (see *Appendix Fourteen*).

Despite Harvard's opposition to the 'brute force, weight and especially shin element', the absence of tripping, holding and pushing hardly suggests it was a particularly violent game that the IFA was after. What is perhaps most important about the 1873 rules is how much

---

[6] We could make an example of Mark Bernstein here, when he uses this Henry Grant quote in his book, one of the most widely read histories of American football's origins. He decides that the words "kicking across field into another's hands" are not needed and edits them out. That's a bit naughty, as a mere six words hardly make much difference to the conciseness. But Bernstein clearly only wants to tell his readers about the "running, dodging and position playing", which all sound close enough to the ethics of American football and rugby, and hides the fact that the focus of the Harvard game was still essentially on kicking the ball.

[7] Henry Grant quoted in *Harvard alumni bulletin: Volume 18* (1915).

[8] William Tyler, class of 1874, in the *Harvard Advocate* (1885).

289

MIKE ROBERTS – THE SAME OLD GAME: CODIFICATION

they resemble soccer – the only major diversion being the throw-up of the ball following fouls and when the ball went out of play. And the ball itself was quite definitely round, the No 6 being the same type endorsed by the London FA.

Like in England and Australia, there were still no strict rules about timing. Play went on as long it had to until somebody scored the required six goals, the visiting team had a train to catch or it was simply too dark to continue. What was certainly missing was any semblance of an offside law, with the Americans apparently as disinterested as the Australians in any such rule, while the tradition of awarding the match ball to the victors survived until as late as 1973, when offenses were allowed to use their own balls.

Soccer's false dawn

The new rules were put into use just a week later, when Yale beat Rutgers 3-1 in front of a crowd of about a thousand, surely the largest to date for a football match on American soil, and with those people all paying 35 cents each to get in, the potential for professionalism was already evident.

For Yale, playing Rutgers and Columbia was one thing, but Princeton was another matter entirely. A month later the two teams that would dominate the first thirty years of college football commenced hostilities. As it turned out, this was to be Princeton's only game that year, but it was one they intended to take seriously, and they even considered the idea of going out jogging each night to get their fitness up. The idea was just that little bit too far ahead of its time, and was unanimously rejected!

Yale had won a coin toss to decide upon the venue, so that was to be Hamilton Park, but the game itself hardly got off to the most auspicious of starts. After half an hour of scoreless football, two players from each side kicked the leather 'pigskin' at the same time and it burst. Left without a ball, the players had to club together to raise the funds to get back to campus and buy a fresh one, and the story goes that while the Yale lads took the time to relax on the grass, the Princeton boys exercised on with the remnants of the defunct football, and the time invested paid off, because they went on to win 3-0. Unfortunately, a dispute over the rules meant Yale and Princeton would not play again for another three years. Things weren't going entirely to plan.

Hamilton Park was also the venue for potentially the most important game in the history of football in America, played on a windy December 1873 afternoon. Yale received a visit from a team calling themselves the Eton Players, and which was mainly made up of former pupils of one of England's most pioneering football schools. The late Sam Foulds wrote that "the so-called American rules were used, which were for all practical purposes a facsimile of the Football Association of England code. The idea for such a contest came about at a reunion of Eton College graduates who were in business or traveling in the United States. Arrangements were made for the game by two members of the Eton group who were visiting New Haven. The English team gathered players from all sections of the United States, including such

THE NOT SO ALL-AMERICAN GAME

distant places as San Francisco and St Louis … Although the Etonians were more skilful and with better ball control than Yale, and showed the home club some new tricks in dribbling and at times resorted to rushing tactics, they were evidently out of condition and tired easily[9]." Yale eventually won 2-1, though the wind was a deciding factor, with all the goals scored by teams playing with it to their backs, and the fourth 'inning' was not completed because the visitors had a train to New York to catch.

The major contribution to American football of that historic encounter was that Eton insisted on playing eleven-a-side, and Yale discovered that the game worked a whole lot better with fewer players. Another plus was that if teams were smaller, it would be easier to get their faculties to grant permission for them to travel to away games, and Yale spent much of the next few years arguing for and eventually convincing the other colleges of the benefits of eleven-a-side football.

But as it turned out, despite all the initial promise, and even a game played against prestigious English opposition, the 1873 Intercollegiate Football Association proved to be a non-starter of little eventual significance. Although a zealous few had managed to agree to some rules, if the actual players could be bothered to read them at all, they simply modified them as they pleased. What hope of convincing other colleges to use the IFA rules when even the founder members weren't taking any notice of them? In 1875, Princeton and Columbia preferred to use the latest version of the FA rulebook, and a season later the two teams decided it would be more fun to kick the ball over, rather than under, the crossbar.

Ultimately, it wouldn't matter too much. So important was Harvard's lack of interest in the IFA that Morton Henry Prince even believed that "if Harvard had not refused it is highly improbable that the modern game played today … would ever have been evolved. Instead, all universities colleges and schools today would be playing the Association Rules – practically soccer." But in 1874, the pattern of football in America was to change its course entirely when Harvard played a Canadian university and were introduced to the wonders of rugby.

What's a rugby?

In 1885, the *New York World* was feeding its readership rewrites of history in the form of such drivel as "when George Washington's father was a boy learning his ABC's the lads of Yale College used to play foot-ball. Long before the blue stars of the American flag were born the boys of Princeton played the same game." Dramatically put, but factually inaccurate. Not even the argument that American football evolved from Harvard and the Boston Game holds up too well in court. The reality is that it grew out of rugby, and had the British dominion of Canada to thank. It's not something they like to make a song and dance about in the United States.

---

[9] Sam Foulds, the former official historian for the United States Soccer Federation in *Soccer Journal* (1988).

291

MIKE ROBERTS – THE SAME OLD GAME: CODIFICATION

Having made his point more than clear in his letter to Yale that he had precious little interest in whatever game the IFA was trying to formalise, Henry Grant, the Harvard captain, continued experimenting in the inter-faculty matches that were gaining in popularity in Cambridge. But what is odd is that despite his aloofness to the IFA, Grant then pounced on a proposal that arrived in the form of a politely put letter from David Roger, the captain of the football team at McGill University in Montreal, Canada. Roger proposed that McGill would travel down to Cambridge for a game played according to the Canadian school's rules (see *Appendix Fifteen*), and later that year, they would play by Harvard's rules in Montreal.

The Canadian colleges were playing something purporting to be English rugby, and Earl Zukerman[10] argues that Harvard's reason for being so keen to play McGill was that they themselves were keen to adopt the game. But they were having trouble getting their heads around the fineries, and felt it might be useful to get some hands-on experience against a team that knew how to play rugby properly.

Despite being in a different country, Montreal lies just over the border and it is no further from Harvard to McGill than it is to most of the other major universities in the New England area. But it was still too far for Harvard, who replied that they would be delighted to play, but would never be able to travel in term time, and that it would be better if both games were played back to back in Cambridge.

The *Harvard Crimson* heralded the arrival of their Canadian guests with the announcement that "the McGill University Football Club will meet the Harvard Football Club on Wednesday and Thursday, May 13th and 14th. The game probably will be called at 3 o'clock. Admittance 50 cents. The proceeds will be donated to the entertainment of our visitors from Montreal."

The Canadian players arrived a day ahead of the match, and as the *Montreal Gazette* later reported, "shortly after their arrival in Boston, the Harvard fellows called on them and exchanged words. In the afternoon they went out to Cambridge, but owing to the great heat only a scratch match was played, six from each side." Some fanciful imaginations have flowered up this particular part of the story. One goes that it wasn't long before a potential problem surfaced. The McGill players, as long as they caught the ball 'on the bound' started running with it under their arms – and the Harvard onlookers explained to them that this was surely a basic violation of the football rules.

It has been said that David Roger and his team maintained that in Canada running with the ball was perfectly legal, and the Harvard players asked just what kind of game it was that they played up there. McGill's answer? Rugby. The PFRA claim that "the Harvard team laughed, but when the McGill players were out of earshot they asked each other nervously, 'what's a rugby?'" Such an exchange is unlikely to have really happened, for Harvard themselves included a certain element of running with the ball in their game, and their

---

[10] On the McGill Athletics website and in a version of events that seems to fit with William Tyler's earlier comment.

292

THE NOT SO ALL-AMERICAN GAME

interest in learning more about rugby was probably the reason they were playing McGill in the first place. Indeed, as Morton Henry Prince remembered, once the challenge had been issued "we at once set to work studying the principles of the Rugby game, practicing plays, and working out what could be done under the rules and particularly what tactics under the Harvard rules could be adapted[11]."

But the first of the two games was played by the local Harvard rules. 250 people turned up to watch, a poor turnout considering the importance of the occasion, and "the officials called the two captains together and tossed a coin to determine the choice of goals. Captain Grant of Harvard, by correctly naming the turn of the coin, set a precedent for all his successors at Harvard. He selected the north-west goal, thereby obtaining the advantage of a slight breeze. Captain Rodger of McGill, who had been carrying his arm in a sling on account of a recent injury, thereupon unconcernedly walked to one of the posts which supported the goal rope, hung his sling upon the post, and called to his players to take the field. The two teams lined up at once[12]."

There was no doubt which of the two teams looked the best kitted out for the occasion. "The McGill men, dressed in the English foot-ball suit, straggled into the field, and, after a few minutes, were followed by a shabby-looking set of men … As it happened, the dilapidated appearance of the Harvard players was quite a boon to the lookers-on, for if they had been respectably clad in a uniform of some kind it might have been quite impossible to distinguish between the two sides; but, as it was, one merely had to notice whether or not a few rags were floating gracefully behind the player to know to which side he belonged[13]."

The *Montreal Gazette* described how "the game commenced shortly before 4 o'clock, and was played in accordance with the Harvard rules. It was arranged that five games should be played, the club winning three to be declared the victor. At the commencement the Harvards won the choice of goals, which entitled the McGills to do the first kick, they playing with the sun directly in their faces. The first game was lively while it lasted, but in less than five minutes the ball was flying over the McGill's goal, and the first game was declared for the Harvards. The second was somewhat longer. The Harvards kept the ball well over on the McGills' side, and after a sharp contest, during which both clubs were several times piled up together indiscriminately, it was again forced over the ropes by the Harvards. In the third game there was more desperate struggling, but the Harvards had it all their own way and again won."

The *Harvard Crimson* was somewhat more damning of the footballing ability of their guests, saying the game was "a disappointment to all who saw it, for the Canadians, from ignorance of the Harvard rules, had failed utterly in resisting the Harvard Ten, who won the

---

[11] Morton Henry Prince in *The H Book of Harvard Athletics* (1923).

[12] *Harvard alumni bulletin: Volume 18* (1915).

[13] This quote is taken from the *Harvard Crimson*'s report of the second match in the series, but could presumably have just as easily been applied to the first.

MIKE ROBERTS – THE SAME OLD GAME: CODIFICATION

three goals so easily that the McGill players seemed standing in the field merely to be spectators of their opponents' excellent kicking." McGill simply couldn't get their heads around the Harvard game with a goal that was just a rope tied four metres above the ground, and despite having some notable sprinters in their side, they were confounded by Harvard's 'only running when under pursuit' rule. It was all over in twenty-two minutes.

It was the second match that would change history. This time, the Canadians would be dictating the rules. $2.50 was invested in a set of proper H-shaped rugby posts, and the Americans were introduced to the oval ball[14] in what is claimed by many to be the first true game of American football ever played, although in reality it was just a simplified form of rugby[15].

The *Harvard Crimson* reported extensively on the game, saying that as it was "played according to the McGill, or rather Rugby rules, it was feared that the result would be quite different – that the Canadians would win the match with little difficulty … For the first half-hour the Harvard men had the wind in their favor. To the agreeable surprise of most of us, the Canadians did not kick the ball over the cross-bar in the first five minutes, and they seemed indeed hardly able to hold their own. The first two half-hours passed without either side winning even a touch-down, although several times it was barely lost; but the last half-hour was the most exciting of all. Both sides were evidently doing their best, though several of the McGill men already showed signs of the rough usage they had received in the first part of the game."

Morton Henry Prince wrote that "we discovered that certain of our own plays could be introduced which, though we had not suspected it, had not been thought of by McGill. When in the match we used these plays, the visitors were dumbfounded, and for the moment questioned their propriety, but at once recognized their legality when it was pointed out by the umpire." This would typify what happened to rugby in the USA – the players took the basics, but applied their own tactics, often based around increased physicality and violence, but also considerable gamesmanship, which would ultimately lead to changes in the laws.

---

[14] Or maybe not, for Mark Bernstein claims that McGill arrived without their own ball, because they had wrongly assumed that they would be able to get hold of one in Boston. However, Morton Henry Prince, who played in the game, remembered that "the ball was the English oval, leather-covered ball, substantially the same as that used today in the present American game."

[15] Contrary to popular belief, the McGill game was not rugby in the strictest sense, but was their own adaptation of the rules, as we shall see in the chapters on football in Canada. Nevertheless, when on October 19, 1974, Harvard and McGill decided to play a game to celebrate the centenary of the historic encounter, it was quite rightly played by the two colleges' respective rugby, not American or Canadian football, teams (McGill, incidentally, won 6-3, and the game is now an annual event).

THE NOT SO ALL-AMERICAN GAME

The *Harvard Crimson* ended by saying that "the end of the half-hour came at last, and the game was drawn. On the whole it was a very successful contest, and it is to be hoped that next year several games may be played between the Tens[16] of McGill and Harvard."

The *Gazette* also explained how "the crowd cheered impartially, and certainly were very patient to remain standing so long. On Friday night the Harvard team entertained the McGill men at a grand dinner at the Parker House. The McGill team came away with reluctance; they would have liked to have stayed another week with the Harvards, they were treated so well and kindly. They carry home with them the pleasantest recollections of their visit, and the courtesy and hospitality of their entertainers."

The fact that the first game was such a one-sided non-event, while the second was a classic encounter, may have been part of the reason why a contributor to the *Harvard Crimson* would later predict that "football will be a popular game here in the future. The rugby game is in much better favor than the somewhat sleepy game played by our men." The *Montreal Gazette* felt that for the rugby match, "the crowd was very much greater." It had raised expectations, several college and civilian papers deemed it worthy of mention, and the crowd reportedly included some Yale footballers that were keen to witness both Harvard's induction into intercollegiate football, and the chance to see this rugby game whose praises were being sung so widely.

In the wake of that one match, Harvard immediately confined the Boston Game to the history books, and also changed their tune regarding the possibility of a rematch with McGill. In November 1875, they were on a train for Montreal in search of more of the same. They were rugby converts. Now it was just a small matter of converting the rest of the nation.

Harvard spread the word

Harvard's first meeting with a fellow American college was against Tufts at Medford, just outside Boston, in June 1875. As the *Daily Globe* reported the following day "the play opened briskly, and ere long five or six Tufts men found themselves laid on their back so violently that they imagined it was evening by the stars they saw." But Tufts soon repaid the compliment, and actually went on to win 1-0 in one of the greatest upsets in college football history. The game is generally overlooked in the American football history books. But not at

---

[16] Several American football histories say this game was played eleven-a-side, and there is a widely accepted belief that the reason American football has eleven players instead of rugby's fifteen was because that was all McGill had that day. Yet this game was not even played eleven-a-side, and neither would fifteen-a-side be stipulated in English rugby until two years later. In fact, McGill's house rules for the rugby game said that "the number of players on each side shall be not more than 20, or less than 10. The definite number to be settled by the Captains before each match." Despite this ten-a-side game, American football would go on to be played fifteen-a-side for many years, and as we shall see later, it was a very persistent Yale that eventually convinced the American football world that eleven would be a better number.

MIKE ROBERTS – THE SAME OLD GAME: CODIFICATION

Tufts, where they are fiercely proud of winning what was arguably the first 'proper' game of football between two US teams.

Harvard's next meeting with a fellow American college meant a lot more for the bigger picture. The Crimsons were finally going to take to the field against their biggest athletic rival. With football's popularity growing by the year, it was unthinkable for Harvard to go much longer without taking to the same field as Yale. That's big. So big in fact that nowadays it is simply known as The Game.

It was inevitably going to need some preliminary discussion over the rules, and an important discussion that would be. Harvard and Yale were such massively influential institutions that whatever they settled upon, the rest of America was very likely to follow. Yale defended the cause of the soccer-like game they had devised along with Princeton and Rutgers, but Harvard were still bleary-eyed about the wonderful things they had learned from the Canadians, so the respective camps decided to agree on 'concessionary rules'. As usual, Harvard played the bully, and came away with most of what they wanted.

The concessionary rules seemed more rugby than soccer in that the ball could be caught on the bound or fly and then carried, and the carrier could be tackled or shouldered (but not hacked, throttled or pummelled). There were scrums and a player was considered offside if he went over to his opponent's side or got in front of the ball. It was fifteen-a-side rather than the eleven Yale had proposed, it had H shaped goals, and in fact, if there were any concessions to Yale at all, it's hard to spot what they were. The ball wasn't even round. It was oval. Well, oval-ish. The drawing on the cover of the match day programme shows something that was a not-quite-round shape in much the same way as an apple is.

Henry Grant had obviously been doing a bit of research into the proper rugby rules, rather than McGill's liberal interpretation, and successfully put forward the idea that although you could only score by kicking the ball over the bar, scoring a touchdown gave you the chance for a free 'try on goal'.

Yale's Hamilton Park was the venue in November 1875, and about two thousand spectators paid 50 cents each to get in, netting a tidy $500 per team. The number included some 150 Harvard students that travelled from Cambridge in support of a team that had learned from Canadian fashion sense and this time turned up dressed to the nines in sparkling crimson shirts, while Yale had also invested in proper uniforms, looking dashing in their dark trousers, blue shirts and yellow caps.

It was not the tidiest of games. The *Harvard Crimson* reported that "the adopted rules were not fully understood by either team." Yale found it particularly hard to understand what was going on, and despaired as Harvard scored three normal goals, and also converted one of their four touchdowns, which went down in the record books as a 4-0 win. Tailgate parties after the Yale-Harvard game got off to an early start. The *New Haven Register* lamented how that evening seven Harvard students were arrested "for creating disturbances by hooting and

THE NOT SO ALL-AMERICAN GAME

singing in the public streets. They all gave fictitious names and deposited their watches and other articles of jewelry as security for a fine of $5.29 in each case."

Despite defeat, the Yale players were sufficiently impressed with what they had seen to consider that perhaps the Harvard game was the way ahead after all. What's more, among the watching throng were two Princetonians, Earle Dodge and Jotham Potter, who liked it so much they raced back to Mercer County and persuaded the rest of the college to learn the new rules and start training for battle with Yale and Harvard.

It was Dodge and Potter who decided to call a second meeting of the Intercollegiate Football Association, announcing that despite their attempt to create a soccer-style game, "it is generally understood that all the colleges have adopted the Rugby Union Rules, but that each is playing them with some slight variations. The specific object of this call is to establish a system of rules by means of which the colleges shall be enabled to compete with one another at football upon a uniform and satisfactory basis."

Giving rugby a try

It all made sense. Yale and Harvard were keen as rabbits in a carrot field to play the rugby game, while Columbia also accepted the invitation to meet at Massasoit House in Springfield, Massachusetts on November 23, 1876. Poor old Rutgers, who had played a pivotal role in early football, were presumably no longer considered important enough to share such illustrious company. And so it was that Dodge and Potter of Princeton were joined HC Leeds and CS Eaton from Harvard, EW Price and CD Brewer from Columbia, and Eugene Baker and JB Atwater from Yale. An eight-man committee that was not, contrary to common belief, about to rewrite the rules of football, but would perhaps rewrite the history of American football. At the Massasoit meeting, and in one evening, these eight young men are said to have drawn up a list of 61 laws, twenty-two of which are still in force in college football today, and twenty-three in the NFL.

They didn't. The rules were not their work. They were the work of three other gentlemen, Rutter, Holmes, and Maton, five years earlier. Rule one said "a drop kick or drop is made by letting the ball fall from the hands and kicking it at the very instant it rises." Word for word the same as rule of for rugby union at the time. Rule two was "a place kick or place is made by kicking the ball after it has been placed in a nick made in the ground for the purpose of keeping it at rest." Again, word for word the same as rule two of the Rugby Football Union. As was rule three "a punt is made by letting the ball fall from the hands and kicking it before it touches the ground", and also rule four, "each goal shall be composed of two upright posts exceeding 11 foot in height from the ground and placed 18 ft 6 inches apart with a cross bar 10 feet from the ground…"

The 1876 rules for American football do not appear in the Appendixes of this book. They would go on for pages, and it would be a complete waste of paper. When Parke H Davis listed the rules in his seminal *The American Intercollegiate Game* of 1911, he called them

MIKE ROBERTS – THE SAME OLD GAME: CODIFICATION

sixty-one "changes and additions." But there are so few changes that they are effectively the same ones listed at the end of this book as *Appendix Seven*, the laws of the RFU drafted in London in 1871. One wonders why they didn't just call the game 'rugby football' full stop, and Harvard actually made a case for that, but happy enough with the way the meeting had turned out for them, they didn't push the point.

Rule 59 was modified. That was the one in rugby about the two captains settling disputes, while in America "there shall be two judges, one for each side, and also a referee, to whom disputed points shall be referred, and whose decisions shall be final." There are also the additional rule 60 that "the grounds shall be 140 yards long and 70 yards wide" and rule 61 that "the number of players shall be limited to fifteen upon a side", but these were rules that the RFU had added themselves that year, and which look much more similar to the size of a rugby field and team these days than a modern day American football one does.

There was only one major change that the Springfield Convention made, but it has to be said that it was a big one. They changed the scoring system. The RFU's rule 6 that "a goal can only be obtained by kicking the ball from the field of play" was totally revised. Harvard had played Yale a week before the 1876 convention, and despite scoring three touchdowns they had missed all of their conversions, and ended up losing 1-0 to one measly goal kicked from the field. Miffed at the injustice of their recent defeat, Harvard proposed that touchdowns should be included directly in the scoring, regardless of whether they were converted or not, an idea that Yale was strongly opposed to. The colleges eventually came to the indecipherable compromise that "a match shall be decided by a majority of touchdowns. A goal shall be equal to four touchdowns, but in the case of a tie, a goal kicked from a touchdown shall take precedence over four touchdowns." One has to agree with David Nelson that understanding what that meant "would defy Euclid, a battery of chancery lawyers and Frank Merriwell" but long before the RFU decided to do the same, the American colleges were going to give a certain value to touchdowns even if they weren't actually converted. From the outset, it was clear that although the Americans were going to adopt the English rules, they weren't in the slightest bit averse to making a few changes. Nobody piped up to ask whether what they were doing might cut them off from the international rugby fraternity and affect their chances at the inaugural Rugby World Cup in 1987. Organising games with neighbouring colleges was all they cared about for now.

There was a further proposal for modification. Beaten on the touchdown issue, Yale also made a case for eleven-a-side, and when they were outvoted on that one too, they went off in a sulk, and decided they were going to pull out of the association.

American football historians invariably describe the 1876 rules as being 'inspired' by rugby, and prefer not to let on, or are blissfully unaware, that they were, in fact, an almost total carbon copy of the English game. That is despite the so-called 'Father of American football', Walter Camp, opening his 1891 book *American Football* by clearly admitting that "it is from the Rugby Union Rules that our American intercollegiate game was derived,"

THE NOT SO ALL-AMERICAN GAME

which he follows with a highly knowledgeable analysis of the way rules and tactics had evolved not just in the American game, but the English one too.

"Rugby was merely a transplanted English game, hardly a pastime to gain widespread popularity in a young nation just celebrating its centennial and beginning to view itself as superior to its European origins" is the PFRA's somewhat misguided view. The 'new' rules had nothing to do with any wave of American patriotism as it sought to create its own identity. If anything, it meant quite the opposite.

After all, if the foundational footballers had been that opposed to Englishness, then what they doing replacing their own games with a set of laws written in London? There is no evidence anywhere of a deliberate effort to dilute the British origins of the game or make it more 'American', whatever that means. Although over the following years the rules would gradually be amended, these changes were introduced to deal with technical issues, the same issues that the RFU was going to have to address too. Walter Camp was quite frank about it when in 1891 he wrote, "being bound by no traditions, and having seen no play, the American took the English rules for a starting-point, and almost immediately proceeded to add and subtract, according to what seemed his pressing needs. And they were many. A favored few, whose intercourse with Canadian players[17] had given them some of the English ideas were able to explain the knotty points to a small degree, but not enough to really assist the mass of uninitiated players to an understanding. Misinterpretations were so numerous as to render satisfactory rulings almost out of the question and explanatory legislation imperative."

Yale's non-membership was more about making a point than wishing to isolate themselves from the blossoming football brotherhood, and they went ahead and played their matches regardless, making the most of both worlds, for against Princeton they stuck to their guns and insisted on eleven-a-side and no touchdowns in the final score and managed to get away with it. Well, they weren't official members, so they were free to use whatever rules they fancied! They won that game, and beat Columbia and Harvard too, and thanks to that sweep Yale are sometimes considered America's first college champions even though they weren't officially members of the association!

But the new IFA was hardly on a mission to spread the football gospel around the country. Rather than encourage expansion, they made sure of adding a rule that new teams would only be accepted into the association with the unanimous consent of its members[18]. So, although the University of Pennsylvania, dressed in white even though the college had recently adopted its famous red and blue colours, did face Princeton under the 'new' rules twice that season, losing 6-0 both times, these were not counted as official games. Anything but bitter, after being treated to supper after their game in New Brunswick, one Penn player remarked

---

[17] Hey, steady on their Walter!

[18] An attitude typified by the way Columbia, who had dropped out of the Association, were met with what Parke Davies calls "dismay rather than rejoicing" when they sought readmission in 1880.

299

MIKE ROBERTS – THE SAME OLD GAME: CODIFICATION

how they "almost feel that if the result of being beaten is such delightful treatment, we would be willing to stand a great deal of it without complaint or murmur."

Other colleges gradually got involved with the new craze. Amherst was one, and in 1878 it was them who gave Brown their first proper game, crushing them by four tries and one goal to nothing, with the *Brunonian* trying to blame it all on the wind.

Dartmouth were reluctant to see their Old Division game modified for the sake of what they considered to an inferior game, Scott Meacham mentioning a report in their college paper that nobody could make neither head nor tail of the rugby rules and explaining how Tufts College, enthused by their first experience of rugby against Harvard, challenged Dartmouth as early as 1875 but were met with a negative response. Nevertheless, by 1878 there was a rugby community emerging at Dartmouth, posts were erected and games were played, living an uncomfortable coexistence with the college's own form of football. The new sport grew in popularity and it is interesting to note that in 1879, there was no Old Division football match between the Frosh and the Sophs, but they did play rugby, with the freshmen winning by one goal and two touchdowns to nothing.

In 1881, Dartmouth got its first taste of intercollegiate football, which was met with an enthusiastic response from one of the players, Charles Weston, who wrote home to say that "this has been quite an exciting week for Dartmouth. We played a game of foot-ball Wednesday with Amherst, it was the first game we ever played. We beat them one touchdown to nothing. Surprising everyone. I 'spect I was the hero of the occasion. I made the touchdown and several good runs, and at the end of the game the boys rode me around the campus on their shoulders. Everyone was nearly crazy during the game. The Professors ran around, clapped their hands, shouted, jumped up and down and fairly went mad … One of the Amherst players complimented me on my playing and said I could play as well as Camp of Yale. Camp is the best player in the country."

He was indeed a fine player that Camp, a Connecticut man who had made his footballing debut as a halfback on the Yale team that swept all-comers in 1876. However, it is not for his achievements as a player that he is revered today, but for the role he played in introducing so many new ideas to what used to be rugby, but was about to become American football. The history of the game can be divided in two. Football before and football after Walter Chauncey Camp.

13 DOWN ON SCRUM
Walter Camp and American football in the making

Interfering with the rules

Almost from the moment they saw them, the Americans started playing around with the rugby rules, so as the 1870s drew to an end, it wasn't so much rugby as it was an *interpretation* of rugby that was becoming more and more popular at their universities. Rather like learning to play the guitar from a book, they did the basics just the way they were told, and let their imaginations do the rest.

We also have to appreciate the practicalities. The FA's rules for soccer were simplicity itself. It may have taken a while to get to grips with offside, but the rest of the laws could be read and digested in a matter of minutes. Understanding the RFU's laws for rugby was a different matter entirely, and even if anybody could perform the almost impossible task of making complete sense of them, getting the message across to a mob of several dozen bodies scrummaging in the slush required martial abilities of Napoleonic proportions.

And despite the regular presence of two officials from each side and a neutral referee, the games were downright violent. The *New York Times* noted how the Princeton and Yale match in 1877 involved an incident whereby "when one man was knocked down by others and obliged to bear their combined weight for a minute or so, he maintained the utmost good humour, and, upon regaining his footing immediately helped to knock down another man and sit on him." Meanwhile, one Princeton player "received a kick in the stomach which demoralised him badly for a few seconds."

Princeton became notorious in the early years for bending the rules to their own benefit, and it was their 'innovations' that were largely responsible for making it clear that the RFU's laws were lacking in several respects. Their game with Harvard in 1879 proved particularly noteworthy. For a start, they developed the idea of the 'onsides kick'. The established principle in rugby was to start the game with a long kick downfield towards the opposing, or receiving, team, but the rules merely said that for a kick-off, "the opposite side must stand at least 10 yards in front of the ball until it has been kicked," but nothing about how far the ball had to travel. Princeton introduced a bit of gamesmanship, and opted just to give the ball the tiniest of kicks forward, and pick it up themselves. It may have gone against the spirit of the game, but not against the rules, and football stayed that way for fifteen years before the rule was introduced that the ball had to travel a certain distance.

But more important in the long term was Princeton's use against Harvard of what has gone on to be known as interference[1], and which as good as constitutes the moment when American football really started making its break from rugby. The original rules state that "a

---

[1] A ploy we know they had first used in their historic meeting with Rutgers in 1869.

MIKE ROBERTS – THE SAME OLD GAME: CODIFICATION

tackle is when the holder of the ball is held by one or more players of the opposite side," the implication being that you can't tackle anybody who isn't holding the ball, and you certainly can't go running in front of the ball carrier and taking other players out of the game, which in any case would have been offside. But the 1871 rules didn't make any of that too clear, and against Harvard, Princeton demonstrated that they were going to exploit that ambiguity.

The referee, a Yale man, did issue Princeton a warning, but allowed them to carry on regardless. Rather than call a penalty, he seemed to be of the opinion that it was actually quite a neat idea, and later that year started getting his own Yale players doing exactly the same thing. His name was Walter Camp.

Setting up camp

America loves its national heroes, and in Walter Camp there is one. Writing an obituary for him in the *1925 Football Guide*, Parke Davis said that "great as he was as a player, he was still greater as an architect of the American intercollegiate game … it was his resourceful mind that conceived and constructed the majority of the basic changes which made a distinctly American game … It has been said that it is as glorious to have written a country's songs as to have fought a country's wars or to have formulated a country's laws. Walter Camp performed an equally large and useful public service by establishing the amateur sports of the country upon a sound and wholesome basis. As the leader of Yale in the years when Yale was the leader of the colleges of the country, Walter Camp stood forth so vividly and so correctly for the best in intercollegiate sport that he deeply impressed his ideals upon the outdoor games of the country. His standard, full high advanced, was ever the standard of honor, nobleness and manliness."

Powerful words indeed. Richard Borkowski also waxes lyrical about the great man when he says "Camp was instrumental through writing and lecturing in attaching an almost mythical atmosphere of manliness and heroism to the game not previously known in American team sports[2]."

Camp has been heralded down the years as the Father of American Football, a title bestowed upon him not after he died, but originally in the 1890s while he was still very much alive and involved in the game. To claim that he actually invented the game is stretching things too far, for American football was essentially a development of rugby, which in turn owed its origins to many other games, but when each of the major changes were made to the structure of the American game, Camp was very rarely not involved in some kind of way. His was no fleeting involvement. Football was his life. As a student, he was playing for Yale in the very first season that the rugby laws were used in 1876. He soon rose to prominence not only as a player, but also as a referee and administrator, and he stayed on the Rules Committee until his dying day, after 50 years of involvement in the game.

---

[2] Richard Borkowski *Life and Contributions of Walter Camp to American Football* (Temple University, 1979).

DOWN ON SCRUM

The son of a schoolteacher, he was born just up the road from Yale in the town of New Britain. He was educated at Hopkins Grammar School in New Haven, and enrolled at the university in 1876. By all accounts he was one of those people who was annoyingly brilliant at everything he did. At school he was top of the class in just about every subject, he excelled as a poet, he was dashingly handsome, he was an eloquent speaker, and on top of all that, he was a genuinely sincere and nice guy who would later in life "gave generously of his time to the civic and charitable movements of the city of New Haven[3]."

But it was in sport that he really excelled. A fitness freak, as soon as he could walk he was off on cross country runs every evening after school, he was a rower, he was a wrestler, he was a swimmer, it is said that the modern hurdling stride was his invention, and he was Yale's first ever representative in a tennis tournament. At baseball he was a brilliant curveball pitcher, and the story goes that in his first game for Yale, he hit three home runs off the first three balls, and eventually collected the highest batting average in the Intercollegiate Association.

But football was his first love. He had already played the game soccer-style at school, and on entrance to Yale, was naturally dying to get his teeth into rugby. Before his debut against Harvard, the opposing captain, Curtis, was shocked that they were going to let a tiny kid like that play in a rugby match, to which Yale's captain Gene Baker replied "look to your business. He is young but he is all spirit and whipcord. He'll take care of himself – and you, too[4]." Indeed he did. Camp threw Curtis to the ground in one of the first plays of the match, and the biggest college football legend of them all was born.

The story goes that he was so obsessed with getting the hang of handling the bulky ball that he would carry it wherever he went. But no analysis of Camp's playing career seems complete without a mention of his remarkable series of unfortunate incidents. In 1877, he flew through the Princeton defence on two occasions to score enormous touchdown runs, but neither ended up counting because the conversions were missed. Then there was his amazing 35 yard drop kick in the last seconds of a game against Harvard. The goal would have won the game, but the whistle for time went while the ball was in the air, and it wasn't counted, and neither was an even longer 45 yard kick against the same team in 1879, which would have been the only score of the game, had the referee not made a dubious call for an earlier infringement.

Camp was not the biggest of players, and he was certainly not remembered for taking a particularly rough approach to the game. In fact, two of his favourite catchphrases in later life were "mind will always win over muscle," and "what a gentleman wants is fair play, and the best man to win." A doyen of sportsmanship, it is remarkable that in 1885, when Yale played Princeton, the opposition actually asked Camp to referee the game! It is somewhat

---

[3] Obituary in *Football Guide* (1925), which Camp himself had founded.

[4] John Stuart Martin *Walter Camp and his Gridiron Game* (*American Heritage Magazine*, October 1961).

paradoxical, given that view, that he ended up having such a hand in turning the American code into the most violent of all the different versions of football.

It wasn't long before he was made captain of Yale, which in those days meant he was effectively head coach as well. He ruled with an iron first. As Amos Alonzo Stagg relates in his memoirs "catching Johnny Moorehead sneaking back from the theater one night late, Camp called every man out of bed and quit on the spot. Moorehead offered his own resignation instead, and Camp reconsidered. As Moorehead played in the Princeton game, he seems to have been restored to grace."

After completing his first four years at Yale, he stayed on to do a two-year postgraduate in medicine, but after failing anatomy and surgery he gave up on his medical career, later admitting that he couldn't stand the sight of blood. So, he was on the team for six years, there being no eligibility requirements back then. In fact, players did not strictly speaking even have to be students at the college they played for, but merely connected to it in some way, so he could have carried on playing for longer. But with his usual penchant for fair play, he retired in support of a motion he was mooting for there to be a five-year limit on college footballers (the rule nowadays is a four-year maximum).

Although he would go on to become one of America's best paid non-fiction authors thanked to the nigh on 30 books he penned on his favourite game, Camp never sought to make his career out of football. In 1893, he wrote that "no matter how winding the road may be that eventually brings the sovereign into the pocket … a gentleman never competes for money, directly or indirectly[5]."

So it was to clocks that he turned for business, using family connections to get a job at the New Haven Clock Company, and as perfect as ever, he rose through the ranks to eventually become chairman in 1902. It is an obligatory observation at this point of all American football histories to note how he worked in such a precise art as clock-making, and was also such a perfectionist regarding football, but it was a fitting coincidence, and little else.

John Stuart Martin wrote that "as a football legislator, Walter Camp did not have a particularly bold or inventive mind. But he was keenly analytical, laboriously methodical, and crafty enough to keep his own counsel until others had said their say. When they got around to saying, 'Let's hear what Walter thinks about it,' he was ready with closely reasoned proposals … He had a patent on football. It was Camp's game and he made up the rules as he went along[6]."

He couldn't have come at a better time. The IFA was crying out for a leader. As Yale were still sulking in the shadows over the eleven-a-side issue and Columbia were as apathetic as ever, it was effectively just Harvard and Princeton, who were failing to agree on anything. When the governing teams returned to Massasoit House in Springfield for their second

---

[5] *Walter Camp's book of college sports* (1893).
[6] Frederick Trevor Hill cited in Harford Powel Little *Walter Camp, the father of American football: an authorized biography* (Brown and co, 1926).

DOWN ON SCRUM

convention in October 1878, they had a new force to contend with. Yale, who politely asked to be accepted back as members, was represented by Walter Camp.

In his first meetings, however, there was little suggestion of the man who would almost single-handedly revolutionise the game. He put forward the motion in favour of the eleven-a-side game, but he was merely carrying a message Yale had been harping on about for years. In any case, he was soundly voted down, as he would be a year later when (and you have to admire Yale for their persistence) he proposed the idea yet again.

In 1879, Camp was also instructed by his Yale colleagues to propose a second amendment – that if a ball-carrier was tackled in his own end zone, then that should count as a score, what we know today as a safety[7], but that motion was also rejected, as was Yale's request for the field to be made bigger.

The eleven players issue had originally been raised by Yale, probably inspired by their game with the Old Etonians, because they felt that the smaller the team, the easier it was to arrange road trips. But Camp had also spotted other benefits. Rugby had become a clumsy, crowded game. It was often little more than one lumbering scrum moving up and down the field, with little space for manoeuvre. The 1879 game between Princeton and Yale was particularly unbecoming. It ended 0-0, making Princeton that year's champions, but nobody was impressed by the way it happened. The *New York Times* reported that "Yale gained a foot and lost it. Then Princeton did the same, and for 10 minutes a writhing mass of legs and arms turned and twisted 20 ways at once, while the ball was not moved three feet."

The increasing pressure to switch to eleven players was not going down too well at Princeton, where in September 1880, *The Princetonian* explained that "if we play with our usual team, it is highly probable that we can prevent our opponents from scoring anything, even if we ourselves are not able to make the game a decisive one. As it now stands, a draw game means a victory for us, inasmuch as we would, in that case, still retain the championship. Why, then, should we, merely for the gratification of the spectators, risk what it has cost us so many hotly contested games to secure?"

At the Springfield 1880 convention, Camp was one of three Yale representatives that for the umpteenth time put to committee the proposal for eleven-a-side football, and this time, at long, long last, it was accepted. And whether Princeton liked it or not, taking eight players off the pitch (four from each side) did open the game up considerably, cut out at least some of the chaos, and interestingly, fifteen years later when the breakaway English rugby clubs in Yorkshire and Lancashire turned professional, one of the first things they did to make their game more attractive to the paying public was to downsize teams from fifteen to thirteen. It

---

[7] The safety was not Camp's innovation. It came from the idea of 'minors' that were being experimented with in northern English rugby, whereby if a defending team under pressure touched the ball down behind their own goal line, this was counted in the favour of the attacking team, originally as a tie-breaker but for a while was even included in the score.

MIKE ROBERTS – THE SAME OLD GAME: CODIFICATION

would not be the last time aspects of American football would be adopted, maybe directly, maybe indirectly, by English rugby.

That meeting also accepted Camp's suggestion to reduce the playing area from 140 by 70 yards to just 110 by 53 yards, making the American football pitch the smallest in any code. But those two changes were minor affairs compared to something else that Camp and his Yale colleagues had up their sleeves, and this idea really would mark America's divorce from rugby.

Camping up the scrum

Legendary coach Fielding Yost, who made Michigan the first non-Ivy League power in college football, wrote how "the English rules were found to be ambiguous in some cases, and difficult of comprehension in others. The novelty of the game, also, was productive of many suggested alterations and it was one of these which is really accountable for the wide difference which now exists between Rugby and American football[8]."

He was referring to what happened to the scrum, which in the 1880s was nothing like what is seen in modern day rugby union. There was no orderly binding at all. The players just gathered in two groups (while always having to having to stay 'on their side' behind the ball), and hacked away as they tried to move the mass of bodies up the field or somehow kick the ball out of the mass of bodies to a runner, although as soon as that player was tackled and brought to ground, it would inevitably lead to yet more scrummaging. No doubt great fun for those involved, but tediously dull from a spectator's point of view. Not only was it unsightly, but it didn't seem to offer anything in the way of tactics.

All handling of the ball was strictly disallowed during a scrum, as was kicking it backwards to a team-mate, so it is difficult to imagine how on earth the ball ever got out into the open. Camp explains one method, whereby "the Americans started with the English scrimmage, kicked at the ball, and pushed and scrambled for a season, until it was discovered that a very clever manifestation of the play was to let the opponents do the kicking – in fact, to leave an opening at the proper moment through which the ball would come, and a man a few feet behind this opening could always get the ball and pass it while the men who kicked it were still entangled in the scrimmage."

Alexander M Weyand wrote that "an article concerning Rugby at about the time we started playing it stated that it was just as poor sportsmanship for a forward to spread his legs and allow an opponent to kick the ball through. I can't imagine young Americans passing up an advantage like that because of some old British custom[9]." But the British weren't quite as noble as Weyand thought. Montagu Shearman described in 1888 how at English clubs "to

---

[8] Fielding Yost *Football for Player and Spectator* (1906).
[9] In a letter quoted in *How to train the Quarterback* (Prentice-Hall, 1960) by legendary Rams, Bears and Redskins coach George H Allen.

DOWN ON SCRUM

this day many think it admirable play for the forwards to open their legs to let the ball through."

However, American footballers soon got wise to this idea and Camp goes on to say that "after a little of this, no one was anxious to kick the ball through, and the rushers began to roll the ball sidewise along between the lines … soon an adventurous spirit discovered that he could so place his foot upon the ball that by pressing suddenly downwards and backwards with his toe he would drag or snap the ball to the man behind him." To help with this, teams started playing with only a single line of scrimmage, which Frank Cosentino mentions when citing that "in 1879, the University of Michigan in a game with the University of Toronto team, Varsity, introduced a major innovation. Michigan lined up with their forwards in a single line, and the ball was snapped out to the backs."

None of these methods fell fully within the bounds of the 'no kicking backwards in the scrum' rule, but the Americans were at liberty to change the rules as they wished, and had the advantage of not being surrounded by English public school old boys commenting on the travesty they were committing. Camp put this down to "the absolute lack of any existing foot-ball lore or tradition on American soil. The English game was one of traditions. 'What has been done can be done; what has not been done must be illegal' answered any question which was not fully foreseen in their laws of the game."

In fact, rugby's solution to the same problem was to disregard its own rule too. The RFU eventually created a more orderly form of the scrum, in which a limited number of players bound into a pack[10], and were allowed to 'heel out' the ball backwards. Although Weyand wrote how "it was unthinkable for a British forward to heel the ball to one of his backs," something the English originally considered a heinous act of gamesmanship became a legally accepted part of the game.

On the other side of the ocean, the solution was the brainwave of Walter Camp. At one fell swoop, the clockmaker from Yale produced his *coup de grace*. He wanted to do away with the scrummage entirely, and replace it with what he called a 'scrimmage'[11] as defined by one

---

[10] As it now stands, there are three players in the 'front row' (the hooker in the middle and two props on either side), who bind together, and behind them are four others, the two locks in the middle and the flankers on the outside, and behind them, the number eight brings up the rear. The players crouch forwards, and the opposing front rows 'engage' by linking heads and shoulders to form a tunnel between them, where the ball is placed. It's essentially the job of the hookers to gain possession of the ball using their feet (no use of the hands in the scrum) and from their position it now defies all logic to attempt to kick it forwards and back to other team. They either keep the ball among them and drive against the other team to gain ground, or feed it back with their feet and eventually out to a player called the scrum half, who is allowed to pick up the ball and get it into open play.

[11] This was no crime against the English language. 'Scrimmage' had been around for many more years than 'scrummage' as a word for any kind of noisy, contentious, confused struggle (derived from the 14th century Old French *escarmouch* and a bastardised form of 'skirmish', which dates back to at least 1470). 'Scrummage' as an alternative form in relation to rugby first appeared in *Tom Brown's Schooldays* in 1857, which is probably why it came into such common use, although in the English *Football Annual* of 1876 it is noted that "scrummage, by-the-bye, is still the official term, though the public speaks of scrimmage."

of the most innovative statements in footballing history. "A scrimmage takes place when the holder of the ball puts it on the ground before him and puts it in play while on-side either by kicking the ball or by snapping it back with his foot. The man who first receives the ball from the snap-back shall be called the quarter-back and shall not rush forward with the ball under penalty of foul."

As simple as that. Bang. In the space of two sentences, rugby has disappeared and American football has appeared in its place. Walter Camp himself said of the subject that "in this lies the backbone to which the entire body of American football is attached." And in many ways he is right.

One of Camp's concerns was that in rugby's scrums and lineouts the team that puts the ball in has very little advantage when it comes to retaining the possession it has supposedly won. He felt a team in possession should be able to start new plays uncontested, and wrote that "in the English game, when the ball is held and put down for what they call a 'scrummage' … there is a deal of pushing and hacking and some clever work with the feet, but the exact exit of the ball from the 'scrummage' can not be predicted or anticipated. When it does roll out, the man who is nearest endeavors to get it and make a run or a kick. The American scrimmage, while coming directly from the English play, bears now no similarity to it. Instead of an indiscriminate kicking struggle we have the snapback and quarter-back play[12]."

"The American quarter-back stands behind the scrimmage and gives a signal, immediately after which he knows the ball will come directly into his hands to be passed for a run or a kick. What is, therefore, in the English game a matter of considerable chance is 'cut-and-dried' in the American game; and the element of chance being eliminated, opportunity is given for the display in the latter game of far more skill in the development of brilliant plays and carefully planned manoeuvres."

Nicholas Mason puts it in a nutshell. "It meant, a British chorus would now argue, the death of open, seesawing play, of defence turned by brilliant inspiration into attack, of sudden, thrilling turn of fortune. On the contrary, a million Americans would retort, it meant the development of brilliantly conceived, dazzlingly executed attacks countered by finely inspired, perfectly drilled defence."

Fielding Yost agreed that scrimmaging was "a procedure not tolerated in the original form of the game, but the additional interest which it imparted was immediately seen, and the superiority of this plan for putting the ball into play over the English method of kicking it about in scrimmage was so apparent that it was eagerly embraced."

Montagu Shearman is an excellent example of what the typical English traditionalist made of the American innovation, when he explains how he took a critic fresh from college in America to see Richmond play Blackheath in 1888. The American versed footballer was astonished at the scrimmaging, and explained to Shearman how the game was now played in

---

[12] In his *Intercollegiate Foot-Ball in America* (November 1889), the quote in the following paragraph is from *American Football* (1891).

DOWN ON SCRUM

the States. In response, the writer muses that "what such a game as Rugby football without scrimmaging would be like is hard to conjecture: the very suggestion would seem a heresy to most players."

But in the USA, the 1880 Convention loved it. It was voted in unanimously, and from then on scrums were no longer part of American football. And with the line of scrimmage in place, the American game soon developed its iconic T formation. The bulk of the players formed the line in front, and behind them there was the quarterback, who was now the brains of the team and the orchestrator of almost every play. Waiting behind him were three running backs (two half backs, and the full back bringing up the rear). With different rules introduced over the following years to determine how many players should and shouldn't stand in the line of scrimmage, and plenty of tactical innovations to follow, this pattern was in for several changes, but the T formation was still the basic arrangement for American football offences for most of the early 20th century[13].

Originally the centre would 'inch-kick' the ball and then hand it to the quarterback, who would be kneeling just behind. Of course, nowadays the 'snap' is almost always thrown back through the centre's legs to the quarterback, who is standing. It was said to be Yale's Bert Hanson in 1889 who started bouncing the ball to the quarterback, while the modern 'lift-up' snap was reputedly the invention of Chicago coach Amos Alonzo Stagg[14].

Interestingly though, it is only in Canadian rules that the procedure is actually an obligation. In American football the centre can actually quite legally pick up the ball himself and make the quarterback an eligible receiver, although you won't see that happen too often.

Dull as ditchwater

Camp's revelation had created a new take on rugby, and it looked like all the problems had been solved. But the rugby rules were the result of decades of experimentation on the pitch, and there was a very good reason why most of them existed. Rather like trying to complete a

---

[13] The introduction of the forward pass particularly influenced change, as wide receivers became a fundamental part of the game, but even so, all the aces, double wings, shotguns, pistols and wishbones that you will see in the modern game are really only adjustments to the original T formation.

[14] A fitness freak who apparently once believed that the only way to true health was to live on a strict diet of crackers and water, and ended up getting beriberi for his efforts, Amos Alonzo Stagg was also a champion baseball player (they say he invented the batting cage) and was included in the first ever basketball Hall of Fame in 1959, after captaining one of the nine-a-side teams that played the very first public game of James Naismith's new invention in March 1892, and being instrumental in the decision to make America's new indoor sport a five-a-side game. But despite his contributions to basketball and baseball, it is for football that Stagg is best remembered. If there was anybody to rival Walter Camp in the innovation stakes, then that man was Stagg, who is also credited with such inventions as the tackling dummy, the huddle and the idea of printing player's names on the backs of their shirts. As late as 1943, and at the ripe old age of 81, he was named Associated Press Coach of the Year when at Pacific. The 'grand old man' of American football finally departed our world aged 102, just two years before the first Super Bowl in 1967. He really had seen it all.

MIKE ROBERTS – THE SAME OLD GAME: CODIFICATION

Rubik's Cube, if you move one piece, you find other pieces have moved too, and Camp was going to have to start looking up his sleeve for another ace.

Taking the element of chance out of the scrummage meant one team now had uncontested possession of the ball, and as long as they didn't do anything silly, like go off on heroic solo runs or punt the ball and risk losing the ball to a fumble or interception, they could simply hang on to the it for as long as they fancied.

If there was ever a way of bending the rules, then you could count on Princeton to find it, and they did just that when they met Yale in the 1880 championship decider. As usual, the Tigers had cruised unbeaten through the season, but when it came to the Elis, they knew they would need to find that something special. They came up trumps. It was simple. All Princeton did was simply cling onto possession for as long as they could, making no attempt whatsoever to kick upfield.

And neither were they particularly concerned if they were forced back towards their own end zone, because once they were there, they knew that all they had to do was touch the ball down for a safety, and the 'penalty' for such a negative approach to football was an instant restart from the twenty-five yard line! They took eleven safeties in that game (Yale hardly acquitting themselves with six of their own), and the game ended 0-0. Princeton claimed that they should retain their 1879 championship title, but the IFA took a dimmer view, and declared the championship void.

The new rules weren't working, but rather than retreat, American football went down new alleys as it sought to find solutions, and in the process distanced itself more and more from the original rugby code.

The obvious realisation was that Walter Camp had a point with that 'safeties' idea of his. At their next meeting, the Rules Committee decided that in the future, in the case of a tie, the team that had conceded the fewest safeties (unless they had conceded less than four) would be declared the winner.

It looked like the IFA had put an end to Princeton's cunning ploys, but they hadn't. Safeties only counted in the end zone, but not to either side of it, and the Elis were once again to be the victims of a Princeton loophole. As soon as they were pushed back behind their goal line, rather than touch the ball down for a safety, Princeton merely chucked the ball out of the sides. Technically, this was recorded as a 'touch in goal', and so it was back to the twenty-five yard for more of the same. Like at the previous year's game, the spectators were disgusted, hailing abuse, littering the field with anything they could lay their hands on, and claiming repayment of entrance fees and wagers.

What became known as the 'block game' was going nowhere, and after a tedious 0-0 first half, in which Princeton apparently never even attempted to gain more than ten yards, any hope that things might improve when Yale got possession in the second period were laid to rest when the Elis simply copied the same trick! It was the third consecutive goalless game between Princeton and Yale, but due to the peculiar system of deciding the championship, it went to Yale because they had beaten Harvard (hardly in epic fashion, that game having ended 0-0, but Yale had won due to Harvard having resorted to four safeties).

"This proved the dullest and most uninteresting period of American football, and it is only fair to say that the game would hardly have survived another season of it" remembered Walter Camp[15]. The simple solution was to adopt an extremely sensible suggestion made by Harvard that the touch in goal should also be counted as a safety. Other voices felt all this scrimmaging had been great in principle but hadn't quite worked out the way they had planned, and perhaps it mightn't be a bad idea just to go back to rugby. But Walter Camp had another revolutionary idea.

Get down on it

Camp wanted to go forward, both metaphorically in terms of the sport's march away from the old rugby rules, and physically by encouraging teams to stop coming up with daft ways of avoiding having to go on the offensive. 1882 was going to be another milestone year for American football, because that was when Camp invented, or rather reinvented, the idea of 'downs'. We say reinvented, because the term comes from rugby's 1871 rule that "in the event of any player holding or running with the ball being tackled and the ball being fairly held he must at once cry down and there put it down."

To encourage positive football, Camp's idea was that "if on three consecutive fair tries or downs a team shall not have advanced the ball five yards, nor lost ten, they must give up the ball to opponents at the spot of the fourth down. When a team advances five yards, it will receive a first down and have as many tries as is required to progress the ball another five yards." Basically, as long as a team could advance a reasonably attainable distance, then they reached a 'safe haven', and if they failed to do so after a set number of attempts, possession was turned over to the other side.

Although the idea is now almost entirely attributed to Camp, Parke Davis claims that the downs and yards system was first put on the agenda by an anonymous *Letter of an Englishman* that appeared in several papers saying that "the block-game is an unmitigated evil. It can be remedied by allowing a team only four scrimmages, the ball then to change opponents, who may put it down or punt. A touch-in-goal should count the same as a safety." The *Princetonian* had also proposed a similar suggestion that "it might be agreed that when one side has had the ball twice in succession the half-back on the third down should be compelled either to kick or to forfeit the ball."

But even if the idea wasn't entirely his own, Camp was the man who saw it went through. In a 1908 article in *Baseball Magazine*, he explains how the idea "generated a lively discussion, and many hands went up in horror. Much serious discussion ensued, and the suggestion was not generally approved, but finally one of the Harvard delegates joined with

---

[15] In a 1908 article in *Baseball Magazine* titled *Recent Changes in Football Tactics*.

me, and as a result the rule was tentatively adopted with the proviso that if upon the occasion of the next meeting, which was to be held in October, the rule had not proved a success, it should be abandoned."

The immediate problem spotted at the IFA meeting was that referees were going to find it nigh on impossible to work out whether the ball had been advanced five yards or not. A fair point, and as Camp himself wrote in his 1908 article, "this very nearly sealed the fate of the proposed innovation. The objection was brought forward that we should have to have two men with a tape line on the field all the time." But Camp was on flowing form by now, and never one stuck for an answer, came up with "my suggestion of marking off the field at the distance of every five yards with white lines." The story goes that Ned Pearce of Princeton scoffed that "the field will look like a gridiron!" To which Camp replied: "Precisely."

Whether that exchange was really made, we cannot be sure, but Camp himself admitted that the term 'gridiron' was originally coined in derision[16]. But although the odd lines on the pitch and the system of downs meant major changes to the essence of the game, the idea was a resounding a success, Camp claiming that "never did a rule in any sport work so immediate and satisfactory a reform as did this five-yard rule." When, as had been planned, the idea came up for review at the October 1882 meeting of the IFA, it was unanimously accepted, and as Camp wrote "the principle has continued ever since as a governing factor in the game."

The divorce from rugby

Whether October 1882, and the introduction of downs, was the moment when American football really became a game in its own right is a matter of opinion. The PFRA says it is, and Mel Smith agrees when he classes all games played up until that date as 'American rugby style' and only from 1882 does he believe it appropriate to consider the American code a game in its own right.

Others place it earlier with Walter Camp's scrimmage idea of 1880. Others still say it was when Harvard learned the rugby game in 1874, and others will even go back to the Rutgers vs Princeton game of 1869. But rather like trying to find the fifth paw on a cat, it is pointless trying to find an exact moment, because there simply was no specific date when American football was 'born'. The safest bet would be to say that the change happened between 1880, with the introduction of the line of scrimmage, and 1882, when the downs rules was added to make it work.

Many reports in the contemporary American press support that proposal. It was then that the *Harvard Crimson* observed that a "new form of foot ball has been formed" with articles in the *Boston Globe, Montreal Gazette, Brooklyn Eagle* and *New Brunswick Fredonian*

---

[16] It's also important to note that although in the British Isles and Australasia the term is commonly used even today as the name of the sport itself, this was never the case in America, where 'gridiron' is only used to describe the field.

DOWN ON SCRUM

making similar observations in late 1882. There were now three kinds of football being played in the country. There were the Association and Rugby games, but also this new kind, which for the time being was going to known as the 'American Collegiate Game'[17].

The five yard minimum was expanded to the current ten in 1906, while the three attempts to gain five yards became the modern day four in 1912. And despite the strange rule that a team also won a first down by losing ten yards, the 1882 reformation also played around with the scoring system, for safeties were no longer quite such an attractive proposition now that they were no longer used just for tie breaks, but at long last were actually counted in the score, being equal to two touchdowns for the opposition. The loss of yards was no longer a matter to take quite so lightly.

Four touchdowns still equalled one goal from the field, which was all becoming a rather convoluted way of saying that a goal scored 4, a touchdown 1, and a safety 2. However, one area that wasn't clear at all was the difference in value, if any, between a goal scored from the field and a goal scored from a conversion after a touchdown. Parke Davis wrote that "a prolific source of disputes was the complicated system of scoring, which in several important games left to the referee the decision as to the proportion in which touchdowns, goals, and safeties should be valued against one another."

For instance, when Harvard played Princeton in 1882, Harvard scored a touchdown but missed the goal attempt, and later kicked a goal from the field. Princeton also scored one touchdown, but unlike Harvard, did make the conversion. Harvard was awarded the game because, as a *New York Times* article in 1920 explained, "the Crimson's goal was from the field and Princeton's goal from a touchdown, the former counting more than the latter."

Princeton refused to accept this verdict and maintained their claim to victory for many years, and with good reason it seems for a modification to the rules in 1881 had stated that "in case of a tie, a goal kicked from a touchdown will take precedence over a goal otherwise kicked."

It was clearly a mess, and in 1883, numerical values for each different type of scoring were finally added to the rules. A field goal was now boosted to five, a touchdown scored two, and a goal after touchdown scored four (so a converted touchdown now scored six, and was therefore slightly more valuable than a goal kicked from the field). Safeties, meanwhile, were devalued to one point.

Like in rugby, there would be considerably more tweaking of the scoring system as the years progressed, with a dramatic swing away from what was originally the only accepted form of scoring, kicking the ball over the posts, to the newer addition of scoring by running the ball over the line. Just one year later, in 1884, the touchdown was raised from two to four

---

[17] Eventually, the names 'association football' and 'rugby football' would be shortened to simply 'soccer' and 'rugby', paving the way for the collegiate game, by the turn of the century by far the biggest of the three codes in the USA, to claim sole property of the 'football' label throughout the country (while remaining 'American' football in the rest of the world).

points, while the goal following touchdown went down from four to two (basically inverting their values so that the touchdown was now worth more than the conversion that followed it[18]).

From its five points in 1883, the field goal dropped to four points in 1904 and to its current value of three in 1909. Touchdowns gained in value in 1897, when they were worth five (the same as a field goal at the time), with the conversion worth just one, and by 1912, touchdowns already had their current value of six. What's curious to note here, and a chance for another dig at the rugby union boys that maintain how theirs is the truly 'traditional' form of the game, is that American football was decades ahead of the English game in devaluing field goals and encouraging tries/touchdowns. Rugby union's drop goals scored four points until 1948, while tries were not raised in value from three to four until 1971 … showing that at least in terms of the most important aspect of the game, how you score points, it was rugby union that followed America's lead, and not vice versa, although another code, rugby league, was ahead of both, for it had made tries worth three points and all other forms of scoring just two way back in 1897.

The rules being those of the RFU, touchdowns in America originally had to be literally touched down, for it said in the 1876 rugby rules that "a touch down is when a player putting his hand upon the ball on the ground in touch or in goal stops it so that it remains dead or fairly so." It was not until 1889 that all an American player had to do was hold the ball in the end zone.

As for the conversion, just like in rugby today, the ball had to be kicked from a position in line with the point where the touchdown was made. And as was also the case in rugby until the 1880s, if the distance was considered too difficult, the ball could be punted back into play from that point, and if caught fairly, the catcher could then attempt the kick from there. That might seem odd from a modern point of view, but even nowadays it is a fine art to convert from the wings, so it should go without saying that trying to kick the cumbersome 19th century ball over a bar ten feet off the ground from at an angled distance of 50 yards while wearing the hefty boots of the period was nigh on impossible even in the fairest of weather.

All of this was eliminated in 1920, and the point-after-touchdown is now the simple matter of a practically unmissable kick in front of the posts. Walter Camp explained the logic for this to the *New York Times*. "The extra point will not depend upon any individual player. It is made as easy as possible by giving the scoring team the option of making the kick from directly in front of the posts. A team would not need a brilliant kicker, for even the worst kicker could hardly miss. Moreover, the value of a touchdown will overbalance, as it should, the value of two field goals … the case with which a team can score the extra point from a touchdown gives the team with the greater rushing powers the desired advantage."

---

[18] The same revision of the system returned the safety to its previous value of two.

Champions that weren't

The Ivy League colleges were not the only ones with a football culture by the 1880s. The game was expanding rapidly all over the country, but still owed almost all of its major innovations to the Yale-Princeton-Harvard trivariate, and especially the former two, who went on to dominate the game in frightening fashion for its first two decades. From 1883 to 1892, Yale won 112 of their 117 matches, 100 of those without conceding a point, while Princeton's 95-8-2 record for the same period was not to be sniffed at either. Harvard were also traditionally strong, but when it came to the crunch, always seemed to be lagging a bit behind the veritable giants of early intercollegiate football. From 1876 to 1893, Yale and Princeton held a duopoly on the national championship that Harvard could only once interrupt in 1890. Pennsylvania became the first champion from outside of the Big Three to win in 1895, and in 1898 and 1899 Harvard finally came of age with back to back wins.

Until the turn of the century, it is unlikely that there were any sides that could have topped any of Yale, Princeton, Harvard or (later) Pennsylvania, but it soon became difficult for any of the elite north-eastern colleges to be able to rightfully claim that they were 'national champions'. American football was being played coast to coast, but there was no national structure for the game. How could a team claim to be champion when so many great teams never even got the chance to play them?

Probably the first person to name what he considered to have been the best side in the country was journalist Caspar Whitney in 1901, who went for Harvard first, Yale second, and then Michigan, Wisconsin and Army, with Princeton way down in sixth. Much later, in 1926, Frank Dickinson, an economics professor at the University of Illinois, came up with a mathematical system for determining the winner, which for that year was Stanford. Knute Rockne, then coach of Notre Dame, took an interest in Dickinson's idea, and asked what would happen if the same system was applied to the earlier 1924 system, and got the answer he had wanted, for it turned out that his own Notre Dame would have been, by Dickinson's method, the national champs, before Dartmouth in 1925.

Dickinson continued announcing his winners through to 1940, but rather than settling arguments, he had simply created a new one. In 1929, Dick Dunkel came up with his alternative mathematical method, Paul Williams revealed his in 1932, followed by Edward and Frank Litkenhous in 1934, while it was the Associated Press in 1936 that devised the brilliantly subjective idea that journalists should simply vote who they thought was the best team – an idea that proved so surprisingly successful that it is still in use today!

This may sound like an odd system to anybody who is not familiar with college football in America, but unlike basketball, baseball and most other sports, a proper national championship is something they never quite got around to organising. The NCAA to this day involves a series of different Bowl finals played around the country, and the national champions are simply decided by a panel of sportswriters and other non-players. Outsiders generally agree that the NCAA method is a rather antiquated and frankly daft one, and several college football enthusiasts would agree, but with so much market force now behind the different Bowls, the situation is unlikely to change in the foreseeable future.

But if that isn't bad enough, US college football also has a craze for retro-ratings, which is the idea of using similarly subjective methods to work out who the champions were in the early years of college football. It's as bizarre as trying to name winners of Rugby World Cups prior to New Zealand's victory in the inaugural tournament in 1987, but among the American college fraternity, these things are taken seriously.

Historian Parke Davis, in 1933, was the first to do this when he went back and scoured his sources to decide who had won every championship played to date, starting by claiming that Princeton were the first NCAA Division One champions in 1869 because they beat Rutgers. The fact that was really a 'soccer' match didn't seem to matter!

Three years later, in 1936, the Helms Athletic Foundation was formed and voted on the champions all the way back to the year they felt American football was born, which was 1883, the year after the downs rule came in, as well as the (more or less) modern scoring system. Curiously, in 1901, they gave the title to Michigan, who may have gone 11-0-0 that year, but had yet to ever beat any of Yale, Princeton, Harvard or Pennsylvania, having lost all seven of their meetings with those sides to date, and who wouldn't get around to claiming any of those scalps until they overcame Penn in 1909. It is all particularly ridiculous when we note that Caspar Whitney, who was actually there at the time, clearly placed Harvard and Yale ahead of Michigan!

The modern day NCAA system is odd enough as it is, but applying it to history is painting a picture of the past that did not exist, and applies modern values to games that should be left in their contemporary context. There are serious gaps in the data covering the early years of college football. There may have been hundreds of games played for which no record survives, and in the games that were played, we cannot be sure whether the colleges were fielding their strongest sides – and in many cases we cannot even be sure what kind of football they were playing!

We could be heroes

In his memoirs, Amos Stagg describes how, in 1881, he sent a letter to the President of Yale College, Noah Porter, asking for funds for the football team. The response from the top was that "to good scholars the college has given from the Ellsworth Fund $175 a year. Beyond this the college, as such, can do little or nothing; but opportunities for self-help present themselves and are soon discovered by those who keep their eyes open to discern them." Prophetic words indeed.

From a contemporary point of view, the 1882 convention's decision to introduce downs was probably not as important as the carried suggestion that an annual Thanksgiving Game should be played in New York City. From an essentially private game to be played within the college walls, football was going to be taken to the masses, and they were going to love it.

DOWN ON SCRUM

Within a decade, the Thanksgiving Game alone was raking in a financial windfall of around $10,000 for each team. Yale and Princeton attracted just 5000 spectators to their game in 1880, but by 1893, there were 40,000 in the crowd, with small fortunes being made from black market and forged tickets, and betting on every imaginable aspect of the match.

In 1883, Joseph Pulitzer purchased the *New York World*. It was a relatively low-key newspaper, but he took mere months to turn its fortunes around and become the number one read in the city. He pioneered a sensationalist tabloid approach featuring comics, gossip pages, the world's first Sunday colour supplement and something unheard of at the time – extensive sports coverage. Baseball and horse racing may have been the nation's first loves, but once the seasons were over, there was precious little sport to write about. College football filled that hole nicely, and match reports were intertwined with the Ivy League rivalry that caught the general's public's imaginations hook, line and sinker.

The other newspapers soon followed suit, even the generally sombre *New York Times*. As Bernstein puts it "they presented the Ivy colleges, particularly Princeton and Yale, as the ideal – socially, athletically and morally. By presenting college football … to its readership, many of whom only had the faintest idea of college life, the press helped perpetuate the ideal of the Ivy colleges as something grand. Such attention connected not only football, but football fans, with the social elite. These schools became not just fine academic institutions, but someplace special, thus feeding the other schools' conceptions of themselves as such. The Ivy League reputation as we know today was burnished on the pages of the New York press."

From the basic paragraphs published in the 1870s that merely announced games or provided a few column inches giving the result and a brief summary, the papers were now publishing multi-page spreads giving every detail of college matches, and often painting a far more romantic and dramatic picture of the game than it really was. Here's the *New York World* on the 1892 game between Harvard and Yale: "An Aetna of humanity, bellowing with the combined thunder of a dozen tornadoes. A huge quadrangular crater filled to the brim with the hoarse tumult of human passions and blazing with blue and crimson fires. In this crater great black drifts, that heaved and swayed and rolled like earthquake-shaken hills, and under all the deep diapason of voices, the thousand inarticulate cries of grief and joy and quick, sharp shrieks of rage. A battery of 40,000 feverish eyes focused with the intensity of burning glasses on a bare plot of withered turf, where twenty-two gladiators were fighting the fag end of a royal battle."

That's a football match they are on about! The popular press put the players in another realm, and took readers into a fantasy world of hero athletes, which cannot be better reflected than the tales of Frank Merriwell, the fictional comic-strip hero created by Gilbert Patten who first appeared in the "ideal publication for American Youth", *Tip Top Weekly*, in 1896. When he wasn't performing heroics on the football pitch, the non-smoking, non-drinking fitness freak went about solving campus mysteries and righting wrongs, typifying the

317

idealistic mystique the press wanted to associate to a bunch of students thumping each other and running around after a ball.

The fascination was the same, but while early football in Britain was built around identification with the community's football club, in America it was built around the local college team. It would not really be until the Super Bowl era of the 1960s onwards that professional football enjoyed the same popularity as the college game, although even today you will not find any single football league in any code in any country that is watched live by more people a season than the NCAA Division 1A, with a total yearly attendance in the region of 36 million[19].

Tramps and cakes

The colleges themselves did not take long to get wise to this surge of interest in their scrimmages and downs. By 1903, football was generating Yale University $106,000 a year, more than one eighth of the institution's entire income, and more than it spent on either law or medicine. So it is easy to understand why the men at the top started realising that as well as providing an education to the great and good of the nation and investing in research programmes, it was as much in the interests of any aspiring academic institution to have a good football team.

The win-at-all-costs mentality was soon causing all kinds of controversies in a reality that was often very far removed from the glorious ideals being presented to the public in the form of Frank Merriwell and his friends.

Yards-to-go having settled the rules issue for the time being, the bone of contention in the 1890s was playing eligibility. These were meant to be matches between college teams, but it became increasingly questionable how many of their players were proper students at all. It had once been a game for sons of the social elite, and the line-ups of the early Ivy League teams reflected that, with most of the surnames being those of the northeast's wealthy landowning families. But by the 1890s, we find German, Irish and other surnames becoming increasingly more prominent, and despite the discrimination against them being as rife as ever, African-American players in college teams were no rarity. Their presence was not the problem, it was the suspicions about how these young men from underprivileged and usually uneducated backgrounds had ended up representing the country's most selective universities.

The use of professional coaches to oversee a college's football programme was already commonplace. In fact the guy responsible for the football programmes was often the biggest earner on the college payroll. Harvard coach William Reid, for example, earned a salary of $3500 plus the same again in 'expenses', which was twice what your average professor was

---

[19] By way of comparison, the highest figures for a season in any other code are those of soccer's English Premiership, with around 13 million. If its average rather than total figures you want, the NCAA Division 1A does well with around 46,000. Figures vary, but the German Bundesliga (soccer) and Aussie Rules' AFL clock in high with around 38,000 a game, while the NFL gets a whopping average of 67,000 a match.

DOWN ON SCRUM

on and even 30% more than the esteemed president, Charles Eliot. That the coaches were on fat salaries was impossible to hide any more, but rumours were soon circulating that there were professional players too.

College sports were plagued by the phenomenon of 'tramp athletes', sportsmen that switched from college to college, often only vaguely trying to present the image that they were actually studying something. For years, it was widely quoted in American football histories that the first case of a player receiving pay to play was John Brallier of Indiana College in Pennsylvania. In return for turning out for a non-school team, Latrobe, against neighbouring Jeannette in September 1895, Brallier was quite happy to take $10 and 'cakes', which was not a voucher to spend at the local Dunkin' Donuts, but a slang term used at the time for expenses.

It was not the first case. It was the first case anyone knew of. But plenty more would have been successfully hushed up. Indeed, it would take eighty years before the accounts sheet was discovered for a game between the Allegheny Athletic Association and Pittsburgh Athletic played in October 1892. It clearly states that Pennsylvania's Pudge Heffelfinger was paid $500 to play – a handsome sum indeed for the time, and which he repaid by scoring the only touchdown of the game.

Penn was on the receiving end of many an accusing finger, where its dental school, which didn't require any entrance exams, was a particularly handy place to fast-track young men into the college who you really wouldn't trust to go poking around any cavities in your mouth, but would be more than relieved to have standing next to you when slamming headfirst into tightly constituted packages of ogre flesh. The average age of the Penn squad in 1894 was twenty-four, with some players much older than that, and one allegedly had an eight-year old son! On February 24, 1894, the *New York Times* wrote that they were sarcastically known as the All America Eleven, rather than a college team, and that "players were induced to come from colleges and academies in all quarters to strengthen the team." New regulations had just been brought in to put at stop to all this nonsense, which prevented players from receiving payment or from being enrolled purely on the basis of their football rather than academic skills. It spelt bad news for Penn, and the *Times* felt the rules were bound "to have a disastrous effect upon athletics at that institution of learning in the future, although they may benefit a certain number of students in the class rooms who have been neglecting their studies in the past by devoting too much of their time to sport."

But although Pennsylvania were involved in such dealings as those with Andy Smith, who between 1902 and 1904 seemed to drift between Penn and Penn State depending on which college's needs (and pay packets) were biggest, they were by no means the only college at fault. There was, for instance, Fielding Yost, who would go on to coach Michigan to become one of the strongest football colleges of the early 20th century. He studied at West Virginia, but in 1896 was curiously 'transferred' to Lafayette, just in time to assist them to a famous victory over Pennsylvania before returning to West Virginia finish his law degree.

319

MIKE ROBERTS – THE SAME OLD GAME: CODIFICATION

Over in Chicago, the great Amos Alonzo Stagg had set up a handy little trust fund to wave dollars at the top footballers and lure them towards his college, having been told in a letter from the president of the institution, William Rainey Harper, to "develop teams which we can send around the country and knock out all the colleges. We will give them a palace car and a vacation too." Chicago's Walter Eckersall was one of the first great quarterbacks in the game, but much less of a star when it came to his studies (although he did go on to carve out a brilliant career as a sportswriter on the *Chicago Tribune* before his life in the fast lane finally burnt him out at the age of 43). Stagg was his coach, and although Eckersall was constantly failing his grades and almost always absent from class, the obliging Professor Thatcher always saw to it that he was given a C. In 1906, as a deliberate ploy to crack down on pros, a new rule was brought in limiting players to just three years, meaning Eckersall's professional career was up and he was merely using up space. He was immediately thrown out of college.

Even the staunch defender of the amateur ethos, Walter Camp, seemed quite happy to play the money game he so publicly denounced. It was Clarence Deming, the same man who gave us that delightful little piece on the 'first age of football', who blew the lid big-time by revealing to *Outlook* in July 1905 that Yale's football man kept a $100,000 slush fund.

Born in Tipperary, Ireland, James J Hogan was from a poor background, but a devastatingly good footballer. He started high school at Exeter aged 23, where he received sufficient education to enrol at Yale at the ripe old age of 27! Benjamin Rader writes that "the renowned captain of the Yale team, reputedly lived in a style befitting a prince. He enjoyed free tuition, a free suite in the swank Vanderbilt Hall, free meals at the University Club, a $100 scholarship, a ten-day vacation to Cuba paid for by the Yale Athletic Association, a monopoly on the sale of scorecards at games, and the exclusive commission to handle the products of the American Tobacco Company on the Yale campus."

In 1905, *McClure's Magazine* explained how, when asking about this rather curious choice of sales rep, an ATC spokesman responded that Hogan's peers "appreciate and like him. They realise that he is a poor fellow, working his way through college, and they want to help him. So they buy our cigarettes, knowing that Hogan gets a commission on every box sold in New Haven." How very considerate of everybody. Once his football days were over, Hogan started working as deputy for the New York Street Cleaning Company, but his life came to a sad early end in 1910 when he fell victim to Bright's Disease.

Watterson also tells the story of Princeton's Charles Patterson, whose job was to scour the region finding potential footballers of whatever social class, age or educational ability, fund their passage through prep school so they could at least spell their names correctly, and enrol them in the elite universities. At Andover, during Princeton's entrance examinations in 1902, one candidate was nowhere near the level required, but he coolly explained that "at the top of the paper I wrote my weight, 205 pounds. I guess I'll pass all right."

DOWN ON SCRUM

In response, the colleges were keen to wave figures at the press declaring how well all these football playing students were doing in their studies, but Columbia found it hard to find any defence in 1900 when the scandal came to light that only three of their team were undergraduates, and two of the players, Larendon and Miller, made the startling confession to the *New York Sun* in March 1900 that "eighty seven dollars were paid by the football management to the university in order that our names would appear on the rolls, and thus make us eligible to play for the team. We did not receive tuition for playing football, as has been stated, as it is a well known fact that we did not attend lectures and never had any intention of so doing."

It was college football but in a candid way it was also professional football. While in other countries, university and old boy competitions soon faded from the public eye as the people turned instead to the higher quality professional teams, in America it was the colleges that had the support base, that had the infrastructure, that had the coaches, and that had the money and the desire to promote a successful football team. And so it was on the college doors that footballers of all social ranks were knocking. If college football had been limited to 'real' students, one wonders whether the public would have maintained the same intensity of interest.

Bastions of tradition

The arrival of the 'American collegiate game' did not mean an immediate death for 'British' rugby in America. While the elite American colleges were under no obligation to play the game the way the British did, neither was the rest of America obliged to play the game the way the colleges did.

Some communities supported the innovations of the American Intercollegiate Association, but there were 'traditional' rugby clubs such as the British influenced New York City FBC that were most upset to see such wholesale changes being made to the sport, and on April 29, 1882, the rugby community even managed to get Walter Camp to meet them and hear their side of the story before introducing the downs rule. They failed to make their case.

But the USA is a big country, and not everybody was quite so quick to pick up on the new innovations. It was anything but a smooth switch from one code to the next. In such states as Virginia, Iowa, Minnesota and Wisconsin, the big colleges all seemed to still be playing soccer. 1882 was the first year Berkeley played football, and they started with the rugby rules, playing their first games against two non-academic clubs, the Merions and the Wanderers, and winning both. Colorado College, meanwhile, was flirting with soccer and then moved on to rugby, while even in Washington DC the new rules didn't have an immediate foothold. The US Naval Academy and Johns Hopkins of Maryland played a game using downs in 1883, but even so most other clubs in the region were still quite happy with the original rugby rules, while Lincoln University in Pennsylvania seemed content enough with their own curious blend of rugby and soccer called 'rabble'.

321

MIKE ROBERTS – THE SAME OLD GAME: CODIFICATION

Over the following decade, colleges all over nation started drifting towards lines of scrimmage and downs. Beyond 1899, Mel Smith is unable to find any record of a college still using the original rugby rules. But outside of the educational institutions, there is no evidence of any athletic club at all using the college rules until 1884, when a small scattering had emerged around New York.

As if to make one last stand against the rising tide of the gridiron, an exhibition match was played in November 1882 between the New York RFC and Britannia FBC of Canada. It was not a big success. Only a few hundred people showed up to watch and few were convinced by what they saw. When the American Rugby Football Union was formed in 1890, it only had four members, New York, Philadelphia, Newark and Paterson, and its activities were largely ignored by the fans and the media, who were far more interested in what was going on at the colleges.

Yet by the turn of the century, we start seeing British rugby in its 'original' form remerging in the USA. It's shared roots with the American game already unknown to many, rugby was now treated as if it was a new and entirely different sport! Students at Yale and Pennsylvania started playing English rugby again in 1906, and in February of that year, New York even played New Zealand, who were on their way home from the historic first ever All Blacks tour of Britain, and beat the Americans 46-13.

Less affected by developments in the east, an alternative rugby culture managed to hold on in California, boosted when the big colleges, especially Berkeley and Stanford, rejected the collegiate game because of its associations to professionalism and the fear of violence. In 1905, Berkeley president Benjamin Ide Wheeler wrote to Columbia to say that "we shall make our own game, probably rugby, with 'socker' as a substitute."

In 1906, most colleges in the north of California switched to the rugby rules, and in the following seasons, colleges further south, and also in Nevada and Oregon did likewise. For a while, it looked like a completely separate football culture was going to emerge on the Pacific Coast. In 1910, the western universities of California, Nevada and Stanford even managed to combine forces for a twenty-match tour of Australia and New Zealand, creating something of an upset by beating both Rotorua and Auckland. In 1912, Australia toured the west of the USA and Canada, and lost their matches against both Berkeley and Stanford. A year later, a full strength New Zealand team toured California. The All Blacks not only beat the All-America team 51-3 at Berkeley, but easily won its other twelve games too, and it is said that the humiliation had a devastating effect on American enthusiasm for the game. Following the First World War, by which time American football had done a lot to clean up its act, the colleges started abandoning rugby for the American game.

Nevertheless, American rugby's finest hour had yet to come. That was in 1920, when the Californians raised the money to travel to Antwerp to play in the first ever Olympic tournament. Sadly, the rest of the rugby world was less inclined to make the effort, and the only game of the tournament saw the Americans goings like lambs to the slaughter against

France. But they pulled off one of most extraordinary upsets in the game's history by winning 8-0.

The USA was back in 1924, this time in Paris itself, and after both the Americans and the French had seen off Romania, they faced each other in front of some 35,000 partisan Parisians in the Stade de Colombes. Once again the French were hot favourites to win, and just in case the mishap of four years earlier should repeat itself, they refused the American team any training pitches, forcing them to make do with a local park. As the players practiced, their French attendant failed to notice that all of their clothing, containing $4000 worth of cash and possessions, had been stolen. The French press had stirred up a hate campaign against the US side that even saw them being abused and spat at in the streets, but that only served to stir up a passion like never before in the American rugby side.

It was never going to be a pretty final. France's Adolphe Jauguery was carried off the pitch unconscious and bleeding, and American reserve Gideon Nelson was flattened by a walking stick. But the Americans denied France yet another Olympic gold with a 17-3 win. To this day, the USA can consider itself Olympic champion, for the game never appeared in the Games again, although rugby sevens has been accepted as a new discipline from 2016.

There is now a professional league in the States, attracting a mild following, while the national side, the Eagles, are considered a decent 'second tier' nation and have appeared at all but one World Cup to date. But it is in the women's game where American rugby really comes to the fore, with many colleges considering rugby to be a better alternative for the fairer sex than the 'man's' game of American football. The USA won the first Women's Rugby World Cup in 1991, and were finalists again at the next two.

Soccer USA

There are many alternative scenarios for the way the American game could have gone. What would rugby be like today if the Americans had not decided to transform it into a different game? The presence of the USA as a superpower and the NFL as rugby's strongest competition would have implied a major shift in the balance of power. And the Americans would surely have sided with the professionalism of rugby league, with who know what implications for that code's role in the sporting world…

But what if Harvard had accepted the invitation to join the fledgling intercollegiate body in 1873? The chances are they would never have ended up playing that game with McGill, and the United States would have become a soccer playing nation. But if America had decided to go with soccer, would it have accepted the London FA's regulations? Totally different forms of soccer emerged in Australia and Ireland, and probably would have done in America too. As Harvard president Charles Eliot said in 1905 after seeing a match, "it is very pretty as they played it, but our American college boys would spoil it in five minutes … There is plenty of opportunity for brutality in socker."

MIKE ROBERTS – THE SAME OLD GAME: CODIFICATION

But although the colleges did not embrace soccer, that did not mean the death of the code on US soil. Walter Camp wrote in 1891 that "of the Association game one can say but little as regards its American following. It is quite extensively played in this country, but more by those who have themselves played it in Great Britain than by native-born Americans. Its popularity is extending, and at some day it will very likely become as well understood in this country as the derived rugby is to-day."

While the Americans made wholesale changes to the rugby game, they continued to play soccer by the London FA's rules, and never swayed from them. This may partly be because soccer was the plaything of more recent European immigrants, but also the sheer simplicity of the kicking game, as opposed to rugby's almost incomprehensible clauses, meant there was less need to modify the rules of the former.

In 1883, the Western Football League of America was founded in St Louis, Missouri, where the names of the three top teams clearly suggest their British or Irish roots (Hibernians, Thistles and Irish Americans). A year later, the American Football Association was formed at Newark in New Jersey and by 1894 the short-lived American League of Professional Football[20] predated any of the pro competitions on the gridiron, established by the baseball clubs as a way to keep their fans fishing into their pockets during the off season. It wasn't a huge success, not helped by the fact that the clubs included baseball stars in their soccer rosters, which may have been a nice gimmick for the spectators, but was hardly the groundwork for a serious competition.

From the 1890s, clubs like Brooklyn Wanderers and Fall River Rovers were probably as good as any others in the world, but the papers were giving them a wide berth. But despite existing in almost utter anonymity, by 1890 there were 15 senior soccer leagues in America. That may sound like excellent progress, but these were largely a mishmash of poorly organised inter-squabbling associations, and when the ambitious Open Challenge Cup was finally created in 1912, it turned out to be an excessively large, costly and diluted fiasco.

Professional soccer in America enjoyed something of a golden age in the 1920s, mainly thanks to the American Soccer League set up in 1921[21]. That competition drew heavily on ethnic (Bethlehem Steel, New Jersey Celtics, Hakoah Brooklyn...) and industrial (Indiana Flooring, Clam Diggers, Boston Wonder Workers...) roots, but failed due to all the usual mismanaged internal divisions and ultimately the financial collapse of its players, fans and clubs in the aftermath of the 1929 Wall Street Crash. The soccer leagues were finished, and unlike American football, there were no massively supported college teams to ensure their survival.

---

[20] Note the use of the word 'football' and not 'soccer' in all these titles. The US Football Association, formed in 1913 did not adopt the wrongly supposed Americanism of 'soccer' until as late as 1945, when it became the US Soccer Football Association, not dropping the 'Football' until 1974.

[21] Stefan Szymanski and Andrew Zimbalist tell the full story in their book *National Pastime: How Americans Play Baseball and the Rest of the World Plays Soccer* (Brookings Institution Press, 2005).

DOWN ON SCRUM

The American Dream was all about the home-grown sports of baseball, basketball, ice hockey and, of course, the gridiron. Soccer was an unwanted intruder, but rather like in Australia, it has always been there, hiding in the background. The USA was one of just 13 countries to enter the inaugural World Cup in 1930 and made the semi finals, and in 1950 the national team caused one of the greatest upsets in soccer history by beating England 1-0 in Brazil. The North American Soccer League arrived with much hype in 1968, attracting such stars as George Best, Ruud Krol, Franz Beckenbauer and Bobby Moore, and crowds of 40,000 to watch Pele at the New York Cosmos. It had the potential to become the biggest soccer league in the world, but the NASL tried to run before it could walk and had fizzled away to nothing by 1984. Yet World Cup attendance records were shattered when the USA hosted the competition in 1994, and the Major League Soccer project that followed in its wake has proved a massively greater success than almost anybody had predicted, and not just among the Latino population. Since the 1990s, the US national side has become established as one of the strongest in the world, and when they drew 1-1 with the creators of the game, England, at the 2010 World Cup, few eyebrows were raised and some were even surprised they didn't win. Exhibitions by touring European teams still pack American stadia, showing that the potential of the soccer market in the USA is strong, but has yet to be fully exploited.

Mark Salisbury puts it brilliantly when he says (American) "football was never a participation sport. It was a battle for survival, weeding out the lesser men through a contest that demanded stature, strength, character, and the ability to play with pain. Soccer was all-inclusive; a game where everybody could enjoy the benefits of outdoor, physical exercise. Though it was a good argument for a gym class, it stripped soccer of its ability to create collegiate heroes like the football gods worshipped weekly in the popular press[22]."

For your average North American, football is a game for watching heroes, not being one. But most soccer fans don't just watch their game from the safety of the terraces or an armchair. They play the game too. In many ways, it's a game millions of young Americans can identify with more than their own national code, but they still have to endure scathing remarks from the likes of Bernie Lincicome of the *Chicago Tribune*, who reckoned the only good thing about soccer is that junior high gym class kids "are free to use their hands to push their glasses up their nose."

Soccer's struggle to be accepted into the US mainstream looks to be finally ending, after long having been the most widely played football code in the country. It has managed to survive in hostile territory, as has the rugby game. In fact, rather than these two, the code that probably came the closest to dying out among Americans was the one that they themselves had created. There were still more problems to be solved before American football truly became the game we know today…

---

[22] Mark Salisbury *American Attitudes toward Soccer* (US Soccer History Archives, 1995, maintained by Dave Litterer).

14 THE KILLING FIELDS
American football and the issue of violence

Power plays

The introduction of the line of scrimmage and downs-to-go in the early 1880s was designed to create the most beautiful form of rugby ever devised. Teams in possession were now spared the ugliness of interminable scrummages, and instead the ball was immediately provided to the backs to delight everyone with flowing passes and delicate punts. And that was the case for a while, but that progress was thwarted by the American footballer's obsession with interference. Described by Walter Camp, this is "the assistance given to a runner by a companion or companions who go before him and break a path for him or shoulder off would-be tacklers."

Though generally considered an American innovation, we could go all the way back to English poet Henry Peacham and his poem *Minerva Britanna* of 1612, which goes that:

"The country Swaines, at footeball heere are Seene,
Which each gapes after, for to get a blow,
The while some one, away runnes with it cleane,
It meetes another, at the goale below.
Who never stirrd, one catcheth heere a fall,
And there one's maimd who never saw the ball"

There is certainly a twang of interference in the way the maimed guy never even got to touch the ball. However, such antics were deemed illegal by the laws of rugby, where any player that was ahead of the ball could not take any part in the game, which included any kind of tackling. Indeed, as Camp himself noted, "this, to the Englishman, would be the most detestable kind of off-side play, and not tolerated for an instant upon any field in the United Kingdom." That is not to say that players hadn't attempted it. AG Guillemard, writing on early English rugby, said that "as to the off-side laws, they were either not understood or flagrantly contravened by a large majority of the minor clubs in 'the sixties'. The Blackheath School boys were terrible offenders in this respect, and it was quite common to see the forwards charging down the ground as an advance guard to ward off opponents from the back who was in full run with the ball behind them."

Despite Blackheath's attempts, when the RFU published its rules in 1871, it outlawed any such tomfoolery. But both American teams and referees tended to be more relaxed about the issue, although Camp does say that "even into this the Americans did not plunge suddenly, but rather little by little they stepped in, until it was necessary to do one of two things – either legalize what was being tacitly consented to, or penalize it heavily. The result was that it was legalized."

THE KILLING FIELDS

When the line of scrimmage was introduced in 1880, as soon as the ball was snapped back to the quarterback, all of the players on the rush line were technically offside, and therefore found themselves in the almost ridiculous position of not being able to do anything to prevent the opposing line from charging through to sack the quarterback. Not surprisingly, defensive lines took the law into their own hands, and from 1881 the rule committee started introducing different types of warnings against "intentional offside playing," although it does not appear that referees were particularly strict in their application.

By 1884, Princeton were already getting away with their famous 'V trick', first tried in a game with Pennsylvania[1], whereby the players would group around the ball-carrier and protect him with interference. Its inventor, Richard Hodge, told Parke Davis how it had happened. "It suddenly struck me that if the rush-line would jump into the shape of a V with the apex forward and with Baker inside, the formation ought to gain ground. A consultation immediately was held, and upon the next play the formation tried, Baker ploughing forward within the V from midfield to the five-yard line. We then reserved this formation for the Yale game, Lamar making within it a long gain on the opening play. The next year the V was not used, but was revived in 1886. By 1888 it had come into general use throughout the country and in 1889 was the standard opening play with every eleven."

The rules committee had decided to bow to the inevitable, and in 1889 announced that "the side which has the ball can interfere with the body only, the side which has not the ball can use hands and arms heretofore." Interference was legal, along with the blocking that is so typical of the modern game, but as Michael Oriard states mathematically: "possession + five-yards-in-three-plays-for-a-first-down + interference = mayhem," especially considering that in 1888 tackling from the waist downwards had also been legalised. The focus of football switched from an open passing game to a chess-like battle to develop strategies to bash through the rival defence, take out opponents and generally spoil any attempt to do anything creative. Half the players no longer even had the remotest intention of actually touching the ball.

As the great player and coach John William Heisman wrote in 1932, "very little scientific thought had been put into that department of play before the dawn of the present century. Nearly all linemen, as a rule, lined up squarely against those who played the same positions on the opposing team. They didn't crouch or squat or play low. They mostly stood bolt upright and fought it out with each other hammer and tongs, tooth and nail, fist and feet. The fact is, you didn't stand much chance of making the line those days unless you were a good wrestler and fair boxer[2]."

---

[1] Although the same college had actually done something very similar way back in 1869 in the historic 'soccer' match with Rutgers.

[2] Cited in Wiley Lee Umphlett *Creating the Big Game: John W Heisman and the Invention of American Football* (Greenwood Press, 1992).

This was not an all inclusive game. This was a game of brute force for only the bravest and fittest, and unlike today, games lasted 90 minutes with no substitutions. Protective clothing was almost unheard of, other than the tendency to grow long hair to soften the impact of the many blows to the skull. Whether carrying the ball or punting it forward, the basic 'skill' was to charge through the opposing line. With just five yards to gain off a down, American football degenerated into little more than one group of bodies trying to barrage its way through another, but while Rugby purists would have sighed with dismay, spectators of the college game watched on in enthrallment as teams devised frighteningly devious methods to achieve the goal.

Harvard epitomised this in the second half of their 1892 game with Yale by unveiling the infamous 'flying wedge'. This was the same tactic that had been used in military manoeuvres for centuries. The Ancient Greeks called it *embolon* and the Romans gave it the colloquial name *caput porcinum* (boar's head) and it is a basic part of riot police training today for breaking through a group of people. Rather than attack side-by-side in a straight line, a flying wedge involves forming a V shape and attacking one specific point, thus dividing the enemy lines.

It was neither a player nor a coach who saw the potential of applying the method to football. It was a Bostonian businessman named Lorin Fuller Deland, a fanatic of both chess and military strategies, who explained to *Harper's Weekly* in December 1893 that if Napoleon "could mass a large proportion of his troops and throw them against a weak point of the enemy, he could easily defeat that portion, and gaining their rear, create havoc with the rest." The Crimsons were about to apply the idea to football to devastating effect, with the ball carrier snugly placed inside the group.

The idea went down a storm. The *Boston Herald* said it "sent the football men who were spectators into raptures." Amos Alonzo Stagg called it "the most spectacular single formation ever", and Parke Davis believed that "no play has ever been devised so spectacular and sensational." The *New York Times* was equally impressed, but also noted how "a surgeon is called upon to attend the wounded player, and the game continues with renewed brutality."

Despite the vicious nature of the wedge, it was just the kind of thing the American audience wanted, and "as much as it was considered a producer of manliness, the flying wedge was hailed by some as a positive reflection of scientific thinking applied to football … With no frontier left to conquer, football produced rugged men and virile leaders. The game of football, then, might not only be a substitute for war, but a palliative for a nation in danger of losing its pioneering spirit[3]."

---

[3] Scott McQuilkin and Ronald Smith *The Rise and Fall of the Flying Wedge: Football's Most Controversial Play* (in *Journal of Sport History,* Spring 1993).

Harvard's revolutionary tactic caused such a stir that it is often overlooked that they lost the game, 6-0, while despite the alarm at the viciousness of it all, the only casualty of the day was the onlooking Pudge Heffelfinger, who got so excited that he jumped over a fence, got tangled in it, and needed the help of three policemen to break free!

Other colleges were soon adopting the flying wedge, or variations on it, like the 'turtle-back' created by Alonzo Stagg, which involved up to nine players hunching all around the ball carrier and ramming their way through the opposing line, or Penn's 'flying interference', which was a human chain moving just ahead of the ball, and which they used to majestic effect to put an end to Yale's incredible run dating back to 1890 of 1,355 unanswered points in no fewer than 35 consecutive shutouts.

The ball carrier's duty often amounted to little more than following on behind to take the ball into whatever space his forwards could create for him, or otherwise clinging tightly onto the ball as the rest of team concentrated on pushing and pulling to get the man, rather than the ball, over the required distance. Heisman writes that "some backs had leather straps, like valise handles, sewed or riveted on the shoulders of their jackets and on the hips of their trousers, so as to offer good handholds for their team-mates."

Other resourceful minds found other solutions. Yale once invented one of almost comical brilliance. Rather than take the challenge head on, they simply stepped aside and allowed the wedge to run straight through, and then toppled the ball carrier instead! And Springfield YMCA once managed to score against Harvard of all teams when one of their players fell out of their tight unit, seemingly injured. The two lines continued to do battle, Harvard ignoring the 'injured' player and noticing too late that he was actually hiding the ball and about make a touchdown run.

Fever pitch

Football may have been booming, but not everybody liked the way it was going. Games were won not by skill but by brute force, colleges were making a mockery of the system by fielding players that weren't even students, and the Intercollegiate Football Association, which by 1894 was effectively just Yale and Princeton, was proving hopelessly inept at keeping any kind of control on what was going on. Better structure was required, and it was here that the University Athletic Club of New York stepped in with the idea of disbanding the IFA and overseeing its replacement with what it called the Intercollegiate Rules Committee (IRC). The UAC was widely represented on the committee, especially by its president and staunch supporter of the amateur ethos, George Adee, but the men who did most of the talking were a panel of experts from the main colleges.

Naturally, Walter Camp, the "foremost authority in this country", as the *New York Times* called him in March 1894, was there in all his glory. He was joined by Alexander Moffat of Princeton, William Brooks of Harvard, John Cromwell Bell of Pennsylvania, and Paul

Dashiell of Lehigh, a fine mix of the cream of former footballers, and present-day coaches and umpires, and all of them extraordinarily well educated gentlemen. Bell was a firm proponent of reducing the violence in the game, but his colleagues seemed less inclined to do so, and their failure to properly modify the rules in that respect was one of the main reasons why the decade that followed would see football not just causing a remarkable number of injuries, but also deaths.

When the Committee issued its revised laws in May 1894, it was probably somewhat reluctant about outlawing what it called 'mass momentum' plays, defined as "one in which more than three men group for that purpose more than five yards back of the point where the ball is put in play." The new rules also specified that "no player shall lay his hands upon an opponent unless he has the ball. Players of the side in possession may obstruct with the body only" and "there shall be no piling up upon the runner after he has cried down or the referee has blown his whistle."

But eliminating the flying wedge and similar plays did little to curb the violence. Harvard and Yale's first meeting after the rules had been revised, rather than displaying a return to open play and flowing ball skills, was remembered as the Hampden Park Blood Bath. It was a big enough a story to make the European press, the German *Münchener Nachrichten* saying that "the football tournament between the teams of Yale and Harvard ... had terrible results. It turned into an awful butchery. Of twenty-two participants, seven were so severely injured that they had to be carried from the pitch in a dying condition. One player had his back broken, another lost an eye, and a third lost a leg ... the indignation of the spectators was powerful, but they were so terrorised that they were afraid to leave the field."

There was obviously some poetic licence at work there, and even more so in *The Nation*'s claim that the casualty rate was higher than that of Napoleon's defeat at Waterloo, but there were indeed both a broken back and collarbone, and other casualties, and Yale's Fred Murphy was indeed feared dead, but eventually came out of a seven-hour coma. The Harvard administration held a referendum and agreed 2-1 to abolish football for good. However, as the *New York Times* noted, $11,000 in revenue for the teams, and plenty of side benefits for other parties, such as $75,000 for the railroads who had transported 15,000 fans to the match meant the people directly involved in the game were not complaining in the slightest, and under pressure from the athletic committee, with the support of the Harvard Corporation, who really ran the show at the university, the vote was overruled.

All but three of the Yale squad were back in training by Monday, ahead of the next weekend's showdown with Princeton. There were mutterings that the game would not go ahead, but there was never really any question of that happening, although NYPD superintendent Byrnes did advise his men to immediately put a stop to it if "it proved to be anything else other than a scientific contest between two college teams." As it happened, the game passed off without major incident, and Yale claimed the championship with a 16-0 win.

THE KILLING FIELDS

Harvard, meanwhile, was disgruntled following the events at Hampden and waiting for an apology from Yale. They didn't get it, so the two colleges severed relations and would not meet again for three years. Elsewhere, similar events in the Army-Navy game saw that encounter suspended from 1884 to 1898. Princeton and Pennsylvania's game sunk to such depths that the aftermath saw students and townspeople involved in riots in the streets and it would take over forty years for the two colleges to make their peace!

The game in 1894 was not in a healthy situation. Walter Camp, who amazingly considering its importance had not even been there to see the infamous Yale vs Harvard game (he was coaching in California at the time), was once again assumed to be the man to turn to in times of trouble. He was asked to form a commission to investigate the brutality in football, which emerged in the form of the highly controversial *Football Facts and Figures* (1894).

Cleaning up the act

One gets the impression that the researchers had already decided what the outcome of their study was going to be before they had even started. Camp concluded that "we find that the almost unanimous opinion of those who have played the game of football at Harvard, Yale or Princeton during the last eighteen years is that it has been of marked benefit to them, both in the way of general development and mental discipline; also that they regard the injuries sustained as generally unimportant and far outweighed by the benefits."

They had also polled other colleges, who came back with the same glowing reports, and also their professors, who were unanimous in proclaiming that "the sport has been beneficial to the physical development and discipline of the school and that the consensus of opinion is that scholarship has certainly not suffered." The finding that 20 per cent of players had suffered some kind of injury playing the game was pooh-poohed on the grounds that more than half of that percentage were no more serious than broken noses or swollen fingers. Penn coach George Woodruff made the comment the anti-soccer brigade would appreciate today that "there should be less delay of game. Less sponging during a game, less fuss about injuries already received. If the hurt is great the player should leave the field; if small he should smile and play harder."

Historians argue about how much of the content of the infamous *Facts and Figures* was an accurate representation of the facts. It certainly reeks of spin-doctored bias, containing letter after letter from almost every field in the sport imaginable, but censoring anything like the letter from former Princeton player Luther Price, who had once had to quit a game "due to sheer weakness and loss of blood." Just how much else Camp and his cronies overlooked in filing that report we will never know, but whether it was because he shared the wish to spread the IRC's propaganda or because he was completely taken in by it, the *New York Times*' reviewer was gushing with praise and felt "every parent who is troubled with doubts and fears about a son's participation in the game ought to read this book, and a perusal of it

MIKE ROBERTS – THE SAME OLD GAME: CODIFICATION

would be extremely beneficial to writers who are tempted to make conclusions of insufficient information."

The game muscled on, with the main colleges at constant loggerheads over personal issues, violence and eligibility. In 1895, Columbia was in no mood to break the habit of a lifetime and once again decided to pull the plug on football[4]. Cornell, Pennsylvania and Harvard turned their backs on Yale and Princeton entirely and formed their own organisation, with rules that brought back the mass momentum plays regardless, and Walter Camp added that there were also "many teams which did not trouble themselves with the alterations made by either of the two prominent parties but stuck to the rules as they had been laid down the previous year. Then there were offshoots of the two main sets of rules, which grew up in peculiar ways … But the most exasperating part of this multiplicity of rules lay in the agreements necessitated in the less important matches[5]," whereby teams would trade rules to suit their own interests. Meanwhile, unimpressed with what was happening in the east, the presidents of Chicago, Illinois, Michigan, Minnesota, Northwestern, Purdue, and Wisconsin gathered to form their own association[6].

Nobody was quite sure what the IRC's role was any more, and in 1896 the big eastern colleges decided to make a fresh start by reforming the former IFA (although Yale and Harvard still refused to play each other). They immediately set about revising the rules yet again to insist that at least five players take their place on the line of scrimmage, thus dissuading mass plays, and at the same stated that "no player of the side in possession of the ball shall take more than one step towards his opponent's goal before the ball is in play without coming to a full stop." Both rules are still in the game today, although it would take three decades before they finally got round to rephrasing the 'without coming to a full stop' bit, which if read textually, actually meant quite the opposite to what it was meant to say.

The efforts the different rules-making boards went to over the years to tone down the violence do more to show how little they cared about reforms than any real concern. The laws were revised on an annual basis, but other than a token meddling with the numbers on the line of scrimmage, very little was done to properly address the problem, and as the 20th century dawned, it was getting worse.

The matter returned to the headlines in 1897, when the University of Georgia's Richard Vonalbade Gammon was killed playing what the *Atlanta Journal* called the 'Death Knell of

---

[4] They'd be back again in 1899, and with a vengeance, as they shocked the nation by beating Yale 5-0. That win came courtesy of a Harold Weekes touchdown, a player who starred in what might be the most spectacular football tactic ever invented in any code. As Bernstein describes "the 210 pound fullback would climb up on the shoulders of two teammates, who would then catapult him over the line, where he would try to land on his feet and keep running." Defences apparently responded by catapulting their own men to meet the human missile in the air.

[5] Walter Camp's *Review of the Season of 1895* in Volume 29 of *Outing* (October 1896).

[6] What would end up being the Western Conference, or 'Big Ten' after Iowa and Indiana (1899) and Ohio State (1912) were added. In the 1940s, Chicago was replaced by Michigan State.

THE KILLING FIELDS

Football'. The outcry was such that the authorities decided to ban football outright in the state, a decision that was only vetoed by Governor Atkinson when he received a letter from the late Gammon's mother Rosalind defending the sport and pleading they "grant me the right to request that my boy's death should not be used to defeat the most cherished object of his life."

But Gammon was not going to be the last player to lose his life on the football field. The level of violence was never put better than John Lawrence Sullivan, a champion heavyweight boxer who had taken plenty of punches in the ring, which itself was considerably more brutal than it is now. But football? No way. "There's murder in that game" he said. "Prizefighting doesn't compare in roughness or danger with football. In the ring, at least you know what you're doing. You know what your opponent is trying to do. He's right there in front of you. There's only one of him. But in football – there are 11 guys trying to do you in!"

Mend it or end it

Criticism of football famously reached its peak in 1905, when the national press was almost unanimous in turning its back on something that had supplied it with so many column inches over the years. Instead, they started highlighting both the financial and the physical evils in the game. One notorious event for the anti-football brigade was the game between Swarthmore and Pennsylvania, in which Penn decided to get their revenge on a giant of a lineman called Robert 'Tiny' Maxwell[7], who had played well against them the year before. On each play, at least three Penn players combined forces to savage Maxwell, who bravely soldiered on, even though he had a broken nose, was dripping with blood, and could barely see out of his swollen eyes. Maxwell himself never complained but others were less impressed, and photos of his battered face the day after the Pennsylvania game were splashed across the papers, and one of the people who saw them was the president of the nation. Football was in crisis, and this was no longer a matter for Walter Camp. This was a matter for the White House.

The popular legend goes that Theodore Roosevelt threatened to abolish football in the USA, but that's a misconception. There is no contemporary evidence that he ever did such a thing, and in fact he had always been a huge fan of the game. His son played for Harvard, to whom he wrote in 1903 that "I am delighted to have you play football. I believe in rough, manly

---

[7] He went on to become what Walter Camp described as the fairest referee in the game, and was a brave and noble man to the end. In 1922 "Bob Maxwell was in a fatal car accident. The accident caused Bob to be pinned beneath the car. He had seven broken ribs, a dislocated hip and other injuries, but those who were there told of his command, 'get the others out. I can wait.' The others lived, but Bob died the following morning." (Richard Pagano *College Football Historical Society Newsletter* (May 1988)).

sports[8]" and in an 1895 letter to Walter Camp, a man he deeply admired, he said "I would a hundred fold rather keep the game as it is, with the brutality, than give it up."

It was the his son's headmaster at Groton School, Endicott Peabody, who reputedly got Roosevelt involved, telling him to "get the coaches of Harvard and Yale and Princeton together, and persuade them to undertake to teach men to play football honestly[9]." Roosevelt agreed, and all three colleges[10] were summoned to the White House on October 9, 1905. It was a bit like the three colleges being sent to their own headmaster and being told they had all been naughty boys. Representing Yale, Camp "was slippery and did not allow himself to be pinned down to anything" and despite the accusations of corrupt coaching methods, the colleges basically denied they had ever done anything wrong.

But Roosevelt wanted none of this 'it wasn't me it was him' nonsense, and sent the three colleges away to do their homework. On the train home, they were to work out a formal statement to offer to the press, which announced how "at a meeting with the president of the United States, it was agreed that we consider an honorable obligation exists to carry out in letter and in spirit the rules of the game of foot-ball, relating to roughness, holding, and foul play, and the active coaches of our universities being present with us, pledged themselves to so regard it and to do their utmost to carry out that obligation."

The *New York Times* heralded Roosevelt's achievement as equalling his Nobel Peace Prize winning mediation in the Russo-Japanese War, but it was more akin to getting a class of ten-year-olds to write out a thousand times 'I will not throw footballs in class'. The statement itself did not say anything whatsoever about writing new rules, just that they were going to see to it more carefully that the ones already in place were applied.

College football was under the microscope in 1905, but a Harvard player requiring surgery after being continually singled out as a target by Yale, probably because he was Teddy Roosevelt's own son, suggests that absolutely nothing had changed. The new law-abiding football for a family audience ended its season with the *Chicago Tribune* famously revealing the outcome of "18 football players dead and 159 seriously injured!" As far as documented statistics can prove, it was the most tragic American football season ever. So much for governmental intervention. Despite maintaining close contact with the colleges all season, Roosevelt achieved nothing, and never really showed any major concern for the issue again.

Far away in California, the mood was summed up by Berkeley president Jack Wheeler, who was quoted in the *New York Times* in September 1906 as saying "I do not believe the present experiment in American college football can survive … in my opinion, the whole country

---

[8] Though he did add that "I do not believe in them if they degenerate into the sole end of any one's existence … I have not a doubt that the British officers in the Boer War had their efficiency partly reduced because they had sacrificed their legitimate duties to an inordinate and ridiculous love of sports."

[9] James McLachlan *American boarding schools: a historical study* (Scribner, 1970).

[10] Columbia also fancied an invite, but it was refused, Roosevelt feeling that if they were invited, then he'd have to invite Penn too, and then who knows who else.

THE KILLING FIELDS

will within five years be playing the rugby game." It was largely thanks to his institution and Stanford that the USA came close to becoming a major force in that code in the early 20th century. Other colleges, such as Massachusetts Institute of Technology, Northwestern, Trinity and Duke followed Columbia's lead and abandoned football entirely, and the big sports story of the time was Harvard tackle Karl Brill quitting a game he felt had descended into "a mere gladiatorial contest."

In December, Columbia folded their football team for the umpteenth time. Its Professor Hebert Lord revealed to the *New York Times* that "the reasons for this action need no explanation. They must be evident to the minds of everyone acquainted with the game as it is played now. Only by such radical action can … college life be rid of an obsession … which has proved itself harmful to academic standing and dangerous to human life."

Not everybody at Columbia was impressed with the decision. The students organised protests and the now former coach, 'Wild Bill' Morley, was shockingly unaffected by the year's horrific death toll, which he didn't think was any worse than it had been the season before. "When you consider that during the football season some 100,000 players are involved in the game, the death rate is wonderfully small. And I believe it is considerably smaller than in such sports as automobiling, steeplechasing, hockey on horseback and other strenuous sports." It's called 'polo', Bill.

Even one of the most outspoken opponents of football, Harvard president Charles Eliot, was blasé about the situation. "If injuries, even deaths, occur in the game, that is not an argument against it. It is not over these things that I find fault … that cheating and brutality are profitable is the main evil[11]."

The colleges that wanted to see football banned outright were still the minority. However, there was widespread agreement that it could not continue in its current form. A widely published chain letter started at St John's Academy, Manlius, NY described football as "a great game gone to the bad. Let us resurrect its best features and save a noble sport. We want more game and less profession about it; more sport and less playing for blood; more open and less mass plays; more interference and less holding; more umpire and less slugging; more sprinting and less bucking; more brawn and less beef. Mend it or end it."

Sentiments shared by Henry McCracken, the chancellor of New York University, who was moved into action when a mass play in a game against Union College led to one of the latter's players, Harold Moore, dying of a cerebral haemorrhage. But he "would not intrust the reformation of the game to the present Rules Committee." He was fed up of seeing the violence issue left in the hands of the Walter Camps of this world who just floundered along looking for excuses and producing timid responses in the form of minor adjustments of the rules. The moment had come for the Big Three to step aside, and let the younger members of

---

[11] *New-York Observer* (Volume 84, 1906).

MIKE ROBERTS – THE SAME OLD GAME: CODIFICATION

the football fraternity dictate the game on their terms. Sheer weight of numbers was going to oust the elite from the monopoly they held over the governance of the game they created.

On December 8, 1905, McCracken managed to muster thirteen colleges together in New York. So many rival governing bodies had been formed over the years that they were running out of names to give them, but this one was called the Intercollegiate Athletic Association (ICAA). Five of the founder members hardly got things off to the most positive of starts by voting to abolish football outright, but the ICAA eventually decreed that it was "football as now played" that had to go. When the ICAA held its second meeting later that month, attendance was up to 68, and another sixty-or-so colleges were members but did not send delegates. The football community was fed up with taking orders from Yale, Princeton and Harvard but although the ICAA considerably outweighed their rival in terms of sheer force of numbers, its membership included practically no colleges of any particular influence.

The two rival committees, the new ICAA and the old guard of the IRC, held sessions on the same January 12, 1906 in nearby hotels in New York. The former was ready to clean up football, the latter was what Columbia's Francis Bangs described as "self-perpetuating, non-representative, pig-headed, oblivious to public opinion and obstinate[12]."

It was here that Harvard coach William Reid did something most unexpected. Knowing his president Eliot was itching for the chance to banish football from Harvard for good, and with a series of proposals for reform, he explained to the IRC that "rules go through or there will be no football at Harvard, and if Harvard throws out the game, many other colleges will follow Harvard's lead, and an important blow will be dealt to the game." He melodramatically stormed out of the meeting and walked straight across to the ICAA, and by the end of the day had become its secretary.

The ICAA got on the phone to Camp and invited him to join their negotiations, and the great man was left with little other option than to accept. The compromise was that the ICAA and IRC would form some form of coalition, originally agreeing that each organisation would be equally represented, an uncomfortable coexistence that still gave the upper hand to the IRC, which had fewer members but greater prestige.

The ICAA only lasted four years. In 1910 it was rebranded as the National Collegiate Athletic Association, its constitution stating that its mission was "the regulation and supervision of college athletics throughout the United States, in order that the athletic activities in the colleges and universities of the United States may be maintained on an ethical plane in keeping with the dignity and purpose of education."

The NCAA was born, the gargantuan body that now oversees the entire realm of college sports in the USA, including basketball, ice hockey and baseball. It would take the NCAA decades to round up all the other colleges and get them under its wing. Camp and his IRC refused to go away, and although they were generally supportive of everything the NCAA

---

[12] Ronald Smith *Harvard and Columbia and a Reconsideration of the 1905-06 Football Crisis* (in *Journal of Sport History*, Winter 1981). Also the Reid quote in the next paragraph.

THE KILLING FIELDS

did, there was plenty of early scepticism. But by 1911, Chicago and Harvard had changed sides, which took a lot of the power and relevance away from the dwindling IRC. Finally, in 1915, Yale took a deep breath and switched to the NCAA, leaving just Navy behind them. Suddenly feeling very lonely and pointless indeed, Navy followed the year after. They turned the lights off as they went.

Fast forward

But so much for the politics, how was all of this going to make the game any more acceptable to the nation? Bernstein hits the nail on the head when he says "agreeing to do something was not the same as agreeing on what to do."

It was Harvard's Bill Reid who had the ideas this time, which he had collated in consultation with his college's Graduate's Athletics Association, and his proposals formed the basis for the ICAA's reforms. His first idea was to reduce the time of the game from seventy minutes to sixty. Well, it was a start. Reduce the length of the game and by logic you will reduce the number of injuries, although the reasoning behind the suggestion was that the reduction would help cut down on the injuries caused through tiredness.

Walter Camp had been scratching his head coming up with a brilliant plan to get rid of the violence without really changing anything, and once again it was a technical change that he was mooting. He felt that when all you had to do was gain five yards, there was no particular incentive to do anything other than gather in a group and barge your way through to gain the ground needed, especially when they got three tries to do it. It hardly made for the most entertaining of viewing, but why send the ball into the open where you were far more likely to lose it? He had long been arguing that "more open play would be forced on the teams by requiring ten instead of five yards in downs. That would change the character of the injuries. It is true that an open hand tackle is the hardest kind of a tackle. But in open field play the injuries are usually a sprained ankle or a broken arm. That is much better than a blood clot on the brain or other injuries which occur in the heavy line plays … In open play the slugging and dirty work sometimes done in scrimmages would be impossible, because it would be seen … What slugging there is now goes on because the crowd can't see it." So five yards became ten.

Having previously insisted that five players should take their place on the line of scrimmage to put a limit on the numbers involved in the mass plays, the figure was increased by one more to six, and to help matters further, a neutral zone was opened up between the two lines, which apart from anything else, made it easier for officials to keep an eye on what was going on.

These may have been technical changes to discourage contact, but the ICAA's 1906 rules tackled the violence issue too. Personal fouls were defined as including but not limited to "striking with the fist or elbow, kneeing, kicking, meeting with the knee and striking with

MIKE ROBERTS – THE SAME OLD GAME: CODIFICATION

locked hands by linemen breaking through." There was a fifteen yard penalty for any of this, as there was for what they considered "unnecessary roughness", which included "tackling, piling up, hurdling[13] and other such acts."

But of all the rules introduced in 1906, there was one that was set to completely revolutionise the game. It was the biggest change to the basic principles of rugby that American football ever made, and completed its transition to the game it is now. Something that would have been unthinkable before 1906 has since become the iconic image of the game.

John Heisman, after whom the prestigious award for the best college player of the season is named, claimed that North Carolina had invented the forward pass as a last ditch touchdown attempt in an 1895 game with Georgia, which was cleanly caught by one George Stephens. There is no reason not to believe the story, but it was a dumb thing to do, considering it was completely illegal at the time. But it would have got Heisman thinking that if the forward pass was made legal, just how much better the game American could be.

That's just one of the theories for the origins of the play, and there is quite some debate on this issue, but what we know for sure is one great football pioneer, Amos Alonzo Stagg, didn't like the idea in the slightest and sensed the sport turning into "a parlor game." This was also the one major innovation that was not the working of Walter Camp, who was also firmly opposed to its introduction, which is curious considering he may have been the first player to successfully make one. Albeit in very different circumstances, the incident occurred in the famous Yale game with Princeton in 1876, when Camp passed the ball forwards to Oliver Thompson, who scored a touchdown. Princeton naturally protested, but the score stood, the umpire reportedly basing his decision on the toss of a coin!

As a counter-solution to Harvard's proposal to the ICAA, Camp immediately came up with an alternative suggestion that they should make the pitch forty feet wider, and encourage open play that way. Judging from the congested way the game was played in the vintage footage of early American football, it is difficult to imagine how a bigger pitch could have done anything other than make it even harder for the spectators to see what was going on, and that suggestion was soon voted down when Harvard pointed out that they had just invested $325,000 in a new stadium, the largest reinforced concrete structure in America at the time. Could anybody suggest how they were going to move that back twenty yards on either side? Of course not. Not one of Camp's better suggestions, but who knows, maybe it was the Harvard Stadium that 'saved' American football.

Camp lost the battle, and the forward pass went into the rulebook. But this didn't mean the ball suddenly being thrown in all directions. Only one forward pass was allowed in any single down, the exact wording being that "one forward pass shall be allowed to each

---

[13] 'Hurdling' was defined as the practice of "jumping over or attempting to jump over an opponent who is still on his feet", while tackling below the knees was also prohibited unless "the tackler makes contact above the knees and slides down."

THE KILLING FIELDS

scrimmage, provided such a pass be made by a player who was behind the line of scrimmage when the ball was put into play, and provided the ball, after being passed forward, does not touch the ground before being touched by a player of either side."

But despite experts like Saint Louis coach Eddie Cochems predicting in student magazine *Fleur de Lis* that the forward pass would "develop many beautiful spectacular plays before the season closes," the early impact was not as immediate as one might imagine. That was partly because it almost impossible to implement because of the severe restrictions. The ball had to be thrown from at least five yards behind the line of scrimmage, which it had to cross more than five yards to the left or right of the position where it had been put into play. And if a forward pass went out of bounds, possession went to the first team to touch the ball, which takes us back to a method that soccer and rugby had eliminated half a century earlier.

Worse still, an incomplete pass resulted in a hefty fifteen yard penalty, so not surprisingly, it was a risk most teams simply didn't want to take! It seems the forward pass was brought in to appease the critics, yet at the same time was actively discouraged by the rules, and speaking about just that in September 1906, the *New York Times* observed that the "risk of dropping the ball is so great as to make the practice extremely hazardous and its desirability doubtful."

Forward passing was also a very different matter when the ball was what they called the 'blimp', a watermelon-like object that was usually passed underarm or basketball-fashion. The kind of passes we see today weren't really possible until the smaller, more streamlined ball was introduced in the 1930s.

The play was only used as a last resort and very few eastern teams made it a regular part of their game. Perhaps because they were less inclined to respect tradition, it was in the Midwest colleges that the idea most caught on. The aforementioned Eddie Cochems at SLU saw the potential early, and his was one of the few sides that regularly put the play into use in the first season it was permitted. Cochems wrote that after closely examining the ball, he "discovered, of course, that it had been designed to fit the instep of the shoe for kicking and the pit of the arm for carrying. Then I lit on the seven lacings as the only physical part of the ball for finger purchase in throwing the ball on its long axis[14]." He took his players on a training camp at Lake Beulah, and "just before the first practice I told the players to put their fingers between the two lacings nearest the end of the ball, where the diameter was shortest, and throw it with a twist of the wrist, on its long axis ... Robinson, all excited, came back and said, 'Coach, I can throw the danged thing 40 yards!'"

Cochems was speaking about Bradbury Robinson, who is widely quoted as being the first player to complete a forward pass on September 5, 1906 when SLU were at Carroll College, Wisconsin. His first attempt failed, which meant an immediate turnover under the rules at the time, but his second throw was caught by Jack Schneider, and SLU went on to win 22-0.

---

[14] Quoted by Allison Danzig *The history of American football* (1956).

David Nelson described how they stunned Iowa 31-0, in a game in which "eight passes were completed in ten attempts for four touchdowns." Although Iowa did "attempt two basketball-style forward passes", they obviously had no idea how to exploit the rule like St Louis did, and paid the price severely.

But Missouri was way off the map as far as influencing the football world was concerned, as was Kansas, where Emporia were basing almost their entire game on the tactic, and bamboozled Pittsburgh State by a frightening 107-0.

It was not until Notre Dame started using the play that the rest of the football world was made aware of the gift horse whose mouth they had been gazing dumbly at for the best part of a decade. Knute Rockne and Gus Dorais had spent the summer lifeguarding by Lake Eerie, and with a shortage of lives to guard had dedicated most of their time to perfecting the forward pass. They revealed the results of that work in a famous 35-13 defeat of Army in November 1913. Rockne would seize on any gaps in the field and leg it up the field, and Dorais would send immense throws his way. The country sat up and took note. A relative nobody from a Catholic college in Indiana had got the better of one of the powerhouses of the game. "Notre Dame Open Play Amazes Army" yelled the *New York Times*. Rockne and Dorais had shown that with a bit of practice what had first appeared to be little more than a suicidal gamble could be lethal. One thing was for sure. Up and down the country, from that day on, teams would be working on taking the forward pass to even more remarkable limits.

Rugged rugby

There was plenty of muttering and nodding of heads that the forward pass, ten yards per down, the neutral zone and six on the line of scrimmage were set to do the trick. But despite the new regulations that were supposedly there to do something to ensure no season would ever have to witness anything like the 18 deaths from football in 1905, mass plays continued regardless.

Although figures vary, the death tolls for the next few seasons were still in the double figures. In 1909, no fewer than 30 people surrendered their lives on the football field. Two of these were particularly well known in the football world, Navy's Early Wilson and Army's Eugene 'Icy' Byrne, while another fatality was Virginia halfback Archer Christian, who died from head injuries in a momentum play against Georgetown, whereby both teams called an end to their seasons. Public schools throughout Washington DC and New York City decided to abolish the game outright.

It was history repeating for the umpteenth time, and even Amos Alonzo Stagg was beginning to realise it had to stop, and wrote to Walter Camp saying "we have certainly got to do something, Walter, for the season has been a mighty bad one for a number of individuals as well as for the game."

The move back to traditional rugby in California was proving successful, and David Starr Jordan of Stanford felt it was time for the east to follow their lead, condemning the American

THE KILLING FIELDS

game as "rugby's American pervert … the heaviest burden yet borne by higher education in America" and urged that "the farce of 'football reform' of five years before should not be repeated[15]." Even the president of Princeton, Woodrow Wilson, who a few years later would become president of the nation, was heard to mutter that perhaps it was time for the Tigers to take up rugby too.

On December 11, 1909, less than a month after the first Grey Cup final had been played, the *New York Herald* managed to get the Hamilton Tigers and Ottawa Rough Riders down to New York City for an exhibition game. It was a chance for those responsible for finding a suitable balance between spectacular sport and barbaric violence to prove or disprove the rumour that the Canadians had got it right. The *New York Times* was theoretically correct to call rugby as it was played in Canada "the game from which the American college game was evolved", but by this stage, the Canadians had already imported several innovations from the American game, and very few from Britain, so what was seen in Van Cortlandt Park by 15,000 curious onlookers, the biggest crowd any of the Canadians had ever performed for, was hardly rugby in the purest sense.

The inquisitiveness the game aroused in the US was startling. Almost every influential name in American football gathered at the ground, including Walter Camp and Amos Alonzo Stagg. There were mixed opinions. The *New York Times* reckoned that "it was the almost unanimous opinion of the many prominent American football players past and present" that the Canadian game "would entail a bigger hospital list and possibly more fatalities." All that manic throwing of the ball back and forth between the players, the wanton punting of the ball, the way that "the ball is not dead until there is no possibility of advancing it further", and the flying kick that was "so slick and easily performed that numerous notebooks were pulled out of American breast-pockets" were all very impressive, but the Americans were doubtful whether the Canadians offered any real solutions for their own game.

Played as it was by the Canadians it looked fine, but "if we played this game in our colleges, it would be stopped by the police within one month as too great a menace to life. It's a good enough game if played slowly and phlegmatically, but it would never be safe to allow our college men to indulge in it with their keen and ever present desires to win."

Another *New York Times* article reproduced a letter from an American football enthusiast, OWK, now living in Ottawa, who wrote off the Canadian game as crude and amateurish. "In regard to the matter of running without interference, which the Canadians claim is the cause of their lack of fatalities, there seems no reason to suppose that our [American] players are hurt on this account. It is rather that they play the game for all there is in it, efforts to which the Canadians are entirely foreign."

But what the American observers seemed blissfully unaware of was that the reason there were no excessively high, low or dangerous tackles on the Canadian football field was not so

---

[15] Quoted in the *Grinnell College Review* (1908).

MIKE ROBERTS – THE SAME OLD GAME: CODIFICATION

much because the Canucks were pussies as it was because such practices had been deemed illegal! The Canadian game was not soft. It just didn't allow the violence to reach the extremes it had escalated to in the USA. As commented in the *Toronto Globe* in 1909, "if fond mammas want their youthful pride and hope to grow up like a banana plant in a greenhouse, there is little sense in arguing the point. The game is too rough for molley coddles. On the contrary, if the boy is to be taught to fight his way in the great battle of life, there is no game that will teach him how in a better way. He'll get plenty of knocks and raise many a crop of healthy bruises but he gains stamina and the knocks he gets, if he is an ordinary cuss in later life, will be equally as hard."

The end of Camp's road

In all seriousness, it is difficult to believe that the Americans would ever have swapped their version of football for the Canadian one. But the scathing press reports also suggest the belief that the real problem was not the violence of the American rules but the violence of the American players, and deep in their hearts, they wanted to keep their game rough and tough, and they did.

Camp is frequently commended on his brilliant sporting mind, but his solution for this latest crisis was another token gesture, and a poor one at that. He suggested restricting forward passing to the area directly behind the line of scrimmage, and also 15-yard downs. This was just going round in circles and it is hard to believe that it would have done anything to improve the fate of lives and limbs.

There were just as many divisions of power in 1909 as there were in 1905, and once again it took a series of negotiations first to work who was going to make the decisions, and then what decisions they were going to make, eventually settling for yet more reform in 1910, with the number of offensive men required on the line of scrimmage moved up to seven, a total ban on interlocking interference in an attempt to quash momentum plays once and for all, and a removal of almost all the petty restrictions that had previously been imposed on forward passing. It was also that meeting that divided the game into four fifteen-minute quarters.

Another rule change was that a player could retire from the field if injured, fatigued or sick, but was able to return in a later quarter. The American game was heading towards the game it is now, whereby when a team has possession it can, and at the professional level invariably does, use a completely different eleven to the team it fields when defending, and even wheels out specialist kickers that otherwise play absolutely no part in the game. However, 1910 was only the start of the process, and it was not until 1949 that totally unlimited substitutions were trialled, to be definitively accepted in 1950.

The latest reforms did little to impress Walter Camp, a man who was moving more and more out of favour in the American football world. In a damning condemnation, Princeton coach William Roper wrote to Woodrow Wilson in June 28, 1910 to say that "Mr Camp is

THE KILLING FIELDS

violently opposed to the new rules for one single reason, because Yale's style of play is practically destroyed, there being no further pulling or pushing of the runner allowed. As this practically eliminates the old bucking game, at which Yale has been so proficient, and which to my mind is the dangerous part of football, naturally Camp is opposed to the rules as changed, not on the score of safety, but because his style of play will be greatly weakened."

It has to be said that from their introduction, the new rules hurt Yale. In 1909 they not only won every game, but didn't concede a single point and only three times did any team even get within 22 yards of the Eli goal. A year later, and following the rules modifications, not only did they lose to Brown for the first time ever, a humiliating 21-0 drubbing, but they were even held to a tie by little Vanderbilt. They would not win another championship until 1927, and that would be their last.

Camp didn't like losing matches. Camp didn't like losing power. Officially his own affiliation to Yale was in the guise of treasurer of the Yale Financial Union, a post from which he finally resigned in October 1914. In his final years, he distanced himself more and more from the college he loved, but not from the game. He wrote copiously on the subject and his All America elevens were always a big talking point. Reporting on one of these in December 1913, the *New York Times* observed how his picks showed "a change of mind on Mr Camp's part concerning new and old football. He has come to believe that the forward pass is a logical scoring play, and in choosing his mythical team, he has picked men who are proficient at this play."

Camp remained on the NCAA rules committee until midnight of March 14, 1925. When that meeting adjourned until the following morning, he returned to his hotel. The following morning, the secretary's seat was mysteriously empty.

The next day, the *New York Times* would be reporting that "Walter Camp, veteran authority on football and sports, was found dead in his bed at the Hotel Belmont yesterday shortly before noon. He apparently had died of heart disease probably without waking from sleep. He was in his sixty-sixth year."

Padding the game out

Football moved on. In 1912, there was a further overhaul of the rules, when the kick off was moved midfield to the 40, the value of the touchdown was raised to six, an extra down was added to the offence to bring it into line with today's four[16], and the pitch itself was reduced to its modern day length of 100 yards.

Play may have opened up, but none of the major reforms of the rules really managed to prevent American football from remaining as violent as ever, and the essence of the game has

---

[16] Very important that one for those who mock Canada's three downs. It is Canada that has stayed faithful to the originally American tradition.

343

barely changed since the forward pass was introduced in 1906. It was not so much improved regulations as improved body protection that ultimately solved the problem.

As a military man, Admiral Joseph Mason Reeves had such a distinguished career that his name was given to two different naval airfields in California, while in his younger days he was no less the hero as a tackle for Navy. In 1883, his doctor told him that if he took any further kicks in the head, he would either die, or at the very least go insane. Rather than risk such fate, Reeves turned to an Annapolis shoemaker to make him a moleskin helmet to protect his ears and head. To the best of anyone's knowledge, this was the first American football helmet.

There was a similar story surrounding George Barclay of Lafayette, who was developing an embarrassing cauliflower ear due to football, and in order to safeguard his chances with the ladies, he got an upholsterer to help him design a simple 'head harness' in 1896. But people taking such precautions were few and far between. Wearing any kind of protection was simply not the done thing in the macho world of American football.

Some kind of shoulder or thigh padding was reasonably commonplace from relatively early on, but the idea of helmets took a lot longer to be accepted. This could be compared to rugby today, where padded headgear is becoming more widespread, and widely recommended by the injury experts who know what they are talking about. Yet many players would never sink to such sensible depths, in much the same way that many countries still struggle to get motorcyclists to respect new helmet laws. It is like that today, and it was like that then. It was football's alleged first pro, Pudge Heffelfinger, and Yale champion of the turn of the 19th century, who once scorned that there was "none of that sissy stuff for me. The players wore very little protective armor. I just let my hair grow long and pulled it through a turtleneck sweater[17]."

What may have led to a greater acceptance of headgear was the 1898 invention of the rubber nose guard. That idea went down an absolute storm as it lent a warrior-like air to the wearer. Protective clothing was suddenly a whole lot more fashionable. In 1917, Illinois coach Robert Zuppke issued his players with his own design, a 'cradled' helmet, which separated the skull from the actual helmet by a sponge lining, providing not only ventilation, but also shock absorption. There was a market for these things, and Rawlings and Spalding were among the companies that latched onto the idea of mass produced football helmets, although they did not become mandatory until 1939 in the college game, and 1943 in the NFL.

It was in the 1940s that there was another innovation, the plastic helmet, which helped spread the shock more evenly but was a controversy from the start, as not only did the it provide protection to the user, but was also a danger in itself to other players, an issue that is still burning today.

---

[17] Quoted in Roland Lazenby *Pictorial History of Football* (Smithmark, 1987).

THE KILLING FIELDS

Helmets, faceguards and shoulder pads are now standard issue in American football, and it is largely these that managed to reduce the fatality count. Even so, you still won't see many quarterbacks or running backs making it through a season without some kind of injury, and the National Center for Catastrophic Sport Injury Research reported that from 2000–05, twenty-eight American footballers, mainly at high school, died directly from injuries sustained playing the game, and an additional 68 died indirectly.

American football has now drifted so far from rugby that although followers of the two modern sports are usually aware of the vague similarities between both codes, they would be surprised to learn that they were both derived from the very same set of laws written in 1871. Laws that may never have even become popular in the USA had Harvard not played McGill in 1874. But on the other side of the border, it could be asked what might have happened had McGill not played Harvard. While the USA developed its own code, Canada stuck with rugby. But US influences are hard for Canadians to keep at bay. American football ideas would eventually creep into their 'pure' form of rugby too, and it is with the curious case of Canadian football that we shall end our story.

15 SLEEPING WITH AN ELEPHANT
The early years of football in Canada

True north strong and free

At the time of writing there are eight teams in the Canadian Football League, the country's only professional championship[1], which involves roughly twice as many games as the NFL, leading up to the CFL's equivalent of the Super Bowl, the Grey Cup. That match draws bigger TV audiences than even ice hockey's Stanley Cup, with one third of the country glued to the television screen every November, while the average attendance for regular season matches is in the region of 30,000.

Few players make their fortune from playing it – and many players top off their income with other jobs outside of football. As a recent CFL promo video announces, it's the game where "you can hug a running back."

But opinions of the CFL are diverse. Its fans swear by it, and consider it not just uniquely Canadian, but also superior to the American game. But in the States, the CFL is constantly on the butt end of unfair jokes and there are even Canadians that scorn it, and ask why they have to have this silly three-down abomination that appears to be different simply for the sake of being different and dream of one day having 'proper' football instead.

"We Canadians live in a blind spot about our identity. We have very strong feelings about who we aren't but only weak ones about who we are. We're passionate about what we don't want to become but oddly passive about what we should be." That's a poignant quote from publisher John Cruikshank, which could very easily be applied to the story we'll be telling in the next two chapters.

The Canadian identity crisis is a direct result of its peculiar standing with respect to its neighbour to the south. "Canada is a country whose main exports are hockey players and cold fronts. Our main imports are baseball players and acid rain" was one of the many gems we were left by Pierre Trudeau, president of Canada from 1968 to 1979. He knew that whether Canada liked it or not, sharing the longest land border in the world with the USA influences his nation in almost every department. He told an American audience in 1969 that "living next to you is like sleeping with an elephant; no matter how friendly and even-tempered is the beast, one is affected by every twitch and grunt" and speaking in the Soviet Union in 1971, at the height of the Vietnam War, which Canada opposed, he commented that the overwhelming American presence in his country was "a danger to our national identity from a cultural, economic and perhaps even military point of view."

---

[1] The Eastern Conference features the Hamilton Tiger-Cats, Montreal Alouettes, Toronto Argonauts and Winnipeg Blue Bombers, and the four Western franchises are the British Columbia Lions (Vancouver), Calgary Stampeders, Edmonton Eskimos and Saskatchewan Roughriders (Regina). A new and as yet unnamed franchise from Ottawa is likely to be added soon, probably in 2013.

SLEEPING WITH AN ELEPHANT

Canada is like its football. Similarities to the USA are only to be expected, but exact imitations are best avoided. Its stronger adherence to British and colonial values, coupled with years of unease with anything that came up from the United States, meant Canada stuck to rugby. But the US influence could not be kept at bay, and ultimately, Canada changed the rules of the game so much that it ended up being almost identical to the American code.

Perhaps we had better go back to the start, because to understand the reasons for Canadian football, we have to understand the reasons for Canada.

OK, so the Vikings and who knows who else had been there earlier, but the first major European settlement in the modern day territory was a French one at Port Royal in 1605, while five years later the British found a new land in which to set up fishing villages, and decided to call it Newfoundland. Anglo-French relations were strained at the best of times in Europe, and in the Great White North they were not going to be any better. The French were setting up colonies all the way down to Louisiana, while the British were arriving in even greater numbers, and the Intercolonial Wars that followed were partly fuelled by territorial conflicts and were partly mere continuations of the same wars that were happening at the same time in Europe. Along with Dutch and Spanish involvement, there was the added spice of Native American nations, whose own conflicts were dragged into the European ones, some siding with the English and others with the French. The ones that picked the English generally made the wiser choice – French power in North America suffered a resounding defeat. The Treaty of Paris that brought an end to the wars in 1763 was a landmark event in determining the present day linguistic map of North America, and involved France renouncing its claim to territories on the mainland, and preferring instead to keep little Guadeloupe and its valuable sugar plantations. Excellent forward planning by the French there.

There was still a huge population of French settlers left in what had come to be called Canada[2], and especially the French speaking enclave of Quebec, but these were now British subjects, and if any of them had any pretence to a place in public office, they had to renounce their Catholic faith first.

It may have looked like the British had come off with the best deal, but as it happens the Treaty of Paris was going to spell a lot of trouble. Now that the French were less of an issue, the settlers further south found they had less need of British patrimony any more, and started getting ideas of independence. The American Revolution was stirring.

It was generally assumed that the French would join the revolution, but Britain's immediate response was to issue the Quebec Act of 1774, which offered enough new rights to convince them than they were better off siding with the British than being swallowed up by what was

---

[2] There is a theory that the name Canada comes from ancient Spanish explorers, who unimpressed by what they found simply wrote on their maps *acá nada* ('nothing here'). It's mildly amusing, but not half as convincing as a note by French explorer Jacques Cartier who around 1535 said of the local tribes that "*ilz appellent une ville 'canada'*" (they call a town a '*canada*'), and it went from there.

347

set to become the United States of America, where it looked like their Catholic, francophone culture was in for an even rougher ride.

In 1775, Canada was 'invaded' when the rebel United Colonies expected to draw on the support of the settlers in the north, and particularly Nova Scotia, as they sought to oust British rule for good. But things didn't go quite as planned. They encountered far less support than they had expected among the northern populace. The French, rather than join the revolution, defended themselves against it, and there was very little support for the insurgents among the English speakers either, who preferred to defend their British identity than be governed by the 'Patriots'.

The United States got their independence, but the Canadian colonies remained loyal to the Crown, and that sentiment was furthered as defeated loyalists vacated their lands in the south and made their way north to what remained an extension of the British Empire.

Having the nation from which they had fought to be independent staring down their throats from so close was not a comfortable situation in the States, and the tension reached the point that in 1812, the USA invaded Canada. But that is viewing things from a modern perspective. What they were really doing was going to war with the British Crown, and it was a good time to do it, because the Brits had enough on their plate, being tied up with the Napoleonic Wars and all.

The Americans had hoped to convince the Canadians that they should take a stand against British control of their affairs, but once again the northerners were less cooperative than they had expected. Even those who were unhappy living under British rule tended to be more comfortable with that than potentially becoming part of the USA. Rather than bring Canada under US rule, what the 1812 war did most was instil a stronger nationalistic feeling than ever in the 'true north strong and free'.

Canada never really had much of a problem with Britain. But as the country grew, it became only logical for it to become more interested in governing its own affairs than remaining tied to the motherland, and both politically and economically the country started taking matters into its hands, and dealing with them very nicely too. Canada eventually agreed peaceful terms for its independence in 1931, but is still part of the British Commonwealth to this day[3]. The monarch was never deposed as the ultimate head of state, and the dear face of Elizabeth II appears on all Canadian banknotes, even though neither her nor her government have any real say in what goes on in the country.

Since 1812, relations between Canada and the US have improved considerably. When the two nations fought side by side in the Second World War, they were brought together once and for all. We're all friends now. The USA and Canada are the world's biggest trading partners, and although they don't always see eye to eye on foreign policy, acid rain or seal-slaughtering issues, they work together in almost every area from defence issues to research.

---

[3] Newfoundland would not become an official part of Canada until as late as 1949.

SLEEPING WITH AN ELEPHANT

In Canada, there are reminders that the United States lie just to the south wherever you tread. It may be the second biggest country in the world, but there is a lot of tundra up there, and 72% of the population lives less than 150 kilometres (95 miles) from the US border. Canadians speak like Americans, eat like Americans, watch much of the same TV as Americans – in fact, to most outsiders they are just the same thing. Which is something Canadians detest, hence whenever they set off any travels, they always make sure they have a massive maple leaf emblazoned on everything they carry in order to avoid the utter indignity of being mistaken for Yanks.

No matter how similar they are in everybody else's eyes, a Canadian is not an American. And no matter how similar they are, Canadian football is not American football.

Similarly different

So what exactly is Canadian football, and is it really so dissimilar? To the outsider it may seem like a spot the difference puzzle, and a hard one at that. The uniforms look the same, the field looks the same, and the plays feature all the same ideas of downs, scrimmages, interference, quarterbacks, forward passes and touchdowns. In fact, the games are so similar that the Canadian Football League (CFL) quite happily includes the statistics of seasons played in the NFL when calculating all-time records for players, which is how Warren Moon, who started out with the Edmonton Eskimos (1978–1983) set an all-time record for passing yards, even though 17 of his seasons were played in the NFL.

But there are differences, the most obvious being the number of players. As opposed to the American eleven, Canada has twelve. As the numbers on the line of scrimmage are the same for both codes, that means the Canadians can gain an extra receiver. Also, while in American there are four downs to advance the ball ten yards, in Canada there are just three, which naturally tends to put more emphasis on kicking in the Canadian game.

The Canadian field is ten yards longer, and also slightly wider, which proved something of a stumbling block during the failed CFL expansion into the US in the early nineties. No solution could be found for the Memphis Mad Dogs at the Liberty Bowl, and they ended up getting special dispensation to play on a normal American football field instead! Also, while the American posts are positioned at the back of the endzone, in Canada they are at the front, on the goal-line[4].

The scoring in both games is identical apart from the Canadian addition of a single point, or 'rouge', which is awarded for kicking the ball through the opposing end zone without it being touched, either from a punt or a missed field goal attempt, or when the ball goes into the end zone and the receiving team does not manage to get it out.

---

[4] It was for reasons of safety that the NCAA in America decided to move the goal posts to the rear of the endzone in 1927, although the NFL didn't follow suit until 1972. The change was never applied in Canada.

MIKE ROBERTS – THE SAME OLD GAME: CODIFICATION

There are also notable differences in what the defence and offence can and can't do when it comes to kicking the ball up and down the field, which originate from the reforms designed to make American football safer in the early decades of the 20th century.

The Americans were concerned about how, when a defender attempted to intercept a punted ball, he was easily caught off his guard by opposing players storming in. Without the protective clothing, players being charged while catching balls was one of the prime causes of injury. So, in 1901, they were offered the option of claiming a fair catch, which means clearly signalling with an outstretched arm that the claim is being made, whereby opposing players have to allow him the chance to make the catch unimpeded[5] – the downside being that after a fair catch, the ball cannot be run, but re-enters play via a snap[6].

When a ball has been kicked in the USA, no player on the kicking side is allowed to touch it again until it has been touched by one of the receiving team (the kick off is one exception). Basically, there are not too many benefits to kicking the ball forwards in American football. As long as the defence doesn't touch the ball, there is nothing the kicking team can do, and it just rolls dead to end the play. Throwing it broadens your options considerably.

The situation is very different in Canada, where there is no fair catch rule and there is no need to wait for the defence to touch the ball following a punt. There is a limitation. Like in rugby, only the kicker and anybody else who was behind him at the moment the kick was made, and therefore onside, is allowed to touch the ball or tackle the catcher. Players that were ahead of the kicker must maintain a distance of at least five yards until the ball has been touched. This makes kicking a much handier feature of Canadian football. The likes of rugby's 'up and under' play are feasible tactics, whereas in American football they would be illegal.

On a similar note, in American football, players can only kick the ball from behind the line of scrimmage, but in Canada, like in rugby, the ball can be kicked from anywhere. So, a player can quite legally advance with the ball as far as he can and then punt it, and even attempt a drop-kick if he wants.

There are other differences. Canadian football is much stricter about how fast a play starts once the referee's whistle has blown, making it much harder to run down the clock as Americans do, and even if there is just a second left at the end of the quarter, the Canadian game, like rugby, will still allow one full play to be completed before it is over.

In the American line of scrimmage, only one backfield player can be in motion before the snap. In Canada, every player but the quarterback can move around as much they like and try

---

[5] It's basically the same principle as being able catch a mark inside your own 22 in rugby.

[6] There is also the rarely taken option of a 'fair catch kick' at the posts – something which you will only ever see about once every five years in the NFL, and no fair catch kick has been scored in the NFL since 1976 (by Ray Wersching for San Diego). Effectively it's the same thing as the 'goal from mark' that rugby union did away with in 1971.

to thwart the offence's game plan. Also, the American line of scrimmage is just eleven inches apart, in Canada it is a full yard.

The respective balls also have a slightly different size, shape and tolerance, and although that slightly is so slightly that mere mortals would barely notice, professional quarterbacks do claim to be able to feel the difference, in much the same way that North Americans can tell the difference between Pepsi and Coca Cola even when blindfold, while for the rest of the world they taste exactly the same.

Other than these and other subtle differences, Canadian football imported almost all the changes to rugby that were made in the United States. But rather like the way the NCAA and NFL have different rules, the Canadians were selective in their choices, which even non-Canadians might argue were good ones. Canada never went quite so far as to adopt the American rulebook word for word, and for the foreseeable future it seems highly unlikely that that is going to happen. And neither should it have too, for the Canadian version has just as much history behind it, and most of its differentiating features are actually the truest to the way both rugby and American football were originally played.

Histories of Canadian football are thin on the ground. "Anyone who has tried to research Canadian football history will be quickly struck by the absolute dearth of printed resources; the amount of literature written on the subject in the past half century likely falls short of the annual output of material on the NFL alone." That's the Canadian Football Historical Association saying that. And they're right.

When it comes to the origins of the game, that's especially so. Perhaps that's partly because it's not a story that Canadians particularly want to hear, for it is hardly one of standing ground in the face of US cultural imperialism. The forward pass? Well, we got that from American football. And the line of scrimmage? Well, err, yeah, that was American football too. And the downs? The helmets? Quarterbacks? OK, OK, so we did borrow one or two of their ideas…

Yet American football may never have existed if it hadn't been for the Canadians. When Harvard met McGill of Montreal in 1874, the United States was inducted to rugby. The USA has Canada to thank for the origins of its game. But rugby was not a Canadian thing. Before we look at what happened to the Canadian game after 1874, we need to go further back and find out how it came to pass that a Canadian university was playing rugby in the first place. It had come from Britain, of course.

Furry balls

By the late 16th century, at any one time there could be as many as half a thousand European fishing vessels hovering around the Newfoundland coast, but these often took as much interest in using European commodities to bargain for local furs as they did in scaly creatures with gills and fins. Canadian colonial history began with the fur traders. Much of the discovery of the barren lands of North America was the work of these pioneering souls, who forged trading links with the Native American tribes – exchanging skins for their own goods, and in particular metallurgy, and even more particularly knives, while the natives also took an immediate liking to the terrific drinks these white men brought with them, which made you laugh a lot and do silly things.

These early traders brought with them the games they knew from back home. The earliest record dates as far back as New Year's Day, 1734 at Prince of Wales Fort, Churchill. Michael Payne describes how "alcohol consumption was the most popular recreational activity at the fort, and often it was associated with other activities. For example, company employees and Indians were inveterate gamblers, and often the stakes were alcoholic. Games of skill, like shooting at a mark or football, were played on holidays, sometimes with alcoholic prizes to the victors[7]."

Records from the Hudson's Bay Company provide some useful source material. This is the oldest corporation in North America, and is still around today, best known for its department stores throughout Canada. So important was the HBC in the 18th century that it was the *de-facto* government in much of the dominion, and it was at its headquarters at York Factory on December 25, 1823 that in temperatures of -30° "part of the men and some of the gentlemen turned out to a game of football which was not kept up with much spirit probably from the severity of the weather combined with a previous too free use of the bottle." It seems football was not encouraged by the York Factory officers, for the workers were only allowed to play the annual Christmas game in 1845 in reward for their moderate drinking of late.

The festive associations with football and the presence of large numbers of Scottish settlers suggest that these games were probably reproductions of Shrovetide ba' games back home. These early matches in 'British North America' were unlikely to have been particularly sophisticated, but more structured ideas would soon be brought across by the constant stream of new settlers, including the educators and the educated from British academia. Though separated by the North Atlantic, Canadian schools and universities were effectively British schools and universities, and would embrace its sporting traditions too.

Quebec

Where the rugby form of football gained its first foothold on Canadian soil seems to have been in Quebec[8], and particularly its major city, Montreal. In 1864, the *Montreal Gazette*

---

[7] Michael Payne *The Healthiest Part in the Known World: Prince of Wales's Fort As Fur Trade Post and Community in the Eighteenth Century* (Manitoba Historical Society, 1978).

[8] For the sake of those unfamiliar with Canadian geography, it might be useful at this point to briefly explain the make-up of the country. The two most populous provinces are Quebec and Ontario, which are home to almost two thirds of the Canadian population, and that bias was even stronger in the 19th century. As late as 1871, the westernmost province of British Columbia had a mere 36,247 people. Alberta, Saskatchewan and Manitoba lie in between, while way out east there are Nova Scotia, New Brunswick, and Prince Edward Island, collectively known as the Maritimes, and in the largely frozen north, what are now known as Yukon, Nunavut and Northwest Territories even today have a collective population of only about 100,000. Hence, almost all of our

SLEEPING WITH AN ELEPHANT

mentioned a game played by artillerymen in the November snow in Champs de Mars park, where within a year matches were a common affair, arranged by a group calling themselves the Montreal Foot and Baseball Club. Back in England, rugby and soccer were still mulling over their divorce documents, and these relatively informal games played between scratch 'blue flag' and 'red flag' teams seem to have been undecided between those two codes, or what they called the American rules, by which they possibly meant something similar to the Boston Game played by the Oneidas and their peers.

It was at McGill University[9] that the seeds of Canadian rugby were sown. McGill rugby's own website claims their club was established in 1863, the evidence being a letter RD McGibbon sent to the *Toronto Globe* in 1875 in which he says rugby had been played at McGill University "for the last ten or twelve years." As McGibbon was there at the time, we can probably take his word for it.

In 1865, a game was apparently played to the English tradition between officers from the British regiments garrisoned in Montreal and the local 'Civilians', who were seemingly almost all drawn from the ranks of McGill University[10]. The British military-men quite feasibly played an early form of rugby, but this was six years before the formation of the RFU and the publication of the first official laws, and the Winchester game was also a favourite among the military.

As the 1860s led into the 1870s, the Montreal game was gradually shaped by ideas imported by people who had played the game in Britain, and most specifically, Scotland[11]. But although there was a strong rugby culture among Scottish academies at this time, they rarely knew the proper rules, and struggled to understand them when they did, so it was not the 'purest' kind of rugby that they were taking to Canada. Gordon Currie may have an additional point when he says the "structured, disciplined life of Britain was a reason for many men escaping to Canada and the US and it seems they did not take kindly to suggestions that they organise and formalise their sports."

---

attention on early Canadian football will be focused on Ontario and Quebec. There were isolated cases of football activity in other parts of country, but almost all of the relevant developments took place in these two main provinces.

[9] Named for James McGill, a prominent local merchant of Glaswegian origin who bequeathed £10,000 and his estate to the Royal Institution for the Advancement of Learning, which would eventually lead to McGill University in 1821. It was always something of a sore point in Montreal society, being a bastion of the English language and education system in the heart of French speaking Quebec. As late as the 1960s, only three per cent of its enrolment was French speaking, leading in 1969 to the McGill Français movement, which eventually won its battle to see the university take more consideration of its francophone setting.

[10] As described by R Tait Mackenzie in an article called *Rugby Football*, which wasn't actually written until 1892.

[11] As explored by Gerald Redmond in *The Sporting Scots of Nineteenth-Century Canada* (Associated University Press, 1982).

MIKE ROBERTS – THE SAME OLD GAME: CODIFICATION

As the years wore on, three separate football cultures emerged in Montreal: that of the soldiers at the garrison, that of the civilians, and that of McGill University – but all three groups regularly engaged in matches with each other, and there seems to have been a gradual adoption of a more rugby than soccer based tradition, with a reference to a 'try' as early as 1866.

Unlike Australia, where the Victorians had little choice but to create their own rules, by the time the Canadians starting thinking about formalising its football, they already had established rulebooks to refer to. In April 1874, the *McGill University Gazette* stated that "until a few years ago, the methods of playing football were varied and numerous, but the game has finally settled into two distinct styles – the Rugby rules and the Association rules … the object of the Association code is to encourage 'dribbling', and simplicity has also been carefully studied by the abolition of all clauses and technicalities calculated to prevent the easy comprehension of the rules; the Rugby laws are much more extensive and elaborate, and the main idea is to encourage speed of foot with a minimum of kicking, besides, there being an atmosphere of danger in the 'hacking' and 'mauls' so dear to every player more Rugbeinsi."

The first big city club was the Montreal Foot Ball Club[12], which was founded on April 8, 1872 in the McGill's Mechanics Hall building, which clearly suggests some kind of student origin. An 1894 article explained that "in order to encourage the game the Montreal Club in 1873 offered a Challenge Cup for competition and this trophy for a number of years was the emlilem of supremacy on the Football field[13]." It was awarded the first time when MFBC played the first game on record involving a side from outside Montreal, a 0-0 draw with Quebec City on the latter's Esplanade in October 1873, using Montreal's rules. The same two teams met again a fortnight later, this time in Montreal using Quebec's rules, but "Quebec tried unsuccessfully to wrest the coveted prize from Montreal," losing by four touchdowns to one goal[14]. However, Montreal would soon face a new challenge, for "the most active competitor the Club has had, is the Britainia Football Club, formed in 1875[15], and which for some years forced the Montreal to take second place honors."

The use of different rules in Montreal and Quebec City clearly shows that these teams were not following the RFU's laws by the book, to the extent that McGill felt obliged to declare that their own interpretations "disagree very materially with the rules of the Canadian

---

[12] In a roundabout kind of way, this is the same team as the modern-day Westmount Rugby Club, making it the oldest active rugby club in North America.

[13] *Our city and our sports: souvenir and official programme of the 12th annual meet of the Canadian Wheelmen's Association, Montreal* (July, 1894). Also the two other quotes in this paragraph.

[14] Quebec disputed the win. Under the RFU's rules, a touchdown was worthless unless it was converted, meaning their solitary goal won the game. Other rules did count touchdowns, but only as a tie-breaker. However, some Canadian clubs, like Montreal, had the rule that three touchdowns equalled a goal.

[15] This year is also supported by an article in the *Montreal Gazette* in November, 1882, which says that the Britannia Football Club had played 39 matches since 1875.

SLEEPING WITH AN ELEPHANT

Association, and while we regret our exclusion from playing for the Champion Cup we feel bound, both by honour and inclination, to stick to our own game, which seems always to have suited our men peculiarly well."

McGill's rules of 1874 (see *Appendix Fifteen*) clearly show the RFU's influence, and many of the laws are lifted word for word from the rules originally laid out in London. But they were considerably simplified, with rugby's 59 laws being whittled down to just 23, generally eliminating the most unnecessarily complicated bits. In particular, there is not one mention of any of the mauls, fair catches, marks or knock ons that the RFU detailed with all manner of complex clauses. They also insist that the only way of scoring a goal was by kicking the ball over the crossbar direct from the field, and there is no mention of rugby's 'try on goal' following a touchdown, which at least implies that this basic element of the game had been removed. The McGill rules never once explain what a touchdown was or how you were supposed to score one, yet do state that the result of a game "shall be decided by the majority of goals, or in the event of no goals being obtained by the majority of touch-downs; three touchdowns counting as one goal." In whatever case, it is curious to note that it was not until November 1875 that the English RFU introduced a similar law that "a match shall be decided by a majority of goals, but if the number of goals is equal or no goals be kicked, by a majority of tries."

McGill clearly wanted the emphasis to be on the kicking game, something that was more of a mix and of soccer and rugby, and that seems to be the reason why, despite their reluctance to integrate with the townspeople, in May 1874 they did accept an offer to travel all the way south to Cambridge, in another country entirely, and play against Harvard, which had no rugby tradition whatsoever, and played the soccer-rugby hybrid known as the Boston Game. As we know, it was thanks to this meeting that the Ivy League colleges first learnt of the rugby game that they would use as the basis for what would eventually become American football. Although contemporary reports suggested that Harvard and McGill played each other at rugby, they clearly did not. It was a hybrid. But when they joined forces with Yale and Princeton to form an American association, the IFA did not adopt McGill's game. They preferred to refer to the official laws published in England, and instead produced their own adaptation. If only the rugby rules had been a bit more straightforward, perhaps none of this would have ever happened!

But despite their amazing job of convincing the normally uptight and self-centred Harvardians to so readily embrace an English idea imported via Canadians, back home in Canada, McGill were hardly rugby pioneers. There was interest from their fellow Canadians over in Ontario to get some games up, but early approaches by both Queens and the University of Toronto were turned down. The McGillians were convinced that their particular style of play wasn't suited to games with anybody other than themselves. It was the kind of stubbornness that would stifle the country's rugby culture for decades and slow the development of a truly national game.

355

Ontario

Ontario's football culture had been developing in isolation from Quebec, but in a more or less parallel fashion. The state obviously had some kind of football from the 1850s, for Galt Grammar School, which was opened in 1852, was already playing it a year later, and in Toronto in 1859, a team of Irishmen played the St George Society. In 1861, the first properly documented game anywhere on Canadian soil was a 'football kick' between Arts and Science versus Law students at the University of Toronto, where one of the captains was William Mulock, later the University's Chancellor, and a senior politician who earned himself a knighthood. In 1864, we have the first Canadian game for which we actually know the result: the University College beat the Medics by a 'game' to nil, and from this year onwards, Mel Smith presents records of several games played by different academic institutions in Toronto, while the Toronto Lacrosse Club laid their rackets aside for the occasional game of football from 1869. By 'game', they usually meant playing simply until the first team scored, but several games could be played back-to-back. In 1867, Trinity played the College of Arts, won the 'game', and then the two teams "partook of college cheer," which presumably meant some form of alcoholic refreshment. Out of that grew a decision to play the rematch there and then, presumably a fair bit more raucously than the first, although the result was another win for the Artsmen. By around 1870, it seems to have been a widely accepted tradition throughout Ontario that football should be played on a 'best of three' basis.

What became known as the 'Old University Game' followed the general trend of football anywhere in the world at the time and made up rules of its own. Writes Mel Smith, "these rules allowed charging from behind, hacking and tripping. Players would bounce the ball along the ground with their hands."

In Ottawa, there was a game in 1867 between the Rough Riders and the Senators[16] and another was played between the Upper Canada College and the Trinity College School in Port Hope in 1872. But as Currie writes, in those days "they were not organized clubs; they were not disciplined groups with the avowed aim of promoting excellence and the popularity of the game. It was still largely a willy-nilly business, with each game almost an accidental happening." A 'football game' was no more scientifically defined than a 'throwing contest' or a 'running race'. The rules were makeshift depending on whatever playing field or ball they could find, how many players there were and what they did or did not feel like allowing.

Things started getting more serious in 1869, when a group of players gathered in a room above George Lee's Fruit Store to form the Hamilton Football Club, who would later be nicknamed the Tigers because of their orange and black uniforms. The Maple Leaf Baseball Club Grounds on Upper James Street was the venue for early football in Hamilton, and the

---

[16] The Rough Riders were named after the lumberjacks that rode logs down the river, and it was probably many of those players that chose the same name for the city's club when it formed a decade later, to eventually fold in 1996. The Senators had no relation to the ice hockey team, which was formed in 1912.

Hamilton Spectator notes that they already had over a hundred members in their inaugural season of 1869, which began with their first ever match against the 13th Battalion in December.

It is claimed that this makes the Hamilton Tiger-Cats the oldest team in the CFL, but others argue that the modern team didn't really exist in its modern form until 1950, when after years of competing for local support with the newer Wildcats franchise in the same city, the two clubs decided the most sensible thing would be to simply merge.

Those 'others' who argue about the Tiger-Cats' vintage are mainly fans of the Toronto Argonauts, who were formed four years later, in 1873, by an Englishman by birth, HT Glazebrook, and his fellow members of the Argonaut Rowing Club. The Argos are at least right with their claim to be the oldest professional football team anywhere in North America with a continuous history and that has always kept the same name. Their nickname, 'the Boatmen', still honours the rowing club that originally formed the side, and their dark and light blue colours honour those worn by the Oxford and Cambridge crews. Not that the club was limited to rowers. Their foundational documents allowed "gentlemen who are not members of the Argonaut Rowing Club to become members of the Argonaut Football Club on paying the subscription of one dollar, after their names have been approved by the committee of the rowing club." That name-approval process suggests a certain vetting of potential associates of their elite institution.

It is not clear from the evidence whether the early games played in Ontario were rugby or some kind of soccer, but when the Rowing Club played their first game, the fact that they lost by one try and one goal to nil[17] leaves no doubt that they were playing the former. Their vanquisher was the University of Toronto, and that's curious. The University was also recorded playing Queens from Kingston on the eastern end of Lake Ontario a year later, in 1874, yet it is always said that the emblematic Varsity Blues didn't come into being until 1877, when JH Mayne Campbell, who had played rugby in Edinburgh, finally managed to persuade his peers that rugby was the way ahead. But the University had clearly been playing some form of rugby for longer than that.

A week after facing the students, the rowers then received a historic visit from the Hamilton club. Toronto won the first game by a goal and a try to nil, and a week later returned the favour by travelling to the Hamilton Cricket Ground, where the home side got "a goal, a try and a touch in goal" and the visitors got "two goals and two trys." Toronto had one more try and one more goal than Hamilton, but Hamilton had a touch in goal, which for some inexplicable reason meant they won the match!

An odd twist came a month later, in November 1873, when the Argonauts plus a handful of players from the University played against an 'English team', and beat them by one goal and three touchdowns to nothing. It has been assumed that this game was rugby, but it's

---

[17] Counting unconverted tries directly in the scoring was way ahead of its time compared to both Britain and the USA.

MIKE ROBERTS – THE SAME OLD GAME: CODIFICATION

intriguing to wonder what kind of football this English team was really versed in, and even more intriguing to note that this was just a month before Yale, down in the USA, played a game against a team of Old Etonians.

In 1875, the Argonauts were again playing a team with British connections, the Old Country Men, with the visitors storming to a win with three goals, three touchdowns and three rouges. That's the first ever mention of a rouge in Canadian football, and it's fascinating to wonder where that word might have suddenly sprung from. We can only guess here. The Eton field game has something called a 'rouge' as had Sheffield Rules football until 1868, and now that weird word was surfacing in the Ontario football scene? Those Etonians playing Yale in 1873 and the mysterious English teams that played in Toronto may have had something to with it.

Quebec and Ontario

The rouge crept into Ontario football at more or less the same time that the province was beginning to forge its first links with Quebec. Together, they formed the Football Association of Canada in 1873, which is the date given on the cover of an 1876 copy of the rules held at the National Library of Canada. The main reason for forming the Association was probably to organise the first interprovincial match, which was played on the Montreal Cricket Grounds in October 1874 by selected players from the two provinces. Ontario won that by four touchdowns to one goal[18], but the FAC doesn't appear to have actually held a proper meeting until October 9, 1875, when eight teams, more or less the pick of the Canadian crop at the time, four from each province, sat down at a table together in Toronto to set out on what would be a long, troubled and confusing road towards nationalised Canadian football.

Ontario was represented by the Toronto Argonauts, the University of Toronto, Hamilton and Queens, while Quebec had Quebec City, Montreal, Britannias and McGill. Unlike in the US, at this first meeting of the FAC, just three of the eight teams were collegiate. Civilian athletics clubs were involved from the start, and as the results panned out over the ensuing years, generally had the upper hand. Unlike in America, college football was not the focus for the origins of the Canadian game.

Heading the Montreal delegation was James Creighton, best known for his contributions to ice hockey[19]. It was apparently he who proposed that they should do the logical thing and adopt the same rules as the RFU in England. But when the two provinces took to the Toronto Cricket Grounds a week later for another Ontario v Quebec game, in which the home side

---

[18] If they had been using the 'official' RFU rules for rugby drafted two years earlier, under which unconverted tries were worthless, the Quebecois would have won!

[19] Some writers, keen as ever to put a face to society's creations, have even gone as far as to say Creighton invented ice hockey, which is probably going a bit far. He was instrumental in organising the first documented 'official' match in Montreal in 1875, and is considered to have been the man who drew up the first set of rules in 1877, although these didn't really amount to much more than the rules of field hockey moved onto the ice.

scored the only goal by converting a try, it was also noted that the home side had a massive fourteen rouges compared to Quebec's one. This was a year before the FAC endorsed its first major breakaway from the rugby rules by declaring that with "no goals having been obtained in a match … rouges should count." Chances are that the Ontarians, who as far as we know were the only province to have used the rouge system before, racked up that enormous fourteen in the 1875 game because their guests were less used to the idea, or perhaps didn't even know about it!

Other than endorsing Ontario's rouges, the 1876 meeting of the FAC also accepted McGill's idea of including touchdowns in the scoring – one goal being equal to three touchdowns. Canada was leading the way on English rugby here, because a year earlier, the RFU had rejected the same proposal that "three tries should equal one goal."

However, a historic game in October 1876 at the Montreal Cricket Grounds "was played with the understanding that goals alone should count[20]." That was when Harvard travelled up to face an All Canada team, which featured players from Toronto, London, Ottawa, McGill, Montreal and the Britannias. It is great to see the Ontario and Quebec clubs cooperating so nicely, but benefitting from all of its players being used to playing together, Harvard won by two goals (and four touchdowns) to nothing.

Meanwhile, over in the Maritimes, rugby was progressing from its mishmash beginnings, with quite a scene developing in and around Halifax, although these teams, rather like their geographical position, were somewhat out on a limb, and as yet made no contact with the new FAC. In fact, in isolation from the rest of the dominion, and even more so from the US, the provinces on the eastern coast played almost no part in the growth of the Canadian game, but instead helped maintain a rugby union playing culture in Canada that is still strong today.

The Dominion Football Association was founded in 1877, using the FA's soccer rules, but it posed little threat. It was rugby, not soccer, that was most on the rise throughout Canada in the late 1870s. It had always been the major code in Quebec, and Mel Smith notes that on a single weekend in October 1878, there were 83 games of football played in Ontario, and 59 of these were rugby.

The FAC formed, the cream of Quebec and Ontario playing interprovincial matches, and those in turn combining as an All Canada team to play to Harvard suggested promising beginnings. Sadly, it was a false dawn. For the period from about 1876 to 1883, there was hardly any interaction between Ontario and Quebec. The FAC was ultimately a non-starter and folded in 1878.

Stuck at a crossroads

The FAC had made a great start by getting all the big clubs to agree to use the RFU rules, but as Mel Smith puts it, many of those teams "only used the new rules if it looked like they

---

[20] *Harvard Crimson* (November 3, 1876).

would benefit from them." Rather than harmony, the game was still in utter confusion, a situation that would be maintained for several decades. Ontario did one thing, and Quebec would do the other. It was the same with the colleges and the athletic clubs. Canadian football was appallingly disjointed and haphazard, which made it especially susceptible to the constant flow of new ideas spreading north from the US colleges. This was only natural. Montreal, Ottawa, Toronto and Hamilton are all closer to the US border than they are to each other. Quebec has New England on its doorstep, and Toronto is much closer to Pennsylvania, Ohio and Michigan that it is to Montreal.

We could note that it was at this same time that the Australian and New Zealand rugby communities were considering making their own changes to the rugby game, but these were stalled when they realised that if their game became too different, then that would be the end of all the tour matches with the British teams, which were one of the best things about the sport. Canada was in a different situation. If they fancied widening their playing horizons a little, they had the whole of the United States on their doorstep. Getting fixtures was never going to be a problem as long as the Canadians and Americans were playing a similar enough game.

In 1880, Walter Camp abolished the scrummage and brought in the line of scrimmage in America. This was also the year that games between Canadian and American teams became fairly commonplace, with Harvard and Michigan being popular rivals. It was in a game with Michigan, for instance, that the University of Toronto first came across the new line of scrimmage idea, liked it, and tried persuading fellow clubs in Canada to take up the idea too.

Contrast that to the Britannias. In 1879, they played two games with Harvard and also challenged Yale, but their offer was declined. But despite this interest in playing American sides, in 1880, and following the introduction of the line of scrimmage, they started protesting against American ideas invading the rugby game, and tellingly, when they next travelled south, it was to New York to face the British Rugby Club and attempt to remind the world what the game should look like.

Mel Smith observes that there was an undercurrent in Canada "trying to get Americans to stop all changes and get back to the rugby game." But the squabbling factions reacted to the American ideas in different measures, and there was no central body to control the way things were going, which further distorted the Canadian game and made it harder still to create any kind of national footballing unity.

But a pan-North American football culture never happened. Generally speaking, over the next three or four decades, Canadian teams ummed and ahhed as to whether they should go with the flow and adopt the USA's continuous innovations, or stay with their own games, which were neither wholly American football nor wholly rugby union. Canada would be left in a limbo in between.

The FAC had failed, but Canada was in dire in need of a central governing body for football, and Ontario and Quebec finally got their heads together in June and September 1880 to form the Canadian Rugby Football Union (CRFU). They devised rules that featured both British and American influences and decided to hold an interprovincial final for their respective champions. The Ontarian clubs were well up for it, but only the Britannias from Quebec responded. Nobody took any notice of the new rules, no interprovincial final was ever played and the idea came to nothing.

This was not so much down to rivalry as to the fact that most people involved in the game saw no particular need for structured organisation. As Gordon Currie says, the real "internal bitterness and politicking" had yet to come. "In 1882 the sport was young and, happily, lacked an establishment, sacred cows and power politicians." Games were still relatively informal affairs on open fields, and although people did gather around the pitch (and often on it) to watch, they would have been stunned if anybody suggested they should have to pay for the privilege!

It may have been great fun to play, as long as you didn't mind being kicked in the shins every thirty seconds, but it was "relatively dull to watch when measured against the American game" writes Currie. "There were no definite downs and no five-yard limit, and as a result the ball could, and frequently did, remain locked in a heaving scrimmage almost indefinitely ... The scanty rules and the scarcity of organised teams or clubs, made it a game for individuals, for prima donnas. A man would simply do the best he could, which often meant a player would seem to be playing against his own side as well as their collective opponents."

There was a second attempt to form the CRFU in 1882, and despite enthusiasm from McGill, this time it was the Britannias, at the peak of their crusade to get teams to quit copying America's silly line of scrimmage idea, who persuaded the Quebec clubs to stay away. Ultimately, the Britannias were fighting a lost cause. In 1883, their disgust at the Americanisation of rugby was such that they started dabbling in soccer instead. By the end of the year, they had folded.

Having failed to conjure up support in Quebec, Ontario decided to go it alone. In January 1883, sixteen teams gathered at Gus Thomas' English Chop House, one of the most popular eateries in Toronto, and established the Ontario Rugby Football Union (ORFU). Their American influenced rules included the innovation of a points-based system, which the Americans were in the process of implementing around the same time, and several years before the RFU in England. A touchdown would be worth four points, and there would be a whopping four more if it was converted. Goals from the field netted a healthy six points, there was one for a rouge, and they also toyed with the American idea of two points to the opposition following a safety.

Not to be outdone, just ten days later, "a meeting was held ... for the purpose of forming a Quebec Rugby Football Union[21]." With just five founder members, Quebec's game was more

---

[21] *Montreal Gazette* (Jan 18, 1883).

faithful to the English rules. There was no line of scrimmage, and they stuck to the traditional system of only recording goals scored over the posts or from converted tries, although touchdowns did come into play as tie-breakers.

The first championship

Just when Canada was heading for footballing division, in 1884, the third attempt to get the CRFU off the ground actually made some progress. A major factor in this could have been the fact that McGill had just turned their backs on their own Union and adopted the ORFU's rules, and also the work of the ORFU president, AH Campbell of Toronto, who was thanked in the minutes of the first meeting "for his energy in forwarding the formation of the union[22]." That meeting in Montreal in February 1884 merely laid the groundwork, and it was in July 1884, at Rossin House, Toronto, that they really got down to business.

It was here that they methodically perused the latest edition of the RFU's rules and the ORFU's own set, and ticked off the changes. Out went the "tedious, rough and unsatisfactory" maul, along with any heeling out of the scrum, which meant there would be no place for the American line of scrimmage for the time being, and the ORFU scoring system was adopted in its entirety, apart from drop-kicks being devalued from seven to six points.

Extraordinarily, the QRFU had given in almost entirely to the ORFU's ideas, which were applied in November to the first ever end-of-season game between the respective champions of each province. Playing at home and felt to have the stronger side, the Ontario champion, the Toronto Argonauts, were expected to be too much for Montreal, but the Quebecois stunned them 30-0 to win bragging rights as the first 'Dominion Champion'.

Sadly, this was not the dawn of a new era for a unified game in Canada either. The following year, 1885, they reverted to 'all-star' Quebec and Ontario teams for the end-of-season interprovincial game, and although Quebec won 3-0, thanks to three rouges, the Ontarians claimed a team had to score a minimum of four points to win. They really should have sorted that point out before they started playing, but as far as Ontario were concerned the game had been a tie. These championship matches weren't going quite as smoothly as hoped.

The two regional bodies and the CRFU (which was basically what the ORFU and QRFU became whenever they held joint meetings) agreed on almost everything apart from the fundamental matter of the rules. In 1886, the QRFU insisted on "passing the ball back through the scrimmage," which upset the folk in Ontario[23], who also wanted a game between the provincial champions rather than another all-star game as Quebec were proposing. No game was played. A year later, and following controversies over the same two issues, ORFU

---

[22] He was made secretary of the CRFU, and another Toronto player, William Hamilton Merritt, was the president. The Argonauts were clearly an influential lot.

[23] This is an odd one, as it was usually Quebec that was most insistent about keeping American ideas at bay.

champions Ottawa College were eventually persuaded to play (and beat) Montreal for the 1887 championship, but Ontario's interest in the CRFU was floundering, and yet another national body was as good as defunct by the end of the year.

Rather than an annual affair, the Quebec vs Ontario game became something that was only played if anybody proposed it, and then only if the respective unions could agree terms, which they usually didn't. In the absence of the CRFU, Ottawa and Montreal arranged a championship match of their own accord in 1888, and 2000 people turned out watch the game end 0-0. Montreal fancied overtime. Ottawa didn't. The game was declared a tie and there would be no Dominion Championship game for another three years.

Ontarian rugby was fast heading more towards the American game, and for the next half decade or so, the two provinces largely went about things in their separate ways. The way Robert Sproule sees it "the Quebec Rugby Football Union was always considered that 'other' union and was somewhat of a mystery. It seemed isolated and different from the rest of Canada ... It should be noted that several articles written on the Quebec Union gave the impression that it was the leader in establishing major milestones on Canadian football when, in actual comparison with the ORFU, research shows that the Ontario Union was the one that brought about important changes to the game. It was the Ontario Union that was the leader and the Quebec Union the follower ... it was the Ontario union that was most productive of rules changes and innovative play. The Quebecers were die-hard traditionalists and were content to play the game as their fathers before them had." But that view depends on the side of the fence you are sitting on. Rather than being conservative, the QRFU was merely more inclined to support rugby rather than American football, and ours is not to judge which is the better game.

The line of scrimmage was gradually becoming a regular thing in Ontario, where it became known as the 'open formation' as opposed to rugby's 'closed formation'. Perhaps so the Canadians could feel more comfortable with their copying of American ideas, the terminology was different, but the idea was the same. Likewise, the two 'guards' that stand on either side of the centre who snapped the ball back were known in Canada as 'scrim-supports'. To help confuse matters, the American 'touchdown' was called a 'try', while the Canadians continued to use the term 'touchdown' but to refer to a ball that had been ruled dead.

The turning point for the divide in Canadian rugby came in 1890, when Quebec themselves adopted the line of scrimmage. They too were beginning to shift towards the American game, and in November 1891, Montreal and ORFU champions Osgoode Hall made arrangements for the first interprovincial match in three years. The success of those games (it went to a replay) may have been the impetus for the rival provinces to mend their differences at a meeting a month later. The dormant CRFU was condemned to the history books, and in its place came the Canada Rugby Union, based in Toronto. Think Monty Python, the Judean People's Front and the People's Front of Judea and you get the picture.

MIKE ROBERTS – THE SAME OLD GAME: CODIFICATION

The CRU tried to make some sense of the madness and settled on a set of laws that were largely concessions to the Ontarians, helped no doubt by its president, AH Campbell, being a member of the Toronto Football Club, and reflected by the result of the 1892 interprovincial game ending in a 45-5 rout of Quebec's Montreal FC at the hands on Osgoode Hall (played in six inches of snow and in -35° temperatures) [24].

The CRU's rules dictated fifteen men, two 45 minute halves (reduced to forty in 1895), no blocking below the knees (which would not be a rule in America until 1906), a fair catch rule, no throwing the ball forward or knocking it on, and a scoring system whereby "a goal kicked from a try shall score 6 points; from a drop kick 5 points; from a flying kick or free kick 4 [reduced to 2 in 1895]; a try shall score 4; a safety touch 2, and a rouge 1."

But perhaps the most important endorsement made by the CRU was that of the American line of scrimmage rather than the scrummage. Rather than a major change in the Canadian game, it was more of an official sanctioning of what was already a widespread practice anyway. But it put the seal on a process that would be mirrored as most of the American innovations crossed the border.

Down in America, Walter Camp had heralded the line of scrimmage as the solution for all the game's ills, but the unwanted side effect was that it meant teams could hold onto possession *ad nausea*. But although the Americans did not take long to see their folly, and fixed the error by introducing the system of downs in 1882, the Canadians didn't seem to mind and persevered with scrimmages but no downs for a decade and a half. But as the scores for games played over next decade remained remarkably high, one assumes the dirty tactic of hogging possession was less of an issue in Canada.

Perhaps the rouge can be thanked for that. There was a tendency not to worry too much with the scrimmage, but to go for a punt immediately, even off the first down. Why slowly gain small amounts of yards at a time when you had the option of simply kicking the thing? You could have a crack at scoring between the posts, and even if you missed, you still got a single. Kicking the ball forwards was generally discouraged by the American rules, and was only employed as a last gasp measure on the final down. Not so in Canada, where games from the 1880s onwards were often little more than punting duels – one side punts it one way, the other side punts it back, and the gaining of yards depended as much on how far you could kick the ball than anything you could gain by rushing.

Another aspect where the Canadian game was remarkably different to America's was in the aspect of safety. Interference had been eliminated altogether, and was penalised by loss of possession; and any kind of tackling below the knees or above the waist, what they called

---

[24] The theory that this was the really the first Canadian championship, as opposed to the first Grey Cup in 1909, is based on the logic that the CRU is effectively the same body that now runs the CFL. But the 1892 game didn't really enjoy any greater status than the Dominion Championship matches that had been played in previous seasons, and it would also be more accurate to say that the CRU became Football Canada, which has been the governing body of amateur Canadian football since 1967.

'scragging', was also forbidden. By all accounts the Canadians were far more effective at eliminating the violence that was plaguing the American game, and if the referee felt any player was being excessively rough, he could be sent off.

Utter confusion

With the foundation of the CRU and the establishment of rules, it would seem the problems with Canadian rugby were solved. Wrong. Things were unclear enough for the championship games, but for games played between clubs within their own provinces, they continued to play by whatever rules they fancied. The CRU wanted to clamp down on this, and in 1894 made the statement that "it is in the interests of football that the game in Ontario and Quebec be played under the same rules" and that the provincial unions should "amend their respective constitutions so as to provide in each case that the rules of play be those from time to time adopted by the CRU."

That was easier said than done, especially as only a small handful of clubs were affiliated to the CRU anyway. What about the rest? The more conservatively minded collegers were far more insistent on sticking to 'pure' rugby, and there was an ongoing feud between them and the 'city teams', that seemed to be taking the game in a completely different direction. Keeping both parties happy was not going to be an easy affair. It wasn't just a rules issue though. By now big matches could attract paying crowds of 4000 or more. There was money to be spent. In 1897, the McGill president said in that year's college annual that "the intercollegiate union is the only thing that is saving the life of football as an amateur and gentlemanly game." What he meant was that the 'city' game was starting to turn professional – which was not just immoral, but also meant an unlevel playing field.

It was time for yet another new body to appear. The Canadian Intercollegiate Rugby Football Union (CIRFU) was formed in Kingston to bring the colleges under a single wing[25], and made no secret of their intention to form a stronger body to defend their own ideas. One of the first things the colleges did was seek admission to the CRU, in the hope of influencing the city teams to come round to their ideas. The plan didn't work. The students insisted on playing by their own rules and when Varsity, the winners of the Yates Cup, the new intercollegiate tournament, played off against ORFU champions Ottawa, they were so unhappy at losing 7-3 to what seemed to be a bunch of professionals that with "deep regret" they and the CIRFU immediately terminated what had only ever been a very loose association with the CRU, and headed off in their own direction again.

The colleges could not be subdued, but the CRU was more concerned at the time with settling the differences between the ORFU and the QRFU. In 1896, they tried to set the record straight by publishing the *Constitution, Rules of the Championship Competitions and*

---

[25] The founder members were McGill and Bishop's College (Lennoxville) from Quebec, and the University of Toronto (by now commonly known as the Varsity Blues), Queen's College (Toronto), the Royal Military College (Kingston), McMaster (Toronto) from Ontario.

Rules of the Game, which included the specification that the size of the field would be 110 by 65 yards, but only with very limited success.

Canadian football was heading for the 20th century, and yet it was still a largely confused and directionless affair. Despite the national pride that now surrounds the game, in the 1890s it didn't really exist. Rugby, soccer, American football, Australian rules and even Gaelic football were all firmly established by this point. But all Canada had was a number of erratic amalgamations of British rugby, American football and local variations, with very little in the way of effective and centralised control. If Canada wanted to believe it had a national form of football, then it was high time that Canadians made it clear just what that game was. Otherwise, there was a very real danger of it being swallowed up by the American game entirely.

16 CANADIAN CLUBS
20th century Canadian football

Burning issues

In the 1880s, no Canadian in their wildest of dreams would have imagined that before the century was out, there would be over 4000 people watching Queens face Varsity, or that, albeit in the form of voluntary donations, there would be over $1500 in gate takings. That was for the intercollegiate championship, and the game was won by Varsity, captained by John Thrift Meldrum Burnside.

That was only the start of Burnside's contributions to the Canadian game. He was often described as one of its great visionaries and what became known as the 'Burnside Rules', which he unveiled in 1901, were set to be the biggest revolution yet in Canadian football. But very little of what they said was really new. He'd done a fair bit of tweaking, but Burnside's rules were conspicuously influenced by the rules Walter Camp and his friends had already been using for years in the USA.

He was proposing that the American snapback using the heel should be adopted, and that the offensive team was "to have six men on the line of scrimmage" rather than the previous eight. It was also time to abolish Canada's rugby-style lineout, and replace it by taking the ball to the scrimmage as in America. He also ordered that all goals from the field "whether by placement, drop kick, free kick from penalty[1] or mark" should be downgraded to two points, which was felt would encourage the rushing game, and "on all kicks players to line back ten yards from their opponents, while kicker kicks from mark."

Burnside also felt that fifteen-a-side was too many. Ever since 1880, when Walter Camp finally won Yale's ongoing battle to make football teams smaller, the American game had been played eleven-a-side. Burnside suggested Canada fielded twelve. Perhaps teams of eleven would have made it too laughingly obvious that he was not far short of suggesting a wholesale imitation of the game that was going down a storm in the States.

Which is basically what he was doing with the most revolutionary suggestion of all. He wanted Canada to adopt the idea of three downs, although teams were required to gain ten yards, not five as in America. Of course, in the USA, it's now about gaining ten yards as well, but the Canadians were first with that one. And more poignantly, those Americans that scoff at the Canucks for having three downs not four 'just to be different' should note that originally it was three on both sides of the border. Although the Americans threw in an extra fourth down, the Canadians stuck to the traditional three, and have done ever since.

The Burnside Rules were intended to sort out Canadian rules once and for all. As Currie writes, games almost always ended in complaints "usually about a bungling referee, and this

---

[1] Note how offences were originally castigated with a penalty kick, as they still are in modern rugby.

367

MIKE ROBERTS – THE SAME OLD GAME: CODIFICATION

was grossly unfair since the rules that did exist left so much to on-the-spot interpretation by the referee – and the middle of a rugby field amid a heaving crowd of shouting players each claiming to be right is no place to produce a decision worthy of Solomon." The game needed a single set of common rules, but was Burnside, with his blatant Americanisation of Canadian rugby, going to successfully convince the nation? It was a big ask.

Although there was some initial scepticism, his ideas soon gained popularity in inter-faculty games at his own University of Toronto. Soon, Ontario in general was latching onto the Burnside way of thinking, and in December 1902, the ORFU voted 19-5 to rock the Canadian football boat by accepting snap-backs, downs, 12-a-side … the lot.

Although the Burnside Rules finally put paid to any possible pretence that the Ontarians were playing the same kind of rugby as the rest of the world, the ORFU remained just that, a 'rugby' union. Predictably enough, none of the rival bodies seemed over-inclined to make wholesale changes to their own games. Rather than solve any differences, the ORFU's latest tampering exercise had Canada potentially headed for its biggest division ever, for the rules were now so darned different that championship games were no longer even the remotest of possibilities. But there was an unexpected shift in attitudes. The more teams experimented with Burnside's ideas, the more they started seeing that they did make sense. The downs rule was already well known from the American game. The QRFU had mooted the idea as early as 1894, as had the CRU in 1897, although both those bodies had rejected it.

A practice game between Varsity and McGill in late 1902 turned out to be a landmark occasion. Despite initial opposition from the latter, they ended up playing a game that experimented with concessions to both colleges' rules. It was described as one of the finest games of football Toronto had ever seen, and McGill, who won 15-11, were forced to swallow their pride and accept that this Burnside chap did have some valid points after all. It wouldn't be long before McGill themselves were introducing elements of the Burnside rules to their own inter-faculty games.

Ontarian rugby was moving towards American football, and Quebec and the colleges were moving towards the Ontario game. Just two years after the ORFU started using downs, the QRFU did likewise, although just to be awkward, they required teams to make five yards in three downs, rather than Burnside's ten. Once again, Canada was gradually heading towards uniformity, and Ontario was ready to compromise and did revert from the six to the eight-man line of scrimmage, and thus move back in line with the other unions. Perhaps the Ontarians were realising that their unilateral law changes were only serving to isolate themselves from the game. Indeed, Hamilton had such a fine season in 1904 that in their desperation to play a championship game, they went as far as suggesting to Quebec champions Ottawa City that they played one half by each union's rules. Ottawa refused.

The Big Four

Snaps and downs soon caught on almost everywhere, but the issue of whether it was five or ten yards that teams had to gain was still unclear. Some rules stipulated that the game should be played as halves, others were moving towards four fifteen minute quarters. The fair catch rule was coming and going, and not even the height and width of the goalposts were uniform. Ontario had downsized its teams, and the announcement that Quebec was also going to reduce numbers in 1903 may have offered a ray of hope, but that hope dimmed when it was revealed that they had settled for fourteen, as opposed to the Ontarian twelve.

To confound the issue, 1905 was also the year that the Intercollegiate Union decided to rejoin the CRU, in theory a positive move, but now there were three unions playing three different types of game vying for the same championship. The CRU, in their usual wisdom, came up with the 'perfect' solution, the same one Hamilton had offered a year earlier, and one which paints a decent picture of the perplexity in Canadian rugby. "Championship games will be one hour in length, divided into four quarters of fifteen minutes each, unless otherwise agreed upon by the captains of the two teams. The first two quarters shall be played under the rules selected by the team winning the toss, and the last two under the rules selected by the team losing the toss." And that's for the championship! They even needed two separate referees, one for each set of rules. But the CRU wouldn't allow any Camp/Burnside influenced Ontario teams to challenge for the title, so it was down to intercollegiate champions Varsity to face Ottawa Rough Riders in front of what must have been 6000 pretty confused spectators. The first half was played the way Quebec wanted it, with three downs to make five yards, four points for a try and two for a goal. Then the intercollegiate rules took over for the second half, with considerably less interference, three downs to make ten yards and the value of tries raised to five and goals reduced to one. Varsity's speed eventually overcame Ottawa's brawn, and they edged it 11-9.

There was only one thing for it. Time to form another union! In September 1907, the Interprovincial Rugby Football Union was formed. Fed up of the petty regional differences, and aware that trying to get everyone to agree was getting nowhere, it was time for a select few to start leading Canadian football forward. The four breakaway clubs were the Hamilton Tigers, Toronto Argonauts from Ontario and Montreal FC and Ottawa Rough Riders from Quebec[2], known almost immediately as the 'Big Four' and who formed the basis of what is the CFL East Division today[3].

There were other reasons for the Big Four going their separate way. These teams were dominating all-comers in their respective states. Montreal FC had recently put 72 points on the board against poor St Patrick's and the Ottawa Rough Riders had routed Westmount 67-6. Such one-sided games were doing the sport no favours. The only real challenge for the Big

---

[2] Ottawa is in Ontario, but was playing in the Quebec union at the time.

[3] Although there is no real connection between Montreal and the modern-day Alouettes, and the Rough Riders sadly disbanded in 1996.

Four, other than each other, came from the major college teams, but the IRFU and the students were constantly at loggerheads, mainly over the professionalism issue.

In fact, that very concern would rear its ugly head in the very first game played by the Big Four. Toronto were on their way to play Montreal, when the Canadian Amateur Athletic Federation, and probably testing the waters of their relationship with the breakaway body, decided that Toronto would be suspended if they played the game, because the Montreal side included a 'convicted' professional by the name of Ernie Russell, the ice hockey superstar who that season amassed an incredible total of 43 goals in only nine games for the now defunct Montreal Wanderers. Toronto was being chastised for playing *against* a *hockey* pro! Their sponsors, the Argonaut Rowing Club, agreed that they should refuse to travel. The footballers saw no cause for alarm, but the rowers did when the former simply announced that they were breaking away from the Rowing Club and were going to rename themselves the Torontos. Times had changed. The boatmen had more to gain from an association with football than football had from one with rowing. By the time the game went ahead, which for the record Montreal won 17-8, the Argos were the Argos again, and the matter was conveniently forgotten. Football now had financial, as well as physical, muscle.

It was the formation of the Big Four in Canada that would pave the way for the professional game. They commanded the bulk of the paying supporters, and were considered the supreme teams. This, in turn, diminished the influence of the colleges, and at the same time that of the ORFU and the QRFU, who had both lost their most influential teams, and would find themselves relegated to the status of 'intermediate' leagues. But for the good of the game, the Big Four were quite happy to go along with the CRU rulebook, at least for the time being, which helped enormously to streamline the confusion.

As they governed the rules played by the Big Four, the CRU was now by far the most influential rulemaking body, but they also took a surprisingly sensible attitude and made a few concessions to the intercollegiate game and also to the ORFU, to the extent that in 1907, the ORFU also accepted the CRU rules in their entirety. Meanwhile, the QRFU withdrew in a sulk from senior competition, but now they had lost Montreal and Ottawa to the Big Four and McGill to the Intercollegiates, it barely mattered in terms of the bigger picture.

Going grey

1909 was the year that Canadian football really started ironing out its regional differences. And it had good reason to do so, because that was when the Grey Cup was first contested. Albert Henry George Grey, the 4th Earl Grey[4], was a former British MP who before arriving in Canada had worked extensively throughout the Empire, and particularly India, generally promoting social reform and earning a grand old name for himself. Governor General of

---

[4] The grandson of British politician Charles Grey, the 2nd Earl Grey, whose many achievements included the Reform Act of 1832, but who for reasons that have never been made entirely clear is best remembered for an aromatic blend of tea.

CANADIAN CLUBS

Canada from 1904 to 1911, among his main concerns were improving relations with the United States and promoting national unity among the English and French speaking communities, but though his intentions may have been good, they often did little more than antagonise the French nationalists.

He did take an interest in sports. *Busy Men's Magazine* in 1909 described how "he skis, showshoes or curls. In the summer he plays golf, cricket and does not disdain a good game of bowling. He is a good traveller, fond of fishing and an enthusiastic patron of the turf. During an evening he enjoys a good game of billiards or a rubber of bridge." There was a horse race in his name until 1916, the Earl Grey Trophy, and Montreal had a skating club named after him, but nowhere is there any particular evidence that the man whose name will forever be associated to Canadian football ever took any interest in either playing or watching the game!

All Grey really ever did for football was donate the trophy that CFL teams still compete for today. He was merely following a tradition – his four predecessors, Stanley, Minto, Connaught and Dufferin, had previously donated trophies to the champions of ice hockey, lacrosse, soccer and curling. Grey picked rugby because it was just about the only sport that was still lacking a trophy! Even then it was a close call. The *Toronto Daily Star* in January 1909 reported that "the Governor General Earl Grey may give a cup to be competed for by amateur clubs of the whole Dominion to stand to the amateur clubs as the Stanley Cup does at present to the professionals." There was no mention of rugby or football; it was ice hockey he was talking about!

Some political advisor murmured in the Lord's ear that he might like to consider giving it to the champion football team, but it was easier said than done. The game had the Big Four, the ORFU, the QRFU, the intercollegiates … but were the irregular championship matches they played on an adhoc basis really the grounds for deciding the champions of the whole dominion? The *Toronto Star* in 1908 certainly didn't think so, and explained the lie of the land nicely when it said "we talk of the Canadian Rugby Union and the Canadian Championship when we mean virtually the championship of the provinces of Ontario and Quebec. In time perhaps it will be possible to extend the field of the CRU so that the Canadian Championship may actually be a Dominion title. Out in British Columbia they have a number of good rugby teams. Way down East they have good teams also. Yet under the present conditions teams from neither section are playing for the Canadian Championship. Of course, there is the difficulty about the rules. Rugby is played in the extremes of the continent more or less largely under the old (British) rugby rules." The article goes on to mention the problems with the long distances involved and also the shortness of the season, which made it awkward to find anywhere to fit such ambitious games into the schedule.

The Earl himself didn't seem to have any particular views on the issue. He was off back to Blighty, and all he was concerned about was ensuring his name would never be forgotten. It was the fitting way to end any Governor General's five-year stint in Canada, and he left the matter in the hands of a board of trustees. On April 2, 1909, one of those, the Reverend DB Macdonald stated that "His Excellency proposes to give a Challenge Cup for the Rugby Football Championship of Canada" which "must remain always under purely amateur conditions." Amateurism, underlined here as in the original, seemed to be the only major concern of the Earl, but was one that would not be heeded in the slightest! Even as those words were penned, the Big Four were wandering clandestinely between amateurism, shamateurism and outright professionalism.

Unsure who on earth they were meant to award the trophy to, the trustees went for the simplest solution in May 1909 by announcing that "it is our idea to give the cup to the winner of the Canadian Rugby Union this year, and then challenges can be sent to us." Although the first championship would be contested by the CRU members, this was only a stopgap, and the ultimate desire was for unaffiliated teams, and even clubs playing more 'traditional' rugby, to also get a look in at a later date. This, of course, never happened.

But the CRU shouldn't really be criticised for that. A few members of the upper class may have provided them with a $48 lump of metal, but it didn't really give them any right to start telling the football community how they should go about organising their affairs. The CRU were pretty blasé about the whole thing, and it would take a good two decades of championship matches before the Grey Cup trophy in its physical self acquired any particular symbolic value or would even be mentioned in most press reports.

In the case of the first Grey Cup match this is hardly surprising, as the cup wasn't even there to be presented. Just two weeks before the game, one of the trustees, HB McGivern, wrote to the Governor General to express his concern that "you might respectfully suggest to His Excellency that the Cup should be in the hands of the trustees as soon as possible."

As it happened, after paying for the pot, the Earl was given a one-year extension to his mandate, which following the death of Edward VII became two. Which is probably why the trophy was suddenly not such an urgent issue after all, and as a series of letters exchanged between the protagonists reveal, there was plenty of faffing about among the appointed trustees, but very little in the way of any silverware being handed to any footballers.

On went the letters, with various queries about what the inscription should say, then there was the problem that "the base sent out from the Old Country was quite inadequate, being too small. The cup did not look well on it, and it would have been quite impossible for the winning team to have affixed shields recording their names. The new base I have had attached to the cup so that they will not become readily separated and the cup will not be in danger of being knocked off and thus injured." Such attention to detail was most thoughtful, but sadly by the time the cup was ready, it was the spring of 1910, three months after Varsity had won the final.

The footballers themselves probably didn't care less where the trophy might or might not be. They had other concerns. Ottawa had beaten Hamilton in November to claim the Big Four's Interprovincial Championship, played in neutral Toronto, where the local *Globe*

CANADIAN CLUBS

reported that "no man who had red blood in his veins" had turned down the opportunity to travel from the capital with their team and "it was as big a football day as has been seen in Canada for many a year." Ottawa were the Big Four champions, and it was generally assumed that a game with intercollegiate winners Varsity would decide the national championship.

The Ottawa and Varsity match grabbed everyone's attention, along with disputes over the referee being a former Toronto student and players threatening to refuse to play over a problem that remains familiar today. Although there were over 10,000 tickets on sale for the match, a huge chunk of them been snapped up by executives. The players themselves had none to offer their friends. The game eventually went ahead among much pomp, with Varsity winning and each side making the princely sum of $3100 from the experience.

But in the Grey Cup trustees' eyes, that was not good enough, for they had decided to recognise the Ontario union, and for any team to be outright champions of Canada, they would have to beat the ORFU champions too. A week later, Varsity had to go back onto the field to take on the unfancied Parkdale Canoe Club. Just 3800 people, not even half the crowd for the Ottawa game, turned up to see what was expected to be a pointless mismatch for the sake of an inexistent trophy. Even so it still managed to generate $2616 in gate takings, and as it happened Parkdale proved stronger than most had expected. They were only 6-5 down at half time, and eventually lost by a respectable 26-6, especially as George Barber's 50 yard run for a try came in the very last second[5].

A year later, the scene was very different when the Varsity Blues defended their title with a 16-7 win over the Hamilton Tigers. The general public had taken to football like never before. Something in the region of 12,000 people, including about 5000 that had travelled down from Toronto, flocked to the Hamilton Cricket Grounds, where the authorities had installed 4475 seats in a hastily constructed grandstand. The touts were flogging tickets for over $100 a pop, and there were hundreds of disgruntled supporters left outside. It turned into a riot, and not even the Mounted Police could do anything to prevent hundreds from forcing their way in for free. The excitement was such that as the game drew to a close, it was held up for seven minutes as the crowd, eager to get a view of the action, started encroaching onto the pitch.

A year later, 1911, the Varsity Blues made it three in a row against local rivals Toronto Argonauts in their brand new Varsity Stadium – and stadiums don't come much more brand new that ones that are completed just 90 minutes before the game kicked off in front of 13,687 spectators, a new record for a Canadian football match.

---

[5] There is a certain controversy over whether Varsity really were the first ever champions. Among the shields on the base of the cup is one commemorating the Hamilton Tigers' win in 1908, a year before the cup existed. This has puzzled CFL historians ever since. However, Peter Cosentino provides evidence that at least as late as 1929 there was certainly no Hamilton 1908 shield on the cup, so it must have been added later by some meddling Tiger, though nobody is quite sure how or when

MIKE ROBERTS – THE SAME OLD GAME: CODIFICATION

There would be trouble in 1912 though. For the first time, Varsity failed to make the championship game, which would be between Hamilton Alerts and the Argonauts. Varsity, however, insisted that it was meant to be a 'challenge cup', and that the championship decider should, by definition, be played against the current holders. They duly refused to hand over the trophy. They stuck to their guns, too. That was the only time the Hamilton Alerts ever won the Grey Cup, but there was no Grey Cup for them to win, nor was there for the 1913 final, won by the team with which the Alerts would merge a year later, the Hamilton Tigers. In 1914, perhaps thankfully, Varsity did make the championship match, and lost to the Argonauts, which meant they were now happy and willing to finally part company with the cup[6].

American dad

Canada's first professional football coach, Frank Shaughnessy, was making a controversial name for himself at McGill. Originally from Illinois, he had captained Notre Dame before going on to make a name for himself as both a baseball and football coach and administrator. But as happens to the best of us, love for a woman dragged him away from it all and up to Ottawa in 1912. There was no football as he knew it in Canada, but nevertheless he contacted the Rough Riders and negotiated a $500 contract to coach them for the season. Striking a deal to pay an American bred on the American game to coach a Canadian team was an unprecedented move, but McGill got wind of it, thought it was neat idea, and offered to match Ottawa's bid and double it to $1000 if he won them the intercollegiate championship. Shaughnessy accepted, and did indeed take McGill to the championship and in doing so fostered even greater Americanisation of the Canadian game than ever[7].

The American observers of the 1909 exhibition match in New York had been concerned what might happen if their own minds had been let loose on the Canadian game, and Shaughnessy was going to be living proof. Unpopular enough for being an American and a pro, his art was not breaking the rules, but spotting loopholes in them, and especially cunning ones that allowed his players to use interference, which strictly speaking was illegal. It was said that "Coach Shaughnessy, the professional advisor, has evidently not studied the Canadian Code of rules, as all his line plays were based on the American system of off-side interference. Every kick and every run was protected in the most glaring manner[8]."

---

[6] That was not the only case of Varsity trophy-hogging. In 1911, they won the Yates Cup, the intercollegiate championship, for the fourth time in a row, and invented a rule that nobody was aware of, not even its creator Dr HB Yates, that a fourth consecutive win meant they were allowed to keep the trophy outright.
[7] There can be no doubting that Shaughnessy had a genius of a sporting mind, later he even coached Ottawa's ice hockey team, and even though he had absolutely no previous experience of the game, he led them to the Stanley Cup!
[8] As noted in an Ottawa newspaper of the time, quoted by Gordon Currie.

CANADIAN CLUBS

Another of the reasons for McGill's great season win was the way Shaughnessy spotted that if a team had a decent kicker, they were already half way there. And to fulfil that role he brought in somebody who had even less experience of Canadian football than he did, a lad called Eric Billington, who had only just arrived from Britain, but was a neat soccer player. He turned out to be one of the best kickers the game has ever seen, once scoring from 55 yards in the final minute of the game. Tragically, Billington would lose a leg in the First World War, and his football days were over.

Shaughnessy's many critics accused him of going against the spirit of the game with his win-at-all-costs mentality, but he was actually a staunch stickler for the rulebook. And where he gained countless brownie points at McGill was his insistence that all of his squad had to pass their exams, and he was even willing to squander chances of winning the championship if it posed any threat to his players' academic schedules. While Shaughnessy was around, there would be no fast-tracking of underachieving students through the college system just because they could pack a punch on the football field, and yet he still managed to ingrain the kind of competitiveness in his teams that was so often missing in Canada. McGill's tactics so changed the shape of the college game that the Intercollegiate Union ended up making interference legal in 1914, even though they wouldn't be able to use it when they played the city teams for the championship.

Ten years after the first Grey Cup and there was still no consensus, the *Toronto Globe* in 1919 pointing out for the umpteenth time that football should "establish playing rules embodying the best offered by the Unions. When the rules have been standardised, there will, it is expected, be better football." A year later the same paper was quoting a player called Bill Hoare saying "not more than fifty per cent of the players really know the rules under which they are playing."

In 1920, there was a surprisingly twist when the Big Four adopted the interference-endorsing Intercollegiate Rules. Why did the supposedly more powerful body cast aside its own methods to play like the students? Well, in a rare case of objectivity when it comes to rival sets of football rules in any code, Interprovincial President James Dixon claimed "it was not a case of following the leader, it was simply a case of recognising the best rules." But just when football looked to be heading towards uniformity in Canada, a totally new divide emerged. It was no longer Ontario versus Quebec ... it was Eastern Canada versus the new provinces of the West.

West side story

Up until the first Grey Cups, the major developments towards modern Canadian football had taken place in Ontario and Quebec. In the 1870s, Ontario was pretty much the last frontier of colonial Canada, but by the 1910s, the dominion's demographics had changed considerably. People were moving west to populate 'The Prairies', and they were taking football with them. Manitoba, the first province moving west from Ontario, was a relatively

375

MIKE ROBERTS – THE SAME OLD GAME: CODIFICATION

early starter with the Winnipeg Rugby Club forming in 1879, but it would not be until 1888 that the province formed its first union, and became an honorary member of the CRU in 1892.

In Saskatchewan, Regina North West Mounted Police faced Winnipeg FC twice in 1890, but the first club of note in the province was Regina Rugby Club, formed much later in 1910.

In Alberta, Calgary and Edmonton played each other at rugby as early as 1891 in the rather dramatic sounding Alberta Total-point Challenge Series. But compared to the East, the football community west of Ontario was an isolated, scattered affair that exerted very little influence, and normally based its game on English rugby, which is understandable enough when we note that the provinces didn't even become an official part of the Canadian Confederation until 1905. Teams based in Manitoba, Saskatchewan and Alberta[9] joined forces to form the Western Canadian Rugby Football Union in 1911 to try to coordinate their different efforts.

Importantly, the WCRFU turned its back on English rugby and readily adopted the CRU's rules when it set about organising its own championship. A trophy was donated by Winnipeg gentleman Hugo Ross[10] and would almost certainly have been won by the Regina Rough Riders had their game with the Winnipeg Rowing Club not been called off due to the bitterly cold weather. Much to Regina's fury, Winnipeg declared themselves the winners by default, and went on to play the Calgary Tigers for the cup, and got their just desserts by losing.

The *Toronto Globe* sent a correspondent, Norman Lambert, on a fact-finding mission to suss out the western football scene, and his report makes for fascinating reading. Lambert noted large numbers of influential names from eastern football that had "lost none of their cunning or enthusiasm through migrating to the west", and observed that "the west has made fairly good headway in nearly every other line of sport, to wit – hockey, lacrosse and rowing. It is not at all inconceivable that some day the west, if it gets the chance it is asking for, may duplicate in Rugby Football the triumphs that it has had recently in these other forms of athletics." He also noted that the prairie crops had been especially good that year, which had a major bearing on the local economy, and was likely to have the knock-on effect of the western teams having the money to travel east to play.

---

[9] From Manitoba, St John's College and the Winnipeg Rowing Club; from Saskatchewan, Moose Jaw, Regina and Saskatoon; and from Alberta, Edmonton, the Calgary Tigers and Calgary YMCA.

[10] Ross' own business ventures had been pretty disastrous, but he was lucky enough to be the son of a successful realtor, whose fortune he inherited. In 1912, a year after he had donated the cup, and following a vacation in the Aegean and Egypt, he fell ill and wrote home to say "we are on the last lap of doing the old lands and ready for Winnipeg and business." He booked an early ship home, but was so sick with dysentery that he spent most of the voyage suffering in his cabin. It was a fellow Canadian, Major Arthur Peuchen, who informed Ross that the ship had struck an iceberg and it would probably be a good idea if he got out of his pyjamas and went up on deck. "Is that all?" was Ross's reply. "It will take more than an iceberg to get me off this ship." That was the last anybody saw of Ross alive. He had perished on the SS Titanic.

CANADIAN CLUBS

Indeed, Calgary issued a challenge to the winners of the 1911 Grey Cup to determine the real Canadian champions. The pedantic CRU rejected the offer on the grounds that the WCRFU could not play until its membership had been accepted at an AGM. The westerners responded that that was fair enough, but would the CRU be so kind as to do that at their 1912 AGM? As it turned out they wouldn't, deciding that "in view of the many difficulties in playing final games owing to the great distances involved, the application of the WCRFU for admission to the CRU be not entertained." The WCRFU were made honorary members but nothing more.

One gets the impression that the Eastern clubs were keen to hold things tight at the fort, and didn't really fancy getting those weird folk out west involved. Despite its name, the Canadian Rugby Union was somewhat averse to unifying Canadian rugby. They would have felt their snobbery was nicely justified when the first major East-West series of games was played in 1913. The Hamilton Tigers embarked on a four-match tour of Western Canada, winning all of their games comfortably, against Winnipeg (26-1), Regina (26-4), Moose Jaw (25-1) and Calgary (19-2).

The Eastern indifference to the west would have a major bearing on how the Canadian game went from there. Had the east taken more interest in them, then the west would probably have played along with the CRU's ideals. Instead, held at arm's length by the east, the western clubs went looking elsewhere for ideas, opposition and talent. And that place was among the US cities and colleges, most of which were geographically much closer than Montreal or Toronto anyway.

Lambert had picked up on the fact that there seemed to be Americans involved in almost every team, and it was the Reverend Bob Pearson of Alberta who in particular set to work on revamping the CRU's rules, most of the ideas clearly being of American influence. Everything from coaches to T formations were imported from the south, and the western clubs would probably have ended up playing American football full stop had events of considerably greater proportions than any occurrence on a football field suddenly transformed the very idea of what Canada meant to its people. The Canadian nation, culture, economy and identity were all about to change. Only 3000 spectators turned up to watch the Hamilton Tigers beat Toronto RAA in the 1915 Grey Cup Final, the last championship for four years. People now had other concerns.

When Britain declared war on Germany, it was effectively speaking not only in its own name, but in that of its whole Empire, and that meant Canada too. There was little opposition to this, especially at first, with former Prime Minister Wilfrid Laurier proclaiming that "it is our duty to let Great Britain know and to let the friends and foes of Great Britain know that there is in Canada but one mind and one heart and that all Canadians are behind the Mother Country."

Canada willingly gave all it had to offer. Its army was but 3000 strong and its navy smaller still, but within two months some 32,000 volunteers had already answered the call. Such was

MIKE ROBERTS – THE SAME OLD GAME: CODIFICATION

the enthusiasm that 3500 Native Americans signed up, and thousands of blacks were left disappointed when they were told there was no place for them in a 'white man's war'. It may seem extraordinary to us now, but the average Canadian couldn't wait to board one of the ships crossing the Atlantic to help topple the Kaiser.

The promise had been that the war would be over in three months. It wasn't. Canada's contribution to the war effort was originally based on volunteerism alone, but as the conflict dragged on and the body count rose, more human resources were required, and Canada started conscripting, which was not a popular decision among many of the French speaking Quebecois.

The Canadians did themselves proud, with British Prime Minister David Lloyd George later acknowledging that "the Canadians played a part of such distinction that ... whenever the Germans found the Canadian Corps coming into the line they prepared for the worst." But such heroics came at a tragic human cost. Of Canada's population of seven million, one in twenty-eight was killed or wounded in World War I, including 24,029 casualties at the Battle of the Somme alone. Of the 619,636 young Canadians that fought in the war, 67,000 would never return. They should never be forgotten, and the war had united Canada like never before.

East meets West

Canadian football had been put on hold while the war took centre stage, and when the game returned in 1920, it was ready to settle its petty differences and do its bit to help build a nation that in a decade's time would be recognised with independence. Many of the arguments from before the war were still there to be settled, but there was a much stronger inclination towards compromise. A Rules Committee was assembled in April 1921 and drafted a series of amendments. The whole country was finally united on the 12-a-side issue, to which there had been a gradual shift since Burnside first recommended the idea no less than 20 years earlier. Teams could now pick from a squad of 18 and make as many substitutions as they liked, and at least five of the attacking team had to be on the line of scrimmage when the ball was put into play.

All told, the new rules were more similar to those already being used by the Western (and more American influenced) Union, and the WCRFU was finally taken seriously by the CRU. Hamilton travelled west for the second time, one of the main reasons being for the distant communities to get a better feel of their differing styles of play. The *Edmonton Bulletin* was gagging for it. "Four thousand people should be at that game on Thursday" it gushed. "Think of it, a game of rugby against the best team in Canada, that has travelled three thousand miles!"

The tour was a resounding success, and knowing that it was time for Canada to start behaving like a country in peacetime too, this time the western offer to play the eastern champion for the Grey Cup was taken up. Canadian football had more or less united as one,

378

and 1921 saw the Edmonton Eskimos become the west's first ever challenger. Neither the Eskimos' solution for the lack of sunlight in winter, practicing with a phosphorous painted ball, nor the fact they had beaten a touring English side despite being obliged to play by the Old Country's rugby rules (showing the two codes were still more or less mutually compatible even then) paid off. As had been feared or hoped, depending on how one looked at things, they were soundly crushed by the Toronto Argonauts 23-0.

It had been a fairly one-sided affair, but Edmonton had certainly not disgraced themselves. It was the occasion more than the result that really mattered, and a "triumph for uniformity of rules", in the words of the *Manitoba Free Press*. Over 9000 people turned out to watch the Eskimos being stunned by the beauty of the passing and handling skills of the Argonauts, who in turn were taken somewhat aback by the unfamiliar American-influenced tactics of the Eskimos, including the T-formation. But it was still early days for the Grey Cup. Lionel Conacher got 15 points including two touchdowns that day, but had left the ground by the final quarter. He had more important things to attend to. A game of ice hockey with the Toronto Aura Lee club[11].

Such batterings were something the western clubs were going to have to get used to. Edmonton returned east a year later, this time to face Queens, who took such a nonchalant attitude to the challenge that they hadn't even bothered training. For a while it looked like they might pay the price for such over-confidence, and they were 1-0 down at half time, but pulled out the stops for the second and cruised home to a 13-1 win.

In ten appearances at the Grey Cup from 1921 to 1934, the Western sides were defeated every time by a combined score of 236–29. On some occasions they didn't even attend. The 1925 incident was the most bizarre of all. The western champions were the Winnipeg Victorias, and the reason they didn't go was because they couldn't agree which train to take! It all came down to the rivalry between the Canadian Pacific and the Canadian National railroad companies, both of which had family connections to the club. Those connections both insisted that the Victorias travel on their own train, and it was impossible to reach a

---

[11] Named Canada's greatest sportsman of the first half of the century, Conacher was born in poverty to a family of ten children, but went on to make his fortune in a bizarrely wide range of different sports. Known as the 'Big Train', his football career, which included a spell of coaching at Rutgers, was a great one, but it was on the ice that he really made his name, going pro for the new Pittsburgh Pirates team in 1925 and scoring their very first goal, before going on to win Stanley Cups with both the Montreal Maroons and Chicago Blackhawks. Baseball? He was a pro for the Toronto Maple Leafs in 1926. Earlier in his career he had hit the winning home run for the Toronto semipro team in the championship final, then casually caught a taxi to play lacrosse with the Toronto Maitlands. They were 3-0 down when he arrived. No problem, Conacher banged in four to win the match, and later went pro in that sport too with the Montreal Maroons. He was also a professional wrestler, and never lost a fight in his career, and in 1921 even took to the boxing ring for four exhibition rounds against legendary world heavyweight Jack Dempsey, and didn't disgrace himself either. He later went into politics, and in 1954 took part in the annual softball match between the MPs and the press. While sprinting to third base, he collapsed and died of a heart attack. He has not been forgotten. The award for the Canadian sportsman of the year is named after the great Lionel Conacher.

compromise, even when the players themselves said they were quite happy to pay their own fares and for each individual to simply take whichever train he felt like. The Victorias eventually decided that the only solution was to call the whole trip off, and would later introduce the crazy club rule that no person connected to either railroad firm was allowed to be a member of the club!

The Regina Roughriders (known since 1948 by their modern day name of Saskatchewan Roughriders, which is more appealing to the province as a whole) were the strongest side in the west in that era, but on more than one occasion had to pass up on their Grey Cup berths due to lack of funds and players not being able to get the time off work.

It wasn't until 1934 that the CRU allowed the Grey Cup match itself to be held in the west. It was a nice concession, somewhat spoiled by their realisation later that year that neither the eastern colleges nor the Big Four had the slightest intention of travelling so far. The CRU backed down on its decision, and obliged Regina to do what they had always done, and make the long slog east to be beaten 20-12 by the Sarnia Imperials. The venue was Toronto, which would host 18 of the next 22 Grey Cups, and it would not be until 1955 that the west finally got the chance to host a final at Vancouver's Empire Stadium in front of what was then a record crowd of 39,417.

In 1935, a major eastern team was beaten by one from the west for the first time, albeit only in an exhibition game. Jubilant newspaper headlines heralded Winnipeg's 3-1 win over Grey Cup holder Sarnia on the back of week-long celebrations in the city in the build-up to the match. But there was better to come that year when the Winnipeg Pegs beat Hamilton to take the Grey Cup west for the first time[12]. The result of Winnipeg's win is forever honoured in the witty name by which that match went down in history: 'The War of 18-12'.

But the Winnipeg triumph hardly set off a flurry of Western victories. After adopting their modern name of the Blue Bombers they managed a couple more wins before Calgary Stampeders became the West's second champion club in 1948 – but it was in 1954 that the balance really started shifting. The Edmonton Eskimos win that year was the first of a three-in-a-row streak that marked the start of a glorious period for the West when they won eight out of eleven Grey Cups. Canadian football was no longer the dominion of the East.

Forward thinking

As the game went national, so did the rules. The Grey Cup grew as an institution, so did the CRU, and the feeling that this was Canada's national game. And this was evident in the way the Canadians dealt with what had been the final defining element of the American game, the forward pass. The play had been introduced to American football way back in 1906, but in the pre-war years, there was no major push to see it included in the Canadian game, which was still squabbling over other matters, such as downs, interference, snapbacks, the number

---

[12]At the time Winnipeg were considered western, although in modern times they play in the Eastern Conference

of players and even the size of the goals, issues that the Americans had largely resolved by the turn of the century.

McGill coach Frank Shaughnessy, as notorious as ever for importing footballing ideas from his native USA, was naturally quick to press for the inclusion of the forward pass. But his efforts got nowhere, partly because the rule changes introduced in 1921 were controversial enough for now, without completely throwing the cat among the proverbial pigeons and adding forward passing to the mix too. The Canadian game tried to hold out against this "baneful influence of the USA" until eventually succumbing to the pressure to allow it in 1929, or at least start to allow it.

The CRU declared in typically fence-sitting fashion that American-style forward passing was acceptable in schools matches and games played by the Western clubs and colleges (many of which were already defying the rulebook and allowing it anyway), and also, somewhat bizarrely, considering none of the major eastern clubs were using it, in the Grey Cup match! The CRU also kept a check on things by limiting its use to only within five yards behind the line of scrimmage, only outside the opponent's 25 yard line, and only six players were eligible receivers. To prevent throwing from completely taking over from kicking, there was to be no forward passing at all on the third and final down.

But despite its introduction, rather like in America, the forward pass didn't mean any overnight transformation in the way the game was played. Western champions Regina only made four forward passes all season on their way to the Grey Cup, and only one of those was completed. And one of the main reasons they beat Calgary to win the Western title was not because of their own forward passing, but because they intercepted one of Calgary's and followed that with a 55 yard run for a touchdown! Hamilton, despite never having faced or used the forward pass in any official game before, still comfortably brushed Regina aside, 14-3, to win the cup for the East.

The following year the CRU decided to back down on its previous decision and only allow the forward pass in the Grey Cup if it was used in all competing unions, and as the East still preferred to go without it, there was no forward passing in the Grey Cup match of 1930.

But following the typical period of procrastination and division, the forward pass was generally accepted across the board the year after, 1931, and officially became part of the Canadian game. But as usual, there were divided opinions, and the exact wording of when and how passes were allowed still differed between various unions.

Money matters

There had been good cause to oppose the inclusion of forward passing. For some time, Canadians had been wary of American footballers coming north to play, preventing locals from getting places on teams. While the forward pass had kept their games separate, and just as importantly had kept the duties of their respective quarterbacks separate, Canadian clubs had been fairly successfully discouraged from looking for recruits south of the border.

Now the forward pass was legal, the concern was that teams would use money to entice American players. Professionalism was not something Canada wanted. Ottawa were particularly troublesome, and hit the headlines over the case of New Yorker Abe Eliowitz in 1933. Having excelled with Michigan State, Eliowitz joined Ottawa, but there were claims in the press that he had previously signed a pro contract with the Brooklyn Dodgers (a football team of no relation to the baseball team now based in Los Angeles). The rumours were never proven and, in any case, he never played a single game for the Dodgers. But it was still enough not only for Ottawa to be potentially expelled from the union, but also any teams that dared to play against them. Lack of evidence against Eliowitz eventually led to the proposal being cast aside.

A year later there were further fun and games with Ottawa. This time the problem was Texan Bohn Hilliard, who was offered a place on their team, but had to be rejected because he had previously played professionally, not as a footballer, but as a baseball player. Hilliard willingly backed down, but recommended his friend Roy Berry as an alternative. Up went Berry, who did indeed prove to be an excellent acquisition, until it was discovered that he wasn't Berry at all! Hilliard had simply assumed his pal Berry's identity, clothing and all, and masqueraded his way into the Ottawa team. All the other Big Four teams had played Ottawa that season, as had Queens and others, and they were all suspended as a result – until common sense finally took over and the bans were lifted.

The doom-mongers that had predicted an American invasion were proven right. Jimmy Riddle, the brilliantly named chief of Montreal, now called the Amateur Athletic Association Winged Wheelers, sought advice from the great Shaughnessy and brought in an American, Warren Stevens, to lead their passing. His contributions had much to do with their undefeated run to the Grey Cup title, the first ever for a Quebec based team. By 1933, Steve O'Brien notes that Toronto already had two Americans, Montreal three and Ottawa five, and in September of that year, the *Toronto Globe* sarcastically commented that "believe it or not, football was once the most amateur of sports in the dominion, and the finger of suspicion was seldom pointed in its direction. Cupidity, the desire to win at any cost and the coming of the forward pass have, however, made a vast difference … Had the pass not been adopted and the United States players barred, the obnoxious conditions that exist at the present time would not have been possible."

It is Canadian instinct to blame the Americans for all their ills, but it was perhaps going a bit far to claim that the 'finger of suspicion' had rarely been pointed at the game before the 1930s. In fact, such was the suspicion regarding Montreal that there had been a joke going around for many years that the Montreal AAA was actually the 'AAAA', standing for the *Almost* Amateur Athletic Association. Way back in 1896, the CRU had issued a rule that "no player shall be eligible to play in any match under the auspices of the union who is not an amateur and in good standing." You just don't go issuing rules like that unless a 'finger of suspicion' had been wagging. It was also declared in 1896 that all CRU players had to be Canadian residents.

The CRU had embarrassed itself in 1898 when its own president, Edward Bayley, was suspended by the Amateur Athletic Association of Canada for "taking money for refereeing games in the ORFU." In Bayley's defence, the CRU's rules only referred to players, and not officials, and they responded by telling them to mind their own business, for "the action of AAA of C is an interference which the CRU considers beyond its jurisdiction."

The financing of the city clubs was an issue. For a start, teams were obliged to pay the union a fee for every game they played, and Hamilton and Kingston were among the teams that complained that they often found they were operating at a financial loss and couldn't even cover their basic expenses. The logical solution was to start operating in a more businesslike fashion by promoting matches commercially and seeking to cover costs by attracting as much paying support as possible. And to attract supporters, you need to attract players…

One may ask whether the $100 gold watches and diamond rings presented to Ottawa players after a good financial year in 1910 were really in the spirit of amateurism. That year saw people queuing overnight for tickets for the championship game, with grandstand tickets going for $5.00 a pop, which was a week's wages for most of the footballers providing the entertainment. Where was all that money going if it wasn't ending up in furtively selected pockets? In December that year, the *Toronto Globe* commented poignantly that "if the sport is to remain an amateur one it is impossible to be too strict … investigations will be instigated that will prove mightily embarrassing for some people … there is no doubt about it; several players in the Interprovincial are professional."

Coaches were already claiming wage packets, even though the practice was widely condemned as immoral. In fact, coaching *per se* was condemned as a form of cheating in the CRU's own laws in 1925, because "the game is to be played by the players using their own muscle and brains. If for example, an onlooker, having seen all the hands in a game of cards, undertook to tell one of the players what card to play, the other players would have cause to object."

Money in the game led to a shift in balance. Folk had always felt that the city game would never be able to compete with the students. Young working men were far too tied up with their jobs, and simply didn't have the time or facilities to train like students did. But in 1912, while the city teams were going from strength to strength, McGill University withdrew early from the championship "in view of the fact that our examinations are fast approaching, and we do not deem it advisable to prolong further an already lengthened football season." The colleges were miffed about the way affairs were going, and an announcement from McGill in 1914 stated that "the club wishes to have as little to do with the Interprovincial Union as possible. In addition to the difference in playing rules … the University players do not want to run the risk of being held up by the CAAU for playing against professionals."

MIKE ROBERTS – THE SAME OLD GAME: CODIFICATION

The college game actually held its own reasonably well over the years, and reached its epitome with the great Queen's side of the early 1920s. When they won their third consecutive Grey Cup in 1924, it came on the back of a 25-0 streak in competitive matches. But that was the last time they would ever get their hands on the trophy. In fact, it was the last time any college team would lift the Grey Cup. The Earl himself may have always underlined his intention that it was a <u>strictly amateur</u> competition, but his wishes would not be the CRU's command, and Canadian football was heading into the professional era.

In 1934, the Intercollegiate Union decided to withdraw definitively from the CRU to concentrate on games between themselves. They went about setting up their own college-specific playoffs and championships, although Queen's did battle on for another year, competing independently. However, when they were bumped off the park 44-4 by Hamilton, it was last we ever saw of a college team competing for the Grey Cup.

The forward pass did not create professionalism in Canadian football, but it was perhaps the turning point for what had until then been a thinly disguised truth to become so blatantly obvious that there was no point living in denial any more. As early as 1932, Canada had its first openly pro team, the Crosse and Blackwell Chefs, which played well-attended exhibition games, and was the brainchild of the great Lionel Conacher.

Keeping it Canadian

The Canadian version of British rugby had become a Canadian version of American football. And it was as streams of Americans came over the border that we really start hearing the first feathers ruffling about the idea of 'our' game and 'theirs'. Until then, most of the disputes and differences in Canadian rugby had been internal, Ontario versus Quebec, college versus city, east versus west. It had hardly been Canada's national game, when the nation was so divided between different factions. Paradoxically, the more Canada adopted American ideas, and the more similar the two games became, the more Canadian football started worrying about keeping its identity separate.

The *Hamilton Herald* wrote in 1931 how "the Canadian Rugby Football Union turned Yankee and accepted the forward pass" the same year former Varsity coach Harry Griffiths was telling the *Toronto Globe* that they had to "keep this a Canadian game. Let us call a moratorium on rule changes for ten years."

Other than their annual Grey Cup meeting, there was very little interaction between east and west throughout the year. The westerners did most of their interacting with the Americans to the south. As Winnipeg coach Joe Ryan said ahead of the 1935 Grey Cup "the west is moving rapidly with its football. We're swinging more to the American code and the customers are with us … we're just about fed up with efforts to keep pace with the authority flaunted over us by the Canadian Rugby Union." Playing their own rules all season, and then playing eastern rules for the Grey Cup, Ryan believed that unless a solution was found, the west would be left with no option but to go with the Americans instead.

CANADIAN CLUBS

As the westerners grew in influence both on and off the football field, it was increasingly more in the East's interests to keep them happy. In a telling comment in the *Winnipeg Free Press* in September 1934, it was noted with glee that "the new Canadian rugby rule book provides some slight reward for officials of Manitoba and other western unions who have battled for so long and so assiduously for progressive changes in the playing code. Every year sees the adoption by the moleskin moguls who comprise the CRU rules committee of some change that has been advocated by the Prairies two years earlier."

Winnipeg's Grey Cup victory in 1935, the first for a Western club, should have paved the way for a new pan-Canadian football culture, but instead the presence of no fewer than nine American players on their roster caused bitter resentment in the east, and the famous 'Resident Rule' was introduced the year after, which insisted that all players had to reside for one year in Canada before they could play their first game. Many Americans did just that, coming north and merely training with the team for a full 12 months before they were allowed to compete. It is a rule that has changed over the years, but that has never quite gone away. Even today teams are limited to 15 foreigners.

In 1936, the CRU effectively endorsed professionalism despite seeming on the outside to be outlawing it. It is unclear whether the glass was half full or half empty when it was declared that teams were restricted to a maximum of five imported Americans, for expressed another way that rule *allowed* five imported Americans. Despite the ruling, several Eastern clubs held out, and refused to sign any on principle, but it didn't last long. The 1947 Toronto Argonauts were the last entirely Canadian team to get their hands on the Grey Cup.

But with its tiny stadiums and tickets that were almost given away free, the game was operating as an amateur institution in a capitalist world, partly embracing professionalism and partly not, and as a result, reeking of unrealised potential. 1950 may have been the turning point. The Ontario government decided that whatever the three local football clubs said, the game was professional enough to be subjected to a 15% amusement tax. Athletic ethos may have implied that football should be amateur, but all the government was interested in was what money was changing hands, and as far as they were concerned, Canadian football was professional. And if the tax office was going to treat football like a professional institution, then the clubs were going to have to start acting like professional institutions too, and it was that same year of 1950 that the CRU finally succumbed to the worst fear of the Earl himself. The Grey Cup would now be contested by professional teams.

Money started flowing into the game – including the arrival of television revenue. CBC paid $7500 to the CRU for the rights to screen the Grey Cup in 1952. The next year, the CRU was asking for $20,500, and by 1957 the figure was up to a massive $125,000. And that was just for the championship game, which had become one of the media events of the Canadian year.

Real rugby

All of this was happening under governance of the Canadian Rugby Union, but the presence of the word 'rugby' in the organisation's name was really just a quirk of history. This was not rugby as any other nation knew it, nor as it continued to be played in the more isolated pockets of the country, especially among the armed forces, in the Maritimes to the east and in British Columbia on the Pacific Coast. But traditional rugby was a small scale, informal operation, with all of the serious competition dominated by the CRU.

After World War I there was a minor resurgence of 'real' rugby in Canada, no doubt influenced by the time spent by so many young men Europe – and the Canadian Services Team toured England, New Zealand, South Africa and Australia in 1919. During the interwar period, the game expanded very little, and any progress that had been made was interrupted by the outbreak of World War II, when the Canadian troops were once again called into battle.

Following the war, in 1945, the Rugby Union of Canada was founded to govern the sport in the country, but it was going to live a difficult, not to say confusing, coexistence alongside the Canadian Rugby Union, which was the ruling body of a completely different version of the same sport, in which tries had become touchdowns, wings had been re-baptised linemen, and players donned padding and helmets (made compulsory in 1949). This curious state of affairs continued for years, but the 1950s and 1960s saw a gradual correction of the misnomer, and the different Canadian associations started replacing the 'rugby' in their names with 'football'.

Rugby union is still a minority sport in Canada. British Columbia is the only province where it really gets a major following, yet the national team has continued to excel on the international stage. They have appeared at every edition of the Rugby World Cup since it was inaugurated in 1987, and in 1991 went as far as the quarter finals after beating Fiji and Romania in the groups, and were by no means played off the park by the All Blacks in the last eight, losing just 29-13. France, Wales and Scotland have all been beaten in recent years, while in the women's game, Canada are consistently among the top four or five nations in the world.

Canada v America

By the late 1950s, both the CFL in structure, and Canadian football as a game, would have been largely recognisable to the modern day fan. The pitch was 110 yards long, the game still had three downs as opposed to the American four, it still had twelve men, it still had its rouge and it still had its enormous 20-yard end zones. These peculiarities of the Canadian game remained.

If American football had ever expanded beyond the United States to become a truly international game, then Canada would almost certainly have had no option but to adopt the complete American rules too[13], for there is no place for regional variations in a sport with pretensions of internationalisation. But low-key amateur leagues and largely unsuccessful World Leagues and NFL Europes aside, American football has never really been much more than a uniquely American game, and Canadian football has never felt that, just because they neighbour America, they should also play football the same way. There was never really a need. In North America, whether American or Canadian, college or professional, sports leagues are invariably organised as closed shops, with a fixed number of teams. Promotion and relegation, continental club competitions, international tests and all the other delights that soccer and rugby clubs can enjoy are foreign concepts. Those sports require international rules and federations; North American football does not.

Both countries had adopted rules from each other, and players had drifted across the border in both directions, but there was very little direct interaction between the two until 1950 saw the dawn of a curious era of preseason games between American and Canadian teams.

The first was in August 1950, reported by the *New York Times* thus: "The New York Giants of the National Football League overcame confusion and Canadian rugby rules today to defeat the Ottawa Rough Riders, 27 to 6. The first half of the exhibition game was played under Canadian rules and the second half under American standards. An estimated 15,000 fans witnessed the novel game at Lansdowne Park."

The same two sides played a rematch a year later, the Giants again winning comfortably, but the experiment would not be repeated until 1959, when the Toronto Argonauts inaugurated their CNE ground with a game against the Chicago Cardinals. This time, rather than play each half to different rules, a set of composite rules was devised, and once again the Americans won. Pittsburgh provided the opposition a year later in a game televised on an experimental network for a $2.00 fee, the first football match in any code to be shown on pay per view. Another lop-sided affair in favour of the American visitors failed to live up the hype, the *Toronto Star* using the words 'sad', 'embarrassing' and 'humiliating' in a write-up that questioned the value of a game that achieved little more than a potential season-threatening injury to the Argonaut's Tobin Rote (which thankfully turned out to be less serious than feared).

1961 saw a veritable flurry as Toronto, Montreal and Hamilton faced the St Louis Cardinals, Chicago Bears and Buffalo Bills within the space of a week, with the Tiger-Cats doing Canada proud by actually winning, although it must be pointed out that at the time, the Bills were in the AFL, the rival and arguably inferior league that had yet to join forces with the more powerful NFL.

These games all went back to the original idea of playing one half by one set of rules and the second by the other. But although it may have seemed at the time that they were destined to become a regular affair, and may even have led to an eventual merger of the two sports, it

---

[13] As indeed they had to when participating in the IFAF World Championship for the first time in 2011 (for which professionals and North American college players are ineligible).

was a false dawn, not helped by the animosity between teams north and south of the border poaching each other's players. America had its own problems to sort out with the rivalry between the NFL and the rising AFL, while Canada also had administrative issues to clear up, and those contests between the two nations are now mere historical anecdotes.

But both the CFL and the NFL went on eyeing each other's markets. Curiously though, despite there always being a fear of American football culture dwarfing the Canadian game, with many Canadians ignoring the CFL and following the NFL instead, the only major attempt to encroach on the other's territory was a Canadian one.

It all started with the World League of American Football, which was first played in 1991, heralded as the start of American football's expansion beyond its borders[14], but which was discontinued after two years. But one of the American WLAF franchises, Sacramento Surge, wanted more, and owner Fred Anderson managed to get his side into the CFL of all things, playing to the Canadian rules and answering to the name of the Gold Miners. It was considered the way forward, and there was even mention of the ultimate objective of a 20-strong CFL, with ten teams in each country. In 1994, three more American franchises were added: the Las Vegas Posse, the Baltimore Colts (later Baltimore Stallions after a legal battle with the Indianapolis Colts), and the Shreveport Pirates, who were in a roundabout kind of fashion the remnants of the Ottawa Rough Riders, who folded in 1994 as a result of dwindling attendances.

It was a confusing time. The American teams were boosted by the advantage of being able to field as many American players as they liked, but were not helped by the absence of any TV contract, and worse still, the general disinterest among the American public, especially once the college season began. Las Vegas lasted just a year, playing to crowds of less than 3000, but Baltimore was an altogether different story. They reached the Grey Cup Final at the first time of asking, and in 1995 became the only non-Canadian team to actually bring the coveted trophy south.

The Birmingham Barracudas and Memphis Mad Dogs were added in 1995, while the Gold Miners moved to become the San Antonio Texans. However, all but two of the new teams

---

[14] Six newly created American franchises played in a tournament along with the London Monarchs, Barcelona Dragons and Frankfurt Galaxy from Europe and the Montreal Machine of Canada. It was met with mild enthusiasm, but Europeans were not fooled by being fed second-string teams in an artificial tournament played by teams almost entirely made up of imported Americans, and not local talent. The WLAF was discontinued after just two seasons and replaced with NFL Europe, which survived until 2007, when it had six teams, five of which were in Germany, the only country that really took it seriously. There were 48,125 in the crowd to see the Hamburg Sea Devils beat Frankfurt Galaxy in the final edition of the World Bowl, but the championship as a whole was losing the NFL a reported $30 million a year. What non-Americans really wanted was the NFL itself, and the NFL has started giving it to them. The first regular season NFL game outside of America saw Arizona defeat San Francisco in Mexico City in 2005 before the highest ever NFL attendance of 103,467, while it is now a regular practice for NFL regular season games to be played at Wembley Stadium in London, and possibly even a Super Bowl in the not-so-distant future.

folded, some before the Grey Cup had even been played, and when the Stallions learned that Baltimore had been selected as the home for the new NFL franchise that would become the Ravens, they relocated to Montreal to become the third incarnation of the Alouettes. The San Antonio Texans were left on their own as the only American side in the CFL, and voluntarily put themselves to the sword.

The CFL USA venture proved an abject failure, and after probably doing more damage than good to the image of the Canadian game, the CFL was once again confined to only Canadian teams. And so it has stayed ever since, with the mid-nineties being viewed now as an embarrassing period when the CFL was in danger of throwing its entire identity out of the window in pursuit of American dollars.

Considering the CFL's attempt to expand into the USA, there is a certain aura of hypocrisy surrounding the fears that are so commonly voiced in Canada of a potential expansion of the NFL into Canada. The three other 'Big Four' professional leagues in North America all have Canadian representation, but baseball, basketball and ice hockey are not treading on any Canadian toes.

Back in 1969, Gordon Currie wrote that the Canadian game had to be "open, fast and as exciting as possible. If the game pales in comparison to the US style of football, then the fans will switch their allegiance and before long the US will be awarding their franchises to Canadian cities. This is a real danger." Four decades later, and a careful eye is being kept on events as the NFL begins its first ever venture to host games in Canada. The Buffalo Bills have always enjoyed a huge fan base just over the border in Ontario – and from 2008, they have played one home game a season in Toronto, always once the CFL season is over. It's a small but important beginning. There is no doubt that cities like Toronto, Montreal and Vancouver offer massive potential for hosting full-on NFL teams, but why set up new franchises when the stadiums, fans and infrastructure are already there? It really is not that inconceivable to see a team like the Montreal Alouettes taking up the lucrative offer of switching codes and joining the NFL.

And once that happens, would it be the death knell of CFL? There is no doubt that plenty of Canadians would welcome the NFL with open arms, but the CFL also has its fervent supporters. The popularity of soccer and rugby in Ireland has done nothing curb the enthusiasm for Gaelic sports, and one hopes the same would be true of Canada, where the people are fortunate that as well as the NFL, they can also enjoy something different, and that is so much closer to home.

Canadian football has had a turbulent history – sometimes its very existence has been in doubt, it has been mismanaged, regional differences hindered its development as a national game, teams have come, teams have gone, and yet it is still there. And although the players may not be as good as they are in the NFL, those who argue that that CFL is the superior game have a very valid argument indeed.

MIKE ROBERTS – THE SAME OLD GAME: CODIFICATION

We'll leave the last word on Canadian football to Steve O'Brien. "For a country so dominated by cultural imports, including professional sports, from the United States, it becomes increasingly harder for Canadians to distinguish what is uniquely their own and to appreciate its own merits … CFL critics attack fans who resist making the game more American. Yet those who clamour for such changes ignore the uniqueness of the CFL game, its rich history and what it means to many Canadians. It is this very diversity which should be celebrated, treasured and maintained. Those who advocate that the CFL eliminate the pesky rouge, go to four downs or to, in many ways, Americanize the game, are sadly deluded. There is no point in replacing Canadian football, with all its eccentricities, simply to have a carbon-copy of American football."

17 THE GAME IS UP
Conclusions

We ended Volume One by examining the lay of the land as British football headed towards standardisation in the mid 19th century. It was becoming normal practice for all sports to be given a more structured form as improved communication and transport transformed a patchwork of local traditions into standard rulebooks that could be used for nationwide competitions. But football was already such a widespread and varied phenomenon that finding a compromise was not going to be easy. The middle class newspapers at the time concentrated more on the different games played at the public schools and universities, but these were only the tip of the iceberg, with countless other types of football being played in towns and villages all over the islands. Cambridge University and Sheffield had already settled rules by the late 1850s, but these were still highly localised, and with so many contrasting views, particularly regarding the amount of violence and use of the hands that should be permitted, there would be no attempt to create a national governing body until the Football Association was founded in 1863, and even so with far less initial success than we are sometimes led to believe.

Convincing the whole of Britain, with so much regional and classist bickering going on, would take time. In the meantime, in an isolated but thriving colony on the other side of the world, the Melbourne Football Club wrote its rules in 1859, which inspired a more established football structure than anything England had created thus far. Before long the whole of Victoria was playing the same game, and by the time the FA had devised its own code, what would eventually be called Australian football was too widely recognized in Victoria for anybody to even consider the idea of replacing it with anything else. Those rules were written before the split between soccer and rugby in Britain, where many of the fathers of Australian football were born or educated, but the Victorians came to similar conclusions to those the Football Association would come to four years later and ignored most of the defining features of rugby to produce a game that resembled the kind of soccer played in the early 1860s. Tough tackling, catching of the ball to claim a mark and crossbar-less goals were all features of soccer that were later changed, but which have remained to this day in the AFL.

So, Victoria had already settled on a unified code when a small gathering of clubs formed the FA to try to the same in London, with an eye to convincing the rest of the country. The original intention was to create a simple, composite code that embraced the principles of all forms of football, rugby very much included. Originally, and despite opposition, they settled for a game that would allow hacking and running with the ball. But when a copy of the Cambridge University laws came into their hands, the members changed their minds. The FA would endorse a kicking game with strong limitations on violence. When Blackheath withdrew their membership as a result, this was hugely symbolic of the way ahead for football. The clubs that endorsed a tough-tackling game in which players could run with the ball were not willing to compromise and would be going their separate way – the rugby way.

2013 has been cited as the year of soccer's 150th anniversary. If there is any date when modern soccer was 'born', then we would probably have to concede that 1863 is indeed the right one. But the road was not a smooth one. Particularly in its first three years, the FA achieved almost nothing, and the handful of members it did have rarely took much notice of its laws. The despondent FA was on the verge of giving up its mission altogether, when new inspiration came in the form of Sheffield FC, who had successfully overseen the development of a game that had been largely standardised in South Yorkshire and beyond, and which shared many of the characteristics of the FA's game. The Sheffielders were veritable football pioneers, and saw in the FA the chance to establish all-important connections in London. It was in 1866 and under Sheffield's influence that the FA made wholesale changes to its game, particularly the elimination of 'tries at goal' and the 'fair catch', which not only made the game unmistakably soccer as we know today, but which also marked the end of the FA's failed attempt to sell its ideas to the rugby clubs. All hope that Britain would have a single football code were abandoned.

Uniting Sheffield and London was the first step towards uniting the nation, but most clubs still felt no particular need to use the FA's rules, and even when they did they adapted them as they fancied, meaning that British football was more of a continuum from pure soccer at one extreme to pure rugby at the other, with no clear dividing line between both. It was not until 1871 and the launch of the FA Cup that this started changing. In order to take part, teams were going to have to fully adhere to the Association's rules, and as the FA Cup and the many other competitions grew in importance, the FA found itself in a stronger position to impose its resolutions.

Clubs that preferred a more physical ball carrying game had carried on regardless up until this point, but a lack of unified criteria, public concerns about violence in such games and the growing might of soccer as a safer alternative encouraged its proponents to pull together in similar fashion and form their own association to promote their own interests. They took the Rugby School game as their basis, and called themselves the Rugby Football Union.

Rugby shunned competitive matches and was also strongly averse to the professionalism that the FA often turned a blind eye to and eventually sanctioned. This led to rugby becoming the game for the gentleman amateur, and without the attraction of cup competition and with its clubs doing next to nothing to commercially promote their sport, soccer was relatively unchallenged in its quest to become a phenomenon for the masses.

But not everybody in the rugby community was happy with the *status quo*. Clubs in Yorkshire and Lancashire did want to turn commercial and compete with soccer, and did want to offer financial compensation to working class players that were otherwise unable to play. The RFU stood its ground, and when the Northern Union was formed in 1895, and endorsed broken time payments, the RFU severed all relations with the rebel body. The NU went against the RFU's principles and set up leagues, hence the name 'rugby league', allowed its clubs to operate as businesses, and would ultimately allow outright professionalism. As it was competing for spectators with the soccer clubs, rugby league felt the need to open up the tedious scrummage-based union game, and introduced changes to make it game more visually appealing. Paradoxically, many of these changes would later be adopted by the RFU, although by 1995, when the RFU finally allowed professionalism too, the two codes had moved so far apart that they were no longer compatible. The schism had caused wounds so deep that many have yet to be healed.

Strangely, though soccer was exported to almost every corner of the world and is now the biggest and most international team sport of all, in the Anglosphere, rugby was a more successful export.

Canada welcomed the game, but almost immediately started playing around with the rules. This was not done for nationalistic purposes, but merely because rugby's 59 rules were so complex and ambiguously written that teams struggled to make full sense of them, and had few qualms about making whatever amendments they saw fit. International tests were unthinkable at the time, and the Canadians were more concerned with local issues and creating a game that Ontarians and Quebecois, and also students and city teams, and later teams from the east and west, were happy to play together. Due to so many conflicting interests, it took over half a century for Canada to establish rugby unity, and during that time, different factions made different changes to the rules in varying measures. By the time the Canadian Rugby Union had managed to get all of its members playing by the same rules, the game was very far removed from the version that was being played back in Britain, and eventually shed its 'rugby' mantle altogether. But the most important of the changes made to Canadian rugby were not home-bred ideas. They had crept north from America.

Rather like she is as a nation, Canada was tied to being a British dominion on the one hand, and the USA's neighbour on the other. Ultimately, it was American rather than British developments in the rugby game that would prevail in Canada, to the extent that nowadays only the uninformed observer would not be able to spot any difference at all between the Canadian and American versions.

Yet if it had not been for the presence of British rugby in Canada, American football may never have come into being. Down in the United States, football had a disjointed history and among its hotchpotch of isolated colonies and immigrants from different nations it was surprisingly undeveloped until well into the 19th century. Different football cultures had emerged among the colleges and the civilian populations, which were generally imported from Britain but without any particularly solid foundation. The Boston Game of the early 1860s and the 'first college fixture' played by Rutgers and Princeton in 1869 were fine examples of more structured football emerging in America, but although these games shared much in common with British soccer, they also revealed a predilection among American

MIKE ROBERTS – THE SAME OLD GAME: CODIFICATION

students for a much more physical game. When the Intercollegiate Football Association was formed in 1873, Harvard's lack of interest for that very reason would be important.

We shall never know what would have eventually become of American 'soccer'. Maybe it would have sided with or even influenced the FA, or maybe the USA would have invented a version all of its own, but a landmark game between Harvard and McGill in 1874 changed everything. McGill was a Canadian college, and they played rugby, and Harvard fell in love with it. Soon the other major colleges were persuaded to switch to the carrying code too, and by 1876 the IFA had tossed its FA influenced rulebook aside and instead adopted the rules of the Rugby Football Union in London.

American football histories often skirt around the fact that the original laws for American football were not a national invention but were, word for word, the same as those used by the RFU. But rugby in that form didn't last long in the USA. In fact, changes in the scoring system were introduced from the outset.

Rugby arrived in the USA just three years after the RFU had drafted its first rules, when it was still a highly congested game that amounted to little more than one continuous scrum of players attempting to kick the ball forwards. It was mainly in their respective ways of dealing with this problem that the two codes went their separate ways. The RFU opened up the game by allowing the ball to be 'heeled out', even though it was a blatant violation of the offside rule, while the Americans replaced the scrummage with the snap in 1880, which removed the random battle for contention and meant the side in possession got to start each play unchallenged. But this method was abused by teams that held onto possession indefinitely, so two years later the downs system was introduced to encourage teams to gain a certain number of yards in a certain number of plays. The gridiron was born. American football continued to be a ferociously violent game, to the extent that it was almost prohibited entirely in 1905, and part of the plans to clean its act was the introduction of the forward pass in 1906. Even so, the violence continued, and ultimately it was the development of helmets and padding, rather than rule changes, that made American football safer. But despite these major changes in rugby's basic principles, it is unfair to accuse the Americans of bastardising the game, for the RFU also made wholesale changes, and the gradual shift of emphasis from kicking balls over the posts to scoring by touchdowns was actually led by American football, and rugby followed.

Most members of the Gaelic football community like to take their game's ancient roots for granted. But although there are records of pre-19th century forms of football being played in Ireland, there does not seem to be any real link between those romantically idealistic allusions to the country's mythological past and the form that was somewhat artificially created by the GAA shortly after its foundation in 1884. Gaelic football was introduced as a reaction to 'cultural imperialism', although the structure of the game was clearly influenced by British rulebooks, and imitated most of its achievements of the previous two decades. In fact, it seems that the people that wrote the first rules for Gaelic football based their work on what they remembered of soccer as it was played in the 1860s, when it was originally codified by the FA as a primarily kicking game with certain concessions to rugby. The inherently 'Irish' traditions like soloing and the H shaped goal were not introduced until the 20th century, as the game developed in its own direction.

This might explain any similarities between the Irish and Australian games, rather than the implausible idea that the Gaelic rules could have influenced Australian football. Tougher tackling and a mixture of kicking and holding the ball were also elements of the Australian game when it was codified, when its creators openly declared that English games were the source of their ideas. It would be another three and a half decades before the GAA wrote laws for the Irish game, laws that were originally almost identical to soccer, and which only later introduced changes that may even have been inspired by the Australian game. It is certainly unlikely to have been the other way round.

We have also examined how, as each of the different codes developed, rivalries were produced between them, and many the arguments are still debated today. From the outset, soccer took deliberate steps to eliminate the more physical aspects of football, and is still looked upon with disdain by players and followers of the other, manlier codes. But rugby's refusal to endorse professionalism and hence its closer association with the gentleman amateurs and supposedly 'Corinthian' attitudes, also made the divide between it and soccer a class issue. That image persists today, although as soccer moved into its 'prawn sandwich' era and rugby finally endorsed professionalism, that division is no longer quite as defined.

The rift between rugby union and rugby league has also started to heal now that the former also allows professionals. After decades of ostracism, there is now plenty of cross-code cooperation, and clubs of both codes would surely now be playing each other again, and rugby would be so much healthier for it, were it not for what, at least for the time being, are impossibility incompatible rules.

We have looked at the adversity among the GAA community to the presence of soccer and rugby in Ireland, and also the suspicious attitude of the British authorities towards the 'rebel' codes. Recent years have seen massive improvements in that relationship too, with rugby, soccer and even Queen Elizabeth II appearing at Croke Park. Irish nationalism is still the essence of why the GAA came to exist in the first place and these connotations are unlikely to ever go away, but the attitudes are no longer anything like as extreme as they were until only very recently.

Australia's footballing make-up has always been a complex issue. The Victorians invented their own rules, and these were adopted elsewhere in the country, but not so Queensland or New South Wales, which became rugby country. Recent decades have seen both codes expand into the other's territory, and although there might have been tension at first, it is curious how the east has embraced AFL and the west has embraced NRL to the extent that the east-west football divide in Australia is rapidly becoming a thing of the past.

At the same time, soccer has continued to become more of a mainstream sport in Australasia, just as it has in North America, where despite always having been surprisingly widespread, the FA's game has often been the focus of derision. But as soccer has become more accepted in both continents, neither of which are the also-rans on the international stage that they used to be, and have also established the kind of soccer leagues that the followers of the game in those countries deserve.

There is little hope of soccer toppling the gridiron as king in the USA, and at the same time, the American game is unlikely to become a major phenomenon outside of its native country – other than in Canada. There, the CFL is as strong as ever, but there is still the fear that NFL expansion could put the Canadian game in danger. However, although it would be all too easy for the NFL to follow baseball and basketball's lead and introduce Canadian franchises, this has yet to happen, and for the sake of the Canadian game, let's hope things stay that way.

Perhaps surprisingly in these times of aggressive globalisation and survival-of-the-fittest market forces, more than ever, rival football codes are starting to work with rather than against each other, and particularly thanks to the force of television, rather than confining themselves to one code, fans and players of one code are taking increasingly more interest in the others. Even clubs now share stadiums and other facilities, schedules are adjusted to avoid matches in one code coinciding with the other, and schools around the world are now teaching games that they would never have done half a century ago.

And so they should. It is for many different reasons that instead of just one form of football, we have so many different codes. Each of them has plenty to be proud of, and each of them should be nurtured and enjoyed. No matter whether there are three downs or four, whether it's a mark or a handball, whether it's play-the-ball, a scrum or a scrimmage, a bounce-up or a throw-up, each of these games deserves to be mutually respected.

As we saw in the first volume, football was never created at any single time or in any particular place, but evolved along with the species that created it. And much as there are many theories for why our ancestors did that, there are none more convincing than the one that says that it was because we love to exercise, we love to play, and we love to compete.

But, for better or worse, it is hard to deny that it was in Great Britain that the roots were sown for all the modern codes of football. Australian settlers took those ideas with them and developed their own game. Canadians and Americans took rugby and shaped them into modern codes. And even Ireland's game ultimately took a British idea and developed an Irish take on it. We're all enjoying the same old game.

Rewriting the football books to deny the role of 19th century Britons in the origins of any of our football codes is an injustice to the now too often forgotten fathers who did so much to turn an old rustic pastime into a game that has played such a huge role in shaping one of the many things that modern society can actually feel proud of. That shape may have been manipulated elsewhere, no doubt in many minds for the better of the game. But criticise us for what you will, at least Britain did give something good to the world.

APENDIXES

Appendix Six: Laws of the Football Association (1863)

1. The maximum length of the ground shall be 200 yards, the maximum breadth shall be 100 yards, the length and breadth shall be marked off with flags; and the goal shall be defined by two upright posts, eight yards apart, without any tape or bar across them.

2. A toss for goals shall take place, and the game shall be commenced by a place kick from the centre of the ground by the side losing the toss for goals; the other side shall not approach within 10 yards of the ball until it is kicked off.

3. After a goal is won, the losing side shall be entitled to kick off, and the two sides shall change goals after each goal is won.

4. A goal shall be won when the ball passes between the goal-posts or over the space between the goal-posts (at whatever height), not being thrown, knocked on, or carried.

5. When the ball is in touch, the first player who touches it shall throw it from the point on the boundary line where it left the ground in a direction at right angles with the boundary line, and the ball shall not be in play until it has touched the ground.

6. When a player has kicked the ball, any one of the same side who is nearer to the opponent's goal line is out of play, and may not touch the ball himself, nor in any way whatever prevent any other player from doing so, until he is in play; but no player is out of play when the ball is kicked off from behind the goal line.

7. In case the ball goes behind the goal line, if a player on the side to whom the goal belongs first touches the ball, one of his side shall he entitled to a free kick from the goal line at the point opposite the place where the ball shall be touched. If a player of the opposite side first touches the ball, one of his side shall be entitled to a free kick at the goal only from a point 15 yards outside the goal line, opposite the place where the ball is touched, the opposing side standing within their goal line until he has had his kick.

8. If a player makes a fair catch, he shall be entitled to a free kick, providing he claims it by making a mark with his heel at once; and in order to take such kick he may go back as far as he pleases, and no player on the opposite side shall advance beyond his mark until he has kicked.

9. No player shall run with the ball.

10. Neither tripping nor hacking shall be allowed, and no player shall use his hands to hold or push his adversary.

11. A player shall not be allowed to throw the ball or pass it to another with his hands.

12. No player shall be allowed to take the ball from the ground with his hands under any pretence whatever while it is in play.

MIKE ROBERTS – THE SAME OLD GAME: CODIFICATION

13. No player shall be allowed to wear projecting nails, iron plates, or gutta-percha[1] on the soles or heels of his boots.

Appendix Seven: Laws of the Rugby Football Union (1871)

1. A drop kick or drop is made by letting the ball fall from the hands and kicking it at the very instant it rises.

2. A place kick or place is made by kicking the ball after it has been placed in a nick made in the ground for the purpose of keeping it at rest.

3. A punt is made by letting the ball fall from the hands and kicking it before it touches the ground.

4. Each goal shall be composed of two upright posts exceeding 11 foot in height from the ground and placed 18 ft 6 inches apart with a cross bar 10 feet from the ground.

5. A goal can only be obtained by kicking the ball from the Field of Play direct (i.e. without touching the dress or person of any player of either side;) over the Cross bar of the opponents' goal whether it touch such Crossbar or posts or not: but if the ball goes directly over either of the goal posts it is called a poster and is not a goal.

6. A goal may be obtained from any kind of kick except a punt.

7. A match shall be decided only by a majority of goals.

8. The ball is dead when it rests absolutely motionless on the ground.

9. A touch down is when a player putting his hand upon the ball on the ground in touch or in goal stops it so that it remains dead or fairly.

10. A tackle is when the holder of the ball is held by one or more players of the opposite side.

11. A scrummage takes place when the holder of the ball being in the field of play puts it down on the ground in front of himself and all who have closed round on their respective sides endeavour to push their opponents back and by kicking the ball to drive it in the direction of the opposite goal line.

12. A player may take up the ball whenever it is rolling or bounding except in a scrummage.

13. It is not lawful to take up the Ball when dead (except in order to bring it out after it has been touched down in touch or in goal) for any purpose whatever - whenever the ball shall have been so unlawfully taken up it shall at once be brought back to where it was so taken up and there put down.

14. In a scrummage it is not lawful to touch the Ball with the hand under any circumstances whatever.

---

[1] Inelastic natural latex, produced from the resin of the *Isonandra Gutta* tree of Malaya. Nowadays its uses include providing the filling for golf balls and fillings for teeth. It was used on football boots as a sneaky way of getting extra grip.

APPENDIXES

15. It is lawful for any player who has the ball to run with it, and if he does so it is called a run - if a player runs with the ball until he gets behind his opponents goal line and there touches it down, it is called a run in.

16. It is lawful to run in anywhere across the goal line.

17. The goal line is in goal and the touch-line is in touch.

18. In the event of any player holding or running with the ball being tackled and the ball being fairly held he must at once cry down and there put it down.

19. A maul in goal is when the holder of the Ball is tackled inside goal line or being tackled immediately outside is carried or pushed across it and he or the opposite side or both endeavour to touch the ball down. In all cases the ball when so touched down shall belong to the players of the side who first had possession just before the maul commenced unless the opposite side have gained entire possession of it.

20. In case of a maul in-goal those players only who are touching the ball with their hands when it crosses the goal line may continue in the maul in-goal and when a player has once released his hold of the Ball after it is inside the goal line he may not again join in the maul and if he attempts to do so may be dragged out by the opposite side - But if a player when running in is tackled inside the goal line then only the player who first tackled him or if two or more tackle him simultaneously they only may join in the maul.

21. Touch in-goal (see plan) Immediately the Ball whether in the hands of a player (except for the purpose of punt out see Rule 29) or not goes into touch in-goal it is at once dead and out of the game and is brought out as provided by Rules 41 and 42.

22. Every player is on side but is put off side if he enters a scrummage from his opponents' side or being in a scrummage gets in front of the Ball, or when the ball has been kicked, touched or is being run with by any of his own side behind him (i.e. between himself and his own goal line).

23. Every player when offside is out of the game and shall not touch the ball in any case whatever, either in or out of touch or goal, or in any way interrupt or obstruct any player, until he is again on side.

24. A player being offside is put on side when the ball has been run five yards with or kicked by or has touched the dress or person of any player of the opposite side or when one of his own side has run in front of him.

25. When a player has the Ball none of his opponents who at the time are offside may commence or attempt to run, tackle or otherwise interrupt such player until he has run five yards.

26. Throwing back. It is lawful for any player who has the Ball to throw it back towards his own goal, or to pass it back to any player of his own side who is at the time behind him in accordance with the rules of on side.

27. Knocking on i.e. deliberately hitting the ball with the hand and Throwing Forward i.e. throwing the ball in the direction of the opponents' goal line are not lawful, As provided by

MIKE ROBERTS – THE SAME OLD GAME: CODIFICATION

the next rule the captain of the opposite side may require it to be brought back to the spot whence it was so knocked or thrown forward and there put down.

28. A Fair Catch is a catch made direct from a kick or a throw forward or Knock-on by one of the opponents' side, or from a punt out or a punt on (see Rules 29 and 30) provided the catcher makes a mark with his heel at the spot where he has made the catch and no other of his own side touch the ball (See Rules 43 & 44).

29. A punt out is a punt made after a touchdown by a player from behind his opponents goal line and from touch in-goal if necessary towards his own side who must stand outside the goal line and endeavour to make a fair catch or to get the ball and run in or drop a goal. See 49 and 51.

30. A punt on is a punt made in a manner similar to a punt out and from touch if necessary by player who has made a fair catch from a punt out or another punt on.

31. Touch (see plan) If the ball goes into touch the first player on his side who touches it down must bring it to the spot where it crossed the touchline, or if a player when running with the ball cross or put any part of either foot across the touch-line, he must return with the ball to the spot where the line the was so crossed, and from thence return it into the field of play as provided by the following.

32. He must then himself or by one of his own side, either (i) bound it out in the field of play and then run with it, kick it, or throw it back to his own side or (ii) throw it out at right angles to the touchline or (iii) walk out with it at right angles to the touchline any distance not less than five or more than 15 yards and there put it down first declaring how far he intends to walk out.

33. If two or more players holding the ball are pushed into touch the ball shall belong in touch to the player who first had hold of it when in the field of play and has not yet released his hold of it.

34. If the ball when thrown out of touch be not thrown out at right angles to the touchline the captain of either side may at once claim to have it thrown out again.

35. A catch made when the ball is thrown out of touch is not a fair catch.

36. Kick-off is a place kick from the centre of the field of play and cannot count as a goal. The opposite side must stand at least 10 yards in front of the ball until it has been kicked.

37. The ball shall be kicked off (i) at the commencement of the game (ii) after a goal has been obtained.

38. The sides shall change goals as often as and whenever a goal is obtained unless it has been otherwise agreed by the captains before the commencement of the match.

39. The captains of the respective sides shall toss up before the commencement of the match, the winner of the toss shall have the option of goals or the kick-off.

40. Whenever a Goal shall have been obtained the side that has lost the goal shall then kick-off.

APPENDIXES

41. Kick out is a drop kick by one of the players of the side which has had to touch the ball down in their own goal or into whose touch in-goal the ball has gone (Rule 21) and is the mode of bringing the ball again into play, and cannot count as a goal.

42. Kick out must be a drop kick and from not more than 25 yards outside the kickers goal line. If the ball when kicked out pitch in touch it must be taken back and kicked out again. The kicker's side must be behind the ball when kicked out.

43. A player who has made and claimed a fair catch shall thereupon either take a drop kick or a punt or place the ball for a place kick.

44. After a fair catch has been made the opposite side may come up to the catcher's mark and (except in cases under rule 50) the catcher's side retiring the ball shall be kicked from such mark or from a spot any distance in a direct line (not being in touch) behind it.

45. A player may touch the ball down in his own goal at any time.

46. A side having touched the ball down in their opponents' goal, shall try at goal either by a place kick or a punt out.

47. If a try at goal be made by a place kick a player of the side who has touched the ball down shall bring it up to the goal line subject to rule 48 in a straight line from and opposite to the spot where the ball was touched down and there make a mark on the goal line and then walk straight out with it at right angles to the goal line such distance as he thinks proper and their place it for another of his side to kick. The kicker's side must be behind the ball when it is kicked, and the opposite side must remain behind their goal line until the ball has been placed on the ground (see Rules 54 and 55).

48. If the ball has been touched down between the goalposts, it may be brought out in a straight line from either of such posts but if brought out from between them the opposite may charge at once (see rule 54).

49. If the try at goal be by a punt out (see Rule 29) a player of the side which has touched the ball down shall bring it straight up to the goal line opposite to the spot where it was touched down and there make a mark on the goal line and then punt out from any spot behind the goal line not nearer to the goalpost than such mark, or from touch in-goal if necessary, beyond which mark it is not lawful for the opposite side who must keep behind their goal line to pass until ball has been kicked (see Rules 54 and 55).

50. If a fair catch be made from a punt out or a punt on the catcher may either proceed as provided by Rules 43 and 44 or himself take a punt on in which case the mark made on making a fair catch shall be regarded (for the purpose of determining as well the position of the player who makes the punt on as of the other players of both sides) as the mark made on the goal line in the case of a punt out.

51. A catch made in touch from a punt out or a punt on is not a fair catch: the ball must then be taken or thrown out of touch as provided by Rule 32 but if the catch be made in touch in-goal the ball is at once dead and must be kicked out as provided by rule 21.

MIKE ROBERTS – THE SAME OLD GAME: CODIFICATION

52. When the ball has been touched down in the opponents' goal none of the side in whose goal it has been so touched down shall touch it or in any way displace it or interfere with the player of the other side who may be taking it up or out.

53. The ball is dead whenever a goal has been obtained, but if a try at goal be not successful the kick shall be considered as only an ordinary kick in the course of the game.

54. Charging i.e. rushing forward to kick the ball or tackle a player, is lawful for the opposite side in all cases of a place kick after a fair catch or upon a try at goal immediately the Ball touches or is placed on the ground; and in cases of a drop kick or punt after a fair catch as soon as the player having the ball commences to run or offers to kick or the ball has touched the ground but he may always draw back and unless he has dropped the ball or actually touched it with his foot they must again retire to his mark (see rule 56). The opposite side in the case of a punt out or a punt on, and the kicker's side in all cases may not charge until the ball has been kicked.

55. If a player having the ball when about to punt it out goes out side the goal line or when about to punt on advances nearer to his own goal line than his mark made on making the fair catch, or if after the ball has been touched down in the opponents' goal or a fair catch has been made more than one player on the side which has so touched it down or made the fair catch, touch the ball before it is again kicked the opposite side may charge at once.

56. In cases of a fair catch the opposite side may come up to and stand anywhere on or behind a line drawn through the mark made by the player who has made the catch and parallel to their own goal line; but in the case of a fair catch from a punt out or a punt on they may not advance further in the direction of the touch-line nearest to such mark than a line drawn through such mark to their goal line and parallel to such touch-line. In all cases (except a punt out and a punt on) the kicker's side must be behind the ball when it is kicked but may not charge until it has been kicked.

57. No hacking or hacking over or tripping up shall be allowed under any circumstances.

58. No one wearing projecting nails iron plates or gutta percha on any part of his boots or shoes shall be allowed to play in a match.

59. The captains of the respective sides shall be the sole arbiters of all disputes.

Appendix Eight: Gaelic Athletic Association Rules for Football (1884)

1. There shall not be less than fourteen or more than twenty-one players a side.

2. There shall be two umpires and a referee. Where the umpires disagree the referee's decision will be final.

3. The ground shall be at least 120 yards long by 80 in breadth, and properly marked by boundary lines. Boundary lines must be at least five yards from fences.

4. The goal posts shall stand at each end in centre of the goal line. They shall be 15 feet apart, with a cross-bar 8 feet from the ground.

402

APPENDIXES

5. The captains of each team toss for choice of sides before commencing play, and the players shall stand in two ranks opposite each other until the ball is thrown up, each man holding the hand of one of the other side.

6. Pushing or tripping from behind, holding from behind, or butting with the head, shall be deemed a foul, and the players so offending shall be ordered to stand aside, and may not afterwards take part in the match, nor can his side substitute another man.

7. The time of actual play shall be one hour. Sides to be changed only at half time.

8. The match shall be decided by the greater number of goals. If no goal be kicked the match shall be deemed a draw. A goal is when the ball is kicked through the goal posts under the cross-bar.

9. When the ball is kicked over the side line it shall be thrown back by a player of the opposite side to him who kicked it over. If kicked over the goal line by a player whose goal line it is, it shall be thrown back in any direction by a player of the other side. If kicked over the goal line by a player of the other side, the goal keeper whose line it crosses shall have a free kick. No player of the other side to approach nearer 25 yards of him till the ball is kicked.

10. The umpires and referee shall have during the match the full power to disqualify any player, or order him to stand aside and discontinue play for any act which they may consider unfair, as set out in Rule 6.

No nails or iron tips allowed on the boots. Strips of leather fastened on the soles will prevent slipping. The dress of hurling and football to be knee-breeches and stockings and boots or shoes.

It would be well if each player was provided with two jerseys, one white and the other some dark colour. The colours of his club could be worn on each. Then when a match was made, it could be decided the colours each side should wear.

Appendix Nine: The Laws of the Melbourne Football Club (1859)

1. The distance between the Goals and the Goal Posts shall be decided upon by the Captains of the sides playing.

2. The Captains on each side shall toss for choice of Goal; the side losing the toss has the Kick off from the centre point between the Goals.

3. A Goal must be kicked fairly between the posts, without touching either of them, or a portion of the person of any player on either side.

4. The game shall be played within a space of not more than 200 yards wide, the same to be measured equally on each side of a line drawn through the centres of the two Goals; and two posts to be call the "Kick off" posts shall be erected at a distance of 20 yards on each side of the Goal posts at both ends, and in a straight line with them.

5. In case the Ball is kicked behind Goal, any one of the side behind whose Goal it is kicked may bring it 20 yards in front of any portion of the space between the "Kick off" posts, and shall kick it as nearly as possible in a line with the opposite Goal.

6. Any player catching the Ball directly from the foot may call "mark." He then has a free kick; no player from the opposite side being allowed to come inside the spot marked.

7. Tripping and pushing are both allowed (but no hacking) when any player is in rapid motion or in possession of the Ball, except in the case provided for in Rule 6.

8. The Ball may be taken in hand only when caught from the foot, or on the hop. In no case shall it be lifted from the ground.

9. When a Ball goes out of bounds (the same being indicated by a row of posts) it shall be brought back to the point where it crossed the boundary-line, and thrown in at right angles with that line.

10. The Ball while in play may under no circumstances be thrown.

An eleventh rule would be added a year later: "In case of a deliberate infringement of any of the above rules, by either side, the captain of the opposite side may claim that any one of his party may have a free kick from the place where the breach of the rules was made; the two captains in all cases, save where umpires are appointed, to be the sole judges of infringements."

Appendix Ten: Rules of Dartmouth College Football (1871)

1. Five umpires, one from each class in the Academical, and one from the Scientific Department, shall be elected annually by the college. The senior umpire present shall settle all disputes which arise concerning the game.

2. The ball shall be warned from the second base of the college grounds and towards the buildings. No warn shall be valid until both parties are ready.

3. Until the ball is kicked the warning party shall stand behind the ball and their opponents in front; the latter at a distance of at least two rods. These positions, and the warn as well, shall be changed each game.

4. No player shall kick, trip, strike, or hold another for any cause during the game.

5. It shall be considered foul when the ball is caught on the bound, or fly, or picked from the ground; when it passes the fence at the north or south end of the common, or at either corner, or when knocked past the east or west fence.

6. In case of a foul the ball shall be tossed up by the umpire at the place where the foul occurs, unless it be within two rods of either fence, in which case the ball shall be brought directly in a distance of two rods before umpiring.

7. The game shall be won when the ball is kicked past the east or west fence.

APPENDIXES

Appendix Eleven: Princeton University Rules (1871)

1. The grounds shall be 500 feet in length by 300 feet in breadth.
2. The goal-posts shall be 25 feet apart.
3. The number for match games shall be 25 to the side.
4. To a game 4 of 7 goals are necessary.
5. The winner of the toss shall have the choice of goals.
6. No player shall throw or carry the ball.
7. Any player catching the ball after it has been kicked or knocked and before it touches the ground shall be entitled to a free kick.
8. Any ball passing the boundary lines shall be kicked or knocked in with full force. If passing the side limits, by the player first touching the ball; if passing the goal limits, by a player of the side defending the goal.
9. No holding shall be allowed except when a player has the ball in his possession not caught on the fly.
10. No tripping shall be allowed, nor shall any player use his hands to push an adversary.

Appendix Twelve: Yale University Rules (1872)

1. The grounds shall be four hundred feet long by two hundred and fifty feet broad.
2. The goal posts shall be eight paces apart.
3. The number of match games shall be twenty to the side.
4. To a game five of nine goals are necessary. To secure a goal the ball must pass between the posts.
5. No player shall pick up, throw, or carry the ball on any part of the field. Any violation of the regulation shall constitute a foul, and the player so offending shall throw the ball perpendicularly into the air from the place where the foul occurred, and the ball shall not be in play until it touches the ground.
6. When the ball is caught in the air an adversary may strike it from the hands of the player so catching.
7. When the ball passes the limits, the person touching it first shall throw it from a spot six paces from, and at right angles to, the boundary line at the place it went over; and the ball shall not be in play until it has touched the ground. Further, the player throwing the ball shall not play upon it until it has been played upon. When thrown, the players shall be between the ball and their goal.
8. When the ball passes the limits within six paces of a goal post, it shall be carried out by the player first touching it fifteen paces in front of the boundary line, and thrown by him into the air under the same conditions as a foul ball (Rule 5).
9. No tripping shall be allowed, nor shall any player use his hands to push or hold an adversary.

MIKE ROBERTS – THE SAME OLD GAME: CODIFICATION

10. The winner of the toss shall have first kick off and the choice of goal. The ball shall be placed fifteen paces from the centre of the field towards the starter's goal. In canting the ball must be kicked, not babied. No player on the canting side shall be in advance of a line passing through the ball and parallel to base line: nor shall any player on the opposite side come within ten paces of this line.

11. No player shall wear projecting nails, iron plates or gutta percha on the soles or heels of his shoes.

12. There shall be two judges for each goal, and a referee, to whom all disputed points shall be referred.

Appendix Thirteen: Rules of the Harvard Game (1873)

1. The number of players upon each side shall not be less than ten nor more than fifteen.

2. The grounds shall not be less than 350 feet nor more than 450 feet in length; and not less than 255 nor more than 325 feet in width.

3. There shall be two end boundaries and two side boundaries.

4. The two end boundaries shall form the goals. To win a game, the ball must strike the ground beyond either goal, passing over it on the fly, but no game can be won on a fair kick.

5. When the ball passes over either side boundary it shall be considered dead, and the player first holding it shall be entitled to a fair kick, and shall carry the ball within bounds at right angles to the boundary line at the spot where it first struck.

6. When the ball passes over either goal in any manner other than to win a game, it shall be considered dead, as in Rule 5, and may be placed anywhere within a line drawn parallel to the goal, and 10 feet distant from it.

7. The winner of the toss shall have either the warning kick or the choice of goals. The warning kick shall be taken from a point half-way between the two goals.

8. Any player is allowed to catch or pick up the ball. No player is allowed to run with the ball or to baby the ball unless pursued by an opponent, and then only while so pursued.

9. No player is allowed to throw or pass the ball to another player unless pursued by an opponent.

10. No lurking, striking, hacking, tripping, nor butting among the players is allowed.

11. Any player when on the adversary's side of the ball must either walk toward the ball, or must walk toward his own goal in a line at right angles with that goal. Any player not complying with this law shall be considered as lurking, and shall not be allowed to touch the ball until he has reached a point on his own side of the ball.

12. A match shall consist of five games. The side winning 3 games out of 5 shall be the winner of the match.

13. Each side shall appoint an umpire who shall select in turn a referee.

APPENDIXES

14. It shall be the duty of the umpires to settle all disputes, see that the rules of the game are complied with, name the victors in all matches, and perform in short all the ordinary duties of an umpire.

15. The referee shall be applied to when the umpires disagree, and his decision shall be final.

Appendix Fourteen: Rules of the Intercollegiate Football Association (1873)

1. The ground shall be 400 feet by 250 feet broad.

2. The distance between the posts of each goal shall be 25 feet.

3. The number for match games shall be 20 to a side.

4. To win a game 6 goals are necessary, but that side shall be considered the victors which, when the game is called, shall have scored the greatest number of goals, provided the number be 2 or more. To secure a goal the ball must pass between the posts.

5. No player shall throw or carry the ball. Any violation of this regulation shall constitute a foul, and the player so offending shall throw the ball perpendicularly into the air to a height of at least 12 feet and the ball shall not be in play until it has touched the ground.

6. When a ball passes out of bounds it is a foul, and the player causing it shall advance at right angles to the boundary-line, 15 paces from the point where the ball went, and shall proceed as in rule 5.

7. No tripping shall be allowed, nor shall any player use his hands to hold or push an adversary.

8. The winners of the toss shall have the choice of first goal, and the sides shall change goals after every successive inning. In staring the ball it shall be fairly kicked, not 'babied' from a point 150 feet in front of the starter's goal.

9. Until the ball is kicked no player of either side shall be in advance of a line parallel to the line of his goals and distant from it 150 feet.

10. There shall be two judges, one from each of the contesting colleges, and one referee; all to be chosen by the captains.

11. No player shall wear spikes or iron plates upon his shoes.

12. In all match games a No 6 ball shall be used, furnished by the challenging side and to become the property of the victors.

Appendix Fifteen: Playing Rules of the McGill University Football Club (1874)

i. Each goal shall consist of two upright posts, 16 feet high and 15 feet apart, with a cross-bar at a distance of 10 feet from the ground. The maximum length of the ground shall be 150 yards; the maximum breadth shall be 75 yards.

ii. The number of players on each side shall be not more than 20, or less than 10. The definite number to be settled by the Captains before each match.

407

MIKE ROBERTS – THE SAME OLD GAME: CODIFICATION

iii. The winners of the toss shall have the option of kick off or choice of goals. The game shall be commenced by a place kick from the centre of the ground, and the opposite side shall not come within 10 yards of the ball.

iv. The ball shall be kicked off (i) at the commencement of the game, (ii) after a goal has been obtained, or (iii) at the end of each half hour.

v. After a goal is won, ends shall be changed, and the losing side shall kickoff. In the event, however, of no goal having fallen to either side at the lapse of half an hour, ends shall then be changed.

vi. The ball may be caught on the bounce and carried; the player so carrying the ball may be "tackled" or "shouldered", but not hacked, throttled, or pommelled. No player may be held unless in actual possession of the ball.

vii. In the event of any player holding or running with the ball being tackled, and the ball fairly held, he may at once cry "have it down"; but he need not do so until his own side comes up.

viii. A goal can only be obtained by kicking the ball from the field of play direct (i.e. without touching the dress or person of any player of either side) over the cross-bar of the opponent's goal, whether it touch such cross-bar, or the posts, or not: but if the ball goes directly over either of the goal posts it is called a poster, and is not a goal. A goal may be obtained by any kind of kick except a punt.

ix. A match shall last for three half hours - it shall be decided by the majority of goals, or in the event of no goals being obtained by the majority of touch-downs; three touchdowns counting as one goal.

x. Every player is on side but is put off side if he enters a scrummage from his opponents' side, or being in a scrummage, gets in front of the ball, or when the ball has been kicked, touched, or is being run with by one of his own side behind him (i.e. between himself and his goal line). Every player when off side is out of the game, and shall not touch the ball in any case whatever, or in any way interrupt or obstruct any player, until he is again on side.

xi. A player being off side is put on side when the ball has been kicked by or has touched the dress or person of any player of the opposite side, or when one of his own side has run in front of him either with the ball or having kicked it when behind him.

xii. It is lawful for any player who has the ball to throw it back towards his own goal, or pass it back to any player of his own side who is at the time behind him, in accordance with the rules of on side.

xiii. If a ball goes into touch, the first player, on his side, who touches it down must bring it to the spot where it crossed the touch line; or if a player, when running with the ball, cross or put any part of either foot across the touch line, he must return with the ball to the spot where the line was so crossed, and then either (i) bound the ball in the field of play, and then run with it, kick it, or throw it back to his own side, or (ii) throw it out at right angles to the touch line.

xiv. The goal line is in goal, and the touch line is in touch.

xv. If the ball be sent beyond the side-bounds and put behind the goal line, it shall be touched down and thrown in from the corner in a diagonal direction by whoever touches it down.

xvi. It is not lawful to take the ball from off the ground for any purpose whatever, unless it be in touch.

xvii. No hacking or hacking over, or tripping up, shall be allowed under any circumstances. No one wearing projecting nails, iron plates, or gutta percha on any part of his boots or shoes, shall be allowed to play in a match.

xviii. In case of any distinct and wilful violation of these Rules of Play, a free kick shall be forfeited to the opposite side from the spot where the infringement took place, but in no case shall a goal be scored from such free kick.

xix. Continued transgressions of Rules by any player, the side to which he belongs shall lose him.

xx. All disputes to be settled by the Umpire, whose decision shall be final.

Appendix Sixteen: Chronology of main events in football history

470 Sidonius Apollinaris writes about a football-like game played in France that was probably very similar to Roman *harpastum*.

1100s Irish mythologies, almost certainly based on older legends, describe ball games that could have been precursors for hurling or Gaelic football.

1180 William Fitzstephen describes boys playing ball games in the streets of London.

1314 Edward II issues prohibition in England of *"rageries de grosses pelotes."*

1303 Earliest known reference to ball play at university, when Irish students at Oxford kill Adam of Salisbury.

1366 The Statutes of Kilkenny in Ireland ban English settlers from indulging in "plays which men call horlings."

1409 Henry IV prohibits "foteball" in England, the first known use of the word.

1430 John Lydgate describes a "campynge ball," the first reference to what would be a rugby-like game played in the east of England."

1441 "Ffooteballeplayers" recorded hiring a hall in London, the earliest evidence of an organised club.

1527 The Galway Statutes in Ireland ban hurling and promote "the great foot balle" in its place.

1530 Earliest record of the rugby-like *calcio* being played in Florence, Italy.

1583 Philip Stubbes writes his vicious condemnation of the evils of football, calling it "a friendly kinde of fight."

1591 Earliest account of ball games at an English public school, Harrow, where pupils were allowed to "toss a handball."

1596 Richard Mulcaster writes a treatise on football, which he deplores as unworthy, but believes that with smaller teams, less violence and a "trayning maister" it offered potential benefits.

1602 George Carew writes an extensive description of Cornish hurling, a structured carrying sport with many similarities to rugby.

1603 George Owen describes a violent form of cross-country football played in Wales with many characteristics resembling rugby.

1609 Henry Spelman writes the first of many accounts of football as played by Native Americans, observing many similarities to the English game, but usually impressed by the refined structure and lack of violence.

1618 James I, the Scot who became King of England, is shocked that his new subjects are forbidden from playing sports and vows that "the common people shall have leave to exercise."

1657 Earliest recorded reference to football among American settlers, where play in the streets was a fineable offence in Massachusetts.

1660 Francis Willughby describes football, a kicking game in which almost all the main characteristics of modern soccer are present.

1720 A Matthew Concanen poem provides an accurate description of football, in which a player holds the ball in his arms and "ran with eager haste," the earliest definite account of football in Ireland.

1734 Earliest reference to football in Canada, played by fur traders in Churchill.

1747 Reference to the "flying ball" is believed to be the earliest mention of football at Eton.

1748 Rugby School purchases a field "for the recreation of the youth," which presumably marks the date of the progress towards modern rugby.

1789 The Marylebone club establishes a nationwide structure for cricket, setting the models and standards that football would later imitate.

1801 Joseph Strutt's description of football closely resembles modern soccer, where "the ball is driven about with the feet instead of the hands." But he also says that "of late years it seems to have fallen into disrepute, and is but little practiced." For the next few decades, football is commonly referred to as an ancient but declining pastime in England.

1823 Edward Moor describes camp-ball in the east of England, with goals at either end of a field and in which the players carry the ball as in rugby.

William Webb Ellis allegedly introduces running with the ball at Rugby School. Though the story is debatable, it was roughly from this date that rugby became a carrying game.

W Pitt writes that although football was rarely seen in England, the game was widespread in Ireland, sentiments that would be echoed in several texts over the next two decades.

APPENDIXES

1824 Earliest known formal records of a football club, organised by Edinburgh lawyer John Hope.

1825 First steam engine runs between Stockton and Darlington – a development that would lead to football teams playing other opposition than local sides and needing common rules.

1829 Earliest record of football in Australia, played at Raffles Bay in Northern Territories.

1830 The Highway Acts imply a ban on street football all over Britain in all but a few exceptionally tolerant or militant communities, where the 'Shrovetide' tradition survived. Football matches are instead moved to fields and other sites away from public highways.

1839 Attempt at Cambridge University for old boys from various public schools to play football together fails due to confusion over different sets of rules.

1841 William Thomas writes an early account of a game played by Australian aborigines that involves kicking the ball in the air and catching it.

1844 First recorded mention of football in Melbourne, played by Irishmen. Several references follow over the next few years of games played at folk festivals.

1845 The first laws of rugby are written by pupils at Rugby School.

1847 First known rules are written for the Eton ball game, with many features in common with soccer.

The Ten Hour Day Act in Britain provides working classes with more time to play games.

1848 Cambridge University students from different public schools meet to draft a simple set of rules for football that they can all play together. Players can catch the ball but not run with it, and these rules would form the basis for the Football Association's first rules for soccer.

1855 First known rules for football at Shrewsbury, the public school game with the most similarities to soccer.

1856 Tom Wills, one of the founders of Australian football, returns to Melbourne after six years of tuition at Rugby School.

1857 Thomas Hughes describes rugby in *Tom Brown's Schooldays*, which helps generalise interest in the game around the Anglosphere, with a notable depiction of the ball being touched down, which is rewarded with a try at goal (conversion).

Sheffield Football Club is formed, the oldest surviving non-academic football club in the world.

1858 First known rules are written for Harrow football, with many features in common with soccer.

The Melbourne Football Club is founded in Australia, the oldest surviving professional club in the world. One of the players, Tom Wills, referees a football match between two schools in the city.

The Sheffield Football Club writes its first laws, which are similar to soccer but have no offside law.

1859 The Melbourne Football Club meets to discuss rules. Unconvinced by the different rulebooks used at English schools, they decide to create "a game of our own." Similar to the soccer that the Football Association would codify four years later, but with no apparent offside law, this game would develop into Australian football.

1862 Richard Lindon pioneers the art of using American Charles Goodyear's invention of vulcanised rubber to create a far superior alternative to inflated bladders, immediately transforming the popular perception of football. He also creates oval balls, which the pupils at the nearby Rugby School take an immediate liking to.

Rugby School writes new rules, which unlike the 1845 version, clearly consider the needs of teams playing the game outside the school itself.

The Oneidas of Boston formed in the USA. Although not the oldest football club in America, their Boston Game, a mix of soccer and rugby, would be taken to Harvard to later influence the attitudes that led to America's adoption of rugby.

1863 The Football Association is formed in London and uses the Cambridge rules as the basis for soccer. The ball can be caught for a free kick, but despite the FA's attempt to embrace all code, the elimination of hacking and running would limit its appeal to players of rugby-like games.

First known use of the rugby rules in Canada, at McGill University.

1865 Australian football allows running with the ball as long as it bounced every ten yards.

1866 The Football Association is still struggling to find supporters, and opts to detach itself from rugby by eliminating the fair catch and try at goal. It starts forging relations with Sheffield's more soccer-like game, and importing several of its ideas.

Australian football uses behind posts for the first time.

Princeton and Rutgers meet for the first major intercollegiate football match in America. Despite essentially being soccer, the use of interference suggests American colleges were after something different.

1867 Charles Barrington arrives at Trinity College, Ireland, where a "desultory" form of football was played, and introduced the rugby rules, which would be the only established rules used in Ireland for over two decades.

Michael Cusack, the founder of the Gaelic Athletic Association, visits his sister in Australia.

1868 The Oneidas issue a challenge to Harvard freshmen, suggesting the violent 'football rush' was developing into a more refined sport inspired by the 'Boston Game'.

1870 A change of rules regarding handling effectively creates goalkeepers in soccer.

1871 The first edition of the FA Cup is a major step towards promoting the soccer rules, which until then only a handful of clubs had adopted, almost entirely in the London

APPENDIXES

area. Queen's Park of Glasgow enter the Cup, thus helping to establish soccer in Scotland.

Clubs in London preferring the carrying game meet to form the Rugby Football Union and three former Rugby School pupils write a new set of laws. Hacking is made illegal, but there is still no score for a try unless it is converted. The first rugby international is played in Edinburgh.

1872 England and Scotland play the first soccer international in Glasgow, which leads to the unification of rules in the two countries.

1873 Princeton, Yale and Rutgers form the Intercollegiate Football Association in America, and write rules that are largely influenced by soccer. Harvard refuse to join, claiming their kicking and carrying game is incompatible. Yale plays a game with former Eton students and sees the benefits of less congested 11-a-side matches.

Clubs in Ontario and Quebec make contact and form the Football Association of Canada to play rugby but struggle to agree on several aspects of the rules.

1874 Sending off and changing ends at half time are institutionalised in soccer.

McGill University in Canada refuses to play in the new Quebec rugby championship because it prefers its modified version of the rules. But they do play Harvard, who immediately fall in love with the game.

1875 Harvard plays Yale under concessionary rules and convinces them that rugby suits American colleges better.

1876 Yale, Harvard, Princeton and Columbia adopt the British rugby laws, but introduce the modification that unconverted tries should be included in the score.

The London and Sheffield FAs amalgamate, effectively nationalising soccer throughout England.

1877 The Melbourne rules are adopted in South Australia, the first colony apart from Victoria to play Australian football. Carlton also play games in Sydney, but New South Wales and Queensland would eventually reject the game and stick to rugby, leading to footballing division in the country.

1878 Whistles introduced to soccer and rugby.

First soccer club formed in Ireland, Cliftonville FC.

1880 American football is effectively created when the scrummage is replaced by the 'snap' and the line of scrimmage and teams are reduced to eleven men.

1882 American football eliminates the problem of teams refusing to risk surrendering possession by introducing the rule that teams have three downs to complete five yards, otherwise possession is turned over. The field gets its 'gridiron' markings.

1883 Michael Cusack forms the Metropolitan Hurling Club in Dublin, which he later claimed was the foundation for the Gaelic Athletic Association.

American football introduces different amounts of points for the different types of score.

MIKE ROBERTS – THE SAME OLD GAME: CODIFICATION

1884 Michael Cusack publishes his Word on Irish Athletics, condemning the Anglicisation of Irish sport, and later that year, the Gaelic Athletic Association is formed in Thurles. The Canada Rugby Football Union is formed, but struggles to maintain unity because Ontario is drifting towards the American idea of the snap and line of scrimmage.

1885 Professional soccer is legalised in England, paving the way for the game to dominate, in commercial terms, the amateur rugby code.
The first laws are written for Gaelic football in Ireland. It is very similar to soccer as it was played in England two decades earlier, with no mention of overs, hand-passes or soloing, and the goals are soccer goals.

1886 Rugby starts counting tries in the score regardless of whether they are converted.
Gaelic football encourages scoring by adding something very similar to Australian football's behind posts.

1888 The professional Football League is formed in Manchester, originally only including teams from the North and Midlands.

1891 The penalty kick is introduced to soccer.
The Canadian Rugby Union is formed and the line of scrimmage generalised in Canada, but differences regarding the rules persist.

1893 Despite mounting pressure, mainly in the north of England, the RFU votes to keep rugby strictly amateur.

1895 Clubs from Yorkshire and Lancashire meet to form the Northern Union, a breakaway rugby association that endorses professionalism.

1897 Australian football starts including behinds in the score, rather than as a a tie-breaker.

1902 In Canada, Ontario accepts the American influenced 'Burnside rules', introducing Canada to the 12-a-side game and three downs to gain ten yards. The rest of the country takes longer to fall in line.

1905 Violence in American football leads Theodore Roosevelt to intervene as the sport comes close to being outlawed.

1906 The Northern Union makes changes to rugby to make it more appealing to the public, including a reduction to 13 players and the introduction of the play-the-ball rule, effectively creating rugby league.
The forward pass is legalised in American football in the hope of opening up the game and reducing injuries.

1907 The 'big four' of Canadian football form the breakaway Interprovincial Union, paving the way for the CFL and professionalism.

1909 Canadian football's Grey Cup is presented for the first time, even though there is still division between the different unions regarding the rules. An exhibition match in New York fails to convince observers that America should adopt the Canadian rules.

1910 Gaelic football's 'behind' posts are moved inwards to create the modern day H-shaped goal.

APPENDIXES

Western clubs are refused permission to play for Canadian football's Grey Cup, leading them to interact with American clubs instead.

1921 Seán Lavan allegedly invents Gaelic football's solo.
Western clubs challenge for Canadian football's Grey Cup for the first time, but their American influences lead to further division just as the game was becoming unified.

1930 Soccer holds the first World Cup in any football code, played in Uruguay.

1931 Forward passing accepted in all Canadian football matches, finally unifying the game across the country.

1939 Helmets made mandatory in American football at college level.

1950 First exhibition match between American and Canadian football teams, a practice that would be fairly commonplace for the next decade or so but later discontinued.

1966 Rugby league introduces the four-tackle rule, influenced by American downs-to-go.

1967 First meetings between Australian football and Gaelic football teams in Dublin.

1971 Tries in rugby union worth more than any other form of score for the first time.
Rugby league four-tackle rule adjusted to six tackles.

1984 Australian football and Gaelic football agree terms for composite international rules football.

1995 Rugby union endorses professionalism.
Baltimore become first and only American winner of Canadian football's Grey Cup.

Appendix Seventeen: Evolution of points scoring[2]

1845	**RUGBY**	Drop goal or converted try: 1 point.
1859	**AUST F**	Goal: 1 point
1863	**SOCCER**	Goal: 1 point
1866	**AUST F**	Goal: 1 point. Behinds counted as a tie-breaker in some competitions but not officially part of the rules.
1871	**RUGBY**	Drop goal or converted try: 1 point. Unconverted tries used as tie-breaker.
1874	**CANADA**	Field goal or converted try: 1 point. Unconverted tries sometimes used as tie-breaker.
1875	**RUGBY**	Goal: 1 point. But unconverted tries used as tie-breaker.
1876	**USA**	Field goal: 4 points. Touchdown: 1 point. Conversion: 3 points.

---

[2] Particularly in the case of early variations on rugby, there was often no numerical scoring system. Certain forms of scoring were deemed equal to a certain number of others. For simplicity's sake, here the scoring systems are described using numerical equivalents. Some of these rule changes did not apply to all sets of rules for a certain code. For example, in America, there were often differences between regional and professional/college rules, and rugby league in Europe and Australia did not follow a united rulebook until 1998.

MIKE ROBERTS – THE SAME OLD GAME: CODIFICATION

1876	**CANADA**	Field goal: 3 points. Touchdown: 1 point. Conversion: 2 points. Rouges counted in case of a tie.
1881	**RUGBY**	RFU rejects a points-based system including points for unconverted tries, although some clubs and minor unions do use such systems.
1881	**USA**	Field goal: 4 points. Touchdown: 1 point. Conversion: 3 points. Safeties used as tie-breaker, unless no team has 4 or more.
1882	**USA**	Field goal: 4 points. Touchdown: 1 point. Conversion: 3 points. Safety: 2 points.
1883	**USA**	Field goal: 5 points. Touchdown: 2 points. Conversion: 4 points. Safety: 1 point.
1884	**CANADA**	Field goal: 6 points. Touchdown: 4 points. Conversion: 4 points. Penalty or free kick: 4 points. Safety: 2 points. Rouge: 1 point.[3]
1884	**USA**	Field goal: 5 points. Touchdown: 4 points. Conversion: 2 points. Safety: 2 points.
1885	**GAELIC**	Goal: 1 point
1886	**RUGBY**	Drop goal: 3 points. Try: 1 point. Conversion: 2 points.
1886	**GAELIC**	Goal: 1 point. Extra posts added 21 feet to either side of goal and a point awarded for scoring between them, but only used as tie-breaker.
1887	**CANADA**	Field goal: 5 points. Touchdown: 4 points. Conversion: 4 points. Penalty or free kick: 4 points. Safety: 2 points. Rouge: 1 point.
1888	**RUGBY**	Drop goal: 3 points. Try: 1 point. Conversion: 2 points. Penalty kick: 2 points.
1887	**CANADA**	Field goal: 5 points. Touchdown: 4 points. Conversion: 4 points. Penalty or free kick: 2 points. Safety: 2 points. Rouge: 1 point.
1891	**RUGBY**	Drop goal: 4 points. Try: 2 points. Conversion: 3 points. Penalty kick: 3 points. Goal from mark: 4 points.
1891	**CANADA**	Field goal: 5 points. Touchdown: 4 points. Conversion: 2 points. Safety: 2 points. Rouge: 1 point. Free or penalty kick: 4 points.
1891	**SOCCER**	Penalty kick introduced, equal to one goal
1892	**GAELIC**	Goal: 5 points. Over: 1 point
1893	**RUGBY**	Drop goal: 4 points. Try: 3 points. Conversion: 2 points. Penalty kick: 3 points. Goal from mark: 4 points.
1893	**RUGBY**	Drop goal: 4 points. Try: 3 points. Conversion: 2 points. Penalty kick: 3 points. Goal from mark: 4 points.
1892	**GAELIC**	Goal: 3 points. Over: 1 point
1895	**CANADA**	Field goal: 5 points. Touchdown: 4 points. Conversion: 2 points. Safety: 2 points. Rouge: 1 point. Free or penalty kick: 2 points.

---

[3] In Ontario. Same system accepted in Quebec a year later. The changes from the 1880s and 1890s relate to the ORFU. Quebec's system often differed.

APPENDIXES

1897	**RUGBY L**	Drop goal: 2 points. Try: 3 points. Conversion: 2 points. Penalty kick: 2 points. Goal from mark: 2 points.
1897	**AUST F**	Goal: 6 points. Behind: 1 point
1897	**USA**	Field goal: 5 points. Touchdown: 5 points. Conversion: 1 point. Safety: 2 points.
1901	**CANADA**	Field goal or penalty: 2 points. Touchdown: 4 points. Conversion: 2 points. Safety: 2 points. Rouge: 1 point.
1904	**USA**	Field goal: 4 points. Touchdown: 5 points. Conversion: 1 point. Safety: 2 points.
1904	**CANADA**	Field goal or penalty: 2 points. Touchdown: 5 points. Conversion: 1 point. Safety: 2 points. Rouge: 1 point.
1905	**CANADA**	Field goal or penalty: 3 points. Touchdown: 5 points. Conversion: 1 point. Safety: 2 points. Rouge: 1 point.
1906	**CANADA**	Field goal or penalty: 4 points. Touchdown: 5 points. Conversion: 1 point. Safety: 2 points. Rouge: 1 point.
1907	**CANADA**	Field goal: 4 points. Touchdown: 5 points. Conversion: 1 point. Free kick: 3 points. Penalty kick: 2 points. Safety: 2 points. Rouge: 1 point.
1908	**CANADA**	Field goal: 3 points. Touchdown: 5 points. Conversion: 1 point. Free kick: 3 points. Penalty kick: 2 points. Safety: 2 points. Rouge: 1 point.
1909	**USA**	Field goal: 3 points. Touchdown: 5 points. Conversion: 1 point. Safety: 2 points.
1910	**GAELIC**	H-shaped goal created. Goal: 3 points. Over: 1 point
1912	**USA**	Field goal: 3 points. Touchdown: 6 points. Conversion: 1 point. Safety: 2 points.
1920	**RUGBY L**	Both goal from mark and field goals abolished in Australia[4].
1948	**RUGBY U**	Drop goal: 3 points. Try: 3 points. Conversion: 2 points. Penalty kick: 3 points. Goal from mark: 3 points.
1956	**CANADA**	Field goal: 3 points. Touchdown: 6 points. Conversion: 1 point. Safety: 2 points. Rouge: 1 point.
1958	**USA**	Option of 2-point conversion introduced[5].
1966	**SOCCER**	Penalty shootout introduced as tie-breaker in cup ties[6].

---

[4] Field goals were maintained in England until 1950, and the goal from mark until 1977.

[5] Only in college football. Professional football adopted the rule in different measures, but it was not used in the NFL until 1994.

[6] This was when FIFA and UEFA endorsed it, although several regional competitions had already used shootouts for several years.

1971	**RUGBY U**	Drop goal: 3 points. Try: 4 points. Conversion: 2 points. Penalty kick: 3 points.
1971	**RUGBY L**	Drop goal: 1 point. Try: 3 points. Conversion: 2 points. Penalty kick: 2 points.
1977	**RUGBY U**	Goal from mark effectively rendered impossible as marking limited to a team's own 22.
1983	**RUGBY L**	Drop goal: 1 point. Try: 4 points. Conversion: 2 points. Penalty kick: 2 points.
1992	**RUGBY U**	Drop goal: 3 points. Try: 5 points. Conversion: 2 points. Penalty kick: 3 points.

INDEX

11-a-side: Aus, 212; Canada, 349, 367; soccer, 20, 37; US, 251, 291, 295, 296, 298, 299, 304, 305

12-a-side, 119, 123, 127, 213, 368, 378, 414; Aus, 212; Canada, 349, 367, 369, 386; GAA, 128, 200; rug lge, 108

13-a-side: rug lge, 108, 112, 305

14th Regiment, 229

15-a-side, 120, 191; Canada, 364, 367; GAA, 162, 196; rugby, 58; US, 261, 295, 296, 298

18-a-side, 191

20-a-side: GAA, 127; rugby, 58, 67, 69; US, 261, 283, 286

25-a-side, 283

Abdülmecid, Sultan, 137

Aberdare, 111, 113

Accrington, 44, 81, 82, 86

Act of Union, 136

Addison, 56

Adee, George, 329

Adelaide, 130, 192, 195, 197, 200, 238, 245, 247, 249

Adelaide Oval, 239

Adelphi Academy, 282

AFL Grand Final, 246, 249

AFL Premiership, 190, 236, 246

Africa, 44, 176, 386

Albert Park, 233

Alberta, 352, 376, 377

Albion Park, 243

Albion Rugby Club, 134

Alcock, Charles, 12, 15, 16, 18, 20, 15–21, 22, 23, 26, 27, 28, 29, 30, 33, 34, 35, 37, 38, 39, 42, 43, 52, 59, 82, 83, 99, 157, 431

Alcock, John, 15, 27

Ali, Muhammed, 186

All Blacks, 112, 113, 322, 386

All Ireland Championship, 160, 162–63, 170, 174, 175, 177, 181, 184, 190, 194, 195, 198

Allaway, Roger, 265

Allegheny Athletic Association, 319

Allesley Park College, 64

Almond, Hely Hutchinson, 67, 68, 71

Amateur Athletics Association of Ireland, 141

American Civil War, 9, 279

American football, 251, 253, 283, 289, 295, 304, 309, 339, 251–345; and Canada, 349, 350, 351, 368, 377, 380, 381, 384, 386, 388, 381–90; and professionalism, 319; and racial issues, 176; and rugby, 62, 291, 294, 297, 298, 297–300, 302, 306; and soccer, 262, 263, 265, 266, 278, 282, 324; beginner's guide, 252; expansion outside USA, 387; in Ireland, 185, 186; padding, 343–45; protective gear, 345

American Football League, 388

American League of Professional Football, 324

American Professional Football Association, 176

American Revolutionary War, 256

American Rugby Football Union, 322

American Tobacco Company, 320

Amherst College, 266, 281, 300

Amsterdam, 254

Anderton's Hotel, 86

Andrews, Peter, 77

Annapolis, 255, 344

Antrim, 128, 143

Antwerp, 322

Archery, 128, 259

Argentina, 44; rugby, 74

Armagh, 135, 173, 181

Army, 315, 331, 340

Arnold, Thomas, 46

Arnold, Thomas (SRFU), 242

Arnott, Walter, 39

Arsenal, 76, 87

Artillery Ground, 127

Ash, Edwin, 13, 55, 56, 55–56, 57

Associated Press, 285, 309, 315

Aston Villa, 64, 75, 81, 85, 86

Athletics: Aus, 212, 237; Canada, 358; GAA, 142, 144, 149, 151, 154

Auckland, 114, 205, 206, 245, 322

Australia, 74, 148, 189–250; AFL, 190, 197, 193–99, 217; Football Association, 247; Football Council, 210, 223; Irish, 136; National Football Council, 192; rug lge, 112–14; rugby, 95; Rugby Union, 240

Australian football, 189–250, 318, 403–4; and other codes, 244–50; early years, 189–221; foundation, 222–29; Irish origin, 136, 189–208; merging with rugby, 192; oval pitch, 226–29

Australian Football World Tour, 195

Austus, 193

Avionel, 134

Baker, Eugene, 297

Balclutha, 206

Balla, 142

Ballarat, 200, 203, 217, 224, 236, 237, 249

Balls, 262; Aus, 229; CFL, 351; FA, 30; GAA, 126, 133; rugby, 61, 108; US, 290, 298

Ballsbridge, 149

Ballymore, 175

Balmoral Academy, 134

Baltimore, 266, 388, 389, 434

Bangs, Francis, 336

Barassi, Ron, 190, 195

Barbor, Sarah Theresa, 217

Barcelona, 158, 388

Barclay, George, 344

Barker, Collet, 211

Barnes, 12, 13, 21, 22, 25, 26, 30, 235

Barnes and Mortlake Regatta, 22

Barnsley, 75, 106

Barnum, Phineas, 257

Barrington, Charles Burton, 61, 131

Barry, 111

Bartlett, Edwin Julius, 278, 287

Bartram, Teddy, 89, 93

Baseball, 85, 176, 193, 256, 258, 263, 281, 282, 303, 309, 317, 324, 325, 336, 346, 374, 382, 389

Baskerville, Albert Henry, 112

Basque Country, 123, 255

Batchelder, Alf, 227, 228

Bateman, Allan, 117

Bath, 52, 118

Batley, 103

Batman, John, 210

Battersea Park, 19, 30

Baxter, James, 114

Beardsell, Harry, 107

Beckenbauer, Franz, 325

Beckett Cup, 106

Beecher, Henry Ward, 266

Behinds, 192, 226, 230; GAA, 207; int rules, 196; Ire., 161; Sheff., 32; soccer, 14

Beitzel, Harry, 194

Belfast, 69, 87, 133, 134, 135, 175, 179, 201

Belgium, 246

Bellaghy Wolfe Tones, 182

419

Belsize Park, 56
Belvedere College, 133
Bendigo, 222, 224, 237
Berkeley, University of California, 286, 321, 322, 334
Berkshire, 36, 46, 56
Berlin, 111, 154
Bernstein, Mark, 289, 317, 332, 337
Berry, Roy, 382
Best, George, 178, 325
Bethlehem Steel, 324
Betts, Morton Peto, 35
Bicycle polo, 159
Billiards, 75, 132, 147, 256, 282, 371
Billington, Eric, 375
Binns, Jonathan, 129
Birmingham, 47, 85; City, 76; prof., 83, 98; soccer, 37, 64, 81
Birmingham and District Football Association, 36, 64
Birmingham Barracudas, 388
Bishop's College, 365
Blackburn, 78; Olympic, 42, 80, 81; Rovers, 40, 78, 80-86
Blackheath, 19, 26, 57; and the FA meeting, 12–19; foundation of the RFU, 55; Proprietary School, 12, 53; rugby, 50, 57, 88, 89, 94, 235, 308, 326
Blackpool, 80
Blackrock College, Dublin, 140
Bladders, 211, 262; Ire., 126
Blainey, Geoffrey, 202, 203, 208, 216, 224, 226
Blake, Dick, 172
Blanchard, John, 270
Blane, William, 258
Block game, 309–11
Bloody Monday, 270, 271
Bloody Sunday, 182–84, 186, 187
Bloomfield Park, 134
Blythe Smart, John, 22, 23, 27
Bolton, 75, 76, 78, 83, 86
Borkowski , Richard, 302
Bosman Ruling, 84, 176
Boston game, 263–66, 279, 291, 295, 353
Boston, Mass., 254, 256, 259, 260, 263, 264–66, 292, 295, 324
Bounce-down, 190
Bouncing the ball, 189, 198, 205, 229, 232, 240, 356
Bournemouth, 80
Bowling, 228, 255, 256, 371
Boxing, 97, 116, 128, 186, 212, 258, 379
Boycott, Charles, 149
Boylan, Sean, 198
Boyne, 123, 201

Bracken, Joseph Kevin, 147
Bradford, 52, 59, 65, 93, 94, 99, 103, 106, 253
Bradford, William, 253
Brady, Liam, 177, 178
Bragg, Melvyn, 21
Brallier, John, 319
Bramall Lane, 33
Bramley, 113
Brasch, Rudolph, 189
Brazil, 188, 325
Brewer, CD, 297
Brighouse Rangers, 103
Bright, Johnny, 176
Brisbane, 111, 114, 119, 216, 243, 244, 245
Bristol, 47, 52
BritanniasFBC, 322, 358, 360
British Amateur Athletic Association, 141, 144
British Columbia, 346, 371, 386
British Football Association, 83
British Guiana, 279
British occupation of Ireland, 141–45, 179–84
British Rugby Club, 360
Brittany, 158
Bromby, John, 214
Bromsgrove, 47
Brooklyn: Dodgers, 176, 382; Polytechnic School, 266; Wanderers, 324
Brooks, William, 329
Broughton Rangers, 92, 103
Brown University, 266, 300, 343
Brown, Charles Wreford, 66
Brown, Sean, 182
Brownlow Medal, 190
Bruce, Alexander, 203, 222
Brumbies, 117
Bryant, Jimmy, 218, 220, 222, 224, 227
Buckingham, James Silk, 259
Buckley, Bill, 109
Budd, Arthur, 59, 89, 94, 98
Buenos Aires, 74
Buffalo Bills, 387, 389
Burdon, Alick, 112
Burnley, 78, 83, 86
Burnside, John Thrift Meldrum, 367
Bury, 81
Butler, Bryon, 22, 81
Butt, Isaac, 138
Caid, 126–28, 155, 175, 199
Calcutta, 51
Calcutta Cup, 67
Caledonian Challenge Cup, 203
Caledonian Games, 148, 149
Caledonians, 133

Calgary, 381; Stampeders, 380; Tigers, 376, 377
Calgary Stampeders, 346
California, 322, 331, 344; State, 268
Camán, 159
Cambridge University, 25, 58, 101, 214, 266; passing, 42; Football Rules, 10, 15, 18, 225
Cambridge, Mass., 268, 355
Cameroon, 44
Camp, Walter, 21, 108, 298-300, 341, 301–43, 360, 364, 367, 369; and forward passing, 338; and professionalism, 320; and violence, 331; at Yale, 304; death, 343; downs, 311; player, 303; scrimmage, 308; soccer, 324
Campbell, AH, 362, 364
Campbell, Dalmahoy, 213–14
Campbell, Francis Maude, 12–19, 57
Campbell, JH Mayne, 357
Canada, 279, 348; Amateur Athletic Federation, 370; fur traders, 351–52
Canadian football, 346–90; US, 340–42, 386–89
Canadian Football League, 346, 349–51; and racial issues, 176; and the NFL, 349
Canadian Intercollegiate Rugby Football Union, 365, 369, 371, 375, 384
Canberra, 117, 244, 246
Canterbury, 46, 48, 435
Capper, Warwick, 244
Cardiff, 40, 52, 70, 92, 93, 117, 185
Carey, Tim, 186, 187
Carlton, 195, 198, 228-229, 235, 238, 240, 242, 244, 413; Oval, 195
Carrick-on-Suir, 144, 147
Carroll College, 279, 339
Carron, 140
Cartwright, Alexander, 281
Cartwright, John Dyer, 10–11
Casey, Tom, 176
Castlemaine, 237
Catholic Emancipation, 136
Cavan, 181
Cavendish, Lord Frederick, 138
Ceasar, WC, 247
Celtic Park, 40
Celts, 139, 164
Chambers, Harry, 83
Champions League, 64, 116
Charging: GAA, 120; soccer, 19, 80; US, 356
Charity Shield, 87
Charleston, 254
Charlton, Jack, 178

INDEX

Charterhouse School, 12, 27
Cheasty, Tom, 177
Chelsea, 113
Cheltenham, 46, 52, 61, 113, 131, 133
Chesterman, William, 29, 31
Chicago, 186, 267, 309, 320, 325, 332, 334, 379, 387
China, 200
Christian, Archer, 340
Christian, JA, 152
Christmas, 8, 93, 253, 254, 286, 352
Church of England Grammar School, 214, 219, 220
Churchill, Winston, 147
Cincinnati Red Stockings, 281
Civil Service, 12, 56
Clam Diggers, 324
Clane, 127
Clapham Rovers, 35, 36, 55
Clare, 135, 140, 206
Clark, JE, 233
Cleckheaton, 92
Clegg, Charles, 34, 39, 42, 97
Cleveland, Ohio, 261, 276
Clifton School, 47, 52, 59
Cliftonville, 133, 134, 173
Clongowes College, 133
Clonskeagh, 160
Clonturk Park, Drumcondra, 175
Clopton Wingfield, Walter, 22
Clowes, Jack, 95
Cnapan, 127
Cobb Morley, Ebenezer, 11–21, 29, 31
Cochems, Eddie, 339
Cock House Cup, 34
Cock-fighting, 256
Cohane, Tim, 287
Collingwood, 213, 217, 235, 244, 245
Collins, Michael, 182
Collins, Tony, 75, 101, 102
Collis, John, 47
Colorado College, 321
Coloured jerseys, 84, 124, 140, 155, 293, 299, 357; US, 296
Columbia University, 266, 275, 282, 285, 287, 289, 291, 297, 299, 304, 321, 332, 335, 336
Columbia, Philadelphia, 266
Combination game, 43, 41–43
Commercials, Limerick, 157, 160, 204
Common, 173
Conacher, Lionel, 379
Conan Doyle, Arthur, 209
Concanen, Matthew, 124–26
Concessionary rules, 296
Connacht, 117, 171, 194
Connecticut, 265, 273, 300
Connell, Anna, 76

Conversion: Aus, 192; Canada, 364; rugby, 62; soccer, 30; US, 252, 303, 314
Conway, Henry, 213
Cooney, Jimmy, 177
Cordner-Eggleston Cup, 220
Corinthians, 95
Corio Bay, 236
Cork, 135, 141, 147, 152, 173, 181, 196; Athletic Club, 147; rugby, 164, 175; University College, 154
Cornell University, 266, 276, 332
Corner kicks, 32, 155-156; GAA, 120; Sheff., 20
Cornish hurling, 127
Corr, Frank, 182
Corry, Eoghan, 140, 148, 152, 170, 176, 178, 179, 184
Cosentino, Frank, 307
Costley, Jimmy, 80
Cottage FBC, 266
Cotton, George, 46, 50
Coulman, Mike, 111
County Championship, 73, 85
Courage Leagues, 73
Coventry, 64, 76, 110
Cowley, Ern, 193
Cray Wanderers, 76
Creighton, James, 358
Cresswell, Edmund, 35
Creswick, Henry, 226
Creswick, Nathaniel, 226
Crewe Alexandra, 64, 76
Cricket, 33-36, 64, 67, 69, 76- 77, 84-89, 93, 129, 144, 150, 176, 212, 256, 371; and Australian football, 226–29; and soccer, 8, 11, 20, 27, 39, 47; Ashes, 69; Ire., 141; Ireland, 140; US, 258, 259
Crimean War, 216
Croke Park, 142, 150, 163, 166, 179, 181, 182–84, 185, 186–88, 194, 195, 196, 197
Croke, Archbishop Thomas, 149–51, 152, 153, 164, 170, 171, 205, 206, 205–6
Cromwell, Oliver (Sheffield), 32
Cronin, Mike, 139
Croquet, 150, 151
Crossbar, 49; Aus, 225, 238, 240; Canada, 355; GAA, 155; rugby, 53; soccer, 11, 19, 29; US, 282, 286, 291, 297
Cross-country football, 126
Cruikshank, John, 346
Crusaders, 12, 30
Crystal Palace, 12, 26, 194
Cudgelling, 159, 173, 256
Cullinlaringo, 216

Culture, Media and Sport Committee, 116
Cumbria: Cumberland and Westmoreland County Union, 52, 99
Currie, Gordon, 353, 356, 361, 367, 374, 431
Curry, Graham, 10, 78, 80
Curtis, Ulysses, 176
Cusack, Michael, 21, 120–67, 177, 204; Academy Football Club, 140; death, 166; downfall and death, 164–66; in Australia, 206; leaves GAA, 165
Czech Republic, 146
Czechoslovakia, 249
Dakota, 24
Dalton, Des, 188
Daniels, Arthur, 111
Dartmouth College, 276–79, 287, 300, 315, 404
Darwen, 78–79, 79, 80, 82
Darwin, Charles, 9, 21
Dashiell, Paul, 330
Davies, Jonathan, 111
Davin, Maurice, 144, 120–47, 157, 169, 171, 176
Davis, Parke H, 302, 311, 316, 328
Davitt, Michael, 142, 148, 149, 165
De Burca, Marcus, 149, 165, 166
Defence of the Realm Act, 181
Deland, Lorin, 328
Delaunay, Henri, 21
Delaware, 254, 433
Deming, Clarence, 261, 260–63, 273, 274, 275, 320
Derby, 28; County, 76, 86
Derry, 179, 182
Dewsbury, 92, 95, 103, 106, 114
Dickinson, Frank, 315
Dingle Peninsula, 126
Dixon, James, 375
Dodge, Earle, 297
Dominion Football Association, 359
Donegal, 173
Donne, John, 272
Donnington School, 35
Dorais, Gus, 340
Doubleday, Abner, 281
Down, County, 181, 195
Downs, 60, 252, 311–12, 349; Canada, 368
Drogheda, 137, 195
Drop goals, 49, 61, 70, 107, 174, 252, 314; CFL, 367; US, 289, 298, 313
Drumcondra, 127
Drummond, Georgie, 83
Dublin, 124, 127, 134-135, 137, 153, 160, 163, 166, 170, 174, 177, 179,

180-186, 190, 194; Athletic Club, 141; Civil Service, 194; University, 52, 121, 130-133, 152, 202, 222, 412
Dumbarton, 40
Dun Laoghaire, 151
Dunbar, Val, 141, 153, 164
Dunedin, 205
Dunkel, Dick, 315
Dunleary, 160
Dunlop, Henry, 141
Dunn, Arthur, 80, 84
Dunton, John, 124
Duration of match: Aus, 191, 219, 230; Canada, 364, 369; GAA, 120, 155; int rules, 196; rugby, 53, 68; soccer, 30; US, 251, 263, 337, 342
Durham, 50, 51, 52
Ealing FC, 65
Earl Grey Trophy, 371
East, Harry, 131
Easter Monday, 180, 201
Easter Rising, 138, 180, 181
Eaton, CS, 297
Ebbw Vale, 111
Eckersall, Walter, 320
Edinburgh, 117, 185; Academicals, 66, 67
Edmonton Eskimos, 346, 349, 379, 380
Edward VII, 372
Edwards, Gareth, 111
Egypt, 168, 182
El Salvador, 44
Eliot, Charles, 319, 335
Eliowitz, Abe, 382
Elizabeth II, 188, 348, 395
Emerson, Ralph Waldo, 259
Emporia, 340
Equestrian sports, 185, 212, 254, 256, 258, 259, 317, 371
Essendon, 203, 232, 235, 243, 244, 246
Eton College, 10; cricket, 35
Eton field game, 14, 61, 131, 202, 223, 224, 230, 235, 291, 358
Eton wall game, 279
European Championship (soccer), 18, 178
Everton, 75, 76, 86, 87
Exeter, 52
FA Cup, 12, 20, 22, 30, 34–37, 38, 39, 43, 55, 72, 78, 80, 81, 82, 84, 86, 87, 89, 90, 134, 162, 392
FA Premiership, 12, 87, 116, 235, 245
Fagan, Sean, 115, 192, 239
Fagging system, 48

Fair catch: Aus, 231; Canada, 355, 364, 369; GAA, 162, 163; soccer, 14, 15, 30; US, 262, 285, 287
Fall River Rovers, 324
Fallowfield, William, 109
Farrell, Patrick, 199
Father Scanlan of Nenagh, 170
Fencing, 259
Fermanagh, 173, 174
Ferris, Father W, 126
Ferriter, Diarmaid, 121, 181
Fettes College, 47, 66
Fevola, Brendan, 198
Field goals, 62, 313, 314, 349
FIFA, 31, 44, 85; World Cup, 18, 21, 73, 162, 172, 178, 185, 248, 249, 325
Fifth Avenue Hotel, 289
Fingal, 124
First World War, 44, 110, 179, 182, 192, 248, 271, 322, 375, 378, 386
Fithian, Philip Vickers, 257
Fitzgerald, Dick, 161
Fitzgerald, Edward, 127
Fitzroy, 244, 245
Flamingoes, 56
Flanagan, Martin, 208
Fletcher, John Walter, 246
Flying wedge, 283, 328, 327–29
Follis, 272
Football as war, 152, 269, 344
Football Association, 8–21, 25–45, 51, 72, 73–87, 397–98; 1866 rules, 29; and professionalism, 74–84; and Rugby School, 54; goes national, 29–40; professionalism, 96; US, 291
Football Association of Canada, 359
Football League, 25, 36, 41, 83; formation, 85–87
Football Players Accident Society, 63
Forest FC, 8, 12, 22, 25
Forward pass, 192, 340, 342; Aus, 226; Canada, 380–81, 381, 382, 384; legalised in USA, 337–40; soccer, 30; US, 343, 344
France, 127, 255, 347; cricket, 27; rugby, 187, 323, 386
Frankfurt, 388
Free kick: Aus, 231, 234; Camb., 10; Canada, 364, 367; GAA, 162; soccer, 34; US, 261, 262, 265, 285, 289
Freemason's Hotel, 203
Freemason's Tavern, 12, 15, 21, 83
Fremantle, 240, 432
Freshmen: Harvard, 268; servitude, 267; Yale, 270, 273
Fulham, 75, 111, 185

Gaelic Athletic Association, 121, 130, 135, 139, 141, 120–88, 198; and politics, 152, 168; and rugby, 185; and soccer, 173; and the British, 180; foundation, 146
Gaelic football, 120–89, 402–3; before the GAA, 145; similarity to soccer, 155
Gaelic League, 139, 177
Gaelic Union, 143, 152, 177
Galahs, 194, 195
Galt Grammar School, 356
Galway, 135, 157, 161, 173, 179, 197, 198
Galway Statutes, 122
Gambling, 75, 97, 173, 254, 256, 257, 258
Gammon, Richard Vonalbade, 332
Gardner, James Alexander, 71
Garnett, Harry, 50
Garnham, Neal, 154
Garrick FC, 63
Geelong, 193, 203, 235–36, 217, 224, 227, 228, 232, 236, 237, 240, 244, 246, 248, 249
George Hotel, 103
George V, 182
Georgetown, 340
Georgia (USA), 260
Geraghty, Graham, 198
Germany, 44, 129, 180, 248, 254, 318, 330, 377, 388; cricket, 27; rugby, 286; soccer, 185, 188, 249
Gibbs, Scott, 117
Gilbert, William, 61, 268
Giller, Norman, 189
Gladstone, William, 138
Glamorgan, 105
Glasgow, 38, 51, 77, 134, 203; Academicals, 38; Celtic, 40, 178, 188, 201; first soccer international, 39; Rangers, 40, 201; rugby, 117
Glasgow Rangers, 40
Glasnevin, 166, 175
Glenbrook North High School, 267
Gloucestershire, 52
Goal from mark, 62, 109, 350
Goal kick: Sheff., 20
Goal nets, 44, 161
Goalkeepers, 29, 32, 36, 44, 155; GAA, 123, 191, 196; rugby, 53; soccer, 176
Goalposts, 397; Aus, 218, 225, 226, 234, 238, 239, 403; Canada, 362, 364, 369, 407; CFL, 349; GAA, 120, 132, 155, 156, 161, 192, 196, 207; Harvard, 288; rugby, 53, 60, 62, 398; soccer, 17; US, 253, 261,

282, 284, 286, 287, 294, 297, 300, 313, 314, 407
Gold Coast, 245
Goldblatt, David, 25
Golf, 129, 132, 255, 371
Goodall, Ken, 111
Goodrich, Charles, 273
Goodyear, Charles, 262
Goole FC, 94, 105
Gordon, James, 128
Gould, Arthur, 93
Graham, Robert, 22, 30, 54
Grangemockler, 184
Grant, Henry, 288, 289, 292, 293, 296
Grattan, Thomas, 259
Gray Butler, Arthur, 46
Gray, Bill, 224
Gray, Edmund Dwyer, 164
Great Awakening, 255
Greece, 164, 179, 248, 249, 255, 328
Green Book, 67
Greenan, Michael, 187
Grey Cup, 341, 346, 370–81
Grey, Earl Albert Henry George, 370–73
Gridiron field, 303, 311–12
Grow, Robin, 226, 228
Guillemard, Arthur, 53, 56, 57, 60, 68, 75, 88, 53, 326
Guinness Premiership, 73
Guy's Hospital Rugby Club, 55, 235
Gypsies, 56
H Smith, John, 108, 109
Hacking, 8; Aus, 233, 234; eliminated from soccer, 17; GAA, 221; rugby, 48, 50-53, 56-59, 63, 68; Sheff., 29, 34; soccer, 11, 14, 15–19; US, 287-288, 308, 354
Haileybury School, 46
Hailwell, 83
Hakoah Brooklyn, 324
Half-time: GAA, 155; Aus, 231; Canada, 373; soccer, 20, 64
Halifax, Canada, 359
Halifax, England, 90, 95, 99, 103, 105
Hallam FC, 32
Halswelle, Wyndham, 280
Hamilton Park, 286, 290, 296, 373
Hamilton Tiger-Cats, 341, 346, 357, 368, 369, 372-374, 377, 378, 381, 387
Hammersley, William, 202, 220, 222, 223-234
Hampden Park, 40
Hampden Park Blood Bath, 330
Hampden Park, Glasgow, 40
Hampstead FC, 56
Hand pass, 162
Handball, 123, 185; Irish, 140

Handling, 155; Aus, 221; soccer, 9, 32, 44; US, 278, 279
Hanover Country Fair, 256
Hardy, Arthur Sherburne, 265
Harlequin FC, 56
Harlequins, 111
Harper, William Rainey, 320
Harrison, Henry Colden, 21, 204, 208, 213, 219, 222, 227, 228, 229, 232, 233, 236, 238
Harrogate, 93
Harrow Chequers, 35
Harrow School, 14, 34, 35, 202
Harte, Owen, 141
Hartford, 260, 265
Hartranft, Chester, 282
Hartshorne, Bertram Fulke, 12
Harvard Stadium, 338
Harvard University, 266, 268–72, 291–97, 352–55, 359; 1872 rules, 288; creation of football, 287–314; demise as football power, 316–37; rejects soccer, 289
Harvard v McGill, 1874, 291–95
Harvard v Yale, 1875, 296–97
Harvey, 26
Harvey, Adrian, 25, 52
Haslam, Arthur, 46
Hawky, 273
Hawthorn, 190
Hay, Roy, 248, 249
Hayes, Johnny, 280
Hayes's Commercial Hotel, 147, 148
Hazing, 267–68
Heading, 31
Headingley, 104
Heap, Moses, 74
Heart of Midlothian, 40, 185
Heckmondwike, 93
Heeley, 77
Heeling out, 59, 307; US, 283, 306
Heffelfinger, Pudge, 319, 329, 344
Heineken Cup, 117
Heisman, John, 327, 329, 338
Helmets, 343–45
Helms Athletic Foundation, 316
Herbert, John W, 282
Heysel Stadium, 44
Hibbins, Gillian, 217
Hibernian FC, 40
Hickey, John, 163, 177
Hill, G Rowland, 62, 68, 71, 97, 100
Hill, Jimmy, 84
Hilliard, Bohn, 382
Hitch and kick, 212
Hobart, 239
Hockey, field, 75, 358
Hockey, ice, 356, 358, 371, 376
Hodge, Richard, 327

Hogan, James J, 320
Hogan, Michael, 182, 184, 187
Hogg, Thomas and James, 74
Holland, 249, 254, 347
Holland, Denis, 141
Holmes, Edward Carleton, 57, 297
Holmes, Oliver Wendell, 259
Holt, Richard, 21, 146
Homer Hall, Benjamin, 267, 268
Honduras, 44
Hone's Every Day Book, 129
Hopkins Grammar School, 303
Houghton, Ray, 178
Houston, 174
Huddersfield, 52, 103
Hudson, Arthur, 90, 91
Hudson, JG, 53
Hudson's Bay Company, 352
Huelva, 74
Hughes, Thomas, 50, 270
Hull, 22, 27, 52, 65, 89, 91, 103, 118
Hungary, 44, 249
Hunslet, 103
Hunting, 22, 143, 212, 256, 258
Hurd, Richard, 273
Hurley, 171, 201, 239
Hurling, 120, 122, 144-145, 150, 152, 154, 159-160, 172, 180, 189; Aus, 201-202; Irish invasion, 171; US, 266
Hutchinson, William, 53, 65
Hyde, Douglas, 139, 159, 177, 179
Ibrox Park, 40
Ice skating, 75, 259, 371
Illawarra, 244
Illinois, 315, 332, 344, 374, 432
India, 370
Indiana, 319, 324, 332
Industrial Revolution, 128, 137
Injuries, 333; Canada, 350; GAA, 122, 127, 130; rugby, 51, 54, 79-88, 97, 107, 108, 114; soccer, 20, 80, 89, 97, 162; US, 330, 331, 334-335, 337, 340, 342, 345
Interchange bench, 162
Intercollegiate Athletic Association of the United States, 336
Intercollegiate Football Association, 287–91, 304, 310, 312, 332, 407; disbanded, 329
Intercollegiate Rules Committee, 329, 331, 332, 336
Interference, 262, 283, 287, 301–2, 326, 335, 341; Canada, 349, 364, 369, 374, 380; flying, 329
International Football Association Board, 43
International Rugby Board, 116

423

International rules football, 120–89,
189–208
Interprovincial Rugby Football Union,
369
Iomain, 123, 126
Iowa, 321, 332, 340
Ireland: rugby, 69, 132; rugby league,
111
Ireland, Stephen, 188
Irish Amateur Athletic Union, 152,
153, 154, 152–54, 164
Irish Champion Athletic Club, 141
Irish Cyclists' Association, 151
Irish Football Association, 44, 134,
187
Irish Football League, 174
Irish Football Union, 69
Irish Hibernians, 260
Irish Home Rule, 138, 139, 170
Irish Hurling and Football Club, 130
Irish Land League, 86, 142, 148
Irish National Athletics Committee,
141
Irish National League, 152, 165
Irish Plea Rolls, 122
Irish Rebellion, 136
Irish Republican Army, 138, 182, 183
Irish Republican Brotherhood, 138,
143, 147, 152, 168–72
Irish Rugby Football Union, 133, 134,
135, 140, 179, 187
Irish Volunteers, 179, 181
Irish War of Independence, 138, 181,
182
Iroquois, 263
Irvine, Robert, 67
Irwin Jenkinson, Henry, 89
Irwin, Tom, 176
Islington, 129
Italy, 248, 249, 280; calcio, 272;
rugby, 74, 117; soccer, 250, 255;
volata, 224
Ivy League, 61, 266–79, 282, 286,
315, 317, 318
James I (VI of Scotland), 255
James II (VII of Scotland), 201
James, David and Evan, 92
Japan, 139, 334
Jenkins, Stitt, 236
Jex-Blake, Thomas William, 46
Johns Hopkins University, 321
Johnson, Chris, 198
Jonson, Ben, 272
Jopling, Michael, 115
Jordan, David Starr, 340
Journée Internationale de Jeux et
Sports Traditionnels, 158
Joyce, James, 167
Kangaroos, 192

Kansas, 340
Kelly, Ned, 200
Kelly, Peter, 171
Kennedy, George D, 238
Kennelly, Tadhg, 190
Kenrick, Jarvis, 35
Kensington Oval, 35, 37, 42, 69, 98
Kensington School, 12
Kensington, Adelaide, 238
Kent, 33
Kentucky, 266
Kerry, 126, 143, 161, 162, 172, 175,
180, 190, 195, 199
Kick off, 231, 240, 277; CFL, 350;
soccer, 14; US, 343
Kick off posts, 225, 230
Kickham, Charles, 168
Kildare, 127, 129, 147, 161
Kilkenny, 161, 166, 181, 409
Killarney, 126, 143, 171
Kiltimagh, 163
King Edward's School, Birmingham,
47
King's College, Windsor, 56
Kingsburgh, Lord Justice Clerk, 72
Kingston, Ontario, 357, 383
Kinnaird, Arthur, 79, 80, 82
Kinsella, Eoin, 122
Kit Burns' Sportsman Hall, 258
Kitchener, Francis Elliot, 48
Knickerbocker Base Ball Club, 281
Knock Lacrosse Club, 134
Knock-on, 14, 49, 71, 154, 155, 192,
376
knock-ons: Knock-on, 107
Kolven, 255
La Trobe, Charles, 211
Lacrosse, 376
Lafayette, 319, 344
Lambert, Norman, 376
Lampeter, 52
Lancashire, 42, 53, 73; Cup, 36; prof.,
80–116; rugby, 65
Lang, James, 77
Lansdowne Road, 180, 186, 187
Las Vegas, 388
Laune Rangers, 175
Laurier, Wilfrid, 377
Lausanne, 56
Lavan, Seán, 163
Law Club, 56
Leeds, 52, 53, 76, 77, 82, 89-93, 99,
103, 104, 106, 113, 119, 297
Lees Club, 175
Leggett, William, 282
Lehigh, 330
Leigh, 101, 103, 105
Leinster, 69, 117, 147, 177
Liffey, River, 127

Ligue Nationale de l'Education
Physique, 146
Limerick, 157, 160, 204
Lincicome, Bernie, 325
Lincoln, 30
Lincoln FC, 14, 26, 27
Lincoln University, 321
Lincoln, Abraham, 188, 279
Lincolnshire, 26, 65
Line of scrimmage, 59, 252, 307, 309,
312, 332, 337, 339, 342, 349- 351,
360, 363-364, 367-368, 378, 381
Lineouts, 19, 49, 155; Canada, 367;
rug lge, 107; US, 308
Linfield, 87
Lisburn, 174
Litkenhous, Edward and Frank, 315
Liverpool, 52, 118; FC, 75; St Helens
FC, 67, 235
Liversidge, 103
Llandovery, 52
Llanelli, 52, 117, 119
Lloyd George, David, 378
Lockwood, Dicky, 93, 109
Lohmes, GL, 276
London, 17, 28, 33, 35, 37; FA
meeting, 12; Irish, 13, 117;
Olympics, 279; prof., 98; Rowing
Club, 22; rugby, 52, 101; rugby
league, 110; rugby union founded,
55; v Sheffield, 1866, 22, 23, 29–
33; Wasps, 56
Long Island, 258
Longford, 134, 179
Lord's Cricket Ground, 35
Loretto School, 66, 68
Louth, 127, 151, 160, 162
Lovett, James, 263
Lowry, John, 161
Luton Town, 87
Lyceum movement, 257
Lynch, Charles, 168
Lynch-Blosse, Sir Robert, 142
Lysaght, Edward, 130
Lyttelton, Alfred, 43
Mac Cuarta, Seamus Dall, 123
Macadam, John, 203, 219
MacCarthy, JJ, 130, 133, 175
Macdonald, Reverend DB, 372
Macken, Peader, 180
MacLaren, William, 53
Magners League, 117
Maguire, Sam, 21, 179, 182
Mahon, Jack, 158
Major League Soccer, 325
Malvern College, 80
Manchester, 92, 96; AFC, 63; City, 75,
76; Free Wanderers, 63; rugby, 47,

52, 67; Rugby Club, 91; soccer, 83, 86
Mangan, James, 223
Manitoba, 352, 375, 376, 379, 385
Manningham, 103, 106
Maple Leaf Baseball Club Grounds, 356
Maradona, Diego, 44
Marindin, Major Francis, 72, 79, 84
Marking, 62, 192, 193, 196, 231–32; soccer, 20; US, 285
Marlborough Nomads, 56
Marlborough School, 10, 14, 43, 46, 50, 51, 238
Marngrook, 189
Marriot, Charles, 59
Marshall, Francis, 67, 70, 93, 99–101
Marshall, Theodore, 233
Martin , John Stuart, 303, 304
Maryland, 255, 321
Marylebone Cricket Club, 11, 89
Mason, Nicholas, 155, 196, 308
Massachusetts, 253, 254, 260, 268, 297; Institute of Technology, 335
Massasoit House, 253, 297, 304
Massasoit, King, 253
Maton, Leonard James, 57, 297
Mauls: rug lge, 107, 108; rugby, 8, 49, 60; soccer, 11, 14; US, 354
Maxwell, Robert, 333
Mayo, 142, 148, 163, 194
Maypoles, 253
McAlery, John, 133
McAnespie, Aidan, 182
McCarron, Patrick, 200
McCarthy, Daniel, 181
McCarthy, JJ, 69
McCarthy, Thomas St George, 147, 182
McCaughey, Francie, 182
McConville, Chris, 199
McCracken, Henry, 335
McDermott, Seán, 180
McGibbon, RD, 353
McGill University, 365, 368, 374–75, 407–9; and Harvard, 291–95
McGill, James, 353
McGivern, HB, 372
McGregor, William, 85–86
McKay, John, 147, 148
McMaster University, 365
McNulty, Sean, 181
Meacham, Scott, 276, 278, 279, 300
Meagher, Thomas Francis, 138
Meath, 123, 127, 172, 179, 195
Mecredy, Richard J, 159
Medford, 295
Meelick, 161

Melbourne, 130, 192-199; Gymnastic Games, 212; Irish, 199–202; settlement, 209–11; soccer team, 248; Storm, 119, 245, 246; University, 235; Welsh, 248
Melbourne Cricket Ground, 192, 198, 217-218, 227-229, 247
Melbourne FC, 190, 212, 218, 220-224, 227-228, 230-37, 239, 243
Memphis Mad Dogs, 349, 388
Merchiston Castle, 66
Merions, 321
Merritt, William Hamilton, 362
Merriwell, Frank, 298, 317
Merthyr Tydfil, 111
Messenger, Dally, 113, 114
Metropolitan Hurling Club, 143
Mexico, 388
Michigan, 276, 306, 307, 315, 316, 319, 332, 360, 382
Mid Rhondda, 111
Middlesbrough, 65, 76
Middlesex, 33, 62
Midwinter, Eric, 28
Milford College, 27
Military, 131, 240, 353, 386; GAA, 169, 183; negative effect of football, 128; tactics, 328
Miller, James, 100, 101
Minnesota, 321, 332
Missouri, 265
Mitchell, Frank, 109
Moffat, Alexander, 329
Mohican, 56
Molony, John, 199
Monaghan, 202
Montreal, 389; AAA, 382; Foot Ball Club, 364; Wanderers, 370
Moon, Warren, 176, 349
Moorabool, 236
Moore, Bobby, 325
Moore, HO, 69
Moorehead, Johnny, 304
Moose Jaw, 377
Moran, Kevin, 178, 191
Morley, 'Wild Bill', 335
Morton, Thomas, 253
Moseley RFC, 64
Mosforth, Billy, 43
Mountjoy Prison, 142
Moyola Park, 134
Muircheartaigh, Micháel Ó, 126, 160
Mullingar, 160
Mulock, William, 356
Munster, 69, 117, 118, 146, 175
Murphy, Fred, 330
Murphy, JF, 175
Murphy, John, 168
Murray, John Fisher, 129

Murrayfield, 185
Muscular Christianity, 46, 47, 67, 75, 99
Musgrave, Sir Richard, 128
Naismith, James, 309
Nally, Pat, 141–42
Napoleon I, 330, 348
Narragansett, 254
National Collegiate Athletic Association, 186, 315, 316, 318, 336, 337, 343
National Football League, 318, 344, 387
National Heritage Committee, 116
National Rugby League, 245, 246
Navy, 186, 321, 331, 340, 344
Neath, 52, 117
Negro Leagues, 176
Nelson, David, 340
Nenagh, 170
Nevada, 322
Neville, WC, 135
New Brunswick, 299
New England, 254, 259, 261, 292
New Hampshire, 276, 281
New Haven, 273, 286, 290, 296, 303, 304, 320
New Jersey, 272, 282, 324
New Orleans, 258
New South Wales, 113, 191, 210, 213, 215, 245, 247, 250; Aus, 241, 243; NSWRL, 192, 193, 245, 246; NSWRU, 109; rug lge, 112; soccer, 243; Waratahs, 117
New South Wales Rugby Football League, 113
New South Wales Waratahs, 242
New Year's Day, 237, 352
New York, 23, 195, 199, 254, 257, 258, 260, 265, 266, 272, 275, 279, 281, 289, 291, 316, 322, 336, 340, 341, 360, 374, 382; City FBC, 321, 322; Cosmos, 325; Giants, 387; University, 335; University Athletic Club, 329
New Zealand, 205, 241, 246, 316; GAA, 195; rug lge, 245; rugby, 74, 95, 112–14, 117, 118, 322, 360, 386; Warriors, 114, 245
Newark, 322, 324
Newcastle, Australia, 247
Newcastle, England, 110
Newfoundland, 347, 348, 351
Newport, 52, 70, 117
Newsome, Mark, 92, 99, 106
NFL Europe, 388
No Names, Kilburn, 12, 26, 30
Norfolk, Sheffield, 32
North American Soccer League, 325

North Carolina, 338
North of Ireland FC, 133
North Queensland Cowboys, 245
Northcott, William C, 214
Northern Ireland, 69, 172, 173, 182;
  rugby, 69, 133; soccer, 40
Northern Territory, 211
Northern Union, 113
Northwest Territories, 352
Northwestern, 332
Notre Dame, 186, 315, 340, 374
Nottingham, 28, 98; Forest, 20, 81, 86;
  Notts County, 36, 39, 42, 81, 86
Nottinghamshire, 65
Nova Scotia, 348, 352
Nowlan, James, 180
Ó Riain, Séamus, 157
O'Brien, Steve, 382, 390
O'Callaghan, Pat, 154
O'Dwyer, Barry W, 199
O'Keefe, Ryan, 198
O'Leary, David, 178
O'Leary, John, 168
O'Malley, Seamus, 163
O'Neill, Pat, 195
O'Rahilly, 180
O'Ryan, Joseph, 147
O'Shea, Kitty, 138
Oakland High School, 286
Offaly, 161
Offiah, Martin, 111
Offside, 225–26; Aus, 192, 203, 225,
  231; Camb., 30; GAA, 190, 207;
  Harvard, 288; rugby, 58, 59, 60;
  Sheff., 29; soccer, 8, 14, 32, 42,
  44; US, 264, 265, 278, 290, 296,
  302, 307, 327
Ohio, 332
Old Carthusians, 76, 84
Old Etonians, 8, 9, 10, 12, 36, 72, 78,
  79, 80, 290, 305, 358
Old Harrovians, 8, 9, 10, 12, 27, 80
Old Rugbeians, 17, 46, 54, 57, 67, 88,
  133, 202
Old Salopians, 8
Old University Game, 356
Old Wykehamists, 11
Oldham, 96, 103
Olympic Games, 116, 149, 152, 154,
  164, 171, 279, 322, 323, 435
Oneidas FC, 263–66, 271, 353
Oneonta, 264
Onsides kick, 301
Ontario, 159, 352, 356–59; ORFU,
  362–70, 373
Open Challenge Cup, 324
Orange Order, 201
Osgoode Hall, 364

Ottawa, 346, 356, 368, 382; College,
  363, 365; Rough Riders, 341, 369,
  372, 374, 382, 387, 388
Oval ball: Aus, 191; GAA, 156, 207;
  rug lge, 109; rugby, 54, 68; US,
  294, 296
Overs, 155, 158, 161
Oxford University, 36, 58, 66, 67, 101,
  266; rugby, 70
Páirc Uí Chaoimh, 196
Pall Mall Restaurant, 55
Parade Hotel, 218, 222, 224
Paris, 112, 116, 323; GAA, 127;
  Treaty of, 347
Parkdale Canoe Club, 373
Parnell, Charles Stewart, 138, 142,
  149, 150, 152, 157, 165, 169, 170
Parramatta, 247
Partick Thistle, 78
Passing: Dublin, 132; rugby, 50, 60, 70
Paterson, 322
Patten, Gilbert, 317
Patterson, Charles, 320
Payne, Michael, 352
Peabody, Endicott, 334
Peacham, Henry, 326
Pearce, Ned, 312
Pearse, Patrick, 180
Pearson, Arthur, 3, 51
Pearson, Charlie, 232
Pearson, Reverend Bob, 377
Pedestrianism, 258
Pele, 325
Pelota, 123
Pember, Arthur, 12, 16, 17, 18, 19, 22–
  24, 27
Penalty kicks, 190, 250; rugby, 62,
  107, 110; soccer, 44, 249; US, 367
Penarth, 111
Penn, William, 254
Pennsylvania, 254, 257, 266, 276, 299,
  315, 316, 319, 321, 322, 329, 331,
  332, 333, 431
Perceval House, 12
Perpignan, 112
Perth, Australia, 192, 195, 197, 198,
  240, 245
Perth, Scotland, 85
Peter, Richard M, 134
Peter, RM, 133, 134, 432
Philadelphia, 265, 266, 272, 322
Phoenix Park, Dublin, 140, 159
Phoenix Rugby Club, 140
Pickford, William, 80
Pietri, Dorando, 280
Pilgrim Fathers, 253–54
Pilgrims FC, 36
Pittsburgh, 186, 319, 340, 379, 387
Play-the-ball, 108, 109

Plymouth Colony, 253
Poland, 177, 248, 255
Polo, 150, 151, 335
Port Adelaide, 198, 236, 238, 245
Port Melbourne, 249
Port Phillip, 201, 212, 236
Porter, Noah, 316
Portugal, 185
Potter, Jothan, 297
Potts, Alexander William, 47, 66
Preston, 40, 65, 72, 78, 81, 82, 86, 87,
  98
Preston Lane, William, 285
Price, EW, 297
Price, Luther, 331
Prince of Wales Fort, 352
Prince, Morton Henry, 271, 288, 289,
  291, 293, 294
Princeton Theological Seminary, 282
Princeton University, 266; 1871 rules,
  287; and Rutgers, 281–85;
  ballown, 272–73; creation of
  football, 296–302; demise as
  football power, 316–37; early
  college matches, 303–14, 315;
  gamesmanship, 301
Professional Football Researchers
  Association, 263, 265, 292, 299,
  312
Professionalism, 145; Canada, 381–84,
  385; Ireland, 176; rugby, 73–119;
  soccer, 27, 40, 41, 73–87, 175; W
  Camp, 304
Prohibitions of football, 128, 254–55,
  260, 270–71, 276, 332–33, 333–
  36; rugby, 55
Pulitzer, Joseph, 317
Purdue, 332
Puritans, 253
Quakers, 254, 255
Quarterbacks, 252, 308–9, 327, 349,
  351
Quebec, 347, 352, 378; City, 354, 358;
  QRFU, 363, 362–70, 433
Queen's House, 56
Queen's Park, 38, 37–42, 51, 133
Queen's Park Rangers, 75
Queens University, 355, 365, 367, 379
Queensland, 210, 241, 242, 246, 247;
  and soccer, 247; Aus fball, 245;
  Australian footbal, 243; Reds, 117;
  rug lge, 114; Rugby Football
  Association, 114
Quidnunces, 134
Quinn, Niall, 178, 191
Quinnell, Scott, 111, 117
Quoits, 94, 256
Rader, Benjamin, 254, 320
Radley College, 47

INDEX

Raffles Bay, 211
Randolph, Thomas, 272
Rashad, Ibrhaim, 168
Rathmines School, 133
Ravenscourt Park, 56
Reading, 36
Real Madrid, 83
Reeves, Joseph Mason, 344
Referees, 155, 196, 249; Canada, 365, 367, 369; FA, 20, 36, 44; rugby, 69, 71, 90; US, 282, 286, 298, 301, 303, 330
Regina, 346, 376, 377, 380, 381
Reid, William, 318, 336, 337
Reigate, 30, 35
Religion and football, 75, 76, 129, 143, 150, 154, 170, 173, 253, 255
Renton, 40
Resident Rule, 385
Rhode Island, 254, 276
Richmond, 13, 26, 55, 56, 57, 81, 117, 308
Richmond FC, Melbourne, 223, 230, 235
Richmond Paddock, 218, 219, 221, 224, 227
Riddle, Jimmy, 382
Rimet, Jules, 21
Ringland, Trevor, 188
Ripon, 46
Robinson, Bradbury, 339
Rochdale, 89, 103
Rockne, Knute, 315, 340
Roger, David, 292
Rokeby, Archbishop, 122
Romania, 195, 323, 386
Romans, 272, 328
Rome: Treaty of, 176
Roosevelt, Theodore, 333–34
Roper, William, 342
Ross, Hugo, 376
Ross, Jimmy, 40, 83
Rosslyn Park, 56
Rote, Tobin, 387
Rouge: Canada, 349, 358, 361, 364, 390; Eton, 10; Sheff., 29
Rouges: Sheff., 32
Rounders, 150, 281
Rouse, Paul, 165, 166, 180
Rowing, 22, 212, 255, 258, 276, 281, 303, 357, 370, 376
Roxbury Grammar School, 260
Royal Engineers, 26, 35, 42, 43, 64, 72
Royal High School, Edinburgh, 66
Royal Hotel, Manchester, 86
Royal Irish Constabulary, 141, 148, 169, 170, 174, 182
Royal Military College, Kingston, 365
Royal Naval School, 14

Royal Park, 233
Rubber, 262, 265, 277, 344; galvanised, 262
Rugby: composite rules, 119; Scot., 38; split from soccer, 18
Rugby football, 398–402; 1871 rules, 57; after the FA, 43; and Aus rules, 241–44; caid, 126; Canada, 352–66, 371, 386; codification, 53–72; Ireland, 176, 185–88; 'rugger', 66; schism between union and league, 46–119; schism with soccer, 8–19; scoring, 61; US, 297–300, 321–23
Rugby Football Union, 19, 45, 53–72, 88–103, 358; and rugby league, 92–110; club competition, 73; conflict with other unions, 70–72; foundation, 46–58; prof., 73–119
Rugby league, 73–119, 176, 185, 192; antipodes, 112–14; Aus, 193, 197, 247; etymology, 66; France, 112; schism, 88–110; Wales, 111
Rugby School, 43, 46, 48, 46–51, 52, 53, 54, 55, 56, 67, 132, 253, 268
Rugby Union of Canada, 386
Rugby World Cup, 73, 116, 316, 323, 386
Rule 21, 184
Rule 27, 177
Rule 42, 185, 186, 187, 188
Runcorn, 103
Running in, 15
Running with the ball, 11, 46, 53, 63, 65; Aus, 232–34, 240; Canada, 292; elimination from soccer, 15–19; GAA, 156, 159; Harvard, 288; Ireland, 127; rugby, 131; US, 261, 264, 294, 311; Yale, 274
Russell, Ernie, 370
Russell, John, 137
Russia, 216, 334
Rutgers University, 285, 286, 288, 289, 296, 312, 316
Rutgers v Princeton, 1869, 281–85
Rutter, Algernon, 56, 57, 297
Ryan, Tommy, 182, 184
Sabbath and football, 126, 128, 173, 254, 257; GAA, 159, 176
Sacramento Surge, 388
Safeties, 61, 253, 305, 310, 311, 313, 364; CFL, 361
Sale Sharks, 52, 235
Salem, 260
Salisbury, Mark, 325
San Diego, 350
San Francisco, 130, 286, 291, 388
Sandhurst, 237
Sandyford, 127
Sarnia Imperials, 380

Saskatchewan, 346, 352, 376; Rough Riders, 346, 376, 380
Schaff, David, 286, 287
Scotch College, 203, 214, 219, 220, 222
Scotland, 47, 93, 129, 213; and professional soccer, 77–79; Aus, 203; Canada, 353; Challenge Cup, 34; combination game, 37–42; Irish soccer, 133–34; rugby, 51, 67, 70–72, 117, 185; rugby league, 111; SFA, 40; SFL, 41
Scotland v England, 1872 (soccer), 38–42
Scrimmage, 306–9
Scrum: rugby lge, 107
Scrums, 50, 58–60, 68; Aus, 192, 234; become scrimmages, 306–9; Canada, 364, 378; eliminated in US, 306–9; etymology, 307; hacking, 51, 57; Ireland, 126, 175; modernisation, 59; rug lge, 107, 110; rugby, 307; US, 296, 305
Second World War, 62, 110, 115, 147, 186, 248, 348, 386
Seddon, Bob, 95
Sending off, 155, 196, 197, 198; Canada, 365; soccer, 36
Separation Sports and Games, 213
Sewell, EHD, 107
Shamrock Classic, 186
Shaughnessy, Frank, 374–75, 381, 382
Shaw, Alfred, 95
Shearman, Montagu, 37, 52, 53, 57, 60, 61, 70, 90, 91, 94, 306, 308
Sheffield, 39, 63, 65, 81; FC, 20–21, 26, 36, 37, 42, 43, 53, 28–34, 64, 77, 83, 235; Hillsborough, 44; merges with FA, 33; rugby, 53, 63; rules, 26, 39, 54, 358; United, 76, 81; Wednesday, 32, 39, 76, 81, 86
Sheffield FC, 226
Sherborne School, 52
Sheridan, Martin, 280
Shillelagh, 201
Shoosmith, GJ, 225
Shrewsbury School, 10
Shropshire: Wanderers, 36, 42
Shrovetide football, 352
Shrule, 168
Simpson, John, 54
Sinn Féin, 138, 177, 188
Six Nations, 73, 115, 187
Six Nations (rugby union), 18
Six-tackle rule, 110
Slane, 123
Sligo Rovers, 178
Smith Miller, Gerritt, 263
Smith, George William, 113

427

MIKE ROBERTS – THE SAME OLD GAME: CODIFICATION

Smith, John H, 108, 115
Smith, Mel, 265, 275, 312, 322, 356, 359, 360
Smith, Thomas Henry, 202, 220, 222, 223
Snapback, 308, 350, 367
Soccer, 8–21, 25–45, 96–97, 97, 100, 397–98; and rugby, 47, 54, 55, 43, 53, 106, 117; Aus, 246–50; etymology, 43, 324; FA Cup, 34–37; first codified games, 19–34; first FA rules, 11–19; GAA, 179, 185–88; Ireland, 133–34, 154–57; prof. and the Football League, 73–87; Scot., 37–42; US, 323–25; USA, 290–91
Soloing, 120, 156, 158, 163, 189, 198
Soule: revivals, 120
South Adelaide, 238
South Africa, 74, 117, 199
South Australia, 200, 238–39, 243, 244, 245; SAFA, 239
South Carolina, 254
South East Lancashire Cup, 61
South Melbourne, 206, 244; Hellas, 248
South Shields, 110
South Yarra, 204, 220, 227, 228, 230, 234, 235
Southampton, 75, 76
Southend, 64
Southern League, 87
Southern Rugby Football Union, 241, 242
Spain, 74, 123, 255, 347; calcio, 272
Spectators: Aus., 213, 226, 228, 229, 241; GAA, 171, 177, 183; rugby, 63, 88, 96; rugby lge, 102, 107; US, 268, 282, 296, 305, 338
Springfield YMCA, 329
Springfield, Massachusetts, 253, 297, 304, 305
St Columba's College, 131
St George FBC, 265
St Helens, 103
St John's Academy, Manlius, 335
St Kilda, 205, 214, 218, 235, 239, 244, 248
St Louis, 265, 291, 324, 339, 387
St Michaels, 160
St Patrick's Day, 200, 260
St Patrick's School, Melbourne, 203
St Paul's School, Birmingham, 47
St Paul's School, London, 56
Stadden, William, 92
Stade de Colombes, 323
Staffordshire, 64, 76
Stagg, Amos Alonzo, 304, 309, 316, 320, 328-329, 338, 340-341, 433

Stanford, 315, 322, 335, 340
Stanley Cup, 346, 371, 379
Stapleton, Frank, 178
Staunton, Steve, 178, 191
Stellenbosch laws, 117
Stephen, Frank, 213
Stevens, John Cox, 258
Stevens, Warren, 382
Stewart, John Huston, 141
Stoddart, Andrew, 62, 95
Stoke, 28, 64, 76, 86
Stokes, Lennart, 70
Stonyhurst College, 129
Stoolball, 253, 281
Strutt, Joseph, 43, 272, 273
Stuart, Angus, 92
Stuttgart, 178
Stynes, Jim, 190
Subiaco Oval, 198
Substitutes: Aus, 162; GAA, 162; rugby, 162; soccer, 18, 20; US, 251, 342
Substitutions: soccer, 35
Sudell, William, 83
Sullivan, John Lawrence, 333
Sunday Observance Act, 173
Sunderland, 27, 36
Super 12, 117, 242
Super Bowl, 251, 309, 346
Super League, 83, 103, 106, 245
Surbiton FC, 12
Surrey, 33, 218, 222; FC, 27
Suter, Fergus, 78, 80, 82
Sutherland, AA, 96
Swansea, 52, 70, 92, 104, 117
Swarthmore, 333
Swindon, 75
Swords, 124
Sydney, 192, 195, 199, 202, 206, 210, 212, 241–44, 246-247; Showground, 193; Swans, 190, 206, 244, 245; University Football Club, 241
T formation, 309, 377, 379
Tackling: Aus, 238; Canada, 364; GAA, 120; int rules, 191, 196; rug lge, 109; rugby, 49, 63, 302; US, 251, 296, 306, 311, 337, 338
Tailteann Games, 149
Tasmania, 239–40, 243
Tees Wanderers, 65
Television, 21, 116, 173, 178, 194, 206, 244, 249, 266, 346, 385, 396
Telstra Dome, 198
Temple, Frederick, 48, 51
Templemore, 147
Ten Hour Day Act, 74
Ten-a-side: US, 295
Tennis, 22, 150, 256, 272, 303

Thanksgiving, 253, 266, 316
Thebarton, 200, 201
Third Lanark, 40
Thompson, James, 202, 222, 223, 229, 234, 237
Thorn, Brad, 117
Thring, John Charles, 8–9, 14
Throw in: Yale, 288
Throw-in, 155; GAA, 162; rug lge, 107; soccer, 19, 34; Thring, 9
Throw-up, 125, 190, 396; US, 290
Thurles, 146, 147-151, 153, 160, 161, 170, 171, 204
Tibbets, Albert Perkins, 287
Tipperary, 135, 144-147, 160-161, 166, 177, 182, 184, 205, 320
Todd, John, 197
Todd, Lance, 114
Tom Brown's Schooldays, 49, 225, 231, 270, 286, 292, 307
Toronto, 356–59; Argonauts, 357–58, 358, 364, 369, 370, 373, 379, 385, 387; Lacrosse Club, 356; University, 307, 355, 358, 360, 365, 367, 368, 373, 384; University, 369
Toronto Argonauts, 346
Toss of coin, 36, 131, 155, 183, 290, 293, 338, 369, 397, 400, 403, 407
Tottenham Hotspur, 75, 81, 87
Touchdowns, 264, 296, 298, 313, 314; CFL, 359, 361; rugby, 60–62, 60; soccer, 30; US, 294
Trains and football's expansion, 65, 87, 100, 174, 282, 290, 291, 295, 379
Tralee, 171
Transcendentalists, 259
Transylvania University, 266
Trautman, Bert, 162
Treherbert, 111
Trent Affair, 279
Tries, 60–62; Canada, 364; GAA, 174; rugby, 61, 62, 67; rugby lge, 107; rugby u, 117; soccer, 20
Tri-Nations, 199
Trinity College School, Port Hope, 357
Trudeau, Pierre, 346
Trueman, Nigel, 58, 118
Try at goal, 49, 58, 240; US, 296
tSléibe, Redmond Murphy an, 127
Tufts College, 269, 295, 296, 300
Tufts, Marshall, 268
Tullabeg College, 133
Tumulty, Brendan, 195
Tunbridge, 56
Turkey, 137, 179, 216
Turnen, 146
Twickenham, 58, 73, 118, 185
Twomileborris, 160

428

Twopenny, Richard, 238, 241
Tyldesley, 103
Tyler, Nathan, 286
Tyrone, 142, 173, 182
Ukraine, 249
Ulster, 69, 87, 117, 123, 171-172, 174, 181, 432
Union College, 335
United Hospitals Cup, 62, 73
United Irishmen, 136
United States of America, 251–345, 251–345; and Britain, 279; Aus, 193; Canada, 346–49, 381–90; creation of American football, 266–97; GAA, 199; Gaelic, 195; hurling, 130, 149, 171; immigration, 23, 137; prof., 316–21; racial issues, 176; rugby, 61, 297–300, 321–23; soccer, 66, 323–25
Universal Football League, 192
University Boat Race, 266, 357
University of Georgia, 332, 338
Upper Canada College, 356
Uppingham School, 14, 214
Upton Park FC, 35, 82, 83
Uruguay, 249
USSR, 346
Van Cortlandt Park, 341
Vancouver, 346, 380, 389
Vanderbilt, 320, 343
Varsity Stadium, 373
Venezuela, 279
Vichy regime, 111
Victoria, 200, 209–44; VFA, 203, 223, 234, 241, 242; VFL, 197, 244
Victoria I, 137
Vietnam, 346
Vigilance Committees, 177
Vikings, 347
Virginia, 256, 319, 321, 340
Volata, 146
Wakefield Trinity, 85, 89, 90, 103, 115
Wales, 27, 148, 185; rugby, 9, 52, 70, 71, 91–92, 93, 117, 118; rugby lge, 92; soccer, 27, 40, 43, 185, 188
Wall, Sir Frederick, 39
Wallsend, 110
Walton, 82
Walvin, James, 66
Wanderers: v Engineers, 1872, 35–36
Wanderers FC, 12, 27, 30, 33, 35, 36, 38, 42
Wanderers, California, 321
Wanderers, Dublin, 131, 132

Waratah, 242
Warburton, SA, 81
Ward Rufus, 90
Warren, Johnny, 249
Warrington, 91, 103, 114
Warwick County, 87
Warwickshire, 27
Washington DC, 321, 340
Washington, George, 256, 291
Waterford, 127, 147, 177
Waterloo, Battle of, 330
Watkins, David, 111
Waukesha, 279
Webb Ellis, William, 18, 21, 57, 126, 163, 232
Wednesbury Strollers, 64
Wellington College, 46, 56
Welsh Challenge Cup, 36
Wembley Stadium, 22, 44, 79, 104, 195, 388
Were, George, 213
Wesleyan Sabbath School, 237
West Bromwich Albion, 72, 81, 86
West Coast Eagles, 245
West Ham, 76
West Kent, 56
West of Scotland Cricket Ground, 39
West Virginia, 319
Western Australia, 240–41, 243, 244, 247
Western Canadian Rugby Football Union, 375–80
Western Football League of America, 324
Western Reds, 245
Westmeath, 159, 200
Westminster Palace Hotel, 100, 101
Westminster School, 10, 27
Weston, Charles, 300
Wexford, 135, 175
Weyand, Alexander, 306, 307
Wheeler, Benjamin Ide, 322
Wheeler, Jack, 334
Wheelock, Eleazar, 276
Whistles, 69, 330, 350
White Benton, Edward, 46
White, Andrew, 276
Whitefield, George, 255
Whitehall Aquatic Club, 258
Whitney, Caspar, 315, 316
Wicklow, 159
Widnes, 103
Wigan, 85, 91, 102, 103, 105-106, 111, 114, 118
Willard, Sidney, 268

Williams College, 281
Williams, Graham, 31, 47, 63
Williams, Paul, 315
Williamstown, 235
Willis, Robert, 22
Wills, Horatio, 216
Wills, Thomas, 201, 202, 212, 216, 219, 222, 225, 214–26, 229-233; and cricket, 217; and Rugby School, 223; death, 217; Geelong, 236
Wilson, Woodrow, 341, 342
Wimbledon, 15, 55
Winchester College, 17, 202, 223, 353
Windsor, England, 134
Winnipeg, 346, 376, 377, 379, 380, 384, 385
Winslow, Edward, 253
Wisconsin, 279, 315, 321, 332, 339
Wolfe Tone, Theobald, 136
Wolverhampton Wanderers, 44, 76, 81, 86
Women, 323, 386; Ire., 124
Woodruff, George, 331
Woolsey, Theodore Dwight, 267
Worcester, 47
Worcester, Massachusetts, 260
World League of American Football, 388
Wray, Thomas, 222
Wrestling: GAA, 126, 150, 173; rugby, 63; US, 256, 259, 268
Wrexham, 36, 185
Wright, John Farrall, 76
Wright, Tommy, 75
Wurundjeri, 210, 211
Wyse-Power, John, 147, 169
Yale University, 261, 266, 267, 273–75, 281, 358; 1872 rules, 287; creation of football, 287–91, 296–302; early college matches, 303–14
Yarra Park, 218, 228
Yarraville, 249
York, 52
York Factory, 352
York Melbourne, 91
Yorkshire, 27, 53, 73, 127; Challenge Cup, 90; prof., 80–116; rugby, 65; Rugby Union, 92, 99, 100, 105
Yost, Fielding, 306, 308, 319
Youdan Cup, 31
Young Irelanders, 138
Yugoslavia, 44, 168, 248
Zuppke, Robert, 344

BIBLIOGRAPHY

Where a source material is used for a very specific detail, it is mentioned as a footnote to the text itself. The source materials detailed in this bibliography are those that have been used more generally as primary sources either throughout the book, or throughout particular sections. Where relevant, and to avoid overloading the text with footnotes, only the name of the author(s) is included in the main body of the book.

Alcock, Charles William *Football: the association game* (G Bell & Sons, 1906).

Austin Smith, Ronald *Sports and Freedom: The Rise of Big-time College Athletics* (Oxford University Press, 1990) .

Bairner, Alan (editor) *Sport and the Irish* (University College Dublin Press, 2005).

Baker, William J *Sports in the Western World* (Rowman and Littlefield, 1982).

Batchelder, Alf *The First Football Matches at the Melbourne Cricket Ground* (Melbourne Cricket Club Library, 2002).

Bernstein, Mark *The Ivy League Origins of an American Obsession* (University of Pennsylvania Press, 2001).

Birley, Sir Derek *Sport and the Making of Britain (International Studies in the History of Sport)* (Manchester University Press, 1993).

Blainey, Geoffrey *The Origins of Australian Football* (Scwartz Publishing, 2003).

Blanchard, Kendall *The anthropology of sport: an introduction* (Bergin & Garvey, 1984)

Blythe Smart, John *The Wow Factor: A concise history of early soccer and the men that made it* (Blythe Smart Publications, 2003).

Brasch, Rudolph. *How Did Sports Begin? A look at the origins of man at play* (David McKay Company, 1970).

Butler, Bryon *The Official History of the Football Association* (Queen Anne Press, 1991)

Camp, Walter *American football* (Harper & Brothers, 1891).

Collins, Tony *Rugby's Great Split: Class culture and the origins of rugby league football* (Frank Cass Publication, 1998).

Corry, Eoghan *An Illustrated History of the GAA* (Gill & MacMillan, 2005).

Cosetino, Frank *Canadian Football: The Grey Cup Years* (Musson Book Company Ltd, 1969).

Cronin, Mike; Murphy, William; Rouse, Paul *The Gaelic Athletic Association* 1884-2009 (Irish Academic Press, 2009).

Currie, Gordon *100 Years of Canadian Football* (Pagurian Press Limited, 1968).

Curry, Graham *Football: A Study in Diffusion* (University of Leicester, 2001).

Davis, Parke H *Football, the American intercollegiate game* (Scribner's sons, 1912).

De Burca, Marcus *Michael Cusack and the GAA* (Anvil Books, 1989).

De Moore, Greg *Tom Wills – His Spectacular Rise and Tragic Fall* (Allen & Unwin, 2008).

Dunning, Eric and Sheard, Kenneth *Barbarians, Gentlemen and Player: A Sociological Study of the Development of Rugby Football* (Martin Robertson, 1979).

Eisen George and Wiggins, David Kenneth *Ethnicity and sport in North American history and culture* (Praeger Paperback, 1995).

Fabian, AH & Green, G (eds) *Association Football Vols 1 to 4* (Caxton, 1960) .

Fagan, Sean. *RL1895 - Rugby League*. (www.rl1895.com).

Fox, Stephen. *Big Leagues: Professional Baseball, Football & Basketball in National Memory*. (Lincoln: University of Nebraska Press, 1998).

Fremantle Media *History of Football, The Beautiful Game* (2004 video).

Gate, Robert *An Illustrated History of Rugby League* (Arthur Barker, 1989).

Garnham, Neal *The Origins and Development of Football in Ireland* (Ulster Historical Foundation, 1999). A reprint of **RM Peter**'s *Irish Football Annual of 1880*.

Giller, Norman *Football and all that: an irreverent history* (Hodder & Stoughton, 2004)

Goldblatt, David *The Ball is Round* (Penguin, 2006).

Gorn, Elliott J and Goldstein, Warren *A Brief History of American Sports* (University of Illinois Press, 1993).

Grow, Robin *More than a game: The real story of Australian Rules Football* (Melbourne University Press, 1998). Edited by Rob Hess and Bob Stewart.

Guttmann Allen *Sports: The First Five Millennia* (University of Massachusetts Press, 2004).

Harris, Tim. *Sport: Almost Everything You Ever Wanted to Know* (Yellow Jersey Press in 2007).

Harvey, Adrian. *Football: The First Hundred Years, The Untold Story* (Routledge, 2005).

Holliman, Jennie *American sports: 1785-1835* (Seeman Press, 1931).

Holt, Richard *Sport and the British: a modern history* (Oxford University Press, 1990).

King, Seamus J *A History of Hurling* (Gill & Macmillan Ltd, 2005) .

Leatherdale, Clive (ed) *The book of football: a complete history and record of the association and rugby games* (Republished by Desert Island Books, 1996, originally serialised 1905-06).

Levinson, David and Christensen, Karen *Encyclopedia of World Sport, From ancient times to the present* (Oxford University Press, 1999).

Lipoñski, Wojciech *World Sports Encyclopedia* (MBI Publishing Company, 2003).

Macrory, Jennifer *Running with the ball: The Birth of Rugby Union* (Collins Willow, 1991).

Mahon, Jack *A History of Gaelic Football* (Gill & Macmillan, 2000).

Mangan, JA *Sport in Europe: politics, class, gender* (Frank Cass, 1999), *Athleticism in the Victorian and Edwardian Public School: The Emergence and Consolidation of an Educational Ideology* (Frank Cass, 2000) and *The Cultural bond: sport, empire, society* (Gainsborough House, 1992).

Marples, Morris. *A History of Football* (Secker and Warburg, 1954).

Marshall, Francis *Football* (Cassell and company, limited, 1892) with **Arthur G Guillemard**, **G Rowland Hill** and **Arthur Budd** contributing particularly relevant chapters.

Mason, Nicholas *Football!: The story of all the world's football games* (Drake Publishers, 1875).

McCarthy, Daniel *Citizen Cusack and Clare's Gaelic Games* (in *Clare History & Society*, Geography Publications, 2008).

Meacham, Scott *Old Division Football, the Indigenous Mob Soccer of Dartmouth College* (Dartmo, 2006) At www.dartmo.com/football.pdf (viewed 1/07/08).

Midwinter, Eric *Parish to Planet: How football came to rule the world* (Know the Score, 2007).

Nelson, David *The Anatomy of a Game: Football, the Rules, and the Men who Made the Game* (University of Delaware Press, 1994).

Northern Bullants FC *Our Game: The Melbourne Rules* (www.northernbullants.com.au).

O'Brien, Steve *The Canadian Football League, The Phoenix of Professional Sports Leagues* (Lulu Enterprises, 2005).

Oriard, Michael *Reading Football: How the Popular Press Created an American Spectacle* (University of North Carolina Press, 1998)

Owl Historian *Sheffield fansite* (www.btinternet.com/~a.drake/2003sheffhist.htm).

Peek, Hedley & Aflalo, FG *The Encyclopaedia of Sport* (G.P. Putnam & Sons, 1898) .

Professional Football Researchers Association (PRFA) *The Journey to Camp: The Origins of American Football* (www.profootballresearchers.org).

Rader Benjamin *American Sports: From the Age of Folk Games to the Age of Spectators* (Prentice hall, 1983).

Rice, Jonathan *Start of Play: The curious origins of our favourite sports* (Prion Books Ltd, 1998)

Sanders, Richard *Beastly Fury: The strange birth of British football* (Bantam Books, 2009)

Shearman, Montagu *Athletics and football* (Longmans, Green, and Co, 1888).

Smith, Melvin I *Early American & Canadian 'Football', Beginnings through 1883/84* (Self-published, 2003).

Spears, Betty and **Swanson, Richard** *History of Sport and Physical Education in the United States 3rd Edition* (Wm. C. Brown Publishers, 1988).

Sproule, Robert *The Ontario Rugby Football Union 1883-1906* and *The Quebec Rugby Football Union 1883-1906* (at www.profootballresearchers.org).

Stagg, Amos Alonzo *Touchdown! - as told by Coach Amos Alonzo Stagg to Wesley Winans Stout* (Longmans, Green, 1927).

Taylor, Matthew *The association game: a history of British football* (Pearson Education Limited, 2007).

Tranter, Nigel *Sport, economy and society in Britain 1750-1914* (Cambridge University Press, 1998).

Trueman, Nigel *Rugby Union History* (www.rugbyfootballhistory.com).

Vamplew, Wray *Pay Up and Play the Game: Professional Sport in Britain, 1875-1914* (Cambridge University Press (2004) .

Walvin, James *The People's Game* (Mainstream, 1995). Revised version of the 1975 edition.

Watterson, John Sayle *College Football: History, Spectacle, Controversy* (Baltimore: Johns Hopkins University Press, 2000).

Williams, Graham *The Code War* (Yore Publications, 1994).

Percy M Young *A History of British Football* (Stanley Paul, 1968).

ABOUT THE AUTHOR

Mike Roberts was born in Aberystwyth, Wales in 1970, and later lived in Okehampton, Devon. He studied at Christ Church University, Canterbury and after moving to Barcelona in 1992 to work at the Olympic Games, he decided to make the Catalan city his home.

He is currently working as a translator for FC Barcelona and the Universitat Autònoma de Catalunya, and recently retired after fifteen years as secretary of the Barcelona International Football League.

Having played rugby at school and soccer as an adult, and followed both sports intently, in the cosmopolitan city of Barcelona, he was drawn into the worlds of what until then had been less familiar football codes to him, particularly Gaelic and American football, and his interest in these was intensified by writing for his self-published sports magazine and also working for a sports travel company.

What started as basic historical research for background articles soon ignited a spark in Roberts' curious mind. Despite all he had been told about Gaelic football, the pieces didn't quite seem to fit. The more he dabbled, the more he came to question the authenticity of several of the generalised claims about ancient ball games and the origins of the modern codes. He also came to realise that no matter how academic the research into different sports, among historians there was widespread lack of knowledge, or of willingness to recognise, the common bond between all the different codes of football. Instead, in each code's self-congratulatory quest to build its individual identity, an inaccurate picture of football's true origins was being presented.

This, his first book, is the result of ten years of dedicated research. In compiling it, he is indebted to the painstaking work of greater historians than he, and hopes he has managed to produce a comprehensive review of the literature as it stands today to paint an accurate and unbiased picture of how all the world's different football cultures link together as the same old game.

Disclaimer

All of the information published in this book is, to the best of my knowledge and following extensive research and verification, correct. However, in such an ambitious project, and with new evidence emerging every week, it is only natural that there may be errors. I would be delighted if readers could bring any of these to my attention in order for them to be corrected in future editions.

Likewise, as often as possible or necessary, all sources have been given. I would be grateful for any information regarding erroneous or missing sources, and to rectify them in future editions, and apologise for any inconvenience unwittingly caused.